Where the Stories Come From

Beginning to Write Fiction

Sibyl Johnston

Longman

New York   San Francisco   Boston
London   Toronto   Sydney   Tokyo   Singapore   Madrid
Mexico City   Munich   Paris   Cape Town   Hong Kong   Montreal

Vice President/Editor-in-Chief: Joe Terry
Acquisitions Editor: Erika Berg
Development Director: Janet Lanphier
Development Editor: Ruth Franklin
Marketing Manager: Melanie Craig
Supplements Editor: Donna Campion
Project Coordination, Text Design, and Electronic Page Makeup: Pre-Press Company, Inc.
Cover Design Manager: Nancy Danahy
Cover Designer: Neil Flewellyn
Cover Art: Detail from "Curve," 1996, © Anne Davey. Oil. 6″ × 5½″
Senior Manufacturing Buyer: Dennis J. Para
Printer and Binder: Courier Corporation
Cover Printer: John P. Pow Company

For Permission to use copyrighted material, grateful acknowledgment is made to the copyright holders on pp. 502–503, which are hereby made part of this copyright page.

Library of Congress Cataloging-in-Publication Data

Johnston, Sibyl.
    Where the stories come from : beginning to write fiction / Sibyl Johnston.
        p. cm.
    Includes index.
    ISBN 0-321-07899-3
    1. Fiction--Authorship. I. Title.

PN3355 .J58 2001
808.3--dc21   2001029268

Please visit our website at http://www.ablongman.com

ISBN 0-321-07899-3

2 3 4 5 6 7 8 9 10—CRW—04 03 02

To all of my students
and to the memory of Arthur Henry King,
teacher, kind friend, exemplar

No one knows where the words are coming from anyway, no one writing sincerely
. . . no one knows where the images and the very story are coming from. We sit at
the desk and try to concentrate absolutely, and concentration takes us to the place
where the words and images and stories are. This is not a place we can reach every
time we want to; it is a strange place. . . . What is art if not a concentrated and im-
passioned effort to make something with the little we have, the little we see?
—Andre Dubus, "Letter to a Writers' Workshop"

Contents

PART FOUR: THE STORIES: AN ANTHOLOGY OF PROFESSIONAL AND STUDENT FICTION   **231**

*Asterisks denote core stories that are excerpted extensively in this book.

To the Teacher

Writing is an intimate act. Creativity is as personal and individual as dreams or fingerprints. Though writers can and should practice skills and techniques, at heart learning to write is based upon understanding one's own nature, skills, and intuitions. It is a combining and recombining of methods and approaches in a continuing search for what works.

With that in mind, *Where the Stories Come From* takes a process-oriented, student-centered approach to teaching beginning writers—that is, it strongly emphasizes revision, and it encourages student writers to participate actively in classroom discussions of their own fiction.

This method, discussed in more detail beginning on page xviii, has developed naturally as I've taught writing; it's what has worked in my classrooms. Some of the ideas in this book are my own; some have been around for a long time; and some have been contributed or improved on by my students, teaching assistants, and colleagues. I've shaped *Where the Stories Come From* for college classrooms, but because of its emphasis on the writing process and on empowering the writer, most of its elements will work just as well in writers' groups or other less formal settings.

Making a Practical, Comprehensive Book

In this book, I've tried to provide what I need in my own classroom: a text that stresses the practical aspects of writing while also offering a clear theoretical overview, combining close attention to the writing process, a detailed discussion of the elements of fiction, and a varied and inclusive anthology.

The Writing Process   Chapters 1, 2, 10, and 11 offer a step-by-step guide through each phase of the writing process, without prescribing a "how-to" approach. Chapter 1, Playing with Words, introduces students to the earliest stages of writing through a variety of intuitive exercises and activities designed to stimulate creativity and generate ideas. Chapter 2, Drafting: Six Ways of Beginning a Story, provides a number of possible starting points for beginning writers: from character, image, setting, voice, event, or theme. Chapter 10, Revising: Linear and Circular Methods, describes systematic and intuitive approaches to revision and includes several revisions of an actual student story. Chapter 11, Working with Readers, offers ideas about how to elicit a helpful reading, emphasizing the unique value of the workshop setting, the importance of thoughtful criticism, how to ask and answer questions about one's own writing and that of others, and the need for students to actively communicate with each other about their writing.

The Elements of Fiction   Chapters 3 through 9 explain the basic concepts of character, plot, point of view, fictional time and verb tense, setting, dialogue, subtext, and theme. These chapters may be read in any order, and complement the writing process chapters by introducing a catalogue of tools and materials—the elements from which students will make their stories. Examples from professional or student fiction from this book's anthology (Part Four) illustrate each concept.

The Stories: An Anthology of Professional and Student Fiction   The anthology features both contemporary and classic stories. To provide clear examples of the elements of fiction, I've included stories that I, like many other teachers, find myself citing often in class. Accompanying each story are a brief introduction of the author and several questions to help students identify some of the story's effects and how the writer has achieved them.

All of the short works quoted from in this book appear in full in its anthology. Twelve of these narratives—eight by professional writers and four by students—are excerpted extensively in Chapters 3 through 9. Each of these core stories (and one personal essay) is asterisked in the table of contents. I have occasionally excerpted novels as well; these are not included in the anthology but are listed at the ends of chapters.

Flexible Organization

The teaching of writing varies according to the teacher, the students, and the moment. Each semester or term is different, so I've tried to offer an abundance of ideas—exercises, questions, alternative approaches—in order to encourage experimentation and to make this book adaptable to a variety of classrooms. *Where the Stories Come From* offers points of departure—assignments, readings, and techniques—that can be adapted as an overall approach or piece by piece, to complement and enhance other teaching methods and to suit individual classrooms.

The structure of this book, like its ideas, is designed to be flexible. Teachers can assign the chapters in a number of ways:

- Assigning chapters on the writing process early in the term and following with elements chapters.
- Assigning writing process chapters one by one as students pass through the phases of generating ideas, drafting, revising, and working with readers.
- Interspersing writing process chapters with elements chapters.
- Assigning elements chapters early in the term in order to help establish a common starting point in academically diverse classrooms.
- Using chapters as resources or supplements by moving back and forth between them.
- Assigning elements chapters to the group as a whole, suggesting them for individual writers with particular interests or challenges, or referring to them as needed by teachers or by writers working independently. These chapters can also provide jumping-off points for lectures or class discussions.

A Process-Oriented Approach

Along with its overview of the writing process and the elements of fiction, *Where the Stories Come From* offers pedagogical ideas that may be new to some classrooms though familiar to others. The techniques described in this section needn't necessarily replace workshop methods that teachers and students are already using successfully; rather, they may supplement effective approaches and provide alternatives where teachers or students are looking for new ideas.

Process Orientation   A writing workshop may be a place where standards are defined and upheld, where stories succeed or fall short. Or it may be a place where writers discover, explore, and respond to the possibilities in each other's work, applying critical standards as the work develops. This book describes "process-oriented" workshops. The book assumes a story emerging through at least two drafts—and a writer developing in the course of that process. Thus, it describes writing problems not as flaws in a manuscript but as characteristics of a work, and a writer, in progress.

It's not uncommon during first-draft workshops to hear comments such as "There's no beginning, middle, and end"; "I can't tell what the central conflict is"; or "What is driving that character?" At such moments, it's essential to a process-oriented approach for everyone involved to remember that this is how people work—doing one thing at a time—and that not everyone does the same thing first. It's a self-evident concept, but it can completely change the tone of a workshop from one of exasperation to one of understanding, and it places a high value on the uniqueness of each story and each writer.

The Importance of Revision   Many writing workshops require students to write a number of separate assignments per term. This approach enables writers to generate a lot of new material and to receive criticism that will help them further develop that work after the course has ended. Students also have an opportunity to respond critically to a large number of manuscripts, gaining experience as readers. Such a structure is useful as well when first drafts prove unpromising or when students wish to work on several short shorts rather than on one full-length story.

But as much as they need to learn how to write a first draft, students also need supervised instruction in the art of revision. So, rather than handing in a number of different stories, students in the process-oriented workshops this book describes submit two or three drafts of the same short story, focusing on each phase of the writing process. Encouraging students to work together in an ongoing way on carefully chosen single stories emphasizes the process, not merely the product. At the same time, it stimulates the class to discuss process-related topics as they come up. Although it takes some patience to read the same pieces again and again, seeing both story and writer progress far beyond the first-draft stage more than compensates. Most important, students express satisfaction and a sense of accomplishment at being able to complete or nearly complete a short story.

Learning Oneself   Emphasizing the writing process profoundly affects the individual writer and the group. Writers feel freer to experiment, knowing that they will submit more than one draft. As they try various approaches and discuss the results in class, they learn what works for them—and for others—at each stage of the writing process. Experimentation opens up new possibilities and leads to respect for and interest in other writers' methods. Revisiting the same stories clarifies these individual methods, so that criticism becomes more and more responsive to the writer and the story. Since everyone is similarly "in progress," a kind of leveling takes places, and, with encouragement, students in such workshops learn to look curiously for potential and to suggest possibilities—to approach critiquing more as coaches than as judges.

The Student-Centered Workshop

The workshopping style this book describes is called "student-centered" not because other approaches don't have students' best interests at heart but simply because the students in this workshop situation take a comparatively active role in the discussion of their own stories. As in most college writing workshops, students read and discuss one another's fiction, gaining experience as writers and as critics. They use a variety of methods, including student critiques, individual conferences, written or spoken questions by the writer or by others, and questioning authors, as well as exercises, reading assignments, discussion of technical or theoretical issues, and adopting new approaches as needs arise. The biggest difference between the workshops this book describes and those used in many other settings is the fact that in these, students lead the discussion of their own work.

Breaking the Silent Author Rule: Giving Student Writers a Voice   Most student-centered workshops don't observe the traditional "silent author" rule, under which discussion of student stories is led by the teacher, who may question the group or raise issues of general interest, while the writer of the story remains silent. After leading the students in a discussion, the teacher in such "silent author" workshops may offer a summary and critique of the story, defining and commenting on the fundamental concepts that have arisen during the workshop, correcting misapprehensions, and suggesting ideas for improvement. In most cases, the writer listens and does not comment; some workshops allow a brief response.

Writers in such workshops quickly learn that their work has to stand on its own. Silencing the writer compensates for the human tendency to react to criticism with defensive speeches, and so it allows readers to respond candidly. It promotes order in the classroom, and it saves time. It enables writers to take careful notes on the discussion, registering points of interest and disagreement for later reference. And it offers them a taste of the undiluted criticism and praise they can expect later in their careers. For these reasons, even those who choose not to use it exclusively do sometimes combine it with other approaches.

Granting all the advantages of the silent author method, there are also good reasons for including the author in the discussion, at least part of the time. Writers need to learn the difficult skill of listening to criticism *and* the equally difficult skill of engaging others responsibly, creatively, and constructively in dialogue about their work. Workshops are more efficient when writers are, at some point, allowed to clarify issues that affect the quality of the criticism: missing or obsolete passages or confusing transitions, as well as larger issues unique to each story. When the writer is not effaced, readers tend to feel accountable to the person herself rather than merely to the task of criticism, and they talk to the writer about the story rather than to others about the story, as the writer watches. With competent leadership from the instructor and genuine effort from students, this attentive two-way communication results in deeper understanding between writer and readers.

Toward these ends, the writer leads the discussion of her own work, using questions she's prepared for the class and following up when necessary. The instructor sets the ground rules and can, in conference or in writing, help form and revise the writer's questions. When necessary, the instructor questions the writer during the workshop in order to bring out her concerns; explains and models the skills of restating readers' remarks and asking follow-up questions; and focuses the discussion, redirecting if necessary and assisting with stage fright.

Once each student has experienced leading a workshop, the ice is usually broken, and student writers gain a lot of confidence as they workshop their second and third drafts. Gradually, they learn to generate and maintain the discussion while the teacher fades somewhat into the background, following closely but quietly, intervening only as necessary. The eventual goal is for students to independently and productively engage readers in useful discussion of their work.

Student-Centered Criticism   Student-centered workshops require responsible criticism. Critics must articulate strengths and problems in a manuscript; they must also learn the skill of communicating these insights in ways the writer can use—and whether they have done so becomes clear immediately, as the writer responds to the criticism. In such a setting, student readers are less likely to slip into using the workshop to display their critical acumen or to vent personal feelings in the guise of criticism. Open communication encourages readers to take the writer's creative process into account as they offer suggestions about the manuscript. As students discover how much they don't know, they also learn what they're already doing well, and how to build on these strengths and to recognize when they're on the right track.

The Benefits of Student-Centered Workshops   Leading their own workshops gives students experience of several kinds. First, they learn to speak articulately about their work and to engage readers in a dialogue. Second, they discover how to draw a good reading out of their classmates, using careful questioning to move the discussion beyond niceties and into an exploration of the topics that concern them. Third, when they are allowed to speak and guided appropriately, students quickly learn from experience that defensiveness only uses up their time and prevents them from getting answers to their questions. Finally, students must take responsibility for identifying areas of interest and concern in their own work, which, along with feedback from the class, teaches them to become more effectively self-critical. Having been doubly on the spot as writer and discussion leader, most are moved by empathy to support other students' work with honest and constructive critiques. Sharing experience at both ends of the workshop process bonds the class. When conducted with care and thought, such a workshop becomes a generous invitation to come along on the creative journey.

Preparing Your Students for a Process-Oriented, Student-Centered Workshop
A few extra steps at the beginning of the semester may help to prepare each student to come up with an idea for a story that she will be able to sustain through several drafts, and to generate the questions and the confidence to lead her own workshop. I've found the approaches below helpful in my classes:

- Asking students to submit and revise several ideas for a story.
- Meeting with each student to discuss the final story idea.
- Asking students to keep track of questions or concerns that occur to them as they work on their stories.
- In conference or through written assignments, helping them to refine these questions in order to ask classmates during their workshops.
- Assigning exercises that allow students to vent anxiety and express hope about their workshops. (See the Workshop Fantasy exercises on p. 225 for some examples.)

Key Pedagogical Features

Where the Stories Come From includes a variety of exercises and activities, study questions, and Idea Boxes. All of these, described below, are designed to apply theory, integrating ideas with the process of writing.

As You Write, located at the ends of Chapters 1–9, offers troubleshooting ideas, alternative techniques and approaches for writers to try out as they work, and questions and activities designed to challenge simple definitions and explanations. It also provides checklists of specific suggestions to help apply chapter material to student stories in progress. Checklists demonstrate such topics as the elements of plot and how to polish your first draft, ask an effective question, critique honestly and sensitively, and evaluate criticism.

Exploration and Discovery, located at the ends of Chapters 1–11, provides several types of pedagogical tools:

- **Ask Yourself** suggests questions for self-evaluation, guiding writers as they apply chapter material to their own story in progress.
- **Ask Readers** offers questions that students or teachers can pose to stimulate group discussion of chapter topics as they apply to students' stories.
- **Wordplay** offers writing exercises and activities based on each chapter's content. Along with the rest of the Exploration and Discovery material, the Wordplay activities become more systematic and goal-oriented as the book progresses. Similar and compatible exercises may be found in The Longman Journal for Creative Writing accompanying this text.
- **Suggested Reading** lists books, stories, and other readings referred to in each chapter, many of which are included in the anthology. Teachers may wish to draw upon these lists for reading assignments to supplement chapter material.

A Self-Challenging Glossary

- **Definitions**, located at the beginning of the book (see gray-tabbed pages), is a mini-glossary, including very simple definitions of terms most often used in beginning creative writing classrooms. Agreeing on these basic definitions at the outset builds confidence that results in more active class discussion.

- **Redefinition**, (see gray-tabbed pages at the end of the book) provides several questions based on each term in **Definitions**. Teachers and students can use these follow-up questions to challenge and expand simple definitions as students' understanding grows over time.

Idea Boxes   These boxed inserts appear throughout the book, containing students' questions about writing along with answers by professional writers and teachers and a number of student writers as well. Contributing writers and teachers include Kim Addonizio, Leslie Epstein, Joseph Hurka, Michael McFee, Bruce Jorgensen, Leslie Lawrence, Jayne Anne Phillips, Lawrence Raab, Jonathan Strong, Patricia Traxler, Norman Rush, and Darrell Spencer.

Appendix: Surviving on Your Own   This appendix contains suggestions for writers working outside a formal workshop. It encourages students to continue writing after college, and it addresses the need for solitude and creative community, including overcoming writer's guilt, and ideas about how to carve out the time and space to write. The appendix also provides a list of issues to consider when forming a writers' group, including practical concerns such as the size and structure of the group as well as subtler issues that affect the quality of group dynamics.

Thanks

My former teacher, Bruce Jorgensen, provided generous and extensive help and support as I developed the readings and commentary in this book. Many people at Longman Publishers supported the project along the way; special thanks to Joe Terry and to acquisitions editors Liza Rudneva and Erika Berg; development editor Ruth Franklin, who smoothed and helped to organize the book and its author during the year of its writing, and to editor Seth Pase, whose kind perseverence in the final hours helped to bring it forth. Charles, Mie, and Leif Inouye sacrificed patiently, tolerating my writing compulsions and occasional need to lie on the floor. I received support from The Ragdale Foundation, The MacDowell Colony for the Arts, and The Critical Thinking Program at Tufts University. Invaluable suggestions came from reviewers Mary Baron, Matthew Benedict, William Boggs, Willard Cook, Greg Garrett, Michael Heffernan, Bruce Jorgensen, Beth Lordan, Nancy McLelland, Elizabeth C. Mitchell, Robert S. Nelson, Mary O'Conner, Karen Rile, Heather Sellers, Jade Quang Hunyh, Connie Wasem, and Anne Williams, and student reviewers Lauren Puccio, James Leon Suffern, Jeannine Thibodeau, and Kelly Zavotka. Paul Fisher and Jeffrey Friedman helped me think through a number of critical issues. The questions in the Idea Boxes throughout each chapter were contributed by Eric Brown, Lizzie Foley, Caitlin McCarthy, Bill Madden, Darragh Murphy, Christopher Pickens, Andrea Potter, Nicole Ruggiery and Patrick Sullivan, all students in my classes at Grub Street Writers, a private school in the Boston area. Responses by Leslie Epstein, director of Boston University's Creative Writing Program, were drawn from an unpublished essay called "Tips," written for his students and used here by permission.

Thanks to my own creative writing teachers, especially Elouise Bell, Leslie Epstein, Bruce Jorgensen, Arthur Henry King, Dennis Packard, Jayne Anne Phillips, and Douglas Thayer. Special thanks to all of my teaching assistants at Emerson College, who contributed and improved many of the ideas in this text: Chris Balzano, Jacobo Bergareche, Andrew Bodenrader, Beth Brewer, Michael Graves, Katy Garfield, Adam Golaski, Kate Milliken, Opus Moreschi, Jeff Paris, Seth Pase, Lisa Phillips, Graham Stevenson, James Suffern, Jeannine Thibodeau, LoraLee Tucker, and Kelly Zavotka.

Sibyl Johnston
sibyl@erols.com

Where the Stories Come From

Beginning to Write Fiction

To the Student

This book is about the process of writing. It won't tell you exactly "how to" write a short story, because in this kind of work, there isn't really a "how to." Instead, this book will explain and illustrate what a good story is. It will offer suggestions and exercises designed to help you develop a basic understanding, skills, and techniques, and to stimulate ideas as you write. And it will expose you to the work of accomplished professional and student writers.

Most importantly, it will help you to discover and develop your own methods and your own answers to some fundamental questions: Where does creativity come from, and how can you develop it? Is writing merely a matter of getting out of the way of one's own inspiration? Or is a more workmanlike view appropriate—approaching this task like any other and just getting down to it? Is there a way of *combining* discipline and inspiration?

The first and last chapters—1, 2, 10, and 11—will guide you through the steps of writing a short story: playing with words (activities to help you warm up and to stimulate ideas), writing a first draft, revising that draft, and working with readers to improve your story.

Chapters 3 through 9 (Part Two, The Elements of Fiction) discuss in detail specific aspects of fiction: character, plot, point of view, verbs and narrative structure, dialogue, subtext, and theme. Each chapter begins by defining a basic concept, which is illustrated with quotations from the The Stories: An Anthology of Professional and Student Fiction (pp. 231–474). Each chapter concludes with ideas to help you apply these concepts to your own stories: As You Write sections offer suggestions to keep in mind; Exploration and Discovery sections provide questions to help you evaluate your work; and Wordplay sections suggest activities and ideas to help you develop your story. (You'll find similiar ideas and exercises in The Longman Journal for Creative Writing accompanying this text.)

Try out the ideas in this book. Use them as starting points, and over time you'll discover what kind of fiction you like, and what, in your own mind, constitutes a good story. As you experiment, you will learn what works for you, and how to adapt and combine exercises, techniques, and approaches to suit your needs and what you are writing at the moment.

The best thing you can do for yourself before you start Chapter 1 is to read the short list of simple definitions that begins on the next page. I've used these terms often throughout the book, and understanding them from the beginning will make your reading much easier.

Finally, I'm interested in your responses to the book. Please feel free to use the Web address on page xxiii to let me know your reactions and ideas. In the best cases, teaching and learning is shared. Your opinions matter a great deal to me and will influence future editions of this book.

Definitions

These very simple definitions will give you a working understanding of terms writing teachers often use, answering some basic questions so you can get started. And they'll deepen your knowledge by raising questions as well. Read through them, but don't stop there. Your understanding of these concepts should and will grow over time. Now or later, turn to **Redefinition** (p. 475), and you'll find questions designed to challenge and deepen each of these definitions.

Abstract description: Description that does not involve the senses but instead relies upon an interpretation or judgment. For example, "The honey was good" is abstract. "The honey was Greek" is concrete. We can all agree on "Greek," but "good" depends on the narrator's interpretation. See also **Concrete description,** below.

Anecdote: A brief retelling of a single incident. Anecdotes lack the formal plot structure of short stories and novels.

Attribution: See **Tags.**

Author: The person who wrote the story. *Not* the same as the narrator, unless the story is nonfiction.

Character: The nature of the story's main actors.

Characters: The people or other main actors in a story.

Characterization: The way a writer conveys characters' personalities and other attributes.

Cliché: An overfamiliar phrase, concept, or image that has, as George Orwell expressed it, "lost force." For instance, the beautiful heroine and the dashing hero are clichés.

Climax: See **Narrative arc.**

Concrete description: Description using one or more of the five senses: sight, hearing, smell, taste, or touch. See also **Abstract description,** above.

Dialogue: Characters' speech. **Direct discourse** refers to speech enclosed within quotation marks; **indirect discourse** refers to summarized or unquoted speech.

Direct discourse: See **Dialogue.**

Events: Incidents that occur in a story.

Exposition: See **Narrative arc.**

Falling action: See **Narrative arc.**

Fiction: A made-up story written according to artistic conventions.

Fictional present: The time frame in which the story's main action takes place. Often called the *novelistic present.*

First person: See **Point of view.**

Foreshadowing: Hints, early in a story, about its eventual outcome. See Flannery O'Connor's "A Good Man Is Hard To Find" (p. 362) for excellent examples of fore-shadowing.

Frame story: A story in which the writer begins at a point late in the narrative arc (see **Narrative arc,** below), or even outside it entirely, and then flashes back to earlier events, building up to and often past those recounted in the first scene. Thus, external events or those that occur later "frame" the rest of the story.

Image: A vivid sensory detail.

Indirect discourse: See **Dialogue.**

Melodrama: A story in which plot predominates over character, and characters are somewhat flat or "stock."

Memoir: An autobiographical work of prose, usually novel-length and often similar to a novel in form.

Narration: What the narrator tells the reader directly, as opposed to what the characters convey through speech and action.

Narrative: A telling of events.

Narrative arc: A simplified way of describing a story's shape in terms of an arc, within which the highest point is the story's *climax*, at which point the main character changes significantly. The arc's upward slope includes *exposition* (background information) and *rising action* (the events that lead up to the climax); its downward slope, after the climax, comprises *falling action* or denouement.

Narrative bridge: Narration used to create a transition between two scenes.

Narrative tension: The momentum that impels the reader into and through the story.

Narrative voice: The personality, tone, or sensibility conveyed by a story's language. See **Voice.**

Narrator: The person or voice that tells the story.

Nonfiction: A telling of real events; prose that isn't fictional.

Novel: A long, fictional work of prose. Contemporary novels generally—but not always—fall between 150 and 500 pages in length, with many at or around 300 to 350 pages.

Novelistic present: See **Fictional present.**

Novella: A short novel, usually around ninety pages. Examples of the novella include Thomas Mann's *Death in Venice* and Andre Dubus's *Voices from the Moon.*

Plot: The pattern of a story's action; what happens; events. These incidents combine with character and other fictional elements to create narrative tension.

Point of view: The perspective from which the story is told. The most obvious examples are the "I" narrator, called *first person*; the usually anonymous narrator describing "he" or "she" (*third person*); or the usually anonymous narrator describing "you" (*second person*).

Prose: Straightforward, direct writing that is not controlled by meter or rhyme as poetry is. Novels and short stories are written in prose.

Rising action: See **Narrative arc.**

Scene: A significant part of a story, specifically located in time and place, and in which characters interact.

Second person: See **Point of view.**

Sentimentality: In writing, an appeal to the emotions by using trite or overfamiliar devices; relying on familiar conventions to evoke feeling rather than achieving it through fresh, accurate writing.

Setting: The environment in which the story takes place.

Short short: A very short work of fictional prose, usually 1500 words or less.

Short story: A relatively short work of fictional prose, usually between 1500 and 20,000 words.

Story: A telling of a sequence of events resulting in a change in the main character.

Subtext: Emotional content that is unsaid but present in a story; unspoken feelings, particularly when the characters are talking to or about each other.

Tags (also called *attribution*):   The words with which the author tells the reader who is speaking when. Example: "he said" or "she said." Gestures or description may function indirectly as tags.

Theme: The main idea or ideas in a story, usually conveyed indirectly.

Third person: See **Point of view.**

Voice: The personality, tone, and sensibility conveyed by a story's language. See **Narrative voice.**

Growing the Story

There are many kinds of writing. Some are carefully polished and intended for publication; others are private, even secret. You're probably reading this book in order to learn the public kind of writing—but the truth is, you won't get there without a secret writing life. Part One explores the writing you do before you actually write a story (Chapter 1), and guides you through the early stages of drafting (Chapter 2). The later stages of writing—revision and working with readers—are discussed in Chapters 10 and 11.

Playing with Words

One should never, at least as a beginner, start off a piece of writing by saying "I am going to write a poem." The magnitude of the task, and the arrogance of attempting it, get in the way of easy thought and easy associational flow. One should simply say "I am playing with words" or "I am doodling in words" or "I wonder what happens if I start off by saying. . . ."

—Robin Skelton

The poet Robin Skelton has referred to the earliest stages of writing as "building the word hoard." This kind of building requires inspiration—a word that suggests an element of revelation. Socrates, Goethe, Byron, Wordsworth, Yeats, and many others have described trance states and automatic writing as a primary source for and expression of their creativity. Some have believed they have been temporarily possessed by the Muse or by other disembodied spirits while in such states; others see these activities more simply and matter-of-factly as limbering-up exercises.

This first chapter is designed to offer you an abundance of ways to begin—the kind of writing that you do before you've committed yourself to a specific project. This sort of writing is often called "pre-writing" or "exercises." Like Robin Skelton, I'd rather call it "playing with words." You'll find here four kinds of playing with words:

Freewriting

Moons and Eggplants: Verbal Still-Lifes

Writing Your Past

Dreamcatching

Instead of stipulating the structure, length, or content of an assigned story, each of these four sections describes an approach to creating or discovering basic material: sensory details, conflicts, associations, memories. These approaches are creative challenges that will help to prepare you for more such discoveries. After each approach, you'll find a number of activities in a section called Wordplay. There are more such activities at the end of this chapter, and you'll also find similar Wordplay sections at the ends of the other chapters in this book.

The writing process is discussed further in Chapter 2, Drafting: Six Ways of Beginning a Story (p. 32), which will guide you into the first steps of actually writing a **story**—a telling of events that result in an important change in an individual. Chapter 10, Revising: Linear and Circular Methods (p. 184); and Chapter 11,

Working with Readers (p. 208) describe the later phases of writing. Chapters 2, 10, and 11 present progressively more linear and systematic approaches designed to encourage the reason, reflection, and organization that usually occurs later on, once you've discovered the story's basic material. But in the beginning there are words, and they're not organized. They are the elements from which you will make your fictional worlds.

Freewriting

Freewriting is a contemporary way of building the word hoard. This basic, useful, and popular form of playing with words is usually presented these days as a warm-up—a practical tool rather than the mystical experience described by Byron, Yeats, and others. Writers of **fiction** (made-up stories written according to artistic conventions) employ freewriting at various points during the writing process. You can use it to prepare for writing, to develop ideas, to work through blocks or problems you encounter as you write, to build **characters** (the people or other main actors in your story) or **setting** (the environment in which the story takes place), to keep a story going, to keep your mind limber and your thinking fluid, or to catch ideas when they're coming too fast to put down in a more structured fashion.

Most writing teachers have their own recipes for freewriting, but the process tends to be similar, emphasizing not a methodical striving toward polished, finished fiction but an opening up—free association, an uncritical gathering of impressions and ideas that can (and must) be sorted out later. Most published descriptions of freewriting suggest putting your pen to paper or fingers to keyboard and writing everything that passes through your mind, without stopping to edit, evaluate, or deliberately develop ideas.

To begin freewriting, try following these "nonrules":

- Find a time and place in which you won't be interrupted. The minutes just before sleep are most productive for a lot of people. As in hypnosis, the drowsy mind tends to be more fluid and closer to spontaneous and associative **images** or sensory details. For similar reasons, some prefer freewriting early in the morning.
- Once you're settled, sit for a few minutes in silence to clear your mind. Then write whatever comes into it, as fast as you can and for a predetermined amount of time.
- If you don't like timing yourself, try setting a page limit instead.
- For the time being, forget spelling, grammar, punctuation, and logical development.
- Don't organize your thoughts into sentences or paragraphs, and don't stop writing until the time is up or the page limit reached. Write whatever you think of. Don't censor yourself. Write with no one else in mind.
- When you're finished, put your freewriting away without re-reading it.
- Do the exercise daily for at least two weeks.

- Increase the time you spend freewriting by five minutes per day, starting at five and working up to twenty minutes. Especially at first, freewriting is a highly disciplined exercise, and twenty minutes will probably be enough for most writers.

- Keep your freewrites together in a notebook or file, and don't look back at them until you've been freewriting for a couple of weeks. Then read through what you've written. Underline images, phrases, ideas that stand out and make you want to write. Keep these in a list for a while, and refer back to it now and then as you work. Wait for things to catch hold.

Shown below is an actual freewrite by one of my former students and teaching assistants, Mary Austin Speaker.

Breaking the Rules

When you first begin freewriting, you may find it difficult to let yourself think in fragments—to catch and record thoughts without processing or developing them into coherent statements or arguments. It's the opposite of what you've probably been taught to do in school, and it involves breaking some taboos. A big one is the taboo against incomplete sentences. When freewriting, shards and scraps and fragments of language are just fine—there's no need to organize them into sentences; in fact, doing so would defeat your purpose.

This doesn't mean that you should simply refrain from capitalizing and leave off the periods. What really makes a sentence is a subject and a verb. That logic, not merely the punctuation, is what you need to discard for the moment. Temporarily dispensing with the step-by-step reasoning that orders formal language will give you practice making intuitive leaps, and once you've mastered these, your thinking will become quicker and more fluid. When you freewrite, you're not writing for anyone but yourself. Instead of clear, explanatory sentences, go for images, phrases, words that fly through your head so fast that you'll miss them if you're not looking. Write quickly and include only what actually passes through your mind—not the explanations that others would need to make it intelligible.

Q: How do you kill (temporarily) the editor in the brain?

A: Here's what I suggest and what I do: Give your inner editor/critic a name. (Mine is Battle Ax.) When you sense her (or him) making you feel self-conscious and insecure, stop and do a freewrite. Let her vent all she wants. Finish your freewrite by telling her to go back where she came from. And you go back to work.

—*Nancy McLelland,
poet and teacher*

Writing Lists   Temporarily giving up sentences may be a lot harder than you expected. Although it may sound contradictory, you'll probably need to practice and refine your freewriting technique a little in the beginning. Check over your first couple of freewrites and underline the subject-verb combinations. If you find yourself sneaking in implied subjects ("Went to convenience store, bought Twinkies"), it may be that writing across the page is making it hard to escape the subject-verb organization of sentences. Vertically *listing* impressions can help to loosen these linear thought processes. If I were going to describe in sentences what's in front of me as I write this paragraph, I might come up with something like this:

> My laptop sits on two large books, which raise it so my neck doesn't get stiff. Behind it is my CD player, now playing Chopin; a lamp; a sewing box made by my uncle and now filled with paper, pens, Post-Its, and whatever I don't want on my table; my printer and my CD's; and behind them, two windows with oak trees outside.

On the other hand, if I were freewriting in list form, the description might read like this:

> Blue screen
>
> Art books
>
> Neck ouch
>
> Incandescent bulb
>
> Blue glaze
>
> Tiny bull
>
> Shaker Uncle Ron
>
> Bach Clapton Smith Parsons Waits Satie

Wavery glass

Ice glittering

No one else could make much sense of that, but I don't need them to.

Your freewrites may not be vertically arranged on the page, but you can probably find the lists in them if you look. Study a freewrite in which you've underlined
the essential images and ideas. These should be mostly nouns, verbs, and modifiers, unorganized. Read them aloud. Next time, try to write *only* essential nouns,
verbs, and modifiers. If that approach feels too controlled or if you still find yourself resorting to the conventional logic of sentences, try simply turning your ruled
paper sideways so the lines run vertically. Then ignore them completely, and polka-
dot the page with random words. That way, even if you do write sentences, you'll
be able to read them in other ways. Or, cut scraps of paper and write your impressions on them. To keep your organization loose for the time being, store them in an
envelope rather than a notebook.

When Freewriting Becomes Writing   After freewriting daily for a little while, you
may find yourself moving spontaneously into a **scene,** or segment of a story, within
a few minutes of beginning to write. Resist this impulse until you can't any longer.
Take some time to explore before committing yourself. Let the creative tension build
so that when you do write the scene, you'll have lots of energy behind it. If you
don't give yourself this time, you'll miss the full benefit of freewriting. Eventually,
the process may lead naturally into the writing of scenes or stories, but be careful
not to rush that transformation. Let your creative energy incubate for a while.

Like practically everything about writing, freewriting can be approached
merely as the means to an end or as a process useful in itself. Writers do come up
with ideas and details for stories as they freewrite, but often the practice itself is
more valuable than anything. Rather than always thinking about what words
or phrases or lines or ideas you can transplant from your freewrites into whatever else you are writing, consider the act itself and how it opens up your thinking—how it feels. Let go.

Breaking the Nonrules: Structured Freewrites   Some writers find the "nonrules rules" for freewriting too restrictive. Be sure to try them out for a couple of
weeks, because it may take that long to get used to the process. But if, after a reasonable trial period, this approach isn't working for you, try the slightly more
structured technique of listing ideas. Make some headings and organize your
thoughts into lists of phrases or sentences. This will still allow spontaneity without forcing you to completely drop all structure—an objective that is sometimes
impossible to accomplish in the beginning. Or, try instead to write out all of your
thoughts about what you're working on at the moment. Write them in the most
linear, rational, step-by-step, and orderly fashion possible. Don't allow yourself to
skip anything. If you do this for long enough, an unstructured approach may start
to feel more attractive.

The main thing to remember about freewriting is the *free* part. Don't edit yourself. Don't avoid scary or emotional topics—but don't force yourself to linger on

any one thing. The point is to follow what is in your mind, not to control it. Like drawings in the margins, this writing is for you, and you only. Use your own personal shorthand any way you like.

Stop making sense. If it makes sense, it's not freewriting.

Wordplay

Below are some variations on the theme of freewriting. Try out these ideas and activities to discover the ways in which freewriting can help as you prepare to write, and also once you've begun a story.

Freewriting into a Scene   After you've practiced freewriting daily for a couple of weeks, try a more flexible version of it. Freewrite for five minutes each day, and relax out of the rules. Allow yourself to write some complete sentences and to put some thoughts together. If scenes begin to form, follow them for as long as they naturally develop (no further). To avoid losing the fluidity, don't edit as you go. Just keep writing—you can put the sentences in order later.

Focused Freewrites   To generate material for a story, try freewriting "on" a character, setting, scene, physical detail, conflict, or anything else that you would like to develop. Write what you see in your mind. Try to stay fluid but keep returning to your focal point, and bounce associations off of it. This approach is a half-step closer to drafting, and can help you to discover material that can then be organized and refined to create or fill out a story.

Freewriting Through a Block   You can use freewriting as a way through writer's block, a problem so common that it's a household word. Blocked writers are often advised simply to behave as though they weren't blocked, and to force themselves to work no matter what. Freewriting can be an excellent alternative for those of us who resist this approach. Sometimes the answer really is to stop trying so hard. Experiment with severely limiting the time you spend writing—allow yourself only five minutes of writing per day, and add to that five minutes of freewriting. Even if more ideas come to you, stick to this schedule, very gradually increasing the time. This should allow your ideas to catch up to your ambition.

Aside from relaxing structural expectations, the biggest problem you may face with freewriting is going blank. This may be your mind stammering, tongue-tied at the sudden freedom. It may be fear of unlimited expectations or of what may surface through this exercise. Be patient. Freewriting unnerves certain parts of the mind, and it won't do any good to berate yourself about that—it's a normal, though frustrating, part of the process. Experiencing and working through it is a big part of how freewriting can help you. Some people suggest writing "I'm blocked" or "nothing" over and over until the block passes. A more positive approach (suggested to me by Seth Pase, a former student and teaching assistant) is to rhyme the last word you wrote until something new comes to mind. Other methods include starting with an object in the room or a bodily sensation, drawing a picture, or writing a favorite word or phrase over and over until your mind relaxes enough to move on.

The Flaming Freewrite   Do you ever find yourself freewriting for an audience? Are you tempted to show off your best freewriting moments? To the extent that you're writing to display, you won't be writing to discover. The purpose of freewriting is to find, develop, and explore your voice and your perceptions. If you find it difficult to relax, try this: for a specified period of time, burn all of your freewrites in a fireplace or other safe location as soon as they're written.

Moons and Eggplants: Verbal Still-Lifes

Another form of word-playing is to focus on describing objects, much as a visual artist might paint or draw a still-life. Contemporary writers tend to emphasize **concrete description**—detail that is mentally seen, heard, smelled, touched or tasted—rather than **abstract description,** which relies upon interpretation or judgment rather than sensory observation. Instead of writing, "It was a nice day," writers try to let readers see the colors of the sky, hear the movements of the trees, and feel the air on their skin. This is because the language of the body is more or less universal. Our opinions, politics, and emotional reactions may vary a lot, but to some degree we all can relate to the green of a parrot, the smell of leaves in the rain or of ginger or rotten meat, the taste of vanilla, warmth or wetness or breath on the skin. Writers create vivid worlds using elements familiar to all of us.

Concrete and Abstract Description

It's not that concrete writing is good and abstract writing is bad. Each has its uses. But without realizing it, beginning writers tend to ask too much from readers, expecting others to accept without question stock descriptions or subjective opinions. This often has exactly the opposite effect, arousing skepticism. Writers must learn how to earn the responses they want.

Most of the time it's less effective to tell readers what's going on than to show them. A writing teacher once told me, "Readers don't care what *you* see—they want to see it themselves." This isn't always true, of course—some people read solely for entertainment and don't welcome challenges to their imagination. The quality of detail is one factor that divides literary fiction from most fiction whose primary purpose is to entertain.

Q: How can I write better description?

A: I can offer two suggestions. First, sketch, in words, often. By sketching, I mean actually look at an object, a person or a setting and write down what it looks like. Don't try to imagine why it looks like that or what the story is behind it, just write a snapshot of it. It's not easy. But if you do it a lot, it will become natural. And second, read poetry. I'm not suggesting this because poetry is always beautiful—that's a silly, romantic misconception—but because poetry is precise in a way that prose should be, but often isn't. By virtue of being precise, you will also be concise and effective.

—Adam Golaski,
editor, New Genre Magazine

This all sounds clear and simple in theory. In practice, it can be more complex. For now, keep in mind that concrete description appeals directly to the physical senses: sight, sound, smell, taste, and touch. Abstract description involves an intellectual process, a judgment. It is an abstract description to say, "The peach is luscious." A more concrete description takes you there—it lets you experience the lusciousness. What does the peach's skin feel like on your lips and tongue and fingers? What does it smell like? What is the sound, the feeling, as your teeth break through it? What color, exactly, is the juice? How does your tongue feel? Show me, take me there, and let me arrive at my own conclusions about the peach.

In this passage from her essay "A Thousand Buddhas" (pp. 329–334), Brenda Miller grounds intense emotion in gestures and physical sensation. Miller is describing a visit from a former lover:

What did my body feel when I placed my hands on Jon's back? My palms curved instinctively to the crook of his shoulders; my own shoulders softened when I asked Jon to breathe, and I inhaled with him, stretching my lungs, and on the exhale my hands slid down his back, kneading the muscles on the downward slide, pulling up long the lats, crossing over his spine, and again and again, until he seemed to flatten and there was no distinction between the flesh of his back or the bones in his arms or the curve of his buttocks—no distinction, in fact, between his breath and mine.

Rather than stating emotion directly ("I massaged Jon and it turned out to be a really intense experience"), Miller describes the massage in language that accurately represents not only the actions involved, but also the rhythms and the sensations. When writers render physical detail as sensitively as Miller does, feeling arises spontaneously through the concrete description.

However carefully you may try to represent your subject accurately, it is important to allow for the sum of the parts to not exactly equal the whole; that is, readers may inform you that the overall effect of your description differs from what you intended: the character's wild gestures are funny rather than fearsome, or the empty white apartment feels bleak rather than chic. This isn't always bad news. Sometimes such a "mistake" illuminates new meanings. You may discover the value of not letting your left hand know what your right is doing—of, like the character Seymour Glass in J. D. Salinger's *Seymour: An Introduction*, not aiming so much. You may learn that meaning emerges and is found rather than being entirely intentional and created.

Rendering the Eggplant: Using Senses and Intellect

This exercise, designed for a group, allows writers to experience the difference between concrete and abstract description. The leader of the group should bring in an object, preferably something organic. I use an eggplant. Other possibilities might include a stone, a dead moth or bird, a twig, or any other inert object that is small enough to touch. Pass the object around. Each person should touch it, feel it, smell it, look at it. The leader then writes two headings on the board: <u>Concrete</u> and <u>Abstract</u>. Each person briefly describes the object. Together, the group decides where to place each description.

Below is a compilation of students' eggplant descriptions over several years. Notice that some of the abstract descriptions are just as vivid as the concrete ones—the difference is in the mental process evoked in the reader. Every semester when we do this exercise, the categories eventually break down and merge as we realize that some descriptions could be placed under either heading. This is particularly true of metaphors, which may appeal to the senses but which are by their nature abstract, requiring an intellectual comparison.

Concrete Descriptions

Cool on my skin

Bottom is a lighter purple, blends into a dark purple, almost black

Rotund

Dry-stemmed

Color is worn on one side

Reflection of room light on black skin

Rubbery

Thumps like a little bongo drum

Lacks a scent

Smells leafy

Mr. Potato Head

Spiked leaves and stem

Holds reflections

Hollow-sounding

Lighter than it looks

Abstract Descriptions

Tastes good cooked in garlic and oil

Deceptive

Solitary

Proud

Pensive

Wanting

Belly button on the bottom

Vulnerable body

Smells like a vacuum

It would work well with veggie baseball

Gerard Depardieu

An object in a still-life, but I can hold it

A blinding depth of purple

I had a boyfriend with skin that perfect

In India the ideal young woman knows one hundred ways to cook an eggplant. (This description inspired a story by its author.)

Describing the eggplant should encourage you to explore descriptive techniques and to become more aware of the level of abstraction in your writing. Although abstract descriptions often fail because they rely on private or too-familiar associations, always remember that the level of abstraction is an aesthetic or technical, not a moral issue. Before getting too rigid about "showing rather than telling," consider when abstract description may be the most appropriate choice.

Very often, the level of abstraction depends upon the pace of the **narrative** or recounting of events. Sometimes the writer needs to convey information without lingering in a paragraph of detailed description. On other occasions, abstract description may reflect the sensibility of the **narrator,** or storytelling voice. For instance, the judgment implied by a description—"Until last August my husband was a virtuous, clean man"—may tell readers more about the speaker than about the person described. Even when the narrator is not an actual character in the story, a few abstract descriptions can suggest something about the main character's thinking: "Henry slammed the door behind him. *The porch was filthy,* cigarette butts and empty cans everywhere. *The whole house was disgusting.*" Notice that the italicized abstract description is supported by some concrete details. How would the effect differ if it were not?

Wordplay

Image Translations   Circle the descriptive passages in a published story, or in a draft of a story you have written. Underline the concrete descriptions in one color and the abstract descriptions in another. Look more closely at the abstract descriptions. Can you think of ways to say the same things through the senses? For example,

- *Abstract*: Mr. Fisher was a very picky eater.
- *Concrete*: Mr. Fisher pushed his green beans to the far side of his plate, scraped the gravy from his meat loaf, and tested the temperature of the milk. Then, folding his reading glasses, he rose and left the table.

Now look at the story's concrete descriptions. Can you paraphrase them in abstract terms? Are you sure?

The Image Log   Keep a record of your senses—what you see, hear, smell, taste, touch. Try to write down at least a few details each day—things that catch your eye, ear, nose, mouth, or fingertips. Collect stuff that you just might use someday. Rereading your lists is a good way of warming up and generating ideas.

Moon Chronicles   This exercise was created by the late Professor Morse Hamilton of Tufts University. A former student of his, Jamie Crawford, has handed down the following version. I have included it here as a way of introducing the elements of change and movement into the act of description.

Keep a journal in which you write your observations about the moon each night. Try to do this for one complete cycle of the moon, and at approximately the same time each night. In your journal, describe the moon and write anything you think of while observing it. If you look for the moon but can't find it, write about that. Describe the clouds obscuring it or the sky lit only by stars in the moon's absence. Pay attention to the effect the moonlight has on objects around you and on yourself. Write about all of this.

Jamie explains, "One thing this exercise inspired me to do was to try to find other cyclical happenings that I could follow and write about—things that are stable yet changing and must therefore be approached differently each time." Some other possibilities, she suggests, might include the subway each morning, the sunrise or sunset, one's own face or body, a single tree, or any window view. The exercise offers a constantly changing view of a single object or phenomenon, reminding writers of the influences of time and circumstances upon the subject and on the writing process.

Writing Your Past

"Write from your experience" has become a writing class cliché. Why should writers choose topics from their own lives? As the previous section explains, concrete description is good material out of which to build a story. When you're familiar with your subjects, you have relatively easy access to the sensory details that will give life and credibility to your writing.

Beginning writers are sometimes tempted by unfamiliar or extreme subjects. While these can be written about well just like anything else, they present difficulties that writers don't always anticipate or know how to deal with. The problem with writing about life on the planet Neptune in the year 2690, or about highly unusual characters like hit men or Tibetan monks, is that no matter what or whom you choose to write about, you're going to have to come up with the sensory detail to create the picture. It's not enough to say, "The city of Atlantis was an eerie place, full of scary zombies." You are going to have to let readers see the place—what color it is, what its buildings are made of, what they feel like, what the light is like under the water, how one can survive there. And if you base those things on movies you've seen or on books you've read, your writing risks becoming clichéd or even plagiaristic. You will need to make your Atlantis different from all other Atlantises in books, movies, and television shows. The zombies, too.

Growing Your Own Details

When you base fiction on your own experience, you have details to draw from. You know what kinds of trees and birds inhabit the place where you grew up or lived, what the clouds looked like, how the people dressed and what they did from season to season. You have all the background information that is so important to narrative credibility, and that must be so meticulously researched if it's not yours to begin with. Writing about what you know gives your fiction another kind of credibility as well: you're already familiar with how certain people have responded to specific events. "What really happened" isn't always the best choice for fiction, but provided you observe and remember well, using it as a starting point can keep you from relying on television or movies and treating the subject in a clichéd way.

Gathering Information   If it's possible to go back to the places or people you're writing about, you can begin gathering information by taking notes. This is invaluable—you'll notice things you otherwise would have forgotten, and you'll focus on detail rather than generalizing. It's a good idea, especially at first, to write down everything you can think of. Later on, you can choose what belongs in each scene. The story, not what really happened, should guide those choices. When writers allow the story to spontaneously diverge from what it's based on, the way a dream goes in unexpected directions, then reading—and writing—becomes a mysterious, pleasurable, and artistically valuable experience. When writers cling protectively to exactly how the actual events occurred, the result is rarely a well-structured story.

A note about research: not all of it needs to go directly into your story. Usually the best way to use it is to assimilate it and let it sift through your mind and into your story. You don't need a lot of documentation in a story. You need the narrative credibility that comes from a few well-chosen details—what the characters would be likely to notice or contend with—slipped in naturally.

If note-taking isn't possible, freewriting or warm-ups like the ones presented throughout this chapter can evoke memories or ideas. You may be able to fill in blanks by talking with friends or relatives. At some point you'll probably find yourself merging events and mixing the past with the present. In any case, it's a good idea to mentally or physically revisit your story's sources often. This will give you layers of observation, resulting in textured, detailed fiction.

Borrowing Details

Writing from your experience doesn't always mean lifting things intact from life and placing them in your story. You can borrow incidents, people, details, traits, places, sounds, smells—any aspect of your experience that is useful. You don't have to use it all. Rather than going straight for the most obviously dramatic events, try looking for whatever matters to you. Think of your childhood or your adolescence. What is the first thing you picture? What's your earliest memory of a sound or smell? When you talk to others about your life, are there any particular stories that you find yourself telling often—events that have been central in some way, or are unusually interesting or entertaining? What places were important to you as a child? These questions may not turn up obvious, highly dramatic material. Instead, they will lead you to what you care about. Ultimately, that will make the most interesting story.

Distancing Yourself

The challenge of basing a story on real events lies in the fact that real events aren't usually as concise as stories, and that their personal impact may skew your sense of their artistic importance. In order to keep your ideas manageable, and to prevent highly emotional or unfamiliar material from distracting rather than enhancing a story, it is crucial to keep in mind what—who, that is—you are writing about, and to detach yourself enough so that you will be able to keep the other elements in place.

Avoiding Melodrama   Even when writing about your own life, you may sometimes find yourself attracted to the exotic: very dramatic events such as the death of a family member, the time you were mugged, your parents' divorce, your first boyfriend, your current boyfriend—especially your current boyfriend. These are all great subjects, but they're such intense experiences that it's quite difficult to step back and to break them down into the concrete details that make good fiction. Often they resist being reshaped into stories with a beginning, middle, and end and remain mere **anecdotes**—recounted single events with no particular artistic structure. This doesn't mean that you can't write about such things, but it does usually mean that one semester is not enough time to do a good job. (See Chapter 2 for more suggestions on choosing topics.)

Drawing Your Family Tree

Family trees are commonly used by genealogists to chart individuals' generational roots, and by therapists to identify family patterns and areas of conflict or agreement. They can offer a broader picture of a person's background, placing events or reactions in a larger context. When you are writing, a family tree can be a sort of crystal ball. As you consider the formations and patterns of your past, you may feel particularly drawn to certain events, people, times, or conflicts. Once you've identified these areas of interest, you can use freewriting, monologue (see the "voice story" described on p. 37), or other methods to focus on and develop them.

Family trees can form the basis for a useful group exercise, breaking the ice and giving participants practice recognizing areas of interest. You can use other people's reactions to your family tree to identify what's particularly intriguing about your experience, and as you think about theirs you'll be practicing the basic critical skills of identifying conflict and recognizing potential stories. Of course, group members should never be forced to share their personal history, so this exercise should be voluntary.

- Reproduced on page 19 is a family tree drawn by a former student, Adam Golaski. Using a blackboard or large sheet of paper, make your own family tree. Draw a symbol for yourself and then add your spouse or companion, children, brothers and sisters, parents, and grandparents on both sides. Generally, circles are used to represent women while squares represent men, but feel free to invent your own symbols as you wish. Deceased family members should be heartlessly crossed out, and people with lengthy or chronic illnesses surrounded by a dotted line. (Alcoholism, mental illness, disabilities, and developmental delays may be circled like chronic illnesses.) Although sharing histories can be good for the group and for individuals, it's worth reiterating that no one should feel obliged to discuss these or other personal matters in the classroom.

- Connect each family member with the others. Different types of lines represent different types of relationships. Generally, a straight line means a satisfying relationship; a jagged line signifies conflict; a dotted line means detachment; double lines signify intensity; and any of these can be mixed or combined or reinvented as you wish.

Family Tree by former student Adam Golaski

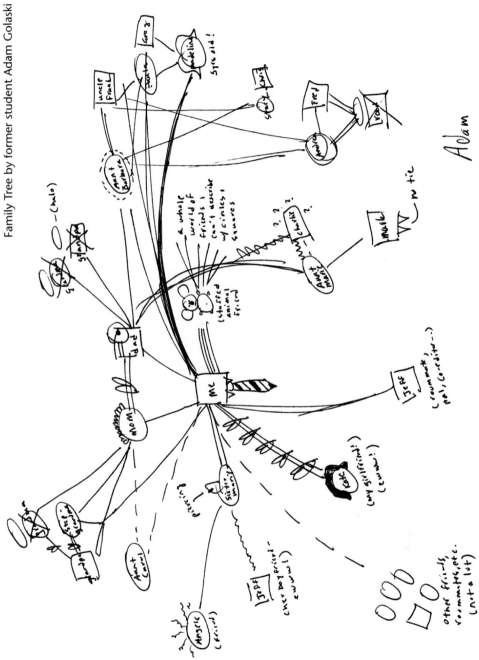

- Stand back from the family tree and ask others in the group some of the following questions:

  What makes you curious? What is it that you want to know? (You don't need to satisfy listeners' curiosity unless you want to—what is important here is their questions, not your answers.)

  If you could choose a story from this chart—something to read about or listen to—what would it be?

  Who on the chart do you wish you could meet?

  Do you see any patterns?

  Where are the conflicts?

- Take notes for discussion. Think about themes that come up in the family—for instance, expectations and compliance, alliances and conflicts, cohesion and autonomy, issues between men and women, secrets, expression of feelings, attitudes about money or children. How are these and other themes played out between family members? What are the potential stories linked to each conflict? How would each story differ if it were told from various points of view, or in different verb tenses or settings? What events come to mind that best exemplify or develop the conflict?

You may want to use freewriting or questions from others to develop the characters or setting related to aspects of your family tree, though it's not necessary that a story emerge from this exercise. The main point is to get you thinking about identifying conflicts and the patterns that express them, and to remember the past, since such memories tend to evoke feelings and images that enrich your writing. This process may suggest material for stories, but its best use is to help you practice the skills you'll need as a writer—listening to others respond to your stories and discovering what interests them and what doesn't. You'll also develop critical abilities, noticing your own reactions to others' stories and learning to recognize your curiosity.

A caution: occasionally, this kind of discussion may start to sound more like a support group than a writing class. Keep in mind that the purpose of this exercise is to develop skills and perhaps to discover stories, not to solve the families' problems—but don't overlook the fact that empathy, compassion, curiosity, and self-knowledge will help writers and writers' groups in their creative and critical work.

Wordplay

Ancestral Image List   This exercise was suggested by a writer who reviewed earlier drafts of this book. It can be used when time is limited or when participants prefer to work privately.

- At the top of a sheet of paper, write the name of a family member about whom you feel strongly. This may be someone you fear, admire, want to be like, or dread resembling.

- Draw a line under the name; then without stopping to think, freewrite a list of images relating to that person. These images may be visual, having to do with the ancestor's appearance, home, clothing, or surroundings. They may reflect the sound of the ancestor's voice, smells you associate with that person, tastes, textures, phrases, places—anything that comes to mind. The list may suggest incidents, details, or moods that will now or later develop into stories. Just be sure to structure the freewrite around the family member.

- If you want, you can take the exercise a step further into the realm of developing characters, introducing a **narrative voice** (the personality, tone, or sensibility conveyed by a story's language) by writing descriptions of the family member in the first, second, or third person.

Compared Memories   Our memories of past events are influenced by our current needs and disposition. Sharing memories adds dimension by drawing upon others' viewpoints.

- Choose an incident from your childhood. Write down some notes about it.
- Now talk to someone who was there and ask them to recall it in as much detail as possible. What are the differences in the two versions? What would be added if you combined or juxtaposed them?
- You can vary this exercise by describing an event from your past to a friend. Have your friend take notes on what you say and how you say it. Now write an account of the event, using your friend's notes.

Dreamcatching

"I shut my eyes in order to see," wrote painter Paul Gauguin. When their work is going well, writers often say that scenes and images seem to spin out before them like a dream. You may have experienced this with freewriting or other forms of early writing: for a time, you lose sight of the world around you and enter the world you're creating. As it unfolds, it feels real to you in much the same way that a good book feels real as you read it, or that a dream is real until you awake, and sometimes for a few minutes afterward.

Dreams and Writing

Readers may also feel the bump from reading into real life as if they were waking from a dream. In his book *The Art of Fiction*, writer John Gardner refers to the power of fiction to compel as "the fictional dream." The poet Rainer Maria Rilke made a similar comparison in his book *Letters to a Young Poet*: "You will experience the great happiness of reading this book for the first time, and will go through its countless surprises as in a new dream." As Gardner has pointed out, mistakes by the writer can be said to disrupt the fictional dream, jolting the reader from "sleep."

Many, though not all, writers and artists have pushed this experience a step further, using actual dreams in their work. Some—fiction writer Isabel Allende and screenwriter John Sayles, for example—have drawn directly from their dreams. Others find they work out solutions to creative problems in their sleep: Stephen King dreamed the ending to his novel *It.* Less dramatic and more common is the experience of "sleeping on it" and finding that last night's impasse is somehow now more bridgeable.

Nocturnal Sources of Creativity   These experiences are not unique to artists, as Brewster Ghiselin's description below of the discovery of the structure of benzene molecules attests. The chemist Friedrich August Kekule von Stradonitz, who had been struggling with this problem for some time, was dozing by the fireplace when the answer came to him. Ghiselin describes the moment in his book *The Creative Process*:

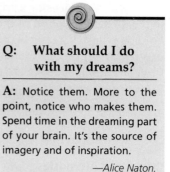

Q: What should I do with my dreams?

A: Notice them. More to the point, notice who makes them. Spend time in the dreaming part of your brain. It's the source of imagery and of inspiration.

—Alice Naton,
poet

> Gazing into the flames, he seemed to see atoms dancing in snakelike arrays. Suddenly, one of the snakes formed a ring by seizing hold of its own tail and then whirled mockingly before him. Kekule awoke in a flash: he had hit upon the now famous and familiar idea of representing the molecular structure of benzene by a hexagonal ring. He spent the rest of the night working out the consequences of his hypothesis.

Dreams are glimpses of the symbols and imagery that make up your psyche. Getting close to them and to your dream state may sometimes give you unexpected and resonant ideas and images for stories. But often it takes great patience and restraint to discover the proper uses of such imagery. More reliably, dreams can give you access to normally silent parts of your mind, thinning the veil between sleep and wakefulness and allowing thoughts to flow more freely. Dreams may affect your writing process as much as or more than they directly influence the story's content. Remembering, telling, and writing them is practice envisioning—practice getting into a creative state of mind. Dreaming is seeing. Recalling dreams means retaining images, and in most cases, to the seer, the acts of seeing and remembering are even more important than what is seen.

Envisioning or Interpreting: Dreams in Creative Work   Robert Bosnak, a Jungian analyst, describes in *A Little Course in Dreams* his feelings of inadequacy when asked to interpret a dream:

> My usual first reaction after listening to a dream is, "I haven't the faintest idea what this is all about. It just proves that dreams are pure nonsense—or maybe my comprehension is just not up to the complexity of the dream world." . . . Dreams seem incomprehensible by nature, nonsensical, an insult to "common sense". . . . Daytime consciousness stumbles when confronted with a kind of logic that is essentially alien to it.

Dreams are elusive. Like any imagery that rings true without being understood, they have a certain sacredness about them. They are elemental and so can't be broken down to an abstract meaning or interpretation. Creatively speaking, it's a mistake to be too reductive about their meaning; once "understood," their beauty may vanish. Psychiatrist Silvano Arieti has written, "When [dreams] are told to others, and even more, when they are interpreted, they are expressed with the usual words and with the ways of thinking of the waking mind. But then they are no longer dreams; they are the translations of dreams." The more you reduce or transmute a dream from an experience to an idea or meaning, the further you move from the original image. There's the danger of imposing ordinary, conscious styles of thought on something original.

Drawing abstract meanings from dreams can be helpful psychologically, but thinking too hard about such interpretations can distract you from the images and limit their artistic possibilities. So you must decide how you want to use the dream—artistically or psychologically—and from there, how deep you want to go. When using a dream creatively, stop short of taking it apart. Remember that you don't have to consciously understand its meaning in order to benefit from it. *Not* analyzing forces you to think of the dream intuitively rather than logically, and this opens the way for connections you might not otherwise make. In fact, you don't have to "use" it at all in order for it to work on you creatively.

It's not uncommon for students in my classes to react to the suggestion that they record their dreams in much the same way Robert Bosnak describes above: a loud sigh, and then, "I'm sorry, but this won't work for me. I just never remember my dreams." Some forgetful dreamers have remembered more by speaking into a tape recorder rather than writing their dreams, or by setting their alarm clocks at odd hours to "catch" dreams. Others begin to notice patterns and learn to nap at times when they're likely to dream vividly. Sometimes writing a description, drawing a picture, or telling someone about the most memorable part of a dream may bring back more of it.

But if you are one of those people, remind yourself: it's the process of remembering and recording dreams that's important here, not particularly the product. The quantity of remembered dreams may be impressive but what will probably be more valuable is simply getting closer to your dreams and becoming more familiar with the dreaming part of your mind. Even just thinking about remembering your dreams is progress. Don't exempt yourself from this useful source, and don't berate yourself for not remembering well. If you can move from remembering nothing to remembering a faint image, a color, a scent, then you've succeeded in thinning the veil, and that is probably the greatest benefit of dreams in writing.

Re-entering Your Dreams

This exercise, inspired by Robert Bosnak's book, *A Little Course in Dreams*, is useful for a group. Group members can bring in noncurrent dreams that they don't mind talking about, and take turns discussing their dreams, using the methods below. Again, the objective is not to analyze the dream, extract its meaning, or make it psychologically useful, though any of those outcomes may be by-products of this exercise. The idea here, based on Bosnak's approach, is simply to re-enter the dream, look around, and say what you see, hear, feel, smell, taste.

- Choose a dream to work with. It should be relatively short and vivid in your memory. You may want to choose dreams whose images intrigue you. The dream should be one you're comfortable talking about in public. (Nightmares or other deeply disturbing dreams are not usually suitable for this exercise.) The dreams that work best for group exercises are those that the dreamer is comfortable discussing and reexperiencing. Here is an example:

> I was in a large, darkened building, something like a museum or public aquarium, in which certain areas were illuminated or spotlighted. These illuminated areas contained displays, scenes, that one could walk into and participate in. A friend of mine was present at first, but soon faded away and I was alone. The first illuminated area contained a chair like that in a dentist's or doctor's examination room. A dark-haired, friendly man in a white coat stood beside the chair. Near him was a tall wooden rack with narrow compartments, something like a typesetter's drawer but vertical. In the compartments were small vials of brilliantly colored liquids. The vials were labeled in an unfamiliar alphabet, perhaps Thai or Arabic. The liquids were some kind of homeopathic medicines or magical potions. The other illuminated area that I saw contained a large, silver branch that lay on the floor. It was shaped in such a way that it could be used as a bench or chair.

- Across the top of a sheet of paper, make a series of headings, each a main character, object, or animal from your dream.

  <u>Room</u>   <u>Chair</u>   <u>Man in white coat</u>   <u>Vials</u>   <u>Branch</u>   <u>Me</u>

- Under each heading, write a series of sentences. The first sentence should say, "I am [supply the name of the person, animal, or object in the heading]." The following sentences should each begin, "I am. . ." and should briefly describe the person, animal, or object. Write at least ten sentences under each heading. Try to get "in character"—to pretend you are the person or thing being described. This sometimes feels clumsy or artificial at first, but it places you mentally in the dream world, close to the character, and it emphasizes that each character is actually an aspect of you, made of and by your mind. This is true of fictional characters as well.

  <u>Branch</u>

  I am the branch.

  I am silver.

  I am softly shining.

  I am bumpy like the branch of a tree, but smoothed out as if by many people touching or rubbing me.

  I am curved so that one part of me is raised. This is where people can sit.

- In as much detail as possible, tell your dream to one or more listeners. Listeners should take notes without interrupting, jotting down details that interest them, questions that occur to them—anything about the dream that arouses emotion or curiosity.

How big was the room?

What did you feel like as you looked at the two displays?

Were there other displays?

Why were you there?

Did the man in the white coat say anything?

How did you feel about being there?

- Listeners tell the dream back, with help from the dreamer. This is the time to look a little more closely at the dream, and to make associations. Listeners should ask questions of the dreamer. Pick out items in the dream that pull at you, and ask for more. Use your senses when you ask questions. What color/shape/texture is it? Can you hear it? Can you smell or taste it? Is it inside or outside? What is the weather like? Ask if there is anything in the dreamer's life that recalls that texture/shape/smell/emotion? You can also use "active imagination," asking the dreamer to "re-enter" the dream and to move around and explore its landscape: to open the door or touch the intriguing object, and see what happens. The dreamer should take notes about connections, images, or ideas that occur during the retelling.

   Here's an example of how active imagination might develop during discussion of a dream:

Q: What colors are the vials?

A: They are brilliant, vivid, electric colors—red, turquoise, green, violet. They remind me of the colors in the paintings of a friend of mine.

Q: Is there any sound in the room?

A: I can't remember any, although it doesn't seem dead silent, either. It's like a public place, with miscellaneous background noises, but nothing specific.

Q: Touch the branch. What is it like?

A: It's smooth, like driftwood, but cool metal. The color is soft. It feels good under my hand, like a massage.

Re-entering a dream can be a strong experience. One of the editors of this book wrote in the margin that she tried this part of the exercise. "As soon as I tried to 'touch the object' I felt suddenly and sharply moved, like a jolt. I couldn't believe how powerful it was!" Reviewing the suggestions below may help you to manage such potentially disconcerting moments:

- Don't violate the dream. Leave it intact, its meaning unspoken. Stop short of identifying themes relevant to the dreamer's personal life, generalizing, or speculating about the dream's "meaning."
- Think of yourself as a traveler in someone else's territory. Ask questions, be curious, but don't trespass.
- Dreamers may refuse to answer a question aloud, but should write down the answer even if they won't speak it. Explore together.

- Avoid reentering nightmares or dreams that touch on very emotional topics.
- Don't participate in this exercise if you are feeling ill or out of sorts.

Wordplay

A Dream Plan   Considering a few basic questions can help you to more consistently remember and write your dreams:

- How often do you remember your dreams?
- Under what conditions are you most likely to remember them?
- Do you need to wake up in the middle of one in order to remember it?
- When you are very tired or go to bed late, is it harder (or easier) to remember?
- Do events of the preceding day influence the vividness of your dreams?

In order to answer these questions, you may need to do a little research and take some notes over a period of time. Using your answers to the first question above, design a plan to help you remember your dreams. Start out with some basic routines:

- Keep a notebook and pen or laptop beside your bed.
- Try out techniques to enhance the likelihood that you will remember. Some people set their alarms every few hours and catch lots of dreams that way. Some report that they remember more by repeating, "I will remember my dreams" three times just as they doze off.
- Be sure to write down the dream immediately upon waking. The reason for this is that the sleeping brain produces chemicals that prevent most dreams from being remembered for more than a few minutes—so don't tell yourself, "I know I'll remember that one in the morning" because you probably won't.
- If you have trouble waking up enough to start writing, try using a tape recorder instead.
- Don't look back at your notes until the two-week period is over. This will allow you to have the exciting experience of discovering dreams you've forgotten and of gaining access to a part of your mind that is usually hidden.

Like freewriting, this exercise is an exploration. Your proper focus should be on the process, not on the actual material produced. Occasionally, you may find that images from dreams turn out to be directly useful as material in a story. More often, it may take you a long time to figure out how to use them. Presented intact, dreams rarely make good stories because they are anecdotal and contextual. Be open to possibilities, but don't make the mistake of canonizing your dreams.

Transmuting Your Dreams   If you're interested in transmuting your dreams into fiction, it's probably a good idea to wait until some time has passed since you recorded them. When you reread them, try underlining the parts that remain particularly vivid or resonant. Because of the dreams' ephemeral and elusive nature, you may find that they develop more interestingly if you allow them to do so at their own pace and in their own directions rather than struggling to make them fit your plans; very often, dreams in fiction are most effective when used obliquely.

As You Write

The point of early writing is that there is no point—writing simply for its own sake helps to free you from the pressure of preconceptions, and from overambitious expectations. As you become comfortable with these processes, you may find your freewrites turning into scenes; you may discover that some of your descriptions apply to a character or setting; elements of your dreams or your family tree may make their way into a developing story, and you may find yourself approaching the next step: writing a first draft. But keep in mind the advice of novelist Jonathan Strong: "Write from what you know toward what you don't know."

This chapter has presented a number of approaches to early writing. Try them out. Identify and adapt the ones that help you warm up and develop ideas. As you experiment, write down variations and combinations. Note what works, and when. Keep a file of exercises and approaches. Remember that not all of your writing will be of comparable quality. The point of these exercises is not the product but the process itself. Do not canonize everything that comes from your pen or keyboard. Don't even try to use it immediately, or maybe ever. This is the stretching, not the dance itself.

To help you get started, try some of the ideas below.

Notebooks   One way to gather what you know, people and places and events you've seen, is to carry a notebook with you everywhere you go. Write in it several times a day. Forget how you used to write in journals: "Today was an okay day. I went to the store and took a nap. Had dinner." Forget about being thorough in that kind of linear, mundane way. Instead, keep a record of the senses: whatever strikes your eye, ear, nose, mouth, skin. Don't write for an audience. Just keep notes: "At the store: large man wearing blue-purple linen shirt, hat. Uncle Maynard. Too many poinsettias. Smelts, fishy salt crystals. Lemon meringue pie." On the other hand, if you feel like writing out something that happened, do that. Let the journal be spontaneous, as close as it can be to what actually crosses your mind—not, as Cecily Cardew puts it in Oscar Wilde's *The Importance of Being Earnest*, "merely the diary of a very young girl, and consequently meant for publication." If you don't carry a notebook, you'll either forget a lot of your ideas or write them down on sales slips, napkins, and phone bills, which you will probably lose. Then you'll spend a lot of time looking for them and it will put you in a bad mood and mess up your writing time.

Some writers swear by one particular kind of notebook: unpretentious spiral, more upscale graph paper or sketchbook, three-ring for easier rearrangement, pocketed, hard-backed blank books. Others don't care or resist forming habits. The problem with getting too hooked on one particular thing is that your needs may change and that sometimes the object of your desire may become unavailable. A certain friend of mine experienced a minor creative crisis when The Gap stopped making their black bound notebooks. The main thing is to recognize what you like, and to be flexible. Needless to say, what you write in the notebook is more important than the book itself.

Daily exercises   Try any two of the following three exercises (or do all three, if you have time) for two weeks:

- Freewrite daily for five to twenty minutes.
- Each night, record your dreams.
- Work on a family tree and chronicle the moon.

Process of elimination   Practice editing your freewrites so that only the essential images or ideas remain. What have you deleted? Next time you freewrite, try to write more simply and directly.

Concrete writing   Look again at this chapter's explanations of concrete and abstract description, which assume that words are the things they describe. Actually, they are symbols. Or, more precisely, they are combinations of letters. Even more specifically, they are ink on paper. What would concrete writing be like if you were to use one of these definitions? Try a little, and find out.

Truth or fiction?   If you've written stories before, try tracing the characters and events to the real-life incidents or people that prompted them. How closely does the fictional version resemble its model? Which details have been preserved and which have been changed or deleted? How did these decisions affect the story? (If you have never written a story, try talking about these questions with someone who has.)

Exploration and Discovery

Ask Yourself

- *As you write, do you find yourself getting ideas—not necessarily for a specific story, but rather, do you find words and images connecting and leading you on to others?*
- *Do you find yourself blocked?* If so, which exercises are the most difficult for you to do? Which are easiest? When doing early writing, try out a variety of exercises and concentrate on those that do not block you; the others may be easier later, or they may not be suitable for you at this time.
- *As you freewrite, are you moving smoothly from thought to thought?* Remember that it's fine to change subjects, and that nothing is taboo.
- *In your freewriting, are you staying away from subject/verb combinations?*
- *In your physical descriptions, are you emphasizing the senses?*
- *As you draw your family tree, are you noticing areas of conflict, and themes that recur?*

- *Does your family tree trigger any particular memories?* These don't have to be dramatic to work well in a story—sometimes the most seemingly innocuous moments provide the best images or scenes.
- *Are you recording your dreams immediately and regularly?*
- *Aside from their "meaning," which dream images stand out most persistently in your mind?* Keep thinking about them—their persistence may be a cue that they are useful.

Ask Readers

Unlike other kinds of writing, those described here—freewriting, verbal still-lifes, family trees, and writing your dreams—are by definition private. Much of what early writing can give you is related to this privacy; if you habitually show it around, you risk dissipating its power. Aside from offering suggestions about how to loosen up structurally, or remarking on interesting images, there may not seem to be much anyone else can or should tell you about your early writing. But sometimes you may find that you get blocked working alone. If all else fails, break the sacred rule and show some of your early writing to someone else. (Be sure to cover or cross out anything you feel uncomfortable sharing.) Below are some questions readers can answer about freewriting, description, family trees, and dream-writing, without violating or disrupting these very personal forms of writing.

- *How would you paraphrase this freewrite?* To the extent that the reader is unable to paraphrase it, your freewriting is succeeding.
- *How many subject-verb combinations can you find in this freewrite?* Marking these is probably the single most helpful thing anyone can do to enable you to see how to loosen up; it's often much easier for others to identify these patterns than it is for the writer.
- *As I retell this story from my family tree, stop me when you want to know more.*
- *What past events or people have I talked about most as I've described my family tree?* You may be surprised at the answers, which may point you toward subjects you didn't realize were so important to you.
- *Which of these descriptions are most striking or evocative?* What associations do they suggest?
- *Which parts of this dream are most vivid and real?* What colors, textures, sounds, smells, or sensations come to mind as you think about these parts?

Wordplay

Letter-writing   Write a letter to someone—either the kind you put in an envelope or the kind you send through cyberspace. Sound out ideas for stories. React to things you've read. Argue, explore. Respond to the person you're writing to—

make your letter a part of a dialogue, as, in another sense, your other writing should be. The key is, write *to* someone. There is a naturalness of thought, flow of ideas, and language in letters that can be extremely hard to achieve under other circumstances. In fact, you may often wind up cutting and pasting parts of your letters or e-mails into your fiction because you said it better when you were writing to someone.

This does not apply to the dutiful kind of letter that supplies expected information: what you've been up to, plans for next week—because the best writing is not merely dutiful. Write to people you care about. Write to them about things that plague, puzzle, delight, or transform you. The clear presence of a reader at the other end of the writing will engage your mind and enliven your voice. Use it to warm up before you write. A letter written to me by a student and teaching assistant, James Suffern, expresses something of this spirit:

> I've always considered [letter-writing] a dialogue of sorts, with one person absent but part of the process nonetheless. I wonder if I would feel, still, that it's a dialogue if I wasn't confident the receiver were going to read to the very end, and likely respond. Often, when I'm writing a letter, especially if it's to someone I'm particularly close to or fond of, I feel like I've spent time with them just by writing. Because they're always with me, in a way. Even if I don't always write about the receiver, or ask questions or write the word "you," they are still, somehow, with me. The whole thing is a performance of sorts, for the audience of One.

An alternative: outlining   Try a completely different approach: plan out your writing. I've suggested starting with freewriting, dreams, and family trees in order to stimulate ideas, and not settling on a structure until those ideas are somewhat developed. This is because beginning writers, trying to write fiction using the same outlining skills that got them through their basic composition courses, often wind up with a page or two of dutiful, uninspired prose, followed by writer's block. The kind of mental and emotional leaps and connections necessary for fiction writing may often be inhibited by a detailed preconceived plan. But there are writers, and stories, that may benefit from some kind of outlining during the beginning stages. Sometimes writers are able to follow their outline toward a finished story. On other occasions, the presence of the outline may inspire rebellion that results in great ideas, just as filling your schedule may prompt you to put off a few commitments in order to write.

There are a number of ways to outline. The two most common are the traditional method we all should have learned in high school or in college composition courses; and clustering, a nonlinear form of outlining in which related words and ideas are clustered on the page and connected with lines. A third, looser type of organization is to start with a list of details, ideas, characters, names—anything that occurs to you about the story. Then you can group these according to the scenes that emerge out of them. Some writers use folders to hold lists for different scenes. This allows them to work on scenes separately and develop the scenes in detail. When it's clear how they fit, they get rid of the folders and put all the details and scenes together.

Suggested Reading

The More Books and Stories section starting on page 496 provides complete bibliographic information for each title listed below.

Robin Behn and Chase Twichell, *The Practice of Poetry*

Anne Bernays and Pamela Painter, *What If? Writing Exercises for Fiction Writers*

Robert Bosnak, *A Little Course in Dreams*

Matthew J. Bruccoli, *The Only Thing That Counts*

Naomi Epel, *Writers Dreaming*

Brewster Ghiselin, *The Creative Process*

Natalie Goldberg, *Writing Down the Bones*

Thomas Merton, *The Hidden Ground of Love*

Anais Nin and Henry Miller, *A Literate Passion*

Flannery O'Connor, *The Habit of Being*

Rainer Maria Rilke, *Letters to a Young Poet*

J. D. Salinger, *Seymour: An Introduction*

Robin Skelton, *The Poet's Calling*

E. B. White, *Letters of E. B. White*

CHAPTER 2

Drafting
Six Ways of Beginning a Story

When you start working, everybody is in your studio—the past, your friends, ene-
mies, the art world, and above all, your own ideas—all are there. But as you con-
tinue painting, they start leaving, one by one, and you are left completely alone.
Then, if you're lucky, even you leave.

—John Cage

The Seeds of a Story

The way you write grows out of your personality and circumstances; the made-up stories that we call **fiction** begin in many different ways. Some writers awake in the middle of the night with a mental image or idea that just has to be written down. Some
feel a need to chronicle changes in their lives, or incidents from their family history.
Others discover ideas through dreamcatching or freewriting. Or, imagination may be
sparked by outside events. Wherever the inspiration comes from and whatever its
timing, once it has struck, the next step is to start the **story**—the telling of events that
will significantly change an individual character. This chapter addresses the task itself: preparing for and writing a first draft. In it, you'll find some descriptions of different ways in which writers actually begin writing: with **character**, the portrayal of
the people or other main actors in a story; with **image**, or sensory detail; with **setting**,
a story's environment; with **voice**, the personality, tone, or mood conveyed by a
story's language; with **event**, what occurs in the story; or with **theme**, the main idea
or ideas in a story. All of these issues are covered in greater detail later in Part Two of
this book. You'll also find questions and exercises that will help you as you begin your
story. Once you've read this chapter, you may want to follow up with the others that
further explore the writing process: Chapter 10, Revising: Linear and Circular Methods (p. 184), and Chapter 11, Working with Readers (p. 208). These will help you to develop and refine the story that you will begin as you read this chapter.

Growing Ideas

"How can I get ideas?" I hate that question. It suggests newspapers, libraries, watching CNN all day and taking notes in a hardnosed quest for "material." It is the wrong
question. Some better questions are, "What do I care about? What random people or
situations or visual details linger inexplicably in the back of my mind?" These seemingly inconsequential hints from your own experience—not what's in magazines or
family albums or on TV—will lead you to what you have to say. It's true that writers

do sometimes get ideas from things that they read, from current events, and certainly from the people around them. But the real subject is not in the newspaper. It's in you; it *is* you—what and how you see. Instead of asking, "How can I get ideas?" think about what you care about, and how to find yourself. Recognize what's already there, in your mind.

The problem with the finding-material approach is that like outlining, it's an A-to-B endeavor. The goal is defined before you reach it, and reaching it is too often reduced to single-mindedly following a preconceived plan. When you are at the draft stage, there are advantages to a more open, fluid, and intuitive approach.

This requires time not always available if you are writing under deadlines, and it requires living with the uncertainty of a work in progress. But even more challenging, an intuitive approach demands that you care about something—that you believe you do contain stories and can find them. If you're listening with the back of your mind, you'll hear them. A person, a place, an event, or even a certain smell, a sound, or the movement of a moth at the window may trigger shadows of memories that can suggest characters, details, moments, and **scenes** or story segments. It sometimes takes courage to acknowledge and believe in what you find this way. It always takes effort to explore and develop your discoveries. But the more practice you give yourself, the easier it will be to discover and recognize the elements that will become your story.

> **Q: Do I need to have an ending in mind before I begin?**
>
> **A:** The answer is easy: yes and no. One must have in mind between sixty-eight and seventy-three percent of the ending. Any more than that percentage and the writer will be in a straitjacket, unable to respond to twists, surprises, and fits of sudden inspiration, or even changes of mind; any less and the project will meander and find itself in danger of sinking into the swamp of indecision.
>
> *—Leslie Epstein, writer and director of Boston University's Creative Writing Program*

Starting from Character

In a sense, all starting points except this one—**character**, the portrayal of human beings or humanlike beings—are back doors into the story. You may not always have a choice about where you begin. Sometimes the front door is locked and you have to sneak in. But if you're lucky enough to find your inspiration in character, you'll be developing the most important thing first. There are a number of ways in which that development can proceed.

Writing Portraits   Sometimes you may be inspired by someone you know. In this case, make the most of having a model. Take notes, from memory or while in the model's presence. List details: appearance, clothing, voice, movements, gestures, and speech. Such lists are useful in three ways:

> First, although you shouldn't feel rigidly tied to "how it really was," you may draw from your notes as you create the character.

> Second, introducing the element of chance by choosing random models dispenses with preconceived notions you may not even realize that you had.

And third, the ritual of writing the lists is a way of practicing the model's style or rhythms—whatever it was that first caught your attention.

After closely observing a person, you may find yourself unconsciously picking up expressions or gestures, or easily identifying clothing, music, food, or surroundings suitable to the character. You may begin to think or talk in ways that remind you of the character. Like its theatrical counterpart, Method acting, this kind of "method writing" can lead quickly to monologues and scenes.

Writing Self-Portraits   Another kind of portraiture is to discover characters within yourself. Models can provide dimension, but literally, the character is a part of the author, voicing feelings or opinions that the author cannot, within the story. In such cases the character becomes the author's alter-ego for certain kinds of statements or actions. This character-as-spokesperson approach can be heavy-handed if it's done deliberately, but when such statements emerge naturally and spontaneously through the character's voice, the character becomes a projection of the author's mind—some aspect of her played out to completion. Thinking of it that way may make it easier to "get in character" as you write—to feel and act through characters rather than constructing them from preconceived notions, lists of traits, or motivations. (For a more detailed explanation of this approach, see Chapter 3, p. 54.)

Growing the Character   Although writers frequently begin by basing a character closely on a friend or acquaintance or on themselves, at some point all successful characters must move away from their models and from their authors' conscious intent. Many writers have described the moment when a character begins to act and speak in surprising ways that don't always conform to the author's plans. This differentiation from the author is an important final phase of character development—the progression from sketch to actual character. Allowing it requires writers to live with uncertainty as they write, exercising faith in their creative processes.

It can be hard to "let a character go." It feels wrong, somehow, almost like a hex, to allow your fictional mother to be seduced by the circus ringmaster or to put her in a car crash or a really unattractive pair of shoes. Beginning writers whose characters have grown from real people are occasionally inflexible when it comes to revising, because, they think, "that's not how it happened." This literal-mindedness prevents characters and situations from coming into their own. As in a dream, some aspect of every character comes from you, anyway—your sensibility is a part of what you observe. Even if you wanted to, you couldn't re-create what happened in a purely objective way; the picture wouldn't be complete without you. If you can avoid trying to "aim so much," as J. D. Salinger's character Seymour says in the **novella** (a short novel) *Seymour: An Introduction*, then the characters in your story will often surprise and delight you as they develop. If you give them time, you'll probably find that they know what they are doing. This might sound touchy-feely or superstitious, but again, remember that characters are products of your mind, which often has a bigger picture than you realize.

Writing Without Models   Sometimes characters may spring from your imagination, appearing in a dream or as you write. Such characters tend to feel very true, but often they're initially somewhat flatter than the life-based ones. The danger with wholly invented characters is that they may *not* be wholly invented—without meaning to, you may find yourself drawing from pop culture, books you've read, or cultural stereotypes. Your characters may tip toward the **sentimental** (writing that attempts to evoke feelings with overused conventions or devices rather than with fresh, accurate language). If this happens, try reversing the usual approach of starting with a model and developing a character; start with a character, then look for a model. Go to a public place and find people who are in some way like the character in your mind—the same age, gender, race, or physical type. Watch them, and take notes. These notes may later give you some of the specifics that can elude you when you're trying to create something from nothing. You may find that a focused freewrite provides further methods for developing characters. (See the Wordplay section on p. 49.)

Writing Composite Characters   Most characters are composites—mixtures of two or more people, with aspects of yourself and your imagination added in. You may find that one character becomes your voice, expressing your ideas, attitudes, or personal style. This character may be able to state certain kinds of things quite directly and gracefully. On other occasions, everything the "me" character says or does may be monitored and critiqued in your imagination by someone you actually know. In this way, your real-life friend becomes a part of the character.

There are great advantages to starting with character. A story that begins with character can then more easily keep character central, as most good contemporary fiction does. This is as much a natural consequence of working outward from the center point as it is a conscious choice or plan; if you allow them to, events, imagery, and other aspects of the story may grow from and in relation to the characters. See Chapter 3, Character (pp. 54–71), for suggestions and activities to further develop fictional characters.

Starting from Image

I wrote a novel that began because of a baby's fingernail. The couple next door had a child who had been severely damaged during birth, and one day they asked me to baby-sit for her. It was a perilous feeling. I'd been left with four or five emergency numbers in case she had a seizure or stopped breathing, and I was afraid to let her out of my sight. When, finally, her parents returned and took her home, I couldn't stop thinking about her. I had no idea what to write about her, but clearly, she was on my mind. Eventually, I wrote in my notebook, "fingernails like little bits of waxed paper." From that small visual detail, the novel grew. Looking back, I can see that the fingernails attracted me because they embodied my awareness of the child's fragility. I didn't need to know that at the time, only to feel that the **image**, the sensory detail, rang true.

Growing the Image   How did this very small image grow into a novel? I began making lists: fingernails, herons that flew by the river I lived near, the sound of the wind in my cabin's roof. Some of what I listed kept coming back to me and made me want to write more. Images became sentences or paragraphs. Other things did not grow, and I put them aside in a folder, to which I returned from time to time.

Many of these images eventually found their place in the book. Others I've saved for the future, and some I threw out.

After a while, I began to sense connections between images on my lists. The heron resonated with the kitchen at dusk; the description of wind connected with a rainstorm. I began sublists, and these eventually became the beginnings of scenes. I kept them in separate folders. Once they all were adequately developed, I began to reason out how they were related—how they might work together to form a story.

In my case, the key to writing from image was being open to impressions and to their potential meanings and places within the developing story. Writing from image is a kind of gathering, sifting, and sorting. It works well for patient writers who are comfortable working with uncertainty and delaying the rational processes of a slow unfolding definition, and for difficult or emotional subjects that demand such an intuitive approach.

Starting from Setting

A story's **setting** or environment evokes feelings through every sense during the process of writing, as well as in the finished story. The Japanese novelist Izumi Kyōka commented about setting,

> I begin with place. . . . Characters must always follow nature. If setting changes, the people in it must also change. For instance, people feel differently on a moonlit night than they do on a dark night. So the way you handle conversation must also change according to whether your characters are in a well-lighted space or in a dark space. In a dark place, it is hard for voices to assume a shape; they sound distant to the ear. But move them to a bright place, and the dialogue appears.

The Significance of Place   Sometimes a place resonates with events that occurred there, or with experiences that are meaningful to the writer. On other occasions, it's hard to say what draws you so strongly to a certain location. The place may exist in the physical world, or it may be imaginary. It may come from a dream, or it may be a composite. Whatever the attraction, trust it.

Growing the Setting   Sometimes you may feel drawn to a setting before you even know what your story will be about. If you indulge and explore your interest in the place, characters and conflicts may grow out of the context that develops. If the location is real, go there. Sit for a while. Notice yourself noticing—what catches your eye, your ear, your sense of smell or touch? (See Chapter 7; Setting, p. 133, for activities designed to develop setting.) If the location exists only in your mind or is otherwise physically inaccessible, a focused freewrite may take you there. Be sure to go more than once, leaving some time in between visits. This will give you a number of perspectives on the place, and should lessen any tendency to veer toward nostalgia. Combined, these multiple perspectives can create a textured and detailed rendering. Because places are so evocative, it's likely that as you develop the setting, other aspects of the story will begin to occur to you, and you'll be on your way. If not, put your notes aside for later and move to the next task.

Starting from Voice

Every story has voices: those of its characters and of its **narrator**, the voice that tells the story. Robert Olen Butler, Darrell Spencer, J. D. Salinger, and many other authors have brilliantly used **voice** as their fictional medium. Voice can also generate story; in fact, if it were possible to choose how to begin your stories, voice would be an excellent way. A strong voice usually indicates the presence of a sensibility—a developed character—who has something to say.

Writer Penelope Bone describes her experience starting a story with voice, the personality, tone, and mood that arises out of the words:

> One night, for apparently no reason, I dreamed about the troubadour's song from Zefferelli's film version of *Romeo and Juliet*. It was running through my head when I woke up the next morning. I laughed at myself for having had such a sappy and seemingly random dream. Then I sat down and drafted (in one sitting—unheard of!) a story called "Juliet. " It didn't have anything to do with the movie or with anything that was in my head to write—instead, it was the story, told by a fourteen-year-old girl, of the purchase and loss of a bird. What I remember most about the story was that it came to me in the form of the girl's voice. It was as if she were speaking through me.

Finding a Voice in "What Killed a Girl"   Once in a while, a story just starts happening and all you can do is write down what you hear in your head. This eventually forms a sort of framework, which can then be filled out or rearranged as necessary. Revision is a delicate process with such stories, since the voice may be broken up or diluted if you tinker too much with it.

You don't need to have a dream that prompts a character's voice. Listen in your mind for your story's voices. Try writing some monologues, getting in character, and telling the story as it occurs to you in the voice that results. Don't edit much as you go; just write out the first draft as you seem to hear it, and save the revising for later on.

Student writer Kelly Zavotka took this approach when she wrote her story "What Killed a Girl" (pp. 465–474):

> It started with a voice that was dropping a lot of g's and felt very fast-paced and slightly volatile or on the edge. It also felt really comfortable. This voice came out easily in the first few pages, which were based on a freewrite. It was very much like my own internal monologues, but not. It was idlike—a voice that didn't censor itself. At that time I was working under the idea of not holding anything back—if something felt like it was going too far, I would put it in the story and look at it later. I would put it all out there and just go nuts. I experimented in that voice with fantasy. I became interested in who this person was and why she was cooking for her dad, and I started wondering where her mother was. I started seeing her as this impossible lightness in really dark circumstances. That was the tension that I was feeling. That's when I thought she was going to be killed, because the more I thought about her character in terms of her surroundings, the more inevitable it seemed that she couldn't be there.

"What Killed a Girl" derives much of its power from the convincing narrative voice that grew out of this process.

. . . Up ahead, through the dark, I can see large sheets of metal clinging to towering steel beams. The light rain like hot needles, pricks me but it's bringing me
out of my trance, enough to drive myself crazy with indecision. Instinct or adventure? I pull myself to Bobby, tight as I can without melting into him, bury
my mouth deep into his skin, close my eyes and try to squeeze my ears shut. I
give up breathing. I can't. I'm hiding. I'm giving myself over to him. I'm on a
roller coaster, at the top of the first hill.

Your story's voice may feel wobbly, inconsistent, or inauthentic at first, but
keep going and it will get stronger. Successful stories that are unified by a single, if
fictional, sensibility often have an unusual fluidity and momentum. Such stories
may spring forth after a time of not writing—suggesting that incubation is a part of
this process. See the Wordplay exercises at the end of this chapter (p. 49) for suggestions about how to develop voice.

Finding Other Voices   The same points apply to **dialogue**, or words spoken by
and among characters. Sometimes you may notice more than one voice forming
at once, and a story may grow out of the interaction of these voices. This kind of
beginning is more complex, and may point to the early development of conflict
and of theme as well as of dialogue. For a more detailed discussion of dialogue,
see Chapter 8.

Starting from Event

Why You Shouldn't Do It   Most writing teachers will correctly advise you not to
begin a story from **event** (an incident or occurrence) or from the patterns of events
that form a **plot** unless you are writing a mystery novel or some other type of fiction
that must be carefully plotted—and even such stories may begin with elements other
than event. The reason for caution with this approach is that stories emphasizing actions rather than characters tend by definition toward **melodrama** and emotional
shallowness. Besides, writing from plot just doesn't always work, because it assumes
foreknowledge about a number of things: how the story will end, how the characters
will change, what events will happen along the way. We simply don't always or even
often know these things before we begin writing. Much of a writing teacher's work
is to convince beginners that it's all right not to know—that eventually these issues
will become clear. Most of the time, trying to write the plot first is working backward.

When It's Okay to Do It   There are exceptions. Some writers actually do benefit
from outlines and storyboards, techniques that will be discussed in Chapter 10
(p. 184). And some writers never begin writing at all until they know the whole story.
Seth Pase, a former student whose fiction appears in this book's Anthology ("The
Father," pp. 372–375), explains his writing process: "My stories incubate for a long
time. I don't start writing until the whole thing is more or less there and ready, so it
comes out as a nearly complete first draft. " As with authors who start from voice,
it may be that such gestational periods are a necessary part of this way of beginning for those whose work emerges relatively well-plotted.

Another author, a friend of mine, wrote to me:

> I never thought I'd advocate this, much less do it myself—I'm not one of those writers who creates detailed storyboards or who even knows the end before they get there. And I've always been proud of that. Sigh. Until, recently, I had the odd experience of having a story emerge event by event, all coming together like a movie or something. And it's not emanating from a conscious place. And it makes me think that even the most left-brained or logical aspects of writing might come through mysteriously.

How to Do It   There's nothing wrong with starting from plot if it helps you to begin writing your story. Certainly, it is reassuring to work within a narrative structure. If you find yourself starting with plot, keeping two issues in mind will help you avoid the potential pitfalls of this approach. First, don't limit yourself by thinking that you know precisely how the story will turn out; much of writing is intuitive, and you may preclude your own success by getting too committed to an outline too early on. It's important to remember that you will discover much of the story as you explore its possibilities. Second, although plot may be where you begin, it should not be where the story ends or centers. Events are important as they form and reveal character. (See Chapters 3 and 4, Plot and Character, pp. 54 and 72, for more on the relationship between plot and character.)

Starting from Theme

The very thought of starting from **theme** (the ideas that underlie a story; see Chapter 9 for more explanation of this concept) is taboo! Conventional writing workshop wisdom forbids it, because doing so is likely to produce idea-heavy, character-light fiction. This is good advice. However, the approach sometimes works anyway. For example, another former student of mine, Ross Kilburn, says he usually starts from theme:

> When I start I focus on an idea. It's not like I say, I think I'll write about racism; what happens when I get the idea for a story is that I'll think of some kind of comment, or a line, or just a vague thought . . . anything like this triggers the story. With one recent story I'd just read the essay "The Serious Writer and the Tired Reader," by Flannery O'Connor and had begun to wonder about the writer who writes for the tired reader. This led to questions about what would happen to a "tired" writer who thinks he's a "serious" writer finding out that he's really pretty damn "tired"?

This author's original idea led quickly to two highly imaginative characters: the tired writer and his companion, an unusually well-spoken wine bottle. When, as in this admittedly unusual case, starting from theme helps you to develop the story's central characters and conflicts, it may serve to focus the story in a highly useful way.

As You Write

Once you've got some images or ideas going, it's time to actually start writing. Don't worry if you feel blocked or frustrated at this point. Often it is difficult to know where in the story to begin, or exactly how. The unwritten story may begin to loom in your mind, and you may be at a loss about how to proceed. The solution is pretty simple: you can only do what you can do. The real challenge is to discover what it is that you can do.

Finding the Open Door

Don't start—or rather, don't think of it as getting started. Don't necessarily begin at the beginning. Go instead with whatever shred of the story persists most strongly in your mind: a scene, a moment, a glimpse of a landscape, a scrap of dialogue. It may not turn out to be on page one—it may wind up deleted. But it's the open door, the way into the story.

Writing intuitively   Taking an intuitive approach as opposed to using an outline or storyboard has its challenges. With no visible guiding map or plan, it's easy to feel frustratingly disorganized and overwhelmed, and to block or bog down. Writers who work intuitively must deal with a lot of uncertainty and with the resulting fear, most of which is reducible to one terrifying suspicion: that the next idea will not come. An obvious tactic is to plant yourself in front of your computer and not leave until something happens. However, this approach may block some writers even further.

Creative receptivity   It's helpful to look at how others have approached creative projects. The mathematician Henri Poincaré, for example, describes in an essay titled "Mathematical Creation" how he developed a key idea:

Q: How do you balance the intuitive flow of your writing with the intent and direction of your narrative?

A: I think while I'm writing. As a result, ideas occur to me *while I'm writing*. When you're actually in the process of writing—when you're "there"—you're better able to make decisions, because you're basing those decisions on what "there" actually is. What I'm saying is that you are just as likely to be wrong—maybe more likely to be wrong—about a story before you start writing it as you are while you are writing it. Besides, if I write a couple of pages of prose that I decide not to use, I store them somewhere else, and later, when I'm stuck for the next scene, or the next story, I often find I've already written it.

—*William Hodgson,
writer and editor*

> For fifteen days I strove to prove that there could not be any functions like those I have since called Fuchsian functions. I was then very ignorant; every day I seated myself at my work table, stayed an hour or two, tried a great number of combinations and reached no results. One evening, contrary to my custom, I drank black coffee and could not sleep. Ideas rose in crowds; I felt them collide until pairs interlocked, so to speak, making a stable combination. By the next morning I had established the existence of a class of Fuchsian functions, those which come from the hypergeometric series; I had only to write out the results, which took but a few hours.

The importance of receptivity in the creative process is very often overlooked by proponents of the action-oriented, nail-your-hand-to-the-keyboard approach, who feel they must be *doing* in order to be making. Poincaré describes the benefits of a more reflective approach:

> Often when one works at a hard question, nothing good is accomplished at the first attack. Then one takes a rest, longer or shorter, and sits down anew to the work. During the first half-hour, as before, nothing is found, and then all of a sudden the decisive idea presents itself to the mind.

The basics about beginning   Remind yourself of a few basic truths as you begin your first draft:

- Imperfection is just fine. It won't come out exactly the way you want it to the first time, and it doesn't have to. That doesn't matter at all. You don't have to show anyone your first draft if you don't want to.
- Incompleteness is in the nature of beginning. You don't have to sit down to write a story. Sit down to discover, explore, and develop the characters, events, and images in your mind.
- There's no need to be afraid to change something you've written. Be flexible. Save your drafts—you can always return to the first one if it turns out to be the best.
- Don't take anything—especially yourself—*too* seriously. Consider Julio Cortázar's short piece, "Instructions on How to Sing":

Begin by breaking all the mirrors in the house, let your arms fall to your side, gaze vacantly at the wall, *forget yourself*. Sing one single note, listen to it from inside. If you hear (but this will happen much later) something like a landscape overwhelmed with dread, bonfires between rocks with squatting half-naked silhouettes, I think you'll be well on your way, and the same if you hear a river, boats painted yellow and black are coming down it, if you hear the smell of fresh bread, the shadow of a horse.

   Afterwards, buy a manual of voice instruction and a dress jacket, and please, don't sing through your nose and leave poor Schumann at peace.

   —Julio Cortázar, *The Instruction Manual*

Critiquing: a preview   By definition, first drafts are incomplete. They develop in all kinds of ways. Some come out as a few intriguing moments with no indication of any overall shape, while others contain excellent dialogue but no description. Still others outline the whole sequence of events, with underdeveloped characters, holes in the plot, and perhaps some clichés or emotional manipulation. Some writers work on one small segment at a time, resulting in a first draft that may be nothing more than one scene or a character sketch.

   Readers in and out of workshops too often overlook the fact that so-called defective stories—those that are vague, incomplete, crowded with detail, inconsistent, obvious, or sentimental—are still in process. The writer has addressed certain issues first and will naturally reserve others for later. Thoughtful criticism acknowledges and respects the writer's process and expresses observations as possible next steps rather than as lists of defects and inadequacies.

   If you're in a workshop where readers will see only one draft of your story, keep in mind that many people tend to hold unfinished stories to the same standard as finished ones. This may seem quite harsh and can leave you feeling that you've walked into the classroom half-dressed. Remind yourself that by critiquing your work as though it were finished, readers will be trying to tell you what remains to be done. They aren't thinking primarily about the writing process but about the product itself. Try to take this in stride.

Readers should try always to see incomplete first efforts—their own and those of others—as what they are: beginnings. This doesn't mean that the standard should be lowered but that readers should assume writers' goodwill and intent to improve, and should offer suggestions in that spirit rather than seeming to condemn or write off the work because it's not finished.

Chapter 11, Working with Readers (p. 208) discusses the critical process in detail; however, it's important to have some idea, before your first workshop, of what you're getting into. This section will help to prepare you for the experience of sharing your work with others.

Shaping Your First Draft

Writing a first draft can feel like wandering in a dark and unfamiliar place; beginning writers often wonder how to evaluate their work, what standards to apply as they make the early choices involved in writing a story. While you shouldn't let such concerns distract you from the work at hand, it can be reassuring to have some idea as you begin. Below are some broad issues to consider and keep in the back of your mind as you draft your story.

Writing from your experience   This is a workshop cliché, but especially at the beginning level, it is excellent advice as you choose your subject matter. It's very hard to write well about having a baby if you've never had one; about being a firefighter if you've never been one; about living in Iceland if you've never been there. Drawing from your experience makes your sources easily accessible, which greatly simplifies the task of coming up with original detail, and keeps you from getting out of your depth.

Distancing yourself from your experience   If you are thinking of using autobiographical material, keep in mind that some situations or characters drawn from real life may be just too loaded. If you find yourself becoming very emotional about your story's subject matter, resisting or overreacting to the thought of others' criticism, or feeling unduly reluctant to deviate from "what actually happened," then the material may be too close to you at this time. If you're planning to work with highly charged personal material, consider talking over your plans with a more experienced writer. Give yourself the extra time you'll need to do an autobiographical project well. This means not only time at your desk

I've watched my mother, who is a painter, as she works. After a while, she puts the painting on a chair across the room and goes about her other chores. That way, she can see it from various angles—literally, she gains perspective. Writers sometimes lose sight of our need to do the same. It's a very good thing to learn to recognize when you're too close to your work to see it, and to give yourself the space you need.

—*Alice Naton,*
poet

actively writing, but time to mull over ideas, to revisit sites, and to feel comfortable with your subject. The more intimate the material is, the more you'll have to say about it, but also the more distance you'll need in order to say it. Changing the names and identifying details of characters and locations may help you achieve enough detachment to write well about an autobiographical subject. When this is most difficult, it is probably most necessary—you're likely too close to the source to fully experience it as fiction. Once you get used to the revised version, you probably won't miss what you deleted, and you will feel much freer to let the story take its own direction.

Avoiding merely lurid or sensational topics, melodrama, and clichés   Certain subjects—murder, rape, incest, adultery, drug addiction—are so neon-bright and scintillating that beginning writers are often attracted to them. Of course, some great works have been written on these subjects. So have countless bad works. Writing credible fiction requires a high level of detail; the more extreme your subject matter, the greater will be the strain on your imagination or your research skills. Too often, flashy stories don't sustain interest because the writer has resorted to an obvious lie or generality—the generic, made-for-TV version of the real experience. A story needn't be extreme in order to be interesting; all human experience, seen from a revealing angle and reported clearly and with feeling, is subject matter for art.

However, even extremely dramatic material is not necessarily a mistake in and of itself. As poet Eve Johnson advises, the writer must determine what subjects are appropriate:

> The subjects that are forbidden are those subjects you forbid yourself to explore. It is worthwhile to try and recognize what those topics are, and maybe eventually challenge your personal censor; to write on a subject that was previously forbidden to you can be very exhilarating! But there will always be subjects you don't explore because you're not aware of how you've censored yourself, or you're not ready to do so (yet).

Q: Are there any subjects that are forbidden—too violent, too sexual, too upsetting, or too personal?

A: The really important issue is not subject matter but attitude. A poem or a story can be about anything as long as its materials are properly handled. The mere appearance of a subject considered shocking or upsetting is unlikely to produce a consequential work of art, even if it generates an immediate response. That such subjects may be difficult to manage does not, of course, make them forbidden. Their cultural weight, however, may easily overwhelm the writer's ability to give them effective shape. Thus the work may appear to exploit its dangerous materials, rather than use, illuminate, or even transform them.

—Lawrence Raab, poet and teacher

But if the events in this early draft are more developed or prominent than the characters, the story may become **melodramatic**—that is, its plot may predominate over character. (See Chapter 4, Plot, p. 72, for a more detailed discussion of melodrama.) For now, remember to keep the focus on how the main character changes. Avoiding lurid or sensational subject matter is the best way to do that.

It also helps to avoid **clichés** or overfamiliar ideas and phrases. If anything—a word, a phrase, a situation, a reaction—feels too familiar, then you've probably seen it before. Try to come up with something unique to this character, this moment. Otherwise, you'll be depending on a standardized stimulus-and-response reaction rather than earning a reader's attention and interest. Intelligent readers will feel and resist the manipulation.

Adapting the form to the idea   At the outset of a project, a lot of writers don't know whether they're working on a **novel** (a book-length piece of fiction), a **novella** (a short novel, usually around ninety pages), or a **short story** (a relatively short work of fiction, usually between 1,500 and 20,000 words). Many beginning writers have not yet learned how much will comfortably fit into these forms, and so they overshoot: the story is set in several foreign countries (or galaxies); the action spans several decades; the writer sets out to deal with the history of Neptune and one boy's search for the meaning of the universe, all in nine pages. Subjects that cover a large time span or involve a number of different locations, themes, or subplots are more suitable for a novel. If you have difficulty reducing the story's scope, try thinking of it as a novel and working on just one chapter of it. If novel excerpts are not acceptable in your workshop, your teacher may have suggestions about adapting the material to fit the short story form.

Limiting the story's scope   Choose one central conflict, one locale, and one reasonably short time span in which the story takes place. Although not all successful short stories are so limited, this kind of definition allows you to explore and develop the story's depth rather than merely its breadth. Accepting some limitations lets you focus on detailing the characters, developing the conflict, creating a richly textured setting, and other essential tasks of writing vivid fiction.

Focusing the story's plot   Sometimes you'll know exactly what the main character's conflict is, what is at stake in its resolution, and how that resolution will change the main character. On other occasions, though, you may surprise yourself: as the story takes on its own life; the emotional intensity may pop up elsewhere. It's possible to adjust the story as you go in order to keep the focus where you want it, but then again, you may know more intuitively than you think you do. Consider letting the story "lead you." Again, don't be afraid to go with what seems most alive. You can always write the other stuff later.

Begin your first draft or assignment early enough to allow time for this basic conflict to develop. If you get close to your deadline and you're still not sure what the story's about, ask for a conference with your teacher and be frank about your concerns. Say, "I need help identifying the central conflict." It's surprising how simply and quickly this problem can often be solved in conference. Alternatively, your teacher may suggest that you not strain in that direction. If she's willing to grant you latitude with early drafts, take it: conflict very often clarifies much later in the process. (For more about plot and conflict, see Chapter 4, Plot, p. 72.)

Including an appropriate amount of background information   Provide enough to create a context for the characters and events, but not so much that the story is weighed down. Until at least the first draft is complete, it can be very difficult to gauge how much information readers need to know in order to understand the action, and when they need it. One way of dealing with the problem is to keep notes, as you write the scenes, on ideas about characters, settings, or situations. Don't even try to put this material into the story at first. Just write down the information itself, then go back to the primary work of establishing the characters, dialogue, setting, and what happens in the scene. Once you have the story drafted, you can insert the background material as necessary. This approach frees you to be mentally in the scene—to really imagine it and focus on it as you write, rather than becoming tangled in logistics.

The best way to evaluate what information is necessary and where to put it is to ask readers. Listen carefully to their confusion and frustration, and resist the impulse to explain or clarify immediately—readers' reactions are excellent signs of what background information may be missing. See this character's Ask Readers section (p. 48) for some specific questions that will help you determine what exposition is necessary.

Looking for signs of crowding   These signs may include more background information than you can handle gracefully, the tendency to skim over or summarize scenes because you feel like there's just not enough time to get it all in, or difficulty imagining how to connect geographically or chronologically distant episodes. This sort of problem may be a cue that you've started the story in the wrong place, or even that you're writing a novel or, perhaps, several novels, rather than a short story. In that case, you can either switch projects or simply reorganize the material into approachable sections and work on one at a time. On the other hand, if you set out to write a novel but find that nothing is happening, that there are not enough events and your characters are standing around looking for something to do with their hands, consider a shorter form where they'll be less at a loss.

Maintaining a consistent point of view   Establishing a clear **point of view** (the vantage point or sensibility from which the story is told) is basic. If you don't do so, readers will feel unnervingly jerked around and won't know how to interpret what is being described. Here again, the main issue is consistency. Generally, it's all right to switch point of view within a story, but not within a scene. Because a scene is a glimpse of a revealing moment, switching point of view within it breaks the reader's engagement with the characters—it breaks up the moment. (See student Mary Austin Speaker's "The Day the Flames Would Stop," pp. 413–418, for an excellent counterexample.) If you choose to switch point of view, don't do it just once. Establish a pattern so readers can feel that you're not losing control of the story.

With respect to your writing process itself, such inconsistencies may suggest that you haven't yet settled on a vantage point from which to tell your story. Try allowing the uncertainty for a while. Follow your instincts and experiment until one point of view feels clearly best. (See Chapter 5, Point of View (p. 90), for more discussion of this topic.)

Keeping the verb tense consistent   There are two issues here. First, you need to establish a consistent tense for the main part of the story. Once you've made that decision, it becomes easier to work with flashbacks. If the story is told in the past tense, use past perfect to work with events in the past. If you choose to write the story in the present tense, use simple past tense to indicate past events.

Here again, "mistakes" may not always be a matter of simple carelessness. Allow yourself to experiment with various approaches: follow your instincts from scene to scene, and wait to standardize the verbs until one tense predominates. But if grammar doesn't come naturally to you, then you'll need to check through your final draft meticulously. Inconsistency on this issue results in glaring and disastrous miscommunication. (See Chapter 6, Time: Verbs and Narrative Structure, p. 109, for further explanation and examples.)

Developing your story's emotional content   As a rule, express emotion subtly rather than overtly. The most obvious ways of indicating characters' emotions and their relations with one another are to state them through dialogue ("'That's so I can eat you better!'") ("Oh my goodness, she thought, how uneasy I am today! And usually I'm so happy at Grandmother's.") or **narration**, what the narrator tells the reader directly, as opposed to what the characters convey through speech and action. It's easy to overlook the subtler but often more effective method of conveying information indirectly, through the characters' actions: The wolf moving closer to Red Riding Hood, Red Riding Hood glancing at the cottage door and drawing her cloak around her. Turning down the emotional volume may enhance your story's emotional texture without extensive rewriting. Similarly, keep narration and dialogue concise and understated—suggestive of meaning rather than explicit—and add descriptive details, gestures, and setting.

When you are beginning a story, rather than choosing details deliberately to prove a preconceived point, trust your intuition: simply imagine the scene as closely as you can, and write what you see. If it contradicts what you thought was your objective, try adjusting that objective to what you see. Before you condemn and throw away a too-obvious first draft, though, consider that it may be a gift: a map of what will later be invisible, the story's **subtext** or unspoken emotional conflict. Conversely, as you replace overt explanations with suggestive detail, be open to new possibilities and meanings that may emerge.

Thinking twice about genre fiction   Science fiction, fantasy, and horror fiction are not bad by definition, but they take a whole lot more work to do well. Of course, good, excellent, profound fiction has been written in these genres. But writing it is a very large task. You're not only taking on the huge job of creating believable characters and voices, writing good dialogue, rendering a vivid and evocative setting, building a compelling plot, and persuading readers to care about all of the above, but you're proposing on top of all that to create the whole world, from the elements on up. Tasks such as accommodating exposition and avoiding triteness are much more difficult in these genres. If you adamantly insist on starting out this way, draw as much as possible from your experience. Simplify all you can. And don't say you weren't warned.

To keep such a story fresh and alive take special care to avoid certain clichés that are unfortunately common in these genres: "types" such as the lovely and spirited heroine, the hardbitten detective, the Han Solo wannabe sci-fi hero; supervaliant heroes and utterly evil villains and ladies who wear filmy gowns and who need rescuing. Watch out for stereotypical reactions and oversimplified conflicts or characters. Look for ways to streamline exposition and insert it subtly. And remember that writing literary-quality science fiction or fantasy will take most writers a lot of extra time. It may be much more doable once a writer has some experience with simpler forms.

It's perfectly natural, in the early drafts of a story, to work on its various aspects one by one. So don't overreact to the resulting unevenness—instead, try to look at it as an indication of what to do next. But do be open to cues from the story itself. If you find yourself developing a supposedly secondary character or conflict, maybe it's more interesting than what you thought was your main subject. If so, consider adjusting your vision of the story. Perhaps the most important approach of all is to consult your own instincts. It sounds like psychobabble, but I can't count the number of times a student has come into my office blocked and frustrated, and I've gone through all kinds of possible solutions and finally remembered to ask, "What usually works for you?" If you already know the answer, try that method first and then move on to others if it's not successful.

Exploration and Discovery

First drafts come in all shapes; some are ready for systematic editing and shaping while others require more time to develop. The questions and suggestions that follow address issues relevant to drafting; for more detailed suggestions on specific topics such as plot, character, theme, and so forth, see the Exploration and Discovery sections in Part Two, The Elements of Fiction (pp. 54–183). Even if you don't want to structure your story early in the writing process, it's a good thing to keep some organizing ideas in the back of your mind as you work—this will save you time later by preventing you from getting way off track in the beginning.

If you're working within the structure of a writing class or group, you may not have the opportunity of presenting multiple drafts of the same story. These questions, ideas, and activities will prepare you to understand readers' reactions and to use them as you begin revising.

Ask Yourself

As you sit down to start writing your first short story, you may feel somewhat overwhelmed. A few key questions can help you sort through your thoughts and find a way of beginning that suits you and your story. Reconsidering these questions once your draft is complete can also help you to self-evaluate.

- *What is most strongly present in your mind?* Do characters, images, settings, voices, events, or themes recur? What do you think about as you fall asleep? Listen to your thoughts; no matter how insignificant they seem, recurring images or ideas may be cues or clues to a developing story. Start there.
- *What images, ideas, phrases, structures, or other elements attach themselves to your original idea?* Where do they lead you?

- *Now that you have begun with one element (character, image, setting, voice, event, or theme), how do the others relate to it?* What voice do you associate with a character? What setting evolves from a chosen theme? What images do you associate with the central event? These questions may suggest ways in which you can branch out and start developing other aspects of the story, related to the one with which you've begun.

- *What remains to be done?* Think of the answers as stopping points on the map of your own creative method, rather than as failings of the current draft.

Ask Readers

Showing your early drafts to others can feel risky, but in the beginning, the benefits tend to outweigh the disadvantages. As you gain more experience, you'll get used to your writing patterns and you'll need to consult with readers less often. But no matter when you choose to share your story with others, certain questions tend to come up. Some of them are listed below.

- *What do you need to know and when do you need to know it?* Were you confused as you read? Where, exactly, and why? The answers to these questions will point to missing information or may suggest meanings or approaches you haven't thought of.

- *Who is the story's main character?* This may seem like an obvious question, but often first drafts are unfocused. You may have inadvertently misplaced the emphasis, causing readers to become distracted by a too-prominent secondary character. Listen to where readers were most interested. The heroine's best friend can sometimes turn out to be your best character.

- *How does that character change in the course of the story?* This question will suggest the story's focus. You can use it to develop the main character and conflict.

- *What if the main character had behaved differently at the climactic moment?* How would the story be different? How did you feel when you reached that moment? While in the drafting phase, it's good to remain open to your story's possibilities. Readers can suggest some that you might not otherwise think of.

- *Can you summarize the story's main action in no more than three sentences?* This commonly prescribed exercise is kind of an unreasonable request, and many readers won't be able to do it. But at the first-draft stage it can quickly reveal misunderstandings or unnoticed potential. Applied to subsequent drafts, this question can help you to focus the story and see what may be extraneous. However, if a story is too easily summed up in this way, it may not be fully enough developed. Think of Andre Dubus's "A Father's Story" (pp. 272–286), James Joyce's "Araby" (pp. 323–327), or Nathaniel Hawthorne's "The Minister's Black Veil" (pp. 311–319). Many of the best stories resist reduction. So answers to this question can point in either direction.

- *As you think back on the story, what images, descriptions, or events stand out?* Don't get too analytical about this question—look for what arrests and intrigues readers. Their responses may provide clues about what is really central in the story.

Wordplay

Developing a writing habit Keep a list of the writing habits and practices that work for you, and another list of things that don't. After a few weeks or months, reread them and look for patterns and preferences. To discover the degrees and kinds of structure that stimulate and sustain your creativity, experiment with the following list of preferences and tendencies:

When you write

Where you write

How long you write at one time

What kind of writing you do first

What reading, music, foods, or other activities make you want to write

How often you write

Learn to recognize what helps you to write, and gradually a system may evolve. Until that time, try out various combinations. For instance, two weeks of the following regimen is enough for many people:

Fifteen minutes of freewriting daily

Recording dreams each night

Carrying a notebook in which to record passing thoughts and observations

In addition, you might consider writing a paragraph or so of a letter or journal entry each day or discussing your writing or nonwriting in your conversations, or e-mails. Such writing and discussion can do a lot to keep you focused on your work.

If you're following the method described above, try not looking back at your writing and notes until the end of the two weeks. By then, you'll have some distance and it will be easier to recognize which details are likely to be useful. Don't set your predilections in stone, but do learn to recognize when something is working, and to try it again. The purpose of this exercise is not to commit you to one way of writing for the rest of your life but to make you more aware of how you

Q: How do you know what to write about?

A: Either I write about what is going on in my life, which usually becomes a long complaining list, or, when things are good, I get an idea somehow. Sometimes the idea will come from a freewrite. Sometimes I'll have a line in my head all day. But it will feel urgent if I have something good. That's how I know it won't be blather.

—*James Leon Suffern, student writer*

work and more able to use that knowledge. (See Chapter 1, Prewriting, p. 6, for more suggestions about this method.)

Focused freewrite   Choose one aspect of your story—a person, a place, a scene, a conflict, anything that you'd like to develop. First, loosely list what you already know about that thing: sensory details, history, lines of dialogue, ideas. Next, picture it in your mind. Now do a freewrite, but stay with the mental image. Keep coming back to it and bouncing associations off of it. If you find a scene beginning, let go of the image and follow the scene.

Monologue   Go to a private space where you will not be overheard. First, think of any events or characters that you have in mind for the story. Now assume the voice of your narrator and talk about them. Ideally, imagine that you are talking *to* someone—another character, or a general audience. Pretending that someone is listening will direct your voice. Try writing this exercise, once you've gotten a feeling for the voice.

If you're interested in further pursuing the topic of voice in fiction writing, you can find a number of excellent exercises in *Finding Your Writer's Voice* by Thaisa Frank and Dorothy Wall.

Reading aloud   Read your own work aloud to check for repeated words or sounds, unintentional rhymes, and other distracting glitches in the language that can wrench it out of its natural rhythm. Reading aloud lets you hear the rhythm of the words, and it forces you to pay attention to each sentence—to notice inconsistencies and other areas that need further development. There are various ways of reading aloud: alone, to a friend or group, asking readers to follow along and mark their own copies as you read. Andre Dubus was known to read his stories into a tape recorder, then play back the recording and read along with it. However you use this exercise, you should build it into your writing habits, because your ears will catch what your eyes don't.

Salvaging   Try writing from memory or from a hard copy of your draft, rather than revising on the screen. At some point in their careers, most writers lose something they've written—notes, a draft, even a whole novel can go up in flames or be accidentally wiped off of your computer. I once stayed up until four in the morning, intermittently cutting and pasting and screaming, because the computer had inexplicably turned my entire novel to word salad; I know this pain. But what you have to remember is that the story is inside you,

> **Q: How can I use reading aloud as I write?**
>
> **A:** Reading aloud, mouthing your words, reading your words closely: each can be helpful, but each requires more discipline than the previous one to be effective. It is best to start with the easiest, composing aloud. This is done by saying your first sentence aloud, writing it down, and then repeating the sentence aloud, over and over, until you are totally at ease with it, in your mind, your mouth, your whole self. Then you are ready to say your next sentence aloud and write it down. Composing wholeheartedly like this will let your emerging story strongly influence you. Nothing, including what you want to accomplish, will be held back.
>
> —*Dennis Packard,*
> *teacher*

the same way it's in the computer or on the paper. You can rewrite it. In fact, many writers deliberately rewrite. Note: always back up your work on a floppy disk and on a hard copy.

Nail your hand to the keyboard Many—though not all—writers swear by the method of forcing themselves to sit down every day to write and not get up for a specified number of hours or pages. For these writers, even if what they write is worthless, the act usually brings something forth. I don't follow this method all the time because my schedule and my creative needs don't allow it. But although people who don't like this sort of routine often talk about it as if it's mechanical and rote and unimaginative, there are other ways to look at scheduled writing: for instance, as a ritual that generates creative power, or a conditioned response on the part of the author. As long as it doesn't make you block, writing on a schedule can create momentum and keep you going.

Suggested Reading

The More Books and Stories section starting on page 496 provides complete bibliographic information for each title.

Jakob and Wilhelm Grimm, "Little Red-Cap"

Julio Cortázar, "The Instruction Manual," in *Cronopios and Famas*

Thaisa Frank and Dorothy Wall, *Finding Your Writer's Voice*

Flannery O'Connor, *Mystery and Manners*

George Plimpton, *Paris Review* interview of Ernest Hemingway

Mary Austin Speaker, "The Day the Flames Would Stop"

The Elements of Fiction

In order to write fiction, you will need to understand a little about what it's made of and how it works. The chapters in Part Two contain simple, brief explanations of some basic elements: character, plot, point of view, time, setting, dialogue, subtext, and theme. There are examples of each from published fiction as well as student writing, and suggestions on how to develop these elements in your own writing.

CHAPTER 3

Character

It's almost like a stress in you that goes on, nibbling and nibbling, gnawing away at you, in a very inquisitive way, wanting to know. And of course while all that's happening you're stroking in the colors, putting a line here and there, creating something which moves further and further away from the original. The truth emerges, the person who is created is a different person altogether—a person in their own right.

—William Trevor, *Paris Review* interview

Character: A Story's Center

What distinguishes a mere made-up story from artistically rendered **fiction**? Writing teachers are very fond of saying that in contemporary literary fiction, **character,** the portrayal of human beings (or, occasionally, nonhuman individuals), is central. In this chapter, you'll find a discussion of how character relates to other elements of fiction, including **plot** (the pattern of a story's action), **setting** (the story's environment), **theme** (the story's main idea or ideas, usually conveyed indirectly), and technique. You'll also explore ways in which you can **characterize** or portray your characters through their physical description, behavior, and speech.

Like any generalization, the idea that character is central isn't always true, but it's an excellent place to start. It's easier to understand if we compare today's fiction with forms that originated in the past, such as the Greek tragedy, in which characters' lives and actions are manipulated by the gods; or the old-fashioned melodrama, which contained no real characters. The suffering heroine, the evil villain, the brave hero—these were stock characters that didn't even attempt complexity. The whole point was the plot, the events. The plots as well as the characters were standardized, and so these stories and plays were thoroughly predictable, but many readers found that predictability satisfying, much as today's readers of romance novels or thrillers enjoy those forms. In contemporary fiction and film, the hero has become conflicted and occasionally weak, the heroine has grown more and more decisive and com-

Q: Must all characters be developed?

A: Even the details you won't be using/revealing in your story should be known to you—heritage, education, geographical background, possibly past traumas and triumphs—because even left unarticulated, such details will contribute to your portrayal of a character, making even your minor characters more truly alive on the page, as well as truly consistent and distinct from one another.

—*Patricia Traxler, poet and writer*

petent, and the villain has become more complex. In literary fiction, there are rarely "good" or "evil" characters, at least in the traditional sense. Conflict is more complex than that; it is the clash of human needs and desires.

Except in certain very deliberate deviations, when a **story**—which, by definition, is a telling of events that result in significant change *for an individual*—veers away from character, the result is almost always something less than contemporary literary fiction.

Character and Plot

If a story emphasizes **plot**—its pattern of events—over character, then by definition it is **melodrama**—a narrative containing lots of exciting action, but somewhat shallow or flat characters. Historically, melodramas were excessively emotional plays with romantic plots and "stock" or clichéd characters. Modern examples include soap operas, most TV dramas, and a lot of Hollywood movies.

What's wrong with melodramatic fiction? It is **sentimental**—that is, it doesn't earn the emotional response it solicits. Rather, it manipulates readers by means of **clichés,** devices or techniques that have become so familiar that they've lost force. What's wrong with being manipulated? Perhaps nothing, if you are aware of it and not taken in by it. But manipulative writing is propagandistic, whether it's on behalf of a political cause or simply the author's bank account. If you lack the ability to understand or care when you are being manipulated, you will be an easy mark for anyone with something to sell.

Plot-Centered Fiction   Certain types of fiction tend to be particularly susceptible to melodrama. Genre fiction—mysteries, love stories, horror stories, fantasy, and science fiction—all can be written well but often are not. This is partly because of the high level of detail required to balance a very dramatic plot with characters that are intriguing enough to drive the story. More often than not, the emphasis in these genres is on colorful plots or settings, and the characters are types. One of the more obvious examples is the monster or alien, a character type that depends all too often on overly familiar and trite **images** or sensory details resembling those in movies or comic books. The effect of these overfamiliar images is bland and ordinary rather than startling and otherworldly.

Usually, the key to creating well-written fantastic creatures and situations is to ground them, as Flannery O'Connor advised, "in concrete, observable reality." The same principles apply to any fiction in which dramatic events may be prominent: plot must not overshadow character, and meeting this requirement depends largely upon the quality of the detail. Gabriel García Márquez provides an excellent example of a fantastic character rendered with skill and care in his story "A Very Old Man with Enormous Wings" (pp. 293–298).

The Fantastic in the Real   Some writers choose to create human monsters, symbols of evil that are fully as frightening as their fantastic counterparts. A student of mine who loved horror fiction once described Flannery O'Connor's classic short story "A Good Man Is Hard to Find" (pp. 362–372) as "the best horror story I ever read." O'Connor's monster—or, more accurately, her fallen prophet—is more or less ordinary in appearance:

> The driver got out of the car and stood by the side of it, looking down at them. He was an older man than the other two. His hair was just beginning to gray and he wore silver-rimmed spectacles that gave him a scholarly look. He had a long creased face and didn't have on any shirt or undershirt. He had on blue jeans that were too tight for him and was holding a black hat and a gun.

The Misfit's monstrousness is shown through his speech and actions, and in O'Connor's language, which recalls the rhetoric of a country preacher:

> "I was a gospel singer for a while," The Misfit said. "I been most everything. Been in the arm service, both land and sea, at home and abroad, been twict married, been an undertaker, been with the railroads, plowed Mother Earth, been in a tornado, seen a man burnt alive oncet," and he looked up at the children's mother and the little girl who were sitting close together, their faces white and their eyes glassy; "I even seen a woman flogged," he said.

The Misfit is fearsome partly because of his behavior, partly because of the sense of inexorableness O'Connor has created through skillful **foreshadowing,** or hints about the story's eventual outcome, and partly because of The Misfit's ordinariness. Far from being a spindly green alien with fins and starlike eyes, he looks more or less like anyone else. The whole incident is entirely believable. The reader is left with the sobering feeling that such a thing might happen anywhere—and so the reader feels rather than merely understands the story's drastic view of redemption and fate. By creating full, believable characters, O'Connor has earned a clear emotional response that a less accomplished writer might try and fail to evoke through manipulating events.

Subordinating Plot to Character   How do writers learn to subordinate events to fully developed characters? There are a number of approaches to this task. One is to avoid extreme or tired subject matter. Death, natural disasters, sensational crime, the illness of the week, the love of a lifetime—such highly dramatic material is likely to overshadow a story's true center: how the main character changes. Consider how other authors have chosen or focused their subject matter. Mary Austin Speaker's "The Day the Flames Would Stop" (pp. 413–418) tells the story of a troubled marriage, but the actual events recounted are simple: the drive across the country to Las Vegas and the wedding. By attending closely to feelings and behavior, Speaker focuses her story on the characters rather than allowing the problems themselves to assume central importance.

Student writer Seth Pase takes a similar approach in "The Father" (pp. 372–375), a story about an abortion. But rather than choosing the most obviously dramatic events—the procedure itself, or the decision to have it—Pase focuses on the drive to the clinic. This approach emphasizes not the event itself but its meaning to and effect on the characters. The same is true of Ernest Hemingway's "Hills Like White Elephants" (pp. 320–323), another story dealing with abortion. Here, Hemingway shows a man and a woman waiting for a train and discussing the prospect of the abortion. By scaling down the events, Hemingway emphasizes the characters and how they change.

Rendering Characters Concretely   In addition to deemphasizing the events, all of these stories employ subtle detail—well-chosen, **concrete** (sensory) description; and distinctive gestures, mannerisms, and speech patterns—that create a vivid picture of the characters, making them individuals rather than types. These authors reveal their characters through their choices or realizations: Mary Speaker's character Alice sees the truth about her imminent marriage—and marries Jim anyway; Seth Pase's character Leo completes the transaction with his girlfriend, for better or worse; Hemingway's couple reaches the impasse that is their differences. In all of these ways—proportion, detail, and change—each of these stories tips the balance away from plot and toward character.

Character and Setting

Emphasizing **setting,** the story's environment, at the expense of character can result in travelogue: "What I Did on My Summer Vacation," or the college version, "My Semester Abroad." Such accounts, if well told, can make good nonfiction. This excerpt from Peter Mayle's *Year in Provence* is an excellent example:

We bought red peppers to roast and big brown eggs and basil and peaches and goat's cheese and lettuce and pink-streaked onions. And, when the basket could hold no more, we went across the road to buy half a yard of bread—the *gros pain* that makes such a tasty mop for any olive oil or vinaigrette sauce that is left on the plate. The bakery was crowded and noisy, and smelled of warm dough and the almonds that had gone into the morning's cakes. While we waited, we remembered being told that the French spend as much of their incomes on their stomachs as the English do on their cars and stereo systems, and we could easily believe it.

The main character in this book is the place itself. The author and his wife are relatively undeveloped, and accounts of their experiences are meant to characterize the place, not them. Rather than building toward the resolution of a conflict, the events build toward a full, detailed portrait of Provence, defining the book as travel writing rather than fiction.

Exotic Settings   Setting-centered writing includes not only travel writing but some genre fiction in which the futuristic city or the lush tropical island where the lovers meet is more developed than the characters. These approaches do not accomplish the goal of literary fiction: telling the story of a person who changes. How the author imagines Atlantis—unless interwoven with descriptions of a character facing a significant conflict—is often more compelling to the writer than to anyone else. Lacking a developed central character and conflict, the story loses tension. Such stories fail to answer the crucial question: "So what?" The author's next step should be to develop the main character and how she changes during the course of the story.

The Details of Place   On the other hand, consider this paragraph describing the setting in Joseph Connolly's "Hard Feelings" (pp. 260–270):

... Their apartment is decorated in the style I call Early College-kid. They say they don't care about material things, and it shows. There's isn't much furniture, and what there is looks second-hand. The dining room itself, which doubles as a library, has brick-and-board bookshelves along one wall filled with every book on self-esteem ever written. The table is rectangular, like a conference table, and looming over it is the world's ugliest light fixture. A single white globe hangs from a wide, clear plastic bell that reminds me of the Cone of Silence on the old T.V. show *Get Smart.* Someone on the show would say, "Lower the Cone of Silence" and this thing would come down over them. It was supposed to prevent eavesdropping on their conversations, but instead it made them unable to hear each other, and they would sit there trying to shout and no noise would come out. We all sat down at the table, and I looked up at the light fixture and said "Lower the Cone of Silence." Neil and Madelyn both turned puzzled stares on me, and Sally wrinkled up her nose and shook her head.

Every detail of this description tells us something about Neil and Madelyn—and on a deeper level, about the **narrator** (the voice that tells the story), whose wit is both entertaining and defensively judgmental. At the end of the paragraph, the author develops the characters by showing them as they react variously to the lamp. In this way, Connolly uses setting in the interest of characterization rather than merely for its own sake.

Character and Theme

One very noticeable difference between a thought-provoking work of fiction and an essay or sermon is the quality of the characters in the former. An essay or sermon may contain anecdotes, but in these the characters exist primarily to illustrate the author's point. Though the best personal essays, such as those of E. B. White, may contain developed individuals with distinctive voices, appearance, gestures, and relationships, the purpose of these nonfiction forms is different from that of a story or novel. Essays explore ideas, and what happens to the characters is illustrative, not in itself the main point.

Fiction explores human experience—how fictional characters change is the main point. Ideas emerge naturally out of that exploration, but if they ever begin to dominate it, the characters will flatten out and intelligent readers will feel manipulated. What pre-

Q: How does one write about characters of different racial or socio-economic groups without violating standards of political correctness?

A: Before you write about someone who is not you, ask why you're doing so. Do you have something valid to say about, or—as is really the case—*with* such a character? When the answer is yes, be smart and be as empathetic as you can be. Do not romanticize. And remember this: we are all human beings. Culture/race/money/religion aside, people's motivations are not so dissimilar as to be impossible to consider and, in a sense, understand—even if you don't agree.

—*Adam Golaski,*
editor, New Genre

sents itself as fiction has turned out to be propaganda. Such stories feel preachy or merely intellectual, and they're too self-consciously crafted to engage readers in a "fictional dream."

Letting Theme Emerge   This isn't to say that ideas have no place in fiction. But since fiction is about people changing, ideas originate and develop through characters and events. During the writing process, it usually works best to forget about theme and let the story develop naturally, even when this entails diverging from ideas you might have had about it. This approach allows for serendipity. Theme *emerges*. Often, the ideas in well-written fiction are so fused with other elements that they are hard to state directly.

If your story involves religion or politics, you will need to come to terms with this subtlety or you'll risk losing readers who don't agree with your beliefs, and even many who do. How directly you can write about theme depends upon the story's **voice**—the personality, tone, and mood conveyed by its language—and on how well you've created the characters. O'Connor's "A Good Man Is Hard to Find" (pp. 362–372) succeeds on a thematic level because the characters are so real. If the family were idealized, the story and its message would be pathetic and sentimental. If The Misfit were drawn in less detail, evil would be present only in theory rather than incarnate. If O'Connor were not true to her characters' natures—if, for example, she forced The Misfit to show mercy, another possible approach to the theme of redemption—the story would express an uncharacteristically sentimental view of religion.

Similarly, the character and voice of Celie, the protagonist in Alice Walker's novel *The Color Purple*, gives life to the author's political convictions. Celie's strong and vivid voice enlivens her experience as an abused and ultimately triumphant girl and woman.

> My little sister Nettie is got a boyfriend in the same shape almost as Pa. His wife died. She was kilt by her boyfriend coming home from church. He only got three children though. He seen Nettie in church and now every Sunday evening here comes Mr. _____. I tell Nettie to keep at her books. It be more then a notion taking care of children ain't even yourn. And look what happen to Ma.

In a kind of sleight of hand, Walker has made a character so compelling that readers are drawn into her life, feel with her, and naturally arrive at the political conclusions without being pushed into them.

In both cases, it's safe to assume that the authors had something to say—O'Connor, about religion; and Walker, about race, class, and gender—yet in each case these thematic matters emerge from between the lines. It is the characters who compel our interest.

Character and Technique

How you write—your style and technical proficiency—is a part of what your writing says; as in speech, voice is a part of the message. However, focusing disproportionately on technique—**point of view** (the perspective from which the story is told), tone, or style—may result in polished fiction that lacks soul. This is often a natural beginning phase, growing out of the writer's experimentation with various tools and approaches. It's good experience for beginning writers to practice specific techniques—for example, telling a story in the second person, playing with verb tense, or writing in dialect. These exercises allow writers to discover what goes into each of these approaches—and what must be done to make them work. But ultimately, most fiction is about people; style should serve character, rather than calling attention to itself.

For instance, when assuming the **second-person point of view,** in which the story is told through the eyes of a character called "you," the writer must find natural-sounding ways of convincing the reader that she is actually experiencing everything that goes on in the story. Two stories in this book, Christine Baxter's "If You Ever Want to Have a Fling" (pp. 233–238), and Eudora Welty's "The Key" (pp. 457–464), provide excellent examples of the second-person point of view; for a more extended discussion and examples, see Chapter 5, Point of View (p. 90).

Similarly, using the present tense offers challenges when the story's action moves back and forth through time. And although it may feel like a novelty to beginners, actually it has become almost as common as the past tense and so lacks some of the extra impact it once had. Beginners must therefore learn to exercise judgment about which tense will tell their stories most effectively. They must choose a verb tense purposefully rather than indiscriminately or because they feel it sounds more exciting. (See Chapter 6, Time: Verb Tense and Narrative Structure, p. 109, for additional discussion of verb tense.)

Kelly Zavotka's story "What Killed a Girl" (pp. 464–474), written during Kelly's senior year at Emerson College, contains many risky imaginative leaps, which succeed because of the author's emphasis on character. In this example from the story's third section, which is not included in this book, the narrator is a murdered girl speaking from beyond the grave to Shell, one of her murderers:

After Karen shot me I lay there in the mud while my body hardened into it. I lost feeling, first in my hands and feet, then arms and legs. Cold until they were numb. You know the sick iciness you get in your stomach when you haven't slept? The feeling you get from too many sit-ups? That was all I could feel, times one hundred. A tornado in my stomach, ripping my spirit from my head, my chest, my thighs and clinging for a while, as if it had tiny octopus fingers fixing sensation to my limbs. But Shell, the twisting and sucking in my belly pulled me in. I guess it's what you would call implosion of the soul. I feel nothing good or peaceful. I'm a storm. Pure hollowness, Shell, and disrest. I'm sickness, only.

Voice, imagery, and skillful rendering of emotion combine to create a startlingly real ghost. Because the character is so clearly felt, it's not a strain to believe in the story's supernatural aspect.

In these and many other ways, a writer's use of technique gives voice and dimension to her characters. A story that allows its readers to enter its characters' lives—to feel and experience through those characters—stands a chance of conveying something universal about human experience, and of engaging readers deeply and meaningfully.

Methods of Characterization

How writers portray their characters varies from author to author and from story to story. Most writers don't consciously apply the methods described in this chapter. Rather, they respond to opportunities that arise naturally within the story. The actual work of writing a character is usually more intuitive than rational, so the techniques listed below—physical description, behavior, and voice—should be seen as elements that may be blended or adapted in a variety of ways.

Physical Description

Physical description is one of the most direct methods of characterization. As in the examples quoted above from Joseph Connolly's "Hard Feelings" and Kelly Zavotka's "What Killed a Girl," a few well-placed observations can convey a lot. Author Norman Rush writes about physical descriptions of characters,

> There is a natural readerly hunger for this information, for understandable reasons (reader identification, social placing). If the reader's desire to visualize a character's physical envelope is to be frustrated, the writer should have a good reason for the maneuver.

In "A Good Man Is Hard to Find," Flannery O'Connor fulfills this need for concrete description by showing her main character in humorous detail:

The old lady settled herself comfortably, removing her white cotton gloves and putting them up with her purse on the shelf in front of the back window. The children's mother still had on slacks and still had her head tied up in a green kerchief, but the grandmother had on a navy blue straw sailor hat with a bunch of white violets on the brim and a navy blue dress with a small white dot in the print. Her collars and cuffs were white organdy trimmed with lace and at her neckline she had pinned a purple spray of cloth violets containing a sachet. In case of an accident, anyone seeing her dead on the highway would know at once that she was a lady.

Characterization by Contrast   In addition to the physical detail—the white cotton gloves, the sailor hat with violets on the brim, the dotted dress with white organdy collars and cuffs, the sachet—O'Connor uses the contrast with an earlier description of "the children's mother, a young woman in slacks, whose face was as broad and innocent as a cabbage and was tied around with a green headkerchief . . . " Because these details are filtered through the grandmother's point of view, they suggest her self-satisfaction and her sense of superiority. The grandmother's thought that anyone seeing her dead on the highway would know she was a lady is both comic and grimly prophetic. The description is precise and vivid, and gives readers a clear impression of the character.

The Narrator's Role in Characterization   Russell Banks's description of Wade Whitehouse early in his novel *Affliction* characterizes Wade. It also suggests some qualities of the narrator, who is Wade's brother:

Let us imagine that around eight o'clock on this Halloween Eve, speeding west past Toby's and headed toward town on Route 29 from the interstate turnoff, there comes a pale-green eight-year-old Ford Fairlane with a blue police bubble on top. Let us imagine a dark square-faced man wearing a trooper's cap driving the vehicle. He is a conventionally handsome man, but nothing spectacular: if he were an actor, he would be cast as the decent but headstrong leader of the sheepherders in range-war westerns of the '50's. He has deep-set brown eyes with crinkled corners, the eyes of a man who works outdoors; his nose is short and hooked, narrow at the bridge, with large flared nostrils. He looks his age, forty-one, and though his mouth is small, his lips thin and tight and his chin boyishly delicate, his lower face, tinged gray by a five o'clock shadow, has the slight fleshiness of a healthy hardworking athletic man who drinks too much beer.

Notice the stubborn concreteness of this description. Rather than saying the town is poor, Banks describes the old car its sheriff drives. Rather than telling readers that Wade works outdoors, he describes his crinkled eyes. The observation that Wade drinks too much hints both that Wade is failing and that his brother, the narrator, is not happy about it. Since the final word or image in any paragraph or sentence receives extra emphasis, this remark subtly suggests an aspect of the story's conflict. Here, point of view combines with physical detail to characterize Wade, his brother, and their relationship.

These two thorough, concentrated physical descriptions occur shortly after each main character first appears in the story. This is a serviceable though somewhat old-fashioned technique that Robie Macauley and George Lanning refer to in their book *Technique in Fiction* as "the introductory portrait." In each of these stories, the approach is justified; in "A Good Man Is Hard to Find," the technique works along with other aspects of the story to suggest the grandmother's pride and propriety, and to establish her voice; in *Affliction*, it conveys some necessary background material, including Wade's relationship with his brother.

Notice that in each case, the introductory portrait accomplishes more than one objective. To be successful, such thumbnail sketches must also be reasonably concise. Although as descriptions, they quickly dispense with the task of conveying certain obvious traits, they must be inserted unobtrusively so that they do not stop the story's action. Introductory portraits must in addition be supported by reminders later in the story so readers don't have to keep flipping back to the descriptions in order to remember who's who. Most contemporary stories are more likely to sprinkle in physical description bit by bit along with other elements so that the characters come gradually into focus. Macauley and Lanning point out that this second technique, which they call "the portrait over time," is more natural than the introductory portrait, and imitates the way we get to know people in life. It is also easier for readers to keep a character in view if the story continues building on the initial impression. Each added detail is a reminder, recalling descriptions that precede it.

Behavior

Overall, characters are defined by their actions: Flannery O'Connor's grandmother reaching out to touch The Misfit in recognition (See "A Good Man Is Hard to Find," pp. 362–372); Luke Ripley in Andre Dubus's "A Father's Story" (pp. 272–286) wrecking the car to cover up his daughter's crime; Alice walking down the aisle with Jim despite her misgivings in student Mary Austin Speaker's "The Day the Flames Would Stop" (pp. 413–418). But sometimes writers choose to work on a smaller scale, using less dramatic behavior to subtly introduce and develop characters. In his story "The Minister's Black Veil" (pp. 311–319), Nathaniel Hawthorne introduces the main character, the minister Mr. Hooper, gradually, by dropping occasional details about his appearance and behavior: he walks slowly and meditatively; he is "a gentlemanly person of about thirty," unmarried, neatly dressed, and wearing a black veil. Student Christine Baxter's "If You Ever Want to Have a Fling" (pp. 233–238) develops its main character similarly:

Q: How much description of characters should I include?

A: Physical description is not always necessary for a character. In fact, sometimes physical descriptions are simply misleading or distracting. Neither hair nor eye color tell you very much about a person's inner life, yet many of my students' first drafts—or my own—could have been written by hairdressers or ophthalmologists, these superficial characteristics are mentioned so often. Red hair, for example, comes up with astonishing frequency.

What makes a character come to life on the page is a sense of the character's attitude toward the world and toward herself. To the degree that physical description helps to convey or suggest that attitude, then it's helpful.

*–Margot Livesey,
writer and teacher*

> You make your way down the stairs and onto the uneven bricks of the sidewalk, your hand moving unconsciously to your skirt and easing the hem below your knees. You step to the right of the entrance and retrieve a cigarette from the pack in your bag. Hands slightly trembling, you fiddle with the matches, attempt to light one and fail.

These actions convey that the narrator is female and that she is alone and somewhat nervous. This sets the scene psychologically for the rest of the story, establishing her discomfort and disadvantage as a woman who is repeatedly and inexplicably accosted by men.

Fantasy and Reality   In his novel *Affliction*, Russell Banks similarly creates psychological context, by building on the introductory portrait of his main character Wade Whitehouse, contrasting his fantasies about his visit with his ten-year-old daughter Jill against his actual behavior:

> Like all the other parents for a change, he could see his kid win a prize in the costume contest, best this or that, scariest or funniest or some damned thing; late for the sleepy drive back to the trailer afterwards, Jill laying her head on his shoulder and falling peacefully asleep while he drove slowly, carefully home.
>
> He tried to explain their lateness to her without blaming himself for it. "I'm sorry for the screw-up," Wade said. "But I couldn't help it that it's too late to go trick-or-treating now. I couldn't help it I had to stop at Penney's for the costume," he said, stirring the air with his right hand as he talked. "And you were hungry, remember."
>
> Jill spoke through her tiger's mask. "Whose fault is it, then, if it's not yours? You're the one in charge, Daddy."

The exchange is painful to read because of the role reversal. In his self-absorption, Wade speaks to his daughter as if she were an adult, and his agenda is self-focused. What begins as an apology quickly turns to self-justification—he's hardly talking to her. Her ability to see through him evokes pain because she shouldn't have to do it, and her precocious accuracy underscores his immaturity. While the first description of Wade is from the outside—his appearance as seen by his brother—the second goes deeper by including speech and interaction.

Voice and Speech

In well-written stories, the words used by characters and narrator create a spoken effect; we seem to hear rather than see them. The resulting voices can indirectly convey much about the characters. In "A Thousand Buddhas" (pp. 329–334), Brenda Miller portrays her main character with telling details spoken by the narrator's soothing, rhythmic voice:

> Light streams through a low doorway into the gazebo, and this young woman leans her back against the deck. The sunlight zeroes into a circle on her belly. Jasmine bush and bamboo are reflected in the glass. The woman bends her head and covers her eyes as if she were about to weep. Steam rises and beads on the glass, obscuring detail and memory.
>
> The woman is not weeping. She is scooping up the water from the tub and splashing it to her face. If this woman is me, she is mumbling some kind of grateful prayer, alchemizing the water into a potion that will heal.

By describing her past self as seen in a photograph, and barely recognizable, this introductory portrait creates a frozen, ambiguous image, as uncertain as a memory. Combined with the narrator's commentary, the passage embodies what she asserts about retrospection, portraying two aspects of the main character: her current voice and the image of her former self. The effect is more than a mere assertion, though—the language evokes a lot of feeling. The verbs alone—*cradles, leans, streams, zeroes, bends, covers, obscuring, weeping, scooping, splashing, mumbling*—suggest gentleness, maternal feelings, an outpouring of emotion, ritual. In this way, the author creates both an introductory portrait and a portrait over time.

Multiple Voices   The novel *House of Sand and Fog,* by Andre Dubus III (son of the author of "A Father's Story"), contains two very distinct **narrative voices** or sensibilities. First, that of Behrani, an Iranian colonel relocated in California:

The fat one, the radish Torez, he calls me camel because I am Persian and because I can bear this August sun longer than the Chinese and the Panamanians and even the little Vietnamese, Tran. He works very quickly without rest, but when Torez stops the orange highway truck in front of the crew, Tran hurries for his paper cup of water with the rest of them. . . . We are up on a small hill. Between the trees I can see out over Sausalito to the bay where there are clouds so thick I cannot see the other side where I live with my family in Berkeley, my wife and son. But here there is no fog, only sun on your head and back, and the smell of everything under the nose: the dry grass and dirt; the cigarette smoke of the Chinese; the hot metal and exhaust of the passing automobiles. I am sweating under my shirt and vest. I have fifty-six years and no hair. I must buy a hat.

In contrast, here is the voice of the book's other main character, Kathy Lazaro, an American woman from Massachusetts:

My husband got to miss all this, that's what I kept thinking, that he didn't have to be around for any of this, and I was stuck at the El Rancho Motel in San Bruno. It was a shitty little one-story L of rooms wedged between an electrical parts warehouse and a truck stop bar near the 101 Freeway ramp. The TV in my room got sound but nothing on the screen, and it was only a Wednesday night but there was a live country band playing at the truck stop and the management must have had all the windows open, so I turned the TV up and listened to an old movie with Humphrey Bogart and in the end he gets shot and his girlfriend weeps and says he's free now, he's free.

The novel's conflicts are implicit in these two paragraphs: Kathy's displacement, her anger, her sense of entitlement, and her depression; Behrani's family, his sense of duty, his dignity and a certain superiority, and his grueling job. Beyond that, readers can sense in the language his formality and discipline. Kathy's bluntness reveals a disregard for convention and an instinctive insistence on her own needs.

Voice in Secondary Characters   By definition, "flat" or secondary characters must be less prominent than main characters. "When you fashion a story," Anton

Chekhov wrote, "you necessarily concern yourself with its limits: out of a slew of main and secondary characters you choose only one—the wife or the husband—place him against the background and describe him alone and therefore also emphasize him, while you scatter the others in the background like small change, and you get something like the night sky: a single large moon and a slew of very small stars." Writers can achieve this, first of all, by not naming secondary characters. "The plumber" or "her mother's friend" is fine for someone who won't reappear in the story. Description of these characters and their speech tends to be brief, proportionate to their importance. In general, a little more "telling" and a little less "showing"—that is, summarizing information rather than dramatizing it—is appropriate for secondary characters. For example, Flannery O'Connor dispenses with Bailey's wife by simply describing a few details of her appearance, as quoted on page 61. In "Hard Feelings" (pp. 260–270), Joseph Connolly is similarly concise when describing his secondary character Reposa:

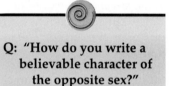

Q: "How do you write a believable character of the opposite sex?"

A: The same question can be asked of exercises in writing believably about characters in other life-circumstances radically different from one's own. (Rich . . . poor; white . . . black; literate . . . nonliterate; bourgeois . . . peasant; old . . . young.) Every attempt to cross such boundaries has to be embraced as an experiment whose success will be judged by members of the invaded community.

—Norman Rush,
writer

> Reposa is simply an offensive person. Every Sunday morning, we go through the ritual of trying to make fair teams out of whoever's shown up that day, and every Sunday morning Reposa says we should play "guineas versus micks." I once made the mistake of pointing out that Neil is a WASP, and Reposa said, "The little fruit looks like a mick to me. You keep him." He goes out of his way to set illegal picks and knock Neil to the floor; if Neil's glasses stay on he'll say "Damn, I'll have to hit him harder next time." Even the other guys, who don't like Neil either, have told Reposa to lay off.

Connolly sums Reposa up in a paragraph by allowing the narrator to comment directly, or "tell" about him, and by covering a number of moments briefly. This keeps Reposa from taking up too much space in the story. Like O'Connor's description of the mother, this one says as much about the point-of-view character as it does about the character being described.

All of the other elements of fiction may be seen as pointing toward character. The most convincing plots feel inevitable because the characters' actions flow from their natures. Ideally, plot is simply the playing out of character's interaction with event: the grandmother's pride and obstinacy and The Misfit's evil nature, combined with an accident, determine the family's fate. Luke Ripley's decision to cover up his daughter's crime grows out of her weakness and vulnerability and his own stubborn honesty, his soft spot for his daughter, personal grace—and another accident. Setting, descriptive detail, and technique are all enlivened by their relevance to character, which is the center point in most good contemporary fiction.

As You Write

Practically speaking, you can approach characterization from a couple of different angles: analytically, looking for ways to convey traits or feelings that you want a character to have; or intuitively, by first envisioning the character and then writing what you see, allowing her to surprise you. In the beginning, a lot of writers veer one way or the other, seeing these ways of working as distinct and incompatible. But that approach can be too rigid. Both methods are useful, and will work in a variety of ways for different writers and projects. Ultimately, most writers wind up using a combination of intuitive and analytical approaches.

How can you combine these methods? Here again, there's no set rule—but it often works well to allow characters some time to form on their own before imposing consciously preformed ideas upon them. Once you have intuitively discovered who the character is and have drafted the events and the main character, you can begin to work more analytically—to look at whether she is coming across and how you can adjust and enhance her characterization. In the beginning, try to focus on imagining the character in as much detail as possible.

But sometimes the best way really is straight through, rather than around; intuitive methods don't work for everyone at all times. Some writers may feel blocked by open-endedness. If, having given intuitive methods a chance, you find yourself unable to put aside your initial impressions enough to allow the fictional character to grow freely, or if you resist change or become angry or tearful at criticism, try something else for a while and come back to it. Here are some ideas that depend more on conscious and logical thought processes:

Writing it out   Write down every action the main character takes in the course of the story. For each action, list several alternative actions that the character might have chosen. List past events that aren't explicitly played out in the story—a history that will shed light on the main character's behavior.

The character in settings   Put the character in various situations—riding a Ferris wheel, driving a truck, buying groceries, on the phone turning down a date—and describe how she would act.

Listing traits   List the main and secondary characters' essential traits—those that lead to her most meaningful actions and realizations—and then quickly write down a number of ways of showing those traits through her actions, appearance, and interactions with other characters. Are any of your lists redundant—that is, are the traits similar enough that it's unclear who belongs to which list? Do any of the characters play similar roles within the story's plot? If so, could these characters' traits be combined in one person in order to tighten the story?

Other writers' characters   Read a story in the Anthology, or any story in which the characters are vividly portrayed. Choose a memorable charcter and picture her in your mind. How does the author convey personality, appearance, and behavior? How much does the character tell us directly? How much does the narrator say directly? Underline everything that contributes to the characterization.

Renaming   If you are finding it hard to imagine characters that are based on people you know, try renaming them. This small change is a symbolic way of giving yourself permission to fictionalize, and it removes constant reminders of real life, thus aiding the process of differentiation.

Defying character clichés   Experiment with using a model to inspire details of your character's clothing, gestures, tone of voice, choice of words, and appearance. Watch the model at home or at work, looking for differences as well as the similarities with your character. This technique works well if a character is hard to envision or if you find yourself relying on stereotypes or clichés such as the hardbitten attorney or the depressive mother or the wacky best friend or the amusing and secondary gay pal.

Thinking it out   Write about your characterization ideas and difficulties or, if possible, talk them out with someone else. Try using the chart in Chapter 11, Working With Readers (p. 218), to keep track of your thoughts. Look especially for signs of the past—places where you are reluctant to let go of a model who may have originally inspired a character but who may now be obsolete.

Reprise   Once you've drafted your story, repeat some of these exercises. This will help you to avoid canonizing early characterizations. Your vision of the story and its characters will be ongoing. If you allow yourself to write in layers, the characterization as well as everything else will deepen and grow richer with each revision.

Exploration and Discovery

Characterization commonly develops over the course of several drafts, but you can enhance that natural process by self-critiquing and by asking help from others. The questions and activities in this section are designed to help you develop well-rounded and believable characters, and to point up the importance of character to your story.

Ask Yourself

- *What elements in your story define the characters?* Does living space convey personality and values, as in the example above from Joseph Connolly's "Hard Feelings"? How about physical appearance, clothing, and speech? Most of all, what do the characters' actions say about them?

- *Are there characters who are only partly visible to you as you work on your first draft?* Are there gaps in what you know about them? It can be tempting to try to quickly reason out how to fill these gaps. But since people are not always reasonable and predictable, this sometimes results in too much con-sistency—in forced or strained characterization. Are there places where what you wrote about a character doesn't ring true? Take notes on all of these thin spots.

- *How do your main character's impulses and desires differ from your own?* In what ways do they conflict with what you want her to do? The characters you create are, literally, both you and not you. Respect the point of divergence: where you notice the character doing things that you don't entirely under-stand but that feel right.

Ask Readers

- *How would you describe the story's main character?* What does her voice sound like? What does she look like? What is she wearing? What does she drive? In each case, what details in the story give you this impression?
- *Do any of the secondary characters distract attention from more important elements of the story?* What questions do these characters raise? Would the story be en-hanced more by further developing these characters, or by downplaying or eliminating them?
- *Is the story's plot focused more on the characters or on the events?*

Wordplay

Who am I?   List your characters' names across the top of a sheet of paper and write "I am . . . " ten times under each character's name. Next, turn each "I am" into a sentence describing the character. Here, as an example, is a description of Lit-tle Red-Cap, the main character of the Grimm's fairy tale:

> I am a girl with short brown hair.
>
> I am innocent.
>
> I am looking forward to seeing my grandmother.
>
> I am a little cold.
>
> I am wearing my red cloak.
>
> I am carrying a basket.
>
> I am hungry—I hope my grandmother will have something for me to eat.
>
> I am a little tired of walking.

Like the dream exercise in Chapter 1, Playing with Words (p. 6), this first-person listing is designed to help you find the character's sources within yourself. As with a dream, granting that the character is you in some sense allows you to feel his or her nature from within.

The other side of the story   Once you've established a character's most prominent traits, round her out. Make another list like that in the exercise above, but this time, use the "I am's" to explore the character's hidden side. Ask yourself, what are the opposites of her most prominent traits? How will those opposite capabilities show up in the character? Nice people are sometimes annoyed. Angry people may also be vulnerable, funny, or unexpectedly forgiving. Aggressors may be fearful or weak or funny or deeply pained. Victims may be vindictive or self-pitying or not so innocent themselves. Intelligent characters may stammer or be emotionally backwards. Red Riding Hood's hidden side might look like this:

> I wish my hair were long and black.
>
> I like to tease people.
>
> Sometimes I'm bored at my grandmother's house.
>
> I like the way the snow feels on my face.
>
> Under my red cloak, I am carrying a pocketknife.
>
> I ate a little of the cake in the basket, being careful to pick it off the sides, where my grandmother wouldn't notice.
>
> My grandmother's cooking sometimes makes me sick.

Random traits   Japanese potters are careful always to include a flaw in their work: a shape that is round but not perfectly round, or a notch deliberately cut into the bottom rim of a tea bowl to indicate imperfection. Like the Renaissance painters who believed a mole on the face heightened beauty, these potters see perfection as ultimately boring. Similarly, a perfectly balanced character becomes unreal and doll-like. Adding random traits can help to dispel overconsistency: Somebody's grandmother might cheat on her income taxes; the county judge may collect dollhouse furniture. On separate scraps of paper, write down a few traits that don't relate directly to a particular character: fingernail-biting; invisible eyelashes; dry lips; small hands; a preference for spicy foods. Scramble your notes; then draw from the pile and try them out on various characters. Experiment with the effects.

Arbitrary models   This exercise will help further develop characters that are thin or stereotypical. Choose a real person who is similar to the character in age, gender, and other basic areas, but don't look for a mirror image. Observe the person closely and take notes on appearance, gestures, clothing, habits of speech, and so forth. Now add those details to the character. How do they change the character? How do they change the story? Try the exercise using several different models, or combining traits from various people.

Sensory freewrite   List the five senses (sight, hearing, smell, taste, touch) across the top of a sheet of paper. Under each heading, list everything you can think of about the character you're working on—appearance, dress, voice, body odor. Do this exercise quickly but thoroughly.

Revoicing   Use monologue as a way of exploring characters. Choose any character in your story, except for the narrator. Taking on the character's voice, rewrite a scene from the perspective of this particular character. Use the first-person point of view; let the character's voice tell about her side of a conflict. Try summarizing the whole story as this character would tell it.

Suggested Reading

The More Books and Stories section starting on page 496 provides complete bibliographic information for each title listed below.

Russell Banks, *Affliction*

Christine Baxter, "If You Ever Want to Have a Fling"

Joseph Connolly, "Hard Feelings"

Andre Dubus III, *House of Sand and Fog*

Andre Dubus, "A Father's Story"

Gabriel García Márquez, "A Very Old Man with Enormous Wings"

Ernest Hemingway, "Hills Like White Elephants"

Thomas Kennedy, "Reality and Other Illusions"

Robie Macauley, and George Lanning, *Technique in Fiction*

Peter Mayle, *A Year in Provence*

Brenda Miller, "A Thousand Buddhas"

Flannery O'Connor, "A Good Man Is Hard To Find"

Flannery O'Connor, "The Church and the Fiction Writer"

Seth Pase, "The Father"

Mary Austin Speaker, "The Day the Flames Would Stop"

Alice Walker, *The Color Purple*

E. B. White, *Essays of E. B. White*

Kelly Zavotka, "What Killed a Girl"

CHAPTER 4

Plot

> *To be whole is to have a beginning and a middle and an end. By a "beginning" I mean that which is itself not, by necessity, after anything else but after which something naturally is or develops. By an "end" I mean exactly the opposite: that which is naturally after something else, either necessarily or customarily, but after which there is nothing else. By a "middle" I mean that which is itself after something else and which has something else after it. It is necessary, therefore, that well-constructed plots not begin by chance, anywhere, nor end anywhere, but that they conform to the distinctions that have been made above.*
>
> —Aristotle, *Poetics*

Plot: The Revelation of Character

Fiction—made-up stories written according to artistic conventions—is about people. But **character,** the nature of the story's main actors, is revealed and developed through action, events—through **plot**. If **story** can be loosely thought of as what happens in a work of fiction (more specifically, as events resulting in change), then plot is how the story is organized and presented—how one event builds upon another, developing a central conflict and leading to the story's climax. In our culture, without a plot of some sort—events ordered by cause and effect and resulting in change—a story will not be told. It becomes pointless, merely an **anecdote** or unstructured retelling of a single incident. This chapter explores the basic elements of a traditional plot: exposition, rising

Q: **Is form important in fiction?**

A: Not to know a hind has no horns, as Aristotle reminds us, is not so serious as to paint it inartistically. God, and art, may be in the details, but the soul of the drama is in the plot, the action, the *agon*—that is, in the intensity of the conflict and of the conviction that you bring to what you do.

—Leslie Epstein, writer

action, climax, and falling action. It also discusses the role of conflict in fiction.

We commonly describe a story on the basis of its events: "It's about a girl who goes into the forest and defeats a wolf"; "It's about a Vietnam veteran coming to terms with his past." Writer Poe Ballantine offers this explanation about the importance of plot in the writing of his story "The Blue Devils of Blue River Avenue":

> I thought this would be the simplest story in the world to write. It was merely about being born into a lucky house and the children across the street being born into an unlucky house, a mood-theme piece rich with droll details and seemingly profound ideas which I thought I could substitute for a plot. However, a story without a plot is often like a mammal without a spine, so the thing went through

vast circus and jelly-roll contortions before ever finding a place to stand and lean its elbow up on the china hutch. . . . For a while it was something like a mininovel with paragraph-length chapters; then, as I continued to excise irrelevant parts, it became a *New Yorker*-style deli-slicer with numbered vignette paragraphs. . . . Gradually it evolved into a story called "1024 Theories of Evil," which was repeatedly turned down by publications of merit (but usually with some positive comment), largely, I imagine, because it still had no plot. Stubbornly and plotlessly, I continued to revise, and finally I submitted a highly polished version to *The Sun*, who said, "Cut out all this Theories of Evil stuff". . . . The Theories of Evil stuff was what held the story together, I thought, but I took it out, and it slid away like an oily gray stomach tumor down the drain; then I put in a plot and realigned the frame to subordinate. About three versions later I came up with what you see.

This experience may be familiar to many readers of this book. It can be hard to understand when readers don't seem to care too much about the thematic implications of a story or the quality of the description. Instead, they want to know what will happen to the main character and—of course—how she will respond and change. The other things will come along and may be appreciated by people who know something about writing, but **narrative tension,** the intrigue of character and conflict, is what engages readers emotionally, pulling them through the pages. Even stories in which the most important movement is psychological or thematic need some kind of ostensible plot—a stage on which these psychodramas or themes can be played out, even if it amounts to a pretext. Though plot is not the heart of a story, putting a well-developed character in a situation, creating a conflict, and building it until it resolves focuses the story on the character and what happens to her, submerging the heavier issues to create a textured and dimensional **narrative** or telling of events.

The Narrative Arc

"Stories are about trouble," writer and critic George P. Elliott said. Conflict and resolution isn't the only way of looking at plot, but it's a good one to start with. Essentially, plot portrays change—what happens to and within a human being. Change is why a story matters, what makes it more than an anecdote and different from an essay. It's why the author has chosen to tell the story of this particular moment. It's the answer to the question, "So what?" In Andre Dubus's "A Father's Story" (pp. 272–286), Luke Ripley, the protagonist, is confronted with a dilemma that forces him to choose between the love and mercy he feels toward his daughter, and his allegiance to religious and civil law. Out of the ensuing struggle with God emerges a fuller, less symmetrical, and more mature faith. In James Joyce's "Araby" (pp. 323–327), a young man learns something of love's elusiveness. In each of these stories, the main character makes a decisive choice or comes to a realization that changes him. The characters' actions build up to that moment of change. Not all change is obvious or easily summarized. But if the story is well told, it can be felt.

Very simply, a traditional plot can be understood as an arc. A simple example—the original Grimms' version of the familiar fairy tale about Little Red Riding Hood (called by the Grimm brothers "Little Red-Cap"; see pp. 298–300)—can be used to explain the narrative, as shown in the illustration on page 74.

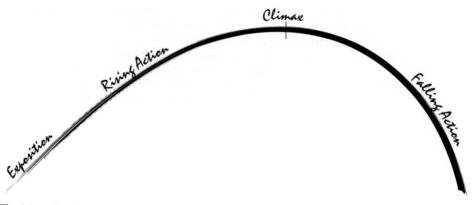

The Narrative Arc

Exposition

The first element of the **narrative arc** (shown above) is **exposition**—whatever background information is necessary for the reader to understand what's going on in the story. One of this book's early reviewers wrote that "Exposition should take place all the time; a good writer will make it as unobtrusive as carpeting." This omnipresence and subtlety make exposition one of the most difficult aspects of writing, and one of the most easily taken for granted. Exposition is something you don't *want* readers to notice. To achieve that, you must study and practice it assiduously.

Background Material: Integrating Exposition Subtly   Exposition may occur at any time in a story before the climax, but naturally, it tends to center around the beginning. What do you need to know in order to understand the story of Little Red-Cap?

> Once upon a time there was a dear little girl who was loved by everyone who looked at her, but most of all by her grandmother, and there was nothing that she would not have given the child. Once she gave her a little cap of red velvet, which suited her so well that she would never wear anything else; so she was always called "Little Red-Cap."

She is a nice little girl who loves her grandmother, and she wears a red cap. This, along with the fact that her grandmother lives in the woods, which is mentioned in the next paragraph, is the exposition in the story of Little Red-Cap.

While some stories, such as fairy tales, present exposition in a straightforward and simple manner, in many cases, especially in contemporary fiction, it is subtly interwoven with the story's action and description. The first paragraph of Akhil Sharma's "Cosmopolitan" (pp. 391–406) supplies directly and indirectly most of the information necessary to understand the story that follows, while at the same time initiating the story's action:

A little after ten in the morning, Mrs. Shaw walked across Gopal Maurya's lawn to his house. It was Saturday, and Gopal was asleep on the couch. The house was dark. When he first heard the doorbell, the ringing became part of a dream. Only he had been in the house during the four months since his wife had followed his daughter out of his life, and the sound of the bell joined somehow with his dream to make him feel ridiculous. Mrs. Shaw rang the bell again. Gopal woke confused and anxious, the state he was in most mornings. He was wearing only underwear and socks, but his blanket was cold from sweat.

Sharma tells us directly the time and place: a little after ten in the morning, in the main character Gopal's living room. He has been asleep on the couch, and as the story begins, he is just awakening. In addition to this logistical scene-setting, Sharma mentions that Gopal has lived alone in the house since his wife and daughter left four months ago; that Gopal wakes every morning confused and anxious; that he has been dreaming, a dream that combines with the sound of the doorbell "to make him feel ridiculous." His anxiety is emphasized by his blanket "cold from sweat." Concisely, this opening paragraph portrays a man who has not quite emerged from emotional chaos.

Emotional Exposition   Because the story is about Gopal's emotional life, much of the exposition conveyed here is emotional information. With this sort of exposition, the writer's task is to find indirect ways of conveying emotion: **concrete** (sensory) details, interesting juxtapositions. The fact that Gopal sleeps in the living room in his underwear and socks, that he now lives alone, that his dreams are troubled, say as much as the adjectives, *ridiculous, confused,* and *anxious.* Because the story is written from Gopal's **point of view** or perspective, these details take on an even more anxious tone: this is how he sees himself.

Here is another example of straightforward but deftly introduced exposition. This one is from student Jeannine Thibodeau's story "Close" (pp. 443–456):

I don't know which direction she's coming from, so my eye wanders up and down the street. As always, my gaze finds them. Every size and every shape, from a firm little lump under a loose blouse to belly bulging, ready to pop. It's not like I seek them out, like I try to spot these pregnant women. I do not try to target them. They're simply everywhere.

I see a flash by the door and look up in time to see Lenore in front of me. "Oh, you cut off all your hair," I say before I can stop myself. Lenore is younger than I, six years, and is beautiful. Today she looks like hell. Her eyes are dark with rings underneath and her cheekbones seem sharper than the last time I saw her, three months ago. Ever since she moved in with Manny, a slouchy guy with long glossy hair and no personality, all she does is party. She says she dropped out of NYU to work on her music. I don't know if she ever picks up her bass anymore.

These first paragraphs tell us that the **narrator** or voice that tells the story is preoccupied with pregnant women; that she is waiting for Lenore; that Lenore is, at least in the narrator's eyes, a college dropout, a nonpracticing musician, living with a deadbeat, and somewhat irresponsible; that something is wrong with Lenore. The narrator's blurted comment about Lenore's hair subtly suggests rivalry. Listed this way, these details are merely a description of a story. It is the narrator's **voice**—her personality, tone, and mood—that gives them life. Try reading these paragraphs aloud and notice how naturally the author has slipped in the background information, and how it combines with the narrator's perspective to reveal not only the past but the sisters' relationship and the narrator's own conflicts.

Even Quieter Exposition   Another student example, from Seth Pase's story "The Father" (pp. 372–375), demonstrates how economically an author can set the scene:

He pulls the car up slowly and puts his blinker on before turning into the driveway. Her father is watching from behind the curtains in the living room with a long cigar hanging from his mouth, unlit. He considers simply honking the horn and waiting in the car, but thinks better of it. He kills the engine, gets out of the car, and, taking a deep breath, climbs the steps to the back door.

Immediately, it is clear that the protagonist is a young man coming to visit a young woman who lives with her father. Readers can sense the protagonist's youth and his caution or reluctance in the way he drives and his observation of the girl's father watching him from inside—a detail that suggests self-consciousness. The young man is somewhat at a loss about how to act. There is a sense as he approaches the house, "taking a deep breath," that he's steeling himself for something momentous. More than the previous example, this story achieves much or most of its effect through what is not said. By hinting at but never explicitly identifying the momentous thing, the author creates interest and curiosity in the reader, and tension in the narrative.

Working with Large Amounts of Exposition   In psychological stories like these, there often are few logistical or physical details that must be conveyed. The necessary exposition consists in large part of mood or state of mind. However, some forms of writing—science fiction, fantasy, legal drama, stories that cover a long span of time—may require large amounts of technical or logistical exposition. In such cases the writer must integrate the exposition without stopping the story's action and thus losing the thread of tension that holds it together and engages readers. Deciding what the story's main events are, what should be placed in the background, and what readers just don't need will determine the story's shape, its emphasis, and its rhythm or intensity. It's often not possible to figure these things out initially—you may need to experiment with different approaches.

Slowing Down the Action   Although long passages of solid exposition will risk sinking your story, you should not feel that any and all interruptions are forbidden; readers of contemporary literary-quality fiction will tolerate some slowing down of the story's action in order to supply hints about the characters' personalities and motivation, and to develop the story's texture and tone. Such readers will generally be willing to participate imaginatively in the story, as long as the gain in depth and complexity is worth the slowing down of suspense and action. This sort of slowing down is one thing that often separates literary fiction from fiction whose sole or primary purpose is to entertain. Plot and character balance each other and may be intertwined. The challenge is to maintain enough narrative tension to sustain readers' interest while keeping the emphasis on the people.

In this book's anthology, perhaps the clearest example of a story with lengthy exposition is "A Father's Story" (pp. 272–286) by Andre Dubus, in which the narrator and main character spends many pages describing the relevant facts of his current and past life as well as his spiritual state, before the story's main action even begins. This long expository section details his daily routines, his prayers, his thoughts of his children and of death, and his work taking care of his horses. It conveys his pain over his broken marriage and the loss of his children, particularly his daughter Jennifer. In addition, it gives some sense of other relationships: the two women he has loved since his marriage, and his friendship with his priest. All of these unhurried details convey the pace and quality of Luke's life and his aloneness, and the spiritual issues that preoccupy him: love, guilt, mercy. This carefully constructed personal and spiritual context allows the story's climax to resonate beyond its immediate, literal significance.

Evaluating Exposition   What do you have in mind about the events and situations that form your story's background? How much of that can readers understand or sense from reading the story? What do readers need to know at the outset? These questions, even the first, may be difficult to fully answer alone. Empathetic responses from readers are often the best ways to find the answers. See the Ask Readers section on page 87 and the Questions and Ideas section at the end of Chapter 11 (pp. 216–224) for some suggestions about how to elicit this information from readers. Take a look at some of the stories in this book and ask yourself what you know about the characters and situations after reading the first paragraph or two. Then ask how you know it. You'll see that in addition to direct explanation, writers use subtle cues, nuances, and descriptive details to convey background information.

Rising Action: The Case of Little Red-Cap

"One day her mother said to her: 'Come, Little Red-Cap, here is a piece of cake and a bottle of wine; take them to your grandmother." The first two words—"One day"—place the story at a specific time and place and signal the beginning of its action. What follows is a series of events—not random, but carefully building up to a peak or climax. Little Red-Cap sets off through the woods for her grandmother's house. She meets the wolf, who finds out where she is going and distracts her, eats the grandmother, and disguises himself in her clothes. Arriving at the house,

---

She was surprised to find the cottage-door standing open, and when she went into the room, she had such a strange feeling that she said to herself: "Oh dear! how uneasy I feel to-day, and at other times I like being with grandmother so much. She called out: "Good morning," but received no answer; so she went to the bed and drew back the curtains. There lay her grandmother with her cap pulled far over her face, and looking very strange.

"Oh! grandmother," she said, "what big ears you have!"

The series of observations and responses that follows brings Little Red-Cap closer and closer to the awful truth. These events, which build up to the story's climax, are called **rising action.** In a simple, traditional plot such as this one, a central conflict—the wolf intends to eat Little Red-Cap and her grandmother, who do not wish to be eaten—is established. Each action that follows—Red-Cap meeting the wolf, revealing her destination, arriving at the house, noticing the door ajar, speaking with the disguised wolf and slowly realizing the truth—advances the conflict. Each rising action **scene** or segment of the story is purposeful, moving the main character "from point A to point B" and toward the story's climax and resolution. What would happen if the author threw in a picnic in the woods, some conversation with friends Red-Cap happened to meet along the way, and then they decided to take in a concert or a movie? The tension created by the developing conflict would be dissipated, and the story would trail off and get lost in irrelevant detail. It would become boring.

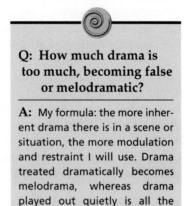

Q: How much drama is too much, becoming false or melodramatic?

A: My formula: the more inherent drama there is in a scene or situation, the more modulation and restraint I will use. Drama treated dramatically becomes melodrama, whereas drama played out quietly is all the more powerful and affecting.

—*Patricia Traxler,*
poet and novelist

Rising Action in Contemporary Fiction   There are a lot of obvious differences between fairy tales and contemporary short stories, but some things are surprisingly similar. Like the rising action in "Little Red-Cap," that in "A Father's Story" begins as the narrator, having finished a long expository passage, locates the story in a specific time and place: "She told me all of it, waking me *that night* when I had gone to sleep listening to the wind in the trees and against the house . . . ." Witnessing his daughter's distress as she recounts the night's events, Luke imagines the sequence of events as clearly as if he had been there: the three girls went to a movie, had some beer, went to the beach, bought more beer, and drove home listening to music and the sound of the wind. At the crest of a hill, a man ran in front of the car and Luke's daughter hit him and kept going, drove home and knocked on her father's bedroom door. After she has finished talking, Luke pours her a drink and drives to the scene of the accident, praying that the young man is still alive, or that if he is dead that Jennifer will not be caught. Holding the man's body, he listens for a heartbeat, finds and then loses it, and then drives back home. In this story, events are intertwined with the protagonist's emotional, moral, and religious conflicts, so that as the tension builds, ideas and feelings explicitly develop, clash, and resolve.

Rising Action and Foreshadowing   Not all stories address readers on the same level. Flannery O'Connor's "A Good Man Is Hard to Find" (pp. 362–372) achieves an almost physical impact from the author's unnervingly clear **foreshadowing** (hints about the story's eventual outcome) in the form of symbols and suggestive

images (sensory details). Like that in "A Father's Story," the rising action in "A Good Man Is Hard to Find" forms a sequence of distinct, dramatic events: Bailey and his family set out on a vacation, with the children bickering and the grandmother trying at every opportunity to thwart the plan. Meanwhile, The Misfit has escaped from prison. Outside Toombsboro, the grandmother makes up a story about a plantation house with a secret panel, designed to throw the trip off course. The children pick up on it, her plan works, Bailey turns down the wrong road, and the family meets up with The Misfit and his partners. By adding to the rising action powerful details such as a family graveyard, Toombsboro, a restaurant owner named Red Sammy, and the early image of the grandmother picturing herself dead on the side of the road, Flannery O'Connor creates a gathering sense of doom, unstated but felt.

Understating the Events   Some stories contain very little action at all; the tension and intrigue is in the nuances of the characters' interactions. In Ernest Hemingway's "Hills Like White Elephants" (pp. 320–323), a man and a woman wait for a train and order drinks. She walks to the other side of the station and returns; he does the same. That's the extent of the physical action, yet by the end of the story both are changed. Here, the conflict and the action are mostly interior. In this subtle story, gestures, changes of subject, or bits of description dropped by characters or narrator advance the conflict as dramatically as do larger events in other stories.

There are obviously many ways to present a story's rising action. But whether your story's action is simple or involved, subtle or dramatic, the writing process itself is more or less the same. When you are beginning to write, try thinking of the events leading up to the climax and its resolution as steps on a staircase rather than as a smooth slope. Each event is clearly defined, and each clearly moves the story's main character one step closer to the climactic moment.

The Climax

When the wolf had appeased his appetite, he lay down again in the bed, fell asleep and began to snore very loud. The huntsman was just passing the house, and thought to himself: "How the old woman is snoring! I must just see if she wants anything." So he went into the room, and when he came to the bed, he saw that the wolf was lying in it. "Do I find you here, you old sinner!" said he. "I have long sought you!" Then just as he was going to fire at him, it occurred to him that the wolf might have devoured the grandmother, and that she might still be saved, so he did not fire, but took a pair of scissors, and began to cut open the stomach of the sleeping wolf. When he had made two snips, he saw the little Red-Cap shining, and then he made two snips more, and the little girl sprang out, crying: "Ah, how frightened I have been! How dark it was inside the wolf"; and after that the aged grandmother came out alive also, but scarcely able to breathe. Red-Cap, however, quickly fetched great stones with which they filled the wolf's belly, and when he awoke, he wanted to run away, but the stones were so heavy that he collapsed at once, and fell dead.

Though it usually occurs toward the end, the **climax** is the central point of the plot. It usually involves a pivotal choice or realization that brings about a change in the main character. In this fairy tale, the change is very simple and circumstantial: because of a fortunate heroic act by someone else, Little Red-Cap and her grandmother are saved. The main character does not make a defining choice or realization, although, once rescued, she does contribute to the wolf's defeat by weighing him down with stones so he can't escape. In "Little Red-Cap," the conflict is resolved through the intervention of an outside force.

Flannery O'Connor uses a somewhat similar device in "A Good Man Is Hard to Find" pp. 362–372: The Misfit intervenes, taking the lives of the main characters. However, at the moment of her death the grandmother has a realization: "She saw the man's face twisted close to her own as if he were going to cry and she murmured, 'Why you're one of my babies. You're one of my own children!'"

The reliance on an outside force to perform or trigger the story's climactic events reflects a belief in fate and, in O'Connor's case, in evil. In both stories, the true subject is not only the main character but also the nature of the world in which she lives. By causing the climax to pivot on another character's action, each writer deemphasizes the protagonist's role in her own fate and in the conflict's resolution.

But the Grimms' version of "Little Red-Cap" contains an alternate ending. "It is also related," the authors add, "that once when Red-Cap was again taking cakes to the old grandmother," she was approached by another wolf. This time, she went straight to her grandmother.

"Well," said the grandmother, "we will shut the door, that he may not come in." Soon afterwards the wolf knocked and cried: "Open the door, grandmother, I am little Red-Cap, and am bringing you some cakes." But they did not speak, or open the door. . . .

In this version, Red-Cap and her grandmother outsmart the wolf and "Red-Cap went joyously home, and no one ever did anything to harm her again." A contemporary version of this story might similarly emphasize the main character's decisions and actions rather than relying on the plot device of a rescue. If we were to conventionally modernize "Little Red-Cap," we might decide that the conflict should be resolved through a revealing choice or decision by the main character as in the alternate ending quoted above, rather than by an outside force, the huntsman. Since Little Red-Cap is the central character, by this standard the decisive action at the point of the story's climax should be hers and she should be the one who changes as a result. We might delete the huntsman entirely and have Little Red-Cap outsmart the wolf. If we did that, Little Red-Cap would change from unsuspecting little girl to hero. Like Luke Ripley in Andre Dubus's "A Father's Story," she would define her character by choosing to do what is necessary to overcome opposition.

A Contemporary "Little Red-Cap"   In fact, that very rewriting has been done in the 1996 film *Freeway*, directed by Matthew Bright. In the film, the story of "Little Red-Cap" is modernized in a number of ways, the most profound of which is the attention to Red-Cap's character and its ultimate results—her actions. Red-Cap is portrayed as an abused child—tough, angry, rebellious, and emotionally honest. In the end it is she, not the police or the legal system, who vanquishes the "wolf," a human predator who picks her up as she hitchhikes on the freeway. Through her actions, her character is revealed and defined. Because she, not an outside force, has made the decisive choice, the film's emphasis is more clearly on character than is the fairy tale's.

Change: The Heart of the Story   A story's climactic moment may be dramatic and physical, or it may be subtle—a shift in sensibility rather than a major event. The essential thing is change, and often that change is emotional. Luke Ripley sees the skid marks, holds the young man as he dies, and confronts his own sins: that he did not call for either priest or ambulance. He returns home, leaving the young man's body to be found—an act he recognizes as a betrayal of his God and his community. He mercifully lies to Jennifer, telling her the man died on impact. With her, he disposes of the beer bottles. After she is asleep, he drives the car into a tree near the church to destroy evidence of her crime. In this protective act he assumes responsibility for her actions and betrays his closest friend, the priest, by implicating him as an innocently false witness. In order to save and protect his daughter, Luke has chosen and acted decisively in a way that has both estranged him from and bonded him to God, family, and community.

The main character in student Mary Austin Speaker's story "The Day the Flames Would Stop" (pp. 413–418) changes in an even subtler way, realizing just after her wedding in Las Vegas that it was a mistake, and why:

> As she walked into the chapel, Nora Keene began playing "Here Comes the Bride" a little too jauntily. She felt a small kick in her stomach. The baby. It knew, too, what they were doing. Was it a soft, approving kick? A warning? Jim gazed at her as she walked; she could see the hope in his eyes. She cast her own down, thinking that she would never tell him that this felt very wrong. In an instant she knew why he loved her, and why she wanted the baby. He thought the flames would stop—she would save him, the baby would save him. She could read it on his face.

No one gets shot or decides to cover up a crime, and yet the moment of change is quietly dramatic and emotionally affecting. The narrative arc in this story is gentler and the changes subtler, but the movement through rising action to a climax and change is the same.

Falling Action

A story's **falling action,** sometimes called denouement, is what happens after the climax: ordinarily not much, just enough to tie up any loose ends and leave the reader with the understanding and the tone the author wishes to convey.

> Then all three were delighted. The huntsman drew off the wolf's skin and went home with it; the grandmother ate the cake and drank the wine which Red-Cap had brought, and revived, but Red-Cap thought to herself: "As long as I live, I will never by myself leave the path, to run into the wood, when my mother has forbidden me to do so."

In Flannery O'Connor's "A Good Man Is Hard to Find," for example, the final conversation between The Misfit and his accomplice Bobby Lee allows the story to coast down from its climactic moment, in which the grandmother, realizing in a terrible moment of grace the connection between herself and The Misfit, reaches out to touch him and he shoots her to death.

Hiram and Bobby Lee returned from the woods and stood over the ditch, looking down at the grandmother who half sat and half lay in a puddle of blood with her legs crossed under her like a child's and her face smiling up at the cloudless sky.

Without his glasses, The Misfit's eyes were red-rimmed and pale and defenseless-looking. "Take her off and thow her where you thown the others," he said, picking up the cat that was rubbing itself against his leg.

"She was a talker, wasn't she?" Bobby Lee said, sliding down the ditch with a yodel.

"She would of been a good woman," The Misfit said, "if it had been somebody there to shoot her every minute of her life."

"Some fun!" Bobby Lee said.

"Shut up, Bobby Lee," The Misfit said. "It's no real pleasure in life."

Some stories contain no falling action. Like many contemporary stories, Mary Austin Speaker's "The Day the Flames Would Stop" ends at the moment of the main character's realization. But as in other such stories, the physical action—in this case, Alice's wedding—has already peaked and the moment of change is emotional, crystallizing during its aftermath.

In addition to the diversity of conflicts and their resolutions, there are many variations of the basic narrative arc itself, such as double plots, subplots, and plot twists. For an example of such fiction, see Christine Baxter's unconventionally plotted story, "If You Ever Want to Have a Fling" (p. 233–238). Baxter's version of her own narrative arc, which she envisions as dragon-shaped, is reproduced on page 83.

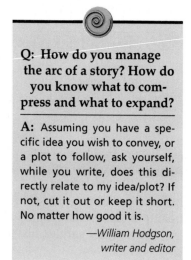

Q: **How do you manage the arc of a story? How do you know what to compress and what to expand?**

A: Assuming you have a specific idea you wish to convey, or a plot to follow, ask yourself, while you write, does this directly relate to my idea/plot? If not, cut it out or keep it short. No matter how good it is.

—William Hodgson,
writer and editor

What holds in all conventional contemporary stories, though, is the focus on a main character who changes in some way, and the build–up and release of tension. This building, peaking, and tapering off of tension is a natural shape—the shape of sex, of a thunderstorm, of life itself. Even in unconventionally structured narratives such as Brenda Miller's essay "A Thousand Buddhas" (pp. 329–334) or Kelly Zavotka's long story "What Killed a Girl" (pp. 464–474) there are definite conflicts with definite resolutions—an accumulation of tension and a release. This organization is a way of demonstrating that what happens matters.

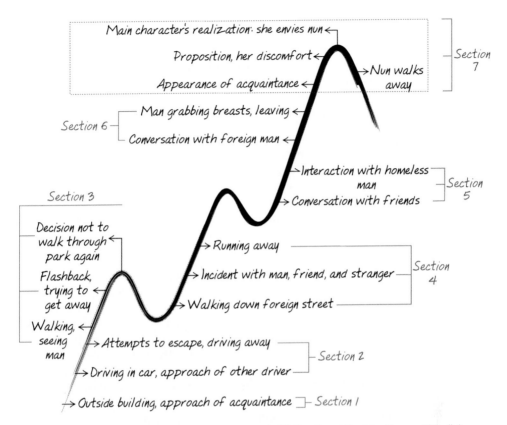

Main character's realization: she envies nun ←
Proposition, her discomfort ←
→ Nun walks away
Appearance of acquaintance ←
— Man grabbing breasts, leaving ←
— Conversation with foreign man ←
→ Interaction with homeless man
→ Conversation with friends
Decision not to walk through park again ←
→ Running away
Flashback, trying to get away ←
→ Incident with man, friend, and stranger
Walking, seeing man ←
→ Walking down foreign street
→ Attempts to escape, driving away
→ Driving in car, approach of other driver
→ Outside building, approach of acquaintance

Section 7
Section 6
Section 5
Section 3
Section 4
Section 2
Section 1

Unconventional narrative arc for Christine Baxter's "If You Ever Want to Have a Fling" (see pp. 233–238. In this diagram, upward slopes represent the rising action; peaks, the climaxes; and downward slopes, the falling action.

As You Write

The narrative arc is a useful, traditional way to chart the overall movement or emotional shape of a story. Writers often deviate from it, as you'll quickly see if you attempt to chart finely written published stories in this way. Writer and teacher Bruce Jorgensen explains this concept:

> It is true that this "arc" seems to be the most durable shape of story we know (whether it ends in tragic or comic or "mixed" denouement or in cognitive "epiphany"). Yet when we look at particular stories, either published or student work, we finally have to get down to far more particular movements than these general phases can specify . . . We have to track the sometimes minute "incidents" . . . deeds and done-to's . . . that actually articulate the larger phases we call rising action, climax, and falling action.

Ultimately, the best way to use the narrative arc is for it to become second nature, so that your fiction grows out of your own natural sense of tension and resolution. But good instincts are usually the result of lots of practice, and of experimentation.

Masked Motivation

Very often, stories contain "masked" conflicts or motivations—somewhat ordinary or mundane elements that account for the characters' strange behavior, allowing readers to more easily suspend disbelief as the writer then slips in the real reason. Student writer and boxing fan Ryan Conroy has likened this kind of "ostensible" motivation to the "rope-a-dope" trick:

> The boxer in question leans up against the ropes with his guard up for a number of rounds, letting his opponent punch and punch him to no avail. He's against the ropes and not throwing many punches so usually his opponent and the audience think he's beaten. Then suddenly after his opponent punches himself out (gets tired from throwing too many punches trying for a knockout), the boxer on the ropes starts his attack. His opponent, now too tired to fight back or defend himself, usually finds himself getting knocked out. This, on a side note, is how Ali beat Forman in 1974.

Writers often do the same sort of thing, creating a surface situation that masks the story's reality. For instance, in J. D. Salinger's "Uncle Wiggily in Connecticut," Eloise and Mary Jane are ostensibly navigating a boozy conversation about their college days as Eloise puts her daughter Ramona to bed. Eloise is irritated by Ramona's attachment to Jimmy Jimmereeno, her imaginary friend. The tipsiness allows just enough emotional hyperbole for the real problem—the loss of Eloise's first love—to become visible without being consciously central, and the imaginary boyfriend provides an effective surrogate, with Ramona's pain mirroring Eloise's.

Stories that deal with the supernatural often employ a similar technique. In these, authors may allow for a rational explanation of events the character and most likely the reader experience as extraordinary. For example, a vision occurs while the character is on drugs or looking at a spectacular sunset and seeing shapes in the clouds. These rationalizations are another kind of literary sleight of hand, allowing skeptical readers to suspend disbelief and thereby enhancing rather than minimizing the story's supernatural or fantastic aspects.

Defining Your Story's Shape

Regardless of the approach you choose, writing good fiction is not a matter of applying a "how-to" formula. As you've probably noticed by now, this book emphasizes the intuitive aspects of the process. Once you've drafted a story, however, it's useful to look at its plot in a more structured way. The following questions will help you begin to define your story's shape, practice plotting, and explore structural possibilities. They may be helpful to you in different ways at different points in the writing process. (The questions and ideas at the end of Chapter 10 take some of these issues further.)

Why this day?   Brett Lot asks this question in his classes at Vermont College. Short story writers don't have as many pages to use as novelists do, and so must choose their time frames strategically. What makes this particular moment more worth telling about than the day before it, or the day after? As you consider what to write about, choose the heart of the story, the point at which change occurs.

Who changes?   In most cases, by definition, this will be the main character. If a secondary character does most of the changing, ask yourself whether making that character primary would improve the story.

How does the character change? What significant choice or decision leads to the change?   These questions will identify the story's central point or climax.

What will be gained or lost by the character's choice?   In other words, so what? Who cares whether the character chooses this course of action or that one? What will be the consequences? The better readers know the main character and others who may be affected by the choice, the more they'll care about the consequences, and the story.

What are the story's main events?   How does each lead to the next—moving the main character from A to B and ultimately to the story's climax—that is, the main character's change? (Notice that these questions are taking you "backward" through the story. That's because defining the moment of change and then working back from it unifies the story, ensuring that everything in it relates to the ultimate outcome. Generally, it's a good idea to begin the story's events close to that moment, even if you then backtrack through some expository material before getting to the climax.)

What's the last straw?   What situation immediately precipitates the character's change? What prompts the decisive choice? These questions are intended to define the story's climax.

What loose ends remain after the story's climactic scene?   If there are more than a very few that need tying up, you may need to rework the story some. Don't spend more time than necessary on falling action.

What background information do readers need?   This will be the story's exposition. Although much exposition occurs early in the story, and some authors write it first, if you put off this task until you've figured out the rest of the story, you may find it easier to judge what readers will need at the outset.

When do readers need to know each bit of information?   Show the story to others if you're not sure.

How can each bit be artfully conveyed?   What parts can be shown, and what parts are better summarized? In general, the essential moments should be developed as scenes in which the characters speak and move around in a specific time and place. Less important moments can be summarized by the narrator.

These questions may not all be useful at the same time. Like the other elements of a story, your story's events will develop throughout the writing process. As you work, notice how this happens. Do you begin with a clear idea of the story's plot, or do you start at some other point? How do plot-related ideas come to you?

Are they prompted by working on a scene? By discussing the story with others? By trying out various possibilities or doing writing exercises? As you discover and cultivate an approach that you're comfortable with, you will learn to develop plots naturally and in proportion to the other elements of fiction.

Exploration and Discovery

Ask Yourself

How do you know if you've constructed a good plot? The answer is not in whether your story conforms to the narrative arc; it is in the tension you've generated. Theories aside, plot is emotional. A good story raises a question: Will Little Red-Cap (pp. 298–300) escape the wolf? Will Luke Ripley in "A Father's Story" (pp. 272–286) turn in his daughter? Will Mr. Hooper in "The Minister's Black Veil" (pp. 311–319) ever show his face? The tension, as readers await the answer to the question, keeps them reading. And the skill or ineptness with which the writer answers the question causes them to wish the story hadn't ended, or to throw the book against the wall. The following questions will help you evaluate whether your story's plot makes emotional sense.

- *What will be the reader's question?* As you think about your story, what is the largest issue that it raises? For instance, in Flannery O'Connor's "A Good Man Is Hard to Find" (pp. 362–372), readers may wonder whether the family will encounter The Misfit, and if so, whether they will escape. On a higher level, they may wonder what it means that this family should, through a series of accidents and foolishness, wind up on the same road as their murderer.

- *What's the character's question?* This is generally somewhat smaller in scope; in O'Connor's story, the grandmother wonders whether she will get to go to Eastern Tennessee, as she has planned, and later, to the old plantation she remembers. Toward the end of the story, she begins to wonder whether the plantation even exists, and at the very end, she wonders about the nature of the man who is about to kill her. The grandmother's questions mirror those of the reader—Toward what fate is this family headed? Will they survive?—but on a literal, concrete level.

- *Have you posed the questions clearly?* It's not uncommon for early drafts to contain a number of conflicts. If these are not carefully managed so that the focus is clear, the story's emotional impact may become blurred. The simplest solution is to cut material so that there is only one conflict; however, many excellent stories develop more than one. Even in these, however, one conflict is usually central, and the others are subordinated.

- *What are the possible answers?* For practical purposes, it makes sense early in the writing process to focus primarily on the character's questions; the answers you suggest will help to convey what is at stake, and will point toward the answers to the reader's questions. (See Chapter 9, p. 167, for a discussion of how to treat emotional and thematic questions in fiction.)

- *What answers does the story give?* Is it clear what happens to the main character at the end of your story? How would the story be affected if you made this clearer? Some endings, such as the one in Gina Berriault's "A Dream of Fair Women" (pp. 239–244) are intentionally ambiguous. If you decide to go this route, be certain that the ambiguity is purposeful. As a rule, physical detail should be clear: who is speaking, who gets shot and when, and so forth. Emotional or thematic detail may be left more open, but consult readers to make sure that your ending is satisfying—intriguing and suggestive rather than merely frustrating.

Ask Readers

For many writers, achieving enough distance to see the story's overall shape is one of the hardest parts of writing; it's easy to get lost in the details as you work scene by scene and moment by moment. The following questions about the story's overall shape focus on readers' emotional responses for a reason. Sometimes writers in a workshop or other group get in the habit of talking about their stories in very technical terms. While this kind of insight is valuable and hard to get elsewhere, it can, if you don't think about it, cause you to lose sight of the real point: the story's emotional center.

- *How would you summarize the story's situation—its rising action, climax, and falling action?* Listen closely. The readers' responses should tell you where any confusion began. Check those places for vagueness, unclear transitions, redundancies, or irrelevancies.

- *Where were you most engaged by the story, and where least? This question should identify spots where the tension sags—very often because the central conflict is out of focus—and what is most compelling in the story.* Sometimes, readers are most interested in something you've thought of as secondary. In that case, ask more than one reader before making a major change, but if you get a consensus, consider refocusing the story or deleting the distracting element.

- *Do you care what happens?* Why or why not? The answers to these questions may surprise you. They should define or redefine what is at stake in the resolution of the story's conflict. If readers say they don't care, there's no point in sulking. Work a little more on clarifying early in the story what will happen if the main character chooses one way or the other. What will be the consequences; what is at stake? More basically, check to be sure that you've given the main character enough scenes and development. See Chapter 3 (p. 54) for suggestions on character development.

- *Did you ever feel lost?* This question should tell you whether you've given enough exposition or other information, and whether the events and the transitions from scene to scene are clear.

Wordplay

Plotting Your Story   Using the narrative arc as described in this chapter, try plotting your own story. Don't start at the beginning, but rather at the peak moment.

First identify the point at which the main character makes a choice and changes in some way as a result (climax). Next, list the events that lead up to that moment (rising action) and that follow it (falling action). Finally, identify the background information provided before the action begins (exposition). Look for a central conflict and a defining change in the main character. Don't get too frustrated if you find it difficult to force the story into the precise shape of the narrative arc; the elements of plot can be variously arranged. "A Good Man Is Hard to Find" (pp. 362–372) for example, conforms to the narrative arc fairly closely, while Andre Dubus's "A Father's Story" (p. 272–286) is shaped very differently, including more than one sequence of events and an extraordinarily long passage of exposition.

A to B: Plot through character   Plot out the narrative arc of a story you have written. Now look at each major event in the story and ask, Does it move the main character "from point A to point B"? Where is "A"? Where is "B"? How has the main character changed by the end of the scene?

Unconventionally plotted narratives   This chapter discusses conventionally plotted stories. As a counterexample, take a look at Brenda Miller's "A Thousand Buddhas" (pp. 329–334) an essay that borrows some techniques from fiction. What events does Miller chronicle? In what order? How are they linked? How would you diagram them?

Alternative methods of plotting   Talking out loud, summarize your story's events. Now try telling the story in another way:

- If you have ordered events chronologically, try instead beginning at the end and flashing back to the beginning. This can often save a potentially melodramatic story by defusing a very dramatic ending; revealing the outcome removes the event-related suspense and readers will look for tension elsewhere—for instance, in how the character arrives at the ending.

- Try telling the story to someone in your head—perhaps one of the other characters. How does your "listener" influence the choice and order of events? Which are emphasized and which summarized? What information is added or withheld?

- Look at the climax—the pivotal scene, the one in which your main character makes a choice and is changed by it. How would the story be different if the character made another choice?

- What would happen to the plot if you changed other elements such as the story's environment, its point of view, or its verb tense? How might such changes influence the events themselves?

Reordering the process   Try working with plot in a new way. If you ordinarily plot out your stories before beginning to write, put that off and start instead with a character sketch or with developing the setting. Allowing other elements to lead the story may open up new plot possibilities. On the other hand, if plot comes last in your writing process, try making an outline and see how this affects the story and its writing.

Outlining after the fact   If you feel your story getting out of control or going off in too many directions, stop where you are, and make an outline after the fact. Go through the story scene by scene and put it into outline form. This will show you the structure and where you may be repeating things or wandering off the point.

A to B and back again   Looking for yet more structure? See the narrative arc on page 83. Get yourself a corkboard, or just a piece of cardboard that you can tape to a wall, and some index cards and thumbtacks. On each card, write an event that occurs in your story. Pin each card along the narrative arc, placing the climax or pivotal choice at the peak of the curve. There. Feel better? Okay. Now, take a risk: move that pivotal choice to the beginning of the arc. What happens next?

Suggested Reading

The More Books and Stories section starting on page 496 provides complete bibliographic information for each title listed below.

Janet Burroway, *Writing Fiction*
Andre Dubus, "A Father's Story"
Jakob and Wilhelm Grimm, "Little Red-Cap"
Ernest Hemingway, "Hills Like White Elephants"
Brenda Miller, "A Thousand Buddhas"
Flannery O'Connor, "A Good Man Is Hard to Find"
Seth Pase, "The Father"

J. D. Salinger, "Uncle Wiggily in Connecticut"
Akhil Sharma, "Cosmopolitan"
Mary Austin Speaker, "The Day the Flames Would Stop"
Jeannine Thibodeau, "Close"
Kelly Zavotka, "What Killed a Girl"

CHAPTER 5

Point of View

Whose story? The answer is so important because it begins the whole sequence of a fiction much like the sequence of the House That Jack Built. There has to be a Jack to build the house before we can have a cat that ate the mouse, before we can have a dog that chased the cat, and so on.

—Robie Macauley and George Lanning, *Technique in Fiction*

Perspective

Point of view is the perspective from which the **story**—the telling of the sequence of events that results in a change within the main **character** or actor—is told. A story is said to be written in the first person point of view if the **narrator**—that is, the storytelling character or voice (*not* always the main character—calls himself or herself "I": "I walked out the door and into the street." A third person narrator refers to the story's main character as "he," "she," or, occasionally, "it": "He walked out the door and into the street." A second person narrator (less frequently seen and more difficult to write) refers to the story's main character as "you": "You walked out the door and into the street."

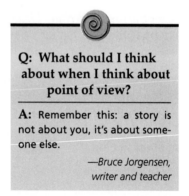

Q: **What should I think about when I think about point of view?**

A: Remember this: a story is not about you, it's about someone else.

—*Bruce Jorgensen, writer and teacher*

In the early stages of writing a story, it may not be at all clear to the author which of these points of view is most appropriate. Writers often draft **scenes** (or story segments), from a number of different perspectives, trying out various approaches until they settle on what is best for the story. This chapter provides examples of the three basic points of view—first person, second person, and third person—and discusses the uses of each.

The First Person

I had always wanted to be a hero. My chance came one fall morning when my mother handed me a basket of goodies and said, "Take these over to Grandma's." I put on my red coat and set out through the pink and yellow maples . . .

First person narrators engage readers directly, creating a sense of intimacy. They can comment on their own experiences and emotions, and readers naturally feel "in the character's head." First person is very economical; the writer can convey the main character's thoughts and personality through the voice. Norman Rush's novel *Mating* is an excellent example. The protagonist, a failed doctoral candidate in anthropology, is shown through her voice and through what she notices and how she describes it to be intelligent, intellectual, sexually eager, and somewhat self-deceived. In the passage quoted below, she has just arrived at Tsau, an all-female utopian community run by the man she loves, Nelson Denoon, who in this ironically romantic scene has grabbed her in the dark and told her not to speak:

The proof that I am a basically empathetic person is that I complied instantly. My essential nature is inclined to violence when someone touches me without being invited, and I am also physically strong. There were things I could have done. However, they would have prolonged the wrestling imbroglio we were in, which would have been okay with me except that the male constitution is a problem, or rather friction is a problem for it. The human penis is a thing like a marmoset or some other unruly small pet they carry around with them. An erection would hardly mean Denoon was in love with me or even desired me qua me, in all my wondrous dimensions. I wanted to spare us embarrassment.

The first thing to notice here is how many words this narrator uses to describe a quick, physical, sexually charged moment. Her editorializing, her irony, her elegant vocabulary, and her patronizing attitude all suggest a person who is somewhat emotionally detached and very concerned with controlling the reader's and perhaps her own interpretation of the events. Her euphemistic references to sex convey a coyness that is at odds with her intellect. Her extended explanation emphasizes her sense of her own control: she could have fought him off but didn't want to make him get an erection, so, graciously, she forfeited the match.

It takes a little time to "find" first person voices and to differentiate them from your own—or rather, to discover which aspect of yourself or your experience is speaking. Once you've found the character's voice, though, first person narration will probably feel very natural to write—after all, we live our lives in the first person.

"Showing" in the First Person   When it's going well, working on first person stories may feel like writing a letter, or like getting in character and delivering a monologue. In fact, you may have to resist the impulse to "tell" all the narrator's thoughts and feelings as though you were chatting with a friend. The technique of narrating thoughts, called interior monologue, is useful in small doses, but perhaps even more than others, first person stories must respect a reader's need to be "shown, not told." Stories that fail to do this can develop a particularly airless quality. In this passage from Andre Dubus's "A Father's Story" (pp. 272–286) the **concrete** (sensory) detail contributes to the reader's image of the character:

> My name is Luke Ripley, and here is what I call my life: I own a stable of thirty horses, and I have young people who teach riding, and we board some horses too. This is in northeastern Massachusetts. I have a barn with an indoor ring, and outside I've got two fenced-in rings and a pasture that ends at a woods with trails. I call it my life because it looks like it is, and people I know call it that, but it's a life I can get away from when I hunt and fish, and some nights after dinner when I sit in the dark in the front room and listen to opera. The room faces the lawn and the road, a two-lane country road. When cars come around the curve northwest of the house, they light up the lawn for an instant, the leaves of the maple out by the road and the hemlock closer to the window. Then I'm alone again, or I'd appear to be if someone crept up to the house and looked through a window: a big-gutted grey-haired guy, drinking tea and smoking cigarettes, staring out at the dark woods across the road, listening to a grieving soprano.

The passage conveys the day-to-day reality of the narrator's life—his occupation, where he lives, what he does in the evenings—but at a deeper level, the details suggest his emotional and spiritual life as well. The horses running in circles embody both beauty and limitation. The headlights briefly illuminating the trees convey Luke's sense of life's transience. The hemlock is a symbol of death. The man sitting in the dark listening to opera suggests sorrow but not dissolution, as it might if he were drinking whiskey rather than tea.

Limitations of the First Person   Although writing in the first person often creates an intimate portrait of the main character, it does not allow writers into the thoughts of other characters without shifting the point of view, except as such material can be shown indirectly, or as the narrator may speculate. Portrayals of secondary characters become complex, since these characters can only be seen through the eyes of the main character.

For example, a first person version of "Little Red-Cap" (pp. 298–300) might be likely to exaggerate the wolf's fearsome qualities—or, if you picture Red-Cap as a bit on the cocky side, to downplay those qualities. She would probably paint a positive portrait of her grandmother and her mother, though in some versions she might be critical of her mother for sending her out into the forest alone. In contemporary writing, such feelings, opinions, and biases are usually conveyed primarily through tone and choice of detail, as in the example above, rather than through direct statements. Effective first person writing creates a context for the narration, using events, reactions by other characters, and descriptive detail to suggest the narrator's accuracy, bias, or misapprehensions.

In order not to violate the first person point of view, it is crucial to show only what the main character would be likely to observe. What a character notices says a great deal about who that character is. However, it can become a particularly delicate operation to indirectly convey information essential to the story but that the first person narrator doesn't know. Such material can be shown through the other characters' actions, or through events. Sometimes it can be conveyed through **dialogue**, characters' speech, though this technique easily becomes artificial or strained.

Some of these approaches are used in Rachel Finkelstein's story "Awakening" (pp. 287–293), written in a beginning creative writing course when Rachel was a freshman at Tufts University. The narrator observes her mother's drunkenness:

She is lying face-down on the couch with her right hand dangling down to the hardwood floor. Her wavy brown hair covers her face and she is only wearing one shoe. As usual, there is a run in her stockings that runs the length of her calf. Next to her hand are the broken pieces of the empty vodka bottle, large chunks of glass and narrow shards scattered between her fingers. Moonlight shines through the window and illuminates the room. I can see blood on her hand where the glass has cut her skin. The blood looks dark, almost black, in the white light of the moon.

Here, the narrator relies completely on physical description—the mother's position and appearance, the broken bottle and her nonresponse to the cut—to convey her stupor. Later in the same story, the narrator recounts her mother's experience as her mother has told it:

They met when she was fifteen, my age. He was twenty-one, she says, and very tall and muscular, with curly black hair and beautiful blue eyes. That part is true; I know because one day I found a shoebox full of pictures of the two of them stashed away in the back of the closet. I knew right away when I saw them that he was my father, even though I'd never seen a picture of him before. It was the eyes, grayish-blue like mine, staring directly at me as if he could see right through to my soul. I stared back intently, trying to make him feel my presence. His smile seemed cold and somehow sarcastic next to my mother's innocent gaze. He isn't looking at her, though. He is looking right at the camera, as if he were the only one in the picture.

This account describes the narrator's father, whom she has never seen. It characterizes her mother's feelings for him through the details she has chosen to describe him. His appearance in the photograph suggests qualities that the narrator may not fully understand.

Although many writers, including Rachel Finkelstein and Brenda Miller, use them well, photographs, like mirrors, are not always the subtlest descriptive techniques. It's best not to employ them often. Generally, it is more graceful to include bits of physical description along with gestures or movement: "I tucked a curl behind my ear"; "the wind made my silk blouse crack and billow." In "Awakening," though, the photograph is given a number of possible interpretations and so portrays all three characters, the viewed and the viewer, and something about their relationships. Its multiple uses allow the author to slip in a physical description of the father without reducing the photograph to an excuse for doing so. This is an example of the virtues of doing more than one thing at a time, discussed elsewhere in this book. It's also one of those infrequent occasions when, by fitting the technique to the moment and using it well, a writer successfully breaks a very sensible rule.

The same story uses dialogue and what is unsaid to convey information that is beyond the narrator's ability to observe:

My father stopped working on the farm while my mom was pregnant with me. I've always wanted to know why, but she won't tell me that, not even when she's so drunk that she doesn't know what she's saying. On those nights, she sits sobbing at the kitchen table with her head in her hands while I make her coffee. She cries about how her life ended as soon as she got pregnant at sixteen, and rambles incoherently about how she used to have dreams, she once thought she could be someone and do something. One night I told her, "You are someone. You're my mother." That only made her cry harder.

Rachel uses dialogue to convey the mother's feelings here, without ever quoting her. Everything she says is conveyed through **indirect discourse**—that is, rather than being quoted directly, it is retold in the daughter's voice. This emphasizes its impact on the story's main character.

Describing the First Person Narrator   It can be quite difficult to convey in the first person the main character's physical appearance or attractiveness. Often direct self-commentary causes the character to seem narcissistic or self-promoting—qualities that may not serve the author's purposes: "I was stunningly lovely, my shining black hair falling in gentle waves over my slender shoulders." This description might work for the evil queen as she consults the "mirror on the wall," since it conveys not only her physical appearance but also her vanity. But because it suggests that trait, it would not work for Snow White. In other words, it's important to think not only about what's being said but also about who's saying it and why.

Once in a while, first person narrators simply describe themselves directly at the outset. In "A Father's Story" (pp. 272–286) Andre Dubus's narrator achieves a successful direct self-description (quoted on p. 92) because the simplicity of the approach reflects the character's honesty, a trait that bears directly on the story's central conflict. Luke Ripley's voice tells us as much as the descriptive details. It is that interaction between the **image** or sensory detail itself and the voice conveying it that makes good first person narration. Here, again, is an author doing more than one thing at a time. When handled well, this complexity can add richness and depth to a story, and the dual focus keeps the technique from being too noticeable.

The first person narrator in Joseph Connolly's "Hard Feelings" (pp. 261–270) is characterized less directly, through his interactions with others:

At one point Madelyn asked Sally—not me, but Sally—whether I was "in touch with my feelings."

"I'm in touch with my parents," I said. "Does that count?"

Neil smiled, but Madelyn just kept looking at Sally, waiting for an answer. Sally, whose hair is straight and brown, and whose brown eyes are always calm, looked right at me and smiled.

"Mark thinks he can tough out emotional problems the way he toughs out his sports injuries," she said.

All three of them looked at me. I felt like I was on display, like a patient in a teaching hospital. They were all wondering if I could be cured. "I hate sports analogies," I said to Madelyn. "Don't you?"

The dialogue and narration in this passage convey Mark's sense of humor and his emotional evasiveness, his not entirely satisfying relationship with his wife, and some sense of the pain beneath his good-natured façade.

Self-Portraiture: Autobiography or Self-Display?   Because it's hard to separate the actual "I" from the fictional one, beginning writers are sometimes tempted to put themselves—real or imagined—on display. It's always embarrassing to readers when they suspect that the handsome, indomitable hero or the fragile yet spirited heroine betrays the writer's fantasy self. Even when writers are not intentionally preening, it can simply feel confusing to write "I" when you are referring to someone else. It's easy to slip out of character when writing in the first person. While it stands to reason that well-written fictional characters present aspects of their writers, there is a point in the development of any successful character when the author feels that it has a life of its own. At that point, the character steps away from the author and becomes whole and convincing. Characters that are merely devices for their authors' self-portraiture can't get there.

Paradoxically, the way to that point is through the author's identification with the character. Like Method actors who "become" their characters even offstage, writers must allow characters to grow out of themselves and must practice and evolve each character's voice until it feels solid and wholly natural. Only then will the character uniquely define itself.

When writers are actually chronicling their own experiences, though, their task is somewhat different, and notoriously difficult. In autobiography or **memoir**, which is often close to the same thing as autobiographical **novel** (a book-length work of fiction), self-description is usually even harder than with a more fictionalized character. It's difficult to see yourself accurately and even harder not to become self-conscious and selective in presenting yourself. But the solution is the same as with other material: as much as possible, try to reveal personality through actions and well-chosen concrete detail rather than through direct explanation by the main character or others in the story. Changing names and identifying traits, whether or not you plan to change them back later, can help a great deal as you seek enough distance to describe an autobiographical character.

Even an autobiographical character will probably move some distance away from an exact self-portrait. No one will prosecute you for that; in fact, autobiography may be the only situation in which writers are entirely safe from prosecution! Remember that even though—or especially because—a character is autobiographical, you don't know her completely. In that sense, allowing her to surprise you is even more important than with an intentionally fictional character.

Regardless of how closely a character is based on you or someone else, when you're in the first person everything you write portrays the character by showing how she sees things. Part of creating a good first person voice is discovering what the character would likely notice and remark on. Although this task can be approached deductively, writers do much of their best work intuitively. Find the part of you that is the character and let it speak.

The Unreliable Narrator   To the extent that a first person narrator's perceptions differ noticeably from those of the author, the narrator is said to be unreliable—that is, the narrator's account of things may be colored by emotion or other factors and so may not be entirely dependable. Because their view of things is not completely trustworthy, unreliable narrators require readers to take an extra interpretive step. Mark in Joseph Connolly's "Hard Feelings" (pp. 260–270) is somewhat unreliable. Between the lines, it can be felt that his wife must be lonelier than he realizes and that behind his wit he hides some complicated feelings, even from himself. Although readers may laugh guiltily at his portrayal of Neil and Madelyn, his wife's flaky friends, and his descriptions of their "Cone of Silence" lamp and their touchy-feely beliefs, we sense that he's not being entirely fair or—more to the point—understanding. Similarly, Angie in Jeannine Thibodeau's "Close" (pp. 443–456) is not completely objective about her sister Lenore. Angie's behavior and her insistent complaints about Lenore suggest that there's more to the picture than Lenore's irresponsibility.

These authors create unreliability by having the character state his or her point of view unequivocally and by showing that point of view to be rather one-sided. Mark's wife Sally occasionally raises an eyebrow at his jibes about Neil and Madelyn. She anticipates his behavior and does some damage control when necessary. Her silence about the painful events in her past provides a subtle backdrop of suffering against which Mark's jokiness takes on a defensive and sometimes insensitive quality. This crack in his credibility is what gives Mark room to change, creating some tension in readers' minds and an internal conflict to be resolved.

Similarly, as readers sense that Angie in "Close" is being a little too critical of her sister, they naturally begin to root for Lenore, which heightens the story's conflicts and their urgency. The physical description of Lenore's gauntness and dark-circled eyes elicits the reader's sympathy, if not Angie's. Skillful use of an unreliable narrator provokes readers' skepticism and causes them to second-guess the narrator's assertions and to arrive by means of rebellion exactly where the author wants them to be.

Suspending Disbelief: Narrating in the First Person   You may sometimes feel awkward stretching a first person voice to perform as a narrator. Adding "he said" to dialogue or allowing such narrators to convey an adequate level of descriptive detail may ring unnaturally bookish to your ear, since "people don't talk that way."

For this reason, you may be tempted when writing in the first person to rely too heavily on summary and indirect discourse, preventing scenes from developing fully. But think about your own experiences as a reader. Have you ever been bothered by "he said"? You can get away with it—and with more description than you might think, too. If you are writing "in character," the details you choose will reveal the narrator as well as whatever else is being described. Readers will naturally suspend a certain amount of disbelief, and curiosity will entice them to overlook slight excesses in the interest of finding out what will happen next.

The Third Person

> Once upon a time there was a dear little girl who was loved by everyone who looked at her, but most of all by her grandmother, and there was nothing that she would not have given to the child. Once she gave her a little cap of red velvet, which suited her so well that she would never wear anything else; she was always called "Little Red-Cap."

There are reasons why so many stories are told in the third person (the main character being "he" or "she" rather than "I" or "you.") It's the freest, most flexible point of view—not only because in its unlimited form it allows the writer to move in and out of a number of characters' minds but also because it offers psychological distance from the characters, freeing the writer to explore and discover them rather than working down from preconceived notions.

Writing in the third person is not simply a free-for-all, though. The degree of access will vary according to how limited the third person point of view is—whether the story's perspective alternates between several characters (third person omniscient), or is primarily that of one character (third person limited). Note that third person stories may be narrated by a character in the story, in which case at least part of the story is told in the first person, or by a disembodied **narrative voice** or sensibility, in which case the point of view is usually that of one or more characters.

Third Person Omniscient   The third person omniscient point of view—a technique in which the narrator is able to move in and out of various characters' minds—gives the author a number of angles from which to tell the story. This makes presenting a balanced picture much simpler. After writing in the first person, switching to third person omniscient can feel like coming up into the air after being underwater—you can, if your story permits, read the minds of your characters, move magically through space and time, walk through walls. Exposition is much easier because the third person omniscient narrator has access to virtually all information and you don't have to devise nearly as many rationales for how the narrator knew this or that as you would if you were writing in the first person.

When a writer tells a story from more than one point of view, establishing a pattern such as alternating scenes or sections from each of the main characters' points of view reduces confusion. In general, although a story written in the third person may include several points of view, each scene should stick with one point of view. As in "The Day the Flames Would Stop" (pp. 413–418) or the stories of Flannery O'Connor, it is possible to slide momentarily in and out of the mind of a given character other than the narrator. But unless this technique is done extremely well, as it is in these stories, it tends to be confusing and to look like a mistake.

Third Person Limited   In the third person limited point of view, the narrator's access is restricted, often to the main character's thoughts. As in the first person, the writer must devise ways of conveying information to which the main character doesn't have access. Still, some aspects of writing a story are easier because of the distance granted by the third person: describing the narrator and her habits feels much more natural, and surprisingly, conveying the main character's thoughts may be easier as well. Although thoughts flow easily in the first person, if the narrator runs on for too long in her head, the effect can be awkward, stifling, or self-conscious.

Free indirect discourse, a subtle variation of third person limited, allows the narrator to veer out to the very limit of the third person point of view, achieving an intimacy ordinarily reserved for the first person. Dorrit Cohn describes this technique, which she refers to as "narrated monologue," in her book *Transparent Minds*:

> [Narrated monologue] may be most succinctly defined as the technique for rendering a character's thought in his own idiom while maintaining the third person reference and basic tense of narration. This definition implies that a simple transposition of grammatical person and tense will "translate" a narration into an interior monologue.

Writer and teacher Darrell Spencer illustrates this concept for his students by changing a first person **narrative** or telling of events to a third person narrative—a process suggested by the opening paragraph of his story "Park Host" (pp. 418–431). Spencer wrote the original version in the first person:

> So me and my wife Rose, we get into these one-on-ones where we lock horns, do these everyday equivalents of Piper Cup open-cockpit wingovers (years back when my wits were quicker and my feel still good, I flew supply drops and the U. S. mail into Nevada mountains and deserts, was expert in the Great Basin the way you are master of the streets you drive to and from work). So anyway, Rose and me, we get into these give-and-takes-and-reverse-your-directions until I say, "You forget, I have my hat on," and she says, "Meaning what, that I'm under arrest?" Borrowed lines from one of the Frankenstein sequels, the movie where Dr. Frankenstein's son returns to his ancestral castle and he's determined he's not going to repeat his father's mistakes, but of course he does.

Then, Spencer explains, "I decided after several revisions that the story needed the twisty skewedness (is there such a word?) that free indirect discourse can bring to language and point of view." With that in mind, he rewrote the story in third person. The result is free indirect discourse—a third person narrative that retains the flavor of the original first person voice:

So Rose and Red Cogsby, they get into these one-on-ones where they lock horns, do these everyday equivalents of Piper Cub open-cockpit wingovers (years back when his wits were quicker and his feet still good, Red flew supply drops and the U.S. mail into Nevada mountains and deserts, was expert in the Great Basin the way you are master of and have down cold the streets you drive to and from work). So anyway, Rose and Red, they get into these give-and-takes, push-and-shoves, these climb-and-stall-and-reverse-your-directions until Red says, "You forget, I have my hat on," and she says, "Meaning what, that I'm under arrest?" Borrowed lines from one of the Frankenstein sequels, the movie where Dr. Frankenstein's son returns to his ancestral castle and he's determined he's not going to repeat his father's mistakes, but of course he does.

To illustrate yet another alternative, here is the passage again rewritten, this time in a more detached and much less colorful "describing and reporting" voice:

Red Cogsby and his wife Rose had arguments that reminded him of piloting. Their conversations reminded him of feats he might have attempted when he was younger and confidently flew supply drops and the U.S. mail into the Nevada desert, but not now. He and Rose argued back and forth until he said, "You forget, I have my hat on," and she said, "Meaning what, that I'm under arrest?" They had borrowed these lines from one of the Frankenstein sequels, in which Dr. Frankenstein's son returns to his ancestral castle mistakenly determined that he will not repeat his father's mistakes.

Free indirect discourse, often combined with the present tense, occurs frequently in contemporary writing. In such stories, the third person narrative voice mirrors that of the main character, allowing readers to identify more consistently with the character, and smoothly integrating action and thought.

Just as the first person can feel confining, so some writers initially feel a bit artificial writing in the third person—"he said" and "she said" seem false, too "written," and can make writers feel distanced from their characters. And it's true that we don't ordinarily speak or think for long in the third person. Doing so in writing, we ask readers to accept a disembodied voice that comes from but is not the writer. We ask them to accept this narrator's omniscience, limited or not, and the implausibility of it going on and on about someone else. Beginning writers, feeling awkward about these conventions, can easily conclude that they are asking too much.

But remember that readers want to suspend disbelief. That's why they read. As long as you don't give them a reason to lose faith, they'll believe. Besides, the chances are that you're not asking too much. If the point of view you have chosen begins to feel awkward, look at a published story that uses the same technique, and ask yourself whether it bothered you as a reader. If so, why? Is there a way to employ it more smoothly? Don't be overawed by techniques in published stories. If a technique is very noticeable, you're being distracted from more important matters and the story is probably not quite working yet.

There are things a writer can do to ensure that a third person point of view does not distance readers from the characters. Staying close to a character's physical senses, as in this passage from "Souvenir" by Jayne Anne Phillips (pp. 376–385) invites the reader to empathize with the character:

There were a few photographs of her and Robert, baby pictures almost indistinguishable from each other, and then Kate's homemade Valentines, fastened together with rubber bands. Kate stared. *What will I do with these things?* She wanted air; she needed to breathe. She walked to the window and put the bundled papers on the sill. She'd raised the glass and pushed back the screen when suddenly, her mother's clock radio went off with a flat buzz. Kate moved to switch it off and brushed the cards with her arm. Envelopes shifted and slid, scattering on the floor of the room. A few snapshots wafted silently out the window. They dipped and turned, twirling. Kate didn't try to reach them. They seemed only scraps, buoyant and yellowed, blown away, the faces small as pennies. Somewhere far-off there were sirens, almost musical, drawn out and carefully approaching.

Here, description combines with action and thought to make the character physically and emotionally present. The story's next scene contains a bit more stated thought and feeling as the third person narrator takes on Kate's voice, shifting into free indirect discourse—still, notice that Phillips always returns to concrete, physical detail, which grounds the emotion and keeps us in the scene:

They stayed up for an hour, watching the moving lights outside and the stationary glows of houses across the distant river. The halls grew darker, were lit with night lights, and the hospital dimmed. Kate waited. Her mother's eyes fluttered and finally she slept. Her breathing was low and regular.

Kate didn't move. Robert had said he'd be back; where was he? She felt a sunken anger and shook her head. She'd been on the point of telling her mother everything. The secrets were a travesty. What if there were things her mother wanted done, people she needed to see? Kate wanted to wake her before these hours passed in the dark and confess that she had lied. Between them, through the tension, there had always been a trusted clarity. Now it was twisted. Kate sat leaning forward, nearly touching the hospital bed.

In contrast, this scene from the same story contains no directly stated feelings, yet the emotional dynamics are clear:

Robert sat down. Their mother was to have surgery in two days.

"After it's over," he said, "they're not certain what will happen. The tumor is in a bad place. There may be some paralysis."

"What kind of paralysis?" Kate asked. She watched him twist the green-edged coffee cup around and around on its saucer.

"Facial. And maybe worse."

"You've told her this?"

He didn't answer.

"Robert, what is she going to think if she wakes up and—"

He leaned forward, grasping the cup and speaking through clenched teeth. "Don't you think I thought of that?" He gripped the sides of the table and the cup rolled onto the carpeted floor with a dull thud. He seemed ready to throw the table after it, then grabbed Kate's wrists and squeezed them hard.

"You didn't drive her here," he said. "She was so scared she couldn't talk. How much do you want to hand her at once?"

Kate watched the cup sitting solidly on the nubby carpet.

"We've told her it's benign," Robert said, "that the surgery will cause complications, but she can learn back whatever is lost."

Kate looked at him. "Is that true?"

"They hope so."

"We're lying to her, all of us, more and more." Kate pulled her hands away and Robert touched her shoulder.

"What do *you* want to tell her, Kate? 'You're fifty-five and you're done for'?"

She stiffened. "Why put her through the operation at all?"

He sat back and dropped his arms, lowering his head. "Because without it she'd be in bad pain. Soon." They were silent, then he looked up. "And anyway," he said softly, "we don't *know*, do we? She may have a better chance than they think."

Kate put her hands on her face. Behind her closed eyes she saw a succession of blocks tumbling over.

In this scene, emotions are not stated directly but shown through gestures and indirectly through dialogue, and through images such as the cup thudding on the carpet and blocks tumbling over. It is clear that brother and sister disagree about how to handle their mother's illness; that neither is fully confident; that beyond the immediate conflict, they see the world differently.

The Second Person

You never expected any trouble. It was a simple errand: deliver a basket of goodies to your grandmother. Yet that morning, as you set out through the forest, the sky seemed darker and the trees blacker than ever before. You hurried along the path, looking neither right nor left . . .

The most obvious attractions of second person narration are its relative novelty and the technical challenges it presents to the writer. When done well, it can be very engaging, involving readers directly in the action. In the best second person writing, the point of view is seamless, natural, and purposeful. For example, student Christine Baxter's story "If You Want to Have a Fling" (pp. 233–238), which depicts a woman who is repeatedly harrassed by men, allows or compels male readers to experience such treatment "firsthand." In this scene, the main character ("you") is driving on the freeway and realizes she is being followed by a man she met at a toll booth.

Traffic lets up slightly and you try to drive away from him, but he changes lanes and comes up on the other side of your car. He's looking down at you, laughing, smiling, and leering. He does the tongue thing again, this time holding his fingers to his mouth in a V and wiggling his tongue between them. Annoyed, you try to speed away again and get up to a good thirty-five miles an hour. You try to concentrate on the road and not the man beside you, then slam on the brakes as the cars ahead come to a sudden stop. He has now gotten behind you, riding close on your bumper. You can see him in the rear-view mirror, sitting forward in his seat and laughing.

The second person point of view is a bold technique to attempt. It's relatively rare, for good reason—readers naturally notice the unusual approach and resist being told what they are doing, thinking, or feeling, and so all of the other elements of the story must be extra sharp to overcome this resistance. Characters and narrator must supply adequate detail and information to persuade at least half the story's readers to suspend enough disbelief to imagine themselves crossing gender. (An exception is when authors direct the second person voice toward a specific character, as in a letter. This implies that the narrator is a character in the story, which means that the point of view is actually first person.)

It's definitely possible to succeed with the second person point of view, but it's hard. Because of the difficulties, many second person narratives read like, and are, writing exercises. When considering point of view, ask yourself what's gained for the story, not just for the author—and what may be lost. Mere novelty is not a good enough reason to choose a particular approach. Second person narration, like any other technique (more so because it's distinctive), must serve the story or it will distract from it rather than enhancing it. Readers may feel dragged into an experiment that may be fun or instructive for the author but is taxing and alienating to everyone else. When second person narration is done well, the technique is not noticeable.

Combining Points of View

Point of view is a complex and sometimes confusing issue. As you begin writing, remember first of all to keep the point of view consistent throughout your story. Readers sense point-of-view violations and are seriously disconcerted by them. When the author "breaks character" in this way, readers feel jerked around, betrayed, disrupted. It may be much harder for writers to sense when they are veering away from the approach they have established. In the beginning, they may feel uncertain how much distance and how many points of view are "allowed," and whether or when they are permitted to deviate from their chosen approach.

The answer isn't simple. When it comes down to it, rules are not really a useful standard. Rather, writers need to identify what will work for the story. There are many possibilities:

Q: How does a writer maintain the point of view, the voice or tone or mood, of a narrative that necessarily must be written over the course of many writing sessions?

A: I think this is hard, but the techniques I use are: Read the story aloud; do five minutes of "tone" warm-up before working on the story; and try to "write" when you are not writing—that is, get to know the voice outside your writing practice.

—Willard Cook,
writer and teacher

- The narrator may be a character in the story or a nonspecific sensibility—the impartial voice that is familiar from many third person stories.

- The narrator may or may not know past and future events.

- The narrator may have direct access to one or more characters' feelings, or may convey such things indirectly.

- The narrator may abide by the highly sensible rule that the story's point of view should be established early on and then maintained consistently throughout.

- Or, occasionally, the author may invent alternative approaches. An example is Andre Dubus III's novel *House of Sand and Fog*, in which a third point of view is successfully added to the two main ones very late in the novel.

As You Write

This chapter presents the basics about point of view and the requirements that govern it. Those requirements are crucial; a story in which the point of view wobbles or wanders lacks narrative authority. It feels unstable and weak. Yet, many of the stories included in this book demonstrate that when writers know their craft, experimenting with techniques such as point of view can result in some very exciting fiction. This section explores some basic questions, and also a few exceptions to the rules.

Which points of view does your story employ?   Look through each scene. Whose impressions and feelings does the narration convey?

Is the point of view consistent throughout your story?   Check each scene. Look for information to which the point-of-view character would not have access, observations she wouldn't be likely to make, emotions she wouldn't have.

If you switch points of view, are the transitions clear?   It may help to use short, simple sentences as you shift points of view, and to include a few details identifying the new point of view early in the scene.

Is the voice consistent?   Read the story aloud and listen for changes in the language: the level of formality, of vocabulary, and of detail; the length and structure of the sentences; the emotional tone. Of course, a good narrative voice will be able to express a range of emotion, but through a variety of feelings, the voice should sound like the same person.

Is the narration consistent?   Look particularly at descriptions of characters and at exposition—these can be tricky.

Is the narrator's knowledge credible? Is it consistent with the story's point of view?   Looking carefully through your story, list the information conveyed by the narrator in each scene. Beside each piece of information, write a brief explanation of how the narrator knows it.

Point of view is more than the skillful use of pronouns—it's the creation of a persona, a fictional voice that tells the story. For examples of first person stories that meet this standard, look especially at "A Father's Story" (pp. 272–286), "Hard Feelings" (pp. 260–270), and "What Killed a Girl" (pp. 464–474). The work of James Joyce, Flannery O'Connor, Darrell Spencer, and many others presents examples of vivid third person narration. Voice is not merely a matter of painstaking consistency; it is fundamentally an emotional project. Below are some suggestions to help you as you further explore the intricacies of point of view.

Multiple points of view   Many third person stories (and some in first person) are written from more than one character's point of view. In these, the point of view generally switches back and forth in a consistent pattern. One of the most challenging technical problems in such stories is how to accomplish the switches between points of view. It helps to look at how other writers handle such transitions. Initially, for example, Alice Munro establishes David's point of view in the story "Lichen" (pp. 347–361) by showing his former wife, Stella through his eyes:

> As David turns the car in to the lane, Stella steps out of these bushes, holding a colander full of berries. She is a short, fat, white-haired woman, wearing jeans and a dirty T-shirt. There is nothing underneath these clothes, as far as he can see, to support or restrain any part of her.

Later in the story, Munro switches to Stella's point of view:

> Down on the beach, at either end of Stella's property, there are long, low walls of rocks that have been stacked in baskets of wire, stretching out into the water.

They are there to protect the beach from erosion. On one of these walls, Catherine is sitting, looking out at the water, with the lake breeze blowing her filmy dress and her long hair. She could be posed for a picture. She might be advertising something, Stella thinks—either something very intimate, and potentially disgusting, or something truly respectable and rather splendid, like life insurance.

The most obvious cue that the point of view has shifted is the phrase "Stella thinks," but Munro uses other transitional devices as well: the description of the beach with details only Stella would know, the choice of detail regarding Catherine's appearance and behavior, and the amused, slightly cynical tone.

Still later in the story there is a more direct switch: "David, in the phone booth, begins to dial Dina's number. Then he remembers that it's long distance. . . ." Obviously, no one else can be in the phone booth with him, so the point of view in this scene is immediately clear. In case there's any mistake, the next sentence takes us inside his mind: "He must dial the operator."

There are many ways of cueing readers about a change in point of view—just remember to do it, and do it early in the scene.

The thing to remember about point of view is that like other techniques, it should serve the story. Some stories clearly benefit from the perspective offered by multiple points of view; others are best tightened and focused by the economy of the first person voice. As you experiment with different points of view, and as you become more intimately acquainted with each new story, it will become easier to identify the appropriate point of view.

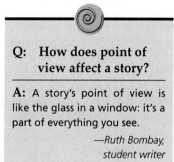

Q: How does point of view affect a story?

A: A story's point of view is like the glass in a window: it's a part of everything you see.

—*Ruth Bombay,*
student writer

Transgressing the boundaries   Occasionally, writers deliberately stretch the boundaries of point of view, creating whole narratives written by characters who were not even present to observe what they are describing. In Russell Banks's novel *Affliction*, for instance, the story is told by the main character's brother, yet it contains many closely described moments when the narrator isn't present, including dialogue and details he could not have observed. Banks gets away with this by first making clear who the narrator is and why he is telling this story. Then the narrator says, "Let us imagine that . . ." and creates a scene and characters so vivid that no reader would want him to stop.

Stories written in the second person obliterate the conventional expectation that the main character should have observed all of the events he or she chronicled. Such narrators presume to suggest that the reader has participated in fictional events. Second person stories must rely on convincing detail and strong narrative tension in order to tempt and persuade readers to believe.

When is violating the point of view a mistake? When it reads like one—when there is no great advantage to doing so, no pattern established, and no convincing rationale or vividness to justify or distract from the violation. This is most of the time.

Animal voices   Usually, the point-of-view character is either an omniscient narrator or a person in the story. But some interesting short stories have been written from the point of view of nonhuman characters. Robert Olen Butler's story "Jealous Husband Returns in Form of Parrot" (pp. 244–249) is told by a man reincarnated as a parrot who, caged in his wife's house, must watch her carrying on with another lover:

I never can quite say as much as I know. I look at other parrots and I wonder if it's the same for them, if somebody is trapped in each of them paying some kind of price for living their life in a certain way. For instance, "Hello," I say, and I'm sitting on a perch in a pet store in Houston and what I'm really thinking is Holy shit. It's you. And what's happened is I'm looking at my wife.

In this story, Butler develops a central trait of the parrot's—its ironic inarticulateness—as an emotional metaphor. This sense of the character's relevant essence, along with careful attention to detail, is necessary to convince readers to suspend disbelief and accept the nonhuman narrator. The physical detail, which in such a story must often be researched, as well as that arrived at through empathy and imagination, persuades us to believe. The intersections of animal and human nature engage through comic delight and a paradoxical sense of truth.

Ghostly voices   Some writers even write voices of characters who are not alive. The first section of student Kelly Zavotka's story "What Killed a Girl" (pp. 464–474) is told in the voice of Cupcake, one of the main characters. The story ends, still in her voice, just after the moment of her death:

Metal barrel two inches from my chest. She must think she's hunting and I'm an animal. I must look like one. Metal looks soft. I wrap my hands around it but it won't bend. Solid.

Quiet is loud. I hear my skin crack.

I fell when it got louder. "Well, that was a fucking blast," Shell says. Her voice comes from inside me laughing.

The precise, concrete detail persuades in much the same way that Gabriel García Márquez's "A Very Old Man with Enormous Wings" (pp. 293–298) persuades us to believe in angels.

Exploration and Discovery

In this section, you will find some suggestions to help you evaluate your story's point of view.

Ask Yourself

- *Whose thoughts and observations, if anyone's, do readers need to know directly?*
- *Is it advantageous in this story to enter the mind of more than one character?*

- *What are you able to write in your chosen point of view?* What knowledge does each scene imply? Is that knowledge consistent with the scene's point of view?

- *Which voices in the story feel most natural as you write?* Pay attention to any voice that comes easily; sometimes this is a sign of an important character, whether in the current story or in a future one.

Ask Readers

- *Was there any place where you wondered how the point-of-view character knew the information being conveyed?*

- *What attitude does the point-of-view character seem to have about the story's events?* What is the tone of the narration, and how does it—or does it not—contribute to the story?

- *Is the voice consistent?* That is, was there any place where you felt that you'd lost the point-of-view character's voice, or that the character had inexplicably changed?

- *Did you notice the point of view?* Where? The answer to this question will help you spot problems or awkward places or possibly a need for a different approach. Ideally, point of view should be so natural that it's not noticeable.

Wordplay

Plot summary   Write a plot summary of your story—one or two paragraphs at most—in the first, second, and third person. How does changing the point of view affect what events you choose to include? Is one point of view more accommodating than the others?

Deliberate inconsistency   Try writing your story's opening paragraph in the first person, then in the third, then in the second. What are the advantages and disadvantages of each? Which feels more natural for this material? When working on a first draft, writers often don't know the answer to this question. Some scenes seem to need to be told in the first person, some in third. Don't decide until you know—just do what feels right in each scene, and worry about consistency later on. This allows you to experiment and discover what is most natural for the story, rather than arbitrarily deciding in advance.

Free indirect discourse   On pages 98 and 99, Darrell Spencer explains how to create free indirect discourse by changing the point of view in a first person scene while leaving other elements intact. Reread this explanation, and then choose one of the first person stories from this book's anthology, and rewrite a paragraph from it in the third person, retaining the original voice. The result should be free indirect discourse. Next, take the exercise a step further by rewriting the paragraph in a more detached third person voice, establishing the narrator's voice as distinct from the character's. Think about the ways in which each point of view serves the story; as you shift the point of view, how is the story changed?

Suggested Reading

The More Books and Stories section starting on page 496 provides complete bibliographic information for each title.

Russell Banks, *Affliction*

Christine Baxter, "If You Ever Want to Have a Fling"

Robert Olen Butler, "Jealous Husband Returns in Form of Parrot"

Dorritt Cohn, *Transparent Minds*

Joseph Connolly, "Hard Feelings"

Andre Dubus, "A Father's Story"

Andre Dubus III, *House of Sand and Fog*

Rachel Finkelstein, "Awakening"

Jakob and Wilhelm Grimm, "Little Red-Cap"

James Joyce, "Araby"

Brenda Miller, "A Thousand Buddhas"

Alice Munro, "Lichen"

Flannery O'Connor, *The Complete Stories*

Jayne Anne Phillips, "Souvenir"

Norman Rush, *Mating*

Darrell Spencer, "Park Host"

Jeannine Thibodeau, "Close"

CHAPTER 6

Time
Verbs and Narrative Structure

The only way round is through.

—Robert Frost

When you can't get through, you might try going around.

—Penelope Bone

Stories and Time

Stories, or **narratives**, exist in time; they begin, continue for a while, and end. The events they chronicle do the same. But in fiction, time is flexible. It may be stretched, compressed, twisted and folded, chopped up, rearranged, or turned inside out. This chapter discusses time in fiction—the use of **scenes** (events dramatized through speech and action) and **narration** (what the writer tells the reader directly). It explains how writers order their stories' events and move from one point in time to another, and it introduces the use of verb tense in fiction.

Some stories, like "Little Red-Cap," by Jakob and Wilhelm Grimm (pp. 298–300); "A Good Man Is Hard to Find," by Flannery O'Connor (pp. 362–372); and Ernest Hemingway's "Hills Like White Elephants" (pp. 320–323), are told chronologically, as events transpire. These take place entirely in the **fictional present**, the time frame that the story's **characters** or main actors would consider the present. (The term *fictional present* does *not* refer to verb tense.) Other stories use flashbacks (relatively brief excursions into the past) or occasionally flashforwards (glimpses of the future), a frame structure (a technique consisting of a story within a story), or other techniques to bend and shape time into functional and appealing forms. Some narratives, like Brenda Miller's essay "A Thousand Buddhas" (pp. 329–334), skip through time, organized instead around **images**

Q: How do writers decide on the structure of their stories—whether to proceed chronologically, use a frame, or employ flashbacks?

A: When you begin to write, locking your characters down to a definite time structure is as unrealistic as having a dinner party and expecting everyone to socialize only around the dinner table, and not in the kitchen when you're getting ready. It may not have been what you planned, but it's much better to let your guests, or characters, teach you where they'd be most comfortable.

—Ruth Andrew Ellenson, student writer

109

(sensory details), **themes** (ideas), or conflicts between or within characters. Some stories are told retrospectively, in the past tense; some contemporaneously, in the present tense; and a very few in the future tense—a choice that presents obvious limitations.

Given all these options, how do you figure out which one to choose? As with almost every issue in writing, the first rule is consistency. Don't jerk the reader around—establish a coherent policy about time. Like the various points of view, each approach to time presents advantages and challenges. The decision between them depends on the story's requirements.

Fictional Time: Narration and Scenes

A fiction writer's most basic forms for organizing time are **scenes,** in which characters are shown doing things and talking with one another, and **narration,** in which the **narrator,** the person or voice that tells the story, conveys information directly to the reader. A story's pace depends most fundamentally upon how and when the author moves to and from the relatively quick pace of narration, the much slower pace of a fully developed scene, or the middle ground of summarized scenes.

How do you know which events to develop into a scene and which to summarize? There are two issues here: the practical question of how long an action takes to perform, and the psychological and artistic issue of how much emphasis the action deserves in the story. In general (though not always), the second factor should take precedence: key moments should be played out while incidental ones may be summarized in narration. If writers try to detail inconsequential background information, the story quickly bogs down. On the other hand, if they withhold or skim over details about important events, the impact may be distorted, as in this line from an otherwise promising student story: "I bring Mom inside and she passes away." Even if the mother did die suddenly, the event's importance demands a little more attention!

There are occasions when writers may deviate purposefully from this general rule—for instance, when they wish to convey a distortion in the passage of time, such as slow- or fast-motion—and there are passages that strike a balance between summary and scene. The scenic and narrative modes may be used together or alone, depending on the desired effect.

Narration

The direct conveying of information by the narrator is an economical technique. Narration is useful for pacing a story and, particularly where the narrator is a character as well, also as means of **characterization** or conveying characters' attributes and personalities.

Narration in *Affliction*   This paragraph from early in Russell Banks's novel, *Affliction* exemplifies effective narration:

. . . Wade was running late, as usual. He had not been able to start the hour-long drive south on the interstate to Concord until finishing work for LaRiviere (besides being Lawford's entire police force, Wade was also a well driller, Gordon

LaRiviere's foreman). Then down in Concord, after stopping at the shopping mall north of the city for a Halloween costume that he had promised but forgotten to purchase and bring with him, he had been compelled—again, as usual—to negotiate certain complex custodial arrangements with his ex-wife, Lillian, after which he had to pick up a Big Mac, strawberry shake, fries and cherry pie to go for Jill's supper, all before even starting the drive back to Lawford.

Now he was late . . .

As shown in this example, narration supplies information relatively quickly and usually without a lot of detail. This narration also establishes the story's **voice** (the personality, tone, and sensibility conveyed by a story's language—in this case, that of Wade's brother) and provides commentary both through direct assertions by the narrator and also more subtly, through the narrator's tone.

Narration in "A Father's Story"   In the following passage from Andre Dubus's "A Father's Story" (pp. 272–286), Luke Ripley, the narrator, describes his daily routine, and also conveys his general mood and attitude.

I sit in the kitchen at the rear of the house and drink coffee and smoke and watch the sky growing light before sunrise, the trees of the woods near the barn taking shape, becoming single pines and elms and oaks and maples. Sometimes a rabbit comes out of the treeline, or is already sitting there, invisible till the light finds him. The birds are awake in the trees and feeding on the ground, and the little ones, the purple finches and titmice and chickadees, are at the feeder I rigged outside the kitchen window; it is too small for pigeons to get a purchase. I sit and give myself to my coffee and tobacco, that get me brisk again, and I watch and listen. In the first year or so after I lost my family, I played the radio in the mornings. But I overcame that, and now I rarely play at all. . . .

Extended narrative passages, like the smaller increments of description and **tags** (words that tell readers who is speaking), offer a change of rhythm, a contrast to the activity of **dialogue** (characters' speech) and interaction. Much contemporary fiction contains relatively little narration, but only a dramatic script—and not all of those—can do without it completely.

Scenes

Like its theatrical counterpart, a scene in fiction dramatizes a single unified action, usually by means of dialogue, gestures, or behavior, and description of characters and **setting** or place. The essential thing is that the point is demonstrated rather than explained. "Write the story," novelist Jonathan Strong advises, "not about the story." Take a look at some of the scenes in stories from this book's anthology. What do you know about the characters and situations after reading each scene? How do you know it? These questions will point up some of the subtle cues, nuances, descriptive techniques, and other scenic elements that writers can use instead of direct explanation. For instance, without fully explaining his actions to the reader or to his daughter, Luke Ripley destroys the evidence of her crime.

Scenes in *Affliction*   Scenes may be summarized by the narrator or a character, or they may be played out in detail. The passage above from Russell Banks's *Affliction* is a good example. With the word *now*, the narrative moves into the fictional present. It then moves into a summarized scene as Wade imagines the rest of the evening:

Now he was late for everything he had planned and fantasized about for a month: late for trick-or-treating with his daughter at the homes of everyone in town he liked or wanted to impress with his fatherhood; late for showing up at the party at the town hall, where, like all the other parents for a change, he could see his kid win a prize in the costume contest, best this or that, scariest or funniest or some damned thing; late for the sleepy drive back to the trailer afterwards, Jill laying her head on his shoulder and falling peacefully asleep while he drove slowly, carefully home.

In the next paragraph, the author makes the transition into a more fully developed scene, using quoted dialogue, gestures, and specific, detailed description:

He tried to explain their lateness to her without blaming himself for it. "I'm sorry for the screw-up," Wade said. "But I couldn't help it that it's too late to go trick-or-treating now. I couldn't help it I had to stop at Penney's for the costume," he said, stirring the air with his right hand as he talked. "And you were hungry, remember."

Jill spoke through her tiger's mask. "Whose fault is it, then, if it's not yours? You're the one in charge, Daddy." She wore a flimsy-looking black-and-yellow tiger suit . . . .

By gradually developing the scene, Banks establishes the background and sharpens the focus on his character.

The Order of Events

In addition to deciding which events your story will chronicle, which it will summarize, and which you should leave out entirely, you must decide what to tell when. Will you begin "once upon a time" and proceed in an orderly fashion through the woods and to Grandmother's house, or will you start with the moment the woodsman bursts through the door, then loop back to earlier events and work your way forward again to where you started? Will your story be organized by means of time, or according to some other scheme such as **point of view** (the perspective from which a story is told) or imagery?

Once Upon a Time: Chronological Stories

Traditionally, a story begins by establishing a time and a place: "Once upon a time, in a cabin in the woods"; "It was a dark and stormy night deep in the heart of central Nebraska." Then after the background information—the **exposition** (p. 74)—has been presented, the **rising action** (what leads up to the climax, p. 77) begins. In such stories, the structure is simple: events are played out in chronological order. "Little Red-Cap" (pp. 298–300), "A Good Man Is Hard to Find" (pp. 362–372), and "Hills Like White Elephants" (pp. 320–323) are examples of chronological stories.

Following the Flow of Time   The success of a chronological story depends largely on whether the author has correctly identified and rendered a significant moment—an important change or realization—and the events that lead up to it. If the central conflict is compelling and well-constructed and the rising action well-defined, the momentum of time will work for it, enhancing the tension and the sense of inevitability, and promoting a natural storytelling voice.

But whether you're basing your story on actual or imagined events, the structural straightforwardness and simplicity of chronological plotting can be deceptive; such stories present their own challenges. Working through the story event by event, you will need to develop the ability to see the parts in proportion to one another rather than getting lost in detail or skimming over moments that deserve more time, and so losing sight of the story's overall shape—its narrative arc. Working with chronology is discussed further in the As You Write section of this chapter (p. 128).

Time Travel: Memories, Background, and Flashbacks

Because the past informs the present and the future grows out of it, even a story whose main action proceeds chronologically will at times refer to events that occurred before or after the story's opening scene. In order to move readers efficiently and smoothly through time, writers must develop techniques such as memories, dreams, fantasies, reveries, or narration. Through these and other such methods, writers create a kind of "time travel," taking readers into characters' memories and experiences. Usually such references are subtle and economical—allusions rather than extended detours into another time and place.

Compressed Memories in "Survivors"   The first sentence of Kim Addonizio's **short short** (a very short story) "Survivors" (pp. 232–233) conveys background material on which a less economical writer might have spent pages: "He and his lover were down to their last few T cells and arguing over who was going to die first." Later in the story, the lovers' life together and its context is concisely suggested by the apartment's decor:

He knew, too, that they all—father, mother, two older brothers—would disapprove of their flat, of the portrait of the two of them holding hands that a friend had painted and which hung over the bed, the Gay Freedom Day poster in the bathroom, all the absurd little knicknacks like the small plastic wind-up penis that hopped around on two feet. . . .

Rather than directly stating that the lovers are gay and then detailing scenes to show their life together, the author reveals this important information by placing a few well-chosen details—their portrait, the poster, and the knickknacks—in the context of family disapproval. This conveys much more than the simple fact of sexual preference—concisely and understatedly, it suggests a whole history.

Background in "Lichen"   The first paragraph of Alice Munro's story "Lichen" (pp. 347–361) contains similar allusions in the form of briefly quoted remarks and narrative summary:

> Stella's father built the place as a summer house, on the clay bluffs overlooking Lake Huron. Her family always called it "the summer cottage." David was surprised when he first saw it, because it had none of the knotty-pine charm, the battened-down coziness, that those words suggested. A city boy, from what Stella's family called "a different background," he had no experience of summer places.

In this paragraph, readers are introduced not only to the story's setting but also to Stella's background and to how she and David differ. Had Munro chosen instead to detail David's first visit to the cottage, the story would have lost tension and focus; this brief flashback conveys the important information while leaving the emphasis where it belongs.

Summarized Flashbacks in "Hard Feelings"   When certain events are particularly important, excursions into the past may be a little more detailed, or even quite extensive. The narrator may summarize a past event in some detail, as in this passage from Joseph Connolly's "Hard Feelings" (pp. 261–270):

> "Let's go," Kevin said. "Let's pick teams." In a minute, we were lined up, guineas versus micks, with Neil an honorary mick on our side. I don't know why, but suddenly I felt good. My first couple of shots went down, and I started to get that elated feeling you get sometimes when everything is coming together. Neil would probably say it was biorhythms. Reposa was covering me, and as soon as he broke a sweat a stale, boozy smell came off him. He smelled like a rug at a frat party. . . . I decided to torture him. I ran everywhere, sprinting on transitions, running him off picks and through crowds, bumping him in the low post and then stepping out and hitting little ten-foot jumpers. When we weren't running, I was needling him about his smell.

The passage provides a particularly good example of maintaining the pacing of the present scene while still including the details from the past—especially difficult in a fast, physical scene such as this one. The key is balancing momentum with the need for information.

As the narrator points out in the story's first paragraph, the characters' weekly basketball game provides an arena not only for athletic competition but also for issues of class and interpersonal conflict. If the author had simply written, "A couple of the guys didn't like each other so the game got a little ugly," readers would be left curious and possibly unconvinced. On the other hand, if he had detailed this scene, quoting every line of dialogue and showing every play, it would have lost the speed of basketball and would have gotten so long that it would seem more important than it is in the story's overall scheme. Summarizing the scene provides a satisfying sense of what exactly happened while maintaining an appropriate pace and length.

Occasionally, authors use dialogue to summarize past events, as in this passage, also quoted above, from Russell Banks's novel *Affliction*:

"I'm sorry for the screw-up," Wade said. "But I couldn't help it that I'm too late to go trick-or-treating now. I couldn't help it I had to stop at Penney's for the costume," he said, stirring the air with his right hand as he talked. "And you were hungry, remember."

Here again, an important scene is summarized rather than being played out in detail. The effect is to compress the events leading up to the present moment—a series of frustrating errands that cumulatively ruin Wade's evening with his daughter—retaining and emphasizing the emotional dynamics by summarizing the errands themselves. By not sinking the story in a blow-by-blow account of essentially boring activities, the author retains the narrative tension. Putting the scene in Wade's voice dramatizes his defensive style rather than the errands, and emphasizes its effects on Jill.

Flashbacks in "Souvenir"   Sometimes, past events are so crucial that the author leaves the narrative mode and recreates them as developed scenes, in the form of flashbacks containing dialogue, gestures, description, and so forth. This passage from Jayne Anne Phillips's "Souvenir" (pp. 375–385) begins such a scene, using the verb *standing* to transition from the past tense to the past perfect, and then shifting back to simple past after the mother's speech:

Standing in the kitchen last summer, her mother had stirred gravy and argued with her.

"I'm thinking of your own good, not mine," she'd said. "Think of what you put yourself through. And how can you feel right about it? You were born here, I don't care what you say." Her voice broke and she looked, perplexed, at the broth in the pan.

The decision whether to allude to, summarize, or play out past events will depend mainly upon their importance to the story's central conflict and its resolution. The more important events are, generally, the more space they deserve.

As suggested by the examples above, though, sometimes other factors, such as the speed with which events occur, the potential for **sentimentality** (trite appeals to emotion) if a scene is drawn out in detail, or the wish to tell events from the voice or perspective of certain characters, lead authors to summarize key moments. Of course, when you turn a story toward the past, you turn it away from the present. In such cases, you will need to judge how long you can afford to keep the reader on pause and at what point the story will lose momentum and the memory become a digression.

The Frame Story

In the frame story, past events are actually more important than what occurs in the fictional present. The writer begins at a point late in the narrative arc or even outside it entirely, then flashes back to earlier events and builds up to and often past what is recounted in the first scene. Thus, external events, or those that occur later, "frame" the rest of the story. This technique sometimes results in a story within a story.

Some Examples of Frame Stories

"A Father's Story" (pp. 272–286), by Andre Dubus, for example, frames a hit-and-run accident within the larger story of the narrator's spiritual life. In "Jealous Husband Returns in Form of Parrot" (pp. 244–249), Robert Olen Butler frames the story of the narrator's marriage within the story of his reincarnation as a parrot. In some other fiction, the current moment is not developed but simply exists as a vantage point from which to recount the past, as in Christine Baxter's "If You Ever Want to Have a Fling" (pp. 233–238), in which an incident of harrassment that occurs in the present frames several similar incidents from the past.

Sometimes writers choose to leave frames open at the end; for example, in "Close Enough" (pp. 335–346), student writer Joseph Moser establishes but then does not return to the retrospective point of view. A few stories, like Raymond Carver's "The Calm" (pp. 249–252), are open at the beginning, though this often isn't evident until the end. In these, the fictional present gives way late in the story to a previously undisclosed time frame. Carver tells the story of an incident in a barbershop, then unexpectedly pulls back for a larger view: "That was in Crescent City, California, up near the Oregon border. I left soon after. But today I was thinking of that place. . . ."

How Frame Stories Work

The frame technique can tighten a loose chronological story. It may also provide a good way to de-emphasize a distractingly prominent **plot** or story line. For instance, by disclosing in the beginning that the main characters in "Survivors" (pp. 232–233) are both dying of AIDS, Kim Addonizio avoids the potential melodrama of revealing such a dramatic plot development at the end of the story, where it would overshadow the particular emotions that are the story's center.

Like any other approach, the frame story has its advantages, but also presents challenges to the writer. It takes a great deal of skill and work to gracefully integrate large amounts of exposition, and usually the best course is to simplify and minimize the backtracking required by a frame; "A Father's Story" is an example of a frame story that successfully accommodates enough exposition to sink most stories. Because of the movement back and forth through time in frame stories, it's necessary to craft transitions carefully (see below) and to avoid the convolutions of flashbacks within flashbacks.

Used appropriately, a frame can tighten and focus your story. When considering this technique, it is important to evaluate whether the gain in concision, flexibility, and emotional emphasis is worth the loss in narrative tension. Sometimes it's not the right strategy to give away the ending. In such cases, it may be possible to begin some time just before the story's end, then flash back and work up to and past where you began. In other cases, the events may be tightly enough rendered in chronological order that there's no need for a frame. The frame structure, like any technique, should be used where it is indicated, rather than gratuitously.

Transitions

Since readers won't initially share your overall vision of your story, they will need a little help moving from scene to scene. When scenes begin and end, readers will need to know where they're being moved in time—back a year, forward an hour? Any changes in point of view or setting also need to be clear as the scene shifts. Such clarifications at the beginnings or ends of scenes are known as transitions.

Seven Ways of Moving from Scene to Scene

A writer may use many methods to move the story from one scene to the next; below are a few.

The Direct Approach   The most obvious type of transition is a phrase such as "I remembered the time," or "she thought about the way her life had been before." Sometimes such a straightforward approach is appropriate. For instance, the plain-spoken narrator in "A Father's Story" identifies himself and moves very directly into the story's exposition in the first line: "My name is Luke Ripley, and here is what I call my life . . ." Later in the story, the narrator locates himself more precisely in time, with similar straightforwardness: "It is late summer now . . . It has been two weeks since Jennifer left . . ."

Suggested Transitions   Unless the story specifically calls for directness, as "A Father's Story" does, it's usually more effective to suggest rather than to spell out the transitions—just do it, don't talk about doing it. The simplest transitions are white spaces—extra space left between paragraphs—as in this scene shift from Raymond Carver's "The Calm"

Q: How can I signal time shifts in my story?

A: Most fiction writers are familiar with the concept of dialogue tags—those *he said's* and *she said's* in dialogue that help the reader follow who is speaking. Many fiction writers, however, don't recognize a second, equally important set: chronology tags. These are the words that, inserted into narrative, help the reader to follow time shifts in the story. "Yesterday . . . ," "Later that afternoon . . . ," "By August of 1904 . . . ," and "On Jenny's tenth birthday . . ." are all examples of chronology tags. As with dialogue tags, clumsily used chronology tags can interrupt the flow of the narrative and confuse the reader. A useful exercise is to go through your story and highlight the chronology tags. Are there enough of them to help the reader follow time shifts? Are they unobtrusive? Attention paid to these tags is well worth the time.

—*Stephen Carson,
writer and teacher*

(pp. 249–252), in which the story moves from the initial scene of men talking in a barbershop to a story recounted by one of them:

"Go on, Charles," the barber said. "Let's hear it."
The barber turned my head again, and went back to work with his clippers.

"We were up on Fikle Ridge. . . ."

The white space creates a cinematic effect, cutting cleanly from one scene to the next.

Using Verbs to Create Transitions   Another very simple transition consists of changing the verb tense (discussed at more length below). For example, the first scene of Akhil Sharma's "Cosmopolitan" (pp. 391–406) describes a meeting between the main character, Gopal Maurya, and his neighbor, with background information inserted as the scene progresses. The use of simple past tense for current events and past perfect for past events keeps the scene clear.

When **he went** back into his house, **Gopal was** too excited to sleep. Before Mrs. Shaw, the only woman **he had ever embraced** was his wife, and a part of him assumed that **it was** now only a matter of time before he and Mrs. Shaw fell in love and his life resumed its normalcy. Oh, to live again as **he had** for nearly thirty years! **Gopal thought**, with such force that **he shocked** himself. Unable to sit, unable even to think coherently, **he walked** around his house.

After a scene break, the story continues with more background information in the past perfect: "His daughter's departure **had made Gopal sick** at his heart for two or three weeks. . . ." (See the section below on verb tense for a more detailed explanation of this type of transition.)

Narrative Bridges as Transitions   When the writer doesn't want a break between scenes but needs a stronger cue than a tense shift will provide, a **narrative bridge**—narration used to create a transition between two scenes—can create a smooth passage, as in the excerpt from *Affliction* quoted above. The following passage from Gina Berriault's "A Dream of Fair Women" (pp. 239–244) moves the story from the previous scene, briefly forward and then to a summarized flashback recounting what happened that afternoon:

While she was at work this night, her lover would take away his possessions—a simple task, there were so few. They had agreed that the most bearable time for both was when she was not there. All afternoon she had raged against the woman he was going to, and now she could not even clear her ravaged throat to see if she still had a voice. And he had held her, he had caressed her, his face confounded. He was like someone dispatched to the ends of the earth, with no idea of what was to happen to him there.

Using Abstractions as Transitions   The passage quoted above also uses an abstraction to move from the present into the flashback scene. Berriault's words "they had agreed" draw attention away from the current actions to the fact of an agreement, which leads naturally into the past scene. Joseph Connolly uses a similar technique in "Hard Feelings" (pp. 260–270):

All three of them looked at me. I felt like I was on display, like a patient in a teaching hospital. They were all wondering if I could be cured. "I hate sports analogies," I said to Madelyn. "Don't you?" I succeeded in changing the subject; Madelyn began talking about how sports and sports talk are used to oppress women in the workplace.

Despite her professed dislike of sports, it was Madelyn's idea that Neil should join our Sunday game. . . .

Here again, the abstraction of Madelyn's dislike for sports moves the story gracefully from a dinner party to the next scene, in the main character's car after a basketball game.

Transitional Words or Images   There are several other simple and standard techniques that move readers through time. Often, as in the passage above from *Affliction*, writers use the word *now* as the time shifts into the fictional present. Robert Olen Butler uses a similar transitional device in "Jealous Husband Returns in Form of Parrot" (pp. 244–249):

In that other life I'd have given anything to be standing in this den with her doing this thing with some other guy just down the hall and all I had to do was walk down there and turn the corner and she couldn't deny it anymore.

But now all I can do is try to let it go. . . .

Other writers use images to link scenes. Juan Rulfo's frame story "Macario" (pp. 387–391) begins with the words "I am sitting by the sewer waiting for the frogs to come out. While we were having supper last night. . . ." At the end of the story Rulfo transitions back to the fictional present by using the word *now* and then recalling the vivid initial image, in almost the same words: "Now I'm by the sewer waiting for the frogs to come out."

Brenda Miller's essay "A Thousand Buddhas" (p. 329) moves similarly back and forth through time, using the image of hands to link the scenes. And in "Jealous Husband Returns in Form of Parrot" the narrator uses an object and a gesture to link present and past:

But I got my giant cage and I guess I'm happy enough about that. I can pace as much as I want. I can hang upside down. It's full of bird toys. That dangling thing over there with knots and strips of rawhide and a bell at the bottom needs a good thrashing a couple of times a day and I'm the bird to do it. I look at the very dangle of it and the thing is rough, the rawhide and the knotted rope, and I get this restlessness back in my tail, a burning thrashing feeling, and it's like all the times when I was sure there was a man naked with my wife. Then I go to this thing that feels so familiar and I bite and bite and it's very good.

I could have used the thing the last day I went out of this house as a man.

The description of the cage ends with the rawhide toy, which elicits a response in the bird that recalls his jealousy in his previous life. The comparison is kept from becoming heavy or sentimental by the comedy of the little parrotlike Hemingway impersonation: "Then I go to this thing that feels so familiar and I bite and bite and it's very good."

Later in the same scene, the narrator's physical reactions to a memory link it to the present time:

. . . the crack in the shade was just out of view and I crawled on along till there was no limb left and I fell on my head. Thinking about that now, my wings flap and I feel myself lift up and it all seems so avoidable. Though I know I'm different now. I'm a bird.

Fantasies as Transitions   Some stories use fantasy to move between scenes. For instance, having moved from the abstract concept of lateness into Wade's imagined evening with his daughter, the passage quoted earlier from Russell Banks's novel *Affliction* eases finally into a more developed scene of the real thing as Wade and Jill discuss his lateness:

Jill spoke through her tiger's mask. "Whose fault is it, then, if it's not yours? You're the one in charge, Daddy." . . .

"Yeah," he said, "but not really. I'm not really in charge. . . . There's damn little I'm in charge of, believe it or not. It is my fault I had to stop for the costume, though, and we got slowed up some there."

In a somewhat different use of fantasy, the narrator of Andre Dubus's "A Father's Story" (pp. 272–286) imagines an incident his daughter has recounted:

She told me all of it, waking me that night when I had gone to sleep . . . told it to me in such detail and so clearly that now, when she has driven the car to Florida, I remember it all as though I had been a passenger in the front seat, or even at the wheel. It started with a movie, then beer and driving to the sea to look at the waves in the night and the wind, Jennifer and Betsy and Liz. They drank a beer on the beach . . . .

. . . She ejected the cassette and closed the window. She did not start to cry until she knocked on my bedroom door, then called: "Dad?"

Her voice, her tears, broke through my dream and the wind I heard in my sleep. . . .

In this case, the main character's imaginings allow readers to see a crucial scene in which he is not present. This provides a way around the limitation of perspective imposed by the first person point of view.

Verb Tense

Is your story told in retrospect, or at the moment its events transpire? Does it follow a simple chronological path, or does it move back and forth in time? However you choose to render time, verbs will be essential to the task.

The Past Tense

One day her mother said to her: "Come, Little Red-Cap, here is a piece of cake and a bottle of wine; take them to your grandmother. . . ."

Fiction writers have tended to use the past tense. The retrospective view is a natural and graceful choice; the past tense implies the narrator's comprehensive vision of the story's events and so brings to the narrative a quiet authority.

A Natural Storytelling Mode   The past tense is the way we commonly tell stories aloud. It lets us convey information in a familiar, natural-sounding way. Perhaps the strongest argument for telling stories in the past tense is its transparency: readers are so used to it that the technique doesn't distract from characters and events.

Most beginning writers find it relatively easy to write in the past tense. This is a matter partly of familiarity, partly of the sense of control granted by a narrator who presumably already knows what happened, and partly of the more flexible verbs and pace of past-tense narratives. Flashbacks make fewer waves when the fictional present is rendered retrospectively by using the past tense, rather than tightly focused on the current moment as in present-tense narratives.

The Present Tense

The girl clutches her basket, draws her red wool cloak around her. She walks a little faster.

The present tense focuses the story on the current moment, making it a good choice when you want to emphasize the immediate action more than its context. It may also be a useful and natural choice in dialogue, when quoting from letters or journal entries, or to establish general truths in a story such as "Hard Feelings" (pp. 260–270), which is introduced in the present tense while most of the action takes place in the past. In this opening passage, the narrator, Mark, explains the intricacies of basketball, one of the story's central metaphors:

From the outside, a pick-up basketball game looks like nothing more than a bunch of guys playing a game, but if you've been in there, especially in there under the basket where most of the bumping and pushing go on, you know that every game is a jumble of little animosities and petty jealousies, and that at least two guys on the court flat out hate each other. It comes out in the banter and the force of the collisions and in whether a guy helps another guy up after knocking him down.

In our Sunday morning game at the King School in Cambridge, the two guys who hate each other are Neil Prentice and Frank Reposa. If they were closer in size, things might get ugly, but Neil is a little guy, about five-eight and skinny. Reposa is around six-four, two-twenty-five, and he does most of his banging on me. I'm not crazy about either of them, but I get caught in the middle because I invited Neil into the game.

In this passage, Connolly uses the present tense exactly as he would if he were telling the story aloud: to establish, explain, and comment on a current situation. The last verb, *invited*, is the first suggestion that the story will go on to chronicle past events. In these paragraphs the present tense allows the narrator's voice a conversational naturalness that is part of how the story succeeds so well. It singles out this passage, which suggests the story's central issues and lays out the situation.

The Present Tense and Immediacy   Writers often use the word *immediacy* to describe the advantages of the present tense. It's true that the present tense can create a sense of immediacy, but it is not the only way to achieve that effect. As Robie Macauley and George Lanning point out in their book *Technique in Fiction*, this device has become common enough that the fresh, startling sense of urgency it once carried is now familiar. Some of the tautness in the sentences above comes from the description. How much immediacy would really be lost if we changed only the tense in the description of Little Red-Cap?

The girl clutched her basket, drew her red wool cloak around her. She walked a little faster.

Other Routes to Immediacy   In recent years, the immediacy of the present tense has sometimes resulted in stories that rely too heavily on this technique and are underdeveloped in other areas. By all means, experiment with verb tense—but remember that the present tense is a shortcut to tension and immediacy, not the only route. It's an obvious method, and unless there are additional reasons for using it in a particular story, it may not be the most interesting solution. Here are some alternatives:

- Descriptive details can do a lot to **foreshadow** or hint at events to come, and to add tension:

Above her, the dark branches shifted heavily and creaked in the wind. Dry leaves scuttled along the ground.

- The story's events can be rearranged or **foreshadowed** to heighten suspense:

There had been rumors of a huge, haggard wolf wandering the forest. "Don't stop for anything," Little Red-Cap's mother warned her.

- The characters themselves can reflect and express tension:

Her mother's hands seemed to shake a little as she fastened the cloak around Little Red-Cap's neck. "Come home quickly," she whispered.

- The rhythm of the prose can be used to reflect the mood of the moment, as in the passage from "A Father's Story" in which Luke discovers the body of the young man his daughter has accidentally killed; here, the long, jerky sentence reflects the narrator's panicky, breathless search:

I climbed, scrambling up the side of the ditch pulling at clutched grass, gained the top on hands and knees, and went to him like that, panting, moving through the grass as high and higher than my face, crawling under that sky, making sounds too, like some animal, there being no words to let him know I was here with him now. . . .

- In other cases, the prose itself may be quite plain, and the intensity arises out of the characters' actions. Flannery O'Connor takes such an approach at the climactic moment of "A Good Man Is Hard to Find"; here, shock and horror is reflected in the bare, straightforward prose. The simple, dramatic action speaks for itself:

His voice seemed to crack and the grandmother's head cleared for an instant. She saw the man's face twisted close to her own as if he were going to cry and she murmured, "Why you're one of my babies. You're one of my own children!" She reached out and touched him on the shoulder. The Misfit sprang back as if a snake had bitten him and shot her three times through the chest. Then he put his gun down on the ground and took off his glasses and began to clean them.

All of this is not to say that you shouldn't use present tense, but to point out that it's not the only option. Your wish to create tension and immediacy isn't necessarily an indication that the present tense is the best possible treatment of time in your story. Putting a story in the present tense is one way to intensify the moment, but not always the most interesting or appropriate one. Like any technique, the present tense should be used where it is the best choice rather than indiscriminately or for the sake of novelty. If you can think of several ways in which it serves the story, it's probably a good choice. If you can't, there are alternatives.

The Future Tense

In the broadest sense, the future is a vital part of any story: readers must feel why the story is being told—what are the consequences of these actions, what is at stake as the main character chooses this way or that. Stories are about choosing and changing, and the dramatic value of a choice depends upon its consequences. Thus, out of love for his daughter Luke Ripley sacrifices his formerly somewhat narrow notions of justice. In a moment of recognition, the grandmother touches The Misfit and loses her life.

Flash-Forwards   Although stories are not usually told in the future tense, at times writers will offer a glimpse into the future in the form of a flash-forward. Writer Bruce Jorgensen describes such moves as "backstitches": "The story—or more usually in my experience, essay—goes on to its end, its conclusion, then loops or stitches back to some salient point in the middle or at least just before the end began."

An excellent example occurs in Andre Dubus III's novel *House of Sand and Fog*. In this scene, the main character watches a mother and child from the window of her hospital room. The scene's main action takes place in the past tense. In order to convey later events without carrying the story beyond this scene, Dubus shifts into a brief flash-forward, orienting the reader by using the present tense to make a comparison ("the way an important dream comes back to you"), and then continues in the present tense as the flash-forward resumes. To ease the flash-forward into a more developed scene, Dubus uses gerunds ("unlocking," "stepping," "filing") to describe the narrator's habitual activities in the prison in which she will soon be confined. The flash-forward finally settles back into the present tense in the next paragraph.

I couldn't see the boy's face anymore, and in the hours and days that followed **I would think of him**, the way an important dream **comes back** to you throughout the day, a day **that begins** at six-thirty, **my door unlocking** electronically, **me stepping out** onto the second tier **and filing downstairs** with black women and white women, Chicanas, all of us dressed in the orange khaki pants and tank tops and overshirts of the San Mateo County Jail, over fifty of us.

On the bottom tier **we sit** at steel tables and eat toast and cold cereal . . .

When written well, as is the one, flash-forwards can add perspective and heighten a scene's emotion. But because the technique demands that readers accept the illogic of "remembering the future," it tends to be distracting and, if not used skillfully, even irritating.

If you plan to use a flash-forward, first be certain that it's necessary, that it will add to the scene in ways other approaches would not, and that what it adds will outweigh the potential distraction. Second, study successful flash-forwards such as the one on page 124 and the one from Russell Banks's *Affliction*, quoted on page 112. Notice the placement of the flash-forward, what necessary objectives it accomplishes, how the author justifies it psychologically, and what verbs the author uses to accomplish the movements through time.

Anticipating the Future   Flash-forwards are by no means the only kind of prophecy writers use. In subtle ways, scenes taking place in the fictional present anticipate the future. Jayne Anne Phillips's "Souvenir" (p. 375–385) ends with the main character's realization of her own mortality, symbolized by a ride on the Ferris wheel:

Q: **What is relevant and what is not? How much of the characters' subjective state—dreams, thoughts, memories—should be included?**

A: The only thing that really interests us about other people is what they say and what they do. After you've told us what they look like and who they are and what the weather is like on the morning they start off on their adventure, you should stick pretty much to those two characteristics. That way you'll never go very far wrong.

—*Leslie Epstein, writer and teacher*

> The sky circled around them, a sure gray movement. Kate swallowed calmly and let their gaze grow endless. She saw herself in her mother's wide brown eyes and felt she was falling slowly into them.

The last line of student Jeannine Thibodeau's unpublished story "Close" (pp. 443–456) affirms the future: "I sit down against the cold metal of the chair and sip my lukewarm coffee. When Lenore opens her eyes, I'll be there, waiting." Similarly, the end of Mary Austin Speaker's story "The Day the Flames Would Stop" (pp. 413–418) implies the probable future as the main character realizes that her wedding is a mistake, "thinking that she would never tell him that this felt very wrong."

Usually, such moments are brief and circumscribed, as in these sentences early in Robert Olen Butler's "Jealous Husband Returns in Form of Parrot" (pp. 244–249):

> For a moment I think she knows it's me. But she doesn't, of course. I say "Hello" again and I will eventually pick up "pretty bird." I can tell that as soon as she says it, but for now I can only give her another hello.

The story ends with a more open look into the future:

A shadow of birds spanks across the lawn. And I spread my wings. I will fly now. Even though I know there is something between me and that place where I can be free of all these feelings, I will fly. I will throw myself there again and again. Pretty bird. Bad bird. Good night.

Since most of this story is set in the present tense, Butler uses the future tense to suggest what will happen later. When the main part of the story or scene is in the past tense, as in the example above from *House of Sand and Fog*, authors can use the gerund, or other verb forms not bound to a particular tense, to transition into a future time. Another example occurs in Kim Addonizio's "Survivors" (pp. 232–233):

. . . maybe, after his lover died, he would put some things away, maybe he would even take the parrot out of its cage and open the window so it could join the wild ones he'd heard of, that nested in the palm trees on Delores Street, a whole flock of bright tropical birds apparently thriving in spite of the chilly Bay Area weather—**he would let it go, fly off, and he would be** completely alone then; dear God, he thought, let me die first, don't let me survive him.

In this example, the author uses the conditional to suggest the main character's dread of what lies in the future. The plea at the end is more dramatic and intense because of the shift from the conditional into the present tense, which signifies the time frame in which the story takes place.

Moving Through Time

Flashbacks and flash-forwards are not the only ways of conveying or suggesting information beyond the present moment; in fact, if you find yourself employing these devices very often, it may be that you need to reconsider your story's scope and when it begins. That said, your story's movement through time will depend in part upon your ability to use verbs smoothly and correctly. This section offers some more suggestions about using verbs as transitional devices.

Moving from Present to Past Tense   Joseph Connolly's "Hard Feelings" (pp. 260–270) begins in the present tense and later moves back in time to recount the events that make up the story's action:

I first met Neil and Madelyn at dinner at their place. In the car on the way over, Sally gave me a brief lecture about how Neil and Madelyn were different from the people I'm used to, and why certain kinds of humor might not go over.

The transition into the past here is very simple: "I first met Neil and Madelyn." Since the first part of the story is written in the present tense, the author uses simple past tense rather than past perfect to convey past events. As explained above, the past perfect (*had gone, had eaten*) is used if the first or main part of the story is told in the past tense. In stories like "Hard Feelings" the narrator may occasionally slide back into the present—"different from the people I'm used to." This reminds us that although the particular events he is telling are in the past, the general situation is current.

Moving from Past Tense to Past Perfect Suppose you decided to begin a past-tense story *in medias res*—in the middle of things—and to flash back on the exposition:

As she walked through the woods, Little Red-Cap thought back on the morning's events. "Take this basket of goodies to your grandmother," her mother had said. So Little Red-Cap had set off from her house in the forest . . . .

When a story is told in the past tense (*she walked*), past events should be told in the past perfect: *had said, had set off*. This will indicate that the incidents took place before the story's main events. Here is an example from *Affliction*, by Russell Banks:

. . . Wade **made** his way across the room to the door. He **arrived** there just as Margie Fogg **entered**. She **wore** a dark-green down jacket over her white waitress's uniform and **was** probably hoping to see Wade here. Not wanting it to seem so, however, to him or anyone else, she **had come** with her boss, Nick Wickham, despite his usual designs on her. The same age as Wade, Margie **had been** one of his girlfriends back in high school, before Lillian—though it was not until years later, when both he and Margie were married to other people, that they **had** actually **ended up** in bed with each other.

Resuming the Original Tense in Long Flashbacks In extended flashbacks, it's an accepted convention once the flashback's tense has been established, to slide out of it and back into the story's original tense. Student James Leon Suffern uses this technique in his story "When the Summer Ends" (pp. 431–443):

A week later that summer **he'd made up** the story of the tornado. **He'd told** them all after a game of 21 down at his house. **Matthews was there** that day, showing off his dumb new pocketknife with the eagle on it.

"It tore up our whole house, and five houses after ours," **Jackson said.** "That's why we had to move to Valtone." **Chad and Scott looked** at each other. **Alan picked up** a free ball and **shot** a lay-up. "It was bigger than the sky itself." **Alan stopped** shooting for a second and **seemed** about to ask something, but then **he turned** back to the basket. Then **Jackson knew** he was safe.

The story's main action takes place in the past tense. As this scene moves further into the past, the tense changes to past perfect ("he'd made up the story"), signaling a flashback. But since the excursion into the past is to be a relatively long one, the writer eases back into the past tense after a couple of sentences: "Matthews was there . . ." Here, the awkwardness of continually using the past perfect tense outweighs the logical inconsistency of slithering back out of it. It's another of those situations in which it's in the reader's best interest to ignore a little inconsistency—who wants to read "had this" and "had that" for the next two pages?

Although the concept is simple, keeping verb tenses straight when moving back and forth through time can be extremely confusing to beginning writers. It helps to visualize this process:

Verb Tense Used in Story's Main Action	Verb Tense Used for Past Events
Present tense: *she goes*	Past tense: *she went*
Past tense: *she went*	Past perfect tense: *she had gone*

Another method is to recite the story out loud and notice which verbs you naturally use. If your spoken English is generally accurate, this will be a reliable guide. If you have doubts, refer to the chart.

In flash-forwards such as the example quoted above from *House of Sand and Fog*, authors may use untensed verbs to blur the story's tense momentarily and allow a relatively unnoticeable transition. In the following example, the verb *to deliver* accomplishes the same purpose:

Little Red-Cap did not come by her fame lightly. She had performed an act of great courage. When just a little girl, she had been asked by her mother **to deliver** a basket of goodies to her grandmother. She set forth through the woods, where she encountered the wolf. . . .

The two important things to remember about verb tense are these:

- Be consistent. When moving back and forth through fictional time, establish one tense to signify the fictional present.
- When moving back in time from the story's main action, use past perfect if the main action is in the past tense. If you are telling the story's main action in the present tense, use simple past tense for past events.

As You Write

Your story's pacing, its emphasis, its cohesiveness, and even, to a large degree, its coherence, all depend upon how well you handle time. Sensing what material should be expanded into scenes and what should be summarized; knowing how to conjugate verbs, how to change tenses to signify time shifts; and developing the knack for changing scenes clearly and unobtrusively—each of these skills is a part of well-written fiction. This section will offer some suggestions for practicing these skills and for self-checking.

When writing scenes, keep in mind the story's sense of time. Think of how it is when people tell stories aloud. Do they move along to what you really want to hear, or do they get caught up in inconsequential detail? If you allow yourself to linger too long in descriptive detail or commentary, or if your characters talk too much, the scene will seem to slow inappropriately. It will become frustrating to read. Unless you are trying for a special effect such as slow motion or intense, compressed action, you should not allow events to take significantly more or less time to describe than they would to observe, within the story's sense of time. In writing as in conversation, such choices are only superficially about the words themselves—providing what readers need, when they need it reflects the writer's sensitivity and engagement.

It may not immediately be clear what to include and what to exclude; it takes some distance to see what is truly relevant. Because it's difficult to edit as you write, the amount of material in your early drafts may exceed what a single story can accommodate. Early drafts often contain material for two or three stories, and it takes some objectivity and sometimes a second opinion to evaluate what belongs where.

As always, you must be willing to sacrifice extraneous detail no matter how attached you are to it, and to alter your original flow of ideas by adding or deleting as necessary. This flexibility will help you avoid long dull passages that exist only because "it's what happened next," as well as confusing transitions, missing information, and frustratingly underdeveloped scenes—all typical problems that cause many early drafts to lack narrative tension, meandering from incident to incident rather than purposefully building and resolving a central conflict.

If you find yourself inserting large amounts of background material or if what's in the background starts developing into out-of-sequence scenes, it may be that you have begun your story at too great a distance from what is essential. Chronological stories must begin close enough to the climactic moment that they won't sag or bog in the middle; for instance, Flannery O'Connor's "A Good Man Is Hard to Find" (pp. 362–372) begins as the family sets out on the journey that will lead them to The Misfit—who appears as well at the very beginning of the story, in a newspaper article. It is also important that the events chronicled stand well enough on their own that they don't require massive amounts of exposition, which would disrupt the flow of time.

You may face other challenges when writing chronological stories—among them becoming tangled in the first few pages, or getting hung up on where exactly to start, or spending too much time detailing logistical transitions. You may also be tempted to "finish off" or resolve individual events, but tying up too many loose ends may give your story an episodic quality. Remember that presenting the events chronologically does not mean that you have to write the scenes in order. If they come out that way, the momentum will probably work for the story; if not, it isn't the end of the world. Work with ideas as they occur to you and polish up the chronology and the transitions later.

Once you've written the first draft, a simple way to edit a story is to imagine the scenes that constitute its rising action as stair steps leading to the moment of change at the story's **climax** or peak—every step must lead toward that moment, rather than rambling away from it. (See Chapter 4, p. 72, for more on this subject.)

As you make the difficult decision to cut extraneous material, keep the deleted stuff in a file rather than discarding it. That way, you can reassure yourself that you're saving rather than losing it. Later, you may find that this discarded material forms the beginning of another story, or you may be able to merge elements of deleted scenes with thin parts of current ones. Layering scenes in this way often results in a more interesting, textured, and less predictable narrative.

Exploration and Discovery

The questions that follow will help you to evaluate your own rendering of time and to solicit readers' responses on this topic. The best way to know whether you've succeeded is to carefully self-critique and then to show the story to a reader and ask for feedback.

Ask Yourself

- *Is your choice of verb tense appropriate to the story?* Why? What are its advantages? Does it feel natural?
- *If you have chosen the present tense, why?* Are you sure the story requires it? If the reason is immediacy, is that particularly important in this story? Why? Can you better or as well convey the same feeling through description, order of events, characterization, setting, foreshadowing, or tone?
- *Is the verb tense consistent?*
- *Are you using the past perfect tense more than you need to?* Where?
- *Are you consistently using the appropriate tense for flashbacks?*
- *Are you moving back and forth through time too often?* Look for ways to simplify the story's movements through time, and to create a pattern that makes sense and that sounds natural.
- *Is the verb tense getting in the way of conveying the necessary information?* Do you feel limited by it? This is often the case with present tense or with past perfect, as may be used in stories with a great deal of past action.
- *Are you all tangled up?* Remain calm and proceed to the next section.

Ask Readers

- *Was it clear when each event happened?* Were you ever confused about time? Where? To ensure that you get specific comments, ask readers to mark the manuscript as they read or to use the chart in Chapter 11 (p. 218).

- *Were there any places where you wanted more (or less) information?* Where?
- *Was each time shift clear?* Did any of them lose or disorient you? Ask readers to mark each change. Most people will come away with a general impression about clarity and may have trouble tracing a problem to specific verbs without prompting.
- *What does the choice of verb tense contribute to the story?* What would another tense contribute?

Wordplay

Shifting tense   Experiment with time in your story. List the story's main events in chronological order. How many of these take place in the story's past? Try making some of them current. Try rewriting scenes or even the whole story in another tense. Outline the story, starting from several different places in time. If you are writing a **frame story** in which later events surround the rest of the story, or if you are flashing back, try writing a draft of the story in strict chronological order. Slow a scene with additional description, actions or gestures, or narrative commentary. Alter transitions. Add lines of dialogue. Speed up a scene by cutting those elements. Try rewriting a scene as narration, or vice versa. What are the effects? Read your story aloud. Where do you have trouble, as you reread your story, following the time sequence? Where do you find yourself tripping over the verbs or getting tired of them?

The voice in time   Using one of the characters as narrator, try telling the story aloud in another time frame—as if it happened very long ago, or as if it were currently taking place, with the narrator located right in the middle of things. How does distance or closeness to the events affect the narrative voice? What do you find yourself doing differently?

Suggested Reading

The More Books and Stories section starting on page 496 provides complete bibliographic information for each title listed below.

Kim Addonizio, "Survivors"
Russell Banks, *Affliction*
Charles Baxter, "Snow"
Christine Baxter, "If You Want to Have a Fling"
Gina Berriault, "A Dream of Fair Women," in *Women in Their Beds*
Gina Berriault, "Lights of Earth," in *Women in Their Beds*
Robert Olen Butler, "Jealous Husband Returns in Form of Parrot"
Raymond Carver, "The Calm"

Joseph Connolly, "Hard Feelings"
Andre Dubus, "A Father's Story"
Andre Dubus III, *House of Sand and Fog*
William Faulkner, "Barn Burning"
Gabriel García Márquez, *One Hundred Years of Solitude*
Jakob and Wilhelm Grimm, "Little Red-Cap"
Ernest Hemingway, "Hills Like White Elephants"
Robie Macauley and George Lanning, *Technique in Fiction*

Brenda Miller, "A Thousand Buddhas"

Joseph Moser, "Close Enough"

Alice Munro, "Lichen"

Flannery O'Connor, "A Good Man Is Hard to Find"

Jayne Anne Phillips, "Souvenir"

Juan Rulfo, "Macario"

J. D. Salinger, "Uncle Wiggily in Connecticut"

Akhil Sharma, "Cosmopolitan"

Mary Austin Speaker, "The Day the Flames Would Stop"

James Leon Suffern, "When the Summer Ends"

Jeannine Thibodeau, "Close"

CHAPTER 7

Setting

Less is more.

—Mies van der Rohe, architect

I've always thought that more is more.

—Janet St. John, poet

A Story's Context

Where does your story take place? The answer to this question will go a long way toward determining the story's nature. This chapter will explain and illustrate the uses of **setting**—the environment in which the story takes place—to convey emotion, to establish and enhance character and conflict, and to create and sustain **narrative tension**, the momentum that impels readers through the story. It will also discuss setting as an element of style, and as a part of the writing process. You'll find examples of how other writers have used their stories' physical and psychological environments, as well as practical suggestions and exercises to help you develop setting in your story.

"Little Red-Cap": The Forest

Even in the simple fairy tale "Little Red-Cap" (pp. 298–300), setting informs the story: the forest suggests Red-Cap's vulnerability, innocence, and bravery, and it influences the outcome of her adventure. How would the tone, Red-Cap's personality, and even the events themselves differ if it took place somewhere else—say, in a village or a city? Red-Cap and her grandmother would be much less isolated. The wolf would have to be more furtive. The woodsman might have another line of work. And the sense of danger might come from anonymous crowds or individuals rather than from the deep forest. How would the story

Q: Does it matter where a story is located? What's the point of setting?

A: Stories *take place.* Get it? They require place. And if you let them, they take it up into themselves; they invade it, colonize it; they get tinctured, tainted with it. To me, place is strongest in a story when its details are not composed in some "set-piece" but gathered into kinetic narrative sentences, swept into the stream of the story's movement, that "profluence" that John Gardner wrote about in his book *The Art of Fiction.* And I think, by the way, that it's the same with what we're used to calling "characterization." (And I'll bet Henry James and Eudora Welty have already said all this better than I can, in *The Art of Fiction* and *Place in Fiction*, respectively. Go read. Memorize some of their sentences: the lightest and most durable baggage you'll ever carry.)

—*Bruce Jorgensen,*
writer and teacher

differ if the descriptions of place had simply been left out? What's lost from the scene below when we delete references to the setting?

So he walked for a short time by the side of Little Red-Cap, and then he said: "See, Little Red-Cap, [**how pretty the flowers are about here**]—why do you not look round? I believe, too, that you do not hear [**how sweetly the little birds are singing; you walk gravely along as if you were going to school, while everything else out here in the wood is merry.**]

Little Red-Cap raised her eyes, and [**when she saw the sunbeams dancing here and there through the trees, and pretty flowers growing everywhere,**] she thought: "Suppose I take grandmother a fresh nosegay; that would please her too. [**It is so early in the day that**] I shall still get there in good time"; and so she ran [**from the path into the wood**] to look for flowers. [**And whenever she had picked one, she fancied that she saw a still prettier one farther on and ran after it, and so got deeper and deeper into the wood.**]

The first bracketed line suggests the wolf's seductiveness. The second conveys his manipulative techniques. The third takes us directly into Red-Cap's thoughts and perceptions, and in so doing indicates the wolf's influence. The fourth portrays her rationalization, and the fifth bracketed description shows her interaction with the place itself—how she gets lost. The edited version is perfunctory and one-dimensional by comparison. It has no context.

Setting and Emotion

Setting grounds a story and helps readers imagine the situation. It provides a backdrop for the action, defining the **characters** (the story's main actors) and events. On a deeper level, setting, like a stage set, creates space in which emotions can resound and reverberate. Adding a few lines about the surroundings paces the story, leaving time for emotional moments to sink in, and awakening and allowing feeling without naming it.

"Yellow Woman": Mystery

In Leslie Marmon Silko's "Yellow Woman" (pp. 406–413), for example, setting interacts with **dia-**

Q: How can I write good description?

A: Description—the condensed selective representation of milieux—is harder to do well when the action is set in locales that are unexotic or over-familiar. What happens is that the writer is too often, in such cases, satisfied to catalog the basic indicators of a scene-type in order to get a recognizable box set up so that the really much more interesting interpersonal stuff can take place within it. But this limits narrative potential, because even an ordinary milieu, when deeply created (perceived, imagined), can yield idiosyncrasies, unexpected symmetries, atmospheres, that can subtly color the nature of the human interactions being portrayed or the reader's reception of them. It's usually worthwhile initially to overdescribe a scene, especially a new one, and then cut it to the resonant essentials. See D. H. Lawrence, especially in his stories, and John Updike, in all his fiction.

—*Norman Rush,*
writer

logue (the characters' speech) and gestures to convey emotion. In this scene, the main character talks with her kidnapper, who calls her Yellow Woman after a legend:

> "Have you brought women here before?" He smiled and kept chewing, so I said, "Do you always use the same tricks?"
>
> "What tricks?" He looked at me like he didn't understand.
>
> "The story about being a ka'tsina from the mountains. The story about Yellow Woman."
>
> Silva was silent; his face was calm.
>
> "I don't believe it. Those stories couldn't happen now," I said.
>
> He shook his head and said softly, "But someday they will talk about us, and they will say, 'Those two lived long ago when things like that happened.'"
>
> He stood up and went out. I ate the rest of the potatoes and thought about things—about the noise the stove was making and the sound of the mountain wind outside. I remembered yesterday and the day before, and then I went outside.
>
> I walked past the corral to the edge where the narrow trail cut through the black rim rock. I was standing in the sky with nothing around me but the wind that came down from the blue mountain peak behind me. I could see faint mountain images in the distance miles across the vast spread of mesas and valleys and plains. I wondered who was over there to feel the mountain wind on those sheer blue edges—who walks on the pine needles in those blue mountains.

The woman's sense of mystery regarding her own identity and that of the man who has kidnapped her is heightened by the sound of the stove and the wind, and the image of the distant mountains as a place inhabited by unknown strangers. Expanses of time and space and silence exist in the description of this place, and convey a sense of wonder and human smallness. The reader, like the writer, doesn't have to make all of these connections on a conscious level in order to feel them.

"A Father's Story": The Dark Night of the Soul

This dramatic scene in "A Father's Story" (pp. 272–286) in which Luke discovers the body of the young man his daughter has accidentally killed, makes use of setting in a more active way, suggesting Luke's emotional turmoil not only through the description of night and wind but also through his interaction with the landscape:

> I started down, watching the tall grass under the trees to my right, glancing into the dark of the ditch, listening for cars behind me; but as soon as I cleared one tree, its sound was gone, its flapping leaves and rattling branches far behind me, as though the greatest distance I had at my back was a matter of feet, while ahead of me I could see a barn two miles off. Then I saw her skid marks: short, and

going left and downhill, into the other lane. I stood at the ditch, its weeds blowing; across it were trees and their moving shadows, like the clouds. I stepped onto its slope, and it took me sliding on my feet, then rump, to the bottom, where I sat still, my body gathered to itself, lest a part of me should touch him.

It would be perfectly possible for Dubus to have set this scene in daylight, in hot weather, in the desert, or in a blizzard. But it would have been a different scene. The blinding darkness and the deafening wind affect its tone, impact, and outcome. Luke's scrambling and sliding down the darkened slope suggest not only his physical responses but his distraught emotional and spiritual state.

"Gooseberries": Happiness

In the joyous scene below from Anton Chekhov's "Gooseberries" (pp. 253–260), descriptions of the physical surroundings and the character's interactions with them convey a moment, however fleeting, of exultation:

Ivan Ivanich emerged from the shed, splashed noisily into the water, and began swimming beneath the rain, spreading his arms wide, making waves all round him, and the white water-lilies rocked on the waves he made. He swam into the very middle of the river and then dived, a moment later came up at another place and swam further, diving constantly, and trying to touch the bottom. "Ah, my God," he kept exclaiming in his enjoyment. "Ah, my God. . . ." He swam up to the mill, had a little talk with some peasants there and turned back, but when he got to the middle of the river, he floated, holding his face up to the rain. Burkin and Alekhin were dressed and ready to go, but he went on swimming and diving.
"God! God!" he kept exclaiming. "Dear God!"

The settings in these two excerpts are quite different—night and day, land and water, Massachusetts and Russia—as are the situations: one man searching for the body of an accident victim and the other going for a swim in the rain. The verbs in these passages convey each character's movements within the setting and suggest the character's frame of mind. Luke Ripley *starts, watches, glances, listens, steps, slides, sits, gathers,* and *contemplates touching.* The leaves and branches *flap* and *rattle.* In contrast, Ivan Ivanich *emerges, splashes, spreads his arms, swims, dives, swims and dives again, exclaims, swims and turns,* and *floats, rocking the lilies with his waves.* Each author's choices of place, time, action, detail, and verbs suggest the character's feelings without ever stating them directly.

Setting, Character, and Conflict

Like negative space—the "background" behind figures or objects in a painting—setting defines characters and their conflicts, showing readers the broad view of the characters' circumstances and positions within a larger context; and in subtle ways, through the choice of detail, it conveys sensibility. For instance, a story's setting can place characters socio-economically, as in the "Cone of Silence" dinner scene from Joseph Connolly's "Hard Feelings" (pp. 260–270), which derives much of its humor from the class warfare and cultural idiosyncrasies of Cambridge, Massachusetts, where it is set.

The Great Gatsby: Privilege

Social and emotional dynamics or conflicts between characters may be further delineated as characters move about and interact within the setting, as in this scene from F. Scott Fitzgerald's *The Great Gatsby*:

The room, shadowed well with awnings, was dark and cool. Daisy and Jordan lay upon an enormous couch, like silver idols weighing down their own white dresses against the singing breeze of the fans.

"We can't move," they said together.

Jordan's fingers, powdered white over their tan, rested for a moment in mine.

"And Mr. Thomas Buchanan, the athlete?" I inquired.

Simultaneously, I heard his voice, gruff, muffled, husky, at the hall telephone.

Gatsby stood in the center of the crimson carpet and gazed around with fascinated eyes. Daisy watched him and laughed, her sweet, exciting laugh; a tiny gust of powder rose from her bosom into the air.

The cool, darkened room carpeted in crimson conveys wealth, privilege, and luxury; the women reclining in it, their central and sheltered status. The characters' positions—the women on the couch "like silver idols," Nick and Gatsby walking in dazzled from outside, Tom preoccupied in the hall on the telephone—suggest social position as well as the emotional alliances and conflicts.

"Hills Like White Elephants": Bleakness

In a narrower, more intimate portrait, the setting of Ernest Hemingway's spare, restrained "Hills Like White Elephants" (p. 320) provides the ostensible point of contention between a couple whose real conflict, as they contemplate the prospect of an abortion, is much deeper:

The woman brought two glasses of beer and two felt pads. She put the felt pads and the beer glasses on the table and looked at the man and the girl. The girl was looking off at the line of hills. They were white in the sun and the country was brown and dry.

"They look like white elephants," she said.

"I've never seen one," the man drank his beer.

"No, you wouldn't have."

In this scene, as in the passage from Chekhov quoted on page 136, the landscape embodies emotion. The **image** or sensory detail of the sun-whitened hills conveys the bleak feelings of the moment visually, allowing for a less specifically defined kind of complexity than if the author had tried to state the feelings directly. Later in the scene, the argument continues:

". . . I said the mountains looked like white elephants. Wasn't that bright?"

"That was bright."

"I wanted to try this new drink. That's all we do, isn't it—look at things and try new drinks?"

"I guess so."

The girl looked across at the hills.

"They're lovely hills," she said. "They don't really look like white elephants. I just meant the coloring of their skin through the trees."

"Should we have another drink?"

"All right."

The warm wind blew the bead curtain against the table.

The hills provide a focal point, allowing the characters to look somewhere other than at each other. The curtain suggests the breeze on a hot day, and the rattle of beads against the table is a small sound that implies silence elsewhere in the scene. These slight details create an understated backdrop against which the couple's unspoken conflict can become the focus.

"The Father": Tension

Student Seth Pase's story "The Father" (pp. 372–375) describes different characters in a similar situation. The enclosed space of the car traps the characters together, magnifies their small movements, and also divides them, placing them in separate seats, turned forward, Leo's eyes on the road.

Leo starts the car while Mary puts on her sunglasses and searches through her purse for some cigarettes. In less than a minute they are driving through the outskirts of town, past the wharf and down the river road toward the city. Mary stares blankly out the window, smoking her cigarette in complete silence. Leo turns down the heater and cracks his window, uncomfortable in the heat and the silence.

Here, the setting—in the car on the way to the abortion clinic—starkly defines the parameters of the story and the conflict.

"A Father's Story": Grief

Because setting, like everything else in a story, is filtered through the characters' sensibilities, the choice of details is part of what defines the point-of-view character. As Luke Ripley notices the dawn sky growing light, the trees taking shape, and the birds awakening, something of his awareness and his aloneness can be felt, as well as the meaning he assigns to his solitude:

. . . Sometimes I try to think of other things, like the rabbit that is warm and breathing but not there till twilight. I feel on the brink of something about the life of the senses, but either am not equipped to go further or am not interested enough to concentrate. I have called this thinking, but it is not, because it is un-intentional; what I'm really doing is feeling the day, in silence. . . .

"When the Summer Ends": Terror

In this scene from student James Leon Suffern's story "When the Summer Ends" (pp. 431–443) the anxiety felt by the main character, Jackson, as well as his outward denial of it, is conveyed through his observations of and reactions to the weather:

A warm breeze ruffled the newspaper, and then cooler wind blew from the other direction. Jackson looked up at the sky. It wasn't black, it didn't seem menacing. The whole sky had a greenish tint lingering over the gray, and even as thin gray clouds criss-crossed quickly above him, the main impression the sky gave was one of immense and awful stillness. Jackson said, "Oh, shit," and spat on the grass, walking inside.

Later on in the story, the extent of Jackson's fear is revealed through this description of the interior landscape:

He read a headline: TWO IF BY LAND, his head shot up, he closed his eyes, a little yelp escaped from his mouth. The headline sparked something inside him, and with his eyes still closed Jackson watched a scene unfold, like a movie projector was rolling in his head. Two funnel clouds cross in the sky and then come down separately within minutes of each other. He watched as the first one dips, travels across some fields, lifts an old hay barn to the sky. It tears a fence out of the earth and then quickly goes back up with no more mischief. The other one lands near a trailer park. It doesn't directly run over anything, but still the homes topple into one another, leaving gaping holes where kitchens and living rooms were. Jackson saw all this from his couch, sort of like a video game, and whenever the tornado got close to buildings or people, he would shift his weight to one side slightly, as if his leaning could control the path.

In this story, character and setting actually merge, the tornado-prone landscape blurring into the character's fantasies.

As a backdrop within a scene, a point of contention, an object or state of fear, or an opportunity for rapture or solitude, setting reveals the nature of the story's main characters. As you develop the setting in your story, notice how the characters react to and within their surroundings, and in what ways the story's environment reflects them. Remember that developing the setting offers you a number of opportunities to show who your characters are and what they feel.

Setting and Narrative Tension

Setting can also affect a story's **narrative tension**— the momentum that impels readers into and through a story. In Christine Baxter's "If You Ever Want to Have a Fling" (pp. 233–238) the **narrator** or character who tells the story is repeatedly accosted in various settings: on the street, at a tollbooth, on the freeway, on a city sidewalk late at night, in foreign countries. With the repeated threats in each new and more unfamiliar setting, the tension escalates. As in "Little Red-Cap" (pp. 298–300), this character's vulnerability is accentuated by the circumstances in which the author has placed her. Similarly, the weather in "When the Summer Ends" grows more and more threatening; the forest in "Little Red-Cap" gets deeper and darker; the family in "A Good Man Is Hard to Find" (pp. 362–372) drives farther and farther into isolated surroundings. In these ways, the setting reflects and contributes to each story's developing conflicts.

"Jealous Husband Returns in Form of Parrot": Powerlessness

In Robert Olen Butler's "Jealous Husband Returns in Form of Parrot" (p. 244), the narrator and protagonist, a man who finds himself transformed into a parrot, is caged and mute, forced to watch his wife cavorting with another man. These restrictions evoke the powerlessness and pain of jealousy, creating tremendous emotional momentum that culminates at the end of the story when the cage is left open:

Q: How can I use setting to develop the other elements in my story?

A: To me, the setting, the *atmosphere* of a story, is another character in and of itself. Your *human* character occupies a place on the stage, but what surrounds your character—a sky, a room, a river, a window filled with a certain light—amplifies the emotion you are trying to present. That doesn't mean if someone in the story is angry the sky has to be dark. But the situation needs to be viewed as an angry person might see it—a bright sky might be "acutely bright," in other words. Flannery O'Connor does this in "A Good Man Is Hard to Find": "The trees," she writes, "were full of silver-white sunlight and the meanest of them sparkled." Once writers concentrate on setting, using it not only to paint a picture, but to present an emotional reality, they have a much clearer idea of what they're writing about: for the writer, the setting can serve as a signpost that points to the deeper nature of the story.

—Joseph Hurka,
writer and teacher

I stand on my cage door now and my wings stir. I look at the corner to the hallway and down at the end to where the whooping has begun again. I can fly there and think of things to do about this.

But I do not. I turn instead and I look at the trees moving just beyond the other end of the room. I look at the sky the color of the brow of a blue-front Amazon. A shadow of birds spanks across the lawn. And I spread my wings. I will fly now. Even though I know there is something between me and that place where I can be free of all these feelings, I will fly. I will throw myself there again and again. Pretty bird. Bad bird. Good night.

Throughout the story the protagonist's confinement, along with his animal nature, defines his interactions with his wife. In the end, he literally hurls himself against his surroundings, choosing self-destruction over continued torment.

"Araby": Longing

The main character in James Joyce's classic story "Araby" (pp. 323–327) is also separated from his beloved.

Every morning I lay on the floor in the front parlour watching her door. The blind was pulled down to within an inch of the sash so that I could not be seen. When she came out on the doorstep my heart leaped. I ran to the hall, seized my books and followed her. I kept her brown figure always in my eye and, when we came near the point at which our ways diverged, I quickened my pace and passed her. This happened morning after morning. I had never spoken to her, except for a few casual words, and yet her name was like a summons to all my foolish blood.

Like the cage and the window in Butler's story, the door, the blind, and the houses themselves divide the would-be lover from the object of his adoration. The sense of separation and unapproachableness builds the momentum toward his eventual attempt to win her love.

Setting need not be static. Consider how the surroundings in your story might change: the weather could get better or worse, the circumstances more or less threatening, comfortable, impoverished, exciting, beautiful, or ugly. The characters' reactions to their circumstances may also intensify or diminish. As the setting evolves, so will the story's tension.

Setting and Style

Understated Description of Setting: "The Calm"

When used well, setting always accomplishes more than one thing at a time. This kind of economy is an important part of any writer's style. Raymond Carver, a contemporary author known for his understated style, conveys a sense of the characters, the place, and the group dynamic, while also establishing the story's tone, from the first paragraph of "The Calm" (pp. 249–252):

I was getting a haircut. I was in the chair and three men were sitting along the wall across from me. Two of the men waiting I'd never seen before. But one of them I recognized, though I couldn't exactly place him. I kept looking at him as the barber worked on my hair. The man was moving a toothpick around in his mouth, a heavyset man, short wavy hair. And then I saw him in a cap and uniform, little eyes watchful in the lobby of a bank.

Of the other two, one was considerably the older, with a full head of curly gray hair. He was smoking. The third, though not so old, was nearly bald on top, but the hair at the sides hung over his ears. He had on logging boots, pants shiny with machine oil.

The barber put a hand on top of my head to turn me for a better look. Then he said to the guard, "Did you get your deer, Charles?"

All the narrator says directly about the setting is that it is a barbershop and that the men are sitting along the wall. The men's appearance and clothing suggest something of the town's economic level, and the situation is intriguing enough that readers will be stimulated to fill in other details. By withholding unnecessary description, Carver creates a tight narrative that entices readers to engage with the story and participate in its creation.

Detailed Descriptions of Setting: "Araby" and "A Dream of Fair Women"

Writers vary a lot in the amount of time and attention they give to describing the places where their stories occur. Some, like Carver, Silko, Hemingway, and Seth Pase, accomplish lots with a few carefully chosen words, engaging readers by providing only essential details. Others, like Chekhov and Dubus, create similarly vivid and affecting pictures with more prominent or extensive physical description. James Joyce provides another such description, of a Dublin neighborhood, in "Araby":

When the short days of winter came dusk fell before we had well eaten our dinners. When we met in the street the houses had grown sombre. The space of sky above us was the colour of ever-changing violet and towards it the lamps of the street lifted their feeble lanterns. The cold air stung us and we played till our bodies glowed. Our shouts echoed in the silent street. The career of our play brought us through the dark muddy lanes behind the houses where we ran the gauntlet of the rough tribes from the cottages, to the back doors of the dark dripping gardens where odours arose from the ashpits, to the dark odorous stables where a coachman smoothed and combed the horse or shook music from the buckled harness.

The situation of children playing outside after dinner is familiar to most people, but aside from evoking childhood and conveying the story's action, the details in this scene resonate thematically and portray the town as dark and colorless. The object of the narrator's desire stands out in contrast:

> . . . if Mangan's sister came out on the doorstep to call her brother in to his tea we watched her from our shadow peer up and down the street. We waited to see whether she would remain or go in and, if she remained, we left our shadow and walked up to Mangan's steps resignedly. She was waiting for us, her figure defined by the light from the half-opened door. Her brother always teased her before he obeyed and I stood by the railings looking at her. Her dress swung as she moved her body and the soft rope of her hair tossed from side to side.

Gina Berriault's "A Dream of Fair Women" (pp. 239–244) includes a particularly lavish setting:

> Light from the candles within the faceted glass globes on the tables glided up and down the waitresses' saris and shimmered along their necklaces, turned ivory the waiters' white turbans, and glinted off the engraved brass trays, large as giants' shields, hanging on the walls. The candles set aglow the faces of the women at the tables, and she saw—more sharply than ever—how, tables apart, women glanced at one another as if by mistake, as if indifferently, to see who was the most beautiful of all.

In this passage, the description is vivid, unusual, and **concrete** or sensory. The candles, the silk saris, the faceted glass globes, the engraved brass trays, and the women's faces—all of these well-chosen details are drawn from and appeal to the senses. All are beautiful, and that beauty is directly relevant to the story's **plot** or story line, and to its **theme,** or main idea.

The details in each of the above examples combine to create a definite mood. But if this were all they did, the writing would be merely pretty. The description in "A Dream of Fair Women" is combined with action: the candles are lit by the waitresses; the light glides and shimmers and glints. The vivid and precise verbs in this passage are as much a part of the description as are the adjectives—and they keep it from becoming a beautiful but static description that would slow the passage of fictional time. Even more important, this description, along with others in the story, develops the idea of beauty's elusive and illusory nature.

Because setting creates the negative space in which everything else transpires, the author's treatment of it is an important part of a story's style. How much detail does the author supply, and how much is left to the reader's imagination? In descriptively rich settings, is the imagery contained primarily in the nouns and adjectives? How do the verbs engage the setting with other aspects of the story? These questions will point to ways of developing the setting in any story so that it is not merely decorative, but also functional—because style, as George Sampson said, "is the feather in the arrow, not the feather in the cap."

As You Write

Writers don't necessarily choose descriptive details in order to create a predecided mood, emotion, conflict, character trait, level of tension, or stylistic approach. Often the process is reversed: almost as if recalling a dream, the writer envisions various elements of the scene and then moves closer to them, adding detail until the entire scene becomes clear. In this way, the scene's final effect is the natural result of the combined details. This more open-ended process is not for everyone, but its advantages are obvious. The more leeway you give yourself, the more likely you are to stumble upon unexpected connections and resonances.

Keeping the setting in view Whether or not your stories grow naturally from setting, it's a good idea to remind yourself periodically to locate characters and action in their physical surroundings. The first reason to do this is so that logistical confusion won't derail whatever else is going on in the scene—if readers can't figure out where the characters are or what they're doing, they will be distracted from deeper issues.

Setting and pacing Try using setting to improve the pacing in your story. Aside from clarity, occasional reminders of the physical surroundings pace a scene in much the same way that **tags** (the words that tell the reader who is speaking) offer

> **Q: How much emphasis (and space) should I give to my story's setting?**
>
> **A:** It varies. And the choice of details matters more than the word count. But one thing is always true: I won't be there until you take me there.
>
> —*Johnny Vickle, student writer*

"breathing room" during long passages of dialogue. Like dialogue tags, setting is often overlooked in early or beginning drafts, because the author has focused first on other issues. It's worth rereading your work in order to specifically check that you haven't inadvertently lost sight of the setting as you've worked on other elements of the story.

Using models for setting Like gestures, setting can be tricky if you're working strictly from memory or imagination. You may find yourself falling back on generalized or stereotypical descriptions, for lack of other ideas. Modeling settings on actual places will provide alternatives to the generic. Even if you can't find a place exactly like the one you're describing, you may be able to use models for such things as weather conditions, the sensation of being in a crowd of people, the way a boat moves on the water, the sounds of traffic, and so forth. Combining the setting from one scene with other aspects of a second scene introduces random elements that will vary a too-consistent picture. See the Wordplay activities on p. 146 for additional suggestions about employing models for setting, and consult the questions on pp. 145–146 to help you evaluate how effectively you are using place in your writing.

Setting and narrative voice Setting profoundly affects **voice,** the personality, tone, and sensibility conveyed by the story's language. In almost any good story, the description reflects the narrator's sensibility. This is sometimes a conscious effort on the author's part, but often it's simply a matter of having found the story's narrative voice—that part of the author that becomes the narrator. If you're true to that voice, appropriate choices will flow from it. Read descriptive scenes aloud and notice what the tone and choice of details reveal about the character from whose point of view the story is told. How does the description double as **characterization** (the way a writer conveys characters' personalities and other attributes)? *Hint:* When describing setting, think not only of what is seen but also of who sees it; setting should convey interior as well as outward landscapes. If you're writing "in character," the voice itself may help you to limit and define your use of setting.

Fantastic settings   Consider how the setting in nonrealistic stories such as Gabriel García Márquez's "A Very Old Man with Enormous Wings" (pp. 293–298) or Robert Olen Butler's "Jealous Husband Returns in Form of Parrot" (pp. 244–249) differs from that in realistic stories such as Andre Dubus's "A Father's Story" (pp. 272–286) or Ernest Hemingway's "Hills Like White Elephants" (pp. 320–323). In what ways is it similiar? Notice that Butler and García Márquez have devoted close attention to physical detail, including the setting. In this way, their fantasy worlds become real.

Setting and emotion   When considering how you can clarify essential elements of a conflict or situation, try adding a little about the setting. The backdrop you create will help to define what's going on emotionally. Experiment with different details; you may be surprised at how much a change in the setting will nuance the tone, the mood, and even the characters' feelings.

Setting as attribution   Vary the **tags** or **attribution** (the words that indicate who is speaking when) in your dialogue. Try substituting brief descriptions of the setting. Notice how these small changes pace the dialogue and suggest the characters' reactions. How does the scene's tone and mood change as you alter the attribution?

Blending setting with dialogue and action   When looking for ways to vary long descriptive passages in your story, try breaking them up and moving some of this description into passages of dialogue and action. This will heighten narrative tension and add vividness to the scenes.

Exploration and Discovery

Ask Yourself

To evaluate how you've used setting in your story, run through the questions below.

- *Have you indicated where each scene is taking place?* Have you referred to the setting consistently throughout the story, and often enough so readers won't forget where they are?

- *Can you envision the setting?* Have you included the relevant details, and do those details draw upon the senses—sight, hearing, smell, touch, and taste?

- *Are the settings related enough to keep the story from breaking apart?* If not, is it possible to relocate some scenes so that radical changes in setting don't disorient readers and create the impression that more than one story is taking place?

- *Are your setting references appropriately integrated into the story's action when possible?* Are there places where long passages of description slow or stop the action in a way that detracts from rather than contributing to the story's impact?
- *What, other than its aesthetic value, does your description contribute to the story?*
- *When in your own writing process do you begin to envision the story's setting?* Is place the first thing you picture, or do you add it in once you've written your scenes?

Ask Readers

- *Without looking back at the story, describe where each scene takes place.* If readers' answers surprise you, you'll have an indication of where you need more or clearer details.
- *Describe the setting in detail.* Again, readers' answers to this question will tell you where you are and are not being clear enough. You may get some new ideas, too.
- *Were there any places where you found yourself skimming through description to get to the action in a scene?* Where? If readers agree on offending passages, it may be a sign that some of the description is superfluous.

Wordplay

Alternate settings   Take a scene from your story, or one from a published story. Underline all description that refers to the setting. Try deleting it. How is the scene affected? Does the situation change? Does the emotional impact or tone shift? Now try changing it—sunshine to rain or sleet, or a brick road to a sidewalk café. What happens to the scene?

Trading settings   Think about the differences between Raymond Carver's "The Calm" (pp. 249–252) and Gina Berriault's "A Dream of Fair Women" (pp. 239–244). How do these two authors choose and construct their settings differently? What similarities do they share? Find a writer or story that describes setting differently from the way you do. Try rewriting one of your scenes in the other writer's style. Try rewriting the other author's scene in your style. Do you see advantages to each? Are there places in your work where you might try another approach?

Layering the setting   Choose an actual place that has some bearing on a story you are writing—someplace that resembles the setting of one or more of your scenes. It may be the location itself that is similar, or perhaps it's the tone of the place, the time of day, or the weather, or the people you're likely to see. Next, go there. Take nothing but a notebook and something to write with. Be sure to go alone. Sit or stand where you can be comfortable and relatively unobtrusive, and spend twenty minutes writing a list of concrete details—colors, smells, people, clothing, trash, the ground, the light, the feel of the air, sounds, anything you notice. Don't try to edit as you go, and don't look back at what you've written. When you've finished, wait a day or two and then return to the same place and repeat the exercise. Finally, wait another day or two and repeat it again. Now reread your lists, underlining details that may be useful to you, and try adding some of them into the scene you're working on.

This exercise will not only help you develop your story's setting; it will also give you experience "writing in layers." Most writers find that revisiting a real or fictional scene adds depth and dimension to their description of it. In a broad sense, the exercise is about revision.

Random elements   A scene that feels "dead" or flat can often be enlivened by introducing a random element, something specifically *not* calculated to create a certain effect. Take notes on various settings—rooms, streets, towns, restaurants—as you go about your daily activities. Keep these details in a notebook or file. Then, as you are working on your story, experiment with injecting these random elements into scenes. How does letting go of your preconceptions in a small way affect the scene's tone, emphasis, and emotional content?

Suggested Reading

The More Books and Stories section starting on page 496 provides complete bibliographic information for each title listed below.

Christine Baxter, "If You Ever Want to Have a Fling"

Gina Berriault, "A Dream of Fair Women"

Robert Olen Butler, "Jealous Husband Returns in Form of Parrot"

Raymond Carver, "The Calm"

Anton Chekhov, "Gooseberries"

Joseph Connolly, "Hard Feelings"

Andre Dubus, "A Father's Story"

F. Scott Fitzgerald, *The Great Gatsby*

Jakob and Wilhelm Grimm, "Little Red-Cap"

Ernest Hemingway, "Hills Like White Elephants"

James Joyce, "Araby"

Flannery O'Connor, "A Good Man Is Hard to Find"

Seth Pase, "The Father"

Leslie Marmon Silko, "Yellow Woman"

James Leon Suffern, "When the Summer Ends"

CHAPTER 8

Dialogue

> *You should never write realistic dialogue. We all talk too much. Look at the short stories of Fitzgerald or Hemingway—they write lines that sound like human speech but it's purified. No one says that little. I try to get a poetic rhythm going and I try to write literary dialogue. We're not trying to be real. We're trying to be better than real. We're trying to be true.*
>
> —Andre Dubus, interview, February 23, 1999

What They Say

The word **dialogue** refers to speech—what a story's **characters** or main actors say aloud. When quoted directly, it is usually enclosed within quotation marks. Whether spare or abundant, quoted or summarized, dialogue is a basic element of most scenes. Because of its subtleties and the technical conventions associated with it, it is also one of the most challenging aspects of writing fiction. This chapter will show you how to manage punctuation, paragraphing, and **attribution** or **tags**—the words that indicate who is speaking when—in passages of dialogue. It will also demonstrate and discuss what makes good dialogue—not only the words themselves but the voices they create, and what is not said. You'll find suggestions about writing dialect and children's speech, as well as exercises and ideas for improving the dialogue in your own stories.

Dialogue is one of the most economical ways to reveal characters. The opening dialogue in Flannery O'Connor's "A Good Man Is Hard to Find" (pp. 362–372), for example, introduces the main characters and their conflicts gracefully and thoroughly, using very little direct **exposition** or background information:

"The children have been to Florida before," the old lady said. "You all ought to take them somewhere else for a change so they would see different parts of the world and be broad. They never have been to east Tennessee."

The children's mother didn't seem to hear her but the eight-year-old boy, John Wesley, a stocky child with glasses, said, "If you don't want to go to Florida, why dontcha stay at home?" He and the little girl, June Star, were reading the funny papers on the floor.

"She wouldn't stay at home to be queen for a day," June Star said without raising her yellow head.

"Yes and what would you do if this fellow, The Misfit, caught you?" the grandmother asked.

"I'd smack his face," John Wesley said.

"She wouldn't stay at home for a million bucks," June Star said. "Afraid she'd miss something. She has to go everywhere we go."

"All right, Miss," the grandmother said. "Just remember that the next time you want me to curl your hair."

June Star said her hair was naturally curly.

The dialogue in this scene, including the silence of those who do not speak, gives the reader a compact and accurate image of this family: the dominant, insistent, self-righteous, and interfering grandmother; the parents who try to ignore her; and the graceless children. In these few lines, the story's emotional dynamics are established.

This clarity is not a matter of making the characters state things directly. The grandmother does not come out and say, "I'm going to get my way no matter what," and Bailey doesn't dispute it. The characters argue over The Misfit and June Star's hair rather than extending the discussion of who will go on the vacation and where they will go. If the author had continued to address these logistical and expository issues directly through the dialogue, the speech would have become dull and unwieldy.

In their book *Technique in Fiction*, Robie Macauley and George Lanning wrote that "Speech, as a way of characterization, moves forward by means of partial concealment, partial exposure." Dialogue is delicate and requires understatement; it's not uncommon for writers to cut most of the speech in a first draft, reducing paragraphs to sentences and sentences to phrases or to silence. Keeping dialogue spare allows readers to imagine what is unsaid, as in this passage from Ernest Hemingway's "Hills Like White Elephants" (pp. 320–323):

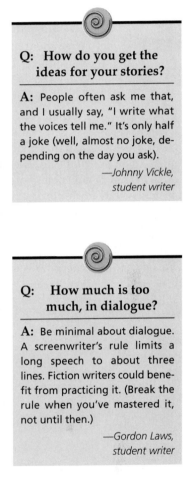

Q: How do you get the ideas for your stories?

A: People often ask me that, and I usually say, "I write what the voices tell me." It's only half a joke (well, almost no joke, depending on the day you ask).

—*Johnny Vickle,*
student writer

Q: How much is too much, in dialogue?

A: Be minimal about dialogue. A screenwriter's rule limits a long speech to about three lines. Fiction writers could benefit from practicing it. (Break the rule when you've mastered it, not until then.)

—*Gordon Laws,*
student writer

"Come on back in the shade," he said. "You mustn't feel that way."

"I don't feel any way," the girl said. "I just know things."

"I don't want you to do anything that you don't want to do—"

"Nor that isn't good for me," she said. "I know. Could we have another beer?"

"All right. But you've got to realize—"

"I realize," the girl said. "Can't we maybe stop talking?"

In contrast, the passage below from *The Krystal Promise*, a popular young adult **novel** (long fictional work of prose) by Blaine M. Yorgason and Brenton G. Yorgason, attempts with less success to convey background information directly through the characters' speech:

"It sure feels good to relax and laugh a little."

"It really does, Ray. Yet I've just been sitting here feeling guilty again. How can I be laughing and having fun when I should be mourning our baby's death?"

"Hmmm. It's interesting that you would say that, honey. Sometimes I feel that way too. How about the fire? Are you still feeling that guilt as well?"

"Yes, Ray. I am. I keep wondering if I acted cowardly during the fire, or if perhaps my carelessness or neglect was the cause of Krystal's death . . . Ray, did my carelessness cause Krystal's death?"

In this passage, the authors use the characters' speech to convey much of the important emotional information: that they are having a good time, that Laura feels guilty over her daughter's death, that Ray has similar feelings, and that Laura holds herself responsible. This technique makes explicit what is ordinarily implicit, particularly in adult literary fiction. Ray and Laura are simply saying to each other what the writer wants readers to understand about them. The result feels scripted; this dialogue is strained and forced, and it flattens the characters. Similar problems occur when writers attempt to convey exposition by means of dialogue, as in the following passage from the same book:

"Hey!" Ray shouted. "Cut that out!"

As the automobile sped down the highway Laura grabbed again at her husband's ribs, doing her best to tickle him.

"Laura, come on!" Ray gasped, grinning. "Do you want me to have a wreck?"

"If you do," Laura replied, smiling mischievously, "it won't be my fault. You don't drive this car any better than you drove that '55 Chevy you had when I met you."

"Wait a minute! I'm known far and wide for my safe driving."

"Oh, you are, are you? What about that night when you rolled your car into the river?"

"The river? I . . . oh, yeah! Listen, lady, I didn't roll it. It rolled itself. In fact, if you will recall, my dear, we were stopped, and you had my mind occupied with . . . uh . . . other things."

"Big deal! One or two little kisses, and you let the car roll into the river. Besides, we'd been married nearly a year."

Here, characters retell events they experienced together. This attempt to convey background information fails because the authors' agenda is too evident; the speech feels stilted and artificial, like the pretext it is.

As a rule, direct exposition is the job of the **narrator**—the voice or character who tells the story. It's too heavy and inflexible to be contained in most dialogue without weighing it down and forcing its speakers out of character and into the role of narrator. When exposition occurs successfully in dialogue, it is usually understated and indicated obliquely. For example, the speech in this passage from student writer Seth Pase's "The Father" (pp. 372–375) conveys a lot of background information, yet it retains the characters' natural voices and the rhythm of the conversation:

"If there's anything else I can do, just let me know," he finally manages. "If you need to stay some place, if you need some money . . ."

"Listen, all I want from you is a ride. I don't want money, I don't even want to see you. They just won't let me leave without a ride. I'd rather've driven myself, but they won't let you do that. You have to relax and sit still afterwards. I shouldn't even leave right away. They want you to stay for at least a little while afterwards. Everyone reacts differently and they like to make sure everything is OK before they let you just waltz out of there, so they don't get anymore bad press, I suppose." She looks down at her hands, out the window, anywhere away from him. "I just need a ride."

Unlike the examples on page 150 from *The Krystal Promise*, this speech conveys the background information—in this case, that Leo and Mary have agreed that she will have an abortion—without stating it directly. The effect is more natural, as if the dialogue has been overheard. More importantly, the background information is not all that is communicated. The speech expresses the characters' feelings in its tone and content, but not explicitly as in the previous examples. It is accompanied by gestures and reactions that communicate more subtly than direct, oversimplified statements such as "Leo, I really resent having this abortion."

Direct Discourse

The two most common forms of dialogue are **direct discourse**—things people say, directly quoted—and **indirect discourse**—things people say, described or summarized rather than quoted. Attribution or tags are the words that directly or indirectly indicate who is speaking.

When Writers Use Direct Discourse   How do writers decide what should be stated directly? Several factors influence this decision, and the results vary from author to author and from story to story. Generally, writers use dialogue as a way of detailing important moments in the story. Crucial events are usually dramatized with scenic elements, including dialogue as well as gestures and description, rather than being summarized. Occasionally, important interactions may be summarized without dialogue. Direct discourse is often somewhat elliptical—which means that the characters' desires and conflicts are ordinarily not stated explicitly. Rather, the characters speak "in evidence"—expressing emotion concretely rather than explaining it, as in this passage from from Joseph Connolly's "Hard Feelings"(pp. 260–270):

"You're a lucky guy," he said. "Sally is so easy to get along with."

"That's true," I said. I felt I should say something positive about his situation, something positive about Madelyn, and my mind raced through everything I knew about her. "Well," I said after a moment, "at least Madelyn's pretty clear about what she wants."

"Sally isn't?"

Rather than saying, "Madelyn's impossible," Mark settles on a patronizing euphemism: "at least . . ." whereupon Neil coolly and perhaps innocently pinpoints the trouble in Mark's marriage, turning the conversational tables. Naming these feelings would deflate the comedy and sink the scene in psychobabble. Dramatizing emotion rather than stating it allows feelings to swell and build beneath the surface rather than being explicitly defined and explained.

Punctuating Direct Discourse   Speech that is directly quoted is ordinarily enclosed within quotation marks. End punctuation—periods, commas, question marks, and exclamation points—is placed within the quotation marks.

> "Thanks to that Volkswagon commercial, *Pink Moon* was actually among the best-selling CDs on Amazon for a while!"

not

> "Thanks to that Volkswagon commercial, *Pink Moon* was actually among the best-selling CDs on Amazon for a while"!

When the spoken words are followed by "he said" or "she said" or similar attributions, the tag—that is, the words identifying who has spoken—is considered part of the sentence. If the spoken words end with a period but you want to attach a tag, use a comma inside the quotation marks at the end of the speech and do not capitalize the tag:

> "I can tell the parakeet likes me," he said.

not

> "I can tell the parakeet likes me." He said.

Technically, in the sentences that follow, the words spoken are the object of the verb *said*—they are what was said. Therefore, they must be contained in the same sentence with the verb. A comma, question mark, or exclamation point inside the quotation marks ends only the remark quoted, not the statement that it was quoted. This is why in all of the examples, the tag should not be capitalized—it is not a separate sentence.

> "Could you be a little less monotonous?" she said.

or

> "You could be a little less monotonous," she said.

not

"Could you be a little less monotonous?" She said.

or

"Could you be a little less monotonous?," she said.

When the spoken words are a direct quotation *preceded* by "he said" or "she said," use a comma after the attribution and capitalize the speech.

He said, "Is this seat taken?"

not

He said "is this seat taken?"

Notice that you don't need a period to end the quoted sentence in this case. That's because *only one end punctuation mark should be used at a time.* When the quote ends the sentence, its punctuation will suffice. To put it more simply, this looks funny:

He said, "Is this seat taken?".

Indirect Discourse

Sometimes speech is described or summarized rather than quoted;

She apologized for being late and went to find her seat.

Of course, if you wanted to quote her (direct discourse), you might do it like this:

She said, "I'm sorry I'm late," and went to find her seat.

But what if you wanted to convey the essence of the speech economically, retaining its tone without quoting it verbatim? In the following passage from "Hard Feelings" (pp. 260–270), Neil explains his argument with his wife Madelyn to Mark, the story's narrator:

Now Neil smiled. "That's what I said. I mean, that's not what I said exactly, but I said that I didn't feel that anger was an appropriate response. I asked her to remove the Mask of Anger." The careful language Neil always used made it sound like he was feeling his way through life on emotional training wheels. "She said she wouldn't," he continued, "because she was angry. She was angry with me for being a victim and angry with herself, she said, because all the men she ever gets involved with are victims. Do you want some water?"

The usual purpose of **indirect discourse** is to convey the content of a speech or conversation relatively quickly. Since indirect discourse is not a direct quotation, it requires no quotation marks.

When Writers Use Indirect Discourse   Indirect discourse and summary are useful when you want to condense less important dialogue or dialogue that would be too time-consuming to quote directly. June Star's last line in the passage above from "A Good Man Is Hard to Find" ("June Star said her hair was naturally curly") is an example, as is this longer passage from student writer James Leon Suffern's story "When the Summer Ends" (pp. 432–443):

The rest of the summer, Jackson would bring up the tornado that ran over his house, adding new flourishes if anyone would let him start talking. One time he called it the strongest tornado in Kentucky history. Hadn't you heard of it? I can't believe you guys don't remember that. Another time, Jackson remembered that he'd run outside and picked up Brimstone while the storm was coming up his street. Sometimes he changed things so they were smaller. It wrecked three houses, not five. It was the strongest one in Kentucky that year.

Combining Direct and Indirect Discourse

Sometimes writers combine direct and indirect discourse. Here, first, is a line of indirect discourse:

> Steve enjoyed juggling oranges, he said, but his favorite fruit was pineapples. He continued, his words tumbling over one another: during a recent stint at a circus, blinded by love, he had dated a knife-thrower.

Now, here it is written as a combination of direct and indirect discourse:

> Steve said he enjoyed juggling oranges, but "my favorite fruit is pineapples." He went on to describe a recent stint at a circus during which, he said, "I dated a knife-thrower."

Notice how the emphasis is distorted if the quoted words are not well chosen:

> Steve said "he" enjoyed "juggling" oranges, "but" his favorite "fruit" was pineapples. . . .

Quotation marks add emphasis, so they have to be used purposefully. Otherwise the effect may be nonsensical or unintentionally ironic. This technique of mixing direct and indirect discourse is often used to save time, when the precise wording is important, or when the writer means to subtly question the speaker's assertions or to distinguish them from the writer's.

> The disappointed plaintiff called the verdict "a travesty."

How They Say It

Tags or Attribution

Tags are the words that tell readers who is talking; for example; *he said* or *she replied*. They are also sometimes referred to as **attribution**. For beginning writers, attribution can be one of the most technically difficult aspects of writing dialogue. Once you get the hang of it, though, it will become second nature. Some basic suggestions can make it easier in the beginning.

Identifying the Speaker   First of all, make sure to attribute dialogue as much as is necessary. Readers need to know clearly who is speaking and to whom. Sometimes it can be hard to figure out when they'll need reminding, so a good rule of thumb is to include some kind of tag every six lines or so, at least. Some beginning writers dismiss this sort of concern as "merely technical" and beneath an artist's consideration. It *is* technical, and it is not the true heart of any writer's effort. But readers have limits. You have to decide where you want them to work: on the substance of what you're saying, or on trying to decipher the logistics of who's speaking when. Once they start counting backward trying to figure it out, you have lost them.

Keeping Tags Simple   There's no need to be fancy. "Said" is a great verb. It's simple, direct, accurate, and unobtrusive. Usually, it's enough. Tags should not be expected to do the main work of **characterization** or conveying characters' personalities and other attributes. This is better accomplished through the dialogue itself or through actions, gestures, and description than through fancy verbs such as "yowled," "spewed," "bespoke," "expectorated," or abuses such as my editor's favorite example from Ring Lardner: "'Shut up!' he explained."

Using simpler verbs in tags has the virtue of requiring the writer to convey tone and feeling in more **concrete** ways, through the senses. Creative tag verbs may be more appropriate in stylized or humorous fiction or with "flat" or minor characters. They're economical where you don't want to linger, but they can seem reductive, judgmental, or simplistic for more important or serious situations or characters. Remember that if the tags distract from the speech itself, the narrator and the author risk attracting more attention than the characters.

Other Methods of Attribution   There are many ways to attribute dialogue. A gesture or bit of description linked to the character is often enough of a nudge to keep readers oriented, and it doubles as characterization. Among the methods writers use to attribute dialogue are

- Including in the speech the name of the person spoken to:

"Those crank calls, Antoinette, were the last straw!"

- Adding a gesture:

Wayne swiveled on his chair. "Where did I put that incense?"

- Adding physical description of the character speaking:

There were snowflakes in Rhonda's dark hair, and her voice was raspy. "I never want to see you again!"

- Explaining the character's thoughts or feelings:

"Enchanted." Roy wished Uncle Bob could see him now.

- Adding some description of the **environment** along with an identifying pronoun:

"Not at all." He ran his hand over the warm wood of the porch rail. The sun was behind the trees, but he could still feel it in the air.

- When a gesture or description identifies the speaker, there is no need to add direct attribution. Double-tagging is redundant, as in this sentence:

"Pass the pepper!" April exclaimed, and pounded the table.

- A simpler version would still be clear:

"Pass the pepper!" April pounded the table.

Some Examples of Attribution   The tags in the following excerpts have been boldfaced to demonstrate various methods of attribution. The first is from Michael Dorris's *A Yellow Raft in Blue Water*:

"Get the hell out of here." **Mom's voice is rough, hard-edged.** Her body twists on the mattress. I can tell she hates to be helpless when Dad's so indifferent.

He watches her as though she's some stranger. "It's not going to work this time. Just give it up."

"You give it up. You! I don't give nothing up."

Dad touches my arm. "Go on now. I have to talk to Christine."

Mom is furious, maddened by the snarled bedclothes. One of her rings hooks in a flaw of the sheet and she tries to rip it free, but the material is too tough.

"I'll call you," **Dad says**, and points a long finger at my chest.

In that scene, the gestures double as tags so there is very little direct attribution. However, every line of dialogue is clearly tagged. It's not always necessary to be this thorough—in the above passage, gestures provide necessary context. The following scene from Ernest Hemingway's "Hills Like White Elephants" (pp. 320–323) attributes less, but it's still clear enough who is speaking:

"We want two Anis del Toro."

"With water?"

"Do you want it with water?"

"I don't know," the girl said. "Is it good with water?"

"It's all right."

"You want them with water?" asked the woman.

"Yes, with water."

"It tastes like licorice," the girl said and put the glass down.

In addition to identifying who is speaking when, tags pace a scene. Without them, readers would not only be confused but wouldn't have a chance to catch their breath and adjust to each new speaker. An extended passage of unattributed dialogue even looks funny on the page—a long, narrow column like a shopping list. Sensitive use of tags, gestures, and description establishes the passage of time visually and to the ear.

Paragraphing in Dialogue

When writing dialogue, your first job is to make clear who is speaking when. In order to do this in direct discourse, there are two basic rules to remember:

- Begin a new paragraph each time you switch speakers.
- Keep each speaker's tag in the same paragraph with his or her speech.

The following sentences provide simple examples of these two rules:

> "What's for breakfast?" Janet asked, cracking her back, one hand against the headboard. "Not eggs Benedict again, I hope?"
> Roger tugged at the window until it opened, then leaned out, testing the air. "Sweater weather." He walked past her to the bathroom. "Whatever you feel like cooking."

not

> "What's for breakfast?" Janet asked, cracking her back, one hand against the headboard. "Not eggs benedict again, I hope?" Roger tugged at the window until it opened, then leaned out, testing the air. "Sweater weather.". . .

or

> "What's for breakfast?"
> Janet asked. Roger tugged at the window.
> "Sweater weather."

Beginning a new paragraph for each speaker is a simple rule, but it's among the hardest to learn. And if you don't get it right—or deviate from it with perfect consistency—it won't matter how brilliant the characters' speech is because it will be incomprehensible. Think of it this way: when more than one character is speaking, paragraph breaks keep them from all talking at once. Each character gets her own paragraph each time she speaks.

This dialogue from "Little Red-Cap" (pp. 298–300) provides a more extended example of simple punctuating and paragraphing:

> "Good day, Little Red-Cap," said he.
> "Thank you kindly, Wolf."
> "Whither away so early, Little Red-Cap?"
> "To my grandmother's."
> "What have you got in your apron?"
> "Cake and wine; yesterday was baking-day, so poor sick grandmother is to have something good, to make her stronger."
> "Where does your grandmother live, Little Red-Cap?"
> "A good quarter of a league farther on in the wood . . ."

An Exception to the Rule   There is one common exception to the rule of beginning a new paragraph each time you switch speakers: occasionally you may read dialogue in which each character's utterances are so brief that the entire conversation may appear in a single paragraph. In the following passage from Joseph

Connolly's "Hard Feelings" (pp. 260–270), the speakers' lines are not divided into separate paragraphs:

Sometimes when Sally is giving me a back-rub she sticks her strong thumbs into a certain spot between my shoulder blades and tears well up in my eyes, tears Sally can't see because I'm face down on the bed, and I know she's disturbed the hiding place of some old, forgotten grief. For a moment, I get that lost-child feeling, like something dark and sad is looming over me, and I say "Not there" and she says "Does that hurt too much?" and I say "Yes."

Condensing the scene in this way allows the author to convey the important moments without slowing down the story; in this example, it also provides a light touch, rather than lingering on an emotional moment that could easily become sentimental or heavy-handed.

Speeches   When one character speaks continuously for more than one paragraph, put quotation marks at the beginning of each paragraph but don't add the final quotation marks until the last paragraph of the speech.

"I was born and raised in Sioux Falls, South Dakota, where my Uncle Maynard ran a small photography studio. He didn't care much about material things, and we lived in an apartment over the studio.

"When I reached adulthood, I learned to drive, and I learned that I liked it. A lot. I traveled to Illinois, Maine, North Carolina—anywhere, so long as it was far away. Eventually, I took a job working at a theme park in Connecticut. Uncle Maynard would have been proud."

Writing good dialogue involves some technical expertise. It's important for beginning writers to remember that all these conventions are not mere pickiness, nor are they "uncreative." Their purpose is to make clear who is speaking and what they're saying. Whether you choose to punctuate dialogue in a traditional manner or to establish your own conventions, as a number of contemporary writers have, consistency is absolutely essential. (See As You Write on p. 160 for more about breaking the rules.)

Writing Dialect

Like other distinctive aspects of a character's speech, the differences of vocabulary, usage, and

Q: How subtle is too subtle? How much should I hold my characters back from saying what they have to say?

A: Let them say it! The reason behind this: over and over in student fiction drafts I will read scenes in which one character or another is thinking something but not saying it, and I suspect that if the writer would let them say it, things would really get out of hand. Of course the writer wants them not to get out of hand. But out of hand is just where the story and characters want to get; and if things do get out of hand, we might have a stronger story on our hands. "Let them say it!" is one of my nontrivial and nonabsolute rules.

—Bruce Jorgensen,
writer and teacher

pronunciation that make up dialect are usually best suggested rather than rendered literally and in detail. In general, writing should be heard and not seen. That is, the words themselves should not distract from the story. The best writing has the quality of speech; it is musical rather than visual. The reader is not conscious of straining to decipher it. This is particularly true of dialect, which usually benefits from a light touch. Flannery O'Connor's advice in a letter to Cecil Dawkins is excellent: "You get a real person down there and his talking will take care of itself, but if you get to thinking about dialect and would he say it this way or that way, then you are going off the track, it's going to sound self-conscious. Concentrate on the meaning." O'Connor's advice reflects her own practice; all of her dialect is exemplary—vivid and yet restrained, as shown in this excerpt from "A Good Man Is Hard to Find" (p. 362–372):

"Now look here, Bailey," she said, "see here, read this," and she stood with one hand on her thin hip and the other rattling the newspaper at his bald head. "Here this fellow that calls himself The Misfit is aloose from the Federal Pen and headed toward Florida and you read here what it says he did to these people. Just you read it. I wouldn't take my children in any direction with a criminal like that aloose in it. I couldn't answer to my conscience if I did."

Understating Dialect   Dialect can be suggested through word choice and speech rhythms and a few phonetic spellings. Any effect you achieve through variant spellings, dropped *g*'s, and so forth will be lost if your technique is more prominent than your characters and what they're saying. Especially, be extremely careful about overusing phonetic spellings in first person colloquial **narration** (what the writer tells the reader directly rather than through **scenic** elements such as speech and action). Such spellings suggest someone must be transcribing, and so undermine the narrative voice. Readers quickly lose patience with characters whose speech is visually confusing or hard to decipher. To the extent that readers become conscious of the words themselves, they won't be swept away into the fictional dream. Readers need to be able to "hear the story"—to forget that they're reading. Because it overemphasizes differences to the point of caricature, a strictly phonetic rendering of dialect is considered demeaning to the character or group in much the same way as is some of the dialogue in books or films such as *Gone with the Wind*. Compare these blatant caricatures with the strong, vibrant voice of Alice Walker's character Celie in the novel *The Color Purple*:

He come home with a girl from round Gray. She be my age but they married. He be on her all the time. She walk round like she don't know what hit her. I think she thought she love him. But he got so many of us. All needin somethin.

My little sister Nettie is got a boyfriend in the same shape almost as Pa. His wife died. She was kilt by her boyfriend coming home from church. He only got three children though. He seen Nettie in church and now every Sunday evening here come Mr. _____. I tell Nettie to keep at her books. It be more then a notion taking care of children ain't even yourn. And look what happen to Ma.

Walker and O'Connor construct clear and convincing dialect not so much by changing the spelling as by re-creating the choice and order of words. This is less a matter of literal accuracy than of catching and rendering the sound and rhythm of the voice. It's more a matter of hearing the voice than of analyzing the elements that comprise it.

Writing Children's Speech

The process of writing children's speech is similar to that of writing dialect. And the mistakes writers tend to make are also similar—among them, using special spelling or featuring "cute things kids say." Like bad dialect writing, such speech focuses on difference, on novelty, rather than on the individual. The principles that govern writing dialect apply here as well. Almost any child appearing in the work of J. D. Salinger will provide an excellent example of children's speech, restrained and unique. Ramona from the short story "Uncle Wiggily in Connecticut" is such a character. Russell Banks's child character Jill in his novel *Affliction* is another fine example. In this scene, she is talking with her father Wade:

"Now I'm a cop, so now I have to listen to all the complaints people make. I'm a police officer," he announced. "I'm not a kid anymore. You change, and things look different as a result. You understand that, don't you?"

His daughter nodded. "You did lots of bad things," she declared.

"What? I did what?"

"I bet you did lots of bad things."

"Well, no, not really," he said. He paused. "What? What're you talking about?"

She turned and looked through the eye holes of her mask, revealing her blue irises and nothing else. "I just think you used to be bad. That's all."

The spareness of the child's dialogue compared to the adult's defensive speech; the accurate detail; and, more than anything, Jill's flat truthfulness, give this scene intense emotion while avoiding **sentimentality** or generic appeals to emotion.

In children's speech, dialect, and dialogue in general, there are two basic rules to remember: first, that the conventions of using tags, punctuation, and paragraphing, as well as the technique of understatement, combine to produce the illusion of real speech. As rules, they are meaningful because they work together that way. The second thing to remember is that before all else, including techniques and conventions, consistency is essential.

As You Write

As a beginning writer, you may find dialogue to be one of the most technically difficult aspects of writing fiction. Once you get the hang of it, though, it will become second nature. Some basic advice can make it easier in the beginning.

Not Saying It All: Voice in Fiction

Fictional dialogue is never a verbatim transcript of an actual conversation. In addition to verbal tics like *ums* and *ahs*, writers delete excess explanation and lines that merely advance the conversation ("You were saying?" or, "Please continue, Georgette!") or the **plot** or story line (for instance, speech used to convey exposition). The final result is not actual speech but rendered speech: the essence or sense of speech as it interacts with the other elements of a scene and story.

This process of elimination applies also to the creation of **voice**, the personality, tone, and mood conveyed by a story's language. In the passage below from a story by student David Ambrosini, one of the most vivid characters is the narrator himself, and much of his personality emerges through his voice. The passage describes a fight that breaks out in a high school classroom. Between the first and second drafts, David made a number of cuts that resulted in a much tighter scene and a clearer voice. In this unedited version, passages that could, with minor changes, be deleted or shortened, have been bracketed.

> [There were] two other football players [in the class. They] sat on the far side of the room. But as soon as they saw Boyer beating on Basley, [the distance shortened between us. These two guys] ran over and jumped on Boyer. Now, what was I gonna do? I couldn't just let them beat on Boyer, even if he did probably deserve it. So I jumped on the back of one [of them].
>
> And from there, it [just] escalated. Four other guys came over [with the intention of breaking] up the fight, but that didn't work. [They just ended up fighting with Boyer, Basley, the two football players and me.]
>
> Somebody had hit me in the right eye, so I couldn't see too well [out of it]. But I [can] remember [seeing] Boyer throw someone against the blackboard. Then [I remember hearing] someone called [out], "Look out!" as a desk [came] crashing down onto [a football player, another guy, and myself]. By this time, Mrs. Teale had run out of the room, screaming.

The edited passage reads like this:

> Two other football players sat on the far side of the room. But as soon as they saw Boyer beating on Basley, they ran over and jumped on Boyer. Now what was I gonna do? I couldn't just let them beat on Boyer, even if he did probably deserve it. So I jumped on one of their backs.
>
> From there, it escalated. Four other guys came over to break up the fight, but that didn't work. They joined it instead.
>
> Somebody had hit me in the right eye, so I couldn't see too well. But I remember Boyer throwing someone against the blackboard. Then someone called, "Look out!" as a desk crashed down onto us. By this time, Mrs. Teale had run out of the room, screaming.

In the revised version, the voice is clearer. Like a letter-writer whose language is shaped and focused by the anticipated reader, this narrator attends closely to the actions he describes. This quality of attention is immediately crucial in quick, active scenes, which sag if description and narration outweigh rather than balance the action. For another excellent example of well-paced physical action, see Joseph Connolly's "Hard Feelings"(pp. 260–270).

Writing Resonant Dialogue

In dialogue as in narration, every line should resonate—serving more than one function. This is perhaps the most frequently used sleight of hand in fiction, directing the reader's eye away from the writer's intent so the prose feels spontaneous rather than obvious. Here is some dialogue from Jeannine Thibodeau's "Close," with my editorial comments in brackets:

"What's taking so long?" I ask. [**Angie is in a hurry. She's abrupt, suggesting tension or anxiety.**]

I'm in the back of a cab, trying to get to the clinic [**something has happened with Lenore's pregnancy**] as fast as possible. [**It might be an emergency. The ambiguity engages the reader in Angie's confusion and anxiety.**] Paul is next to me, our fingers entwined. [**The couple is anxious; it is also clear that they have an intimate relationship.**] My other hand is balled into a fist, my nails cutting half-moons into my palm. [**Angie is tense.**]

Paul raps on the plexiglass divider. "Hey, pal, can you go any faster?" [**Paul's tension is conveyed by the question itself and by his abruptness.**]

Again, the point is that every line of dialogue serves more than one function: characterization or color, subtle exposition, psychological development, or moving the scene along dramatically. Practically speaking, the easiest way to accomplish this richness is simply to cut what you can and work with what is left. Often, the briefer the speech, the more it seems to say.

Breaking the Rules

You may find many stories that bend or break the basic rules for writing dialogue discussed in this chapter. For instance, in "Hard Feelings" (pp. 260–270) Joseph Connolly consistently omits the comma in tags directly preceding speech. Other writers take greater liberties, separating tags from dialogue by starting a new paragraph when the actual speech begins:

In the afternoons our mother would listen to old Rae Veldorah albums and sip her sherry, gazing out the living room window as the light began to fade. When she noticed me standing in the doorway she would smile.

"Join me?"

Similarly, E. E. Cummings used no capitalization, and Cormac McCarthy doesn't use quotation marks. But when these writers deviate from the basic rules, they do so consistently, throughout the work. The reason, as any editor will tell you, is that consistency is the most important principle of clear writing.

To keep these issues in perspective, remember that all of the rules, as well as the emphasis on consistency, support the most basic and necessary objective: clarity. Readers may not know the rules of grammar or punctuation themselves, but clarity and consistency can be felt, and create a foundation for narrative credibility. Once these habits have become second nature, by all means, deviate intelligently. But be sure you have it down cold first. Otherwise your deviation may come across more like wavering.

Exploration and Discovery

Be patient as you learn the many skills involved in writing good dialogue, and remember that the trial and error will sensitize your ear and sharpen your instincts; eventually, writing dialogue will come naturally. The questions and activities below will help you more thoroughly evaluate your work and explore some new possibilities as you write dialogue.

Ask Yourself

In the beginning, you can best improve your dialogue writing by systematically checking your work. The following questions and suggestions summarize what you will need to consider as you evaluate the dialogue in your story.

- *Is the balance of summary and detail appropriate?* Go through your story and underline direct discourse in one color, indirect in another. Now go back through and mark the scenes in which the key developments take place. Are those scenes played out fully and given the space they deserve? If defining scenes are summarized rather than dramatized, what does this contribute to the story? What does it take away? Have you used indirect discourse where appropriate to summarize less important dialogue?
- *Are the characters talking too much?* Delete lines that merely advance the conversation—remarks like "Go on," and "You were saying . . . ?" Just move the scene along, don't make the characters discuss moving it along.
- *Are the characters repeating themselves (or repeating you)?* Telescope redundant speeches. Arthur Quiller-Couch advised writers to "murder your darlings"—that is, don't get so attached to a word or phrase or speech that you keep it in merely because you like it. When you've said something twice, choosing which version to keep is difficult but necessary. When in doubt, try combining the best elements of each.
- *Is the dialogue punctuated correctly?* Circle the end punctuation in every sentence of your dialogue. Is it correct? Mark each time a different person speaks. Have you switched paragraphs? If not, why not? Are you repeating the same punctuation errors again and again? What are they? Write them down and post them where you work.
- *Are your tags working well?* Mark every tag in your story. Are you attributing dialogue at least every six lines or so? Are you varying tags enough so that they don't get monotonous? Are you avoiding pretentious or distracting verbs?

- *Does the dialogue, including dialect, sound natural?* Are you listening to it, rather than relying only on word choice? Say it out loud. Does it sound real? Dialogue's effect depends more upon its sound—its rhythms—than on rendering speech verbatim.

- *Do the characters sound like real people?* They may not always say exactly what you planned for them to say. Remember that you'll be discovering them as you write. Sometimes, if a line rings false, discovering what the character *will* say can redefine the scene.

- *Are you using dialogue to convey exposition?* ("Good afternoon, Colin, as you know it's been seven years since we've met, during which time I've become a shoe salesman and your cousin Fiona, my business partner, has died.") It's unnatural and bogs down the conversation. Exposition is the job of the narrator, not the characters.

Ask Readers

- *Is it clear who is speaking when?* Ask readers to mark places where they were confused. Check to make sure you've attributed adequately.

- *Are the characters' voices distinguishable from each other and from the narrator?* Try reading a line aloud and asking your listener to identify the speaker. Ask readers to describe how each character's speech differs from the others'.

- *Which comes first—voice or content?* Sometimes it moves a draft along to simply write down what characters will say, even if you're not sure exactly how they'll say it. On other occasions, you might feel more comfortable experimenting with a character's voice by writing practice monologues or attending closely to the voice as you draft the dialogue. Notice which approach or combination of approaches works for you, and when. If you understand how you write, you'll be less anxious and guilt-ridden about things you haven't done yet.

Wordplay

Reading dialogue   Read aloud all of the dialogue spoken by the main character in your story. Is it consistent? Overall, does it convey the character's attitudes and personality as you envision them?

Hearing dialogue   Ask someone to read your story aloud to you. Allowing for some awkwardness if the dialect is different from the reader's ordinary speech, make note of each place where she stumbles or stops and has to sort through the sentence to figure out how to read it. Go back to these places and look for ways to simplify sentences and keep them short where possible. Even if you're writing dialect, standardize most of the spelling and avoid dropped letters (as in *twistin'*, *jumpin'*, *'n' shoutin'*).

Punctuating dialogue   Choose a passage of dialogue from a published story or novel. Type it out, removing punctuation and paragraphing. Then rewrite the passage using punctuation and paragraphing appropriately, to indicate who is speaking when. Don't add or take out any words. Remember: each time a new person speaks, begin a new paragraph. Put quotation marks around whatever someone says and keep end punctuation inside the quotation marks. Keep tags or descriptions of a character in the same paragraph as what the character says. Try retyping the passage on your computer, then hitting the return key each time it is clear that a new character is speaking. Then, you can fiddle around with the rest. Don't be surprised if this exercise is more difficult than you expected. Hearing punctuation explained in class is not enough; people really don't get it until they try it themselves. After you've finished, compare your punctuated version with the published original. Where do they differ, and why?

Editing dialogue   Go to a public place—a restaurant, bus, subway, or anywhere crowded, such as a party—taking only a pad of paper and something to write with. Sit or stand unobtrusively where you can overhear a conversation. Write down as much of it as you can, verbatim. Leave nothing out.

Take your notes home and type them. Reread them, noticing where your mind starts to wander. Edit the conversation as if you planned to use it in a story, removing most of the following:

Ums and *ahs*, *you knows*, *likes*, etc.

Redundancies.

Things that don't sound like someone would say them, whether or not someone did.

Mere pleasantries. In written dialogue, things like "Hello" or "It's a nice day, isn't it?" are implied and do not need to be spelled out.

Now type out the dialogue. Hit the return key each time a different speaker begins talking. Add punctuation and tags. Read the dialogue aloud and revise as necessary. You will probably still need to make some cuts for the scene to move naturally without dragging.

This exercise is designed to reveal the difference between written and spoken language. Dialogue as it appears in fiction is not simply transcribed speech—it is the essence of speech. Like a good drawing, dialogue can convey a lot with very few lines. This leaves some of the work to be done by readers, thus engaging them more fully. It also allows room in the scene for emotions to resonate.

Editing dialogue in reverse   Try doing the previous exercise backward: first, type out a tightly constructed scene from a published story and then add *ums* and *ahs*, redundancies, pleasantries, and spelled-out emotions. Reread the finished version; how has the scene's effect been altered?

Suggested Reading

The More Books and Stories section starting on page 496 provides complete bibliographic information for each title listed below.

Joseph Connolly, "Hard Feelings"

Michael Dorris, *A Yellow Raft in Blue Water*

Jakob and Wilhelm Grimm, "Little Red-Cap"

Ernest Hemingway, "Hills Like White Elephants"

James Joyce, "Araby"

Robie Macauley and George Lanning, *Technique in Fiction*

Flannery O'Connor, "A Good Man Is Hard to Find"

Seth Pase, "The Father"

J. D. Salinger, "Uncle Wiggily in Connecticut"

Jeannine Thibodeau, "Close"

Alice Walker, *The Color Purple*

Blaine M. Yorgason and Brenton G. Yorgason, *The Krystal Promise*

CHAPTER 9

Between the Lines
Subtext and Theme

The movies ruined everything. Like talking about something good. That was what had made the war unreal. Too much talking.
—Ernest Hemingway, "On Writing"

A poem is an exploration rather than a disquisition.
—Robin Skelton, *The Practice of Poetry*

Leading the Reader

A good story is the work of both reader and writer—what creates the story is a relationship, a dialogue that consists not of words only but also of the silence between them. The writer leads and, like a good dancer, knows when to pause, when to move back so the reader will come forward. This is a matter of empathy, not manipulation. To engage readers is a kind of wooing: awakening their feelings and enticing them to enter the fictional dream and be absorbed by it, and to bring to the story their powers of imagination. To accomplish this, writers must allow a certain spareness—must leave some things implicit rather than explicit, and must employ covertness rather than overtness. When you learn the art of indirection, you will find space in your scenes for the development of **subtext**, the story's unspoken but implied emotional content, and of **theme**, the main idea or ideas in a story, usually conveyed indirectly.

When written well, a story's unspoken content is subtle and enormously powerful. Beginning writers sometimes feel at a loss when approaching this mysterious, "unwritten" part of writing. This chapter will help you to understand how to work with the silences in your writing, and how to suggest and develop meaning without being heavy-handed. Exercises and activities will help you develop the subtext and the theme in your writing.

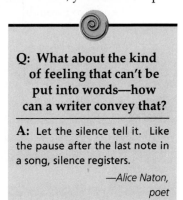

Q: What about the kind of feeling that can't be put into words—how can a writer convey that?

A: Let the silence tell it. Like the pause after the last note in a song, silence registers.

—*Alice Naton,*
poet

Subtext

Writing subtext is the art of using words obliquely to convey more or other than their literal meaning. It is suggesting emotional nuances through verbal indirection, and through techniques such as body language, pauses, gestures, multiple meanings, allusions, and resonances. Broken down in this way, the task can sound overwhelming; but most writers don't plan out the subtext for their stories—rather, it emerges naturally as they attend to the story's **dialogue** (the characters' speech) and surface detail. In the following scene from "Hills Like White Elephants" (pp. 320–323), Ernest Hemingway uses simple, slightly indirect dialogue and well-chosen descriptive detail to generate powerful unspoken emotions.

"You started it," the girl said. "I was being amused. I was having a fine time."

"Well, let's try and have a fine time."

"All right. I was trying. I said the mountains looked like white elephants. Wasn't that bright?"

"That was bright."

"I wanted to try this new drink: That's all we do, isn't it—look at things and try new drinks?"

"I guess so."

The girl looked across at the hills.

"They're lovely hills," she said. "They don't really look like white elephants. I just meant the coloring of their skin through the trees."

"Should we have another drink?"

"All right."

The warm wind blew the bead curtain against the table.

"The beer's nice and cool," the man said.

"It's lovely," the girl said.

"It's really an awfully simple operation, Jig," the man said. "It's not really an operation at all."

The girl looked at the ground the table legs rested on.

"I know you wouldn't mind it, Jig. It's really not anything. It's just to let the air in."

The girl did not say anything.

"I'll go with you and I'll stay with you all the time. They just let the air in and then it's all perfectly natural."

"Then what will we do afterward?"

"We'll be fine afterward. Just like we were before."

"What makes you think so?"

"That's the only thing that bothers us. It's the only thing that's made us unhappy."

The girl looked at the bead curtain, put her hand out and took hold of two of the strings of beads.

"And you think then we'll be all right and be happy."

"I know we will. You don't have to be afraid. I've known lots of people that have done it."

"So have I," said the girl. "And afterward they were all so happy."

Subtext in "Hills Like White Elephants"   The subtext in this scene interacts with the explicit story to create depth and dimension. The withheld information that generates the subtext is simply the characters' feelings, which are suggested rather than explicitly stated as the **characters** or main actors in the story argue without ever naming the source of their conflict—an abortion.

James Suffern, a former student who has worked with me as a teaching assistant, has developed an exercise for my class in which we read "Hills Like White Elephants" aloud, line by line, speaking the subtext as we go. (The exercise is described in detail on p. 180.) Our spoken version of the passage above produces a lot of emotion, some of it very intense—all suggested by the spare, understated prose and none of it nearly so eloquent. Though it isn't always the case, here it does seem that the fewer words used, the more space is left in which the subtext can resonate. When subtext can be felt, readers, required to reach their own conclusions, engage with and participate more fully in the scene.

Subtext in "The Father"   In "The Father" (pp. 372–375), another story about an abortion, student writer Seth Pase withholds almost all stated emotion. As in "Hills Like White Elephants," the word, or even the fact of an operation, is never mentioned by the characters or by the **narrator**, the voice that tells the story. This conspicuous omission aptly conveys that for Leo and Mary, the main characters, the situation is too painful even to speak of. It underscores the sense of emotional subterfuge and guilt implicit in the story's action—the couple hiding their secret from Mary's father, the exchange of money, the unspoken hostility, both characters' wish not to be in this situation. As a student reader commented about "The Father," "This story has secrets." In the passage below, Leo takes Mary to the clinic.

Leo drives on, his hands tensing and relaxing on the wheel. After a moment of deliberation he says, "Are you sure about the money? I've got it, it's no big deal, really. Let me at least give you half." He tries to take her hand.

Mary does not move. She continues to look out the window as the river goes by. She does not take his hand. Finally she says, "Half. Fine, OK. Half and a ride back next week if they want me to come, OK? They probably won't need to see me, but . . ."

"OK," he says. "Whatever you need. I'm there. I mean I'm here."

With this, Leo drives into the city. He takes a breath, drawing the frigid air deep into his lungs. He tightens his grip on the steering wheel and squints at the grey half-light of the afternoon.

Subtext in "Hard Feelings"   Subtext engages readers emotionally. Like a rest in a musical phrase, it quietly attracts attention. Its proper impact requires the writer's subtlety and the reader's sensitivity. When created skillfully, it can suggest things the characters would never say. For example, Mark, the witty and articulate narrator in Joseph Connolly's "Hard Feelings" (pp. 260–270), feels deeply despite his difficulty talking about his emotions. Rather than stating this directly, Connolly demonstrates it in the story's ending:

I was driving my rental car through the dark and sleet back to my hotel, listening to some station from across the river in Kentucky. A song came on about a man who loves his wife and his wife loves him; he dreams his wife has left him and he wakes up crying and reaches out in the darkness to touch her and she's still there. I got back to the hotel and called Sally. She said, "What's wrong? You weren't going to call until eleven." I said "Nothing's wrong," and my voice came out kind of husky and I couldn't say anything else, so she said "What's wrong?" again, and I just sat there with my eyes closed, holding the phone.

Having already begun to suspect this narrator's emotional inarticulateness earlier in the story, readers have become accustomed to second-guessing him occasionally, as in the scene below, which occurs following a basketball game. The other character, Neil, has just experienced a disastrous argument with his wife.

"You're a lucky guy," he said. "Sally is so easy to get along with."

"That's true," I said. I felt I should say something positive about his situation, something positive about Madelyn, and my mind raced through everything I knew about her. "Well," I said after a moment, "at least Madelyn's pretty clear about what she wants."

"Sally isn't?"

For God's sake, I thought, this is supposed to be a good-bye, and he's ready to open up another round of emotional show-and-tell. He was grinning the same way he does on the basketball court when he's thrown in one of his set-shots, as if finding a possible flaw in my relationship with Sally scored him a point in some little one-on-one I didn't even know we were playing. I'd actually started to like him a little, but I stopped liking him as suddenly as I started.

"Sally's fine," I said. "I gotta go." I opened the door and made my escape, promising to pick him up for basketball next Sunday.

I was feeling pretty irritable when I got in the car, but that's not surprising considering how my body felt. My muscles were begging me for Tylenol and sleep.

In this little exchange, Neil, often the loser on the basketball court, prevails emotionally. Mark's psychic pain, unlike Neil's, is unspoken, as is the subtle competition between the two men. These things come across in the body language, in the way Neil contradicts Mark, and through physical sensations. Even Mark's seemingly direct statements that he wanted to leave and that he felt irritated avoid the truth. In leaving, he dodges Neil's question about his wife, and he attributes his irritation to sore muscles (which he plans to treat with drugs and sleep) rather than to his conversation with Neil. He's the kind of character who would be amused and irritated at this interpretation.

"A Thousand Buddhas": Grounding Abstraction   In Brenda Miller's essay "A Thousand Buddhas" (pp. 329–334), readers are prepared to accept a few overt assertions of feeling because the author evokes emotion so vividly through **concrete** or sensory description:

> What did my body feel when I placed my hands on Jon's back? My palms curved instinctively to the crook of his shoulders; my own shoulders softened when I asked Jon to breathe, and I inhaled with him, stretching my lungs, and on the exhale my hands slid down his back, kneading the muscles on the downward slide, pulling up along the lats, crossing over his spine, and again and again, until he seemed to flatten and there was no distinction between the flesh of his back or the bones in his arms or the curve of his buttocks—no distinction, in fact, between his breath and mine. I felt a small opening in my heart, a valve releasing, and an old love—a love aged and smooth as wine—flowed down my arms and sparked on Jon's skin. I knew, then, that sometime in the night I would remember this gushing, and I would be shattered by a sense of tremendous loss, a grasping ache in my palms, and I would cry, but even this certainty could not stop my hands in their circular route through Jon's familiar and beautiful body.

The "sense of tremendous loss" is illustrated in the narrator's physical responses, and "Jon's familiar and beautiful body" is likewise rendered concretely, through physical details, before this generalization is presented. Thus, Miller earns the response these abstractions ask for.

Subtext in "Cosmopolitan"   Whether your style is subtle or forthright, intelligent readers will wonder what's beneath the surface of your characters' interactions, just as they will naturally speculate about the "real meaning" of their interactions with people around them. Because of and through that wondering, there will always be subtext. How you work with it will influence the depth of your writing. As you can see from the examples in this chapter, sometimes the strongest statements are silent and the most direct ones may carry subliminal or even contradictory meanings. Skillful use of subtext is like a whisper—others will unconsciously draw closer in order to hear. The first scene of Akhil Sharma's story "Cosmopolitan" (pp. 391–406) is a good example. The main character, whose wife has recently left him, is visited by his divorced neighbor, Mrs. Shaw:

> "Hello, Mr. Maurya," Mrs. Shaw said, looking at him and through him into the darkened house and then again at him. The sun shone behind her. The sky was blue dissolving into white. "How are you?" she asked gently.
>
> "Oh, Mrs. Shaw," Gopal said, his voice pitted and rough, "some bad things have happened to me." He had not meant to speak so directly. He stepped out of the doorway.
>
> The front door opened into a vestibule, and one had a clear view from there of the living room and the couch where Gopal slept. He switched on the lights. To the right was the kitchen. The round Formica table and the counters were

dusty. Mrs. Shaw appeared startled by this detail. After a moment she said, "I heard." She paused and then quickly added, "I am sorry, Mr. Maurya. It must be hard. You must not feel ashamed; it's no fault of yours."

"Please, sit," Gopal said, motioning to a chair next to the kitchen table. He wanted to tangle her in conversation and keep her there for hours. He wanted to tell her how the loneliness had made him fantasize about calling an ambulance so that he could be touched and prodded, or how for a while he had begun loitering at the Indian grocery store like the old men who have not learned English. What a pretty, good woman, he thought.

As in "The Father," this scene's action and dialogue are deceptively simple. But unlike Seth Pase's story, "Cosmopolitan" provides a great deal of commentary in the way of interior monologue. Although this commentary appears to be straightforwardly stated emotion, the contrast between Gopal's assumptions and interpretations and Mrs. Shaw's reactions to him reveal that his thoughts are often touchingly unrealistic. As the story progresses, both Gopal and Mrs. Shaw are shown to be vulnerable characters whose understanding of love is growing but fragile. The contrast between the extremely restrained dialogue and the outpouring of unspoken and frequently misplaced emotion in the **narration** (what the writer tells the reader directly rather than through scenic elements such as speech and action) creates much of this scene's tension as it unfolds. The occasional pause emphasizes that tension as well as Gopal's pain and Mrs. Shaw's compassion. The brief, evocative descriptions of the surroundings act as emotional lightning rods, drawing and holding the unspoken feelings.

Most writers would acknowledge that good subtext is not entirely within the writer's conscious control. Subtext often evolves unknown by or even in spite of the writer, sometimes as a result of what seem to be accidents. Occasionally readers can apprehend a story's subtext more readily than its writer can. That may be a sign that the writer is working purely by intuition, not aware of what is being accomplished. At some point, most writers learn to define their subtexts and can then shade and highlight appropriately. Still, working with subtext remains largely an intuitive task.

Theme

Many writers say they don't know—and don't want to know—what their story is about, at least not until it's done. For them the ideas contained in a story, like the feelings, emerge after the fact. They write the theme by first *not* writing it. Overthinking theme, especially in the story's early

Q: Does a story need to be about anything?

A: If your story isn't about anything, there's no reason to write it. A story needn't preach or be didactic, but there ought to be something at stake for the writer—a question or concern the writer wants to explore. Anyway, it's impossible to write a story about nothing. What's important is that the writer is passionately interested in some aspect of the story. If the writer isn't interested enough to pursue something—an idea, a character, a series of events—the reader won't be, either.

—*Kim Addonizio, poet and writer*

stages, can make the characters slaves to the author's ideas, lacking the spontaneity that allows them to seem real. As one of my first writing teachers said, "Theme is what the story is about when you've forgotten what the story is about." Intuitive decisions may involve a great deal of trial and error, but they often have an essential rightness about them that for many writers is hard to come by through a more methodical process.

It's often best to avoid thinking about what the story means until the final phases of revision. This deliberate unawareness of theme and subtext is a kind of not letting your left hand know what your right is doing. It is working on one aspect of the story and believing that your mind is meanwhile developing others as well. Taking this approach requires you to allow the fortunate accidents and combinations that are as important to writing as to watercolor painting; in all creative endeavors, the effects arise in part from elements interacting somewhat unpredictably. It's important to recognize that the author is not the last word—the story is.

Does Theme Matter? To say that writers shouldn't necessarily think about theme as they write is not to say that it doesn't exist, that it isn't important, or that the beginning writer in one of my classes who said, "I hate theme!" was justified. Of course, a work of fiction can't be reduced to an abstract statement, or it would *be* one. But hating theme is like hating hydrogen: it's a neutral element, as long as you don't make a bomb with it.

Writing Theme and Subtext So how do you write theme and subtext? I'd say the same thing that I say to most students who ask how to start a story, and for the same reason: Don't. Think about it later. Do first whatever it is about the story that is present in your mind. If you make other decisions well, then when the story is almost done, certain feelings, dynamics, or ideas will start to form a pattern. Later, checking with readers, you can adjust these to bring out the story's subtext and theme.

Q: How can I tell what my story is about—what is its thematic content?

A: A short story isn't unlike a lobster, I tell my students. You have the surface elements—dialogue, plot, character, voice, setting, detail, and so on. But if the reader cracks the surface and doesn't find any emotional meat underneath, the story still isn't "about" anything. A story has to have an emotional heart; through dealing out all the aforementioned elements, the author should try and express some greater truth, whether it's what happens to a family in the aftermath of a death or the corrosive impact of loneliness or something more cheery. We garner material from our own lives—"real" experiences, dialogue, people—and twist it into some fictional form. Then we have to make it real again on the page—believable. And through doing so, we invite the audience to look through our eyes at some aspect of life we find to be true and want to share. That truth, the emotional heart of the story, is what the story is "about." The question to ask yourself, in the second draft, is, What part of the story is the most compelling to me? or, What would I choose to read? What part of the story is giving me the most trouble? That's usually the heart. Starting again from that point will emphasize, both for you and your reader, what your story is about.

—*Jenna Blum,*
writer and teacher

Three Stories About the Nature of Good and Evil

Three of the stories in this book—"A Father's Story" by Andre Dubus (pp. 272–286), "A Good Man Is Hard to Find" by Flannery O'Connor (pp. 362–372), and "The Minister's Black Veil" by Nathaniel Hawthorne (pp. 311–319)—concern some similar themes. Each, in its own way, explores the concepts of good and evil.

Evil in "A Good Man Is Hard to Find"   Traditionally, philosophers have identified two kinds of evil or misfortune: the kind that is done deliberately and the kind that just happens. In "A Good Man Is Hard to Find," both occur. The family takes a wrong turn at the wrong moment; this is chance or fate, though the decision is influenced by the grandmother's willfulness. The Misfit murders them; this is a deliberate act.

Q: Does theme matter to the writer?

A: Writers want (or should want) to know what ideas or feelings readers get from their work. I like people to tell me what they think the story is about. I like to know what moved them and why. I like to know how they react to the vision of life or humanity that I convey.

—*Leslie Lawrence, writer and teacher*

If chance were all there was to this story, we would have unlucky or ill-fated victims and an evil murderer. And so what? If the victims were merely innocent and had no choice in the events that led to their deaths, then the only way to make the story more than an **anecdote** or inconsequential incident—to adequately develop **character**, the nature of the story's main actors, as well as choice and change—would be to make it The Misfit's story. The grandmother, along with the rest of the family, would be acted upon, rather than acting decisively. Her fate would not tell us anything about her. It would tell us something about The Misfit.

Looking more closely at the story's events, we can see that though there is definitely an element of chance or fate, if it were not for the grandmother's obstinacy, the violence would not have occurred. If O'Connor had not written in that choice, the grandmother would lack the irritating qualities that make her so ripe for a change (and that supply much of the story's humor). She would be a pathetic victim rather than a character who acts and changes. The moment of her death would be merely shocking, like a segment of *America's Most Wanted*. Implicating the grandmother focuses the story and gives it import beyond its immediate events.

However, the grandmother is not completely to blame. She does not know that the road she insists upon is the very road on which The Misfit is traveling. Through this dreadful coincidence, O'Connor introduces the concept of fate (ominous hints throughout the story suggest that it is fate and not chance) and a religious rather than merely emotional or psychological level to the story. Because of the story's quality of inexorable doom, the reader is challenged to wonder not only about the nature of the grandmother or of The Misfit, but of the universe.

There are other questions to ask about this story. What if O'Connor had made Bailey and his wife and children and the grandmother more likable and sympathetic? The conflict would be much more simplistic, as in so many Hollywood slasher films: nice family and murderer, rather than annoying family and murderer.

The emotion evoked would be predictable: pity. Not much thought would be required to understand the story—in fact, its implications would be so clear that readers would probably feel manipulated. As it is, O'Connor offers a much more complex situation: the brutal murder of a family we have come to know and feel ambivalent about. This confronts us with the truth that evil does not happen only to the truly evil or the truly good; it is uncontrollable and its nature is ultimately independent of those who suffer it. This truth is more profoundly frightening and thought-provoking than a clearcut heroes-and-villains situation.

Evil in "A Father's Story"   Although Andre Dubus and Flannery O'Connor shared a religious affiliation, there are interesting differences between the two authors' handling of the question of evil. Luke Ripley is a much more thoughtful and introspective character than the grandmother, and so the story and its thematic issues turn on his thinking and conscious actions rather than on the combination of fate, an outside evil, and mere obstinacy. O'Connor suggests a specific view of evil and the human condition: that we are by nature selfish and recalcitrant, and that grace or redemption lies in accepting that we are no less evil than those, or than what, we fear. Dubus presents a more complex character with a more complex choice. Luke Ripley must choose between doing what would conventionally be seen as the right thing—reporting his daughter's crime, which was an accident possibly influenced by alcohol—and covering up that crime out of his love for her. This story pits mercy against justice, pondering the notion of moral certainty. Ripley's choice to protect his daughter reveals him to be compassionate, imperfect, loving: merely and fully human. In this story's world the nature of good and evil, right and wrong, is complex.

Sin, Sorrow, and Ambiguity in "The Minister's Black Veil"   Nathaniel Hawthorne's "The Minister's Black Veil" (pp. 311–319) develops its thematic material subtly and dramatically. First, Hawthorne creates a mystery: a minister suddenly decides to cover his face at all times with a black veil, and will not reveal to anyone his reasons for doing so. This intriguing symbol suggests a deeper mystery, an unknowableness about the man. It does this by raising questions: Why is he wearing a veil? What does it mean? Along with the questions comes a faint sense of dread. It is an unsettling image, suggesting deep grief, or psychological or physical disfigurement.

Next, Hawthorne shows the townspeople's reactions to the mysterious veil. They speculate that there is no face behind it; that "'he has changed himself into something awful, only by hiding his face,'" that he has gone mad. The characters put forth various theories about the meaning of the veil: that the minister is hiding from God; that he fears other people; that he has weak eyes; that he is afraid to be alone with himself; that he is in mourning. The minister replies that we all mourn; and when he is accused of having sinned secretly, he says, "What mortal might not do the same?" He calls the veil a symbol he is bound to wear, confesses his loneliness behind it, and thinks that "the horrors which it shadowed forth, must be drawn darkly between the fondest of lovers." He himself hates the veil and will not look at himself in the mirror. "Thus, from beneath the black veil, there rolled a cloud into the sunshine, an ambiguity of sin or sorrow, which enveloped the poor minister, so that love or sympathy could never reach him."

The minister chooses never to remove the veil, and on his deathbed speaks to those who have gathered at his bedside.

"Why do you tremble at me alone?" cried he, turning his veiled face round the circle of pale spectators." Tremble also at each other! Have men avoided me, and women shown no pity, and children screamed and fled, only for my black veil? What, but the mystery which it obscurely typifies, has made this piece of crape so awful? When the friend shows his inmost heart to his friend; the lover to his best-beloved; when man does not vainly shrink from the eye of his Creator, loathesomely treasuring up the secret of his sin; then deem me a monster, for the symbol beneath which I have lived, and die! I look around me, and, lo! on every visage a Black Veil!"

Simply and systematically, Hawthorne develops the symbol through comments that get progressively closer to the source, the final one being the minister's last words. Neither the minister nor the narrator ever explicitly states the meaning of the veil. To do so would be to undo its mystery, and the mystery of sorrow—the fact that we all suffer, and exist, alone. Rather, a number of possible interpretations are offered, with the minister steadfastly resisting the act of interpretation and asserting that where the veil is concerned, he is essentially no different than others—that there is something inexplicable and unspeakable about all human beings. In the "ambiguity of sin or sorrow," his unspoken experience both sets him apart and affirms his humanity.

As You Write

Perhaps the most difficult part of writing is *not* writing—knowing when to stop, and to allow your words to resound in the silence. This chapter has focused on developing subtext and theme by understating overt emotion and ideas.

The famous directive, "Show, don't tell," has become conventional wisdom in writing classes. This sound and useful suggestion is sometimes taken to an extreme by writers who have come to feel so self-conscious about expressing emotion directly on the page that they tie themselves in knots and utterly confuse readers. Spare dialogue may benefit from occasional emotional signposts, as in this passage from Leslie Marmon Silko's "Yellow Woman" (pp. 406–413):

"Wake up."

He moved in the blanket and turned his face to me with his eyes still closed. I knelt down to touch him.

"I'm leaving."

He smiled now, eyes still closed. "You are coming with me, remember?" He sat up now with his bare dark chest and belly in the sun.

"Where?"

"To my place."

"And will I come back?"

He pulled his pants on. I walked away from him, **feeling him behind me** and smelling the willows.

"Yellow Woman," he said.

I turned to face him. "Who are you?" I asked.

He laughed and knelt on the low, sandy bank, washing his face in the river. "Last night you guessed my name, and you knew why I had come."

I stared past him at the shallow moving water **and tried to remember the night, but I could only see the moon in the water and remember his warmth around me.**

In this passage, Silko sparingly inserts enough explanation to clarify the narrator's responses to an unusual and extreme event. The **setting** or environment reflects the characters' unspoken feelings.

In the novel *Affliction*, Russell Banks goes further toward explicating his main character's emotions—but because he goes as far as he does, we are moved, as in Akhil Sharma's "Cosmopolitan," to suspect more or other than what the narrator says; we sense the narrator's irony and his complex feelings toward the character, Wade Whitehouse. By the end of the paragraph quoted below, Wade's reactions to his daughter's accusations have become so self-justifying that readers will feel his guilt:

He wanted to reach over and remove her mask, find out what she really meant, but he did not dare, somehow. He was frightened of her, suddenly aware of it. He had never been frightened of her before, or at least it had not seemed so to him. How could this be true now? Nothing had changed. She had only uttered a few ridiculous things, a child talking mean to her father because he would not let her do what she wanted to do, that was all. No big deal. Nothing to be scared of there. Kids do it all the time.

What makes this apparently overt passage work is its subtext. In his thoughts, Wade protests too loudly, asserting his innocence with such certainty that he raises questions about it.

Working with Subtext and Theme

There are many ways of developing subtext or theme in your own work. Here are a few to try out.

Toning down   Mark all the emotions or ideas that are directly stated by the narrator or the characters in your story. In any of these cases, would it be possible to suggest or imply the thought or emotion instead? Try it. How does it change the scene?

Reordering the process   If theme or subtext emerges late in your writing process, experiment with identifying it before you write a scene and then writing the scene around it. Conversely, if you ordinarily decide theme or subtext beforehand, try withholding that judgment and writing only what the narrator might observe from the outside. Does this alter the result? How?

People versus ideas   Identify the main character's choice or central conflict, and the consequences—not the philosophical implications but the actual visible consequences—of choosing one way or the other. This is the story's point.

Writing without theme   Write a scene or two of your story without regard for theme. Put it away for a few weeks, then go back to it. Do you see any patterns in the characters' behavior, or in the descriptive detail? What themes seem to be emerging? Try building on these patterns by developing the relevant details and editing out those that distract. But beware of making the story too consistent—that may give it an artificial edge.

Exploration and Discovery

Subtext and theme are perhaps the hardest aspects of a story for writers to evaluate. Often, these elements are out of their control—in fact, many writers have described thematic and emotional content as something to be discovered rather than planned out ahead of time. It's also not uncommon for writers to plan for a certain effect and then to discover that they have accomplished something else entirely—and frequently the result is as good or better than the one first planned. These subtleties make it particularly difficult to know how a story is communicating thematically and subtextually. The questions below are designed to help you evaluate that, and to become more aware of your writing process with respect to theme and subtext.

Ask Yourself

These questions will guide you as you develop the story behind your story—the unspoken emotional and intellectual content that comprises subtext and theme. Use them as a touchstone during your explorations; probably more than any other aspect of a story, emotional and intellectual meaning is something you must discover rather than decide.

- *What don't you know about your characters?* Resist the impulse to find and expose it. Don't try to make everything explicit, even in your own mind. Don't dissect your characters; allow them their secrets. In life, there is sacred space in everyone; so, in fiction, well-grown characters contain an element of mystery, and this must be respected. Focus on what you can easily see: concrete, physical details. Choose these intuitively—because you can just picture the character saying, wearing, doing them—rather than deductively, because they make a point. If you're true to the character, the details will combine to create an impression, though not always the one you anticipated. It's important to "allow your characters to lead you" in this way—otherwise they may turn out one-dimensional—more like puppets controlled by an overriding idea than distinct individuals.

- *What is best left unsaid?* Cut out most explanations of emotion ("He felt sad"; "She became angry"). If you feel reluctant to do so, save the original draft and revise on a copy—you can always go back to the original if necessary. Instead of stating emotion directly, show the characters' feelings through observable details: their actions and interactions, appearance, and so forth. Because it's a reader's instinct to second-guess the narrator and to look for subtext, direct assertions often raise readers' skepticism. In places where the story needs to move more quickly and summary is appropriate, use brief concrete details to demonstrate what you're trying to say.

- *Do scenes feel rushed?* Here and there, create pauses by adding gestures or brief descriptions of the characters or setting. These breathing spaces will allow time for subterranean emotions to resonate and register so readers can mentally see, hear, smell, and feel each moment.

- *Have you laid the groundwork for important scenes?* Consider the scene in "A Father's Story" (pp. 272–286) in which Luke Ripley's daughter tells him about the man she has killed. How would the scene be different if we did not know

  that Luke is a lonely man who has lost his wife?

  that he is in genuine spiritual crisis, caught between his loyalty to an institution and his deep sense of social injustice?

  that his daughter is growing up and moving away from him?

  All of this information makes the moment meaningful rather than generically dramatic. The **exposition** or background material does not merely build up to the climactic scene—it also places that moment in context so that its meaning to the main character is clear and moving. The same can be said about James Joyce's "Araby" (pp. 323–327), Jeannine Thibodeau's "Close," and most of the other stories in this book.

- *Where is the story's **climax** or peak, and how does the main character change?* Can you draw any implications from that change? Are you comfortable with these implications? If so, are they reflected elsewhere in the story? Does anything in the story seem to contradict them?

- *Are you conscious of a theme in your story?* If so, forget about it and consider the main character first. Are her actions true to her nature? Do they feel inevitable? Or are they dictated by your own ideas or philosophy? Where theme and character conflict, consider opening up your conception of the theme.

- *How do subtext and theme develop in your work?* When do ideas occur? When, if ever, do you begin to worry about whether they will occur? How do they evolve from draft to draft? When do you begin to systematically develop them? Does your method work? Can you see places where you might try a different approach? Some writers know at the outset what the characters and the scene "really mean"; many others discover it along the way. Understanding your own process will reduce frustration.

Ask Readers

Readers' impressions and responses are particularly useful as you develop subtext and theme—first of all, because readers can tell you whether your intent is clear, and second, because they can help you to discover patterns you may not have intended but which may enhance your story. Use the questions below to elicit readers' reactions to your story's subtext and theme.

- *Are there places where the scene's emotional or thematic content is confusing?* If so, try to clarify by doing more to show (not tell) the feelings. Then run the scene by a different reader to check yourself.

- *Is there any place where the ideas distract you from the characters?* Readers' responses to this question will help you to identify where you need to tone down thematic elements.

- *Is there any place where the characters behave hyperconsistently?* Do their actions ever seem dictated by a point the author wants to make rather than by their own natures? These problems are signs that you may be trying too hard to develop theme or subtext. Remember to focus first on the characters themselves.

- *Is there any place where you find yourself pulling back or rebelling because of an idea, or because you feel the author is preaching to you?* Where? Emotional reactions are perhaps the most reliable guide to revision of subtext and theme.

Wordplay

Speaking the subtext   This exercise is especially suited to such stories as Hemingway's "Hills Like White Elephants" (p. 320) or Seth Pase's "The Father" (pp. 372–375), or others that contain little overt commentary. Enlist the help of two friends, preferably at least one of whom is of the opposite sex. Each person should choose one of the voices in the story: man, woman, and narrator. Read it aloud, taking your parts. Pause at each line and state the subtext—what the character really means or feels. The narrator should write down these subtextual lines. When you've finished, read the subtext version aloud. What is the effect? Do you feel this version conveys more, or less? When, how, and why? How do you think the author would feel about your "explicated" version?

Writing it all   Try rewriting a subtle scene by adding explanations of all that is unspoken or implied. Now ask yourself what has been gained or lost. Silence, used well, can say more than words. By showing rather than explicating emotion, you will allow subtext to develop. It is not only a deliberate technique but also a giving up of control that results in the story becoming much richer and less predictable, and taking on its own complex meanings that can't always be summed up or paraphrased. With each addition, what has been subtracted?

Acting the scene   Alone or with a friend, put your story aside and role-play a scene in your own words. First, define each character's **point of view** or perspective;

then talk the scene out. As you do so, pay attention not to what you say but to what is unsaid. Watch for gestures, pauses, facial expressions. Once you've finished, quickly take notes. Later, compare the role-played version with the original. Look for ways of showing emotion rather than stating it directly.

Comparing subtexts   Write out the emotion that is indirectly conveyed in a scene you've written, then ask a friend to do the same. Are your results consistent? Are there places where your point is not coming across? Look at them again. Is it possible that your friend's version might be better—that you've accomplished something other than what you intended? Don't be unnerved if the reader sees meanings that are slightly different from but consistent with what you see. This indicates that the scene is alive at a level deeper than your awareness. On the other hand, if the two versions are incompatible, you may need to clarify.

Remembering subtext   Do a focused freewrite (see p. 11) on a scene you've already written. List everything you imagine about it. Include some of these details in your next draft. Remember that setting, including emotional context, provides the backdrop for the action and so defines the characters. Adding a few such details can make a scene much richer. Similarly, adding gestures to dialogue can convey quite a bit of unspoken feeling.

Theme and action   Once you have finished or drafted a story, save it and make a copy. On the copy, change the main character's behavior at the moment of choice. How does this affect the story's impact thematically? What are the implications?

Understating theme   Underline every thought, concept, or idea that is directly expressed in the story—that is, everything that you wrote intending to indicate aspects of the theme. Now tone down each one. Save that version and write another in which you actually delete the ideas. Give these drafts to readers and see whether they make sense. If not, pay close attention to what questions the readers ask, and to when in the story they occur, as you adjust the story's thematic dynamics.

Breaking the rules: writing from theme   Go against the usual advice and write a story from theme. Start with an idea you believe in: pride goes before a fall; kindness is a virtue. Or, choose a more general idea: memory, love, goodness, cruelty, need. Next, design a character and a situation through which this idea can be explored. As you write, keep the theme in mind and structure the story to prove your point or explore your issue. Try putting the story aside after the first draft is written, to give yourself a little distance so that when you return you can more easily discover the story's larger meaning. If this exercise produces a good story, great; if not, why didn't it?

Challenging theme   Copy your story and rewrite it so that it presents the case against your original thematic ideas. Make that case as convincingly as you can. Try combining the two versions. Are there ways in which you can use the opposing point of view to deepen and more thoughtfully explore the story's thematic issues? Be careful to minimize direct statements of theme.

Suggested Reading

The More Books and Stories section on page 496 provides complete bibliographic information for each title listed below.

Russell Banks, *Affliction*

Joseph Connolly, "Hard Feelings"

Andre Dubus, "A Father's Story"

Nathaniel Hawthorne, "The Minister's Black Veil"

Ernest Hemingway, "Hills Like White Elephants"

James Joyce, "Araby"

Brenda Miller, "A Thousand Buddhas"

Flannery O'Connor, "A Good Man Is Hard to Find"

Seth Pase, "The Father"

Akhil Sharma, "Cosmopolitan"

Leslie Marmon Silko, "Yellow Woman"

Jeannine Thibodeau, "Close"

Shaping the Story

Once you've drafted your story, it's time to step back from it a bit. Part Three returns to the writing process introduced in Part One. This section will help you to move from the early stages of prewriting and drafting to the later stages of revision (Chapter 10) and working on your story in a class or group with other writers (Chapter 11). Chapters 10 and 11 present an intensive, hands-on look at the process of refining your short story. You may find the checklists, exercises, and activities in these two chapters especially useful; they contain a detailed review of key points from previous chapters and are designed to help you to evaluate and improve your story, and to prepare to discuss it with others.

CHAPTER 10

Revising
Linear and Circular Methods

A scrupulous writer, in every sentence that he writes, will ask himself at least four questions, thus: What am I trying to say? What words will express it? What image or idiom will make it clearer? Is this image fresh enough to have an effect? And he will probably ask himself two more: Could I put it more shortly? Have I said anything that is avoidably ugly?

—George Orwell, "Politics and the English Language"

I was feeling a story form, slowly. I kept sensing this threshold beyond which I couldn't see, but each time I wrote, I pushed it back just a little: first I could hear a voice, and then I saw someone going into a room. Then a couple of past events hooked on, and I felt a change in mood about to happen. So I could almost see the story, after months of not seeing it. But not quite. And then one morning, just as I woke up, I realized what I was doing wrong: I had gotten to where I was writing and writing and writing, even when I didn't know what I had to say. And so I would get to a certain point and the story just didn't make sense. I wasn't giving it time to breathe and grow between drafts. I was wandering in it, not waiting until I had enough distance. You have to get far enough away to see the curve of the earth—then you know where you are.

—Alice Naton, poet and fiction writer

It *Is* Everything: Methods of Revision

It's a classroom cliché, but true: revision *is* everything. But like drafting, revising is a different job for every story and every writer. Unlike drafting, it isn't always required in writing classes—so, often, beginning writers are unsure how to go about it. If you are in a workshop, you'll have the benefit of readers' comments to guide you as you revise, but you'll still need to discover methods and techniques that you're comfortable with. This chapter picks up where Chapter 2 left off, and explores a variety of approaches to revision—from straightforward outlining to more intuitive methods. It presents several drafts of one of the student stories in the anthology, Rachel Finkelstein's "Awakening" (pp. 287–293). At the end of the chapter, you will find checklists to help you evaluate your draft, and suggestions and exercises for addressing problems and further developing your story.

There's no "one right way" to revise your story; rather, the various approaches to revision may be combined or adapted. Those that are logical, systematic, and linear add order and a sense of control during the early stages of writing a story, and they provide a way of pulling it together and giving it form during revision. Circular methods take a seemingly less direct route to the same end.

Although it's difficult to generalize about something so personal, you may, like many beginning writers, benefit from combining these methods—for instance, taking an open-ended approach to drafting and gradually becoming more structured as you shape and polish your story. Try thinking of revision not as steps toward a preconceived goal but as a continuation of your writing process. Exploring and discovering shouldn't end with your story's first draft. Treat the methods described in this chapter as colors to mix and combine, rather than as a paint-by-numbers map.

> **Q: How can writers free themselves from previous drafts of a story without at the same time starting from scratch?**
>
> **A:** If you have written a draft, you can no longer start from scratch. I learned this from drawing classes. Sketch an apple once; then, on a fresh sheet of paper, draw it again, and you'll be surprised how much your hand, your eye, your mind, retained from the first sketch. If you aren't interested in your revision, you need to have someone else look at it, or, better yet, take some time away from it. I find revision a wonderful way to return to my original voice, to smooth out the voice of my novel. As for what works in the earlier version, why revise what works?
>
> —*Ada Matsui, writer and editor*

Linear Methods

By "linear methods," I mean those that follow a relatively clear-cut and predecided course. Linear methods involve thinking things through and then working according to a plan. They tend to be logical and systematic rather than intuitive. Although this book's bias has so far been toward intuitive methods and away from more logical ones, most writers do combine methods. The later drafts in particular often require a somewhat more systematic approach. Those who have leaned strongly toward intuitive, emotional methods in the early stages of writing a story may find the opposite approach refreshing as they revise.

Questioning Readers   One of the most useful ways of thinking systematically about your story is to decide what it is that you need to improve and then, if your workshop or discussion group allows it, to question readers directly on these subjects. As you approach discussing your story with others, give careful thought to any questions you'd like to ask your readers during or after the discussion, and to the order in which you will ask them. The Ask Readers sections of this chapter (p. 198) and the next (p. 217) provide some specific suggestions.

Whether or not you will be questioning them directly, never approach readers "cold," without thinking over what you want to know. To do so is a waste of time and opportunity. No matter how intuitive your writing process has been so far, you owe it to your story and to your readers to think out what you want from them, besides, often they won't know how best to help you unless you tell them. But how do you know what to tell them? Your questions to readers should address the issues that concern you as you write, should be specific, and should be posed in a way that engages your readers. (See Ask Readers, p. 198, for some examples.)

Outlining   Formal outlining is a very basic linear method in which the writer organizes the story's material in the familiar outline form. While this approach often doesn't work during the drafting phase, it may give perspective during revision. After working intuitively for a while, you may need some distance, an overview of the draft. Rather than assuming that you already know exactly where the story is heading, though, try a reversal of the outlining techniques you may have used for term papers or essays.

The technique of "backwards outlining" involves listing the scenes you've already written, with a brief summary of the key events in each. This approach allows you to map what you've done and to see how to shape it. Repetitions or omissions become obvious and structural patterns may be revealed. Adapt the outline as you revise, moving back and forth between the prose itself and your developing map of the larger story. At every point, the outline should reflect the story, not the other way around.

Working from a Narrative Arc   Some writers, especially beginners, benefit from creating a **narrative arc**, a simplified way of diagramming a plot as they edit and shape their stories. To define your story's narrative arc you'll first need to identify the story's climax—the point at which the main **character** or actor makes a choice or has a realization that leads to a significant change. From there, you can work backwards to determine first which events should build up to the story's climax (**rising action**), then those that should follow it (**falling action**), and finally, preferably with responses from readers in your workshop or writers' group, what background information (**exposition**) is necessary to orient readers adequately. This method is impractical for many first drafts because it requires you to know what will happen before you write it, but it gives perspective as you shape subsequent drafts. See Chapter 4, Plot (p. 54) for a detailed explanation of the narrative arc.

Using a Storyboard   Some writers swear by using a storyboard. This is an especially useful tool for **novels** (book-length fictional works of prose); for long, intricately plotted stories; or for those that

Q: How do you kill the "editor in the brain"?

A: I don't try to kill the editor in the brain. I try to notice it: what it says. When I am writing I allow it to be there but not to interrupt me. For example: if the editor says, "You shouldn't write that because it will create problems later in the story," in a blip of a second I just notice that and keep writing. If the editor is particularly annoying, I simply say out loud, "BACK OFF UNTIL I AM FINISHED WRITING THIS DRAFT." Using such an approach, you can list ideas as they occur to you, then return later and address them systematically.

—*Willard Cook,*
writer and teacher

don't follow the conventional narrative arc. When you are ready to begin defining your story's overall structure, write the main events or scenes on index cards and attach them to a bulletin board or wall. This method can give a sense of order and control to the writing process. For many writers, physically making the overall shape defines it so they are less apt to get lost in detail and wander off course.

As with outlines or the narrative arc, if you use a storyboard, don't let it make you feel prematurely and irrevocably committed—instead, play with it, move things around and try out different possibilities. Use it to reflect where the story is and where it might go, not to dictate where it should be.

Building from Ideas   Another linear method may be particularly useful for those who begin their stories from **plot** (the arrangement of events) or **theme** (a story's ideas). Most teachers discourage students from starting with these elements, for good reason: plot- or theme-centered stories are generally **melodramatic** (that is, inappropriately dominated by plot rather than character) or preachy. But if you find that you are able to naturally and successfully write this way, then your revision process may involve working downward, filling in your framework of ideas or events with characters, setting, and other elements of fiction. It's a good practice to consult an experienced writer before trying this approach—it's hard to do well. See Chapter 2, Drafting (p. 32), for more on writing from theme.

Q: What is the difference between good confusion and bad confusion?

A: Bad confusion remains confusion. Therefore the reader becomes irritated, then angry. Good confusion makes specific demands on a reader that eventually result in clarity and illumination, though perhaps not the kind of illumination the reader at first expected. The important word here is "specific." The writer has to know exactly what those demands are, how they are meant to work, and what effects they are designed to produce. After the initial uncertain provocations of inspiration, the writer cannot afford to be confused, and thus cannot share the state of mind, however appealing, the reader will experience.

—*Lawrence Raab,*
poet

Circular Methods

Circular methods involve a less rational and more emotional or intuitive approach. They are often particularly useful for generating ideas, working through a block, or developing specific aspects of a story. I've called them "circular," but "curved" might be more accurate since they don't always return to where they started—they swerve. If you've written your first draft according to linear methods, switching to circular ones can add depth and dimension to your work as you revise. If, after experimenting over time with both methods, you're extremely uncomfortable with the logic and planning involved in linear writing, circular methods may be best for you all the way through the process.

Gestating   For some writers and at some times, the writing process includes long gestational periods, often mistaken for writer's block. When I first started writing, I worked in bursts, with long blank spells in between, during which I sat at my writing table, stared at pieces of paper, felt intensely guilty, and didn't get ideas.

Every time this happened I was convinced that it was over, I'd never write again. Later, I called these nonwriting periods "writer's block."

Then one afternoon, flying home from visiting friends after six months of "writer's block," I found myself suddenly pouring out thirty fairly complicated pages—the ending to the novel I'd been working on. After that experience, I realized that active creativity isn't the only kind—there is a passive process, a dormant or gestational period that may last a few hours, a week, nine months, or a year. Although recently I've had longer and more structured active periods, I still find that some of my best work develops in the dark, when I'm not looking.

Loosening the Schedule   Even if they don't experience long gestational periods, some writers simply find that it works better to be loose about schedules. Their lives don't always allow them to write daily, or at times there just may not be something to say every single day. Sometimes, they may need to think rather than write—or to enjoy doing something unrelated to writing, for a change. And for some people, deliberately *not* setting aside the time to write takes the pressure off and makes them more eager to work. If you're an orderly sort of writer most of the time, experiment with following ideas exactly as they occur to you, rather than looking for them only when it's time in the story or in your schedule for them to occur. Keep an open mind about where everything will fit in. Once you get good at this, it may actually make your thinking more fluid so that stories begin to come out more whole, and in that sense the process may become more orderly than it was.

If so much openness results in getting nothing done, try the middle course that works for many people: write every day at the same time, but limit that time to as little as fifteen minutes, and be strict about the limit. This removes the pressure of large time commitments, keeps the story in the back of your mind each day, and will probably result in a surprisingly large accumulation of useful notes after a week or two.

Circular Methods and Revision   Circular methods apply also to the specifics of revision. The most obvious example concerns the point at which plotting occurs. Many beginning writers view their stories primarily in terms of plot. For these writers, it is difficult to resist immediately organizing the story's events into a linear sequence. The ability to resist plotting until it's inevitable can feel like being told not to look in *that* corner, whatever you do. For other writers, there is a fear bordering on conviction that the story will never take shape, until it does. Deciding to plot a story last can be a scary way to work, but it ensures that decisions about plot will not be arbitrary—that they will grow from and be a part of the story's other elements.

Working from Lists or Clusters   If you don't feel ready for the structure of a storyboard or outline, you can still get some perspective on your story by revising with looser forms of outlining such as working from lists or clusters. (These forms of outlining are described in Chapter 2, p. 32.) Such approaches offer an experimental step in the other direction for very structured writers. Of course, the point of a looser outline is to allow spontaneous connections and ideas. Some writers make up their own style of outlining, while others find that a strict structure inspires "cheating" or rebelling—illicit bursts of freewriting or listing that often are highly productive.

Dividing Your Time   Writing several stories at once can relieve pressure. When one story isn't moving, don't push it—just go to another one. This method requires you to attach and detach frequently, which can be disconcerting to innately or habitually "monogamous" writers. On the other hand, it can keep you from becoming obsessive or anguished about a story, if you're so inclined. Try waiting until you have a good start on each story—that way, it's easier to keep them distinct.

Sensing When to Revise   How often should you revise, when you're using circular methods? If you're not in a structured workshop, there's no right answer to this question. Sometimes ideas come so fast that you'd lose them if you stopped; sometimes you absolutely must take a break in order to get enough distance to see what you're doing; and sometimes a slow but regular rhythm will move you forward. But letting drafts age a bit between revisions, when possible, will give you perspective, and it allows ideas and images the gestation they need before you're ready, as the poet Rainer Maria Rilke has said, to bring them forth.

Q: How many drafts does it take to finish a story?

A: When I started school (and thus, workshops), I was under the impression that a story went through three or four drafts (I don't remember which number) and that was it, and it was *wrong* if you spent more time on one story. When I learned that some stories take ten, fifteen drafts, I was more than a little surprised. Imagine: we have to write all these different versions just to make it sound like it naturally came out that way.

—James Leon Suffern,
writing student

Writing within the System   The fact that there isn't always time for this gestational period is a built-in problem with workshops and schools in general. Although inspiration cannot be expected to occur according to a schedule, in a classroom there is usually no choice. If you are faced with serious deadlines, be sure to schedule *non-writing* time once a draft is completed. Wait a while and then, after printing it out, reread it. You'll probably see things you missed before.

Guilt   If you're a circular worker, don't assume or let anyone else assume for you that resistance to deadlines is necessarily a sign of laziness, though it may result in negative consequences if you're in school, regardless of its creative significance. Sometimes you do just need to sit down and do it, but on other occasions—lots of them—the work you need to do may be in the back of your mind, not yet formed. If this is the case, talk with your teacher or whoever else is waiting for your work. Sometimes the calendar may bend to accommodate your methods. In other situations, *you* may need to be flexible, or to accept the consequences of not being so.

Discipline   I've said a lot here about indulging your creativity. But keep in mind that this is not the same thing as indulging a lack of discipline. If you worry a lot about whether you're acting with artistic integrity or merely being lazy, you probably aren't being lazy—you probably need to understand and respect your creative needs more, and redefine a work ethic for yourself. You may be worrying instead of writing. On the other hand, if it has never occurred to you that you might be self-indulgent in your disrespect for deadlines and schedules . . . think about it. Consider alternatives. You might get more done if you try handing things in on time, and you might find the results tremendously rewarding.

Of course, most writers employ a variety of methods, and these categories—linear and circular—may in reality blur and overlap. So, varying your methods is a natural and useful approach. If you wrote the first draft of your story chronologically—as sometimes happens in a story that starts from **voice,** the personality, tone, or sensibility conveyed by a story's language (see Starting from Voice on page 37 in Chapter 2, Drafting) or that has incubated for a long time—you may begin feeling bound to that order, either in the writing process or in the story itself. If you find yourself blocking, try skipping around in time as you write, or try rearranging the scenes so they occur out of chronological order.

Conversely, if your first draft came out piecemeal, try revising straight through, scene by scene. This should help you smooth out the transitions between scenes, catch redundancies and inconsistencies, and even out the story's narrative voice. The same thing applies to the creative process itself: if you've so far waited for inspiration to strike before sitting down to write, try revising according to a schedule. If you feel nervous about switching methods, save your drafts—you can always go back to them if you don't like your experiments.

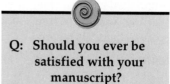

Q: Should you ever be satisfied with your manuscript?

A: Yes and no. I think you should feel confident enough (or even sick enough) of your manuscript to know when it is time to let it go, to sink or swim on its own. Manuscripts often take on a life of their own anyway, seeming to control us more than we tame them. Some poet, when asked which poem was the best they had written, responded, The *next* poem. I like that philosophy because it maintains the element of hope, as well as a driving force toward what is better, and *that* usually leads to discovery. Isn't discovery, after all, what often makes a piece of writing shine? That the writer learns something personally, or about the world, and the reader inevitably also learns through the process of reading that work.

—*Janet St. John,*
poet

The Revision Process in Detail: The Writing of "Awakening"

Virtually all writers use a combination of circular and linear methods. How they use them depends on what they're comfortable with, on the requirements of the workshop or writers' group they are in, and on the nature of each story. This section takes another approach to the revision process. Rather than offering suggestions, it includes several drafts of a scene from an actual story written in a beginning fiction-writing course. The author, Rachel Finkelstein, comments (pp. 191–193) on her writing process from draft to draft. She begins with an overview. The entire finished story is included on page 287 of this book's anthology section.

When I started to write "Awakening," I had just one image in mind. I could see the narrator, a young teenage girl, walking out over a frozen lake, wondering with each step whether she would fall through the ice. I didn't know exactly where this came from, but I wanted to know more about this character: what was going on in her life that would make her do such a thing? Along with that image, I also had in my mind the sound of glass breaking, which seemed to suggest ice shattering. From that point, all I really did was decide what that glass was (a vodka bottle), why it broke (it was dropped), and then who dropped it (the narrator's mother). So my basic strategy was to start with one clear image, sound, or scene, and then ask myself questions about it to come up with more of a plot.

I like writing in the first person, because I feel readers can best understand my character if she talks directly to them. At first, a little of my own personality came out in the narrator as I would ask myself, What would I be thinking in this situation and how might that make me feel? As the story progressed, the narrator became a stronger character, both in my mind and on paper. I felt both that I knew her better and that she was entirely separate from me.

Similarly, the story itself became somewhat separate from me—I did not know how the events would unfold. I knew the ice scene had to figure in somewhere, but I did not have a specific ending in mind. The whole Fat Man incident was completely unexpected, but as I was writing, it just happened as if it were out of my control.

First Draft

The passage that I'm going to examine is from the second page of the story, before any of the action or flashbacks start. I had a difficult time trying to keep the language mysterious to set the mood, while trying to establish the narrator's personality. I wanted to use adjectives that would evoke images of darkness and feelings of fear to foreshadow that something bad will happen soon, although it is not clear at this point in the story exactly what that will be. In the first draft, a lot of the paragraphs are very wordy and logical, which detracts from the emotional impact of what is actually happening in the story.

> I take a step toward the door, then pause. Maybe I should think about this, form some sort of plan. I don't know who's out there. Maybe my mom isn't home yet. I tiptoe over to the window and glance outside. I can hear crickets chirping in the distance. It occurs to me that if I get killed tonight, and my mom isn't home yet, there will be no one to hear me scream. Our house is on a narrow back road, set far back from the road. If we didn't leave the porch light on at night, you could probably drive right past it and never know. But we always leave the light on, since my mother usually comes home very late, and most nights she is still drunk.
>
> I want my mother. She needs me right now but I am so scared. I glimpse myself in the mirror and, considering I just woke up, I don't look too bad. I purposely mess my long hair, trying to make myself look uglier, just in case there is someone out there. I am wearing a long white cotton nightgown that probably makes me look younger than I am.

Second Draft

Revising the first draft, I removed a lot of the phrases that describe the forming of a thought ("It occurs to me that if I get killed tonight . . ." "I want my mother. She needs me right now but I am so scared. . . ."). I left just exactly what the narrator was imagining or doing. I also cut short phrases ("then pause"), as well as full sentences ("Maybe I should think about this . . .") that felt too rational at such a tense moment in the story. Throughout the story, I tried to remove sentences or phrases that were already understood by the reader and therefore unnecessary. I added sentences that showed the emotional state of the narrator in place of ones that told how she felt.

I take a step toward the door, I don't know who's out there. Maybe my mom isn't home yet. I tiptoe over to the window and glance outside. I can hear crickets chirping in the distance. Our house is on a narrow back road, set far back from the street. If we didn't leave the porch light on at night, you could probably drive right past it and never know. But we always leave the light on, since my mother usually comes home very late, and most nights she is still drunk.

If I get killed tonight, and my mom isn't home yet, there will be no one to hear me scream. I glimpse myself in the mirror and try to see myself through the eyes of a burglar. I am wearing a long white cotton nightgown that probably makes me look younger than I am. I purposely mess my long hair, trying to make myself uglier, just in case there is someone out there.

Third Draft

In the third draft I mostly tried to further simplify the language while maintaining the mystery and tension. This is why I made the sentence "If I get killed tonight . . ." a separate paragraph: I wanted extra emphasis on that point because it shows the narrator's fear and sets up the scene for the reader. And I wanted sentences that showed the reader how the narrator felt and what she was thinking, rather than just stating her thoughts one after another.

I take a step toward the door. I don't know who's out there. Maybe my mom isn't home yet. I tiptoe over to the window and glance outside. I can hear crickets chirping in the distance. Our house is on a narrow back road, set back off of the street. If we didn't have the porch light on at night, you could probably drive right past it and never know. But we always leave the light on, since my mother usually comes home very late, and most nights she is still drunk.

If I get killed tonight, and my mom isn't home yet, there will be no one to hear me scream.

Suddenly, the solitude of my room makes my skin crawl. I feel so small and alone, like I am shrinking into the darkness. I long for the comfort of my mother's arms around me, but my feet are rooted to the floor. I glimpse myself in the mirror and try to see myself through the eyes of a burglar. I am wearing a long white cotton nightgown that probably makes me look younger than I am. I purposely mess my long hair, trying to make myself look uglier, just in case there is someone out there.

Final Draft

Revising the third draft consisted mainly of making descriptions more concrete. In this passage, I changed only a few small details. Elsewhere in the story I added details about the mother's bedroom and developed the secondary characters to make them seem more real, and not just stereotypes. Also, certain scenes that seemed too familiar just needed a few specific details about characters or relationships. For example, the narrator doesn't just comfort her mother; she rubs her shoulders and strokes her hair.

> I take a step toward the door. I don't know who's out there. Maybe my mom isn't home yet. I tiptoe over to the window and glance outside. I can hear the wind dragging dry leaves over the pavement. Our house is on a narrow back road, set far off of the street. If we didn't have the porch light on at night, you could probably drive right past it and never know. But we always leave the light on. My mother usually comes home very late, and most nights she is still drunk.
>
> If I get killed tonight, and my mom isn't here, there will be no one to hear me scream.
>
> Suddenly, the solitude of my room makes my skin crawl. I feel small and alone, like I am shrinking into the darkness. I long for my mother's arms around me, but my feet are rooted to the floor. I glimpse myself in the mirror and try to see myself through the eyes of a burglar. I am wearing a long white cotton nightgown that probably makes me look younger than I am. It hangs loosely over my body, and I can't see my breasts unless I stick out my chest. I purposely mess my long hair, trying to make myself look uglier, just in case there is some-one out there.

Summary

As I revised this passage, I realized that understatement is very important. The reader will understand what you mean even if you don't come right out and say it, as long as you show the characters' actions that represent their feelings. By deliber-ately not saying certain things, you can create a more powerful effect for the reader.

No one can tell you exactly how to revise your story. Your approach will be in-fluenced by the story's particular challenges; your own comfort or discomfort with various methods; and, in many cases, the requirements of your writing class or group. This chapter has suggested a few methods that have been useful to others; you will need to decide which of these are helpful to you, and add them to your own discoveries. From all of these approaches, you can then form your own revi-sion method.

Exploration and Discovery

In preparation for Chapter 11's more detailed exploration of the critical process, the rest of this chapter draws from Chapters 3 through 9 to create an extensive review of this book's key questions about character, plot, point of view, time, setting dialogue, subtext, and theme. This section gathers together the central critical questions that will guide you as you revise your early work.

- **Ask Yourself** suggests general questions on a variety of topics to consider before you distribute your draft to others.

- **Ask Readers** reframes these questions to solicit helpful comments from readers. Each of these categories contains a summary of some of this book's key concepts. You won't need to use all of these questions and ideas; rather, choose the ones that apply to your story.

- **Translating Criticism** lists comments that writers frequently hear in workshops, and suggests follow-up questions to encourage readers to be more specific.

- **The Revision Checklist** suggests ways of using the criticism you will receive from others.

- **Wordplay** will give you a chance to try out some revision techniques.

Ask Yourself

As you prepare to show your draft to others, it's a good idea to step back and try to look at it objectively. This will help you anticipate questions that may arise during the workshop or discussion. You may be able to address some of these beforehand; in other cases, you'll be better able to think out what kind of help you want from readers and to prepare for the potentially stressful experience of showing your work to others. The questions in this section review some topics that often come up during discussion of first drafts. For more specific questions on each topic, refer to the Ask Yourself and Ask Readers sections in Chapters 3 through 9. You may want to "check your work" by considering some of the questions that follow before giving your story to others to read.

Structure

- *What is the story's central conflict?* Are all of the events directly related to it?

- *How is this conflict resolved?* Identifying the resolution should help you locate where the story's climax should be.

- *What events lead up to the climax?* These are the rising action; each should move the main character "from A to B" and toward the conflict's resolution.

- *Where does the story's main action begin?* Where are time and place established? Usually, this marks the end of the exposition and the beginning of the rising action. If it's more than a few paragraphs into the story, there's a good chance that some of your exposition would be better sifted in as the story proceeds rather than kept in a block at the very beginning. If this is not possible, you may want to consider starting the story at a different point.

- *What information do readers need to know in order for the story to make sense?* This expository information should be inserted as gracefully as possible, usually toward the beginning of the story.

- *What information is essential after the climax?* This will be the story's falling action.
- *If your story doesn't conform strictly to the narrative arc as described in Chapter 4 (see p. 73), how does it achieve a satisfying sense of tension and release?* What significant change occurs, and how is this change dramatized?

Clarity

- *Have you clearly identified the characters and their relations to one another?* Check to be sure that you've given enough detail to distinguish main characters, that their names are distinctive enough not to be confusing, that you have not named or devoted too much space to secondary characters, and that you have provided subtle reminders of who's who when necessary.
- *Is it clear what is happening?* Is the action simple and direct? Clarify where you can and identify places where you're not sure.
- *Have you punctuated the dialogue correctly?* If not, readers may become confused.
- *When you're "showing rather than telling," is the meaning clear?* Ask yourself what **concrete**, sensory details will get the idea across; if you were watching and listening, what would tell you how to interpret the scene?
- *Are you trying to be mysterious?* If so, when and why? As a writer, you must decide where you want your readers to work. If you deliberately mystify them about basic issues like what's the main character's name or gender, who's who, who's speaking, and what's happening, you're likely to exhaust readers' patience before they get to weightier matters such as theme and subtext. There are lots of ways to create intrigue and complexity; save the mystery for where it's appropriate to be less direct.
- *Are your sentences clear and reasonably short?* Don't be slavish about it, but simplify wherever you can. Think: subject, verb, object, period. Keep adjectives, adverbs, and prepositions to a minimum.
- *Is the vocabulary appropriate rather than distracting?* Here again, simplify. A distinctive narrative voice doesn't require a showy vocabulary. Writer Elsa Lasker Schuller commented, "A real poet does not say azure. A real poet says blue"—a remark that writer Leslie Epstein has called "the single wisest thing ever said about creative writing." Don't let words get in the way—ordinarily, the language should be transparent.
- *Are your verbs clear, appropriate, and consistent?* Remember, in a past tense story flashbacks should be in past perfect; in a present tense story, they should be in simple past.
- *Are the transitions from scene to scene clear and simple rather than labored?* Have you provided basic information such as where and when scenes take place, and who is present? Have you muddied the transitions by giving unnecessary information or trying to summarize the scenes' meanings or tie up inconsequential loose ends before moving on?

Pacing

- *Have you balanced **scenes** and **narration** (what the writer tells the reader directly, as opposed to what the characters convey through speech and actions) appropriately?* Make sure that the amount of space you've devoted to each scene is appropriate to its importance and to the story's sense of time. Watch for sketchy scenes that move too quickly over significant events, and for lingering, wordy, or repetitive descriptions that slow the action inappropriately. As a rule, dramatize the main events—using enough action and dialogue for readers to see the characters rather than merely hear the **narrator** (the voice that tells the story) summarize their actions. Use narration to move quickly over less important events. For instance, in most scenes a character getting out of his car and walking up to the door of his mother's house is relatively unimportant—that is, boring—and should be narrated, while the confrontation itself deserves more extensive detail.

- *Are you being redundant?* Look for dialogue, narration, and description that is repetitive, and make the sometimes difficult choice to cut it. Keep in mind that the reader defines what is redundant. What the reader has already been told by the narrator, for instance, should not be restated by the characters, even though realistically such a discussion might be likely to occur. Make a choice: keep one account and summarize, imply, or skip the others.

- *Do scenes and the story itself begin in the midst of an important event—one that clearly moves the main character closer to the climax and resolution of the conflict? Do they end once the event is completed?* Look for unnecessary trailing in and out of the essential action.

The Quality of the Writing

- *Are the subject matter or plot developments distractingly extreme?* In fiction, such subjects as death, severe illness, kidnapping, passionate love, and financial ruin or winning the lottery are not necessarily the most interesting. More death, severe illness, plus dismemberment, human sacrifice, unusual sexual practices, and spaceships from Neptune are not necessarily even more interesting. The most subtle human developments often signify profound change, thus creating the most interesting reading.

- *Are you explaining too much?* It's necessary to supply basic information that readers could not guess, but beginning writers often do a lot more work than they need to by spelling out what characters are thinking or why they act as they do. Usually, this overtness is unnecessary and actually diminishes a

Q: How much drama is too much drama, becoming false or melodramatic?

A: My formula: the more inherent drama there is in a scene or situation, the more modulation and restraint I will use. Drama treated dramatically becomes melodrama, whereas drama played out quietly is all the more powerful and affecting.

—Patricia Traxler,
poet and writer

scene's impact. If you overexplain, you risk seeming to patronize or even to manipulate readers, and this will cause intelligent readers to disengage from the story. Don't get carried away with logistics; once you have identified the story's key moments, place other things in the background. Check to be sure that the story "shows" rather than "tells" when appropriate. Are there things that are now spelled out but could be more subtly indicated? Have confidence in your ability to reach readers through concrete detail rather than explicit exploration.

- *Are you explaining too little?* A certain level of withholding intrigues readers and engages them in the story, but be careful not to confuse readers about basic information. Be sure you are "telling" where appropriate. Some of the hardest work of writing is to strike a balance between giving so much information that the story lacks mystery and, on the other hand, creating an artificially terse or compressed style that may actually be confusing.

- *Are words, phrases, or situations fresh and distinctive?* Does anything sound overfamiliar or tired? Emotion will resonate most fully in your writing if you avoid relying on situations or language that have been overused by other writers.

- *Does the writing call attention to itself?* Unless you're writing nonfiction, the most important point isn't to portray yourself or to define your style, but to focus on the story itself and to convey something about the characters' thinking or being. You won't look good if you keep jumping in front of your characters.

- *Have you gone overboard with rhetorical devices such as similes and metaphors?* When these are not just right, they're awful, drawing attention to themselves and to you, and away from your story. As writer and teacher Leslie Epstein has said, "Limit your similes to two a page, tops, and *make them count*; that is, be sure they nail down the point you are after, and do so with the swift, short, hard stroke of a hammer on a tack."

Mechanics

"Little" things like incorrect punctuation, sloppy paragraphing, and spelling errors will undermine even the most otherwise brilliant work. People who read many manuscripts (and this includes anyone who participates in a writing workshop) appreciate promptly delivered, readable papers. If you want a thoughtful critique rather than an irritable one, do what you can to avoid tripping up your readers with mechanical problems. Use the list below to improve the technical details in your writing.

- *Double-space your manuscript, and leave at least 1½-inch margins for comments.*
- *Use readable 12-point type.*
- *At the very least, always spell-check.* And remember that spell-checkers miss many errors; there's no substitute for rereading your work and checking it with a dictionary. Once you try this, you'll see how important it is.
- *Number all pages to avoid confusion in class, and in case the story falls to the floor.*

- *Be sure your copies are coming out dark enough to read easily.*
- *If workshop rules permit, attach questions for readers.* This will give them time to think over what you want to know, which will result in better responses. If you're concerned about getting an "absolutely unbiased" reading, ask readers to read and respond to questions *after* they've written their comments.
- *Staple or clip all pages together.*

Pet peeves   Here are a few minor and common errors that will detract from your manuscript. (Your teacher will be able to supplement this list.) These are all easily corrected.

- *Never write "ya" instead of "you," even in dialect.*
- *Remember that "your" is a possessive; "you're" means "you are."*
- *Remember that "its" is a possessive; "it's" means "it is."*
- *Do not use double, triple, or quadruple exclamation points or question marks unless you are writing a comic book.* This practice leads to punctuation inflation: once you start using two or three or four, one just won't feel like enough. Similarly, do not combine exclamation marks with question marks. (?!) As Ernest Hemingway wrote in a letter to Horace Liveright, punctuation "ought to be as conventional as *possible*. The game of golf would lose a good deal if croquet mallets and billiard cues were allowed on the putting green." Generally speaking, avoid relying on punctuation marks, boldface lettering, or capitalization to convey emotion. That is the writer's job, not the keyboard's. If you pay attention to gestures, language, and choice of detail, you will not need typographical gimmicks to add emphasis. Keep in mind that once you've used two exclamation marks, one may never again be enough; overstatement leads to more overstatement, and the story becomes cluttered.
- *Be sure to indent paragraphs.*
- *When writing dialogue, be sure to begin a new paragraph each time a different person begins speaking.*
- *Use a comma when characters address each other directly: "Hi, Don," not "Hi Don."*

Ask Readers

Once you've evaluated and polished your first draft as thoroughly as you can, you will be ready to show it to others. The fundamental questions starting on page 199 follow up on those raised in the previous section by suggesting some ways to elicit the information you need from readers. Chapter 11 (p. 208) provides some more specific guidelines on this topic. As you discuss your story, be careful, at least at first, not to reveal too much about what you are trying to convey. If you do, readers will have a hard time separating what they read from what you said, and you won't be able to determine where you need to make changes.

Conflict

- *What is the story's central conflict?* This usually is not stated directly in the story, but readers should be able to sense it, and they should be able to convey some understanding of it back to you.

- *What is at stake in the resolution of the conflict—what will be the consequences either way and are they significant enough to make you care what happens next?* Readers will care what happens to the extent that it matters. Find out whether the potential consequences of the main character's actions are clear by the time of the moment of choice.

- *What interests you most in the story?* Readers' answers will test your choice of central events and their relation to the main character. It isn't the event itself that creates the fullest kind of interest; it is the character experiencing the event and changing as a result. Almost anything can be riveting if the main character faces a conflict, the resolution of which leads to significant change.

- *How did the main character change as the conflict was resolved—that is, what significant choice or realization occurred?* Here again, even if readers have trouble describing the moment of change precisely, their interpretations should be consistent with your intent. If they're not, you may want to either identify and clarify misunderstood elements or consider adjusting your own ideas about the story.

- *Is it clear from the beginning that the character has room to change?* Wishes, desires, shortcomings, fears—all signs of imperfection—create momentum toward change.

Clarity and Focus

- *Retell the story scene by scene, without help.* Were readers ever confused or curious about the central events? Whether scenes are clearly portrayed is hard to judge without feedback, so listen to what readers say. Question back and forth. Don't let them simply express confusion and frustration. They need to tell you exactly where—on which page and at what paragraph—they felt confused, so that you can figure out what they would have needed to know in order to understand.

- *Is the story communicating as it was intended to?* Beyond the first draft, it's almost never in your best interest to be secretive about your intent. Once readers have seen a couple of drafts, you won't get a completely spontaneous response anyway. Comments will be a lot more specific if you're straightforward about what you're trying to do.

- *Is there too much information in places?* Did readers ever feel patronized? Where you are "telling," readers can be extremely helpful, leading you to a level of concreteness that is vivid and communicative. Always consider the source before simply following this kind of advice, though; inexperienced readers may ask for too much explanation or may adhere slavishly to the "show, don't tell" rule. When in doubt, look for more than one opinion.

- *Put away your copy of the story; now, list and describe the characters and their relationships.* Did readers have any trouble remembering who's who? Asking for specific information will encourage them to respond thoroughly and precisely.

- *Was there any place in the story where the language itself distracted you from the characters and what was happening to them?* Be sure to ask where.

Exposition

- *Did you sense that any background information was missing?* Were there past events or situations that readers needed to know about and didn't? Others can't read your mind—and this makes discussing your work extremely valuable. Listen for signs of confusion; what is evident to you may not be to your readers.

- *Were you ever confused about time or place?* If so, what necessary information is missing? It may help to briefly walk readers through each scene so they will remember.

Falling Action

- *Once the conflict was resolved, did loose ends remain?* Ask whether readers felt satisfied with the ending.

- *On the other hand, did the story seem to trail on longer than it needed to?* Readers can usually tell you exactly where they lost interest, and you should usually stop the story at that point.

Dialogue

- *Were you ever confused about who was speaking? Where?* Ask readers to help you identify where you need to **attribute** dialogue (that is, identify who is speaking) more clearly or frequently.

- *Where dialogue is attributed, do you think you'd recognize the character's voice without being told who was speaking?* Ask readers to help you evaluate whether your characters' voices are clear and distinct.

Pacing

- *Did the story feel rushed in places, or slow?* Be sure to ask where.

- *Did it sound summarized or "told"?* Be sure to ask where.

- *Did you notice any unnecessary repetition?* Readers' responses to these questions can help you evaluate your story's pacing—a very difficult quality to assess by yourself.

Emotion

- *Did you ever find yourself pulling back, withholding belief or sympathy?* This question should help you identify places where you may be straining credibility or where the emotions are not ringing true.

- *Did anything seem overfamiliar or trite?* What, exactly?

Translating Criticism

This section will help you to anticipate some of the comments you're most likely to hear in workshops or writers' groups. If you're discussing your story draft by draft in such a setting, your revision process will not be private. At times, the exchange of ideas between writers and their readers can feel almost like collaboration. It's important to carefully evaluate your readers' responses before making changes. Some will be insightful and particularly useful to your story. There are also certain "stock" remarks (for instance, "The story *really* starts *here*," or "Your piece flows well.") Such comments frequently contain some truth but may be so abstract, general, or trite that it's hard to figure out how to use them, or how to get the critic to be more specific. After "translating" some of these stock criticisms into ordinary English, this section suggests some follow-up questions to help you to identify and solve the problems they hint at.

- *"This is confusing"* or *"I'm not sure what you're getting at."*

   (The reader is asking for clarification.)

   > "Can you tell me exactly where (on which page and in which paragraph) you got confused?"
   >
   > "What is it that you would like to know?"
   >
   > "Let's back up, and you tell me what you *think* is happening."

- *"The prose is tangled and hard to read."*

   (Here again, the reader is asking for clarification—this time, with specific reference to the language.)

   > "Can you underline some examples?"
   >
   > "Do you remember when you first noticed this?" Try to locate the page and paragraph.
   >
   > "Was the problem more severe in some places than in others? Where?"
   >
   > "Are the sentences too long?"
   >
   > "Is the vocabulary confusing or distracting?"

- *"Transitions are weak or confusing."*

   (The reader is asking you to clarify how each scene connects to the next.)

   > "Which transitions confused you?"
   >
   > "Let's go through each transition and you tell me how you think the time and place is shifting."
   >
   > "What did you need to know and when did you need to know it?"

- *"It reads too fast"* or *"It reads too slowly"* or *"It needs expanding in places and cutting in others."*

   (The reader is asking you to adjust the story's pacing by adding or deleting material.)

   > "Were there places where you wanted more detail?"
   >
   > "Were there conversations or scenes that you would have liked expanded?"

"Is there too much narration and are there not enough scenes?"

"Is there too much detail?"

"Does the story contain unnecessary dialogue or description?"

"Are there scenes that are missing or unnecessary?"

"Let's go over the list of scenes and you tell me where you felt rushed or impatient."

- *"The story really begins here"* or *"Begin in medias res (in the middle of things)."*

(The reader is telling you that the beginning of your story drags or is irrelevant.)

"What interested you? What didn't?"

"Let's look through the story page by page, and try to remember where you first began to be interested."

"Is any of the material in the first three to five pages extraneous? What, specifically?"

- *The story is sentimental"* or *"The story is melodramatic."*

(The reader is telling you that the story is not working on an emotional level.)

"Were there places where you felt that the story was asking you to feel things that you didn't feel?"

"Do you think that I intended you to feel what you felt?"

"Did you ever feel annoyed at me or at the story? Where?"

"Do you have a clear sense of the main character and how he or she changes in the course of the story, or did you feel distracted by dramatic events?"

- *"Show, don't tell."*

(The reader is asking for less direct commentary from the narrator, and more sensory description.)

"Please underline places where you felt that I was 'telling.'"

"Please underline places where you felt that I was 'showing.'"

"Please circle places where you think the opposite approach would work better, and indicate why."

- *"The writing calls attention to itself."*

(The reader feels that your writing style is so prominent or unusual that it detracts from the story rather than enhancing it.)

"Please mark paragraphs, sentences, or words where this was a problem."

"Is the vocabulary too flashy or unusual?"

"Are the sentences too long or convoluted—or, on the other hand, too terse?"

"Are there particular techniques or devices such as metaphors or similes that distract from other elements of the story?"

- *"Certain words, phrases, or situations are clichés."*

(The reader is telling you that some elements of your story are overfamiliar.)

"Please mark the passages that you felt were clichés."

"What makes them clichés?"

"What are some other ways of describing the same things?"

Revision Checklist: Using Criticism

Once you've identified the problems in your first draft, it's time to start revising. All writers need critics and editors; still, sitting down to implement their suggestions can feel a little overwhelming, particularly when you've received a lot of feedback all at once. This checklist will take you into the actual revision, suggesting ways to address some of the criticisms in the previous section.

> **Clarifying:** If readers are confused about key moments of the story, consider expanding, simplifying, or defining these sections.

- Use readers' feedback to identify unclear spots and figure out what information is missing. Then supply it, as artfully, simply, and concretely as possible. *Note:* Confusion will occur if you leave out important information, make mechanical errors regarding punctuation or paragraphing, or try too hard to "show rather than tell." The solution is not always to give up on that objective. Try using context, the reactions of other characters, gestures, and description to make your point. If that approach fails, it may be necessary to allow the narrator a minimal explanation.

- To clarify your prose, mark trouble spots that readers have pointed out. Read the story aloud and mark places where you lose your breath. Shorten or change long or fancy-sounding words. Minimize adjectives, adverbs, and prepositions. Simplify sentences. Eliminate the passive voice. Streamline transitions by deleting end-of-scene summaries and the tying up of unimportant loose ends. Think of the scene as a movie, and just cut to the next action.

- Cut redundancies that readers have pointed out. After your second draft is complete, take a little time away from the story, if possible. Then reread it, marking and deleting any remaining repetition.

> **Restructuring:** Use readers' responses to guide you as you evaluate the story's shape and put the parts in place.

- Begin in medias res. Underline the essential action in each scene. Cut trailing explanations from both ends of the scenes. Anton Chekhov explained this process to one of his students:

> Fledgling authors frequently should do the following: bend the notebook in half and tear off the first half. . . . Normally beginners try "to lead into the story," as they say, and half of what they write is unnecessary. One ought to write so that the reader understands the progress of the story, from the characters' conversations, from their actions. Try to rip out the first half of your story; you'll only have to change the beginning of the second half a little bit and the story will be totally comprehensible.

- You may not need to throw away the kind of false beginning that Chekhov describes. Sometimes what's in it can be integrated into the story—just not at the beginning.

- Use readers' responses to reevaluate events' proportion. Identify the story's most important moments and write these out as scenes with dialogue, interaction, description, and gestures as appropriate. Identify the transitions and the events that are of secondary importance. Use the narrator to summarize these.

Restyling: Pay particular attention to readers' emotional responses, and adjust your story accordingly.

- To eliminate melodrama, reduce the number and intensity of dramatic events, and make sure to develop your characters fully. If you've chosen a very dramatic subject, you'll need to give the same attention to developing the characters, which may take a lot of imagination.

- If readers have advised you appropriately to "show, don't tell," the best approach is usually to ruthlessly cut all explaining by the narrator and the characters, and force yourself to find other ways of conveying the information. Where that is impossible, allow the narrator to briefly explain. As novelist Jonathan Strong has said, "Write the story, not about the story."

- Take the ego out of your prose. Give yourself a little time after your workshop. Then, using other writers' responses, ask yourself: have you succumbed to the temptation to use the story to show off your wit, vocabulary, sophistication, toughness, sexual expertise, or drug connections? This ploy is much more obvious than writers sometimes think. Go back through the story and underline places where you're guilty. Be honest. Ask yourself where you're addressing the story's needs and where you're addressing your own. Rewrite when necessary.

- Exterminate clichés. First of all, don't overreact to the word. Most beginning writers and readers don't even realize that they're using a cliché until someone points it out to them, so the criticism shouldn't be made disdainfully. But like all labels, this one can and should be translated into useful information; if the critic hasn't done that, you can. By definition, clichés are elements that have become so familiar that they no longer have much impact. (The "stock criticisms" in Translating Criticism on p. 201 are good examples.) Sometimes writers—and critics—are tempted to rely on timeworn approaches rather than creating characters, events, language, or commentary that are vivid and specific. The result is that anyone who is educated enough to recognize the cliché will feel cheated, manipulated. And that is really where the annoyance comes from. George Orwell offers this advice in his essay " Politics and the English Language": "Never use a metaphor, simile, or other figure of speech which you are used to seeing in print." Instead, look more closely at what it is that you are trying to describe. Underline the passages others point out, and later on ask yourself whether you have seen or heard elements of the writing before somewhere. Look for other, more concrete ways to say the same thing. Some situations are themselves clichéd: The hero triumphing against all odds, or the beautiful woman dying. In this case, look for ways to vary the formula by changing characters or events to make them less typical: the hero triumphs at great cost, perhaps *to others;* the dying woman is neither beautiful nor wholly likable.

Recognizing critical whims. One of the challenges of responding to a reading is discerning good advice from readers' mood swings.

- Look for a consensus on important issues—but remember that it won't always give you more than a homogenized or "cookie cutter" critique. Learn to identify the issues that matter to you and to ask searching questions of your readers.

- Use time. Let advice about which you are uncertain sit for a while before you act on it. This usually allows the issues to clarify.

Respecting the process. Don't try to do all of this at once. Remember that it's completely normal to work on one step at a time; take that into account when you respond to criticism.

The following excerpt from "Tips," an essay written by teacher Leslie Epstein to his students, offers additional thoughts on style, in and out of the classroom:

> Here are some tips for writing and for life. Spell all right as I have here (not "alright"). Keep commas and periods inside quotation marks, semicolons and colons outside; learn the proper usage for each. Don't say *disinterested* unless you mean impartial; say *indifferent* instead. Also, *centered around* should always be replaced by *centered on.* Avoid ellipses, those three dreamy dots at the end of unfinished thoughts; either finish the thought or interrupt it with a dash. As for echoes (the same distinctive or even relatively common word or sound in adjoining sentences, paragraphs, and real purists would even say pages)—watch for them like a hawk, swoop, and eliminate. Do not say such things as "He got out of bed, pulled on his pants" or "She inhaled her cigarette, ground it out." Such constructions, leaving out the "and" or the "then," are not only pretentious—they imply a list that does not exist, and so disconcert the reader. In narrative prose, as opposed to indented dialogue, write, on the average, two and a half paragraphs per page, never six or seven or ten or one. These simple rules, and a few others like them—for instance, not chewing gum in public, and tearing your bread in two before applying the butter—will make you seem sophisticated and glamorous and are by themselves worth your college tuition. . . .
>
> Now if truth be told, I violate a good many of these rules. So may you. But you ought at least to be aware that you are doing so and be able to justify each such decision. It's possible to take everything I've said both with a grain of salt and not lightly. That's the kind of balancing act all good writing consists of. I wish you luck upon the high wire.

Wordplay

On the wall   Adam Golaski, editor of *New Genre,* suggests the following exercise to help evaluate a story's shape: "Tape your story up on the wall, then mark off each scene. You can then literally see how much space each one takes up, and if a less important scene takes up too much space—say, more than an important one—edit it in relation to the more important scene."

Simplifying your style   Readers may get tangled up in your words if the sentences are too long or the vocabulary too fancy. ("The nimbostratuses are cumulating," a beginning student once wrote, to his teacher's dismay.) To streamline your prose, try this painstaking but effective method developed by another student, who used it on her novel: Highlight all uses of the passive voice in yellow; long or over-fancy words in pink; long sentences in orange; and adjectives and adverbs in blue. Next, simplify all of it as much as you can. Type in the corrections, and read it again. This method takes a long, dull time, but it results in much smoother and better-paced prose.

Two exercises for concision   Poet Kim Addonizio writes,

> The best exercise I know for concision is this: pick an arbitrary number of pages or number of words, say about one-third fewer than you have. This then has to become the length of your piece. You'll find that when you are forced to cut, you discover what you absolutely have to say, and you can say it in fewer words. This is how I learned to write short-short stories, by the way; I entered a contest in which the story could be no longer than 250 words. I thought it was impossible and found out it wasn't. I didn't win the contest, but I learned a lot about tightening my work.

Writer and editor Adam Golaski suggests this approach:

> The best exercise for concision that I have come upon is to read poetry and to either write or analyze it. I think most prose writers don't read poetry because somehow they see it as unrelated or look upon it as some sort of impenetrable code. Poetry focuses on language in a way that prose should. As a prose writer who gradually discovered the value of poetry, I can recommend a few contemporary poets whose work appealed to me: Stephen Dunn's *Riffs & Reciprocities*, Charles Simic's *The World Doesn't End*, A. R. Ammons' *Garbage* and Billy Collins's *Picnic, Lightening*. I would suggest that serious writers, no matter what they are writing, should be buying and reading an equal number of poetry books (not anthologies!), short stories (not exclusively anthologies) and novels.

Defining your process   As you revise, take notes on your revision process: what do you do first, second, third? As with drafting, understanding your work habits will help you evaluate your progress in the future and keep you from being unnecessarily self-critical. It may also suggest other possible approaches. Once you've listed the steps of your revision process, experiment with rearranging them and discovering what else might work. Always remember that the revision process, like the drafting process, will probably vary from time to time, story to story, day to day, and mood to mood.

Adjusting the volume   Try turning the volume of your story's central conflict up and down. Write pivotal scenes with exaggerated or minimized intensity, and see what happens. Ask questions: How extreme or subtle are the writer's methods of portraying characters? How high is the emotional pitch? How dramatic are the story's events? How striking is the imagery and description? How direct are the symbols? How outspoken is the dialogue? *Note:* remember that in many cases, a whisper is more emphatic than a scream. And once you've screamed, where do you go from there? Beware of overstatement—it weakens every point you use it to make. Save top emotional volume for the very top moments.

Improvising actions   Write what would happen if the characters in your story reversed their behavior—were silent instead of answering one another, opened the door rather than slamming it, and so forth. Notice the difference that even a small change makes to the emotional import of the moment and the scene. The key to this exercise is to open your mind, rather than remaining fixed on your original decisions. Try out a number of possibilities; they may lead you to more fully understand your story's emotional content.

The two best tools for self-editors are time and readers. When you find yourself unable to cut and shape your own work, remember first that there's nothing wrong with you that isn't wrong with all writers. Don't be harshly self-critical. Just admit that you need a little distance from the story before you will be able to see it clearly enough to shape it. If you can, put it away for a week or a month or six months. Then read it again, and you may find cutting and shaping much easier to do. If that doesn't work or you don't have time, create some objectivity for yourself by giving your story to a reader you trust, and asking where his or her attention wanders, and what seems extraneous. (See Chapter 11 for more specific suggestions about working with readers.) Though over time you'll probably find that you need readers less often, remember that the old saying is true: No writer ever completely outgrows the need for an editor.

Suggested Reading

The More Books and Stories section starting on page 496 provides complete bibliographic information for each title listed below.

Rachel Finkelstein, "Awakening"   George Orwell, "Politics and the English Language"

CHAPTER 11

Working with Readers

The writing of poetry can easily be an egotistical maneuver; maybe it often is. Maybe it almost always is. But the competitive exercise of any skill can be, often is, and maybe always becomes so: we must be alert to preserve the helpful, proper attitudes toward whatever we learn to do with fluency and grace.

—William Stafford

Whenever I had a gun in my hand I was always afraid to death that I would shoot you, and I daresay you were in danger.

—Editor Maxwell Perkins, in a letter to Ernest Hemingway

Why Other People?

Solitude is a need, and a lot of writers crave it more than most people. Some don't want college workshops, writers' groups, or "literary communities." To certain people at certain times, all that activity feels like poison. Some talented and disciplined writers are able to write alone, as this excerpt from Poe Ballantine's author's note in *Best American Short Stories 1998* attests:

> I am forty-two. College dropout. Live in a motel room. I generally move every year, but I am tired of moving and I like this room so I think I will stay another year. I have had lots of odd jobs, mostly cooking. I worked at the radio antenna factory just across the tracks for a while, then sold a couple of stories, so I quit March 5, and if I live on $400 a month and this wisdom tooth coming in doesn't knock the rest of my teeth sideways, I will be able to write until August.

But most people find that they can stand pure solitude for only so long. And in fact, the exceptionally talented writer quoted above received feedback and advice from editors with whom he corresponded—an extremely encouraging sign for a writer. At times, even the most self-sufficient authors find that isolation limits their perspective.

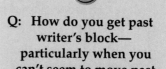

Q: How do you get past writer's block—particularly when you can't seem to move past a certain scene in the story?

A: Step away from your computer and occupy yourself with something else creative for a while. I like to listen to complicated lyrics when I am at a standstill. Singing or reading melodic poetry, paying attention to voice and instruments, helps to release tension. Take a short jog, or a nap, or doodle.

—*Lisa Marie Zambri, student writer*

All the words start to look the same, and self-criticism becomes difficult or even impossible, like trying to see your own face objectively in a mirror.

This creative vertigo is disconcerting but not unusual. It occurs particularly often early in writers' careers, when they need more feedback and may be more open to it. Frequently the confusion can be cleared up with the help of a reader. Like a change of scene when you're bored or tense, a fresh perspective can dispel the hopelessness and stagnancy of writer's block—it can get you out of a rut. Creative dialogue can be motivating, supportive, and stimulating.

This chapter will help you to prepare for that dialogue—for the experience of others reading and responding to your work. It will give you insight and the tools to draw useful criticism out of those who read your work. It will help you to develop the ability to ask good questions about your story and to use the answers that you receive, and to be a good reader yourself. It will provide suggestions to foster a positive atmosphere in writing workshops or groups.

The Reader's Part in the Story   The need for a touchstone aside, your work with readers will affect your voice—how you project your story to others. Have you ever overheard someone, maybe even yourself, talking to an imaginary audience? Because there is no actual listener to hear and respond, there's no real effort to communicate; the speaker and the listener are one. The posturing, the fierce self-concern, is marked and almost comic. The focus is on performance, not contact. It's a very different voice from that used in ordinary conversation—or even in a letter or other writing *to* someone.

This difference can sometimes be felt in even the best authors' writing if we compare their personal letters with prose meant for public consumption. The letters invite and engage; they're warm. This is because the letter-writing persona, if there is one, is usually very thin. In high school acting classes, they sometimes tell you to speak to a point on the far wall. But it's better when you speak to a person at the far wall. What's unique about a letter is that every bit of it is shaped by the writer's consciousness of the other person. So what is said and unsaid form patterns, like light and dark—a record of this particular moment of these writers' lives. A letter is an artifact, in a much more direct way than is fiction. The letter-writer looks toward the one written to, rather than back at her own reflection in the prose. In this subtle but profound way, the reader's existence means everything to the quality of the writing.

In ordinary conversation the speaker relies on the person listening to respond with verbal and visual clues. When comedians, actors, and musicians are performing well, they sustain a kind of dialogue or repartee with their audiences. When that rapport fails, we talk of the performer "dying." I know more than one teacher who—only half-facetiously—measures success in the classroom by the number of laughs from students. Virtually all teachers consider class participation, whether in the form of laughter, talk, or written comments, an important indicator of their ability to connect with students. Writers need cues, too. The way in which you learn to interact with the two different kinds of readers—visible and invisible—will shape what you write or have written.

The Invisible Reader   The invisible reader (the imagined or eventual reader) acts as a sort of conscience that guides you as you write—an anticipated response from within. When you're working on something complicated or hard to understand, stop writing and instead talk, imagining that you're explaining to a listener—preferably, a specific person. This exercise, described in more detail at the end of this chapter (see p. 229), quickly clarifies what is essential and how to say it naturally. If you do it right, you'll be focusing on the anticipated reader rather than merely on the sound of your own voice.

The Actual Reader   Later, by echoing and responding to the story during the process of writing and revising, actual readers can reflect and confirm your intent or suggest new possibilities—a response from without. When commenting on early drafts, readers may express confusion that can be traced to what you have omitted—what may be clear in your mind but not on the page. Conversely, you may inadvertently belabor a point. You may be oblivious of the fact that something you've written is funny (or not funny). A good reader will help you to more objectively see and hear what you've put on the page.

The question when to deliberately bring readers into the writing process depends upon the writer, the reader, and the story. The only real answer is, when you need to and when you can. Most people work more or less alone, sometimes for a long while, before they even begin actually writing a story. The poet Rainer Maria Rilke seems to have referred to this process when he wrote, "*Everything* is gestation, and then bringing forth." The gestational or prewriting period varies in quality and in length—an issue covered in more depth in Chapter 1.

Some people talk out ideas during this period, using long-suffering friends or lovers as sounding-boards. Other writers superstitiously avoid betraying the slightest amount of information about works in progress. Some abhor even thinking consciously about gestating stories, as if exposing the images to light would alter or destroy them. Still others are not even aware that anything is developing until the story appears. Most discover and evolve their process and methods as they go, and for most, some kind of rhythm also evolves, with the writer seeking readers' responses as often as is necessary to keep the work progressing. If you're very lucky, you will find readers whose stamina and sensitivity match your need for response.

The Anonymous Reader   When a story is published, anonymous readers continue in this work alongside authors. Even the reader who remains a stranger to the author ultimately becomes a kind of co-creator. Where the writer suggests, alludes, or understates, the reader is led to imagine, completing the picture. Where the writer asserts or demands, the reader may feel challenged to doubt or question, to seek proof. Much of writing well is

> **Q: How do you read someone else's story?**
>
> **A:** I'm trying to pay attention to all the details, all the sentences, in order to read as justly and mercifully as I can—because I think that is all we ever can do. Our readings reveal as much (sometimes more) about us as they reveal about the texts we read. Our readings always reveal us; our judgments reveal the judges we are.
>
> —*Bruce Jorgensen,*
> *writer and teacher*

knowing what to leave unsaid; learning to engage readers in the story; recognizing when writer, reader, and story have become one. Ultimately, the reader is a part of the book—the real story is a sort of collaboration, existing somewhere between writer and reader.

Writer and Readers: The Role of Writing Workshops   Aside from the creative issues, there are also some very down-to-earth reasons for working with readers. Writer and teacher DeWitt Henry offers these observations:

> The Maxwell Perkins or Edmund Wilson role continues to be as important for to-day's writers as it was for Fitzgerald, Hemingway or Wolfe, but it is to be found in writing programs and in literary magazine editing rather than with literary agents or in the publishing houses, small or large. As the literary editor has been replaced by the acquisitions editor in most mainstream publishing, the editor/writer relationship of nurturing and coaching talent has shifted to the relationship of mentoring writer and apprentice in writing workshops at both the undergraduate and graduate level. Similar teaching relationships are found in adult education centers and in writing conferences. Amy Tan, for instance, developed the material that was to become *The Joy Luck Club* over repeated visits to the Squaw Valley Community of Writers. This is especially true of short story collections and novels. Literary magazine editors on and off of college campuses also count for a reliable standard.

It's possible to hire "book doctors," freelance editors who, for a fee, will contribute expertise on technical or artistic issues as you revise a promising but unfinished manuscript. But most writers can't afford such services and so must rely on workshops, on writers' groups, and on each other for criticism and feedback. For all these reasons writing is more and more a cooperative if not a collaborative art. The networks and the communication skills that writers develop in school and later are often essential to their long-term survival. Group work can become an indispensable aspect of a writer's method, offering a welcome diversion from the sound of silence. In this chapter you will find a few suggestions about beginning and sustaining creative coworking.

Choosing Your Readers

This book is written with college-level workshop classes in mind. But whether or not you're in a class, you'll need to learn to recognize the people you should listen to most carefully. Showing someone a draft puts you at their mercy. It can be tempting to share your unfinished work only with people you know will understand it. But if you give them a chance, some of your best readers may turn out to be those whose personalities complement your own in various ways: where you're systematic, they may be intuitive; where you're detail-oriented, they can see the big picture; where you're emotionally involved, they may be more objective.

Because of such differences, you may find yourself initially resisting these readers' criticism. If you put their comments aside for a while, though, they often seem to grow increasingly insightful. Ideally, you may be able to work with the same readers through several drafts, responding to their comments as they respond to your story. Eventually, you may find that you already know what certain readers will say. The most useful criticism is the kind that teaches, and one of the best things writers can do for themselves is to learn to think like their best critics.

Working with Nonwriters: What to Look For   Don't despair if you don't know another writer who will read your work. You can learn to draw a useful reading out of anyone who is reasonably sensitive and communicative.

Choose your readers carefully, and think about what you want to know from them. Include a list of specific questions along with the manuscript. This is especially helpful when working with nonwriters, who may feel intimidated and unqualified to comment on your work. Clarifying the issues will help them respond coherently and specifically.

When working with inexperienced readers, you may sometimes need to disregard unsolicited and incorrect advice about punctuation, the specifics of description, or other technical matters. Ask questions that focus on emotional issues rather than technique:

How did you feel at certain key points in the story?

With whom did you sympathize?

Was this or that funny or sad or scary or suspenseful?

Where, if anywhere, did you get lost?

Nonwriters are sometimes better than writers at responding to basic emotional issues, because they're less likely to get distracted by your technique and can less easily decipher it and second-guess what you're trying to do. Careful, sensitive work with nonwriters can help keep you focused on the story's heart.

What to Ignore   Learn when not to listen to readers: when there is something basic about the manuscript that they don't understand—for instance, a page is missing or a detail has already been changed since you wrote the draft you gave them; when they propose a sweeping change that goes against the nature of the work (easier to recognize as you get more experienced); when they're clearly having an emotional reaction to you or to the subject matter or technique of your work rather than to the story itself. (Husbands, wives, and lovers may sometimes fit this last cat-

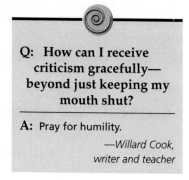

Q: How can I receive criticism gracefully—beyond just keeping my mouth shut?

A: Pray for humility.

—Willard Cook,
writer and teacher

egory.) Ultimately, you will learn to think as your readers do by listening, empathizing, and trying out their suggestions, and by working with them over time.

Reading Others' Work

As a member of a group or class, you will be giving as well as receiving criticism, and often the quality of the readings you get will depend on what you give. The most important thing is always to respond. Follow the group's guidelines and give a well thought-out and substantive critique. If for some reason you're unable to do so on time, be sure to discuss this with the writer and arrange to hand in a written critique or to talk over the story at a later time. If you are unable to attend another person's workshop, always apologize, explain your absence to the writer, and return the manuscript with written comments. Not everyone is sensitive about nonresponses, but those who are often take silence or absence as a slight.

How to Write a Good Critique   As you formulate your response, remember that almost any problem in a manuscript can be seen in two ways: as a flaw in the product or as a stage in the process. Treating incomplete manuscripts as the works in progress that they are shows respect for the writer's process and encourages hope for future drafts rather than despair over the current one. Acknowledge that you're commenting on a draft in progress, and that your suggestions constitute possible next steps rather than what the writer should have done.

As you consider your response, try, as novelist and teacher Jonathan Strong suggests, "to understand what the author is doing, better yet what the story is doing," and don't impose your own notions on either one. To be sure you understand, ask a question before commenting. This not only demonstrates respect for writers and engages them in the discussion, but it may clear up misconceptions and point out aspects of the story that need to be clarified or further developed. If writers are not allowed to speak during their workshops, summarize your understanding of what they're trying to achieve: "I can see that this scene introduces the main character and the story's central conflict, which is. . . ." That way, at least they will be aware of any fundamental misunderstandings.

Once you're certain that you have understood the writer's question, it is time to consider how to express your response. In writer and teacher Willard Cook's words, "The art of criticism is not about one's own ideas but the critic being sensitive to the writer and knowing when and how to say it so the writer can listen." Use your feelings to identify and express your criticism. (For example: This was funny to me; I felt confused here; I wanted to know more there; I found this scene terrifying; I wondered whether the character knew this or that.) Many writers value such emotional responses more than or at least in addition to suggestions about how to solve problems. Critics who can say what they felt as they read, and exactly where, can mirror what the writer has communicated, and in that way, without seeming to impose judgments or solutions, can help the writer to precisely identify problems.

> **Q: What makes good criticism?**
>
> **A:** Effective criticism requires both absolute honesty—which is a sign that you respect the writer—and absolute tact. You want the writer to leave the workshop with a feeling of possibility rather than failure. Be excited about the *potential* story you can glimpse in what the writer has done so far. Challenge the writer to ask more of the story, and convey your belief that he or she is up to the task. If you offer insincere praise for fear of offending someone, you're lowering the bar and encouraging mediocrity. Assume the other person wants to grow, not be patted on the back, and offer your comments accordingly.
>
> *—Kim Addonizio,*
> *poet and writer*

Taking notes as you read will allow you to be specific—page, paragraph, and line. Whether paying a compliment or expressing a reservation, always talk about particular scenes or moments in the story rather than merely making vague, frustrating generalizations such as "It just didn't work for me" or "This character was too extreme." Try more useful approaches: "When I got to the end, I still had these specific questions," or "I found myself not suspending disbelief when he ate the Goliath beetles." But don't harangue the writer by nitpicking. In general, leave the line editing on the page—don't use the workshop to publicly take the writer to task over punctuation or word-specific issues. It wastes the group's time, since presumably the teacher or workshop leader has already corrected these problems, and belaboring them can be humiliating to the writer.

The atmosphere of a workshop should be positive and enthusiastic—a tone of brainstorming or "jamming" rather than displaying erudition or critical acumen, or venting irritation. To the extent that the writer welcomes it, involve yourself in the writing process. While writers need to accept criticism in a professional manner, readers are equally responsible for giving it professionally—which means thoughtfully, keeping in mind that most people rightly have strong feelings about their work. Responding sensitively is not unprofessional, nor should it lower your critical standards. What, precisely, affected you as you read? Expressing criticism in terms of your own responses rather than the story's intrinsic qualities helps to avoid potential damage; although it's never safe to assume that a story is autobiographical, it is always wise to assume that it may be. Think out what you're going to say before you say it, and avoid sarcasm, jokes, and flip remarks, which can misfire. When things get intense, ask a question and listen to the answer.

The Abusive Workshop: What Not to Do

Everyone has heard or told this type of story. It happens regardless of the teaching method and sometimes even in the best of classes: a writer comes out of an intense workshop devastated, demoralized, angry, helpless. Outraged fellow writers present all kinds of theories about why—and what—has happened, and what could have possessed whoever did the damage. But really, nobody knows. It's like being in a dysfunctional family: the devastation is severe and there are no footprints. Abuse just seems to be in the air.

Unfortunately, "trashing" is a regular occurrence in some workshops. It can be hard for group members to understand why. The atmosphere is tense and fraught; everyone's ego is on the line, and confusing unwritten rules abound. There are many possible causes for toxic workshops. With or without realizing it, students may seek to please the instructor at the expense of each other, their work, or themselves. The instructor may be irritable or simply oblivious. There may be personality conflicts and other pressures among the writers. But whatever the cause, the results are the same. A complex and confusing subtext develops. A few people may benefit; many more are harmed.

No-Holds-Barred Workshops: Pros and Cons   Professors and even student writers sometimes justify such an uncontrolled critical atmosphere with John Wayne–style assertions like these: "It's a hard world out there in the literary jungle. You're going to get a lot of rejection before you ever see success. You better toughen up and get used to it." Of course, it's true that anyone who tries to publish can expect some rejection. But not everyone is hell-bent on publishing; it's not the only reason to write. In any case, why start the rejection when writers are freshmen or sophomores in college (or even graduate students)? That's like choosing to raise a child in a war zone.

People who come to a fiction writing class are there because they want to learn—not because they are already hardened professionals. In fact, I'm not sure it's ever a desirable thing to be a hardened professional. The defensive strategies to which writers sometimes resort in order to survive an abusive workshop—callousness, indifference, isolation, extreme detachment, overcompensation, destructive competitiveness, drug abuse—often amount to making oneself an insensitive, emotionally evasive person. These are not ultimately useful traits. Besides, the John Wayne position overlooks the fact that the relationship between professor and student—and that between writer and reader in a workshop—is not an equal one. When the balance of power is unequal, respectful boundaries must be observed or someone will get hurt. Trashing is *un*professional.

Self-Defense   There are definitely things you can do to avoid such incidents. Give other writers the consideration you'd like to receive. Be honest, respectful, and sensitive. Most negative behavior in workshops results from hurt feelings. In a few cases, writers have histories with each other, and this is something to consider about any workshop you join: are you comfortable? If not, can you cope? In other cases, a careless remark early on, a skipped workshop, or a story returned with inadequate or insensitive comments has led to retaliation. Even if you yourself wouldn't react to such things, it's in your interest and the group's to make an effort not to provoke others.

The Importance of Honesty   Trashing a story is unjustifiable, but the best alternative is not for the group to slip into vague denials like "Oh, it was good!" The best criticism, like the best writing, is specific and concrete. In everyday life, you get better results by saying, "When you use my car without asking me I get annoyed," rather than, "You freeloader!" or "Oh, that's okay. . . ." In a workshop, it's more constructive to say, "I've heard that phrase often enough that it doesn't affect me much," than to tell someone, "That's a cliché," or to repeat the notoriously avoidant and useless mantra, "Your piece flows well." *It is necessary not only to articulate the problem but also to communicate it so that the writer can understand, accept, and use it.*

It's perfectly possible, of course, to set and maintain high standards without hurting people. Each semester, when I ask my students to write about their worst fantasy of what their first workshop will be like (see the exercise beginning on page 225), the same two scenarios come up repeatedly: (1) Nobody will tell me what they really think, and (2) I will get trashed. No one wants either fate. But between these destructive extremes there is room for alternatives. Nearly everyone who joins a writing workshop really does want to learn. Most have defenses to overcome, but most also respond to a supportive atmosphere by loosening up a bit.

The Irritation Factor   Students, professional editors, and writing teachers often notice that they become annoyed and even outraged by what they perceive as other writers' inadequacies. There is something exquisitely irritating about errors that the reader (now) knows better than to commit, particularly when that reader is subjected to them manuscript after manuscript, semester after semester. To be fair, the readers who get the most annoyed are likely to be those who genuinely care about the quality of the writing. The irritation isn't always arrogance—it may mask despair or plain exhaustion.

But no matter how hard it may be, group members and teachers must remember that their purpose is to teach and help each other, not to vent frustration. What's required is self-control, empathy, and careful communication—remembering that most mistakes are innocent and will be willingly corrected once the writer understands. To encourage a constructive approach, I've sometimes used the exercise called "Barbara Cartland" (p. 224), in which the class first uninhibitedly critiques a piece of romance fiction, then rephrases the criticism more constructively. The long-term solution, though, is for all members of the group to commit themselves to an energetic and thoughtful exchange. Honesty and sensitivity are not mutually exclusive.

Exploration and Discovery: Preparing for Your Workshop

Whether you're enrolled in a class or working informally with other writers, this section will help you to develop questions to ask readers about your story. It introduces a visual method—a chart—to help you keep track of the problems that arise as you write, and to use them to develop questions. You can then use these questions to elicit helpful responses from readers during discussion of your work, and this will help you to form a plan for revising your story. This section also includes a checklist for working with readers, which summarizes this chapter's main points.

Ideally, your questions for readers should be attached to the end of each draft you distribute. If your workshop allows you to make a statement following the discussion of your work, you might consult the instructor about incorporating some of these questions. If that's not feasible, consider inviting a few readers for a mini-discussion of your story outside of the workshop. It's thoughtful and effective to do something in return: offer your readers dinner, and/or a reading next time they need one.

Another way of getting feedback is to arrange for a conference with your teacher or group leader. Some instructors invite students to discuss their stories privately after the workshop. This is a wonderful opportunity and an excellent chance to ask questions. Even if such an invitation is not extended formally, you can speak with most teachers during their regular office hours. This time is yours. You should never hesitate to use it to discuss your writing before or after your workshop. (Remember also that your teachers will appreciate your making an appointment in advance, and coming in with specific questions.) Occasionally, you may encounter instructors who are less forthcoming than you would like. Teachers don't always realize when they haven't answered your questions. Given the high cost of tuition these days, it's your right to further pursue minimalistic comments like "Good job!" or "Keep on working!"

Writers must learn to go after the responses they need. However you decide to do it, take the initiative to ask questions of readers. This is the first step toward engaging others in a dialogue about your work—an essential skill for writers. Once you've drafted your story, start thinking about how your readers can help you improve it.

Ask Yourself

Although charts might seem too structured for some writers, researchers have found that using such "graphic organizers" makes people more conscious of what issues and questions matter to them, and how they plan to proceed. In other words, a chart can help you to catch and save thoughts while they're still fresh. Many writers also find that solutions are evident once they have carefully formulated the problems. Try making a chart such as the one on page 218, and by the time you've finished the draft you're working on, you'll have a list of questions to ask readers. Use the questions and guidelines below as you fill out your chart.

- *What questions, doubts, fears, or hopes about your story passed through your mind as you wrote?* What were you thinking? What did you wonder? What problems or possibilities arose? Learning to identify and articulate self-criticism is the first step toward revision. Write these thoughts in the second column of your chart.
- *Where—on what page, what line, of your story did each question occur to you?* Write the page and paragraph in the first column of your chart.
- *Once you've charted your questions and when they occurred to you, revise them so that they clearly communicate your concerns and evoke helpful responses from your readers.* Write your revised questions in the third column of your chart.
- *Now that you've formulated your questions, what do you want in response—a detailed list of alternatives, an emotional reaction, brainstorming, something in writing?* If you give your readers practical ideas about how to help you, it's more likely that they will do so. Write your request in the fourth column of your chart.

Ask Readers

The next step, of course, is the workshop or discussion itself. How that goes will depend in part upon the discussion leader and others in the group. But there are some things that you can do to make the most of your workshop:

- *Before you begin questioning, refresh readers' memories.* They may not have looked at the manuscript for several days. Briefly summarize the story's events to ensure that they remember enough to comment accurately. Or, ask another member of the group to summarize the story's main events. Knowing you may do this will keep them reading attentively. Even your instructor will be grateful for the recap. And you may be surprised to learn that your version of the story may differ from that of your readers—useful information, especially if you keep your mind open to new possibilities.

Reader Response Chart

Write the page, paragraph, and line you were working on when the question occurred.	Write the question exactly as it occurred to you.	Revise the question for use in class.	Add a request for specific kinds of help: lists, emotional responses, ideas, etc.
Page 11	Will readers get the ending (especially Duane—he's so spacy)?	If you were going to summarize the ending or to retell it to a friend, what would you say? Duane?	Please write one paragraph retelling the story's ending in your own words.
Page 5, paragraphs 2 and 3	Is the transition between scenes clear? Add indication of time elapsed?	On page 5, there's a break after paragraph 2, and a new scene begins in paragraph 3. Were you confused by that transition? Did you need me to clarify how much time has elapsed?	Please reread paragraphs 2 and 3 on page 5, and tell me how much time you think elapses between these two scenes.
Throughout	Will readers be able to tell what's going on?	As you read, were there any places where you found you needed to reread sections because you were confused?	I'd like you each to write a one-paragraph retelling of the story's main events, and a one-sentence description of the central conflict.
Throughout	Are the characters believable?	How would you describe the main (or other) character?	Please make a list of the characters' traits.
Page 11 and throughout	Is my dialogue realistic? Is it punctuated correctly?	As you read the dialogue, did it seem to you that you could hear the characters' voices? What did those voices sound like? Could you tell who was speaking when?	Please go through the story and write beside each line of dialogue the name of the character who is speaking it.

218

- *Briefly set the scene for each question.* This will further orient readers and remind them of the material you're referring to, while giving them time to think before answering. For example, "If you remember, John is in the shower when Lily flings open the curtain and announces she's pregnant." It may also be helpful to read a paragraph or two of the story aloud. This will bring it back in a very direct way, focusing readers' attention on the sound of the story, something that can be overlooked in more theoretical discussions. Here are a couple of ways to use this technique:

  > "I'll read the last two paragraphs of the story aloud. After I finish, I'd like you to summarize what happened so I can evaluate how well it's coming across."

  > "As I read from page 11, please put away your copies of my story and listen for places where the action/speech/description sounds unconvincing or confusing."

- *Thoughtful, empathic questioning will engage readers not only in the story but also in your writing process.* Once you've listened to their first reactions or received them in writing, it's good to let others in on what you're going through as you work. Personalizing the question connects readers not only with the writer but also with the story. It allows them a sense of how you work, and encourages them to respond more thoughtfully and sensitively, with your writing methods in mind. Here are some examples of personalized questions:

  > "After I wrote the ending, it was hard for me to know whether other people would see what's clear to me. I'd like to ask you to summarize in a few sentences what you think happened at the end of the story."

  > "As a woman, I found it challenging to write from a male point of view. I'd like to focus on that as I revise. Were you convinced of the character's gender? Where did you find yourself doubting it?"

- *Avoid asking too many yes/no questions.* These provide a limited amount of information; this is why lawyers use them during cross-examinations to control what a witness is allowed to say. In a workshop, however, a writer will usually want to get as much information as possible by allowing readers to respond in their own words. Think about the different answers that the following two questions might provoke:

  > Yes/no question: "Did you get the ending?"

  > Open-ended question: "How would you summarize who changed, and how, at the end of the story?"

- *Ask readers about their emotional responses to the manuscript:*

  > "As you read, were there places where you felt confused? Where?"

  > "Were there places where you felt tension, a desire to know what would happen next? Where?"

  > "Did you ever feel bored or that the story lacked tension? Where?"

"Do you remember having a mental image of the main characters? Could you describe them to me now?"

- *Direct some of your questions to specific readers or groups of readers:*

  "Duane, I was wondering whether you felt the ending was clear enough. Did any questions occur to you as you read it? What were they?"

  "I see that several people agree that the ending is clear. What about the rest of you? Did anyone have trouble? Duane? Where?"

- *Encourage specificity by being specific yourself:* "Let's flip through the manuscript page by page, and you tell me where I'm straining credibility. Here on page 1, where Sheila pushes Ed's car off the cliff. . . ." Or, you can read paragraphs or lines and ask what readers felt about a character at this or that point. At other times you may need to change the subject entirely. Ask for what you want:

  "I'd like to ask you briefly to glance again through the story and put an X by any places that confused you. Then we'll talk about them."

  "First I'd like to get a general response from everyone. Let's go around the group and each person summarize your reaction to the story in a few sentences."

  "Thank you for your comments about the transitions from scene to scene. I'd appreciate it if you would mark any places where you got lost. Now I'd like to turn to the issue of characterization. . . ."

- *Some questions are so broad that they are difficult to answer and will probably evoke silence from the class.* Here are some examples, with alternative versions to elicit more helpful criticism:

  "So, what'd you think?"

  Alternatives: "What did you think of the story's main character?" or, better yet, "Make a list of five words to describe the story's main character."

  "Did you like it?"

  Alternatives: "Flip through the story quickly and try to remember your first reaction when you finished it. Did you laugh? Cry? Yawn? Please sum it up in one sentence." If you're worried that some people will hesitate to respond honestly, try having them write their answers and pass them in anonymously.

  "Does it work? If so, why, if not, why not?"

  Alternatives: "When you got to the end of the story, did you feel that it had peaked and that the main character had changed significantly?" or "I meant for the ending to be funny. Did you laugh, or were you confused or unamused?"

  "I'd just like to know any parts that you thought didn't work."

  Alternatives: "Looking at the plot, is the story shaped well enough? Does the action peak as the climax is resolved?" or "What can I do to deepen the characterizations in the story?"

- *Withhold your intent when appropriate.* There are times—usually in the earliest stages of writing a story, or in the first few minutes of a workshop—when the writer may wish to discover what readers perceive in the story before revealing her own intent. Or, the writer may simply wish to keep an open mind about the story's possibilities. On these occasions, it can be useful to ask specifically for readers' impressions: "What do you see as the story's central conflict?" "In this scene, what (or who) changes?" "How would you describe the main character?" "Describe your feeling at the end of the story."

- *Reveal your intent when appropriate.* Once you understand how the story is coming across to readers, it will save a lot of time to be direct: "In this scene, Morris is mad at his mother, but he's trying to hide it. I want the effect to be comic but also to build up to the murder. Did it work as an emotional transition, or did you miss his anger?" By telling others what you were trying to achieve, you will make it relatively simple for them to evaluate how close you got to it.

- *Try not to assume the worst when readers don't answer you immediately.* When I first started teaching, I used to get scared when I'd ask a question in the classroom and get blank stares back. But usually it's all right—people just need a minute to think before they respond. Since some of your questions won't get immediate answers or will use up less time than you expected, it's a good idea to write more questions than you plan to use. You can ease awkward moments a little by talking more, avoiding point-blank questions, and instead letting listeners in on your thought process: "As I worked on the story it occurred to me that. . . ." Try offering several different angles on the question. This reduces the silent-thinking time, and it's more likely that you'll catch listeners' interest and trigger ideas if you give them more than one version of the question. Here are some examples:

  "I'm going to read a paragraph from the airport scene and ask you to write your emotional reaction to it—is it sad, exciting, scary?"

  "As I wrote the cafeteria fight scene I felt unsure about the level of violence. Were you with me, or did you find yourself feeling put off, annoyed, or distracted from more important things? Was it clear who did what and to whom?"

  "What is your mental image of the main character? Can you picture her? Can you hear her voice? What do you see and hear?"

- *Be prepared with three or four follow-up questions for each main question.* You may not get all the responses you need on the first try. Writing answers to your own questions can give you some ideas for follow-ups.

  Question: "I'm going to read a paragraph from the ending and ask you to write your emotional reactions to it—is it sad, exciting, scary?"

  Anticipated response: "It was kind of gory."

  Follow-up: "I wondered as I wrote whether the explicit violence would bother anyone. Did any of you find yourselves pulling back because of that?"

Follow-up: "Let's go around the room and each of you give me a one-sentence reaction."

Follow-up: "Please write some thoughts about your reaction."

Follow-up: "I personally found it funny. Did anyone laugh?"

- *You might ask a friend—preferably someone who's participated in workshops before—for help writing follow-up questions.* Discuss the questions you've written for the class. Notice where your friend is confused or draws a blank. Work on ways of clarifying the questions and focusing the follow-ups, using them to narrow the original question or to suggest another slant on it. Try to anticipate your worst scenario and how you could question readers further to turn it into useful information.

- *Talk over your questions about your story with the workshop leader before the workshop.* The leader can help you identify the issues that are important to you, anticipate class reaction, and design follow-up questions.

- *Consider areas you'd like to avoid or save for later.* If there is anything you particularly don't want to talk about, say so. Sometimes you may already know how to improve a scene and may not want to waste time during the workshop discussing it. Or, a scene may be too unfinished to discuss profitably, or you may need help elsewhere in the story. By closely defining the questioning, you may limit the feedback some, but you will focus the discussion. If you already have specific questions in mind, you should decide and communicate how you want to use your workshop time.

- *Listen to your readers.* Remember that any time you spend defending yourself is lost and may mean that you don't get to ask all of your questions. If you find it difficult to keep from reacting to criticism, try writing down verbatim any comment that particularly provokes or offends you or makes you want to explain. Wait at least a week. Then look at the criticisms again. Can you see ways of addressing them in the manuscript? If not, use them to design follow-up questions for your next workshop or conversation about your writing.

  Ask an open-ended question such as, "I noticed you wrote that the story was boring. Do you remember when you began to feel that way?" Listen to the answer, and write it down. Most people will respond to your openness by trying to be helpful. If that doesn't happen, it's almost certainly the reader's problem. Remind yourself that there will always be one or two people in a workshop who won't respond to or understand what you're trying to do, and next time, remember not to let them get to you. The same thing happens to published authors. Don't waste energy trying to persuade these people, and above all, don't retaliate—nothing will harm the tone of a workshop more.

- *Here are some approaches other writers have used during their workshops:*

  "I'm going to pass around a piece of paper. When it comes to you, I'd like you to write a one-sentence description of how you felt after reading the last line of my story. Then fold the paper over so your writing can't be seen, and pass it on."

"I'd like you to imagine my main character in another situation—taking a shower, or falling asleep, or negotiating a minor traffic accident. Write a brief scene describing what you imagine."

"For the next five minutes I'd like you to freewrite on the main character/the setting/possible plot complications, or other elements of the story."

"I'm going to go out of the room, and when I come back I will be the main character of my story. Please ask me some questions."

A Checklist for Working with Readers

No matter how well you prepare, a workshop is a stressful and demanding experience. Keeping in mind a few basic guidelines about using criticism will help you maintain perspective.

- *Consider the source.* Certain readers will intuitively understand what you're doing, while others will raise questions that don't feel relevant at this time or may even annoy you. Although some misconnection is inevitable, negative reactions to criticism are very often the writer's defensiveness. It's usually a mistake to simply dismiss criticism, and often those who "don't get it" turn out to be the most helpful readers.

- *If you feel you need space, open up or redirect the discussion.* In groups or workshops, consider the following techniques:

    "Would you mind writing that question on the draft? I want to think about it but because of limited time I'd like to bring up a few other things as well."

    "How do other people feel about that issue? Let's go around the room. . . ."

    "If I decide to revise the manuscript with respect to this issue, what are three ways that I could solve the problem that's been pointed out?" (Giving readers a number will encourage them to think of several possible solutions rather than arguing for one "correct" one.)

- *Resist the temptation to explain.* Although it is your right to redirect discussion when it wanders, be careful not to indulge in defensive speeches. Clarifying why you wrote what you wrote wastes the limited time that you have to get others' input; after all, the quieter you are, the more you will hear and learn. Try not to think of these discussions as debates to be won or lost but as times to gather ideas. You are free to accept or reject others' criticisms, but always remember: the real last word is the final draft of your story.

    Defensive reactions:

    "Well, I only put in the bosom-heaving because I wanted to be concrete!"

    "If you notice, I did explain that inconsistency on the previous page."

"Actually, it's a little-known fact that some Brazilian frogs are indeed white."

Nondefensive reactions:

"Let me ask you: What was it, specifically, about the bosom-heaving that bothered you?"

(Rather than dismissing the issue, this question opens up the discussion by asking the reader to be more specific.)

"Does the bosom-heaving itself bother you, or the fact that the character does it only in one place and not consistently throughout the story?"

(Rather than defending against the accusation of bosom-heaving, this question attempts to clarify the problem.)

"Thank you for your comment. Could I also ask you about the monsoon scene on the previous page?"

(This approach may be useful when you'd like to change topics without being abrupt.)

- *Never throw out a critical response.* In a workshop setting you will get a lot of emotionally laden information at once. It's good policy to deflect stuff that you're not ready for, but before you decide to take offense at a criticism or remark about your work, give it some time to incubate—it may become more reasonable. Even when you agree with a reader's comments, you're likely to see more in them once you've cooled off. If, after time has passed, you still feel ambivalent, though, don't hesitate to put some critiques on the back burner and work more actively with others.

- *Encourage continuity.* I learned this technique from one of my students, Chris Pickens: when you are fortunate enough to engage a reader through more than one draft, promote continuity and further dialogue by referring to readers' previous comments in your next round of questions; for example, "When we talked before, you suggested that I smooth out the transitions from scene to scene and make the verb tense more consistent. What do you think of my efforts in these directions? Should I keep working on these issues? If so, where?" This sort of back-and-forth turns critical monologue into dialogue and also helps refresh readers' memories after some time has passed.

Wordplay

Barbara Cartland   This exercise works well in a group. Read the following honeymoon scene from Barbara Cartland's *A Runaway Star,* a popular romance novel.

He came into her room to stand looking at her in the light of the candles that were lit beside the bed.

For a moment neither of them moved. Then he asked:

"You love me?"

"So much . . . so very much . . . my darling Virgil!"

She moved towards him as she spoke and put her arms round his neck.

He pulled her against him, kissing her in a way that she felt was different from the kisses he had given her before.

She knew without being told that everything that was sensitive and spiritual was aroused in him, besides a fire which was very human and at the same time purified by the rapture within his soul.

He took the necklace from around her neck and the stars from her hair.

Then as he held her mouth captive she felt his fingers undoing the back of her gown.

It slipped to the floor and her petticoats followed it.

As he kissed her neck, her shoulders, then her breasts, he said:

"My star, my one precious little star, your love shall lift me into the sky from which you came. I adore you, I worship you, but I want you!"

"I . . . want you . . . too," Gracila tried to say.

But there were no words in which to express the love which carried them as if on a shaft of starlight into the ecstasy of their own Heaven.

After you've read it, discuss the writing. Where does the prose affect you emotionally? Are there any places where the author seems to be overreaching—asking for an emotional response that the prose has not specifically earned? Be frank. Be honest. Don't hold back.

Now stop, and start over. Imagine that Ms. Cartland is present and that she, like all of us, wants to write the best story that she can. (This works well as a role-play, if someone is willing to take the part.) How can you explain the strengths and problems with this or any writing so that the author will understand, and will leave the discussion inspired to return to the story and improve it?

Workshop Fantasy I   This exercise is designed to prepare writers to discuss their work in a group setting: Write your best or worst fantasy of how your first workshop in your creative writing class or group will go. Include concrete detail and description to convey your fantasy vividly. Your Workshop Fantasy should be brief—no longer than two pages—and may be very serious, or comic. Whatever approach you choose, let your fears and hopes play out. Two examples by student writers follow.

Matthew Horvitz
Workshop Fantasy?

No one's in the room except me and eleven copies of my story. A school newspaper is lying on the huge rectangular conference table, out of place in this small room in the corner of East Hall. The intermittent hiss and knock of the water heating pipes reminds me this should have been an anti-perspirant day.

It's a quarter past, and the last latecomer finally eases the ridiculously tall and narrow door shut and looks around for a seat somewhere around the table. Everyone else, in perfect harmony, unzips their bookbags. "Hi, sorry I'm late," emanates from a black puffy quilted jacket, its owner trying to push through the doorway. Everyone exchanges overly happy and enthusiastic smiles. It takes a couple of tries and a blush for the latecomer to get his jacket untangled from the doorknob.

(continued)

A girl with red burns under her nostrils, a surer sign of winter's approach than houses dripping with blinking colored lights and shortages at Toys 'R Us, flips through the newspaper back to front. "My Horoscope says today is a 5!"

Why is she so excited? I've always been suspicious of optimists, especially on dark winter days like today. Wet leaves are stuck to the window and the tree trunks outside are black with moisture.

It's time to start class. The sweet stench of burnt popcorn drifts in from the graduate students' lounge, agitating my insides. Copies of the draft are passed around the table, and I outline questions for my classmates to consider while reading the work. My voice alternates between breathless cracking and phlegm-choked stuttering as I read my draft to the class.

Finally it's over. The door is slightly ajar. My muscles tense and a little voice in my head implores me to flee, but my sweat-soaked shirt is adhered to the wood seat back. I'm stuck here. Time passes and eyes dart around. No one is smiling anymore. They are done with the story, but don't look up at me. My heart slams against my chest.

A guy wearing a watch too big for his slim wrists politely shakes his head. "Um, I, like, well, I need a couple of minutes to think about the story. I can't go first."

The girl on the other side of me nervously taps her fingers against the table rhythmically. "Thanks, I guess it's my turn." She diplomatically tilts her head toward me, "It was nice, but I'm really confused about what's going on with this one."

The tone has been set as everyone takes their turn, basically repeating each other. "Why aren't the characters nicer?" a girl in an enormous cable-knit sweater throws at me. This English AA meeting is a disaster.

It's happening. My brain freezes and the left side of my body goes numb. I can't even mumble a response as I feel myself slipping out of the chair. The hardwood floors are thin in this old building and the speckled brown industrial carpet does little to soften the impact. Have you ever sat in a classroom and heard what sounds like the rumble of thunder overhead? That was my limp body.

"Matthew, it's time to go." I hear my professor's voice as she shuts the door behind her. I'm alone in the room again, lying in the middle of the table with my jean jacket covering me. I sit up. The drafts are neatly stacked on the corner. I grab one and read the comments at the end. My heart slams against my chest, this time with excited energy. Quickly I skim through the rest of the drafts' comments, surprised, noticing that not all of them are stark rejections. Then it hits me; the only disaster of the day is that I will forever be remembered as "that guy." You know, the one who fainted in English class and spent the entire period out cold in the middle of the room. Plodding through wet grass on the academic quad, I realize it's only Monday. Four more days until the weekend.

Kristen Bevilacqua
Workshop Fantasy Exercise

DO tell me if something doesn't sound right or make sense . . .

> . . . and **DO** offer advice on how I can improve these things.

DON'T tell me you "don't get it." Why do you think you don't get it?

𝔇𝔒𝔑'𝔗 let me use clichés / trite metaphors if they're hurting my story.

DO criticize when necessary.

DO tell me if you like something.

DO tell me if you hate something.

DON'T give me a canned review. I don't want to see the same comments on someone else's story.

DO correct mistakes' Spell checker is not God.

DON'T forget to tell me what's different or the same about my paper.

DO tell me if the pace of my story is okay.

Please, one last thing. DON'T tell me my story "flows well." I hate that. It's so abstract, so easy, and besides—my story is not a river.

Workshop Fantasy II   Read the following humorous piece by writer David Carkeet. Using it as a model, write a list of instructions, either humorous or serious, to the readers in your class or writers' group.

Dear Reviewer

To: Reviewers of novels
From: David Carkeet, novelist
Re: The things you do

If you don't know what's going on in the book, quickly send it back to the review editor so that someone else can get the assignment. Don't, of all things, go ahead and write the review.

Don't begin your review with a long discussion of a general truth and then get around to the book by and by.

Don't get all worked up just because you're reviewing a major writer. Don't pump up. Don't slobber. Don't write the history of the world. Forbidden words: "century," "decade," "era," "generation." Oh, and this one: "arguably."

Don't get stuck on what happens in the first thirty pages and give short shrift to the rest of the book.

Don't praise the author's style and quote an example. The example is part of a whole that your reader doesn't share with you, so it never looks as good as you say it does. You might as well whistle two notes of a melody. Don't quote any bad examples either. And don't quote any jokes. What I'm saying is don't quote anything.

Don't steal from the language of the book to make fun of the book. If the author describes a character as "initially fetching, but a let-down after a while," don't you quote it and say the same goes for the book.

Don't use this word to describe the author's style: "riffs."

Yes, the author is a person, but that's no excuse: Don't try to explain things by making guesses. Don't say this part of the novel is better than that part because it's closer to the author's experience. Don't you do that. Don't look at the author's previous publication dates and say she wrote this book too fast. Forbidden words: "I suspect."

Don't say all the writer's work thus far is just a prelude to this book. The opposite is also outlawed—damning the book because of where you think the author should be right now. Maybe, considered all by itself, it's a grand book. Forbidden words: "development," "growth," "disappointment."

If the book is a translation, don't call it "a good translation" unless you've read the original and compared the two. If you mean the translation is pretty, or grammatical, or handsomely punctuated, you may say that. Don't say it's good.

You are permitted, in the course of your reviewing career, to say about one author, and one author only, that he or she is "the most accomplished writer of our time."

Don't use this word to describe a character: "loopy."

Don't give away a single surprise of any kind, big or small. Don't say there is a major surprise at the end that you're being careful not to give away. You may say, "The book is surprising."

Don't laundry list the characters and their salient features. This may be fun for you, but it is tedious as all hell to everyone else.

Come to think of it, don't even say, "The book is surprising."

Don't write your review in the prose style of the novel you're reviewing. Use some other device to tell us that the book is so mesmerizing, so utterly hypnotic, that its enchantment lingers and befogs you, even now as you write. Use a declarative sentence. Don't you go jumping in the writer's river just because it's so pretty. If the writer's style intoxicates you, go dry out before you write the review. Then use your own style.

Don't use these words to describe the book's structure: "cobbled together."

Don't compare the book to anything. Don't compare it to another book. Don't compare it to a movie. Don't compare it to a meal.

Don't write a penultimate paragraph qualifying everything you've said, followed by a last paragraph that begins with, "Still" and reaffirms everything you've just qualified.

Don't stand out in any way. Stay back there where you belong. No, further back. Further still. Further. There.

When you finish your review, send a copy to the author right away. Ask for comments, so that you might improve your craft.

Readers writing   Once you've identified areas you'd like to improve in your story, you may want to use some of your workshop or discussion time to ask your readers to do a little writing. Try assigning them a brief exercise on an aspect of your story; for instance, a focused freewrite (p. 11) based upon a character or setting; an alternate ending; or any of the Wordplay exercises in this book. Asking them to write will focus their thoughts and give you individual feedback. Try some of these, or make up your own:

- Before we start talking, I'd like you to write down a one-paragraph summary of the story's main events.
- Without looking back at the story, write down everything you can remember about the main character/setting/central conflict.
- Write one paragraph about each of these questions: How might the central conflict have been resolved differently? How would the story be changed if it had been?
- Write a paragraph describing the main character's bathroom on a Saturday morning.

Internalizing your critics   Keep your marked-up drafts or, if they've been edited electronically, save them. Go over them carefully, and when you find readers whose advice is especially helpful, do what you can to keep working with them. If comments don't make sense, wait a few days or weeks or even months, and go over them again. After you've worked with good readers for a while, try asking yourself when you run into writing problems what advice they would give you. As you become more able to anticipate readers, you will need less from them and will become able to work more independently.

The imaginary reader   Try reading a draft aloud, imagining the reader's responses. You can try imagining a specific person whose opinion you would value or who might be likely to be critical in ways the story needs, or you can imagine a general audience. This exercise should help you keep readers in mind as you write, which will enliven your prose. A caution: there is a difference between writing to someone to communicate, and writing "for an audience." Attempts to manipulate or "psych out" your "audience" are likely to result in canned-sounding prose.

Silent readers   Read your story aloud to someone whose literary opinion you value. For the sake of this exercise, your listener's response doesn't really matter as much as your own; in fact, it's best if the listener doesn't say anything. Keep a pen in your hand and, as you read, put an X on the manuscript in every spot where you feel embarrassed, uneasy, or mortified, or that the listener might be bored, irritated, or confused. Forbid interruptions; and if you allow any comments afterward, first go back through the story and quickly write down the question or concern that prompted each of your X's. When you have finished, you should have a list of your doubts and hopes about the story. It doesn't matter whether these match the listener's perceptions. Keep the list intact for your workshop; you may add questions relating to the listener's responses if you wish.

Computer exercises   Print out your story. As simple as this may sound, holding your story in your hands and seeing the words on the paper will give you a new perspective. Many writers consider any draft incomplete until they've printed it out and revised it at least once. Try taking it one step further: write a story that you don't revise on-screen; *always* print your drafts, and *always* retype them. You'll find yourself paying attention to every word. (*Hint:* If you're really serious about this exercise, drag the electric typewriter out of the basement and find out what so many writers are talking about when they say it's still indispensable.)

Reducing it to plot   Ask readers to summarize your story in no more than four or five sentences. This is no way to describe a story, but it's a good exercise in seeing your story's shape, and in pinpointing miscommunications.

Suggested Reading

The More Books and Stories section starting on page 496 provides complete bibliographic information for each title listed below.

Ernest Hemingway and Maxwell Perkins, *The Only Thing That Counts*

Thomas Merton, *The Hidden Ground of Love*

Anais Nin and Henry Miller, *A Literate Passion*

Flannery O'Connor, *The Habit of Being*

Rainer Maria Rilke, *Letters to a Young Poet*

E. B. White, *The Letters of E. B. White*

PART FOUR

The Stories: An Anthology of Professional and Student Fiction

Compiling this anthology has been a pleasure. I've been able to include many of my favorite stories—the ones that make me say, "You have *got* to read this!" That delight was my first requirement for inclusion; the second was that each story should clearly demonstrate the elements of fiction discussed in Chapters 3 through 9. The anthology contains contemporary stories as well as classics, and also nine stories by undergraduate writing students. Each selection is accompanied by a brief introduction of the author, and by questions for further study.

Of course, you are free to read the stories as they're assigned in class or to devour them immediately. I have designated as "core stories" the eleven stories (and one essay) from which I've quoted most extensively in the other sections of this book. These are marked in the Table of Contents with an asterisk. The core stories include Robert Olen Butler's "Jealous Husband Returns in Form of Parrot," Joseph Connolly's "Hard Feelings," Andre Dubus's "A Father's Story," "Little Red-Cap," by Jakob and Wilhelm Grimm, Flannery O'Connor's "A Good Man Is Hard to Find," and Akhil Sharma's "Cosmopolitan." Core stories by students include Rachel Finkelstein's "Awakening," Seth Pase's "The Father," Jeannine Thibodeau's "Close," and Kelly Zavotka's "What Killed a Girl." Also in the core group is Brenda Miller's personal essay "A Thousand Buddhas."

Kim Addonizio

Kim Addonizio grew up in Bethesda, Maryland, and now lives in San Francisco. Among the jobs she has held are waitress, office temp, fry cook, portrait photographer, tennis instructor, attendant for the disabled, and college lecturer. She currently teaches writing workshops in the Bay Area and is on the faculty of Goddard College's low-residency MFA in Writing Program. She has a daughter, Aya Cash, who is currently in the BFA in Theater Program at the University of Minnesota.

Addonizio has written three books of poems: The Philosopher's Club, Jimmy & Rita, *and* Tell Me. *She also coauthored, with Dorianne Laux,* The Poet's Companion: A Guide to the Pleasures of Writing Poetry. *"Survivors" is taken from her book of stories,* In the Box Called Pleasure. *Addonizio writes, "In my work I'm interested in getting close to how our experience really feels. I want my poems and stories to have an emotional impact, and to connect with a reader. I'd like to move people the way really good music moves me: I feel, when I hear it, more deeply alive."*

Survivors

He and his lover were down to their last few T cells and arguing over who was going to die first. He wanted to be first because he did not want to have to take care of his lover's parrot or deal with his lover's family, which would descend on their flat after the funeral, especially the father, who had been an Army major and had tried to beat his son's sexual orientation out of him with a belt on several occasions during adolescence; the mother, at least, would be kind but sorrowful, and secretly blame him, the survivor—he knew this from her letters, which his lover had read to him each week for the past seven years. He knew, too, that they all—father, mother, two older brothers—would disapprove of their flat, of the portrait of the two of them holding hands that a friend had painted and which hung over the bed, the Gay Freedom Day poster in the bathroom, all the absurd little knickknacks like the small plastic wind-up penis that hopped around on two feet; maybe, after his lover died, he would put some things away, maybe he would even take the parrot out of its cage and open the window so it could join the wild ones he'd heard of, that nested in the palm trees on Delores Street, a whole flock of bright tropical birds apparently thriving in spite of the chilly Bay Area weather—he would let it go, fly off, and he would be completely alone then; dear God, he thought, let me die first, don't let me survive him.

How It Works

1. What does the first sentence tell you about the characters? What details did the author choose to reveal in this sentence, and what background information do they convey?

2. How would the impact of the details in the first sentence differ if the author had presented them in the first person, or from the point of view of the main character's lover, or from an omniscient rather than a third-person limited point of view?

3. Did this story affect you emotionally? If so, reread it and mark places where you reacted. Identify specific techniques that evoke emotion. How would you describe your feelings to the author?

4. Outline a full-length short story based on "Survivors." Which scenes would be played out and what material would be summarized by the narrator? What elements of fiction could you add? What would be gained by expanding this story? What would be lost?

Christine Baxter

Christine Baxter graduated magna cum laude from Emerson College in 1999. "If You Ever Want to Have a Fling," a story she wrote while in school, began as a first-person narrative but eventually wound up in the second person. "I didn't intend to write this piece in the second person," she has said. "It just came naturally as a way of distancing myself from a topic that was very personal and somewhat disturbing." Baxter has written several short stories and is currently working on two novels.

If You Ever Want to Have a Fling

You are a woman, not particularly attractive, not particularly ugly. You are neither thin nor fat, short nor tall. You are simply an average woman, walking out of a city building early in the evening. You make your way down the stairs and onto the uneven bricks of the sidewalk, your hand moving unconsciously to your skirt and easing the hem below your knees. You step to the right of the entrance and retrieve a cigarette from the pack in your bag. Hands slightly trembling, you fiddle with the matches, attempt to light one and fail.

Your eyes quickly dart around, taking in the lone man on the corner, the homeless woman rummaging through a garbage can, the two children hanging out of a window of the building across the street. And then your eyes fall upon the nun standing alone some ten feet away from you. She seems an odd addition to a college campus, though it is a city campus, but a non-religious one without a single church nearby. You notice the habit she wears, a light shade of blue and shaped like a tent that drapes long and unrevealing to the ground. The white band of the headpiece frames her face, and you see that she wears no makeup at all, her skin smooth and unmarked by any lines or creases. You might guess that her hair is brown, it would fit her features, but the long blue material completely covers her head. For all you know, her hair could be black or blonde, or maybe even a bright, fiery red. It could be short or long, straight or curly, or she might not even have any hair at all.

The sound of a deep voice pulls you from your thoughts. You are suddenly aware of your own obliviousness; your pulse catches in your throat. You realize how you must look standing there gaping at a nun, an unlit cigarette and empty matchbook shaking in your hand. But you see that it is an acquaintance, a cigarette lit and perched between his lips, the flame of a lighter in his outstretched hand.

You are driving in your car, somewhere just past New York City on the way from Pennsylvania to Boston. You slow down as you near the toll booth and your dog pops up from his sleep in the backseat, anticipating a walk as he always does when the speed of the car drops. You roll down the window, hold the dollar bill out and hand it to the man in the booth. He peeks into the car, smiles at your dog, and then turns his smile on you, revealing rows of gold fillings.

"Aaaah," he says, "two pretties." His smile widens and you smile back because he seems a relatively harmless old man.

"Thanks," you say and pull away from the booth. You drive a few miles at a good speed, your dog returning to sleep in the back, when you see the blur of red brake lights stretch out ahead. You slow and settle into heavy traffic, pressing the seek button on the stereo in search of a decent song. You give up, push the cassette into the tape player, and sing quietly along with Frank Sinatra. *Flyyyy me to the moon. Let me plaaaay aa-mong the stars. Let me know what spring is like on a-Jupiter and Mars* . . . A large Ford pickup truck pulls up close beside you, inches away from your car, and you think, *What the hell is this guy doing?* You glance up at him, the eyes staring back at you, the short blond hair in a military-like crew cut. He would be good-looking if it weren't for that stupid grin on his face. You turn your head away and try to ignore him, but he inches even closer to your car. You look again at him and he smiles, sticks his tongue out and moves it back and forth obscenely. You let out a sigh and shake your head, wondering if he knows how ridiculous he looks, wondering if this is the first time he's ever seen a woman in a car. You think about giving him the finger. If he had a smaller car, or you a larger one, you'd like to ram right into him like on some *Dukes of Hazzard* episode. Instead you attempt to move over a lane and away from him, but he only moves into the space you moved out of and pulls up close beside you once again.

Traffic lets up slightly and you try to drive away from him, but he changes lanes and comes up on the other side of your car. He's looking down at you, laughing, smiling, and leering. He does the tongue thing again, this time holding his fingers to his mouth in a V and wiggling his tongue between them. Annoyed, you try to speed away again and get up to a good thirty-five miles an hour. You try to concentrate on the road and not the man beside you, then slam on the brakes as the cars ahead come to a sudden stop. He has now gotten behind you, riding close on your bumper. You can see him in the rearview mirror, sitting forward in his seat and laughing.

Traffic lets up slightly again, just enough for you to weave in and out of the cars, but he sticks firmly to you. He pulls up real close on one side, then real close behind you, then real close on the other side, all the time laughing and smiling. Finally he gets in front of you and slows down as the cars whiz past. You shift to the right at the first chance, but he pulls quickly in front of you. He slows again and you shift left and just get past him. You speed away, see the truck gaining on you in the rearview mirror, and press harder on the accelerator. The signs come up first, and then the toll booth, and you know that you must stop. You slow down and he catches up to you, riding close again on your bumper. You stop at the toll booth, see the man, and hand him fifty cents.

"I know this is going to sound weird," you say, "but could you try and keep the guy behind me for a minute after I go? He's tailing me and just, y'know, acting stupid." The man looks at you for a moment, then smiles.

"Sure, hon."

The gate raises and you speed away, watching as the truck and the toll both turn to tiny indescribable dots in your rearview mirror.

You are walking down a city sidewalk late at night toward your car. You cut through the park, feet weary in their heels, a heavy bag weighing down your shoulder. The click of your footsteps echoes on empty walkways. And then you hear the noise, a rubbing sort of noise. Quickly glancing behind you, you see the dark figure in the moonlight, a man, following closely.

You think of a time, years ago, when you were vacationing with friends. The three of you were sightseeing, snapping pictures as you struck silly poses around statues in some foreign park. You were the first to see him, standing off in the shadows of some trees. In broad daylight he had his fly unzipped, his hand on his penis as he watched you. He watched you watching him and the movements of his hand quickened. Motioning to your friends, you gathered your backpacks and your cameras, his eyes following the three of you as you hurried off.

In the park now, your pace quickens. Glancing again over your shoulder, you see the hand at the crotch of his pants. Your grip tightens on the strap of your bag and you think of the pepper gas your mother made you promise to carry, the pepper gas that is now in the glove compartment of your car. The street opens up before you, beckoning with its bright lights and spattering of pedestrians. You swing around out and onto the sidewalk, exiting the park. A long rush of air, the breath that you've been holding, quickly escapes you.

Separated from him now by a four-foot wrought iron fence, you see him there, still following, lurking in the bushes. His face flashes in the street light just as you reach the car and you see the leer, the slight upturned curve of the lip, the tongue hanging loosely, the bulging of the eyes. Fumbling with the key, you open the door, lock it quickly behind you and sink into the bucket seat. Heart pounding, you tell yourself that you will never walk through the park alone

at night again, no matter how much longer it takes to go around.

You are walking down a foreign street late at night in the general direction of your hotel, giggling at something your friend just said, something that wouldn't be nearly as funny if you weren't so tipsy. You turn the corner and attempt to step around a man who stands in the middle of the sidewalk outside of a neon-lit bar. He moves in front of you, blocking your way as your friend continues on, still laughing.

"Du bist meine." He pokes you hard in the chest with his index finger. From the little German you know, you understand that he is saying *You are mine.* You look beyond him at your friend as she stops and turns around, the smile quickly dropping from her face. You try to brush the man's hand away and step around him, but he blocks your path again and lays his hand hard upon your chest.

"Du bist meine."

"Get away from me." You try to step back and away from him, but he grabs you by the shoulders, his fingers pressing hard into your skin. "Dumkopf!" you yell. It is the worst German word you know, meaning *Dumbhead,* and its effect is apparent as the man laughs in your face and continues to grab at you.

"Du bist meine."

Your friend jumps forward and reaches for him. She tries to pull him away, but he is far too big and far too persistent. He repeats the words again and your friend gets in between you and him. She tries to push him away, but he pushes harder toward you. You feel her falling back against you and then you feel yourself falling toward the ground, landing hard on your butt. He continues advancing toward you, pushing your friend with him, and repeating the words again.

"Heu!" He turns around as a man exiting the bar calls out and grabs his attention. There is a slur of German and then all you hear are angry voices shouting back and forth. Your friend reaches out her hand, helps you to your feet, and the two of you run off into the night, the shrill of your laughter betraying the fear that you feel.

You push through heavy glass doors, squinting in the sunlight. A voice calls your name and when your eyes adjust to the light you see two friends standing against the building. You walk over and join in their conversation.

"Are you coming with us Sunday night?"

"Yeah, I think so," you say.

"It should be a lot of fun. I hear there's going to be . . ." Your friend trails off midsentence and the three of you turn to the sound of a loud banging noise. There, on the corner, a man stands beside the large metal box that houses the traffic signal controls. He kicks it violently again and again, yelling obscenities at the box, then turns in your direction and stumbles up the street. You see your friends' eyes glaze over and their bodies grow stiff, as if concentrating hard on becoming invisible. You lean against the cool concrete of the building, feel it through the thin material of your shirt, and try hard to disappear as well. But you know that he will come up to you, and he does. He stops just inches away, swerving slightly from side to side, and thrusts his face into yours. His eyes are bloodshot, his face marked with cuts and scabs. You smell the sweetly rancid breath as he speaks in a gruff, slurring voice.

"I just wanted to tell you I think you're beautiful."

"Thanks," you mumble, but all you can think about are those heavy construction boots violently kicking your head in.

"I'm going up to Montana, you want to come with me?" He swerves again, this time threatening to fall against you.

"Thanks but I have school, classes, y'know."

"School! What the hell you want school for?" His voice rises loudly and you see your friends flinch in response. "I went to school once and they fucked me up, they fucked me up real bad. They taught me some bad shit. You don't need school."

You let out that giggle that you do when you're nervous, and try harder to sink into the concrete of the building, only trapping yourself against the wall.

"I just wanted to say I think you're beautiful. That's all." He grabs your hand in his and raises it to his lips. You feel the cracked skin, the bristle of his chin hair too long on your fingers. He finally lets go, turns and walks away, muttering under his breath. You hold your hand out and away from you, go back into the building and wash it in the bathroom sink.

"Parlez-vous Français?"

"Excuse me?"

"Parlez-vous Français?"

"No, no, English. Do you speak English?"

"Ah, w-where ees . . ." The man before you struggles with a few words in English, then continues in a rush of French that you do not understand.

"I'm sorry. I don't understand."

"S'il vous plaît. S'il vous plaît. Pleease." He gestures for you to come closer. You glance around at the street, then at your friend beside you. You both know what it is like to be a tourist in a foreign country so you inch closer.

"Habla Espanol?" Perhaps there is another language that could work.

"Sprechen Sie Deutsch?" your friend chimes in.

"No, no. Français. See. See. Loook." He pulls a map from his pocket and opens it before him, pointing to some destination. Your friend and you move closer, surrounding the man, and peer at the map. It drops to the ground and in an instant the man is reaching out both of his arms, grabbing on hard to one of your breasts and one of your friend's, and twisting the nipple between his fingers. You are too stunned to pull away, but your arm moves automatically, swinging your purse up and against the man's body. His hands drop to his sides and he turns, walking quickly away, his laughter trailing behind him.

You stand there staring after him, too astonished to move, too angry to say a thing. You feel the deep flush creep up on your face and the tears threatening to fall. You feel like a child again, on the lawn during the neighborhood block party as Mr. Gordon spotted you doing a handstand, his hands rubbing your ass, and you too young and confused to say or know a thing. And then you hear the words slung back at you, the words in perfect English without even a trace of a French accent.

"Thanks, ladies."

"Hey, were you here last week?" He holds the lighter out for you and you lower your head, your hand on his to steady the flame, and light your cigarette.

"No. How 'bout you? You've missed a lot lately."

"Yeah, I have a lot to tell you. I had a run-in with a Heineken bottle." It is an odd thing to say and you stare at him for a moment, picturing some barroom brawl with tattooed bikers and broken beer bottles.

"What happened?"

"Well, things just got to be too much, y'know. And I cut myself." He says it casually, one hand gently scratching the scruff on his chin, then moving up to the sandy brown curls on his head.

"You cut yourself? What do you mean?" You inhale from your cigarette and stare at him again.

"I cut myself. It's just something I do sometimes, but never this bad. I cut down to the tendon this time and had to go to the hospital, get stitches." He pushes the sleeve of his shirt up. A band of puffy pink skin, nearly four inches long, circles the top of his forearm.

"My God, I'm sorry." Instinctively you reach out and place your hand on his shoulder.

"Yeah, they kept me in a psychiatric hospital for a little while."

"Why?" you ask. "I mean, what happened? Why'd you do it?"

"Things just got to be too much, y'know, work and graduating and having to move. And I was really upset when you said you have a boyfriend."

You catch your breath. You can feel the guilt being forced upon you as he pushes the fallen sleeve up on his elbow, brazenly displaying the scar. You try to think how you might have led this guy on, this guy you've had a cigarette with once a week for five minutes over the past few months.

"Yeah, but I'm doing better now," he continues quickly. "I'm moving back home. And seeing a psychiatrist."

"That's good."

"And I'm just learning to say whatever I think." He looks down at the ground, shifts his feet in the dirt, then looks back up at you intently. "I know you have a boyfriend and all, but if you ever want to have a fling or anything, if you ever want to have a fling with me, let me know."

You let out that nervous giggle of yours, drop your cigarette to the ground and concentrate on squashing it beneath your shoe.

"I'm sorry. I don't mean to make you uncomfortable. It's just that when you asked me if I liked anyone in any of my classes I thought that was weird." He looks at you, as if ready to start a fight.

"But you were talking about how you wanted to meet someone. It just seemed a logical place."

"Yeah, but you asked me if I liked anyone in any of my classes and it just seemed weird. It was like, yeah, you."

"Oh." It is all that you can think to say, and you look away from him. You clasp your hands together to keep them from trembling and concentrate hard on how to get yourself out of this situation. You feel your mouth dry up, any response that forms in your head getting lost on the back of your tongue. And you feel your throat tighten with all those words that you cannot say and you begin to feel sick. You look around you at the traffic, the pedestrians, the trees, and then your eyes fall again upon the nun still standing alone some ten feet away from you. For just a moment you consider that maybe she isn't real at all, maybe just a figment of your imagination, a guardian angel of sorts. But just as soon as the thought hits you, it suddenly departs, and you think that if there really were a God the nun would step in somehow. You wonder how long she has been standing there, whether she's heard the conversation or not, and whether she's counting her blessings that she is who she is. You envy her just then.

"I meant what I said."

You feel the words pressing against you, weighing you down, but you keep your eyes on the nun. She turns from the traffic in the street and slowly comes toward you. The light blue habit moves stiffly with her steps, just barely revealing the shiny black tips of her shoes. The rest of her seems still, silent, but as she passes by a gentle smile floats across her lips. She walks into the building and is gone.

How It Works

1. Underline the details that describe the main character. What has the author chosen to show of her? What has she not revealed? What are the effects of these choices, and how would the story change if she had chosen differently?

2. Christine Baxter based some of the characters in this story on real people. One of those is the nun who appears at the beginning and end of the story. What does this detail from life add to the story? What techniques has the author used to integrate it into this fictional situation?

3. What similarities do the story's seven scenes share? How do they differ from one another? How does each scene build on the preceding ones to advance the story?

4. Were you able to suspend disbelief as you read this story, in spite of the demand (implicit in the use of the second person point of view) to imagine yourself as the main character? How would the story's impact be affected if Baxter had chosen to use a first or third person point of view? Rewrite a scene from this story in the third person. Now rewrite the same scene in the first person. What does the scene lose or gain when the point of view is changed?

Gina Berriault

Gina Berriault was born in 1926, the third child of Latvian and Lithuanian Jewish immigrant parents. She grew up in Los Angeles. Berriault wrote her first stories on her father's typewriter when she was in elementary school. Her formal education ended with high school, and as a writer she was self-taught. After her divorce, she supported herself and her daughter by writing and by working at various jobs, including short-term teaching, "uncredentialed social work," and waitressing. Berriault received a National Endowment for the Arts grant, a Guggenheim fellowship, an Ingram-Merrill fellowship, a Commonwealth Medal for Literature, and a Pushcart Prize. A collection of her short stories, Women in Their Beds, *won the National Book Critics Circle Award, the Pen/Faulkner Award, and the Rea Award for lifetime achievement in the short story. Prominent writers including Grace Paley, Richard Ford, Wright Morris, and Robert Stone admired her work, and Andre Dubus referred to her (along with Nadine Gordimer) as one of his "living gods." In 1984 she adapted one of her most famous stories, "The Stone Boy," for the screen. The resulting film starred Robert Duvall and Glenn Close. Despite four novels, nearly forty short stories, and the high regard of her peers, during much of her career she was overlooked by critics and anthologists, only beginning to be more widely recognized in the years before her death in 1999.*

Berriault's fiction treats complex social, emotional, and psychological issues with subtlety and delicacy, never losing its focus on the human soul. Her style is characterized by precise description and complex resolution. Although never didactic or polemical, her stories are true to a fine sense of social responsibility. She wrote, for instance, progressively oriented stories about women before the feminist movement became prominent; yet, she commented, "My stories about women's plights are stories about men's, inseparably." *Over and over, as writer Bruce Jorgensen has pointed out, "these stories invite us to bear the suffering of others." Berriault's explicit question is implicit in all of her fiction: "Do we slip away from the tragic world for a brief time and even for a lifetime by going about our assigned tasks while the deprived and the denied and the homeless are all around us, and in an inquisition chamber, somewhere, anywhere, one person, man or woman or child, is alone with the enemy of us all?"*

A Dream of Fair Women

Like a night sentry on the border between India and dream country, Singh, the restaurateur, watched her from the little lamplit bar, his post. Over six feet tall, he was made even taller by his emerald green turban, and his Nehru jacket was as white as Himalayan snow. Alma was the last waitress to arrive, and even though she was on time the near-miss must seem to him a portent of ruin. The most famous of roving gourmets was to be his guest this night, a man who would either place the restaurant on the map of the world or obliterate it with a few cruelly chosen words or no words at all.

The tiled cubicle restroom was still fragrant with the colognes of the other waitresses who, by arriving early and lighting the candles on all the tables, were like angels promising a celestial ending to this night. She slipped her costume on, drawing up the long cotton underskirt, smoothing the snug silk vest over her breasts, draping the red silk sari around her waist and over one shoulder, her hands weak with fear over her own night apart from the restaurant's night. While she was at work this night, her lover would take away his possessions—a simple task, there were so few. They had agreed that the most bearable time for both was when she was not there. All afternoon she had raged against the woman he was going to, and now she could not even clear her ravaged throat to see if she still had a voice. And he had held her, he had caressed her, his face confounded. He was like someone dispatched to the ends of the earth, with no idea of what was to happen to him there.

The sitar music began its nightlong spiraling from the stereo in the alcove next to the restroom. She folded her clothes into her canvas bag, carried her coat and bag to the employees' closet, and emerged into the opulent dark of the dining area.

Early diners waited at the bar, and over their heads he signaled her to escort them to their tables. His wife, Lila, the hostess, was in the kitchen, overseeing the preparation of the dishes to be set before the honored guest. A feast was in the making, created by the three silent Indian cooks, women of the same birdlike smallness, the same dark skin, their dark gray hair drawn back into a knot at the nape of their thin necks, their heads always bowed over their tasks.

The restaurant this night was more than ever like a stage, and, to Alma's eyes, unforgivably deceptive. Light from the candles within the faceted glass globes on the tables glided up and down the waitresses' saris and shimmered along their necklaces, turned ivory the waiters' white turbans, and glinted off the engraved brass trays, large as giants' shields, hanging on the walls. The candles set aglow the faces of the women at the tables, and she saw—more sharply than ever—how, tables apart, a room apart, women glanced at one another as if by

mistake, as if indifferently, to see who was most beautiful of all.

At the bar, Singh appeared more Indian than ever, drawn up to his full height by the advent of the famous gourmet. But only Singh and the two waiters and just one of the three waitresses were authentic. None of the patrons—she was sure—suspected that he was born on a dirt farm in the San Joaquin Valley and had never set foot in India, nor that both waiters, flawless as a maharaja's servants, were students enrolled in business administration classes, nor that the one Indian waitress—Kamala, aloof, remote—spoke street language in the kitchen, ridiculing the diners, and was a fervent belly dancer. The rest were impostors. She was one herself, her parents Chilean. Lila was from the Detroit ghetto, but Indian ancestry could easily be imagined for her large eyes, her prematurely white hair and dark skin, her thin little hands. Marlie was ghetto-born, too, but her silky, gold-flecked, flitting presence so mesmerized the patrons that two or three or four men dining together would loudly declare, for all to hear, that Indian women were the most beautiful in the world.

When Alma came to the bar with her little brass tray to order drinks, Singh was gazing out over the tables, losing his way by candlelight, his soft, dark face plump with desire.

"That woman at the corner table," he said. "What a face! Right out of those old movies where they come down those long, curving stairs to breakfast. Who is she? She looks familiar."

Every beautiful woman is always someone waited for and always recognized as someone seen before. Alma had never told him this notion of hers. For one reason, he wouldn't know what she was talking about, and, for another reason, she'd be confessing a bewilderment of her own.

"Remind me," he said, pouring drinks. "Remind me to tell you about a woman I knew in Texas. She looked like that. She almost died when I left. Why I ran out on her I don't know. I was just a dumb kid, knocking around. I thought I had my destiny to look after. She would've left her husband for me. A filthy rich oilman, but she would've left him. In my life nothing synchronizes."

On quiet nights, when his wife wasn't there, and when all the diners had left, then how many intimate things he told her about the women of his past, about what pleased them in bed, what subtle artistry of his. On busy nights when his wife was there, and after the restaurant doors were closed, then the departing waiters and waitresses would pretend not to see what was going on at the bar. Lila, on a stool, was bent low over the counter, fiercely accusing him of present affairs, past ones, and those to come, while he ranged within his small space like a tiger tormented by its keeper.

At the top of the stairs, Lila was welcoming the celebrated columnist, her face endowed by that guest with a brief flare of tender, pleading beauty. Alma, waiting at the bar for a glass to be filled, saw closely how affected Singh was by the famous gourmet—a man unexpectedly brisk, trim and gray, like an executive with no time or talent for savoring—and by his companion, another familiar beauty. Their presence stole away Singh's natural suavity, his air of reserve. He stepped out from behind the bar and, towering over the couple, shook hands with the man and bowed his head quickly to the woman, then gave them back to his wife, who led them to their table, her head high, her silk garments floating.

"What's her name?" he asked Alma. "She's an actress. I've seen her, but I can't remember which movie." With unusually hasty hands he concocted the third Pimm's Cup for her tray, fumbling the long slice of cucumber.

It was in those moments of their arrival that he first appeared to have lost his wits. Alma blamed the loss on the woman of shocking beauty and on the man who could either make or break the restaurant, but, as the evening wore on, the reason for his odd behavior began to seem not so simple. On other evenings he would wander among the diners, shaking hands with steadfast patrons and with celebrities he recognized— a violinist, a comedian, an opera singer—his eyes darkening to a degree in accord with the patron's significance out in the world, and he would chat for only the graceful length of time, longer for the lesser ones, shorter for the greater ones. But this night he remained behind the bar, gazing out to the couple at their table apart.

Hovering over the couple, Lila confided to them the ingredients of each dish as it was set down by their waiter, and the number of seconds, the number of minutes required for two and more ingredients to fuse perfectly.

"He won't talk to them," she complained to Alma in the kitchen, appealingly, as though Alma could persuade him, and resignedly, because the pain of this frustration was hers alone, and out she went through the swinging doors, followed by the waiter, bearing on his tray the evening's most elaborate offering, roast pheasant glazed with gold leaf, a bird of molten gold.

This hours-long homage to the famous guest recalled to Alma the Shah of Iran's great feast for select hundreds of the world's celebrities and dignitaries. The magazine had shown luxurious tents where they slept, and the banquet like no other, and the long parade of waiters bearing peacocks on trays, their fantastic plumage adorning again their roasted bodies. She felt scorn for this guest who was mesmerized by the food set before him and who seemed unaware of time and how it steals away every morsel, like a cunning beggar.

Eventually, Singh gave in. It was at the very end of the meal, which had become a celebration of the lives of the two guests, with gifts from the sea, from earth's black loam, from vine, from tree, from the perfumed air. He stood above them, gazing at the face of the gourmet, a face soothed by the many gifts but tantalizingly withholding gratitude, patches of lacy capillaries like a clown's rouge on cheeks and nose; and gazing, in turn, at the woman's lifted face and at her throat, that lovely channel down which all the bites had slipped, and at her body, languidly sloping under the weight of so much adoration. To Alma, glancing by, all the gifts seemed given to the woman in exchange for just the sight of her. Singh leaned toward them to catch their words of praise, but his face was mournful, as though he had come to confess the failure of his own attempts at a plenteous life.

At his nod, Alma brought out the woman's fur coat from the employees' closet where diners' priceless coats were hung. The woman had come prepared for San Francisco's cold, whipping fogs that often swept in on summer nights. It was customary, when diners were leaving, for Singh or Lila, or both, to signal Alma, if she were free, and she would come to help them put on their coats. The departing guests would stand with their backs to her, and if they were unfamiliar with the courtesy, their shoulders would stiffen; others would slip into their coats with affected ease as if their wraps were held up for them by someone invisible or by the world's esteem. But this extravagant night roused her resistance to this act that humbled her, and her arms refused to hold up the woman's coat. When Singh saw that she was in trouble, he took the coat from her and lifted it to the woman's bare shoulders. The woman turned her head toward him, knowing—Alma was sure—how pristine a profile of beauty appears, like a very brief and partial view granted to mortals. So close was that profile, he seemed to tire instantly.

They were the last to leave. Alma watched them go as she went among her tables, blowing out the candles. On his way out, the gourmet was introduced to the three Indian gentlemen, the restaurant's financial backers, all in dark suits. They stood up at their table, and, unsmiling, shook his hand, afraid perhaps that if they were to smile he might deceive them later. At the bar he was introduced to the restaurant's publicist, Patricia, who had induced him to come, but when she stood up from her stool she began to sway. She had drunk too much, celebrating his presence, and from a distance she appeared to be swaying with religious awe. Then they were gone.

A jostling wave of relief rose up in their wake, doing away with everyone's roles and with all glittering. The only light left was from the brass carriage lamps at the bar and the candles on the table where the three backers sat over their vegetarian delicacies. In this intimate dimness they gathered together for a little party.

Lila poured drinks and carried them to whoever wanted one, while Singh wandered among them, empty-handed, uncritical, uncommending, voiceless. Kamala unwound her green sari, pushed the elastic band of the long underskirt down below her belly, and began her dance. From the stereo rose her delirious music. She danced barefoot, her hands, her arms gliding desirously, her belly moving with many little leaps and undulations. Her husband, who often accompanied her home, came up the stairs and paused at the top, watching her, pleased and uncomfortable. The two waiters, now in their leather jackets, heads bare, feigned indifference.

Marlie, a faux fur jacket over her sari, sat at the low cocktail table, restlessly peeling her nail polish, lifting her eyes only to see if her lover had arrived—a young doctor who would take her to his apartment. Alma, her costume again in the canvas bag, stood close to the stairs. When the dance was over she would leave, and no one would know that she had left and that she had left alone.

"Where is your friend tonight?"

There was so much that was intimidating about Kamala's husband, a high school mathematics teacher—his precise words, his eyes demanding correct answers. He and Alma's lover had often sat together at the bar, waiting to escort their women home. If he were able to understand the garbled language of loss, she might be able to say to him, *I don't know where he is, he's with someone else but I don't know who she is and I don't know who he is anymore and I don't know who I am anymore, either, if I ever knew.*

"A sculpture class at the art school. They stay late," she said.

The three thin women from the kitchen slipped by, passing close to her, their work done, cheap sweaters, old coats over their faded saris. They said good night to no one and were noticed by no one as they went down the stairs and into the night.

Then Singh, among the few who were gazing at the dancer, toppled to the floor, striking against his wife, who fell with him. At once the waiters lifted her, and Marlie ran to the alcove to turn off the music. The three financial backers bent over the man on the floor, and one, still clutching his large white napkin, shouted Singh's name warningly, hoping to alarm him back to life and his responsibilities. When they stepped away, the waiters then knelt by him, softly calling to him, and one laid an ear to his chest and felt for a pulse at his wrist. Nothing. A napkin

wet with ice water was passed from hand to hand and spread over his brow, a jigger of brandy was touched to his lips, and when it was seen that he was far, far beyond these clumsy persuasions, they stepped away from him.

He lay on his side, his turban tipped, his white jacket twisted. Someone had removed his shoes, thinking that would relax him. His trouser legs had slipped up, and narrow shins were exposed above his black silk socks. On some nights after the restaurant closed, he had worn his turban, his Nehru jacket, out into the nightlife, a short walk away, visiting the bars and the amateur strip show, a presence so startling and impressive that people made way for him.

Wailing, Lila roamed the tables, flinging her arms out and crossing them against her breasts, over and over, a ritual of grief and disbelief. The publicist was sobbing, head down on a table. Alma, along with Marlie and Kamala, wept quietly in the kitchen. They had been fond of him, they had exchanged little jokes about him and he hadn't known why they were laughing.

No one left until he had been taken away, and then they left together, down the steps carpeted in persimmon. The cold of early morning broke the group apart. They went off to their cars, Lila to be driven home in her car by one of the Indian backers, the other two to follow in their car. Alma watched her walk away, a very slender woman in a long pale coat, her sari stirring around her ankles, losing its color to distance.

Alma was driven home by the waiter who had served the famous gourmet. At the restaurant he seldom spoke. Now in the car he said, "Terrible, terrible. I think he was only forty." The rest of the way he was silent.

When she entered the dark apartment she did not switch on a light, seeing well enough that her lover's possessions were gone and the apartment empty despite her own things solidly there. She lay down in her clothes, calling on sleep to postpone her confrontation with her own unsolvable loss. An hour later or a minute later she was wide awake, already sitting up. It was not loss lifting her from sleep, it was gratefulness that her lover, no longer there, was taken from her only by the dream, only by that.

How It Works

1. Writers often warn each other against "writing pretty." Is Berriault's description merely pretty, or does it have a purpose? How would the story's thematic and emotional content be different if the description were spare and plain?

2. Underline places in the story where beauty is depicted or alluded to. How do the story's events, descriptive detail, and structure embody this theme?

3. What is at stake on this night—for the narrator, and for Singh and his wife? What do the characters in this story lose? Underline places in the story that depict or allude to loss. How does Berriault express this theme?

4. Go to your own or someone else's place of work and take notes on the setting: the physical space, the people and their interactions. Try writing a story using this setting, or try adding it to a story you've already begun.

Robert Olen Butler

Robert Olen Butler's critically acclaimed fiction is characterized by graceful, precise language, a balance of comedy and pathos, and voices so clear that they seem to be heard rather than read. In the past twenty years Butler has written nine novels and two volumes of short fiction. His 1993 collection A Good Scent from a Strange Mountain *won the Pulitzer Prize for fiction. Butler's stories have appeared in such publications as* The New Yorker, Esquire, Harper's Magazine, Paris Review, *and* Sewanee Review, *and in four editions of* The Best American Short Stories *and seven editions of* New Stories from the South. *A recipient of both a Guggenheim Fellowship in fiction and a National Endowment for the Arts grant, he also won the Richard and Hinda Rosenthal Foundation Award from the American Academy of Arts and Letters and was a finalist for the PEN/Faulkner Award. Additionally, he was awarded the Tu Do Chinh Kien Award by the Vietnam Veterans of America for outstanding contributions to American culture by a Vietnam* veteran. *He teaches creative writing at Florida State University and is married to the novelist and playwright Elizabeth Dewberry.*

Jealous Husband Returns in Form of Parrot

I never can quite say as much as I know. I look at other parrots and I wonder if it's the same for them, if somebody is trapped in each of them paying some kind of price for living their life in a certain way. For instance, "Hello," I say, and I'm sitting on a perch in a pet store in Houston and what I'm really thinking is Holy shit. It's you. And what's happened is I'm looking at my wife.

"Hello," she says, and she comes over to me and I can't believe how beautiful she is. Those great brown eyes, almost as dark as the center of mine. And her nose—I don't remember her for her nose but its beauty is clear to me now. Her nose is a little too long, but it's redeemed by the faint hook to it.

She scratches the back of my neck.

Her touch makes my tail flare. I feel the stretch and rustle of me back there. I bend my head to her and she whispers, "Pretty bird."

For a moment I think she knows it's me. But she doesn't, of course. I say "Hello" again and I will eventually pick up "pretty bird." I can tell that as soon as she says it, but for now I can only give her another hello. Her fingertips move through my feathers and she seems to know about birds. She knows that to pet a bird you don't smooth his feathers down, you ruffle them.

But of course she did that in my human life, as well. It's all the same for her. Not that I was complaining, even to myself, at that moment in the pet shop when she found me like I presume she was supposed to. She said it again, "Pretty bird," and this brain that works like it does now could feel that tiny little voice of mine ready to shape itself around these sounds. But before I could get them out of my beak there was this guy at my wife's shoulder and all my feathers went slick flat like to make me small enough not to be seen and I backed away. The pupils of my eyes pinned and dilated and pinned again.

He circled around her. A guy that looked like a meat packer, big in the chest and thick with hair, the kind of guy that I always sensed her eyes moving to when I was alive. I had a bare chest and I'd look for little black hairs on the sheets when I'd come home on a day with the whiff of somebody else in the air. She was still in the same goddamn rut.

A "hello" wouldn't do and I'd recently learned "good night" but it was the wrong suggestion altogether, so I said nothing and the guy circled her and he was looking at me with a

smug little smile and I fluffed up all my feathers, made myself about twice as big, so big he'd see he couldn't mess with me. I waited for him to draw close enough for me to take off the tip of his finger.

But she intervened. Those nut-brown eyes were before me and she said, "I want him."

And that's how I ended up in my own house once again. She bought me a large black wrought-iron cage, very large, convinced by some young guy who clerked in the bird department and who took her aside and made his voice go much too soft when he was doing the selling job. The meat packer didn't like it. I didn't either. I'd missed a lot of chances to take a bite out of this clerk in my stay at the shop and I regretted that suddenly.

But I got my giant cage and I guess I'm happy enough about that. I can pace as much as I want. I can hang upside down. It's full of bird toys. That dangling thing over there with knots and strips of rawhide and a bell at the bottom needs a good thrashing a couple of times a day and I'm the bird to do it. I look at the very dangle of it and the thing is rough, the rawhide and the knotted rope, and I get this restlessness back in my tail, a burning thrashing feeling, and it's like all the times when I was sure there was a man naked with my wife. Then I go to this thing that feels so familiar and I bite and bite and it's very good.

I could have used the thing the last day I went out of this house as a man. I'd found the address of the new guy at my wife's office. He'd been there a month in the shipping department and three times she'd mentioned him. She didn't even have to work with him and three times I heard about him, just dropped into the conversation. "Oh," she'd say when a car commercial came on the television, "that car there is like the one the new man in shipping owns. Just like it."

Hey, I'm not stupid. She said another thing about him and then another and right after the third one I locked myself in the bathroom because I couldn't rage about this anymore. I felt like a damn fool whenever I actually said anything about this kind of feeling and she looked at me like she could start hating me real easy and so I was working on saying nothing, even if it meant locking myself up. My goal was to hold my tongue about half the time. That would be a good start.

But this guy from shipping. I found out his name and his address and it was one of her typical Saturday afternoons of vague shopping. So I went to his house, and his car that was just like the commercial was outside. Nobody was around in the neighborhood and there was this big tree in the back of the house going up to a second floor window that was making funny little sounds. I went up. The shade was drawn but not quite all the way. I was holding on to a limb with arms and legs wrapped around it like it was her in those times when I could forget the others for a little while. But the crack in the shade was just out of view and I crawled on along till there was no limb left and I fell on my head. Thinking about that now, my wings flap and I feel myself lift up and it all seems so avoidable. Though I know I'm different now. I'm a bird.

Except I'm not. That's what's confusing. It's like those times when she would tell me she loved me and I actually believed her and maybe it was true and we clung to each other in bed and at times like that I was different. I was the man in her life. I was whole with her. Except even at that moment, holding her sweetly, there was this other creature inside me who knew a lot more about it and couldn't quite put all the evidence together to speak.

My cage sits in the den. My pool table is gone and the cage is sitting in that space and if

I come all the way down to one end of my perch I can see through the door and down the back hallway to the master bedroom. When she keeps the bedroom door open I can see the space at the foot of the bed but not the bed itself. That I can sense to the left, just out of sight. I watch the men go in and I hear the sounds but I can't quite see. And they drive me crazy.

I flap my wings and I squawk and I fluff up and I slick down and I throw seed and I attack that dangly toy as if it was the guy's balls, but it does no good. It never did any good in the other life either, the thrashing around I did by myself. In that other life I'd have given anything to be standing in this den with her doing this thing with some other guy just down the hall and all I had to do was walk down there and turn the corner and she couldn't deny it anymore.

But now all I can do is try to let it go. I sidestep down to the opposite end of the cage and look out the big sliding glass doors to the backyard. It's a pretty yard. There are great placid maple trees with good places to roost. There's a blue sky that plucks at the feathers on my chest. There are clouds. Other birds. Fly away. I could just fly away.

I tried once and I learned a lesson. She forgot and left the door to my cage open and I climbed beak and foot, beak and foot, along the bars and curled around to stretch sideways out the door and the vast scene of peace was there at the other end of the room. I flew.

And a pain flared through my head and I fell straight down and the room whirled around and the only good thing was she held me. She put her hands under my wings and lifted me and clutched me to her breast and I wish there hadn't been bees in my head at the time so I could have enjoyed that, but she put me back in the cage and wept awhile. That touched me, her tears. And I looked back to the wall of sky and trees. There was something invisible there between me and that dream of peace. I remembered, eventually, about glass, and I knew I'd been lucky, I knew that for the little fragile-boned skull I was doing all this thinking in, it meant death.

She wept that day but by the night she had another man. A guy with a thick Georgia truck-stop accent and pale white skin and an Adam's apple big as my seed ball. This guy has been around for a few weeks and he makes a whooping sound down the hallway, just out of my sight. At times like that I want to fly against the bars of the cage, but I don't. I have to remember how the world has changed.

She's single now, of course. Her husband, the man that I was, is dead to her. She does not understand all that is behind my "hello." I know many words, for a parrot. I am a yellow-nape Amazon, a handsome bird, I think, green with a splash of yellow at the back of my neck. I talk pretty well, but none of my words are adequate. I can't make her understand.

And what would I say if I could? I was jealous in life. I admit it. I would admit it to her. But it was because of my connection to her. I would explain that. When we held each other, I had no past at all, no present but her body, no future but to lie there and not let her go. I was an egg hatched beneath her crouching body, I entered as a chick into her wet sky of a body, and all that I wished was to sit on her shoulder and fluff my feathers and lay my head against her cheek, my neck exposed to her hand. And so the glances that I could see in her troubled me deeply, the movement of her eyes in public to other men, the laughs sent across a room, the tracking of her mind behind her blank eyes, pursuing images of others, her distraction even in our bed, the ghosts that were there of men who'd touched her, perhaps even that very day. I

was not part of all those other men who were part of her. I didn't want to connect to all that. It was only her that I would fluff for but these others were there also and I couldn't put them aside. I sensed them inside her and so they were inside me. If I had the words, these are the things I would say.

But half an hour ago there was a moment that thrilled me. A word, a word we all knew in the pet shop, was just the right word after all. This guy with his cowboy belt buckle and rattlesnake boots and his pasty face and his twanging words of love trailed after my wife, through the den, past my cage, and I said, "Cracker." He even flipped his head back a little at this in surprise. He'd been called that before to his face, I realized. I said it again. "Cracker." But to him I was a bird and he let it pass. "Cracker," I said. "Hello, cracker." That was even better. They were out of sight through the hall doorway and I hustled along the perch and I caught a glimpse of them before they made the turn to the bed and I said, "Hello, cracker," and he shot me one last glance.

It made me hopeful. I eased away from that end of the cage, moved toward the scene of peace beyond the far wall. The sky is chalky blue today, blue like the brow of the blue-front Amazon who was on the perch next to me for about a week at the store. She was very sweet, but I watched her carefully for a day or two when she first came in. And it wasn't long before she nuzzled up to a cockatoo named Gordo and I knew she'd break my heart. But her color now in the sky is sweet, really. I left all those feelings behind me when my wife showed up. I am a faithful man, for all my suspicions. Too faithful, maybe. I am ready to give too much and maybe that's the problem.

The whooping began down the hall and I focused on a tree out there. A crow flapped down, his mouth open, his throat throbbing, though I could not hear his sound. I was feeling very odd. At least I'd made my point to the guy in the other room. "Pretty bird," I said, referring to myself. She called me "pretty bird" and I believed her and I told myself again, "Pretty bird."

But then something new happened, something very difficult for me. She appeared in the den naked. I have not seen her naked since I fell from the tree and had no wings to fly. She always had a certain tidiness in things. She was naked in the bedroom, clothed in the den. But now she appears from the hallway and I look at her and she is still slim and she is beautiful, I think—at least I clearly remember that as her husband I found her beautiful in this state. Now, though, she seems too naked. Plucked. I find that a sad thing. I am sorry for her and she goes by me and she disappears into the kitchen. I want to pluck some of my own feathers, the feathers from my chest, and give them to her. I love her more in that moment, seeing her terrible nakedness, than I ever have before.

And since I've had success in the last few minutes with words, when she comes back I am moved to speak. "Hello," I say, meaning, You are still connected to me, I still want only you. "Hello," I say again. Please listen to this tiny heart that beats fast at all times for you.

And she does indeed stop and she comes to me and bends to me. "Pretty bird," I say and I am saying, You are beautiful, my wife, and your beauty cries out for protection. "Pretty." I want to cover you with my own nakedness. "Bad bird," I say. If there are others in your life, even in your mind, then there is nothing I can do. "Bad." Your nakedness is touched from inside by the others. "Open," I say. How can we be whole together if you are not empty in the place that I am to fill?

She smiles at this and she opens the door to my cage. "Up," I say, meaning, Is there no place for me in this world where I can be free of this terrible sense of others?

She reaches in now and offers her hand and I climb onto it and I tremble and she says, "Poor baby."

"Poor baby," I say. You have yearned for wholeness too and somehow I failed you. I was not enough. "Bad bird," I say. I'm sorry.

And then the cracker comes around the corner. He wears only his rattlesnake boots. I take one look at his miserable, featherless body and shake my head. We keep our sexual parts hidden, we parrots, and this man is a pitiful sight. "Peanut," I say. I presume that my wife simply has not noticed. But that's foolish, of course. This is, in fact, what she wants. Not me. And she scrapes me off her hand onto the open cage door and she turns her naked back to me and embraces this man and they laugh and stagger in their embrace around the corner.

For a moment I still think I've been eloquent. What I've said only needs repeating for it to have its transforming effect. "Hello," I say. "Hello. Pretty bird. Pretty. Bad bird. Bad. Open. Up. Poor baby. Bad bird." And I am beginning to hear myself as I really sound to her. "Peanut." I can never say what is in my heart to her. Never.

I stand on my cage door now and my wings stir. I look at the corner to the hallway and down at the end the whooping has begun again. I can fly there and think of things to do about all this.

But I do not. I turn instead and I look at the trees moving just beyond the other end of the room. I look at the sky the color of the brow of a blue-front Amazon. A shadow of birds spanks across the lawn. And I spread my wings. I will fly now. Even though I know there is something between me and that place where I can be free of all these feelings, I will fly. I will throw myself there again and again. Pretty bird. Bad bird. Good night.

How It Works

1. Does the narrator convince you that he is a parrot? Underline descriptive details, emotions, and actions that create this impression. List the techniques the author uses to do so.

2. How does the nature and situation of being a parrot reflect the feelings of the jealous husband? What details are common to both situations? Compare this story with "A Very Old Man with Enormous Wings," by Gabriel García Márquez. In what ways do you think these authors might have responded to the frequently given advice to "write from their experience"?

3. This story is funny and also moving. Underline the humorous parts and the emotionally affecting parts. Do they ever overlap? How does humor function emotionally in this story? What can you learn from Butler's use of it here?

4. Pick a nonhuman subject—an animal, flower, place, planet, vehicle, toy—and spend fifteen minutes taking notes on it. In order to add depth to your description, return later and repeat the exercise. Write a scene from the point of view of this subject.

Raymond Carver

Born in 1938 in Oregon, Raymond Carver grew up in Yakima, Washington, the son of a poor family. Carver married when he was nineteen and soon had two children. Like that of Anton Chekhov, his literary mentor, much of his early writing consisted of short fiction and poems written to earn money. Carver has been credited with reviving realistic short fiction, which had suffered a period of decline as more experimental forms came into fashion. His stories about working-class characters have frequently been misunderstood. "I'm not talking down to my characters, or holding them up for ridicule, or slyly doing an end run around them," he said in a 1986 interview. "I do know something about the life of the underclass and what it feels like, by virtue of having lived it myself for so long."

Raymond Carver was a Guggenheim Fellow in 1979 and received two grants from the National Endowment for the Arts. In 1983 he received the Mildred and Harold Strauss Living Award, and in 1985 Poetry magazine awarded him the Levinson Prize. In 1988 he was elected to the American Academy and Institute of Arts and Letters and received an honorary Doctorate of Letters from the University of Hartford. He was awarded a Brandeis Citation for fiction in 1988. Carver lived in Port Angeles, Washington during the last ten years of his life. He died of lung cancer on August 2, 1988.

The Calm

I was getting a haircut. I was in the chair and three men were sitting along the wall across from me. Two of the men waiting I'd never seen before. But one of them I recognized, though I couldn't exactly place him. I kept looking at him as the barber worked on my hair. The man was moving a toothpick around in his mouth, a heavyset man, short wavy hair. And then I saw him in a cap and uniform, little eyes watchful in the lobby of a bank.

Of the other two, one was considerably the older, with a full head of curly gray hair. He was smoking. The third, though not so old, was nearly bald on top, but the hair at the sides hung over his ears. He had on logging boots, pants shiny with machine oil.

The barber put a hand on top of my head to turn me for a better look. Then he said to the guard, "Did you get your deer, Charles?"

I liked this barber. We weren't acquainted well enough to call each other by name. But when I came in for a haircut, he knew me. He knew I used to fish. So we'd talk fishing. I don't think he hunted. But he could talk on any subject. In this regard, he was a good barber.

"Bill, it's a funny story. The damnedest thing," the guard said. He took out the toothpick and laid it in the ashtray. He shook his head. "I did and I didn't. So yes and no to your question."

I didn't like the man's voice. For a guard, the voice didn't fit. It wasn't the voice you'd expect.

The two other men looked up. The older man was turning the pages of a magazine, smoking, and the other fellow was holding a newspaper. They put down what they were looking at and turned to listen to the guard.

"Go on, Charles," the barber said. "Let's hear it."

The barber turned my head again, and went back to work with his clippers.

"We were up on Fikle Ridge. My old man and me and the kid. We were hunting those draws. My old man was stationed at the head of one, and me and the kid were at the head of another. The kid had a hangover, goddamn his hide. The kid, he was green around the gills and drank water all day, mine and his both. It was in the afternoon and we'd been out since daybreak. But we had our hopes. We figured the hunters down below would move a deer in our direction. So we were sitting behind a log and watching the draw when we heard this shooting down in the valley."

"There's orchards down there," said the fellow with the newspaper. He was fidgeting a lot and kept crossing a leg, swinging his boot for a time, and then crossing his legs the other way. "Those deer hang out around those orchards."

"That's right," said the guard. "They'll go in there at night, the bastards, and eat those little green apples. Well, we heard this shooting and we're just sitting there on our hands when this big old buck comes up out of the underbrush not a hundred feet away. The kid sees him the same time I do, of course, and he throws down and starts banging. The knothead. That old buck wasn't in any danger. Not from the kid, as it turns out. But he can't tell where the shots are coming from. He doesn't know which way to jump. Then I get off a shot. But in all the commotion, I just stun him."

"Stunned him?" the barber said.

"You know, stun him," the guard said. "It was a gut shot. It just like stuns him. So he drops his head and begins this trembling. He trembles all over. The kid's still shooting. Me, I felt like I was back in Korea. So I shot again but missed. Then old Mr. Buck moves back into the brush. But now, by God, he doesn't have any oompf left in him. The kid has emptied his goddamn gun all to no purpose. But I hit solid.

I'd rammed one right in his guts. That's what I meant by stunned him."

"Then what?" said the fellow with the newspaper, who had rolled it and was tapping it against his knee. "Then what? You must have trailed him. They find a hard place to die every time."

"But you trailed him?" the older man asked, though it wasn't really a question.

"I did. Me and the kid, we trailed him. But the kid wasn't good for much. He gets sick on the trail, slows us down. That chucklehead." The guard had to laugh now, thinking about that situation. "Drinking beer and chasing all night, then saying he can hunt deer. He knows better now, by God. But, sure, we trailed him. A good trail, too. Blood on the ground and blood on the leaves. Blood everywhere. Never seen a buck with so much blood. I don't know how the sucker kept going."

"Sometimes they'll go forever," the fellow with the newspaper said. "They find them a hard place to die every time."

"I chewed the kid out for missing his shot, and when he smarted off at me, I cuffed him a good one. Right here." The guard pointed to the side of his head and grinned. "I boxed his goddamn ears for him, that goddamn kid. He's not too old. He needed it. So the point is, it got too dark to trail, what with the kid laying back to vomit and all."

"Well, the coyotes will have that deer by now," the fellow with the newspaper said. "Them and the crows and the buzzards."

He unrolled the newspaper, smoothed it all the way out, and put it off to one side. He crossed a leg again. He looked around at the rest of us and shook his head.

The older man had turned in his chair and was looking out the window. He lit a cigarette.

"I figure so," the guard said. "Pity too. He was a big old son of a bitch. So in answer to your question, Bill, I both got my deer and I didn't. But we had venison on the table anyway. Because it turns out the old man has got himself a little spike in the meantime. Already has him back to camp, hanging up and gutted slick as a whistle, liver, heart, and kidneys wrapped in waxed paper and already setting in the cooler. A spike. Just a little bastard. But the old man, he was tickled."

The guard looked around the shop as if remembering. Then he picked up his toothpick and stuck it back in his mouth.

The older man put his cigarette out and turned to the guard. He drew a breath and said, "You ought to be out there right now looking for that deer instead of in here getting a haircut."

"You can't talk like that," the guard said. "You old fart. I've seen you someplace."

"I've seen you too," the old fellow said.

"Boys, that's enough. This is my barbershop," the barber said.

"I ought to box *your* ears," the old fellow said.

"You ought to try it," the guard said.

"Charles," the barber said.

The barber put his comb and scissors on the counter and his hands on my shoulders, as if he thought I was thinking to spring from the chair into the middle of it. "Albert, I've been cutting Charles's head of hair, and his boy's too, for years now. I wish you wouldn't pursue this."

The barber looked from one man to the other and kept his hands on my shoulders.

"Take it outside," the fellow with the newspaper said, flushed and hoping for something.

"That'll be enough," the barber said. "Charles, I don't want to hear anything more on the subject. Albert, you're next in line. Now." The barber turned to the fellow with the newspaper. "I don't know you from Adam, mister, but I'd appreciate if you wouldn't put your oar in."

The guard got up. He said, "I think I'll come back for my cut later. Right now the company leaves something to be desired."

The guard went out and pulled the door closed, hard.

The old fellow sat smoking his cigarette. He looked out the window. He examined something on the back of his hand. He got up and put on his hat.

"I'm sorry, Bill," the old fellow said. "I can go a few more days."

"That's all right, Albert," the barber said.

When the old fellow went out, the barber stepped over to the window to watch him go.

"Albert's about dead from emphysema," the barber said from the window. "We used to fish together. He taught me salmon inside out. The women. They used to crawl all over that old boy. He's picked up a temper, though. But in all honesty, there was provocation."

The man with the newspaper couldn't sit still. He was on his feet and moving around, stopping to examine everything, the hat rack, the photos of Bill and his friends, the calendar from the hardware showing scenes for each month of the year. He flipped every page. He even went so far as to stand and scrutinize Bill's barbering license, which was up on the wall in a frame. Then he turned and said, "I'm going too," and out he went just like he said.

"Well, do you want me to finish barbering this hair or not?" the barber said to me as if I was the cause of everything.

The barber turned me in the chair to face the mirror. He put a hand to either side

of my head. He positioned me a last time, and then he brought his head down next to mine.

We looked into the mirror together, his hands still framing my head.

I was looking at myself, and he was looking at me too. But if the barber saw something, he didn't offer comment.

He ran his fingers through my hair. He did it slowly, as if thinking about something else. He ran his fingers through my hair. He did it tenderly, as a lover would.

That was in Crescent City, California, up near the Oregon border. I left soon after. But today I was thinking of that place, of Crescent City, and of how I was trying out a new life there with my wife, and how, in the barber's chair that morning, I had made up my mind to go. I was thinking about the calm I felt when I closed my eyes and let the barber's fingers move through my hair, the sweetness of those fingers, the hair already starting to grow.

How It Works

1. At what point in this story does the main character change? How would you describe that change? What techniques does the author use to convey it?

2. What events lead up to the main character's change? How are these events crucial to the change?

3. How did you feel when you read Carver's description of the barber's hands in the main character's hair? Trace your feelings to the words—what concrete details provoke the emotional response?

4. Without looking back at the story, write a brief description of the place. Now compare your description with Carver's. Does yours contain any details that are not explicitly described in the story? What about the story suggested these to you?

Anton Chekhov

Anton Chekhov is generally credited with having invented the modern short story. He was born in 1860 in Taganrog, Russia, into the first free generation of a family of emancipated serfs. While in medical school, Chekhov began writing fiction in order to support his parents and his brothers and sisters. Later, he devoted himself to a literary career. A subtle, understated writer, Chekhov was often misunderstood by Stalinist critics, and even by close friends. Although he was quietly activist, mostly through his work as a medical doctor and through the occasional anonymous editorial, Chekhov's fiction is concerned with individual people at a complex emotional and moral rather than an explicitly political level. Chekhov's subtlety, his attention to nuance, and his ability to illuminate his characters' souls make him a "writer's writer"; many contemporary fiction writers consider him unparalleled. His stories reflect his skill as a dramatist, his understanding of human nature, his fine sense of irony, and his steadfast acknowledgment of life's uncertainty and irresolution. Anton Chekhov died in 1904 of tuberculosis.

Gooseberries

translated by Ivy Litvinov

The sky had been covered with rain-clouds ever since the early morning; it was a still day, cool and dull, one of those misty days when the clouds have long been lowering overhead and you keep thinking it is just going to rain, and the rain holds off. Ivan Ivanich, the veterinary surgeon, and Burkin, the high-school teacher, had walked till they were tired, and the way over the fields seemed endless to them. Far ahead they could just make out the windmill of the village of Mironositskoye, and what looked like a range of low hills at the right extending well beyond the village, and they both knew that this range was really the bank of the river, and that further on were meadows, green willow-trees, country estates; if they were on the top of these hills, they knew they would see the same boundless fields and telegraph-posts, and the train, like a crawling caterpillar in the distance, while in fine weather even the town would be visible. On this still day, when the whole of nature seemed kindly and pensive, Ivan Ivanich and Burkin felt a surge of love for this plain, and thought how vast and beautiful their country was.

"The last time we stayed in Elder Prokofy's hut," said Burkin, "you said you had a story to tell me."

"Yes. I wanted to tell you the story of my brother."

Ivan Ivanich took a deep breath and lighted his pipe as a preliminary to his narrative, but just then the rain came. Five minutes later it was coming down in torrents and nobody could say when it would stop. Ivan Ivanich and Burkin stood still, lost in thought. The dogs, already soaked, stood with drooping tails, gazing at them wistfully.

"We must try and find shelter," said Burkin, "Let's go to Alekhin's. It's quite near."

"Come on, then."

They turned aside and walked straight across the newly reaped field, veering to the right till they came to a road. Very soon poplars, an orchard, and the red roofs of barns came into sight. The surface of the river gleamed, and they had a view of an extensive reach of water, a windmill and a whitewashed bathing-shed. This was Sofyino, where Alekhin lived.

The mill was working, and the noise made by its sails drowned the sound of the rain; the whole dam trembled. Horses, soaking wet, were standing near some carts, their heads drooping, and people were moving about with sacks over their heads and shoulders. It was wet, muddy, bleak, and the water looked cold and sinister. Ivan Ivanich and Burkin were already experiencing the misery of dampness, dirt, physical discomfort, their boots were caked with mud, and when, having passed the mill-dam, they took the upward path to the landowner's barns, they fell silent, as if vexed with one another.

The sound of winnowing came from one of the barns; the door was open, and clouds of dust issued from it. Standing in the doorway was Alekhin himself, a stout man of some forty years, with longish hair, looking more like a professor or an artist than a landed proprietor. He was wearing a white shirt greatly in need of washing, belted with a piece of string, and long drawers with no trousers over them. His boots, too, were caked with mud and straw. His eyes and nose were ringed with dust. He recognized Ivan Ivanich and Burkin, and seemed glad to see them.

"Go up to the house, gentlemen," he said, smiling. "I'll be with you in a minute."

It was a large two-story house. Alekhin occupied the ground floor, two rooms with vaulted ceilings and tiny windows, where the stewards had lived formerly. They were poorly furnished, and smelled of rye-bread, cheap vodka, and harness. He hardly ever went into the upstairs rooms, excepting when he had guests. Ivan Ivanich and Burkin were met by a maidservant, a young woman of such beauty that they stood still involuntarily and exchanged glances.

"You have no idea how glad I am to see you here, dear friends," said Alekhin, overtaking them in the hall. "It's quite a surprise! Pelagea," he said, turning to the maid, "find the gentlemen a change of clothes. And I might as well change, myself. But I must have a wash first, for I don't believe I've had a bath since the spring. Wouldn't you like to go and have a bath while they get things ready here?"

The beauteous Pelagea, looking very soft and delicate, brought them towels and soap, and Alekhin and his guests set off for the bathing-house.

"Yes, it's a long time since I had a wash," he said, taking off his clothes. "As you see I have a nice bathing-place, my father had it built, but somehow I never seem to get time to wash."

He sat on the step, soaping his long locks and his neck, and all round him the water was brown.

"Yes, you certainly . . ." remarked Ivan Ivanich, with a significant glance at his host's head.

"It's a long time since I had a wash . . ." repeated Alekhin, somewhat abashed, and he soaped himself again, and now the water was dark blue, like ink.

Ivan Ivanich emerged from the shed, splashed noisily into the water, and began swimming beneath the rain, spreading his arms wide, making waves all round him, and the white water-lilies rocked on the waves he made. He swam into the very middle of the river and then dived, a moment later came up at another place and swam further, diving constantly, and trying to touch the bottom. "Ah, my God," he kept exclaiming in his enjoyment. "Ah, my God. . . ." He swam up to the mill, had a little talk with some peasants there and turned back, but when he got to the middle of the river, he floated, holding his face up to the rain. Burkin and Alekhin were dressed and ready to go, but he went on swimming and diving.

"God! God!" he kept exclaiming. "Dear God!"

"Come out!" Burkin shouted to him.

They went back to the house. And only after the lamp was lit in the great drawing-room on the upper floor, and Burkin and Ivan Ivanich, in silk dressing-gowns and warm slippers were seated in armchairs, while Alekhin, washed and combed, paced the room in his new frock-coat, enjoying the warmth, the cleanliness, his dry clothes and comfortable slippers, while the beautiful Pelagea, smiling softly, stepped noiselessly over the carpet with her tray of tea and preserves, did Ivan Ivanich embark upon his yarn, the ancient dames, young ladies and military gentlemen looking down at them severely from their gilded frames, as if they, too, were listening.

"There were two of us brothers," he began. "Ivan Ivanich (me), and my brother Nikolai Ivanich, two years younger than myself. I went in for learning and became a veterinary surgeon, but Nikolai started working in a government office when he was only nineteen. Our father, Chimsha-Himalaisky, was educated in a school for the sons of private soldiers, but was later promoted to officer's rank, and was made a hereditary nobleman and given a small estate. After his death the estate had to be sold for debts, but at least our childhood was passed in the freedom of the countryside, where we roamed the fields and the woods like peasant children, taking the horses to graze, peeling bark from the trunks of lime-trees, fishing, and all that sort of thing. And anyone who has once in his life fished for perch, or watched the thrushes fly south in the autumn, rising high over the village on clear, cool days, is spoiled for town life, and will long for the countryside for the rest of his days. My brother pined in his government office. The years passed and he sat in the same place every day, writing out the same documents and thinking all the time of the same thing—how to get back to the country. And these longings of his gradually turned into a definite desire, into a dream of purchasing a little estate somewhere on the bank of a river or the shore of a lake.

"He was a meek, good-natured chap, I was fond of him, but could feel no sympathy with the desire to lock oneself up for life in an estate of one's own. They say man only needs six feet of earth. But it is a corpse, and not man, which needs these six feet. And now people are actually saying that it is a good sign for our intellectuals to yearn for the land and try to obtain country-dwellings. And yet these estates are nothing but those same six feet of earth. To escape from the town, from the struggle, from the noise of life, to escape and hide one's head on a country-estate, is not life, but egoism, idleness, it is a sort of renunciation, but renunciation without faith. It is not six feet of earth, not a country-estate, that man needs, but the whole globe, the whole of nature, room to display his qualities and the individual characteristics of his free soul.

"My brother Nikolai sat at his office-desk, dreaming of eating soup made from his own cabbages, which would spread a delicious smell all over his own yard, of eating out of doors, on the green grass, of sleeping in the sun, sitting for hours on a bench outside his gate, and gazing at the fields and woods. Books on agriculture and all those hints printed on calendars were his delight, his favorite spiritual nourishment. He was fond of reading newspapers, too, but all he read in them was advertisements of the sale of so many acres of arable land and meadowland, with residence attached, a river, an orchard, a mill, and ponds fed by springs. His head was full of visions of garden paths, flowers, fruit, nestling-boxes, carp-ponds, and all that sort of thing. These visions differed according to the advertisements he came across, but for some reason gooseberry bushes invariably figured in them. He could not picture to himself a single estate or picturesque nook that did not have gooseberry bushes in it.

"'Country life has its conveniences,' he would say. 'You sit on the verandah, drinking tea, with your own ducks floating on the pond, and everything smells so nice, and . . . and the gooseberries ripen on the bushes.'

"He drew up plans for his estate, and every plan showed the same features: (a) the main residence, (b) the servants' wing, (c) the kitchen-garden, (d) gooseberry bushes. He lived thriftily, never ate or drank his fill, dressed anyhow, like a beggar, and saved up all his money in the bank. He became terribly stingy. I could hardly bear to look at him, and whenever I gave him a little money, or sent him a present on some holiday, he put that away, too. Once a man gets an idea into his head, there's no doing anything with him.

"The years passed, he was sent to another province, he was over forty, and was still reading advertisements in the papers, and saving up. At last I heard he had married. All for the same purpose, to buy himself an estate with gooseberry bushes on it, he married an ugly elderly widow, for whom he had not the slightest affection, just because she had some money. After his marriage he went on living as thriftily as ever, half-starving his wife, and putting her money in his own bank account. Her first husband had been a postmaster, and she was used to pies and cordials, but with her second husband she did not even get enough black bread to eat. She began to languish on this diet and three years later yielded up her soul to God. Of course my brother did not for a moment consider himself guilty of her death. Money, like vodka, makes a man eccentric. There was a merchant in our town who asked for a plate of honey on his deathbed and ate up all his banknotes and lottery tickets with the honey, so that no one else should get them. And one day when I was examining a consignment of cattle at a railway station, a drover fell under the engine and his leg was severed from his body. We carried him all bloody into the waiting-room, a terrible sight, and he did nothing but beg us to look for his leg, worrying all the time—there were twenty rubles in the boot, and he was afraid they would be lost."

"That's a horse of a different color," put in Burkin.

Ivan Ivanich paused for a moment, and went on. "After his wife's death my brother began to look about for an estate. You can search for five years, of course, and in the end make a mistake and buy something quite different from what you dream of. My brother Nikolai bought three hundred acres, complete with gentleman's house, servants' quarters, and a park, on a mortgage to be paid through an agent, but there were neither an orchard, gooseberry bushes, nor a pond with ducks on it. There was a river, but it was as dark as coffee, owing to the fact that there was a brick-works on one side of the estate, and bone-kilns on the other. Nothing daunted, however, my brother Nikolai Ivanich ordered two dozen gooseberry bushes and settled down as a landed proprietor.

"Last year I paid him a visit. I thought I would go and see how he was getting on there. In his letters my brother gave his address as Chumbaroklov Fallow or Himalaiskoye. I arrived at Himalaiskoye in the afternoon. It was very hot. Everywhere there were ditches, fences, hedges, rows of fir-trees, and it was hard to drive into the yard and find a place to leave one's carriage. As I went a fat, ginger-colored dog, remarkably like a pig, came out to meet me. It looked as if it would have barked if it were not so lazy. The cook, who was also fat and like a pig, came out of the kitchen, barefoot, and said her master was having his after-dinner rest. I made my way to my brother's room, and found him sitting up in bed, his knees covered by a blanket. He had aged, and grown stout and flabby. His cheeks, nose and lips protruded—I almost expected him to grunt into the blanket.

"We embraced and wept—tears of joy, mingled with melancholy—because we had once been young and were now both grey-haired and approaching the grave. He put on his clothes and went out to show me over his estate.

"'Well, how are you getting on here?' I asked.

"'All right, thanks be, I'm enjoying myself.'

"He was no longer the poor, timid clerk, but a true proprietor, a gentleman. He had settled down, and was entering with zest into country life. He ate a lot, washed in the bathhouse, and put on flesh. He had already gotten into litigation with the village commune, the brick-works, and the bone-kilns, and took of-

fense if the peasants failed to call him 'Your Honor.' He went in for religion in a solid, gentlemanly way, and there was nothing casual about his pretentious good works. And what were these good works? He treated all the diseases of the peasants with bicarbonate of soda and castor-oil, and had a special thanksgiving service held on his nameday, after which he provided a gallon of vodka, supposing that this was the right thing to do. Oh, those terrible gallons! Today the fat landlord hauls the peasants before the *zemstvo* representative for letting their sheep graze on his land, tomorrow, on the day of rejoicing, he treats them to a gallon of vodka, and they drink and sing and shout hurrah, prostrating themselves before him when they are drunk. Any improvement in his conditions, anything like satiety or idleness, develops the most insolent complacency in a Russian. Nikolai Ivanich, who had been afraid of having an opinion of his own when he was in the government service, was now continually coming out with axioms, in the most ministerial manner: 'Education is essential, but the people are not ready for it yet,' 'Corporal punishment is an evil, but in certain cases it is beneficial and indispensable.'

"'I know the people and I know how to treat them,' he said. 'The people love me. I only have to lift my little finger, and the people will do whatever I want.'

"And all this, mark you, with a wise, indulgent smile. Over and over again he repeated: 'We the gentry,' or 'Speaking as a gentleman,' and seemed to have quite forgotten that our grandfather was a peasant, and our father a common soldier. Our very surname—Chimsha-Himalaisky—in reality so absurd, now seemed to him a resounding, distinguished, and euphonious name.

"But it is of myself, and not of him, that I wish to speak. I should like to describe to you the change which came over me in those few hours I spent on my brother's estate. As we were drinking tea in the evening, the cook brought us a full plate of gooseberries. These were not gooseberries bought for money, they came from his own garden, and were the first fruits of the bushes he had planted. Nikolai Ivanich broke into a laugh and gazed at the gooseberries in tearful silence for at least five minutes. Speechless with emotion, he popped a single gooseberry into his mouth, darted at me the triumphant glance of a child who has at last gained possession of a longed-for toy, and said:

"'Delicious!'

"And he ate them greedily, repeating over and over again:

"'Simply delicious! You try them.'

"They were hard and sour, but, as Pushkin says: 'The lie which exalts us is dearer than a thousand sober truths.' I saw before me a really happy man, one whose dearest wish had come true, who had achieved his aim in life, got what he wanted, and was content with his lot and with himself. There had always been a tinge of melancholy in my conception of human happiness, and now, confronted by a happy man, I was overcome by a feeling of sadness bordering on desperation. This feeling grew strongest of all in the night. A bed was made up for me in the room next to my brother's bedroom, and I could hear him moving about restlessly, every now and then getting up to take a gooseberry from a plate. How many happy, satisfied people there are, after all, I said to myself. What an overwhelming force! Just consider this life—the insolence and idleness of the strong, the ignorance and bestiality of the weak, all around intolerable poverty, cramped dwellings, degeneracy, drunkenness, hypocrisy, lying. . . . And yet peace and order apparently prevail in all those homes and in the streets. Of the fifty thousand inhabitants of a town, not one will be found to cry out, to proclaim his indignation aloud. We see those who go to the market to buy food, who eat in the daytime and sleep at night, who prattle away, marry, grow old, carry their dead to the cemeteries. But we neither hear nor see those who suffer, and the terrible things in life are played out behind the scenes. All is calm and quiet, only statistics, which are dumb, protest: so many have gone mad, so many barrels of drink have been consumed, so many children died of malnutrition. . . . And apparently this is as it should be. Apparently those who are happy can only enjoy themselves because the unhappy bear their burdens in silence, and but for this silence happiness would be impossible. It is a kind of universal hypnosis. There ought to be a man with a hammer behind the door of every happy man, to remind him by his constant knocks that there are unhappy people, and that happy as he himself may be, life will sooner or later show him its claws, catastrophe will overtake him—sickness, poverty, loss—and nobody will see it, just as he now neither sees nor hears the misfortunes of others. But there is no man with a hammer, the happy man goes on living and the petty vicissitudes of life touch him lightly, like the wind in an aspen-tree, and all is well.

"That night I understood that I, too, was happy and content," continued Ivan Ivanich, getting up. "I, too, while out hunting, or at the dinner table, have held forth on the right way to live, to worship, to manage the people. I, too, have declared that without knowledge there can be no light, that education is essential, but that bare literacy is sufficient for the common people. Freedom is a blessing, I have said, one can't get on without it, any more than without air, but we must wait. Yes, that is what I said, and now I ask: In the name of what must we wait?"

Here Ivan Ivanich looked angrily at Burkin. "In the name of what must we wait, I ask you? What is there to be considered? Don't be in such a hurry, they tell me, every idea materializes gradually, in its own time. But who are they who say this? What is the proof that it is just? You refer to the natural order of things, to the logic of facts, but according to what order, what logic do I, a living, thinking individual, stand on the edge of a ditch and wait for it to be gradually filled up, or choked with silt, when I might leap across it or build a bridge over it? And again, in the name of what must we wait? Wait, when we have not the strength to live, though live we must and to live we desire!

"I left my brother early the next morning, and ever since I have found town life intolerable. The peace and order weigh on my spirits, and I am afraid to look into windows, because there is now no sadder spectacle for me than a happy family seated around the tea-table. I am old and unfit for the struggle, I am even incapable of feeling hatred. I can only suffer inwardly, and give way to irritation and annoyance, at night my head burns from the rush of thoughts, and I am unable to sleep. . . . Oh, if only I were young!"

Ivan Ivanich began pacing backwards and forwards, repeating:

"If only I were young still!"

Suddenly he went up to Alekhin and began pressing first one of his hands, and then the other.

"Pavel Konstantinich," he said in imploring accents. "Don't *you* fall into apathy, don't *you* let your conscience be lulled to sleep! While you are still young, strong, active, do not be weary of well-doing. There is no such thing as happiness, nor ought there to be, but if there is any sense or purpose in life, this sense and purpose are to be found not in our own happiness, but in something greater and more rational. Do good!"

Ivan Ivanich said all this with a piteous, imploring smile, as if he were asking for something for himself.

Then they all three sat in their armchairs a long way apart from one another, and said nothing. Ivan Ivanich's story satisfied neither Burkin nor Alekhin. It was not interesting to listen to the story of a poor clerk who ate gooseberries, when from the walls generals and fine ladies, who seemed to come to life in the dark, were looking down from their gilded frames. It would have been much more interesting to hear about elegant people, lovely women. And the fact that they were sitting in a drawing-room in which everything—the swathed chandeliers, the armchairs, the carpet on the floor—proved that the people now looking out of the frames had once moved about here, sat in the chairs, drunk tea, where the fair Pelagea was now going noiselessly to and fro, was better than any story.

Alekhin was desperately sleepy. He had got up early, at three o'clock in the morning, to go about his work on the estate, and could now hardly keep his eyes open. But he would not go to bed, for fear one of his guests would relate something interesting after he was gone. He could not be sure whether what Ivan Ivanich had just told them was wise or just, but his visitors talked of other things besides grain, hay, or tar, of things which had no direct bearing on his daily life, and he liked this, and wanted them to go on. . . .

"Well, time to go to bed," said Burkin, getting up. "Allow me to wish you a good night."

Alekhin said good night and went downstairs to his own room, the visitors remaining on the upper floor. They were allotted a big room for the night, in which were two ancient bedsteads of carved wood, and an ivory cruci-fix in one corner. There was a pleasant smell of freshly laundered sheets from the wide, cool beds which the fair Pelagea had made up for them.

Ivan Ivanich undressed in silence and lay down.

"Lord have mercy on us, sinners," he said, and covered his head with the sheet.

There was a strong smell of stale tobacco from his pipe, which he put on the table, and Burkin lay awake a long time, wondering where the stifling smell came from.

The rain tapped on the windowpanes all night.

How It Works

1. Underline the descriptions of the setting in this story—those by the narrator and also those that are incorporated into the story's dialogue. Notice particularly how the char-acters interact with and are affected by the setting, including the weather. How would you describe the author's method in each case?

2. Chekhov's choice of title provides some focus for the story. What other titles might he have considered? Where are gooseberries men-tioned in the story, and what does this partic-ular choice suggest about the author's intent?

3. After watching his brother eat the goose-berries, Ivan Ivanich tells his companions, "There had always been a tinge of melan-choly in my conception of human happi-ness, and now, confronted by a happy man, I was overcome by a feeling of sadness bor-dering on desperation." Do you see this mix of feelings expressed and developed else-where in the story? What does it mean, in this story, to be happy? Find several places where Chekhov explores this question. How does he do it?

4. Take a scene you're working on and round out the emotion: add "a tinge of melan-choly" to happiness, desire to hatred, pity to anger, resentment to admiration.

Joseph Connolly

Joseph Connolly was born May 3, 1957, in Urbana, Illinois. He now lives near Boston with his wife, Joan, and their daughter, Emma. He is currently a stay-at-home dad. Connolly writes, "I began my college career as a religion major, because I thought I was going to be a Presbyterian minister. When I turned my attention to fiction writing, I had some trouble getting beyond the notion that a story should be preachy and important, like a grim sermon. My sense of humor was a leisure time toy, like my record collection and my jump shot. As a result, I didn't enjoy writing, and rarely wrote at all. The breakthrough, if it can be called that, came when I spent some time looking through old college notebooks and realized that the stuff I wrote when I was just fooling around was fresher and more enter-taining than what I wrote when I was trying to be "se-rious." Writing "Hard Feelings" felt like a guilty plea-sure, because I'd allowed myself to let two of my favorite activities, laughter and basketball, into the story." Connolly has published one other short story, "Heinie Manush Tries for Third," which appeared in Elysian Fields Quarterly.

Hard Feelings

From the outside, a pick-up basketball game looks like nothing more than a bunch of guys playing a game, but if you've been in there, especially in there under the basket where most of the bumping and pushing go on, you know that every game is a jumble of little animosities and petty jealousies, and that at least two guys on the court flat out hate each other. It comes out in the banter and the force of the collisions and in whether a guy helps another guy up after knocking him down.

In our Sunday morning game at the King School in Cambridge, the two guys who hate each other are Neil Prentice and Frank Reposa. If they were closer in size, things might get ugly, but Neil is a little guy, about five-eight and skinny. Reposa is around six-four, two-twenty-five, and he does most of his banging on me. I'm not crazy about either of them, but I get caught in the middle because I invited Neil into the game. The only weapon he brings to the game is an ugly, old-fashioned set-shot. He holds the ball over his right shoulder, as if he wants you to compare it to his head, and then he pushes it up with his whole arm. Kevin Wolfe says he looks like he's trying to throw a pumpkin over a fence. It goes in with irritating frequency, and occasionally you'll hear some guy mutter that a shot that ugly shouldn't count.

Neil is a relative newcomer to our game. He's been playing with us for about a year and a half, and the rest of us have been at it for twelve. My wife, Sally, has suggested a few times that, at thirty-six, I'm going to have to start thinking about putting away the sneakers for good. I tell her I'll quit when she gets pregnant or when I blow out my other knee, whichever comes first. "Thanks, Mark," she says, "I'm glad to see I fit into the equation." Maybe I shouldn't joke about Sally getting pregnant, not when we're thinking about going to a doctor for help. Sally is thirty-five, and getting anxious. I'm not quite as eager as she is, I guess. Having a child would astonish me. Sometimes I feel like I'm still a kid myself, that being an adult is just a face I put on in the morning with my jacket and tie. Even with a job that takes me all over the country and a house that Sally and I own, it all feels like a big game, like I'm playing grown-up. Sally thinks that's why I still play ball, because I don't want to admit I'm an adult.

Neil's girlfriend's name is Madelyn, but I call her the Madwoman. She met Sally at the food co-op and latched onto her the way unstable people sometimes do when they meet someone who is stable, patient, and kind. Madelyn thinks that anyone who hasn't been through therapy must be as screwed up as she was before she started. Sally is all right, I guess, because she saw a counselor for a while in high school after her parents were killed in a traffic accident. Madelyn is always using words like "wellness" and "empowerment," and she and Neil jump on every New Age or self-help bandwagon that comes along. Sally told me that Madelyn and Neil have masks they wear when they have arguments, real masks they made themselves with paint and papier-mâché. They call them the Masks of Anger. I almost fell off my chair laughing, picturing the two of them wearing Punch and Judy masks and bitching at each other about who didn't balance the checkbook or whose underwear was all over the floor. Sally said it wasn't such a crazy idea; it was just a way of putting anger behind them when they were through fighting. Nothing's that simple, I said, and Sally agreed. Sally and I deal with anger in more traditional ways, which sometimes means we don't deal with it at all. We just get quiet for long stretches of time, then we get over it.

Anyway, I made my own mask by cutting a Jack-o-lantern face out of a paper plate. I keep it on my beside table, and I pick it up any time I want to announce a change in my state of mind. "This is the Mask of Horniness," I say, or "This is the Mask of Having to go to the Bathroom Real Bad." Sally laughs and tells me I'm mean.

I first met Neil and Madelyn at dinner at their place. In the car on the way over, Sally gave me a brief lecture about how Neil and Madelyn were different from the people I'm used to, and why certain kinds of humor might not go over. She should have said *any* kind of humor. Their apartment is decorated in the style I call Early College-kid. They say they don't care about material things, and it shows. There isn't much furniture, and what there is looks second-hand. The dining room itself, which doubles as a library, has brick-and-board bookshelves along one wall filled with every book on self-esteem ever written. The table is rectangular, like a conference table, and looming over it is the world's ugliest light fixture. A single white globe hangs from a wide, clear plastic bell that reminds me of the Cone of Silence on the old T.V. show *Get Smart.* Someone on the show would say, "Lower the Cone of Silence" and this thing would come down over them. It was supposed to prevent eavesdropping on their conversations, but instead it made them unable to hear each other, and they would sit there trying to shout and no noise would come out. We all sat down at the table, and I looked up at the light fixture and said "Lower the Cone of Silence." Neil and Madelyn both turned puzzled stares on me, and Sally wrinkled up her nose and shook her head.

Dinner was the predictable vegetable stir-fry with rice and herbal tea, during which Neil and Madelyn eagerly told us their whole emotional histories, their never-ending quest for what I believe they called "integration." After my Cone of Silence blunder I retreated into nod-and-smile mode. Sally, as usual, was gracious and engaged, and acted as if nothing could have fascinated her more than the dependencies and degradations of Madelyn's romantic history. Madelyn's hair is wild, reddish, and frizzy, and I couldn't help thinking it got that way from being so close to her brain. I don't mean to be callous; it's just that she seems so smug about her suffering. She believes we all have the same wounds, but that she and Neil are special because they *know* they are suffering, and the rest of us are kidding ourselves.

At one point, Madelyn asked Sally—not me, but Sally—whether I was "in touch with my feelings."

"I'm in touch with my parents," I said. "Does that count?"

Neil smiled, but Madelyn just kept looking at Sally, waiting for an answer. Sally, whose hair is straight and brown, and whose brown eyes are always calm, looked right at me and smiled.

"Mark thinks he can tough out emotional problems the way he toughs out his sports injuries," she said.

All three of them looked at me. I felt like I was on display, like a patient in a teaching hospital. They were all wondering if I could be cured. "I hate sports analogies," I said to Madelyn. "Don't you?" I succeeded in changing the subject; Madelyn began talking about how sports and sports talk are used to oppress women in the workplace.

Despite her professed dislike of sports, it was Madelyn's idea that Neil should join our Sunday game. She asked Sally to ask me to invite him, and I did, and I've been sorry ever since. He acts like he's an anthropologist among savages, analyzing every move on the court in terms of power relationships, psychic wounds, and lost connections to our fathers. The other guys don't have to listen to this stuff, but I get it when I pick him up before games and when I drive him home and on the too frequent occasions when Sally and I get together with the two of them.

"I've noticed," he said once, just before I dropped him off, "that you say 'My fault' a lot during the game." His little pop-psych lectures always begin with "I've noticed."

I said, "Yeah, what about it?"

"Well, I don't want to make a big deal of this, but it seems to me that 'fault' is a highly charged word."

"Oh, please," I said. "Look, if I start to cut to a spot, and my teammate passes to that spot and the ball goes out of bounds because I stopped cutting, my teammate looks bad because he's thrown the ball out of bounds. I say 'My fault' to acknowledge that my teammate has done the right thing. It's a courtesy."

He considered for a moment. Then he said, "Nobody else says it."

I pulled to the curb in front of his apartment and kept my foot on the clutch while I waited for him to get out. "I'm an exceptionally courteous person," I said.

I told Kevin about the sensitive-male spin Neil puts on everything, and soon Neil was being subjected to some fairly friendly ribbing from some of the brighter guys on the court. After a flagrant foul, Kevin might say "I sensed some hostility in that foul" or "You guys should hug now, to show there's no hard feelings." Reposa is not one of the brighter guys on the court, and it took him a while to figure out what was going on. Occasionally he would mutter something like "You guys have all turned into faggots all of the sudden." When he finally realized that Neil was the butt of these jokes he jumped in with both feet, and he wasn't friendly or subtle.

Reposa is simply an offensive person. Every Sunday morning, we go through the ritual of trying to make fair teams out of whoever's shown up that day, and every Sunday morning Reposa says we should play "guineas versus micks." I once made the mistake of pointing out that Neil is a WASP, and Reposa said, "The little fruit looks like a mick to me. You keep him." He goes out of his way to set illegal picks and knock Neil to the floor; if Neil's glasses stay on he'll say "Damn, I'll have to hit him harder next time." Even the other guys, who don't like Neil either, have told Reposa to lay off.

What puzzles me is why Neil keeps showing up. It's clear he hasn't been playing basketball his whole life, as the rest of us have, and I don't think he gets out of it what we get out of it. He wants to analyze everything, and I play to get away from analyzing, to get out of my brain. During the week, work piles up, bills come due, somebody cuts me off in traffic or some smelly drunk leans over me in the subway, maybe Sally and I get testy with each other over some little thing, and my brain takes all these little setbacks and passes them on to my muscles for storage. That's the way I see it. I don't know how it works, but I swear it's true: muscles have their own memory. Sometimes when Sally is giving me a back-rub she sticks her strong thumbs into a certain spot between my shoulder blades and tears well up in my eyes, tears Sally can't see because I'm face down on the bed, and I know she's disturbed the hiding place of some old, forgotten grief. For a moment, I get that lost-child feeling, like something dark and sad is looming over me, and I say "Not there" and she says "Does that hurt too much?" and I say "Yes." So when I play basketball, I'm trying to empty the week's tensions out of my muscles. It starts with the stretching I do before the game, bending and pulling until the knots come out and I feel loose enough to play. Then I put on the battle gear I need to hold my thirty-six year old body together—a leather brace for my right ankle, a leather and metal brace for my left knee, hundred and fifty dollar leather shoes. Sometimes some guy will shake his head and remind us of the cheap canvas shoes we all played in back in high school, when our bodies were light and quick and we moved up and down the court like a cluster of sparrows. Now we have thicker bodies and thinner hair, and our game is an earthbound game of cunning and collisions.

It's not a game for Neil. He doesn't have the strength, or the experience he needs to make up for his lack of strength. But every week he shows up, takes his punishment, hits a couple of his ugly set-shots, and presents me with his post-game psychoanalysis on the way home. He seems to enjoy it, so what the hell.

This Sunday morning I pulled my car into Neil and Madelyn's driveway and they both came out of the house, and Neil climbed into the back seat and Madelyn got in front.

"I'm coming to watch," she said, and smiled. I glanced back at Neil, and he gave me a kind of what-can-I-do shrug. I didn't say anything. There was no rule, spoken or otherwise, about bringing wives or girlfriends to watch our game. It's just that nobody ever did. If someone had to break that pattern, it didn't seem like Neil was the right person to do it. I also couldn't think of anyone who would be more out of place at our game than Madelyn. Our games aren't very pretty, and sometimes the talk gets a little raw. It was hard to imagine her having a good time.

The court in the downstairs gym at the King School is considerably shorter than regulation, but it's plenty long enough for a bunch of weekend athletes like us. There are no bleachers, so Madelyn had to sit in a little plastic chair

that was probably designed for a fourth grader. Things were quieter than usual during our pre-game warm-up. Guys were making furtive glances at Madelyn. Reposa, who was red-eyed and surly, kept looking back and forth between Neil and Madelyn, and you could almost see his little brain working, trying to find something obnoxious to say. The best he could do was "Bet she doesn't shave her legs."

"Why should she?" Neil said.

"Let's go," Kevin said. "Let's pick teams." In a minute, we were lined up, guineas versus micks, with Neil an honorary mick on our side. I don't know why, but suddenly I felt good. My first couple of shots went down, and I started to get that elated feeling you get sometimes when everything is coming together. Neil would probably say it was biorhythms. Reposa was covering me, and as soon as he broke a sweat a stale, boozy smell came off him. He smelled like a rug at a frat party. When you're in your twenties, you can stay out late and get hammered and still get up in the morning and make your body go, but the body of a man approaching forty is less forgiving. I decided to torture him. I ran everywhere, sprinting on transitions, running him off picks and through crowds, bumping him in the low post and then stepping out and hitting little ten-foot jumpers. When we weren't running, I was needling him about his smell.

"Jesus, Frank," I said, "when did they make Jack Daniels the breakfast of champions?"

"Shut the fuck up," he said.

"Hey," I shouted, "don't anybody light a match near Frank!" He started taking me under the basket and pounding me with his elbows, but his legs were pretty rubbery and he couldn't put much into it. We took a break after the first hour, and Reposa left the gym, probably to find a bathroom.

Neil spent the break sitting on the floor next to Madelyn, while the rest of us gathered around Mike Costa's cooler. Mike always brought a cooler full of juice and ice water. Madelyn was whispering something to Neil, and he was nodding and smiling. I couldn't help feeling we'd all just been reduced to caricatures—hulking, tribal males in a ritual of dominance. I wanted to walk over there and say "Look, it's a game. It's fun."

When we started again, Reposa was covering Eddie Monahan, and Mike Costa was on me. Mike is rangy and quick, and I knew I was going to have trouble scoring for the rest of the day. The guy who took up the scoring slack, to everyone's surprise, was Neil. He was hitting his shot, and he even started cutting through the lane like I'd been urging him to do for months. We started setting picks for him and feeding him the ball, giving him a chance to show off for his girlfriend. With about ten minutes left, I had the ball on the right side and Neil ran his man off a pick near the top of the circle and headed for the basket. I hit him with the pass, and as he turned to put the ball up, Reposa stepped over from the left side and clotheslined him—raked his forearm across Neil's face and laid him out flat. The lenses of Neil's glasses skittered across the floor.

"What the hell was that?" I shouted at Reposa.

"Weak side help," he said, and grinned.

It was Kevin, surprisingly, who went after Reposa, shoving him repeatedly and swearing at him. I ran over to get between them, but Reposa turned and walked away. "Fuck all you guys," he said.

Meanwhile, Mike Costa was tending to Neil. Neil's nose was bleeding, and Mike had gotten him up on his knees, bent over with his face in his hands. His hands were full of blood,

and blood spilled over onto the floor. Mike kneaded Neil's shoulders and whispered to him. I walked over, and Mike looked up at me. "There's a towel in my bag," he said.

I jogged over to Mike's bag to get the towel. Madelyn was standing with her toes on the out-of-bounds line, watching the scene on the court with an expression I couldn't quite pin down. It could have been fear, or anger, or contempt, and it might have been all three.

"It's just a nosebleed," I said. "He's all right." She turned her strange expression on me for a full second, then looked back out at the court. Hell, I thought, she looks that way most of the time.

The game was over. Reposa grabbed his stuff quickly and left without saying anything else. Neil had to stop up his nose with toilet paper, but other than that he seemed fine. Our games usually end with handshakes, and Neil isn't always included in the ritual, but on this day everybody shook his hand or patted his butt and said "Good game." He'd had a good game, too. It was probably the best he ever played.

When Neil went over to Madelyn to pick up his stuff, she put a hand on his chin and gave his face a good looking over, but the look on her face didn't change and she didn't offer any sympathy or express any concern. The drive home was quiet. Madelyn sat in back this time, and Neil sat up front with me.

"You had your shot going today," I said, to break the silence.

"Yeah," he said. "Yeah, it felt good."

I stopped the car in front of their house and they both opened their doors and got out. Neil looked back in at me.

"Good game," I said.

"Yeah," he said. "Good game." Madelyn closed her door without saying anything and went ahead of him to the house.

When I got home, I took four Tylenol capsules and sat down on the edge of the bathtub to take off my shoes and the braces on my ankle and knee. Sally stood in the doorway, leaning against the frame, and I told her what happened between Neil and Reposa, and about Madelyn's silence in the car.

"Why is Reposa such a jerk?" she said.

"I don't know. He's just a little man in a big man's body."

"Why don't you just tell him not to come anymore?"

I peeled off the knee brace and ran a finger along my surgery scar. "I'd love to," I said. "But he's been in the game from the beginning. It would be an awfully unpleasant scene."

"More unpleasant than what happened this morning?" This question was an example of what I once would have called "oversimplifying the situation" and Sally called "cutting through the crap." I had as much as admitted I'd rather confront Reposa physically on the court than emotionally off the court, and as long as I was on my post-game adrenaline high, that attitude felt right to me. I also knew the rightness of it would fade as the post-game ache invaded my muscles and joints. "No," I said. "You're right."

Then we just looked at each other. Women, it seems to me, aren't satisfied with just being right. Once they've established that they're right, they expect you to do something about it. Sally and I both knew I wasn't going to say anything to Reposa, that there would have to be more, and greater, violence before anybody thought to try to kick him out of the game.

"You're right, you're right," I said.

"Take your shower," she said, and she left.

About an hour and a half later, Sally and I were in the living room, reading the Sunday paper, when the doorbell rang. Sally got up to answer it. It was Madelyn, and she was crying.

Right away, Sally was comforting her, stroking her hair and asking her what was wrong.

"Neil hit me," she said, staring accusingly at me.

Sally steered Madelyn to the couch and sat her down. After a moment of silence, Madelyn announced that she wanted to be alone with Sally.

"Okay," I said, quietly, pushing myself with some effort out of my chair. I was sore now, and my knee crackled as I stood. "I guess I'll go for a drive." Sally just nodded at me, and I walked out the still-open front door, and closed it gently behind me.

I drove back to Neil and Madelyn's apartment. Neil didn't seem surprised to see me. His eyes were puffy and red, but I couldn't tell if it was from crying or from the shot he took from Reposa. He had a bit of a mouse under his left eye. We sat down at the dining room table, under the Cone of Silence, and Neil apologized for not having any beer.

"Madelyn says you hit her," I said.

He started to say something, then stopped. He looked defeated, which was not unusual for Neil, but now it was worse than ever. He shook his head and started out the window.

"Did you hit her?" I said. I thought of the tee-shirt Neil sometimes wore at basketball, a shirt with "Another Man Against Violence Against Women" emblazoned on the front. It always struck me as a kind of shallow boast, like saying you were against child molesting or something.

Neil seemed to be gathering the strength to make an assertion. It appeared to be difficult for him to paint a picture of reality different from the one Madelyn painted. I had to push him.

"Yes or no," I said.

"I did not hit her," he said.

"Why does she say you did?"

"Look," he said, and then he started to blush. "Look, Mark, do you know about the Masks of Anger?"

Oh Jesus, I thought. Yes, I told him, I knew about the Masks of Anger.

"Well," he said, "when I got out of the shower this afternoon, Madelyn was sitting here at the table, wearing the Mask of Anger."

I didn't laugh, and I didn't roll my eyes. I kept my faced fixed in a look of seriousness and concern, but the scene was comic to me, comic and sad. The poor bastard was not having a good day. First a big moron tried to rip his head off, then he'd had to stuff his nose full of toilet paper to keep from bleeding to death, and finally he gets out of the shower to find his girlfriend sitting at the dining room table with a damn mask on her face, a mask that, to him, meant he was in trouble.

"What was she mad about?"

"She said," he began, and then he had to take a deep breath. "She said she was disappointed in me for not standing up to Reposa."

"That's ridiculous," I said. Neil's face brightened. "What did she want you to do, take a swing at him?"

"She said I have to stop being a victim."

I sat there a moment, gazing up at the Cone of Silence. Then I remembered that my own paper plate mask was propped up against the lamp on my bedside table. Please God, I thought, keep Madelyn out of the bedroom. To Neil, I said "I take it Madelyn doesn't have a Mask of Mild Disappointment, and that's why she had to go straight to anger?"

Now Neil smiled. "That's what I said. I mean, that's not what I said exactly, but I said that I didn't feel that anger was an appropriate response. I asked her to remove the Mask of Anger." The careful language Neil always used made it sound like he was feeling his way

through life on emotional training wheels. "She said she wouldn't," he continued, "because she was angry. She was angry with me for being a victim and angry with herself, she said, because all the men she ever gets involved with are victims. Do you want some water?"

"Yes," I said. "Please." Neil popped out of his chair and went into the kitchen. Suddenly he was energetic and almost cheerful. I seemed to have offered him the opportunity to believe he might not be in the wrong, a belief I'm not sure he allowed himself. From the kitchen I heard the *shoosh* sound of bottled water being opened. He came back into the dining room with two glasses of water with ice and little lemon wedges in them. I drank half of mine, then set it down on the table.

"Look, Neil," I said, "if you didn't hit her, why is she saying you did?"

The phone rang. Neil jumped out of his chair again, this time looking nervous. Madelyn's suggested presence filled the room. Neil excused himself and answered the bedroom phone with a tentative hello. After a minute or so I heard him say that he was not a homeowner. "No, really," he said. While Neil struggled to get off the phone, I looked at the shelf full of self-help books and wondered what it would be like to be Neil. He has to walk pretty softly around Madelyn to make sure he doesn't tread too heavily on any of her emotional tender-spots. No wonder he seems nervous. One of the remarkable things about Sally is her tolerance. I don't have to feel like I'm living my life on tip-toe, the way Neil does. Then again, I don't always know when I've let Sally down. Neil finally got off the phone, and when he returned to the living room he apologized for the interruption. I asked him again why Madelyn said he hit her.

"I was just coming to that," he said. He sipped at his water. "I asked her again to take off the mask. In fact, what I said was—" He put down his glass with a thump. "Hell, I didn't feel like a victim today, you know? I played real well today. With her there watching, I played one of the best games I've ever played in my life. And just because some jerk whacks me over the head, I mean—I mean *screw* him! Screw Reposa! He's not worth the trouble."

"Right," I said. "Right on all counts." Neil gave me a look that seemed to ask if I really meant it, and I nodded yes, and he went on.

"So what I said to her—I said, 'I can't talk to you if you're going to wear that stupid mask,' and I reached out to take it off her face and she kind of moved her head to one side and—and I guess it could have seemed to her like I hit her, but I was only reaching for the stupid mask." He was crying now, not sobbing, just letting the tears run down his face. "I was only reaching for the mask." After another pause, he said, very softly, "I broke its nose."

I clapped my hand over my mouth and looked at the floor. I was going to lose it any second. I took a deep breath, then looked up at Neil and said, as solemnly as I could, "You broke the nose on the Mask of Anger?"

There was a short silence. Then a little smirk appeared behind the tears on Neil's face, and we both broke out laughing, Neil mixing his laughter with what might have been little sobs. We laughed for what seemed like half a minute, longer than we would normally laugh over a little thing like a broken mask. Then we were quite for a while. Neil got up and found himself some tissues. When he sat down again, he said "What would you have done? I mean about Reposa, if he'd hit you like he hit me?"

The truth was that Reposa would never pull a stunt like that on me, because he's a coward who picks on little guys. "I'd have done exactly what you did," I said.

Neil nodded. It was what he'd hoped to hear. "You know," he said, "it's easier for guys like you."

"I beg your pardon?"

"For big guys," he said. He was settling down now, and I was afraid he was about to give one of his wounded-male lectures. I was right.

He launched into a lengthy and obviously well thought out speech about how, on the playgrounds and in the gym classes and locker rooms of our youth, where guys like me were in training to become what our society calls real men, guys like him were in training to become our victims. He told me about the teasing and the torture he'd been through because he was small, because his arms and legs could never seem to come together to work in concert, because a ball thrown to him was as likely to hit him in the face as to land in his hands. I usually try to deflect or break up his lectures with jokes, but he'd had a tough day, and I figured he deserved a break. It struck me, as I sat there listening, that he wasn't using his usual ready-made phrases and other psycho-props. What he was saying didn't come from the bookshelf or from something Madelyn told him. He was talking about his life.

He got up in the middle of it to get us some more water. He handed me a glass and asked me whether what he was saying made sense. It wasn't a question he normally asked.

"It does," I said.

He went on to say that we—we, the big guys—always made it clear to everyone else that the world was ours, that all the women were ours, and that guys like Neil were lesser creatures who would be left with nothing but the things we didn't want. He even started to tell me there was a price I must pay for staying in the brotherhood of the big and the tough and the cool. Then I interrupted him, and said something that startled us both.

"It's fear," I said.

Neil had been looking out the window throughout much of his speech, but now he looked at me. "What's fear?" he said.

I put my glass down on the table and looked at the floor. I wasn't sure why I'd said what I'd said. I wasn't even entirely sure what I meant.

"Fear of emotion?" Neil said.

That wasn't it, and I felt a flicker of anger go through me at the suggestion. Then I realized what it was. It wasn't fear of emotion. It was fear of being treated the way Neil was treated, by Madelyn, by the guys on the basketball court, even by me. It was fear of having the woman you love scrutinizing your inadequacies and comparing you to other men whose inadequacies she can't see because she doesn't know them like she knows you. I had looked at Neil for a moment without the lens of contempt through which I generally saw him, and I'd found him sympathetic and, when he dropped the pop-psych talk, even insightful. But I didn't want to be him, or to live with the constant threat of humiliation he lived with. We—the big guys, as he called us—did what we did out of fear that at the first sign of weakness the whole world would turn on us and treat us the way we treated him.

"Fear of emotion?" I said. "I guess you could say that."

"Yeah," he said. "That's what I thought."

We sat quietly for a while. Finally I muttered something about how he and Madelyn needed to talk, and he said all they ever did was talk, and we both laughed. Then I got up to leave.

"If Madelyn's still at your place," he began, then shrugged. I offered to tell her his side of the story, and he thanked me. I wanted to ask him if she was worth the trouble, but it didn't seem like a nice question to ask, so I kept my mouth shut. As we walked to the door, I asked him if he hurt as bad as I did.

"How do you mean?"

"I mean your body," I said. "After we play, I feel like I've been hit by a truck."

"No," he said. "Actually, I feel pretty good." We stopped at the door and faced each other. "And I'm the one who got hit by a truck."

We laughed again, and then I shook his hand and wished him luck.

"You're a lucky guy," he said. "Sally is so easy to get along with."

"That's true," I said. I felt I should say something positive about his situation, something positive about Madelyn, and my mind raced through everything I knew about her. "Well," I said after a moment, "at least Madelyn's pretty clear about what she wants."

"Sally isn't?"

For God's sake, I thought, this is supposed to be a good-bye, and he's ready to open up another round of emotional show-and-tell. He was grinning the same way he does on the basketball court when he's thrown in one of his set-shots, as if finding a possible flaw in my relationship with Sally scored him a point in some little one-on-one I didn't even know we were playing. I'd actually started to like him a little, but I stopped liking him as suddenly as I'd started.

"Sally's fine," I said. "I gotta go." I opened the door and made my escape, promising to pick him up for basketball next Sunday.

I was feeling pretty irritable when I got in the car, but that's not surprising considering how my body felt. My muscles were begging me for Tylenol and sleep. I tuned the car radio to a country station. Country music seemed like the perfect antidote to Neil and Madelyn and their need to intellectualize everything, although its emphasis on tears and slamming doors is more suited to them than to Sally and me. You don't get too many good country songs about people who get along just fine. I did hear a country song, once, that fit us pretty well. It was last winter, when I was out in Ohio on business. I was driving my rental car through the dark and sleet back to my hotel, listening to some station from across the river in Kentucky. A song came on about a man who loves his wife and his wife loves him; he dreams his wife has left him and he wakes up crying and reaches out in the darkness to touch her and she's still there. I got back to the hotel and called Sally. She said, "What's wrong? You weren't going to call until eleven." I said "Nothing's wrong," and my voice came out kind of husky and I couldn't say anything else, so she said "What's wrong?" again, and I just sat there with my eyes closed, holding the phone.

How It Works

1. Was this story funny? When? Underline the parts where you laughed—do they include jokes, rejoinders, wisecracks, images, irony? What else was amusing? Go back to each of these moments and consider what, other than entertainment, the author's wit adds to the story's characterization, its events, its sense of setting, its point of view, and its thematic content. Look particularly at how humor and seriousness interact in the scene between Mark and Neil at the end of the story. Why do they laugh so hard together?

2. Underline the passages in which Mark mockingly describes Neil's and Madelyn's beliefs. Do any of these beliefs reappear in any form later in the story? For instance, Mark laughs at Neil's opinion that psychic pain resides in the body, yet when his wife massages him in certain ways, he cries. Can you find other similar examples of disparities between this character's professed opinions and his experience? What is the emotional impact of this technique?

3. Look at passages that refer to Mark's wife, Sally. How would you describe her? Connolly depicts her with minimal detail. How does this decision, combined with the story's point of view, contribute to our picture of what is going on?

4. For a week or two, carry a notebook. Write down things that make you laugh: jokes, coincidences, mistakes, anything that strikes you as funny. Try inserting some of these into scenes you are working on. What is the effect?

Julio Cortázar

Julio Cortázar was born in Brussels, Belgium, in 1914, and later returned with his parents to their home in Argentina. In 1935, he graduated from a teachers' college in Buenos Aires with a degree in literature. Cortázar refused a job at the University of Buenos Aires because he opposed the regime of Juan Perén, and he later donated his Prix Medicis (an important prize) to the United Chilean Front. He is considered one of the greatest Latin American writers. The poet Pablo Neruda wrote that "Anyone who doesn't read Cortázar is doomed. Not to read him is a serious invisible disease which in time can have terrible consequences. Something similar to a man who has never tasted peaches. He would quietly become sadder . . . and, probably, little by little, he would lose his hair." Julio Cortázar died in 1984.

Instructions on How to Sing

Begin by breaking all the mirrors in the house, let your arms fall to your side, gaze vacantly at the wall, *forget yourself.* Sing one single note, listen to it from inside. If you hear (but this will happen much later) something like a landscape overwhelmed with dread, bonfires between rocks with squatting half-naked silhouettes, I think you'll be well on your way, and the same if you hear a river, boats painted yellow and black are coming down it, if you hear the smell of fresh bread, the shadow of a horse.

How It Works

1. Underline the images in this short piece of writing. What feelings or emotional tone do they convey? Is this always easy to paraphrase?

2. How does the tone or mood change as the piece progresses? What images, verbs, adjectives, and other devices does the author employ to achieve this movement?

3. Do you notice a tonal shift between sentences? How would you describe it?

4. Reread "Instructions on How to Sing." Now, choose a relatively innocuous activity such as singing, cooking, running, eating dinner, or anything you might do in the course of an ordinary day, and write your own set of instructions. Keep them brief; let your concise descriptions of the activity convey its nature and its implications, as in the example below:

My Own Instructions for Crying
With Apologies to Julio Cortázar
Penelope Bone

Sit on your bed. It should be disheveled; it probably is, anyway, right? Be honest. Look at it. Look at it! The crooked spread, the lumps of sheet beneath and the untucked blankets! Look around, see everything: the lint on the floor, the balls of hardened Kleenex. It is all revealed by the spring sunlight, which you are trying to soften by not raising the blinds. Aren't you?

The cry won't come, like the sneeze, the traveling itch you, frantic, can't even find. Say it: like the climax.

When you were a kid, clattering down the attic stairs dragging a peacock fan or a pair of gilt angel wings, a mask in the shape of a dog's head, calling down to someone you could almost see, whirling around the corner you smacked your skull on the sharp-angled ceiling that overhung the stairs. You cried then, fast and hard like rain that fell while the sun still shone. It hardly hurt until later, and you laughed, the tears still on your face.

What you think of now, to force the tightening in your throat, is of course, the man in question. But which man—the current, the recent, or the deep past? Go for the jugular, the aorta. Bite deep, remember, whatever it is: cut of cheekbone, glint of hair; phrase of music, slant of light. Skin on your skin and his voice, resonant in your bones. Let the taste of him fill your body and then turn sharply back to this place, your morning room.

It's not even his absence—it's the freefall of having had him, the lunge off the step you thought was there.

If all that proves merely dreary, think this: you and he are beyond gender, two human hearts, two souls in proximity, half-visible to one another but not touching, not able to touch, sliding discreetly past each other on the stairwell. Don't think, how can that *be?* Think, that's why one doesn't cry.

Andre Dubus

Andre Dubus was born in 1936, in Lake Charles, Louisiana. He served in the Marine Corps and attended the Iowa Writers' Workshop, later teaching literature and creative writing at Bradford College in Massachusetts. A dedicated teacher, Dubus held additional free workshops in his home. Dubus's critically acclaimed realistic fiction portrays the complexities of love, faith, and class in accurate, generous, and compassionate detail. Although, for much of his life, his work was relatively unknown outside the literary community that treasured it, he wrote steadily and his stories set a high standard for serious writers. In its subtlety, empathy, and depth of feeling, his fiction is reminiscent of Chekhov's.

In 1986 Dubus was struck in a hit-and-run accident while helping another driver by the side of a freeway in Massachusetts. As a result of the accident, he lost the use of his legs. This physical and emotional loss resulted in a period of writer's block but eventually found its way into his fiction and nonfiction writing. Throughout his career, however, his compassion extended his vision beyond his own experience to the suffering and grief of women and men in a variety of situations including rape, bereavement, and loss of innocence. Always, there is a redeeming sense of meaning, humor, and above all, love.

Before his death of a heart attack in 1999, Dubus published ten works of fiction and two collections of essays. He was awarded the PEN/Malamud Award, the Rea Award for excellence in short fiction, the Jean Stein Award from the American Academy of Arts and Letters, the Boston Globe's *first annual Laurence L. Winship Award, and fellowships from both the Guggenheim and MacArthur Foundations. He was also a finalist for the Pulitzer Prize for Literature and the National Book Critics Circle Award.*

A Father's Story

My name is Luke Ripley, and here is what I call my life: I own a stable of thirty horses, and I have young people who teach riding, and we board some horses too. This is in northeastern Massachusetts. I have a barn with an indoor ring, and outside I've got two fenced-in rings and a pasture that ends at a woods with trails. I call it my life because it looks like it is, and people I know call it that, but it's a life I can get away from when I hunt and fish, and some nights after dinner when I sit in the dark in the front room and listen to opera. The room faces the lawn and the road, a two-lane country road. When cars come around the curve northwest of the house, they light up the lawn for an instant, the leaves of the maple out by the road and the hemlock closer to the window. Then I'm alone again, or I'd appear to be if someone crept up to the house and looked through a window: a big-gutted grey-haired guy, drinking tea and smoking cigarettes, staring out at the dark woods across the road, listening to a grieving soprano.

My real life is the one nobody talks about anymore, except Father Paul LeBoeuf, another old buck. He has a decade on me: he's sixty-four, a big man, bald on top with grey at the sides; when he had hair, it was black. His face is ruddy, and he jokes about being a whiskey priest, though he's not. He gets outdoors as much as he can, goes for a long walk every morning, and hunts and fishes with me. But I can't get him on a horse anymore. Ten years ago I could badger him into a trail ride; I had to give him a western saddle, and he'd hold the pommel and bounce through the woods with me, and be sore for days. He's looking at seventy with eyes that are younger than many I've seen in people in their twenties. I do not remember ever feeling the way they seem to; but I was lucky, because even as a child I knew that life would try me, and I must be strong to endure, though in those early days I expected to be tortured and killed for my faith, like the saints I learned about in school.

Father Paul's family came down from Canada, and he grew up speaking more French than English, so he is different from the Irish priests who abound up here. I do not like to make general statements, or even to hold general beliefs, about people's blood, but the Irish do seem happiest when they're dealing with misfortune or guilt, either their own or somebody else's, and if you think you're not a victim of either one, you can count on certain Irish priests to try to change your mind. On Wednesday nights Father Paul comes to dinner. Often he comes on other nights too, and once, in the old days when we couldn't eat meat on Fridays, we bagged our first ducks of the season on a Friday, and as we drove home from the marsh, he said: For the purposes of Holy Mother Church, I believe a duck is more a creature of water than land, and is not rightly meat. Sometimes he teases me about never putting anything in his Sunday collection, which he would not know about if I hadn't told him years ago. I would like to believe I told him so we could have philosophical talk at dinner, but probably the truth is I suspected he knew, and I did not want him to think I so loved money that I would not even give his church a coin on Sunday. Certainly the ushers who pass the baskets know me as a miser.

I don't feel right about giving money for buildings, places. This starts with the Pope, and I cannot respect one of them till he sells his house and everything in it, and that church too, and uses the money to feed the poor. I have rarely, and maybe never, come across saintliness, but I feel certain it cannot exist in such a place. But I admit, also, that I know very little, and maybe the popes live on a different plane and are tried in ways I don't know about. Father Paul says his own church, St. John's, is hardly the Vatican. I like his church: it is made of wood, and has a simple altar and crucifix, and no padding on the kneelers. He does not have to lock its doors at night. Still it is a place. He could say Mass in my barn. I know this is stubborn, but I can find no mention by Christ of maintaining buildings, much less erecting them of stone or brick, and decorating them with pieces of metal and mineral and elements that people still fight over like barbarians. We had a Maltese woman taking riding lessons, she came over on the boat when she was ten, and once she told me how the nuns in Malta used to tell the little girls that if they wore jewelry, rings and bracelets and necklaces, in purgatory snakes would coil around their fingers and wrists and throats. I do not believe in frightening children or telling them lies, but if those nuns saved a few girls from devotion to things, maybe they were right. That Maltese woman laughed about it, but I noticed she wore only a watch, and that with a leather strap.

The money I give in the church goes in people's stomachs, and on their backs, down in New York City. I have no delusions about the worth of what I do, but I feel it's better to feed somebody than not. There's a priest in Times Square giving shelter to runaway kids, and some Franciscans who run a bread line; actually it's a morning line for coffee and a roll, and Father Paul calls it the continental breakfast for winos and bag ladies. He is curious about how much I am sending, and I know why: he guesses I send a lot, he has said probably more than tithing, and he is right; he wants to know how much because he believes I'm generous and good, and he is wrong about that; he has never had much money and does not know how easy it is to write a check when you have everything you will ever need, and the figures are mere numbers, and represent no sacrifice at all. Being a real Catholic is too hard; if I were one, I would do with my house and barn what I want the Pope to do with his. So I do not want to impress Father Paul, and when he asks me how much, I say I can't let my left hand know what my right is doing.

He came on Wednesday nights when Gloria and I were married, and the kids were young; Gloria was a very good cook (I assume she still is, but it is difficult to think of her in the present), and I liked sitting at the table with a friend who was also a priest. I was proud of my handsome and healthy children. This was long ago, and they were all very young and cheerful and often funny, and the three boys took care of their baby sister, and did not bully or tease her. Of course they did sometimes, with that excited cruelty children are prone to, but not enough so that it was part of her days. On the Wednesday after Gloria left with the kids and a U-Haul trailer, I was sitting on the front steps, it was summer, and I was watching cars go by on the road, when Father Paul drove around the curve and into the driveway. I was ashamed to see him because he is a priest and my family was gone, but I was relieved too. I went to the car to greet him. He got out smiling, with a bottle of wine, and shook my hand, then pulled me to him, gave me a quick hug, and said: "It's Wednesday, isn't it? Let's open some cans."

With arms about each other we walked to the house, and it was good to know he was doing his work but coming as a friend too, and I thought what good work he had. I have no calling. It is for me to keep horses.

In that other life, anyway. In my real one I go to bed early and sleep well and wake at four forty-five, for an hour of silence. I never want to get out of bed then, and every morning I know I can sleep for another four hours, and still not fail at any of my duties. But I get up, so have come to believe my life can be seen in miniature in that struggle in the dark of morning. While making the bed and boiling water for coffee, I talk to God: I offer Him my day, every act of my body and spirit, my thoughts and moods, as a prayer of thanksgiving, and for Gloria and my children and my friends and two women I made love with after Gloria left. This morning offertory is a habit from my boyhood in a Catholic school; or then it was a habit, but as I kept it and grew older it became a ritual. Then I say the Lord's Prayer, trying not to recite it, and one morning it occurred to me that a prayer, whether recited or said with concentration, is always an act of faith.

I sit in the kitchen at the rear of the house and drink coffee and smoke and watch the sky growing light before sunrise, the trees of the woods near the barn taking shape, becoming single pines and elms and oaks and maples. Sometimes a rabbit comes out of the treeline, or is already sitting there, invisible till the light finds him. The birds are awake in the trees and feeding on the ground, and the little ones, the purple finches and titmice and chickadees, are at the feeder I rigged outside the kitchen window; it is too small for pigeons to get a purchase. I sit and give myself to coffee and tobacco, that get me brisk again, and I watch and listen. In the first year or so after I lost my family, I played the radio in the mornings. But I overcame that, and now I rarely play it at all. Once in the mail I received a questionnaire asking me to write down everything I watched on television during the week they had chosen. At the end of those seven days I wrote in *The Wizard of Oz* and returned it. That was in winter and was actually a busy week for my television, which normally sits out the cold months without once warming up. Had they sent the questionnaire during baseball season, they would have found me at my set. People at the stables talk about shows and performers I have never heard of, but I cannot get interested; when I am in the mood to watch television, I go to a movie or read a detective novel. There are always good detective novels to be found, and I like remembering them next morning with my coffee.

I also think of baseball and hunting and fishing, and of my children. It is not painful to think about them anymore, because even if we had lived together, they would be gone now, grown into their own lives, except Jennifer. I think of death too, not sadly, or with fear, though something like excitement does run through me, something more quickening than the coffee and tobacco. I suppose it is an intense interest, and an outright distrust: I never feel certain that I'll be here watching birds eating at tomorrow's daylight. Sometimes I try to think of other things, like the rabbit that is warm and breathing but not there till twilight. I feel on the brink of something about the life of the senses, but either am not equipped to go further or am not interested enough to concentrate. I have called all of this thinking, but it is not, because it is unintentional; what I'm really doing is feeling the day, in silence, and that is what Father Paul is doing too on his five-to-ten-mile walks.

When the hour ends I take an apple or carrot and I go to the stable and tack up a horse. We take good care of these horses, and no one rides them but students, instructors, and me, and nobody rides the horses we board unless an owner asks me to. The barn is dark and I turn on lights and take some deep breaths, smelling the hay and horses and their manure, both fresh and dried, a combined odor that you either like or you don't. I walk down the wide space of dirt between stalls, greeting the horses, joking with them about their quirks, and choose one for no reason at all other than the way it looks at me that morning. I get my old English saddle that has smoothed and darkened through the years, and go into the stall, talking to this beautiful creature who'll swerve out of a canter if a piece of paper blows in front of him, and if the barn catches fire and you manage to get him out he will, if he can get away from you, run back into the fire, to his stall. Like the smells that surround them, you either like them or you don't. I love them, so am spared having to try to explain why. I feed one the carrot or apple and tack up and lead him outside, where I mount, and we go down the driveway to the road and cross it and turn northwest and walk then trot then canter to St. John's.

A few cars are on the road, their drivers looking serious about going to work. It is always strange for me to see a woman dressed for work so early in the morning. You know how long it takes them, with the makeup and hair and clothes, and I think of them waking in the dark of winter or early light of other seasons, and dressing as they might for an evening's entertainment. Probably this strikes me because I grew up seeing my father put on those suits he never wore on weekends or his two weeks off, and so am accustomed to the men, but when I see these women I think something went wrong, to send all those dressed-up people out on the road when the dew hasn't dried yet. Maybe it's because I so dislike getting up early, but am also doing what I choose to do, while they have no choice. At heart I am lazy, yet I find such peace and delight in it that I believe it is a natural state, and in what looks like my laziest periods I am closest to my center. The ride to St. John's is fifteen minutes. The horses and I do it in all weather; the road is well plowed in winter, and there are only a few days a year when ice makes me drive the pickup. People always look at someone on horseback, and for a moment their faces change and many drivers and I wave to each other. Then at St. John's, Father Paul and five or six regulars and I celebrate the Mass.

Do not think of me as a spiritual man whose every thought during those twenty-five minutes is at one with the words of the Mass. Each morning I try, each morning I fail, and know that always I will be a creature who, looking at Father Paul and the altar, and uttering prayers, will be distracted by scrambled eggs, horses, the weather, and memories and daydreams that have nothing to do with the sacrament I am about to receive. I can receive, though: the Eucharist, and also, at Mass and at other times, moments and even minutes of contemplation. But I cannot achieve contemplation, as some can; and so, having to face and forgive my own failures, I have learned from them both the necessity and wonder of ritual. For ritual allows those who cannot will themselves out of the secular to perform the spiritual, as dancing allows the tongue-tied man a ceremony of love. And, while my mind dwells on breakfast, or Major or Duchess tethered under the church eave, there is, as I take the Host from Father Paul and place it on my tongue and return to the pew, a feeling that I am thankful I have not lost in the forty-eight years since my first Communion. At its center is excitement; spreading out from it is the peace of certainty. Or the certainty of peace. One night Father Paul and I talked about faith. It was long ago, and all I remember is him saying: Belief is believing in God; faith is believing that God believes in you. That is the excitement, and the peace; then the

Mass is over, and I go into the sacristy and we have a cigarette and chat, the mystery ends, we are two men talking like any two men on a morning in America, about baseball, plane crashes, presidents, governors, murders, the sun, the clouds. Then I go to the horse and ride back to the life people see, the one in which I move and talk, and most days I enjoy it.

It is late summer now, the time between fishing and hunting, but a good time for baseball. It has been two weeks since Jennifer left, to drive home to Gloria's after her summer visit. She is the only one who still visits; the boys are married and have children, and sometimes fly up for a holiday, or I fly down or west to visit one of them. Jennifer is twenty, and I worry about her the way fathers worry about daughters but not sons. I want to know what she's up to, and at the same time I don't. She looks athletic, and she is: she swims and runs and of course rides. All my children do. When she comes for six weeks in summer, the house is loud with girls, friends of hers since childhood, and new ones. I am glad she kept the girl friends. They have been young company for me and, being with them, I have been able to gauge her growth between summers. On their riding days, I'd take them back to the house when their lessons were over and they had walked the horses and put them back in the stalls, and we'd have lemonade or Coke, and cookies if I had some, and talk until their parents came to drive them home. One year their breasts grew, so I wasn't startled when I saw Jennifer in July. Then they were driving cars to the stable, and beginning to look like young women, and I was passing out beer and ashtrays and they were talking about college.

When Jennifer was here in summer, they were at the house most days. I would say generally that as they got older they became quieter, and though I enjoyed both, I sometimes missed the giggles and shouts. The quiet voices, just low enough for me not to hear from wherever I was, rising and falling in proportion to my distance from them, frightened me. Not that I believed they were planning or recounting anything really wicked, but there was a female seriousness about them, and it was secretive, and of course I thought: love, sex. But it was more than that: it was womanhood they were entering, the deep forest of it, and no matter how many women and men too are saying these days that there is little difference between us, the truth is that men find their way into that forest only on clearly marked trails, while women move about in it like birds. So hearing Jennifer and her friends talking so quietly, yet intensely, I wanted very much to have a wife.

But not as much as in the old days, when Gloria had left but her presence was still in the house as strongly as if she had only gone to visit her folks for a week. There were no clothes or cosmetics, but potted plants endured my neglectful care as long as they could, and slowly died; I did not kill them on purpose, to exorcise the house of her, but I could not remember to water them. For weeks, because I did not use it much, the house was as neat as she had kept it, though dust layered the order she had made. The kitchen went first: I got the dishes in and out of the dishwasher and wiped the top of the stove, but did not return cooking spoons and pot holders to their hooks on the wall, and soon the burners and oven were caked with spillings, the refrigerator had more space and was spotted with juices. The living room and my bedroom went next; I did not go into the children's rooms except on bad nights when I went from room to room and looked and touched and smelled, so they did not lose their order until a year later when the kids came for six weeks. It was three

months before I ate the last of the food Gloria had cooked and frozen: I remember it was a beef stew, and very good. By then I had four cookbooks, and was boasting a bit, and talking about recipes with the women at the stables, and looking forward to cooking for Father Paul. But I never looked forward to cooking at night only for myself, though I made myself do it; on some nights I gave in to my daily temptation, and took a newspaper or detective novel to a restaurant. By the end of the second year, though, I had stopped turning on the radio as soon as I woke in the morning, and was able to be silent and alone in the evening too, and then I enjoyed my dinners.

It is not hard to live through a day, if you can live through a moment. What creates despair is the imagination, which pretends there is a future, and insists on predicting millions of moments, thousands of days, and so drains you that you cannot live the moment at hand. That is what Father Paul told me in those first two years, on some of the bad nights when I believed I could not bear what I had to: the most painful loss was my children, then the loss of Gloria, whom I still loved despite or maybe because of our long periods of sadness that rendered us helpless, so neither of us could break out of it to give a hand to the other. Twelve years later I believe ritual would have healed us more quickly than the repetitious talks we had, perhaps even kept us healed. Marriages have lost that, and I wish I had known then what I know now, and we had performed certain acts together every day, no matter how we felt, and perhaps then we could have subordinated feeling to action, for surely that is the essence of love. I know this from my distractions during Mass, and during everything else I do, so that my actions and feelings are seldom one. It does happen every day, but in proportion to everything else in a day, it is rare, like joy. The third most painful loss, which became second and sometimes first as months passed, was the knowledge that I could never marry again, and so dared not even keep company with a woman.

On some of the bad nights I was bitter about this with Father Paul, and I so pitied myself that I cried, or nearly did, speaking with damp eyes and breaking voice. I believe that celibacy is for him the same trial it is for me, not of the flesh, but the spirit; the heart longing to love. But the difference is he chose it, and did not wake one day to a life with thirty horses. In my anger I said I had done my service to love and chastity, and I told him of the actual physical and spiritual pain of practicing rhythm: nights of striking the mattress with a fist, two young animals lying side by side in heat, leaving the bed to pace, to smoke, to curse, and too passionate to question, for we were so angered and oppressed by our passion that we could see no further than our loins. So now I understand how people can be enslaved for generations before they throw down their tools or use them as weapons, the form of their slavery—the cotton fields, the shacks and puny cupboards and untended illnesses—absorbing their emotions and thoughts until finally they have little or none at all to direct with clarity and energy at the owners and legislators. And I told him of the trick of passion and its slaking: how during what we had to believe were safe periods, though all four children were conceived at those times, we were able with some coherence to question the tradition and reason and justice of the law against birth control, but not with enough conviction to soberly act against it, as though regular satisfaction in bed tempered our revolutionary as well as our erotic desires. Only when abstinence drove us hotly away from each other did we receive an urge so strong it lasted all the way to the drugstore and back; but always, after release, we threw away the remaining condoms; and after going through this a few times, we knew what would happen, and from then on we submitted to the calendar she so precisely marked on the bedroom wall. I told him that living two lives each month, one as celibates, one as lovers, made us tense and short-tempered, so we snapped at each other like dogs.

To have endured that, to have reached a time when we burned slowly and could gain from bed the comfort of lying down at night with one who loves you and whom you love, could for weeks on end go to bed tired and peacefully sleep after a kiss, a touch of the hands, and then to be thrown out of the marriage like a bundle from a moving freight car, was unjust, was intolerable, and I could not or would not muster the strength to endure it. But I did, a moment at a time, a day, a night, except twice, each time with a different woman and more than a year apart, and this was so long ago that I clearly see their faces in my memory, can hear the pitch of their voices, and the way they pronounced words, one with a Massachusetts accent, one midwestern, but I feel as though I only heard about them from someone else. Each rode at the stables and was with me for part of an evening; one was badly married, one divorced, so none of us was free. They did not understand this Catholic view, but they were understanding about my having it, and I remained friends with both of them until the married one left her husband and went to Boston, and the divorced one moved to Maine. After both those evenings, those good women, I went to Mass early while Father Paul was still in the confessional, and received his absolution. I did not tell him who I was, but of course he knew, though I never saw it in his eyes. Now my longing for a wife comes only once in a while, like a cold: on some late afternoons when I am alone in the barn, then I lock up and walk to the house, daydreaming, then suddenly look at it and see it empty, as though for the first time, and all at once I'm weary and feel I do not have the energy to broil meat, and I think of driving to a restaurant, then shake my head and go on to the house, the refrigerator, the oven; and some mornings when I wake in the dark and listen to the silence and run my hand over the cold sheet beside me; and some days in summer when Jennifer is here.

Gloria left first me, then the Church, and that was the end of religion for the children, though on visits they went to Sunday Mass with me, and still do, out of respect for my life that they manage to keep free of patronage. Jennifer is an agnostic, though I doubt she would call herself that, any more than she would call herself any other name that implied she had made a decision, a choice, about existence, death, and God. In truth she tends to pantheism, a good sign, I think; but not wanting to be a father who tells his children what they ought to believe, I do not say to her that Catholicism includes pantheism, like onions in a stew. Besides, I have no missionary instincts and do not believe everyone should or even could live with the Catholic faith. It is Jennifer's womanhood that renders me awkward. And womanhood now is frank, not like when Gloria was twenty and there were symbols: high heels and cosmetics and dresses, a cigarette, a cocktail. I am glad that women are free now of false modesty and all its attention paid the flesh; but, still, it is difficult to see so much of your daughter, to hear her talk as only men and bawdy women used to, and most of all to see in her face the deep and unabashed sensuality of women, with no tricks of the eyes and mouth to hide the pleasure she feels at having a strong young body. I am certain, with the way things are now, that she has very happily not

been a virgin for years. That does not bother me. What bothers me is my certainty about it, just from watching her walk across a room or light a cigarette or pour milk on cereal.

She told me all of it, waking me that night when I had gone to sleep listening to the wind in the trees and against the house, a wind so strong that I had to shut all but the lee windows, and still the house cooled; told it to me in such detail and so clearly that now, when she has driven the car to Florida, I remember it all as though I had been a passenger in the front seat, or even at the wheel. It started with a movie, then beer and driving to the sea to look at the waves in the night and the wind, Jennifer and Betsy and Liz. They drank a beer on the beach and wanted to go in naked but were afraid they would drown in the high surf. They bought another six-pack at a grocery store in New Hampshire, and drove home. I can see it now, feel it: the three girls and the beer and the ride on country roads where pines curved in the wind and the big deciduous trees swayed and shook as if they might leap from the earth. They would have some windows partly open so they could feel the wind; Jennifer would be playing a cassette, the music stirring them, as it does the young, to memories of another time, other people and places in what is for them the past.

She took Betsy home, then Liz, and sang with her cassette as she left the town west of us and started home, a twenty-minute drive on the road that passes my house. They had each had four beers, but now there were twelve empty bottles in the bag on the floor at the passenger seat, and I keep focusing on their sound against each other when the car shifted speeds or changed directions. For I want to understand that one moment out of all her heart's time on earth, and whether her history had any bearing on it, or whether her heart was then isolated from all it had known, and the sound of those bottles urged it. She was just leaving the town, accelerating past a night club on the right, gaining speed to climb a long, gradual hill, then she went up it, singing, patting the beat on the steering wheel, the wind loud through her few inches of open window, blowing her hair as it did the high branches alongside the road, and she looked up at them and watched the top of the hill for someone drunk or heedless coming over it in part of her lane. She crested to an open black road, and there he was: a bulk, a blur, a thing running across her headlights, and she swerved left and her foot went for the brake and was stomping air above its pedal when she hit him, saw his legs and body in the air, flying out of her light, into the dark. Her brakes were screaming into the wind, bottles clinking in the fallen bag, and with the music and wind inside the car was his sound, already a memory but as real as an echo, that car-shuddering thump as though she had struck a tree. Her foot was back on the accelerator. Then she shifted gears and pushed it. She ejected the cassette and closed the window. She did not start to cry until she knocked on my bedroom door, then called: "Dad?"

Her voice, her tears, broke through my dream and the wind I heard in my sleep, and I stepped into jeans and hurried to the door, thinking harm, rape, death. All were in her face, and I hugged her and pressed her cheek to my chest and smoothed her blown hair, then led her, weeping, to the kitchen and set her at the table where still she could not speak, nor look at me; when she raised her face it fell forward again, as of its own weight, into her palms. I offered tea and she shook her head, so I offered beer twice, then she shook her head, so I offered whiskey and she nodded. I had some rye that Father Paul and I had not finished last hunting

season, and I poured some over ice and set it in front of her and was putting away the ice but stopped and got another glass and poured one for myself too, and brought the ice and bottle to the table where she was trying to get one of her long menthols out of the pack, but her fingers jerked like severed snakes, and I took the pack and lit one for her and took one for myself. I watched her shudder with her first swallow of rye, and push hair back from her face, it is auburn and gleamed in the overhead light, and I remembered how beautiful she looked riding a sorrel; she was smoking fast, then the sobs in her throat stopped, and she looked at me and said it, the words coming out with smoke: "I hit somebody. With the *car.*"

Then she was crying and I was on my feet, moving back and forth, looking down at her, asking *Who? Where? Where?* She was pointing at the wall over the stove, jabbing her fingers and cigarette at it, her other hand at her eyes, and twice in horror I actually looked at the wall. She finished the whiskey in a swallow and I stopped pacing and asking and poured another, and either the drink or the exhaustion of tears quieted her, even the dry sobs, and she told me; not as I tell it now, for that was later as again and again we relived it in the kitchen or living room, and, if in daylight, fled it on horseback out on the trails through the woods and, if at night, walked quietly around in the moonlit pasture, walked around and around it, sweating through our clothes. She told it in bursts, like she was a child again, running to me, injured from play. I put on boots and a shirt and left her with the bottle and her streaked face and a cigarette twitching between her fingers, pushed the door open against the wind, and eased it shut. The wind squinted and watered my eyes as I leaned into it and went to the pickup.

When I passed St. John's I looked at it, and Father Paul's little white rectory in the rear, and wanted to stop, wished I could as I could if he were simply a friend who sold hardware or something. I had forgotten my watch but I always know the time within minutes, even when a sound or dream or my bladder wakes me in the night. It was nearly two; we had been in the kitchen about twenty minutes; she had hit him around one-fifteen. Or her. The road was empty and I drove between blowing trees; caught for an instant in my lights, they seemed to be in panic. I smoked and let hope play its tricks on me: it was neither man nor woman but an animal, a goat or calf or deer on the road; it was a man who had jumped away in time, the collision of metal and body glancing not direct, and he had limped home to nurse bruises and cuts. Then I threw the cigarette and hope both out the window and prayed that he was alive, while beneath that prayer, a reserve deeper in my heart, another one stirred: that if he were dead, they would not get Jennifer.

From our direction, east and a bit south, the road to that hill and the night club beyond it and finally the town is, for its last four or five miles, straight through farming country. When I reached that stretch I slowed the truck and opened my window for the fierce air; on both sides were scattered farmhouses and barns and sometimes a silo, looking not like shelters but like unsheltered things the wind would flatten. Corn bent toward the road from a field on my right, and always something blew in front of me: paper, leaves, dried weeds, branches. I slowed approaching the hill, and went up it in second, staring through my open window at the ditch on the left side of the road, its weeds alive, whipping, a mad dance with the trees above them. I went over the hill and down and, opposite the club, turned right onto a side street of houses, and parked there, in the leaping shadows of trees. I walked back across the road to the club's parking lot, the wind behind me, lifting me as I strode, and I could not hear my boots on pavement. I walked up the hill, on the shoulder, watching the branches above me, hearing their leaves and the creaking trunks and the wind. Then I was at the top, looking down the road and at the farms and fields; the night was clear, and I could see a long way; clouds scudded past the half-moon and stars, blown out to sea.

I started down, watching the tall grass under the trees to my right, glancing into the dark of the ditch, listening for cars behind me; but as soon as I cleared one tree, its sound was gone, its flapping leaves and rattling branches far behind me, as though the greatest distance I had at my back was a matter of feet, while ahead of me I could see a barn two miles off. Then I saw her skid marks: short, and going left and downhill, into the other lane. I stood at the ditch, its weeds blowing; across it were trees and their moving shadows, like the clouds. I stepped onto its slope, and it took me sliding on my feet, then rump, to the bottom, where I sat still, my body gathered to itself, lest a part of me should touch him. But there was only tall grass, and I stood, my shoulders reaching the sides of the ditch, and I walked uphill, wishing for the flashlight in the pickup, walking slowly, and down in the ditch I could hear my feet in the grass and on the earth, and kicking cans and bottles. At the top of the hill I turned and went down, watching the ground above the ditch on my right, praying my prayer from the truck again, the first one, the one I would admit, that he was not dead, was in fact home, and began to hope again, memory telling me of lost pheasants and grouse I had shot, but they were small and the colors of their home, while a man was either there or not; and from that memory I left where I was and while walking in the ditch under the wind was in the deceit of imagination with Jennifer in the kitchen, telling her she had hit no one, or at least had not badly hurt anyone, when I realized he could be in the hospital now and I would have to think of a way to check there, something to say on the phone. I see now that, once hope returned, I should have been certain what it prepared me for: ahead of me, in high grass and the shadows of trees, I saw his shirt. Or that is all my mind would allow itself: a shirt, and I stood looking at it for the moments it took my mind to admit the arm and head and the dark length covered by pants. He lay face down, the arm I could see near his side, his head turned from me, on its cheek.

"Fella?" I said. I had meant to call, but it came out quiet and high, lost inches from my face in the wind. Then I said, "Oh God," and felt Him in the wind and the sky moving past the stars and moon and the fields around me, but only watching me as He might have watched Cain or Job, I did not know which, and I said it again, and wanted to sink to the earth and weep till I slept there in the weeds. I climbed, scrambling up the side of the ditch, pulling at clutched grass, gained the top on hands and knees, and went to him like that, panting, moving through the grass as high and higher than my face, crawling under that sky, making sounds too, like some animal, there being no words to let him know I was here with him now. He was long; that is the word that came to me, not tall. I kneeled beside him, my hands on my legs. His right arm was by his side, his left arm straight out from the shoulder, but turned, so his palm was open to the tree above us. His left cheek was cleanshaven, his eye closed, and there was no blood. I leaned forward to look at his open mouth and saw the blood on it, going down into the grass. I straightened and looked ahead at the wind blowing past me through grass and

trees to a distant light, and I stared at the light, imagining someone awake out there, wanting someone to be, a gathering of old friends, or someone alone listening to music or painting a picture, then I figured it was a night light at a farmyard whose house I couldn't see. *Going,* I thought. *Still going.* I leaned over again and looked at dripping blood.

So I had to touch his wrist, a thick one with a watch and expansion band that I pushed up his arm, thinking *he's left-handed,* my three fingers pressing his wrist, and all I felt was my tough fingertips on that smooth underside flesh and small bones, then relief, then certainty. But against my will, or only because of it, I still don't know, I touched his neck, ran my fingers down it as if petting, then pressed, and my hand sprang back as from fire. I lowered it again, held it there until it felt that faint beating that I could not believe. There was too much wind. Nothing could make a sound in it. A pulse could not be felt in it, nor could mere fingers in that wind feel the absolute silence of a dead man's artery. I was making sounds again; I grabbed his left arm and his waist, and pulled him toward me, and that side of him rose, turned, and I lowered him to his back, his face tilted up toward the tree that was groaning, the tree and I the only sounds in the wind. Turning my face from his, looking down the length of him at his sneakers, I placed my ear on his heart, and heard not that but something else, and I clamped a hand over my exposed ear, heard something liquid and alive, like when you pump a well and after a few strokes you hear air and water moving in the pipe, and I knew I must raise his legs and cover him and run to a phone, while still I listened to his chest, thinking *raise with what? cover with what?* and amid the liquid sound I heard the heart, then lost it, and pressed my ear against bone, but his chest was quiet, and

I did not know when the liquid had stopped, and do not know now when I heard air, a faint rush of it, and whether under my ear or at his mouth or whether I heard it at all. I straightened and looked at the light, dim and yellow. Then I touched his throat, looking him full in the face. He was blond and young. He could have been sleeping in the shade of a tree, but for the smear of blood from his mouth to his hair, and the night sky, and the weeds blowing against his head, and the leaves shaking in the dark above us.

I stood. Then I kneeled again and prayed for his soul to join in peace and joy all the dead and living; and, doing so, confronted my first sin against him, not stopping for Father Paul, who could have given him the last rites, and immediately then my second one, or, I saw then, my first, not calling an ambulance to meet me there, and I stood and turned into the wind, slid down the ditch and crawled out of it, and went up the hill and down it, across the road to the street of houses whose people I had left behind forever, so that I moved with stealth in the shadows to my truck.

When I came around the bend near my house, I saw the kitchen light at the rear. She sat as I had left her, the ashtray filled, and I looked at the bottle, felt her eyes on me, felt what she was seeing too: the dirt from my crawling. She had not drunk much of the rye. I poured some in my glass, with the water from melted ice, and sat down and swallowed some and looked at her and swallowed some more, and said: "He's dead."

She rubbed her eyes with the heels of her hands, rubbed the cheeks under them, but she was dry now.

"He was probably dead when he hit the ground. I mean, that's probably what killed—"

"Where was he?"

"Across the ditch, under a tree."

"Was he—did you see his face?"

"No. Not really. I just felt. For life, pulse. I'm going out to the car."

"What for? Oh."

I finished the rye, and pushed back the chair, then she was standing too.

"I'll go with you."

"There's no need."

"I'll go."

I took a flashlight from a drawer and pushed open the door and held it while she went out. We turned our faces from the wind. It was like on the hill, when I was walking, and the wind closed the distance behind me: after three or four steps I felt there was no house back there. She took my hand, as I was reaching for hers. In the garage we let go, and squeezed between the pickup and her little car, to the front of it, where we had more room, and we stepped back from the grill and I shone the light on the fender, the smashed headlight turned into it, the concave chrome staring to the right, at the garage wall.

"We ought to get the bottles," I said.

She moved between the garage and the car, on the passenger side, and had room to open the door and lift the bag. I reached out, and she gave me the bag and backed up and shut the door and came around the car. We sidled to the doorway, and she put her arm around my waist and I hugged her shoulders.

"I thought you'd call the police," she said.

We crossed the yard, faces bowed from the wind, her hair blowing away from her neck, and in the kitchen I put the bag of bottles in the garbage basket. She was working at the table: capping the rye and putting it away, filling the ice tray, washing the glasses, emptying the ashtray, sponging the table.

"Try to sleep now," I said.

She nodded at the sponge circling under her hand, gathering ashes. Then she dropped it in the sink and, looking me full in the face, as I had never seen her look, as perhaps she never had, being for so long a daughter on visits (or so it seemed to me and still does: that until then our eyes had never seriously met), she crossed to me from the sink and kissed my lips, then held me so tightly I lost balance, and would have stumbled forward had she not held me so hard.

I sat in the living room, the house darkened, and watched the maple and the hemlock. When I believed she was asleep I put on *La Boheme*, and kept it at the same volume as the wind so it would not wake her. Then I listened to *Madame Butterfly*, and in the third act had to rise quickly to lower the sound: the wind was gone. I looked at the still maple near the window, and thought of the wind leaving farms and towns and the coast, going out over the sea to die on the waves. I smoked and gazed out the window. The sky was darker, and at daybreak the rain came. I listened to *Tosca*, and at six-fifteen went to the kitchen where Jennifer's purse lay on the table, a leather shoulder purse crammed with the things of an adult woman, things she had begun accumulating only a few years back, and I nearly wept, thinking of what sandy foundations they were: driver's license, credit card, disposable lighter, cigarettes, checkbook, ballpoint pen, cash, cosmetics, comb, brush, Kleenex, these the rite of passage from childhood, and I took one of them—her keys—and went out, remembering a jacket and hat when the rain struck me, but I kept going to the car, and squeezed and lowered myself into it, pulled the seat belt over my shoulder and fastened it and backed out, turning in the drive, going forward into the road, toward St. John's and Father Paul.

Cars were on the road, the workers, and I did not worry about any of them noticing the fender and light. Only a horse distracted them from what they drove to. In front of St. John's is a parking lot; at its far side, past the church and at the edge of the lawn, is an old pine, taller than the steeple now. I shifted to third, left the road, and, aiming the right headlight at the tree, accelerated past the white blur of church, into the black trunk growing bigger till it was all I could see, then I rocked in that resonant thump she had heard, had felt, and when I turned off the ignition it was still in my ears, my blood, and I saw the boy flying in the wind. I lowered my forehead to the wheel. Father Paul opened the door, his face white in the rain.

"I'm all right."

"What happened?"

"I don't know. I fainted."

I got out and went around to the front of the car, looked at the smashed light, the crumpled and torn fender.

"Come to the house and lie down."

"I'm all right."

"When was your last physical?"

"I'm due for one. Let's get out of this rain."

"You'd better lie down."

"No. I want to receive."

That was the time to say I want to confess, but I have not and will not. Though I could now, for Jennifer is in Florida, and weeks have passed, and perhaps now Father Paul would not feel that he must tell me to go to the police. And, for that very reason, to confess now would be unfair. It is a world of secrets, and now I have one from my best, in truth my only, friend. I have one from Jennifer too, but that is the nature of fatherhood.

Most of that day it rained, so it was only in early evening, when the sky cleared, with a setting sun, that two little boys, leaving their confinement for some play before dinner, found him. Jennifer and I got that on the local news, which we listened to every hour, meeting at the radio, standing with cigarettes, until the one at eight o'clock; when she stopped crying, we went out and walked on the wet grass, around the pasture, the last of sunlight still in the air and trees. His name was Patrick Mitchell, he was nineteen years old, was employed by CETA, lived at home with his parents and brother and sister. The paper next day said he had been at a friend's house and was walking home, and I thought of that light I had seen, then knew it was not for him; he lived on one of the streets behind the club. The paper did not say then, or in the next few days, anything to make Jennifer think he was alive while she was with me in the kitchen. Nor do I know if we—I—could have saved him.

In keeping her secret from her friends, Jennifer had to perform so often, as I did with Father Paul and at the stables, that I believe the acting, which took more of her than our daylight trail rides and our night walks in the pasture, was her healing. Her friends teased me about wrecking her car. When I carried her luggage out to the car on that last morning, we spoke only of the weather for her trip—the day was clear, with a dry cool breeze—and hugged and kissed, and I stood watching as she started the car and turned it around. But then she shifted to neutral and put on the parking brake and unclasped the belt, looking at me all the while, then she was coming to me, as she had that night in the kitchen, and I opened my arms.

I have said I talk with God in the mornings, as I start my day, and sometimes as I sit with coffee, looking at the birds, and the woods. Of course He has never spoken to me, but that is not something I require. Nor does He need to. I know Him, as I know the part of myself that knows Him, that felt Him watching from the wind and the night as I knelt over the dying boy. Lately I have taken to arguing with Him, as I can't with Father Paul, who, when he hears my monthly confession, has not heard and will not hear anything of failure to do all that one can to save an anonymous life, of injustice to a family in their grief, of deepening their pain at the chance and mystery of death by giving them nothing—no one—to hate. With Father Paul I feel lonely about this, but not with God. When I received the Eucharist while Jennifer's car sat twice-damaged, so redeemed, in the rain, I felt neither loneliness nor shame, but as though He were watching me, even from my tongue, intestines, blood, as I have watched my sons at times in their young lives when I was able to judge but without anger, and so keep silent while they, in the agony of their youth, decided how they must act; or found reasons, after their actions, for what they had done. Their reasons were never as good or as bad as their actions, but they needed to find them, to believe they were living by them, instead of the awful solitude of the heart.

I do not feel the peace I once did: not with God, nor the earth, or anyone on it. I have begun to prefer this state, to remember with fondness the other one as a period of peace I neither earned nor deserved. Now in the mornings while I watch purple finches driving larger titmice from the feeder, I say to Him: I would do it again. For when she knocked on my door, then called me, she woke what had flowed dormant in my blood since her birth, so that what rose from the bed was not a stable owner or a Catholic or any other Luke Ripley I had lived with for a long time, but the father of a girl.

And he says: I am a Father too.

Yes, I say, as You are a Son Whom this morning I will receive; unless You kill me on the way to church, then I trust You will receive me. And as a Son You made Your plea.

Yes, He says, but I would not lift the cup.

True, and I don't want You to lift it from me either. And if one of my sons had come to me that night, I would have phoned the police and told them to meet us with an ambulance at the top of the hill.

Why? Do you love them less?

I tell Him no, it is not that I love them less, but that I could bear the pain of watching and knowing my sons' pain, could bear it with pride as they took the whip and nails. But You never had a daughter and, if You had, You could not have borne her passion.

So, He says, you love her more than you love Me.

I love her more than I love truth.

Then you love in weakness, He says.

As You love me, I say, and I go with an apple or carrot out to the barn.

How It Works

1. Underline places where the events in this story drive the characters. Now underline places where the characters drive the events. On the continuum between plot-centered and character-centered fiction, where would you place the story? How does the author balance these two elements, preventing the story from tipping too far toward plot (and becoming a murder mystery) or too far toward character (and losing momentum in its examination of Luke's spiritual and emotional life)?

2. Reread the story's first paragraph. *How* does it characterize Luke Ripley? What do we learn or sense about him from that paragraph? Trace those perceptions to the words on the page: what details and information does Dubus provide that lead you to your conclusions?

3. Where does the exposition begin and end in this story? Writers are often told to minimize exposition. Does this story successfully break that rule? If so, how? What steps does the author take to prevent the exposition from deflating the narrative arc? If you were discussing this story in a workshop and someone said there was too much exposition, how would you respond?

4. Listen to a recording of this story. (Author recordings are easy to find at your college or local library; if you can't find this particular story, try another in this book.) Read along. Listen for nuances conveyed by the author's voice. Reread the story. Do you feel that you understand it better?

Rachel Finkelstein

Rachel Finkelstein was a junior at Tufts University as this book went to press. She has always enjoyed writing stories, although since entering college, she has found it difficult to make time to write. "Awakening" was written during her freshman year, and was later published in a student literary journal. She wrote this story, which stemmed from a single image of a frozen lake, all at once: "It just poured out and I didn't want to stop until I had it all out on paper." She feels that her main challenge as she wrote it was trying to keep the narrator believable even as the events in the story became more and more unusual and traumatic. She felt a strong bond with this character and has said that in some ways the narrator's personality is reflective of her own.

Awakening

Sleep draws me in against my will, beyond the darkness to a place where jumbled images collide and soundlessly drift apart, floating on silence. It is a restless sleep tonight, filled with demons that lure me with their soothing, hypnotic voices, promising an escape from reality. They lead me into their dreamlike world and then vanish when the dark curtain of night is flung open to the light of a new day. The demons are strong, as long as they are invisible.

A loud crash breaks through the silence, and the images of dreams shatter like broken glass. I can even hear the splintering noise; it sounds so close that my eyes open and hazy visions dissolve as easily as if they had never been. I turn over in my bed and the blackness melts into shadows and slivers of moonlight. The room is dark and quiet, so the demons are still here. I can feel their presence in the way the air sits heavily on my skin; I can hear them in the rustle of my curtains in front of the open window.

The fuzzy red glow slowly transforms into the numbers on my digital clock. It is 3:24 a.m. As my sleepy mind struggles back to the waking world, I look around the room, confused. I can't remember what I was dreaming about. The sound of glass breaking echoes in my head, and suddenly I realize that the crash I heard was real, and it came from downstairs.

I strain my ears but hear nothing. I don't even know what I'm listening for: the heavy footsteps of an intruder, or maybe another loud crash? A scream from my mother's room?

My mother! I sit straight up in bed. Has she come back yet? These days, I don't even know what time she gets home. I stand up, trying not to let the old wood floor squeak. It is 3:26. Is two minutes long enough to break into a house, find a bedroom with someone in it, and kill her?

I take a step toward the door. I don't know who's out there. Maybe my mom isn't home yet. I tiptoe over to the window and glance outside. I can hear the wind dragging dry leaves over the pavement. Our house is on a narrow back road, set far off of the street. If we didn't have the porch light on at night, you could probably drive right past it and never know. But we always leave the light on. My mother usually comes home very late, and most nights she is still drunk.

If I get killed tonight, and my mom isn't here, there will be no one to hear me scream.

Suddenly, the solitude of my room makes my skin crawl. I feel small and alone, like I am shrinking into the darkness. I long for my mother's arms around me, but my feet are rooted to the floor. I glimpse myself in the mirror and try to see myself through the eyes of a burglar. I am wearing a long white cotton nightgown that probably makes me look younger than I am. It hangs loosely over my body, and I can't see my breasts unless I stick out my chest. I purposely mess my long hair, trying to make myself look uglier, just in case there is someone out there.

I could die tonight. The thought gives me goosebumps. A tiny smile pulls at my lips as I imagine my mother screaming when she sees my lifeless body sprawled out on the floor. She hides her face in her hands and falls to her knees, wailing. A pool of blood forms beneath me, leaving a dark red stain on my nightgown. When the police come, they will have to undress me, probably.

I quietly slide open my top drawer and take out the pair of silky blue Victoria's Secret panties that a friend of my mother's once left here by accident when she came to visit last year. They feel so nice and smooth against my skin. After removing my boring white cotton bikini briefs, I slowly slide the satin panties up my legs. When the police find my body, my mom will be surprised; I don't think she knows I kept these. She will wonder how many other secrets I have.

Now there can be no more stalling. I open my door slowly, hoping the hinges won't squeak. They do. There is no one in the hallway. My mom's door is ajar and the bed is empty. The blankets and pillows are strewn about and the laundry basket is tipped over, dirty clothes scattered across the mauve carpet. Her glasses are carefully folded on top of the book she is halfway through. She's supposed to wear them all the time.

Suddenly I hear another noise, downstairs. It sounds like a person sighing. My mouth goes dry and I reach for the banister. I swallow hard and take a deep breath. With each step, a new image of my mother's body floats in front of my eyes. Strangled, stabbed, raped . . . I gasp so hard that I nearly choke. At the bottom of the steps I hesitate, unable to move. Finally I turn the corner and stop short. Someone in the living room.

She is lying face-down on the couch with her right hand dangling down to the hard wood floor. Her wavy brown hair covers her face and she is wearing only one shoe. As usual, there is a run in her stocking the length of her calf. Next to her hand are the broken pieces of the empty vodka bottle, large chunks of glass and narrow shards scattered between her fingers. Moonlight shines through the window and illuminates the room. I can see blood on her hand where the glass has cut her skin. The blood looks dark, almost black, in the white light of the moon.

I wonder how long she has been sitting by herself in the dark room. I used to keep her company late at night while she sobered up. She would talk and talk, telling me stories of when she was young and happy, stories about her and my father from before I was born. Most of what I know about my father I learned from my mother late at night. She won't talk about him when she's sober.

They met when she was fifteen, my age. He was twenty-one, she says, and very tall and muscular, with curly black hair and beautiful blue eyes. That part is true; I know because one day I found a shoebox full of pictures of the two of them stashed away in the back of the closet. I knew right away when I saw them that he was my father, even though I'd never seen a picture of him before. It was the eyes, grayish-blue like mine, staring directly at me as if he could see straight through to my soul. I stared back intently, trying to make him feel my presence. His smile seemed cold and somehow sarcastic next to my mother's innocent gaze. He isn't looking at her, though. He is looking right at the camera, as if he is the only one in the picture.

He used to work on my grandfather's farm, and my mom used to watch him working, without his shirt on, lifting heavy things. One day she followed him into the stable and let him feel her breasts. After that day, they had sex almost every day. That's what my mom told me.

Sometimes when I can't sleep at night I think about them in the stable. It's still there, out behind our house, only it's empty now. I imagine my mother, young and pretty, standing in one of the empty stalls facing the sexy man from the photo. Then, in my imagination, I become my mother, and it's me standing there, slowly lifting up my shirt, first just enough to let him catch a glimpse, then more until he reaches out and pulls it off over my head. I stand motionless while he cradles my small bare breasts. His hands feel rough and callused, and a little bit sweaty. Gently he runs his fingers over my nipples. He inches closer until we are standing right up against each other, breathing deeply. He smells like hay and horses and his breath is hot against my cheek. I can feel him pushed hard against me.

My father stopped working on the farm while my mom was pregnant with me. I've always wanted to know why, but she won't tell me that, not even when she's so drunk that she doesn't know what she's saying. On those nights, she sits sobbing at the kitchen table with her head in her hands while I make her coffee. She cries about how her life ended as soon as she got pregnant at sixteen, and rambles incoherently about how she used to have dreams, she once thought she could be someone and do something. One night I told her, "You are someone. You're my mother." That only made her cry harder.

I never used to mind rubbing her shoulders, holding her thick hair back if she had to throw up, stroking it while she lay with her head in my lap, sitting with her until she fell asleep. The sound of her even breathing relaxed me as I ran my fingers through her dark, shiny curls, gently untangling them. I would close my eyes and slow my breathing until it matched hers and then watch our chests rise and fall in unison.

Then once she was tucked into bed, I would go back downstairs and throw away tear-soaked tissues or sweep up broken glass. One night she threw my favorite seashell at the wall and it shattered into tiny pieces. I had found the beautiful white shell years ago on the shore of the lake by our house. I sat and ran my fingers over its smooth, shiny surface and then brought it back as a present for my mom. She said it was the best gift anyone had ever given her. I don't think she meant to throw that.

I stopped waiting up when my mother starting bringing men home. I don't want to get in the way or anything. I guess I should be happy for her, but I'm not. Knowing that she is not alone in her bed just makes me even lonelier in mine. Sometimes when I'm trying to fall asleep I can hear my mother rolling around in her bed, breathing heavily. I hear the bed squeaking, and the loose headboard rattles against the wall. Sometimes my mother moans, and other times she just giggles. I don't try to listen, but I can't help it. Once I was sleeping over at a friend's house and we were watching an R-rated movie. I'd never seen one before. The couple in the movie was having sex. "That's what my mom sounds like," I said.

"When she's fucking, you mean?" Jen looked at me, amazed, and then broke into a fit of giggles.

Since then, when I hear my mother making those noises I pretend she is with my father and they are out in the stable. And then in my mind, it's me moaning and panting, feeling his strong arms wrapped around me, our sweaty naked bodies pressed together. I press my hand hard against my crotch, pretending my fingers are his. Sometimes I let my fingers wander inside my panties, moving them to the same rhythm as the breathing in the next room. Then when my mother's room is quiet, I stop too, and wait for sleep to pull me back through the darkness.

I've never met any of the men my mother brought home; they're always gone by the time I wake up in the morning. I've only seen one of them and that was two weeks ago. Now I picture his face on all the men I hear but never see. I don't know his name. I call him the Fat Man because that's what he was. I was lying in my bed, on the very edge of sleep, about to fall into my dreams and let them carry me away, when the Fat Man came into my room.

I didn't hear him until he sat down heavily on my bed. In the darkness I could only make out his massive frame at the foot of the bed, and I opened my mouth to scream, but he clamped his fat hand down over my face. I couldn't breathe, and I started hitting him with both hands, as hard as I could. He moved his hand and I screamed, "Mom!" as loud as I could even though I knew she was probably passed out downstairs.

When I screamed, he slapped me and I was so startled that I stopped shouting. "That's a good girl," he mumbled. Then he pressed his mouth on top of mine and slid his hand under my T-shirt and over my breasts. He tasted and smelled so strongly of alcohol that my stomach churned and I swallowed hard to avoid being sick. His sweat-soaked undershirt reeked of cigarettes and beer, and the stubble on his cheeks burned against my skin. His tongue penetrated my lips even though I had been clamping them tightly shut. I pushed at his arm, trying to get his hand off me, but he was huge and I couldn't budge him. I shut my eyes tight in order to avoid seeing his fat ugly face. When he finally removed his mouth from mine, I took a deep breath and shoved my knee into his balls with all my might.

"Fucking bitch," he groaned and rolled over, lying on top of my legs so that I couldn't move. He was so damn fat! I yelled for my mother again, knowing it was pointless, but screaming my throat raw just the same. I struggled, but I couldn't free myself from under him. He was coming at me again and I burst into tears. I just didn't know what else I could do. I hated the Fat Man, but I hated her more for bringing him into the house and then disappearing drowsily into her dreams.

I continued to struggle against him, but I knew I was defeated and the Fat Man knew it

too. I cried and cried as he pushed himself inside me, crushing me with his overflowing belly. It was the worst pain I had ever known. I felt like he was splitting me in half. I knew this was sex, but it was nothing like how I thought it would be, nothing like the way it was in my dreams of my mother and father in the stable. I couldn't imagine the man in the picture being so rough and causing that wide-eyed young girl such pain. But I can tell from the way she talks and cries about him that he broke her heart, and maybe that hurts her even more than the Fat Man hurt me.

I haven't told my mom about the Fat Man. Every time I see her, I just want to shout at her, to grab her by the shoulders and shake her, to slap her so hard I leave a handprint on her cheek. I want to scream, "Look what you did!" But I don't want to see the guilt in her eyes.

The morning after it happened, I couldn't even look at her. I thought that if we made eye contact, then she would see through me and know. But then I realized that she would never know, because she doesn't see me.

The day after the Fat Man came in my room, I opened the closet and found the shoebox of pictures. I stared at my father and he stared back with my eyes. He knew. He saw me.

And now I see my mother lying on the couch amidst shattered glass. I mean I really see her, the way she can never see me. A sob rises up inside me, but I swallow it. I walk over to her and tap her gently on the shoulder. "Mom," I whisper into the darkness. "Come on, Mom, let's go upstairs and get you into bed." I know she won't wake up.

I go to the medicine cabinet in the bathroom and the tiles are cold against my bare feet. In the mirror I stare at my reflection. My knotted hair sticks out in all directions, covering my face. How could I have thought such a pathetic shield would offer me any protection? Would messy hair have stopped the Fat Man?

I reach for some rubbing alcohol and gauze bandages. Back in the living room, I carefully wash my mother's bleeding hand. The sting of the alcohol penetrates her sleep and she moves away and moans, but does not awaken. When I finish, I sit back and watch her sleep. I wonder what my mother dreams about.

From across the moonlit room I glare at her, and the image of her motionless body freezes in front of my eyes. I feel like if I stare at her long enough, I can enter her body and then suddenly I do. I can see myself as she sees me, not as a person, not as a daughter, but as a living reminder of what she once had and lost. I am the shade of the stable roof, the feel of hay under her bare feet, the smell of horses. My eyes are his eyes and that is why she cannot look at them.

Slowly, as if in a dream, I rise from my chair in the darkened corner of the room and step into the patch of light in front of the window. I can see the moon watching me. I find myself kneeling on the floor, my face inches from my mother's. I move in slow motion, smoothing her matted hair away from her face, leaning in to kiss her cheek. When I feel my lips on her skin, I pull away and examine her face, looking for some physical sign of my kiss. I could tell her that I love her right now, but she wouldn't hear me.

My hand grazes the floor between the chunks of broken glass. I look down and find the biggest, sharpest piece. Its rough edge glistens in the light of the moon. My hand reaches out and picks it up. Slowly, gently, I run the jagged edge over the thin skin of my wrist. Again and again I slide the glass across my veins, very faintly, just enough to make a light scratch. When I do break the skin, I carefully set the glass shard back on the floor, while watching my blood spill out in a neat little line. Not a lot of blood, just a few drops at first that quickly run together and form one solid line across my pale wrist. I watch, fascinated by my red blood glistening in the moonlight. I want to taste it. I raise my arm to my mouth and stick out my tongue, slowly running it over the cut, letting my own warm, salty taste fill my mouth. It makes me weak, and my entire body feels hot and cold at the same time. I am dizzy, like I'm floating. I can't see. I can't breathe.

The screen door slams behind me as I run out onto the porch, into the frigid night. I can't stop running, and I gulp the air, drinking it like water. The ground is hard and frozen beneath my bare feet. When I reach the gravel driveway, I keep running even though the rocks are sharp. The pain feels good, sharp bursts that bring me back to myself; I feel like I am waking from a deep sleep to the cold, wonderfully refreshing air.

I know exactly where I'm going. I run across the narrow road and into the woods. My feet find the familiar path, worn smooth over the years. Dry leaves crackle beneath my heels and an occasional twig snaps, but beyond that it is completely silent. I push my long hair out of my face but don't bother to wipe away the tears coursing down my cheeks. How long have I been crying?

Soon I see light as the path comes to an end at the other edge of the woods. I stand still, taking the night air into my lungs. I stare out at the frozen lake, a vast white sheet surrounded by dark forest. The trees and the sky are so black that they blend together. It's a clear night, and stars pierce the darkness while the full moon waits overhead.

"Well what did you want me to do?" I shout at the sky, and I hear my own words echo across the lake. "It's her! I couldn't—I mean, I just—" I'm sobbing now, so hard that I can barely breathe. I fall to my knees by the shore of the lake and cover my face while I cry. I hate her! I really do! My hand reaches around, groping for something, anything I can throw. I find a rock, stand up, and hurl it with all my might at the lake. It hits the ice, skids across the surface, and comes to rest. The moon seems to smirk.

An outraged scream erupts from deep inside of me, and I bend and pick up more and more rocks, throwing them as hard as I can out onto the ice. Finally, I pick up a stone that is bigger and heavier than the others. It takes both hands, but I manage to heave it out over the frozen lake. Mesmerized, I watch it sail through the air, its path a perfect arc, before it crashes through the ice with a tremendous splintering sound.

I hear it crash over and over in my mind. The sound of glass splintering rings in my ears and I picture that rock, plummeting through the freezing water, straight down to the bottom. I wonder how long it will take to get there. I wonder how cold the water is. I see myself in the water, plunging to the bottom just like that rock. I see myself, and I am not afraid.

Cautiously I place one foot on the ice and then the other. I am slightly surprised that the ice is supporting my weight; I half-expected to fall through immediately. I confidently take a few more steps away from the shore. My steps grow larger and quicker and soon I am walking at an almost normal pace. I close my eyes and concentrate on the feel of the ice beneath my feet. It is not slippery or cold; it doesn't feel much different from the hard wood floor of my bedroom. With my eyes closed, I can even convince myself that I am there, walking over to the window to look for my mother. I will not wait up for her anymore. I will not listen to her cry, letting her misery seep through my skin.

I don't know how many steps I've taken and I refuse to look back. With each step, a surge of

energy tingles from my head to my feet, forcing me to take another. My face feels funny, like it's made of rubber, and I realize that it's because I'm smiling. I can't remember a time in my life when I've ever felt this free. I open my eyes and take in every detail.

Stars glisten over the treetops and a slight breeze moves through the trees. My long cotton nightgown flutters and the ruffled bottom tickles my legs. The material suddenly feels heavy and restrictive, so I stop walking and slowly slide my nightgown over my head, tossing it onto the ice. I put my hands over my breasts and run them slowly up and down, squeezing them gently, enjoying my own caress. My nipples are hard from the cold. I think it's the first time I've touched myself without pretending my hands are really the hands of the man in the picture. The breeze lifts strands of my hair and tickles my face with them. I stretch my arms up to the sky and stand still for a minute, reaching for the moon's embrace and then I smile, hugging my arms around my naked body.

Now a calm settles over me, and I take another step forward. And then I hear the ice moan underneath me. I look down and am shocked to see how thin it has become. I had almost forgotten where I was. I stare at my feet and I can see the black water beneath the ice, so thin that it is almost transparent.

I listen to the wind breathing in the woods. My own breath comes out like puffs of smoke and I shiver. I'm tempted to look behind me and see how far I've come, but if I do that I'll only go back. So here I stand, staring out into the trees across the ice and listening to the stillness that surrounds me.

The sky has gotten lighter. I can still see the moon but she's not as bright as before. Soon she will disappear, and although I will not be able to see her, I will know she is there, waiting.

I take a step forward and with a huge groan the ice swallows me whole. I hit the water laughing.

How It Works

1. Describe the story's events first in chronological order, then in the order in which the story presents them. What does the story gain by the author's choices regarding sequence? Imagine she had chosen to put the events in a different sequence—what would the effect have been?

2. This story contains a lot of concrete description. In her account of writing the story (see page 190), the author mentions images that occurred to her very early in the writing process, and she emphasizes the importance of being concrete in her revisions. Underline repeating images. How does the author use these concrete images to heighten emotion?

3. It would be easy to sentimentalize this narrator—a distraught, abused teenaged girl with an alcoholic mother. What steps does the author take to avoid this pitfall?

4. Take a look at the author's notes on her writing process (see page 190). Take similar notes on your own process through several drafts of a story. What changes did you make between the first and second drafts? Between the second and third?

Gabriel García Márquez

Gabriel García Márquez, one of the most important authors in the history of Latin American literature, was born in Aracataca, Colombia, in 1928. He was one of sixteen children. He worked for a time as a reporter, then began writing fiction. After writing a number of short stories and three novellas, all deeply indebted to Franz Kafka, García Márquez suffered a period of writer's block. This block ended when he suddenly saw the first chapter of his next novel, which would chronicle several generations of a Colombian family in the style known as magic realism, which explores the subjective nature of reality by depicting supernatural and fantastic occurrences in a very concrete, nonmystical manner. He wrote the book One Hundred Years of Solitude *(1967), in eighteen months. Other works by García Márquez include* Leaf Storm *(1955),* No One Writes to the Colonel *(1958),* The Autumn of the Patriarch *(1975),* Chronicle of a Death Foretold *(1983),* Collected Stories *(1984),* Love in the Time of Cholera *(1988), and* The General in His Labyrinth *(1989). Gabriel García Márquez was awarded the Nobel Prize for Literature in 1982. He lives in Mexico City.*

A Very Old Man with Enormous Wings

translated by Gregory Rabassa

On the third day of rain they had killed so many crabs inside the house that Pelayo had to cross his drenched courtyard and throw them into the sea, because the newborn child had a temperature all night and they thought it was due to the stench. The world had been sad since Tuesday. Sea and sky were a single ash-gray thing and the sands of the beach, which on March nights glimmered like powdered light, had become a stew of mud and rotten shellfish. The light was so weak at noon that when Pelayo was coming back to the house after throwing away the crabs, it was hard for him to see what it was that was moving and groaning in the rear of the courtyard. He had to go very close to see that it was an old man, a very old man, lying face down in the mud, who, in spite of his tremendous efforts, couldn't get up, impeded by his enormous wings.

Frightened by that nightmare, Pelayo ran to get Elisenda, his wife, who was putting compresses on the sick child, and he took her to the rear of the courtyard. They both looked at the fallen body with mute stupor. He was dressed like a ragpicker. There were only a few faded hairs left on his bald skull and very few teeth in his mouth, and his pitiful condition of a drenched great-grandfather had taken away any sense of grandeur he might have had. His huge buzzard wings, dirty and half-plucked, were forever entangled in the mud. They looked at him so long and so closely that Pelayo and Elisenda very soon overcame their surprise and in the end found him familiar. Then they dared speak to him, and he answered in an incomprehensible dialect with a strong sailor's voice. That was how they skipped over the inconvenience of the wings and quite intelligently concluded that he was a lonely castaway from some foreign ship wrecked by the storm. And yet, they called in a neighbor woman who knew everything about life and death to see him, and all she needed was one look to show them their mistake.

"He's an angel," she told them. "He must have been coming for the child, but the poor fellow is so old that the rain knocked him down."

On the following day everyone knew that a flesh-and-blood angel was held captive in Pelayo's house. Against the judgment of the wise neighbor woman, for whom angels in those times were the fugitive survivors of a celestial conspiracy, they did not have the heart to club him to death. Pelayo watched over him all afternoon from the kitchen, armed with his bailiff's club, and before going to bed he dragged him out of the mud and locked him up with the hens in the wire chicken coop. In the middle of the night, when the rain stopped, Pelayo and Elisenda were still killing crabs. A short time afterward the child woke up without a fever and with a desire to eat. Then they felt magnanimous and decided to put the angel on a raft with fresh water and provisions for three days and leave him to his fate on the high seas. But when they went out into the courtyard with the first light of dawn, they found the whole neighborhood in front of the chicken coop having fun with the angel, without the slightest reverence, tossing him things to eat through the openings in the wire as if he weren't a supernatural creature but a circus animal.

Father Gonzaga arrived before seven o'clock, alarmed at the strange news. By that time onlookers less frivolous than those at dawn had already arrived and they were making all kinds of conjectures concerning the captive's future. The simplest among them thought that he should be named mayor of the world. Others of sterner mind felt that he should be promoted to the rank of five-star general in order to win all wars. Some visionaries hoped that he could be put to stud in order to implant on earth a race of winged wise men who could take charge of the universe. But Father Gonzaga, before becoming a priest, had been a robust woodcutter. Standing by the wire, he reviewed his catechism in an instant and asked them to open the door so that he could take a close look at that pitiful man who looked more like a huge decrepit hen among the fascinated chickens. He was lying in a corner drying his open wings in the sunlight among the fruit peels and breakfast leftovers that the early risers had thrown him. Alien to the impertinences of the world, he only lifted his antiquarian eyes and murmured something in his dialect when Father Gonzaga went into the chicken coop and said good morning to him in Latin. The parish priest had his first suspicion of an impostor when he saw that he did not understand the language of God or know how to greet His ministers. Then he noticed that seen close up he was much too human: he had an unbearable smell of the outdoors, the back side of his wings were strewn with parasites and his main feathers had been mistreated by terrestrial winds, and nothing about him measured up to the proud dignity of angels. Then he came out of the chicken coop and in a brief sermon warned the curious against the risks of being ingenuous. He reminded them that the devil had the bad habit of making use of carnival tricks in order to confuse the unwary. He argued that if wings were not the essential element in determining the difference between a hawk and an airplane, they were even less so in the recognition of angels. Nevertheless, he promised to write a letter to his bishop so that the latter would write to his primate so that the latter would write to the Supreme Pontiff in order to get the final verdict from the highest courts.

His prudence fell on sterile hearts. The news of the captive angel spread with such rapidity that after a few hours the courtyard had the bustle of a marketplace and they had to call in troops with fixed bayonets to disperse the mob that was about to knock the house down. Elisenda, her spine all twisted from sweeping up so much marketplace trash, then got the idea of fencing in the yard and charging five cents admission to see the angel.

The curious came from far away. A traveling carnival arrived with a flying acrobat who buzzed over the crowd several times, but no one paid any attention to him because his wings were not those of an angel but, rather, those of a sidereal bat. The most unfortunate invalids on earth came in search of health: a poor woman who since childhood had been counting her heartbeats and had run out of numbers; a Portuguese man who couldn't sleep because the noise of the stars disturbed him; a sleepwalker who got up at night to undo the things he had done while awake; and many others with less serious ailments. In the midst of that shipwreck disorder that made the earth tremble, Pelayo and Elisenda were happy with fatigue, for in less than a week they had crammed their rooms with money and the line of pilgrims waiting their turn to enter still reached beyond the horizon.

The angel was the only one who took no part in his own act. He spent his time trying to get comfortable in his borrowed nest, befuddled by the hellish heat of the oil lamps and sacramental candles that had been placed along the wire. At first they tried to make him eat some mothballs, which, according to the wisdom of the wise neighbor woman, were the food prescribed for angels. But he turned them down, just as he turned down the papal lunches that the penitents brought him, and they never found out whether it was because he was an angel or because he was an old man that in the end ate nothing but eggplant mush. His only supernatural virtue seemed to be patience. Especially during the first days, when the hens pecked at him, searching for the stellar parasites that proliferated in his wings, and the cripples pulled out feathers to touch their defective parts with, and even the most merciful threw stones at him, trying to get him to rise so they could see him standing. The only time they succeeded in arousing him was when they burned his side with an iron for branding steers, for he had been motionless for so many hours that they thought he was dead. He awoke with a start, ranting in his hermetic language and with tears in his eyes, and he flapped his wings a couple of times, which brought on a whirlwind of chicken dung and lunar dust and a gale of panic that did not seem to be of this world. Although many thought that his reaction had been one not of rage but of pain, from then on they were careful not to annoy him, because the majority understood that his passivity was not that of a hero taking his ease but that of a cataclysm in repose.

Father Gonzaga held back the crowd's frivolity with formulas of maidservant inspiration while awaiting the arrival of a final judgment on the nature of the captive. But the mail from Rome showed no sense of urgency. They spent their time finding out if the prisoner had a navel, if his dialect had any connection with Aramaic, how many times he could fit on the head of a pin, or whether he wasn't just a Norwegian with wings. Those meager letters might have come and gone until the end of time if a providential event had not put an end to the priest's tribulations.

It so happened that during those days, among so many other carnival attractions, there arrived in town the traveling show of the woman who had been changed into a spider for having disobeyed her parents. The admission to see her was not only less than the admission to see the angel, but people were permitted to ask her all manner of questions about her absurd state and to examine her up and down so that no one would ever doubt the truth of her horror. She was a frightful tarantula the size of a ram and with the head of a sad maiden. What was most heart-rending, however, was not her outlandish shape but the sincere affliction with which she recounted the details of her misfortune. While still practically a child she had sneaked out of her parents' house to go to a dance, and while she was coming back through the woods after having danced all night without permission, a fearful thunderclap rent the sky in two and through the crack came the lightning bolt of brimstone that changed her into a spider. Her only nourishment came from the meatballs that charitable souls chose to toss into her mouth. A spectacle like that, full of so much human truth and with such a fearful lesson, was bound to defeat without even trying that of a haughty angel who scarcely deigned to look at mortals. Besides, the few miracles attributed to the angel showed a certain mental disorder, like the blind man who didn't recover his sight but grew three new teeth, or the paralytic who didn't get to walk but almost won the lottery, and the leper whose sores sprouted sunflowers. Those consolation miracles, which were more like mocking fun, had already ruined the angel's reputation when the woman who had been changed into a spider finally crushed him completely. That was how Father Gonzaga was cured forever of his insomnia and Pelayo's courtyard went back to being as empty as during the time it had rained for three days and crabs walked through the bedrooms.

The owners of the house had no reason to lament. With the money they saved they built a two-story mansion with balconies and gardens and high netting so that crabs wouldn't get in during the winter, and with iron bars on the windows so that angels wouldn't get in. Pelayo also set up a rabbit warren close to town and gave up his job as bailiff for good, and Elisenda bought some satin pumps with high heels and many dresses of iridescent silk, the kind worn on Sunday by the most desirable women in those times. The chicken coop was the only thing that didn't receive any attention. If they washed it down with Creolin and burned tears of myrrh inside it every so often, it was not in homage to the angel but to drive away the dungheap stench that still hung everywhere like a ghost and was turning the new house into an old one. At first, when the child learned to walk, they were careful that he not get too close to the chicken coop. But then they began to lose their fears and got used to the smell, and before the child got his second teeth he'd gone inside the chicken coop to play, where the wires were falling apart. The angel was no less stand-offish with him than with other mortals, but he tolerated the most ingenious infamies with the patience of a dog who had no illusions. They both came down with chicken pox at the same time. The doctor who took care of the child couldn't resist the temptation to listen to the angel's heart, and he found so much whistling in the heart and so many sounds in his kidneys that it seemed impossible for him to be alive. What surprised him most, however, was the logic of his wings. They seemed so natural on that completely human organism that he couldn't understand why other men didn't have them too.

When the child began school it had been some time since the sun and rain had caused the collapse of the chicken coop. The angel went dragging himself about here and there like a stray dying man. They would drive him out of the bedroom with a broom and a moment later find him in the kitchen. He seemed to be in so many places at the same time that they grew to think that he'd been duplicated, that he was reproducing himself all through the house, and the exasperated and unhinged Elisenda shouted that it was awful living in that hell full of angels. He could scarcely eat and his antiquarian eyes had also become so foggy that he went about bumping into posts. All he had left were the bare cannulae of his last feathers. Pelayo threw a blanket over him and extended him the charity of letting him sleep in the shed, and only then did they notice that he had a temperature at night, and was delirious with the tongue twisters of an old Norwegian. That was one of the few times they became alarmed, for they thought he was going to die and not even the wise neighbor woman had been able to tell them what to do with dead angels.

And yet he not only survived his worst winter, but seemed improved with the first sunny days. He remained motionless for several days in the farthest corner of the courtyard, where no one would see him, and at the beginning of December some large, stiff feathers began to grow on his wings, the feathers of a scarecrow, which looked more like another misfortune of decrepitude. But he must have known the reason for those changes, for he was quite careful that no one should notice them, that no one should hear the sea chanteys that he sometimes sang under the stars. One morning Elisenda was cutting some bunches of onions for lunch when a wind that seemed to come from the high seas blew into the kitchen. Then she went to the window and caught the angel in his first attempts at flight. They were so clumsy that his fingernails opened a furrow in the vegetable patch and he was on the point of knocking the shed down with the ungainly flapping that slipped on the light and couldn't get a grip on the air. But he did manage to gain altitude. Elisenda let out a sigh of relief, for herself and for him, when she saw him pass over the last houses, holding himself up in some way with the risky flapping of a senile vulture. She kept watching him even when she was through cutting the onions and she kept on watching until it was no longer possible for her to see him, because then he was no longer an annoyance in her life but an imaginary dot on the horizon of the sea.

How It Works

1. Underline the concrete physical descriptions in this story. What does each one contribute to the story?

2. How does García Márquez's angel differ from other angels you've heard about? What was your initial reaction to him? How did that feeling grow or change over the course of the story? Would the story have affected you differently if the angel

had been more conventionally rendered? How does García Márquez work with and against convention to engage readers in this unusual situation?

3. What images remain in your mind after reading this story? What feels most real? Do the realistic parts of the story feel more real than the fanciful parts? Why or why not? What does this story teach you about rendering the fantastic?

4. Pick another kind of fantastic creature—a ghost, a demon, a fairy, a gremlin—and render it unconventionally. Use concrete descriptive detail to make it real.

Jakob Ludwig Carl Grimm
Wilhelm Carl Grimm

Jakob Ludwig Carl Grimm and Wilhelm Carl Grimm were born in Hanau, Germany, in 1785 and 1786, respectively. Their parents died just as the two brothers reached adulthood. Influenced by the cultural, political, and social changes of their times and by the German Romantic movement, the Grimm brothers came to value the literature of the past as a source of national pride and purpose, and together collected a number of folktales, publishing them as the Kinder- und Hausmärchen (Children's and Household Tales), *the title of which implied that the stories were meant for adults and children alike. These stories, which came to be known as* Grimm's Fairy Tales, *presented folklore in a readable form and were eventually published worldwide. In 1840 the brothers became members of the Academy of Sciences in Berlin and professors at the University of Berlin. They remained in Berlin until their deaths.*

Little Red-Cap

Once upon a time there was a dear little girl who was loved by everyone who looked at her, but most of all by her grandmother, and there was nothing that she would not have given to the child. Once she gave her a little cap of red velvet, which suited her so well that she would never wear anything else; so she was always called "Little Red-Cap."

One day her mother said to her: "Come, Little Red-Cap, here is a piece of cake and a bottle of wine; take them to your grandmother, she is ill and weak, and they will do her good. Set out before it gets hot, and when you are going, walk nicely and quietly and do not run off the path, or you may fall and break the bottle, and then your grandmother will get nothing; and when you go into her room, don't forget to say, 'Good-morning,' and don't peep into every corner before you do it."

"I will take great care," said Little Red-Cap to her mother, and gave her hand on it.

The grandmother lived out in the wood, half a league from the village, and just as Little Red-Cap entered the wood, a wolf met her. Red-Cap did not know what a wicked creature he was, and was not at all afraid of him.

"Good-day, Little Red-Cap," said he.

"Thank you kindly, wolf."

"Whither away so early, Little Red-Cap?"

"To my grandmother's."

"What have you got in your apron?"

"Cake and wine; yesterday was baking-day, so poor sick grandmother is to have something good, to make her stronger."

"Where does your grandmother live, Little Red-Cap?"

"A good quarter of a league farther on in the wood; her house stands under the three large oak-trees, the nut-trees are just below; you surely must know it," replied Little Red-Cap.

The wolf thought to himself: "What a tender young creature! what a nice plump mouthful—she will be better to eat than the old woman. I must act craftily, so as to catch both." So he walked for a short time by the side of Little Red-Cap, and then he said: "See, Little Red-Cap, how pretty the flowers are about here—why do you not look round? I believe, too, that you do not hear how sweetly the little birds are singing; you walk gravely along as if you were going to school, while everything else out here in the wood is merry."

Little Red-Cap raised her eyes, and when she saw the sunbeams dancing here and there through the trees, and pretty flowers growing everywhere,

she thought: "Suppose I take grandmother a fresh nosegay; that would please her too. It is so early in the day that I shall still get there in good time"; and so she ran from the path into the wood to look for flowers. And whenever she had picked one, she fancied that she saw a still prettier one farther on and ran after it, and so got deeper and deeper into the wood.

Meanwhile the wolf ran straight to the grandmother's house and knocked at the door.

"Who is there?"

"Little Red-Cap," replied the wolf. "She is bringing cake and wine; open the door."

"Lift the latch," called out the grandmother, "I am too weak, and cannot get up."

The wolf lifted the latch, the door sprang open, and without saying a word he went straight to the grandmother's bed, and devoured her. Then he put on her clothes, dressed himself in her cap, laid himself in bed and drew the curtains.

Little Red-Cap, however, had been running about picking flowers, and when she had gathered so many that she could carry no more, she remembered her grandmother, and set out on the way to her.

She was surprised to find the cottage-door standing open, and when she went into the room, she had such a strange feeling that she said to herself: "Oh dear! how uneasy I feel today, and at other times I like being with grandmother so much." She called out: "Good morning," but received no answer; so she went to the bed and drew back the curtains. There lay her grandmother with her cap pulled far over her face, and looking very strange.

"Oh! grandmother," she said, "what big ears you have!"

"The better to hear you with, my child," was the reply.

"But, grandmother, what big eyes you have!" she said.

"The better to see you with, my dear."

"But, grandmother, what large hands you have!"

"The better to hug you with."

"Oh! but, grandmother, what a terrible big mouth you have!"

"The better to eat you with!"

And scarcely had the wolf said this, than with one bound he was out of bed and swallowed up Red-Cap.

When the wolf had appeased his appetite, he lay down again in the bed, feel asleep and began to snore very loud. The huntsman was just passing the house, and thought to himself: "How the old woman is snoring! I must just see if she wants anything." So he went into the room, and when he came to the bed, he saw that the wolf was lying in it. "Do I find you here, you old sinner!" said he. "I have long sought you!" Then just as he was going to fire at him, it occurred to him that the wolf might have devoured the grandmother, and that she might still be saved, so he did not fire, but took a pair of scissors, and began to cut open the stomach of the sleeping wolf. When he had made two snips, he saw the little Red-Cap shining, and then he made two snips more, and the little girl sprang out, crying: "Ah, how frightened I have been! How dark it was inside the wolf"; and after that the aged grandmother came out alive also, but scarcely able to breathe. Red-Cap, however, quickly fetched great stones with which they filled the wolf's belly, and when he awoke, he wanted to run away, but the stones were so heavy that he collapsed at once, and fell dead.

Then all three were delighted. The huntsman drew off the wolf's skin and went home with it; the grandmother ate the cake and drank the wine which Red-Cap had brought, and revived, but Red-Cap thought to herself: "As long as I live, I will never by myself leave the path, to run into the wood, when my mother has forbidden me to do so."

It is also related that once when Red-Cap was again taking cakes to the old grandmother, another wolf spoke to her, and tried to entice her from the path. Red-Cap, however, was on her guard, and went straight forward on her way, and told her grandmother than she had met the wolf, and that he had said "good-morning" to her, but with such a wicked look in his eyes, that if they had not been on the public road she was certain he would have eaten her up. "Well," said the grandmother, "we will shut the door, that he may not come in." Soon afterwards the wolf knocked, and cried: "Open the door, grandmother, I am little Red-Cap, and am bringing you some cakes." But they did not speak, or open the door, so the grey-beard stole twice or thrice round the house, and at last jumped on the roof, intending to wait until Red-Cap went home in the evening, and then to steal after her and devour her in the darkness. But the grandmother saw what was in his thoughts. In front of the house was a great stone trough, so she said to the child: "Take the pail, Red-Cap; I made some sausages yesterday, so carry the water in which I boiled them to the trough." Red-Cap carried until the great trough was quite full. Then the small of sausages reached the wolf, and he sniffed and peeped down, and at last stretched out his neck so far that he could no longer keep his footing and began to slip and slipped down from the roof straight into the great trough, and was drowned. But Red-Cap went joyously home, and no one every did anything to harm her again.

How It Works

1. Read the story aloud. Where is the its climactic moment, and when did you first start to feel it coming? How does the author signal it?

2. Using that moment as the peak, diagram the plot using the narrative arc as explained on page 73. Add in each event. Notice how everything that happens in this story has a function on the arc. Now look at the alternative ending discussed on page 300. Draw another arc, using that ending instead of the standard one. What changes on the arc? If you were discussing this story in a workshop, how would you express the pros and cons of each possible ending?

3. Does the main character in this story make a decisive choice? Do other characters? How do the characters change as a result of their choices? How does the author signify these changes? How does the main character's change in this story differ from those that occur in other stories contained in this anthology?

4. Write the name of each character across the top of a page. Under each name, list that character's personality traits. Are your lists long or short? Are the traits simple or complex? How does the story differ in this respect from others in this book? Try tinkering with these qualities, making them more or less dramatic, adding opposite or neutral traits, trading qualities from character to character. How do these exercises change the story and its import?

Garnette Hall

Garnette Hall is a painter and writer currently living in Los Angeles. She attended the School of the Museum of Fine Arts in Boston and Tufts University, where she received the Morse Hamilton Fiction Award for her story "8 Mountains." About that story, she writes: "'8 Mountains' began as random scraps of paper. While waiting for or riding on the train I scribbled down the memories that drifted into my mind. Each memory developed intensely and carefully as an individual scene and then I later arranged them within a structure. For me, structure seemed to be the greatest obstacle because memories flow in a way that is both connected and random. I was inspired by the paragraph structure in Brenda Miller's essay 'A Thousand Buddhas.' The sections of her essay conjured up vivid sensations although their relationship wasn't immediately clear. '8 Mountains' began from what I knew, and from that expanded into what I believe: that a memory of a past experience exists only in a fictionalized state. My writing is fiction because what I write is no longer a reality."

8 Mountains

4 Years

An ash green cabin, with a small yard and a pathway round the back made of thin pieces of slate, northern New Jersey. The trees were tremendous pillars whose branches formed blankets of shade. The Red Maples sent down spinning pinwheels in autumn. I would much rather have lived in the house down the road, whose exterior was white with exposed dark-beam supports, like a German gingerbread house. Our cabin was small, which made us cozy in the winter, like a family of birds in the tender enclosure of a nest. In snowy evenings by the fire, I would quietly rearrange soft objects to create a niche for slumber while my sister held chatty conversations with her dolls.

I was born the eldest daughter to an engineer and a nutritionist. At first my hair was an inky black, but each year the sun lightened it more and more to a shade of red, like my mother's. Mother liked to point it out to her grocery store acquaintances and say, "Look how Garnette's hair is getting more red like mine." And they would say, "Oh, yes, very pretty, her hair has gotten very pretty, like *yours.*" It is not a disappointment to me that my eyebrows have been left unaffected from those many summers I spent at the ocean and bicycling in the sun. They are black and thick, startlingly so against the paleness of my face.

For four years, the first four of my life, we lived in the ash green cabin, snuggled between other like-sized cabins. The neighborhood was built as a summer retreat for wealthy New Yorkers some forty years ago, but now families lived there year-round. The cabins were on a steep hill, and at the base of the hill was a lake, which was polluted. The pollution didn't keep people from swimming in the lake. There was an enclosed section next to the sailboat dock where children could come for lessons in the summer. Once the lake rid Mother's foot of a plantar's wart modern medicine had failed to cure. Mother's feet are massive with small toes, like the illustrations of Neanderthal men's. I inherited them. Mine are larger, but still have the abnormally short pinky toe that has been the cursed gene of women in my family.

My friend Jenny lived in the cabin next door. We ate a lot of mint chip ice cream together, even in the winter. At her house the mint was white, at my house it was green, and at that time I much preferred the green. This was before I learned that the green color was food dye and usually meant artificial flavoring.

The inside of our cabin was filled with mahogany furniture, dark and heavy-looking, with little feet sticking out beneath mammoth facades. My room was pearlescent pink, like a mermaid's shell, but that's all I can remember about it.

My most vivid memory is of Nagle's candy shop. It was a real life Hansel and Gretel house, with cheap foil-wrapped chocolates, barrels of novelty candies, and glass cases filled with handmade vanilla creams. The exterior had colorful glass windows, the old kind that are almost opaque and slump thicker at the bottom from age. Mother purchased a collection of plastic chocolate molds for every holiday there. She would melt down bars of chocolate and spoon them into molds of bunnies, jack-o-lanterns, mittens, shamrocks, hearts. When I was young she made a big fuss for the holidays. At Easter I would search for baskets—not one, but one for each room—filled with marshmallow eggs, orange jelly beans, pastel shelled candies, Cadbury cream eggs, molded chocolate rabbits, and sugar-speckled chicks, all laid carefully in a bed of green plastic grass.

I loved to visit my grandmother, who lived in the farming area of northeast New Jersey. I wanted a house like hers—clean and comfortable, with antique clocks that chimed on each hour, even in the middle of the night. The bed sheets were soft and still white after years of washing, the wood furniture polished from the wear of four generations of children. My grandmother would sit in a grand armchair and tell stories while my sister and I sat on the couch, wrapped in a white-flowered quilt. The back screen door of the house was always open in the summer, leading out onto a pear orchard. We always entered through the back door, into the marvelous scents of her kitchen. The back door was intimate, a place of greetings and smiles. I never knew anyone to use the front door, which faced the road. Her bathroom was my favorite room, decorated in delicate shades of blue and white—cobalt blue jars and bottles filled with talc and lavender, white linen curtains, oversized towels that smelled like a turbulent ocean. A room in a hundred-year-old house, with cracking ceilings like that of a fragile egg, doors slightly ill-fitted from settling, yet so beautifully clean.

13 Years

A barn-shaped house, light blue with brown shutters, suburban Maryland, two floors, four bedrooms, quarter-acre of land. I shared a bedroom with my younger sister, Alyssum. Our bedroom was pink, with strawberry print bedspreads and curtains, two dark wood bureaus with glass knobs, and five wide shelves of picture books. Our bathroom was also pink, and remained so for sixteen years, until I came home on a visit from college and found Alyssum had painted it white. She told me it had taken her four coats to get rid of all the pink, as if the pinkness was a disease, as if her past girlhood was a disease. My half of our shared room was always clean. I kept my shoes in neat rows and my dolls arranged in a bassinet. Once I got up in the middle of the night to clean up my toys, to surprise Mother in the morning. Mother found me awake and spanked me.

At age ten I got my own room and a set of heavy oak furniture. My bedroom was small and had one window overlooking a Christmas tree farm. Because the room was small I rearranged the furniture every few weeks for several years until I found the most space-efficient composition.

Mother often warned me about my grandmother's compulsion to throw away important things. "Could be of value to someone. Nana throws away things that are perfectly good, nothing wrong with them. She just throws them away."

"Mm-hmm," I would mumble, trying to feign attention as she paced the room in agitation, readjusting the position of the phone, the stacks of bills, the couch pillows.

"She doesn't even think if anyone would want them. She threw away all my toys, all the dolls from my childhood. She didn't even ask me if I wanted them. I know you're happy I saved all your toys in boxes down in the basement, because someone's been rummaging through them lately, it must have been you."

I had gone down in the basement to explore the things Mother had saved so diligently. There were mail-order cosmetics, still in their boxes, from the short time she had spent as an Avon lady. There was a hope chest and a woodland painting that covered up a huge hole in the foundation. When I was seven I had asked my father to cement the inside of the hole so that I could make a secret room, but he said the basement was too damp to play in. In the far corner were Mother's outdated nutrition books from college and Father's collection of protractors and drafting equipment. There were boxes full of holiday decorations—not one box for each but a huge semi-conglomerate of Halloween costumes, plastic Easter eggs, three plastic Christmas trees (two green and one silver), broken glass ornaments, a web of tinsel and silver beads, children's birthday favors. And I found my toys. They had a permanent musty smell from when the basement had flooded. Some of them had been packed away so long I couldn't remember when I got them or even playing with them, only that I felt a powerful attachment to them. I carried several boxes to my bedroom. I sorted them, gently washed them and placed them in plastic storage boxes according to type: stuffed animals, plastic figures, or trinkets. When I finished I had three large and four small plastic containers filling half of my closet. They are still there, but I took a few important treasures with me when I left home—a brown gingerbread perfume bottle with lavender icing details, a white and cobalt unicorn print bottle my father gave me, and a chocolate-colored Pound Puppy I had named Chocolate. When I come to Maryland for visits I sort through the boxes, eliminating a few of the items that seem trivial, caressing the ones that remind me of when they were my most valuable possessions.

My brother Devin was born in 1985, when I was six. He was my best friend, and I adored him. He had opal skin and thick hair the color of beach sand. His heart was as fragile as butterfly wings. I used to pretend he was my baby. He died when I was ten. Mother kept the marble urn by her bed, refusing to put it in the ground. She continued to set the table for five. She stopped going to church because infant baptisms made her weep; the sweet voices of the children's choir crumbled her. I wished it had been me in the marble urn, because I knew he had been her favorite. Updated photos of Alyssum and me transformed beside his unchanging one. Our images went through stages of awkward braces and brattiness, while his continued to smile. After Devin died we had a brilliant, caring father and a mother who existed

only in moving shadows. It seemed as if us being alive was not as important to her as him being dead. She saved all his toys, his clothes, even hamburger wrappers he had scribbled on. Then it expanded to old coupons, yellowing newspapers, used tissues and Q-tips, molding food. She said she couldn't let go of them, she was afraid of losing something important. Slowly all the rooms started to fill. Doors wouldn't open or close, the cats would go unseen for days. The food in the pantry was expired and had bugs in it. Even sealed plastic chip bags and soda bottles—the maggots managed to worm their way into everything that was edible. Mother stopped cooking meals after Devin died but sometimes she would try and serve me food from the pantry, saying, "Not all of the food has bugs in it," but I always refused to eat. She was a homemaker and a nutritionist, but she never taught my sister or me how to cook, and with the state of the kitchen I never asked.

My father took her to a doctor who gave her pills. Mother pretended to take them but we knew she flushed them down the sink each day. Alyssum and I would try to sneak bags of trash out on Monday mornings without her waking. She would rush down the driveway in her nightgown just as the garbage men arrived and pull the trash cans into the house. She would search through empty milk cartons and eggshells and opened envelopes, and then upon finding something of value, like the back of an earring, she would say, "See! you were going to throw this out, you're lucky that I rescued it." Outdated school newsletters and worn-out tee shirts I had disposed of would be redelivered to my room months later. The years of garbage collected in layers. If I dug from the ceiling to the carpet I would find a cross-section of experiences: Girl Scout cookie boxes, spelling tests, baseball mitts, training bras, board games. Malleable mountains of the past formed barriers over closets and heating vents, exposing certain memories while burying others. As I got older I stayed away from home as much as possible. I slept over at my friends' houses often, but never invited them to mine. I saw how clean my friends' mothers kept their houses and I believed they must love their daughters more. I was bitter and angry at Mother for floating away from us and I showed her by pushing her further away, excluding her from the passioned talk about dreams and plans and experiences I happily divulged to my sister and father.

When I turned sixteen I started having a persistent dream about Devin. I was back in middle school. Devin's wrapped corpse was in my locker. I was supposed to bring it home, but when I went to my locker at the end of the day I forgot, and his body became crushed under books at the bottom of the locker. It started to smell. Each day I remembered my duty but each day I forgot. I felt a tremendous guilt for having forgotten him.

For six of the thirteen years that I lived in that house I was chronically ill—strep, pneumonia, mononucleosis, sinus infections, asthma. In bed, surrounded by empty soup bowls and flat ginger ale, I would recall my past illnesses and try to determine the worst. Once I woke up in the middle of the night with my throat so swollen I couldn't swallow. Father had to crush penicillin into a paste with applesauce to try and push it down my throat. It hurt more to cry because it contracted my throat, but I was in tremendous pain and couldn't stop. It lasted for five days. After being able to eat nothing but popsicles for that time, nausea set in. It was a nausea that never culminated in vomiting, although I desperately hoped it would, to end the dizziness. I spent midnights and mornings seated on the cold bathroom tiles by the toilet, waiting for something to happen.

1 Month

In the early morning I could hear the Italian religious parades passing through the narrow alleys, shrines flourished with dollar bills and followed by a six-piece marching band. On the corner of one alley was a 24-hour Italian bakery, which I never visited until after I moved out of the apartment. In passing I could see cases filled with strawberry cakes topped with white icing, chocolate chip cannolis, moon pies filled with gelatinized whip cream, and Boston creme cakes.

The stairwell was steep and wound like a whelk shell, poorly lit, finding each landing was a surprise. There were three doors at each, but only one opened with a key. The rooms of the apartment connected like a chain, one into the other. Mine was the smallest, with a glass door that I covered with a blue flowered curtain, and two French style doors that led out the other side to my roommate's room. My room was shaped like a triangle. It was an uncomfortable space, like a hallway. I felt cornered at every position in the room. I lived with two girls, each an only child, both a full foot shorter than I. *You're gonna get it, Garnette. I'm telling you, you're gonna pay for this.* One was Russian and one was from New Hampshire. The girl from New Hampshire had an Irish boyfriend who liked to use the word *fucking* as an adjective. I temporarily adopted a foul mouth from him, and it didn't suit me well at all. I always felt like I was forcing the words. *You're driving me fucking crazy! I can't fucking stand it! Get the fuck away from me or I'll throw you out that goddamn fucking window!* The floors were hardwood. I missed the carpet of home, among other things.

I had brought a lot of stuff with me to Boston. Too much. Even with so many belongings, I didn't feel as if I was in a home. I felt transient, waiting for the next thing, a better thing. One month was agonizing, wanting to be in transit.

11 Months

An apartment in a converted three-floor home with a colonial blue and white exterior, Jamaica Plain, Massachusetts. I lived with an acquaintance from high school on the second floor of the building, which was an enormous two-and-a-half-bedroom apartment. The landlord lived on the first floor with his wife and brother. When the wife cooked each day the pungent aroma of Middle Eastern food would engulf the hallway, striking me with a painful hunger, even after I'd just eaten. There was a long hallway directly after entering the apartment that narrowed as I walked toward the kitchen. It had a kind of *Alice in Wonderland* effect, I always felt fatter and wider as I entered the kitchen and slimmer and more elegant when I left. The kitchen windows overlooked a family's backyard. The family was bratty and had noisy patio gatherings but I envied them. I longed for the stability of a chosen path that seemed too many years in my future to be real. I nested in my room, stringing up white Christmas tree lights and collecting nature and memories abundantly in boxes. I had collections of seashells and polished stones and photos and jewelry box ballerinas and bird feathers. I filled the boxes tightly—filling them as if I was filling myself. The floors were hardwood and collected dust easily, and so I swept my bedroom methodically each day. Mother rarely sent packages, but when she did the contents were a variety of drug store commodities—vitamins and grocery brand chocolates, coupons, shampoo, newspaper articles.

My roommate hated his mother and as it turned out, strong women in general. He had five televisions, each of which received one channel with reasonable reception. He left sticky jam residue on the kitchen table and on the telephone. He left all the lights on and sometimes the stove when he went out in the evening.

I didn't cook often, but I stockpiled food in expectation of a blizzard, the tremendous Boston type I had been promised. To be snowed in with a cup of cocoa and chicken soup seemed glorious, but it never happened. The grocery store was forty minutes away by bus. My friend and I would make the trek on Sunday mornings. I adored the grocery store, the act of collecting and recollecting each week. I would write lists, read nutritional content, compare prices by weight.

While living in that apartment, in the eighteenth year of my life, I started eating in indulgent repetitions. At the time my current breakfast favorites were strawberry yogurt (the thick kind), not-from-concentrate orange juice, a hardboiled egg, and an English muffin with cinnamon and sugar. I ate these foods, usually in that order, every day for eleven months. Then one day I was disgusted by the thought of that combination. So then for one year I ate strawberry yogurt, not-from-concentrate orange juice, a hardboiled egg, and a half bowl of cream of wheat. After that it was strawberry yogurt, not-from-concentrate orange juice, bran flakes, and buttered toast. The combination change often coincided with a move, but not predictably.

Packing was fun. I could look at each thing, scrutinize it, ponder its potential necessity and importance. Each time I moved I looked forward to this ritual, often starting two and three months ahead of the move date, in anticipation of a new and better home, a more perfect home. I felt like I was giving myself an examination, discerning from what is me and not me. I had read a book on the art of Feng Shui, and it said that you should only surround yourself with things that you can say you *absolutely* love. At that time I thought that if I surrounded myself with more things it meant I had found many things in life to love. And so along with my treasured belongings I kept things that I thought one day could mean something, could be important, even if they weren't yet.

9 Months

An immaculate house. I didn't read, paint, work, or relax until my home was clean and organized. Living by myself for the first time, I immersed myself in the responsibility of caring for my own kitchen, bathroom, living room, and bedroom. The walls were pure white and the floors a newly lacquered pine that smelled of polyurethane. My childhood oak furniture filled up the rooms like heavy building blocks, with drawers pillowed full of wool winter sweaters and blue bed sheets. There were four rooms and I filled them all with plants. I rescued a scorched ficus and palm that had been set out as garbage. I made it my duty to resurrect them from their neglected condition. The strong smells of peppermint and oregano and lavender and marjoram and meadow rue and basic plants filled the rooms. I visited them, my babies, each morning before breakfast: watering them, checking for insects, fluffing their soil. The street was quiet on a hill with trees, at the end of the orange subway line in Forest Hills, Massachusetts. School was thirty minutes away by train, and so coming home became a salvation. I would steam white rice and watch pointless television shows on one of the five channels.

I had a collection of maps. World maps: physical, political, topographical. U.S. maps, state maps, celestial maps, maps of whale migration patterns. They covered the walls in abundant blueness. It was a beautiful color—right in between the blue of the sky and the blue of the ocean. My bed was pale blue and white and so I was able to hover in-between, like a low-lying cloud. The bathroom had small blue and white tiles, a blue sink and bathtub, a white toilet, and a blue and white checkered shower curtain. The blue was a pale tone nearly devoid of pigment. The room was encapsulating, fifteen feet long and three feet wide, with no windows and a fluorescent light, like a tunnel with terry cloth towel buffers on either end. The kitchen had shiny maple wood cabinets with robin's egg blue doors, which had white knobs with pink and blue flowers. I had a ridiculous collection of kitchen accessories—a potato masher, a garlic crusher, ice tongs, different sized mesh strainers—collected with the intention of teaching myself how to cook. My idealization of the task, at least, was genuine. I had mismatched wood chairs for the kitchen table and the back porch. The porch had a view of the arboretum in summer and the highway in winter, depending on the density of the oak leaves that surrounded the porch. In the kitchen I also had a wood table with a green picnic cloth, which always had a napkin holder and glass salt and pepper shakers on top. The bedroom and kitchen in the back of the apartment were icy in winter, even with plastic insulation and heavy blankets for curtains. The front rooms beamed with direct morning sunlight, as if there were no walls to shade. It was an effortless greenhouse. In the winter the temperature never fell below eighty degrees even if the bedroom was fifty.

The most pitiful thing I ate in shameless abundance was cold macaroni and cheese. I actually liked it better left over. This was not the reason that people didn't come to see me often, it was just that I was far away from everything, and I preferred it that way.

On Saturday I would paint all day in my studio at school. The room would always be empty except for another painter named Sia, who talked to me sometimes. Eventually I looked forward to seeing his feet under the partition. He took walks at night to look at the moon, and after two months of talking with him, he invited me to go with him. I led him to the North End of Boston where I used to live, to the 24-hour bakery. I had a moon pie and he had a baguette. We walked past midnight, long after the train stopped running. He offered to walk me home, even though it took four hours. I let him sleep in my bed until the morning when the train started running again.

A few years earlier, I had discovered the pleasure of washing laundry. I found the transformation from dirty to clean satisfying. But the laundromat was down the hill and turned laundry back into a chore. So I decided to keep moving in search of the perfect home, the perfect town. Each time I moved I learned a little about what's important. A grocery store nearby and a laundry machine in the same building, especially if it snows often. Carpeting is preferable to hardwood floors because you can walk around barefoot. Gas stoves cook more evenly than electric and are less expensive. The higher the floor in an apartment building the better the view and less street noise you hear. Elevators are important if you want to live above the second floor. I felt that if I knew what made the perfect nest, the perfect home, I could discover myself within that nest.

5 Months

I moved in with Sia, who after four months of night walks, had seduced me. Or maybe it was I who seduced him. His apartment was dark and mysterious, with black blankets and black furniture, so different from my light blue apartment. The blackness was enveloping, but was not as dark as the depth of his eyes, which were bright and dark like eclipsed suns. The apartment consisted of one small room, a kitchenette and a bathroom. The front of the building overlooked a park and a magnificent rose garden, but all his windows overlooked an alley. Nevertheless, he raised phalaenopsis orchids on the windowsill. He carved my initial into the mahogany molding of his doorframe next to his own. I started baking, not always successfully, but I enjoyed it and it amused him. He cooked gourmet for me. Not the creamy French foods I savored—but biting, sour Persian foods. Tart pickles, dried limes, dill yogurt. He ate meat, which I hadn't tasted for five years, twice a day. The tiny kitchen was filled with bottles of precious saffron, rose water, and wine. The sabzi herb mix he used often in cooking was intense. Its potent aroma lingered long after the food was eaten, clinging to my clothes and to the bed sheets like a heavy perfume.

He is a transient. A true transient, whereas I have only have been impatient with homes these past few years. His family fled the Iran/Iraq war when he was seven. They moved westward, to refugee camps in Turkey and Germany. After arriving in America they never stayed in one place for more than a year. He has traveled over countries, continents, states, and oceans. He is like a hawk and I a finch; he sweeps across mountains, whereas I am still hopping across small ponds.

One evening Sia rushed home with a baby sparrow that he had found abandoned on the ground outside the rose garden. "He must have fallen out of his nest, he's too young to even open his eyes yet," he said, out of breath. "He's hurt badly. There's a scrape on his head and a hole under his left wing." Sia placed the bird gently on the bed and then quickly gathered socks to set up a makeshift nest. The sparrow opened and closed his mouth and made barely audible noises. Sia mixed cornmeal with water to feed him. I watched the helpless sparrow into the night, knowing and fearing his fate. The sparrow must have been lying on the ground for awhile before Sia found him, for flies had already laid eggs in his wounds, and by morning his insides were taken over by maggots. Sia buried him in the rose garden.

2 Months

I moved with Sia to a new apartment. One with beige carpet. A dishwasher. Laundry in the hallway. A working heater and elevator. It was seductively modern, like a hotel. We didn't need to clean when we moved in, it came like a package, twenty years old but seemingly just built. The apartment had two rooms. I had sent my oak furniture back to Maryland so they were divinely empty. We had a bed and a small round table but mostly we sat on the floor. Six stories high but closer to the earth. When I lived alone I used to sleep facing the wall. With Sia I find I always face out—towards the door, as if away from sleep.

One autumn afternoon I was lying on the bed, playing with Sia's prayer beads and staring at the vast whiteness of the wall. Sia was seated on the edge of the bed, watching the birds out the window. He turned to me and said, "Isn't it beautiful? When ducks migrate to the south they don't need to take anything with them. Their destination, their flight patterns, it's all internal."

I thought of my younger self, en route to my grandmother's for the weekend, stuffed in the backseat with poorly-folded maps, suitcases, and a cooler full of iced tea. I glanced over to Sia. He seemed to be lingering in the possibility of weightlessness.

He continued, "I want to be free like that. Coasting from place to place. When I fled Iran, all I had was a backpack. I don't have any physical proof of that time, but I remember it more vividly than any other."

It occurred to me that all my life I had been collecting dead things, vessels, boxes, papers to document something that had already passed me by. I had collected so many containers full of memories—letters, photographs, gifts, sketchbooks, things that would outlive me. If I sat down to review them all it would take up the rest of my lifetime, and so truly how many years would I have lived then? Half my life spent living, half my life spent remembering how I lived.

For Thanksgiving I cooked all day. I remembered why I had never cooked meat for myself. It's the color of blood and of raw poultry skin, the rubbery feel of it that disgusted me. I rubbed down a twenty-pound turkey with lemons and bay leaves and garlic. I baked pumpkin bread and cinnamon yams and scalloped potatoes and stuffing and gravy from long recipes. I was triumphant. The two weeks of meals it produced fell like heavy stones in our stomachs—after each one we could do nothing but nap for an hour. I was so proud. I had accomplished what I had always admired in my grandmother— the deliverance of a masterful meal, perfectly arranged to arrive all components from the stove and the oven to the table simultaneously. On that day I embraced what I had learned a home should be, but in my mind shed the necessity of it. I could have just as easily ordered a pizza.

1 Month and Counting

I have two months until we leave. Everything I do now seems in anticipation of flight—true flight—a suitcase, a 3,000 mile destination and us two, Sia and me. To a new home, only this time on the other side of the country. We visited California this past January, one month ago. It has since taken over my mind, my commitments, my desires. It was the first time I felt the pleasure of a breath. I spent all day just breathing the air and never felt as if anything were lacking. All this time I have been searching for a box, a box with the right-colored walls and the right amount of sunlight. A box to put all my belongings, to make a material arrangement of my existence. I had a fifty-pound collection of books that I believed defined me. I had four winter coats. I had bottles and baskets full of peppermint foot lotion Mother sent me from the drugstore that I had never used. I'm selling what's left of my furniture, most of my books, tapes, clothes, other excesses. I'm letting go of my mountainous seashell collection and keeping those most precious ones in a thimble box.

Sia talks about California often and with great excitement, to keep our spirits up during the constant gray weather. "Remember how it felt when we were swimming in California? It was winter, but your face was glowing with freckles. When we inhaled, we breathed in the smell of flowers and trees. Palm trees, pine trees, flowering trees, the weeping willow outside the patio door. We were surrounded by nature. I never want to live in a city again. Full of black snow and buildings and cars, everything unnatural." "There is nothing surrounding me now that I will miss," I say, and smile.

Temporarily we are living in a room, a shared apartment with four others. The apartment is on the second floor of a house. The house is situated on a traffic circle. But the rent is cheap and it is only temporary, till I graduate from school in May. What I know now is that I am alive, and I want to enjoy living. I eat, and I enjoy eating. I love, and I enjoy loving. I wear proof of my existence in my bruises and wrinkles. I am a creature without wings but I can nest in air.

How It Works

1. How has Garnette Hall dramatized her feelings about place in this story? How many settings does the story describe? By including so many different locations, the author risks fragmenting the story. What techniques does she use to link one scene to the next? Does she succeed in unifying the story?

2. Like Brenda Miller's "A Thousand Buddhas" (pp. 329–334) this story describes a spiritual journey that includes several emotional conflicts. What are the "stories within the story," and how are they unified?

3. The main character and the author share the same name. Did this influence the way you read the story? What questions does it raise? What does the author's identification with the character contribute to the story? Does it detract in any way? How do you think students or teachers in a workshop would react to this technique?

4. List all of the places in which you have lived. Freewrite a bit on each one. What do these descriptions suggest about your life at the time? What changes do differences between the settings suggest?

Nathaniel Hawthorne

Nathaniel Hawthorne was born in Salem, Massachu-setts, in 1804. He graduated from Bowdoin College in 1825, and then returned to Salem, where he continued writing, mostly short fiction until The Scarlet Let-ter *established his reputation as a major writer. He went on to write four more novels and many short sto-ries. Hawthorne's fiction grew out of his New England Puritan heritage, with which he was not comfortable; he was haunted by the acts of his ancestor John Hathorne, who was a judge during the Salem witch trials. Rejecting persecution, hypocrisy, and denial, Hawthorne explored what he called "the depths of our common nature," touch-ing as well on themes of morality, sin, and redemption. His fiction was remarkably unsentimental compared to most of what was popular at the time. Hawthorne worked at the Boston Custom House in 1839 and 1840, and later was surveyor of customs in the port of Salem. In 1842 he married Sophia Peacock and moved with her to Concord, Massachusetts. Hawthorne lived for a time in England and in Italy, eventually returning to Concord. He died in 1864.*

The Minister's Black Veil

A Parable

The sexton stood in the porch of Mil-ford meeting-house, pulling busily at the bell-rope. The old people of the vil-lage came stooping along the street. Children, with bright faces, tripped merrily beside their parents, or mimicked a graver gait, in the con-scious dignity of their Sunday clothes. Spruce bachelors looked sidelong at the pretty maidens, and fancied that the Sabbath sunshine made them prettier than on week days. When the throng had mostly streamed into the porch, the sexton began to toll the bell, keeping his eye on the Reverend Mr. Hooper's door. The first glimpse of the clergyman's figure was the signal for the bell to cease its summons.

"But what has good Parson Hooper got upon his face?" cried the sexton in astonishment.

All within hearing immediately turned about, and beheld the semblance of Mr. Hooper, pacing slowly his meditative way to-wards the meeting-house. With one accord they started, expressing more wonder than if some strange minister were coming to dust the cush-ions of Mr. Hooper's pulpit.

"Are you sure it is our parson?" inquired Goodman Gray of the sexton.

"Of a certainty it is good Mr. Hooper," replied the sexton. "He was to have exchanged pulpits with Parson Shute, of Westbury; but Parson Shute sent to excuse himself yesterday, being to preach a funeral sermon."

The cause of so much amazement may ap-pear sufficiently slight. Mr. Hooper, a gentle-manly person, of about thirty, though still a bachelor, was dressed with due clerical neatness, as if a careful wife had starched his band, and brushed the weekly dust from his Sunday's garb. There was but one thing remarkable in his ap-pearance. Swathed about his forehead, and hanging down over his face, so low as to be shaken by his breath, Mr. Hooper had on a black veil. On a nearer view it seemed to consist of two folds of crape, which entirely concealed his features, except the mouth and chin, but probably did not intercept his sight, further than to give a darkened aspect to all living and inanimate things. With this gloomy shade be-fore him, good Mr. Hooper walked onward, at a slow and quiet pace, stooping somewhat, and looking on the ground, as is customary with abstracted men, yet nodding kindly to those of his parishioners who still waited on the meeting-house steps. But so wonder-struck were they that his greeting hardly met with a return.

"I can't really feel as if good Mr. Hooper's face was behind that piece of crape," said the sexton.

"I don't like it," muttered an old woman, as she hobbled into the meeting-house. "He has changed himself into something awful, only by hiding his face."

"Our parson has gone mad!" cried Goodman Gray, following him across the threshold.

A rumor of some unaccountable phenomenon had preceded Mr. Hooper into the meeting-house, and set all the congregation astir. Few could refrain from twisting their heads towards the door; many stood upright, and turned directly about; while several little boys clambered upon the seats, and came down again with a terrible racket. There was a general bustle, a rustling of the women's gowns and shuffling of the men's feet, greatly at variance with that hushed repose which should attend the entrance of the minister. But Mr. Hooper appeared not to notice the perturbation of his people. He entered with an almost noiseless step, bent his head mildly to the pews on each side, and bowed as he passed his oldest parishioner, a white-haired great-grandsire, who occupied an arm-chair in the center of the aisle. It was strange to observe how slowly this venerable man became conscious of something singular in the appearance of his pastor. He seemed not fully to partake of the prevailing wonder, till Mr. Hooper had ascended the stairs, and showed himself in the pulpit, face to face with his congregation, except for the black veil. That mysterious emblem was never once withdrawn. It shook with his measured breath, as he gave

out the psalm; it threw its obscurity between him and the holy page, as he read the Scriptures; and while he prayed, the veil lay heavily on his uplifted countenance. Did he seek to hide it from the dread Being whom he was addressing?

Such was the effect of this simple piece of crape, that more than one woman of delicate nerves was forced to leave the meeting-house. Yet perhaps the pale-faced congregation was almost as fearful a sight to the minister, as his black veil to them.

Mr. Hooper had the reputation of a good preacher, but not an energetic one: he strove to win his people heavenward by mild, persuasive influences, rather than to drive them thither by the thunders of the Word. The sermon which he now delivered was marked by the same characteristics of style and manner as the general series of his pulpit oratory. But there was something, either in the sentiment of the discourse itself, or in the imagination of the auditors, which made it greatly the most powerful effort that they had ever heard from their pastor's lips. It was tinged, rather more darkly than usual, with the gentle gloom of Mr. Hooper's temperament. The subject had reference to secret sin, and those sad mysteries which we hide from our nearest and dearest, and would fain conceal from our own consciousness, even forgetting that the Omniscient can detect them. A subtle power was breathed into his words. Each member of the congregation, the most innocent girl, and the man of hardened breast, felt as if the preacher had crept upon them, behind his awful veil, and discovered their hoarded iniquity of deed or thought. Many spread their clasped hands on their bosoms. There was nothing terrible in what Mr. Hooper said, at least, no violence; and yet, with every tremor of his melancholy voice, the hearers quaked. An unsought pathos came hand in hand with awe. So sensible were the audience of some unwonted attribute in their minister, that they longed for a breath of wind to blow aside the veil, almost believing that a stranger's visage would be discovered, though the form, gesture, and voice were those of Mr. Hooper.

At the close of the services, the people hurried out with indecorous confusion, eager to communicate their pent-up amazement, and conscious of lighter spirits the moment they lost sight of the black veil. Some gathered in little circles, huddled closely together, with their mouths all whispering in the center; some went homeward alone, wrapt in silent meditation; some talked loudly, and profaned the Sabbath day with ostentatious laughter. A few shook their sagacious heads, intimating that they could penetrate the mystery; while one or two affirmed that there was no mystery at all, but only that Mr. Hooper's eyes were so weakened by the midnight lamp, as to require a shade. After a brief interval, forth came good Mr. Hooper also, in the rear of his flock. Turning his veiled face from one group to another, he paid due reverence to the hoary heads, saluted the middle aged with kind dignity as their friend and spiritual guide, greeted the young with mingled authority and love, and laid his hands on the little children's heads to bless them. Such was always his custom on the Sabbath day. Strange and bewildered looks repaid him for his courtesy. None, as on former occasions, aspired to the honor of walking by their pastor's side. Old Squire Saunders, doubtless by an accidental lapse of memory, neglected to invite Mr. Hooper to his table, where the good clergyman had been wont to bless the food, almost every Sunday since his settlement. He returned, therefore, to the parsonage, and, at the moment of closing the door, was observed to look back upon the people, all of whom had their eyes fixed upon the minister. A sad smile gleamed faintly from beneath the black veil, and flickered about his mouth, glimmering as he disappeared.

"How strange," said a lady, "that a simple black veil, such as any woman might wear on her bonnet, should become such a terrible thing on Mr. Hooper's face!"

"Something must surely be amiss with Mr. Hooper's intellects," observed her husband, the physician of the village. "But the strangest part of the affair is the effect of this vagary, even on a sober-minded man like myself. The black veil, though it covers only our pastor's face, throws its influence over his whole person, and makes him ghostlike from head to foot. Do you not feel it so?"

"Truly do I," replied the lady; "and I would not be alone with him for the world. I wonder he is not afraid to be alone with himself?"

"Men sometimes are so," said her husband.

The afternoon service was attended with similar circumstances. At its conclusion, the bell tolled for the funeral of a young lady. The relatives and friends were assembled in the house, and the more distant acquaintances stood about the door, speaking of the good qualities of the deceased, when their talk was interrupted by the appearance of Mr. Hooper, still covered with his black veil. It was now an appropriate emblem. The clergyman stepped into the room where the corpse was laid, and bent over the coffin, to take a last farewell of his deceased parishioner. As he stooped, the veil hung straight down from his forehead, so that, if her eyelids had not been closed forever, the dead maiden might have seen his face. Could Mr. Hooper be fearful of her glance, that he so hastily caught back the black veil? A person who watched the interview between the dead and living, scrupled not to affirm, that, at the instant when the clergyman's features were disclosed, the corpse had slightly shuddered, rustling the shroud and muslin cap, though the countenance retained the composure of death. A superstitious old woman was the only witness of this prodigy. From the coffin Mr. Hooper passed into the chamber of the mourners, and thence to the head of the staircase, to make the funeral prayer. It was a tender and heart-dissolving prayer, full of sorrow, yet so imbued with celestial hopes, that the music of a heavenly harp, swept by the fingers of the dead, seemed faintly to be heard among the saddest accents of the minister. The people trembled, though they but darkly understood him when he prayed that they, and himself, and all of mortal race, might be ready, as he trusted this young maiden had been, for the dreadful hour that should snatch the veil from their faces. The bearers went heavily forth, and the mourners followed, saddening all the street, with the dead before them, and Mr. Hooper in his black veil behind.

"Why do you look back?" said one in the procession to his partner.

"I had a fancy," replied she, "that the minister and the maiden's spirit were walking hand in hand."

"And so had I, at the same moment," said the other.

That night, the handsomest couple in Milford village were to be joined in wedlock. Though reckoned a melancholy man, Mr. Hooper had a placid cheerfulness for such occasions, which often excited a sympathetic smile where livelier merriment would have been thrown away. There was no quality of his disposition which made him more beloved than this. The company at the wedding awaited his arrival with impatience, trusting that the strange awe, which had gathered over him throughout the day, would now be dispelled.

But such was not the result. When Mr. Hooper came, the first thing that their eyes rested on was the same horrible black veil, which had added deeper gloom to the funeral, and could portend nothing but evil to the wedding. Such was its immediate effect on the guests that a cloud seemed to have rolled duskily from beneath the black crape, and dimmed the light of the candles. The bridal pair stood up before the minister. But the bride's cold fingers quivered in the tremulous hand of the bridegroom, and her deathlike paleness caused a whisper that the maiden who had been buried a few hours before was come from her grave to be married. If ever another wedding were so dismal, it was that famous one where they tolled the wedding knell. After performing the ceremony, Mr. Hooper raised a glass of wine to his lips, wishing happiness to the new-married couple in a strain of mild pleasantry that ought to have brightened the features of the guests, like a cheerful gleam from the hearth. At that instant, catching a glimpse of his figure in the looking-glass, the black veil involved his own spirit in the horror with which it overwhelmed all others. His frame shuddered, his lips grew white, he spilt the untasted wine upon the carpet, and rushed forth into the darkness. For the Earth, too, had on her Black Veil.

The next day, the whole village of Milford talked of little else than Parson Hooper's black veil. That, and the mystery concealed behind it, supplied a topic for discussion between acquaintances meeting in the street, and good women gossiping at their open windows. It was the first item of news that the tavernkeeper told to his guests. The children babbled of it on their way to school. One imitative little imp covered his face with an old black handkerchief, thereby so affrighting his playmates that the panic seized himself, and he well-nigh lost his wits by his own waggery.

It was remarkable that of all the busybodies and impertinent people in the parish, not one ventured to put the plain question to Mr. Hooper, wherefore he did this thing. Hitherto, whenever there appeared the slightest call for such interference, he had never lacked advisers, nor shown himself averse to be guided by their judgment. If he erred at all, it was by so painful a degree of self-distrust, that even the mildest censure would lead him to consider an indifferent action as a crime. Yet, though so well acquainted with this amiable weakness, no individual among his parishioners chose to make the black veil a subject of friendly remonstrance. There was a feeling of dread, neither plainly confessed nor carefully concealed, which caused each to shift the responsibility upon another, till at length it was found expedient to send a deputation of the church, in order to deal with Mr. Hooper about the mystery, before it should grow into a scandal. Never did an embassy so ill discharge its duties. The minister received them with friendly courtesy, but became silent, after they were seated, leaving to his visitors the whole burden of introducing their important business. The topic, it might be supposed, was obvious enough. There was the black veil swathed round Mr. Hooper's forehead, and concealing every feature above his placid mouth, on which, at times, they could perceive the glimmering of a melancholy smile. But that piece of crape, to their imagination, seemed to hang down before his heart, the symbol of a fearful secret between him and them. Were the veil but cast aside, they might speak freely of it, but not till then. Thus they sat a considerable time, speechless, confused, and shrinking uneasily from Mr. Hooper's eye, which they felt to be fixed upon them with an invisible glance. Finally, the deputies returned abashed to their constituents, pronouncing the matter too weighty to be handled, except by a council of the churches, if, indeed, it might not require a general synod.

But there was one person in the village unappalled by the awe with which the black veil had impressed all beside herself. When the deputies returned without an explanation, or even venturing to demand one, she, with the calm energy of her character, determined to chase away the strange cloud that appeared to be settling round Mr. Hooper, every moment more darkly than before. As his plighted wife, it should be her privilege to know what the black veil concealed. At the minister's first visit, therefore, she entered upon the subject with a direct simplicity, which made the task easier both for him and her. After he had seated himself, she fixed her eyes steadfastly upon the veil, but could discern nothing of the dreadful gloom that had so overawed the multitude: it was but a double fold of crape, hanging down from his forehead to his mouth, and slightly stirring with his breath.

"No," said she aloud, and smiling, "there is nothing terrible in this piece of crape, except that it hides a face which I am always glad to look upon. Come, good sir, let the sun shine from behind the cloud. First lay aside your black veil: then tell me why you put it on."

Mr. Hooper's smile glimmered faintly.

"There is an hour to come," said he, "when all of us shall cast aside our veils. Take it not amiss, beloved friend, if I wear this piece of crape till then."

"Your words are a mystery, too," returned the young lady. "Take away the veil from them, at least."

"Elizabeth, I will," said he, "so far as my vow may suffer me. Know, then, this veil is a type and a symbol, and I am bound to wear it ever, both in light and darkness, in solitude and before the gaze of multitudes, and as with strangers, so with my familiar friends. No mortal eye will see it withdrawn. This dismal shade must separate me from the world: even you, Elizabeth, can never come behind it!"

"What grievous affliction hath befallen you," she earnestly inquired, "that you should thus darken your eyes forever?"

"If it be a sign of mourning," replied Mr. Hooper, "I, perhaps, like most other mortals, have sorrows dark enough to be typified by a black veil."

"But what if the world will not believe that it is the type of an innocent sorrow?" urged Elizabeth. "Beloved and respected as you are, there may be whispers that you hide your face under the consciousness of secret sin. For the sake of your holy office, do away this scandal!"

The color rose into her cheeks as she intimated the nature of the rumors that were already abroad in the village. But Mr. Hooper's mildness did not forsake him. He even smiled again—that same sad smile, which always appeared like a faint glimmering of light, proceeding from the obscurity beneath the veil.

"If I hide my face for sorrow, there is cause enough," he merely replied; "and if I cover it for secret sin, what mortal might not do the same?"

And with this gentle, but unconquerable obstinacy did he resist all her entreaties. At length Elizabeth sat silent. For a few moments she appeared lost in thought, considering, probably, what new methods might be tried to withdraw her lover from so dark a fantasy, which, if it had no other meaning, was perhaps a symptom of mental disease. Though of a firmer character than his own, the tears rolled down her cheeks. But, in an instant, as it were, a new

feeling took the place of sorrow: her eyes were fixed insensibly on the black veil, when, like a sudden twilight in the air, its terrors fell around her. She arose, and stood trembling before him.

"And do you feel it then, at last?" said he mournfully.

She made no reply, but covered her eyes with her hand, and turned to leave the room. He rushed forward and caught her arm.

"Have patience with me, Elizabeth!" cried he, passionately. "Do not desert me, though this veil must be between us here on earth. Be mine, and hereafter there shall be no veil over my face, no darkness between our souls! It is but a mortal veil—it is not for eternity! O! you know not how lonely I am, and how frightened, to be alone behind my black veil. Do not leave me in this miserable obscurity forever!"

"Lift the veil but once, and look me in the face," said she.

"Never! It cannot be!" replied Mr. Hooper.

"Then farewell!" said Elizabeth.

She withdrew her arm from his grasp, and slowly departed, pausing at the door, to give one long shuddering gaze, that seemed almost to penetrate the mystery of the black veil. But, even amid his grief, Mr. Hooper smiled to think that only a material emblem had separated him from happiness, though the horrors, which it shadowed forth, must be drawn darkly between the fondest of lovers.

From that time no attempts were made to remove Mr. Hooper's black veil, or, by a direct appeal, to discover the secret which it was supposed to hide. By persons who claimed a superiority to popular prejudice, it was reckoned merely an eccentric whim, such as often mingles with the sober actions of men otherwise rational, and tinges them all with its own semblance of insanity. But with the multitude, good Mr.

Hooper was irreparably a bugbear. He could not walk the street with any peace of mind, so conscious was he that the gentle and timid would turn aside to avoid him, and that others would make it a point of hardihood to throw themselves in his way. The impertinence of the latter class compelled him to give up his customary walk at sunset to the burial ground; for when he leaned pensively over the gate, there would always be faces behind the gravestones, peeping at his black veil. A fable went the rounds that the stare of the dead people drove him thence. It grieved him, to the very depth of his kind heart, to observe how the children fled from his approach, breaking up their merriest sports, while his melancholy figure was yet afar off. Their instinctive dread caused him to feel more strongly than aught else, that a preternatural horror was interwoven with the threads of the black crape. In truth, his own antipathy to the veil was known to be so great, that he never willingly passed before a mirror, nor stooped to drink at a still fountain, lest, in its peaceful bosom, he should be affrighted by himself. This was what gave plausibility to the whispers, that Mr. Hooper's conscience tortured him for some great crime too horrible to be entirely concealed, or otherwise than so obscurely intimated. Thus, from beneath the black veil, there rolled a cloud into the sunshine, an ambiguity of sin or sorrow, which enveloped the poor minister, so that love or sympathy could never reach him. It was said that ghost and fiend consorted with him there. With self-shudderings and outward terrors, he walked continually in its shadows, groping darkly within his own soul, or gazing through a medium that saddened the whole world. Even the lawless wind, it was believed, respected his dreadful secret, and never blew aside the veil. But still good Mr. Hooper sadly smiled at the pale visages of the worldly throng as he passed by.

Among all its bad influences, the black veil had the one desirable effect, of making its wearer a very efficient clergyman. By the aid of his mysterious emblem—for there was no other apparent cause—he became a man of awful power over souls that were in agony for sin. His converts always regarded him with a dread peculiar to themselves, affirming, though but figuratively, that, before he brought them to celestial light, they had been with him behind the black veil. Its gloom, indeed, enabled him to sympathize with all dark affections. Dying sinners cried aloud for Mr. Hooper, and would not yield their breath till he appeared; though ever, as he stooped to whisper consolation, they shuddered at the veiled face so near their own. Such were the terrors of the black veil, even when Death had bared his visage! Strangers came long distances to attend service at his church, with the mere idle purpose of gazing at his figure, because it was forbidden them to behold his face. But many were made to quake ere they departed! Once, during Governor Belcher's administration, Mr. Hooper was appointed to preach the election sermon. Covered with his black veil, he stood before the chief magistrate, the council, and the representatives, and wrought so deep an impression, that the legislative measures of that year were characterized by all the gloom and piety of our earliest ancestral sway.

In this manner Mr. Hooper spent a long life, irreproachable in outward act, yet shrouded in dismal suspicions; kind and loving, though unloved, and dimly feared; a man apart from men, shunned in their health and joy, but ever summoned to their aid in mortal anguish. As years wore on, shedding their snows above his sable veil, he acquired a name throughout the New England churches, and they called him Father Hooper. Nearly all his parishioners, who were of mature age when he was settled, had been borne away by many a funeral: he had one congregation in the church, and a more crowded one in the churchyard; and having wrought so late into the evening, and done his work so well, it was now good Father Hooper's turn to rest.

Several persons were visible by the shaded candlelight, in the death chamber of the old clergyman. Natural connections he had none. But there was the decorously grave, though unmoved physician, seeking only to mitigate the last pangs of the patient whom he could not save. There were the deacons, and other eminently pious members of his church. There, also, was the Reverend Mr. Clark, of Westbury, a young and zealous divine, who had ridden in haste to pray by the bedside of the expiring minister. There was the nurse, no hired handmaiden of death, but one whose calm affection had endured thus long in secrecy, in solitude, amid the chill of age, and would not perish, even at the dying hour. Who, but Elizabeth! And there lay the hoary head of good Father Hooper upon the death pillow, with the black veil still swathed about his brow, and reaching down his face, so that each more difficult gasp of his faint breath caused it to stir. All through life that piece of crape had hung between him and the world: it had separated him from cheerful brotherhood and woman's love, and kept him in that saddest of all prisons, his own heart; and still it lay upon his face, as if to deepen the gloom of his darksome chamber, and shade him from the sunshine of eternity.

For some time previous, his mind had been confused, wavering doubtfully between the past and the present, and hovering forward, as it were, at intervals, into the indistinctness of the world to come. There had been feverish turns, which tossed him from side to side, and wore away what little strength he had. But in his most convulsive struggles, and in the wildest vagaries of his intellect, when no other thought retained its sober influence, he still showed an awful solicitude lest the black veil should slip aside. Even if his bewildered soul could have forgotten, there was a faithful woman at his pillow, who, with averted eyes, would have covered that aged face, which she had last beheld in the comeliness of manhood. At length the death-stricken old man lay quietly in the torpor of mental and bodily exhaustion, with an imperceptible pulse, and breath that grew fainter and fainter, except when a long, deep, and irregular inspiration seemed to prelude the flight of his spirit.

The minister of Westbury approached the bedside.

"Venerable Father Hooper," said he, "the moment of your release is at hand. Are you ready for the lifting of the veil that shuts in time from eternity?"

Father Hooper at first replied merely by a feeble motion of his head; then, apprehensive, perhaps, that his meaning might be doubtful, he exerted himself to speak.

"Yea," said he, in faint accents, "my soul hath a patient weariness until that veil be lifted."

"And is it fitting," resumed the Reverend Mr. Clark, "that a man so given to prayer, of such a blameless example, holy in deed and thought, so far as mortal judgment may pronounce; is it fitting that a father in the church should leave a shadow on his memory, that may seem to blacken a life so pure? I pray you, my venerable brother, let not this thing be! Suffer us to be gladdened by your triumphant aspect as you go to your reward. Before the veil of eternity be lifted, let me cast aside this black veil from your face!"

And thus speaking, the Reverend Mr. Clark bent forward to reveal the mystery of so many years. But, exerting a sudden energy, that made all the beholders stand aghast, Father Hooper snatched both his hands from beneath the bedclothes, and pressed them strongly on the black veil, resolute to struggle, if the minister of Westbury would contend with a dying man.

"Never!" cried the veiled clergyman. "On earth, never!"

"Dark old man!" exclaimed the affrighted minister, "with what horrible crime upon your soul are you now passing to the judgment?"

Father Hooper's breath heaved; it rattled in his throat; but, with a mighty effort, grasping forward with his hands, he caught hold of life, and held it back till he should speak. He even raised himself in bed; and there he sat, shivering with the arms of death around him, while the black veil hung down, awful, at that last moment, in the gathered terrors of a lifetime. And yet the faint, sad smile, so often there, now seemed to glimmer from its obscurity, and linger on Father Hooper's lips.

"Why do you tremble at me alone?" cried he, turning his veiled face round the circle of pale spectators. "Tremble also at each other! Have men avoided me, and women shown no pity, and children screamed and fled, only for my black veil? What, but the mystery which it obscurely typifies, has made this piece of crape so awful? When the friend shows his inmost heart to his friend; the lover to his best beloved; when man does not vainly shrink from the eye of his Creator, loathsomely treasuring up the secret of his sin; then deem me a monster, for the symbol beneath which I have lived, and die! I

look around me, and, lo! on every visage a Black Veil!"

While his auditors shrank from one another, in mutual affright, Father Hooper fell back upon his pillow, a veiled corpse, with a faint smile lingering on the lips. Still veiled, they laid him in his coffin, and a veiled corpse they bore him to the grave. The grass of many years has sprung up and withered on that grave, the burial stone is moss-grown, and good Mr. Hooper's face is dust; but awful is still the thought that it mouldered beneath the Black Veil!

How It Works

1. As you imagine the minister in his black veil, what sort of emotion does the image evoke? What emotions—as opposed to judgments—do the townspeople and his intended wife Elizabeth feel about the veil? How does Hawthorne use those reactions to develop the story's theme?

2. Reread the story and underline each possible reason given by the townspeople for the black veil worn by the minister. List them.

3. All the way through this story, the minister resists others' attempts to make him explain the veil's meaning. Write out, in simplified form, the questions and his responses. How does Hawthorne use this dialogue to develop the story's theme? How does it develop the minister's character?

4. What makes a good symbol? List the qualities that contribute to the veil's symbolic import. As you think about the elusiveness of this symbol, consider how a less subtle writer might have used it. Try rewriting a few passages, articulating the symbol's meaning more explicitly. What is the effect?

Ernest Hemingway

Born and raised in Oak Park, Illinois, Ernest Hemingway began his career early, writing for his high school newspaper and literary magazine. Rather than going to college, he accepted a position as a reporter for the Kansas City Star, *where he learned the value of a plain, direct writing style. Hemingway left the* Star *to serve during World War I as an ambulance driver in Italy. In 1921 he moved to Paris. Although Hemingway's fiction often depicts colorful adventures such as war, bullfighting, and big game hunting, it usually centers on emotional and spiritual issues such as love, dignity, political responsibility, and trauma. After some initial rejection, Hemingway's early novels,* The Sun Also Rises *and* A Farewell to Arms, *brought him immediate fame and stature. In 1953 his novella* The Old Man and the Sea *was awarded the Pulitzer Prize, and in 1954 he received the Nobel Prize for Literature. His fiction is known for its short declarative sentences, crisp dialogue, understated description, and subtextual depth. He did not like talking about writing, but his advice to writers is the source of much conventional workshop wisdom. During the last decade of his life, Hemingway suffered from physical and mental illness. He committed suicide in 1961.*

Hills Like White Elephants

The hills across the valley of the Ebro were long and white. On this side there was no shade and no trees and the station was between two lines of rails in the sun. Close against the side of the station there was the warm shadow of the building and a curtain, made of strings of bamboo beads, hung across the open door into the bar, to keep out flies. The American and the girl with him sat at a table in the shade, outside the building. It was very hot and the express from Barcelona would come in forty minutes. It stopped at this junction for two minutes and went on to Madrid.

"What should we drink?" the girl asked. She had taken off her hat and put it on the table.

"It's pretty hot," the man said.

"Let's drink beer."

"*Dos cervezas,*" the man said into the curtain.

"Big ones?" a woman asked from the doorway.

"Yes. Two big ones."

The woman brought two glasses of beer and two felt pads. She put the felt pads and the beer glasses on the table and looked at the man and the girl. The girl was looking off at the line of hills. They were white in the sun and the country was brown and dry.

"They look like white elephants," she said.

"I've never seen one," the man drank his beer.

"No, you wouldn't have."

"I might have," the man said. "Just because you say I wouldn't have doesn't prove anything."

The girl looked at the bead curtain. "They've painted something on it," she said. "What does it say?"

"Anis del Toro. It's a drink."

"Could we try it?"

The man called "Listen" through the curtain. The woman came out from the bar.

"Four reales."

"We want two Anis del Toro."

"With water?"

"Do you want it with water?"

"I don't know," the girl said. "Is it good with water?"

"It's all right."

"You want them with water?" asked the woman.

"Yes, with water."

"It tastes like licorice," the girl said and put the glass down.

"That's the way with everything."

"Yes," said the girl. "Everything tastes of licorice. Especially all the things you've waited so long for, like absinthe."

"Oh, cut it out."

"You started it," the girl said. "I was being amused. I was having a fine time."

"Well, let's try and have a fine time."

"All right. I was trying. I said the mountains looked like white elephants. Wasn't that bright?"

"That was bright."

"I wanted to try this new drink: That's all we do, isn't it—look at things and try new drinks?"

"I guess so."

The girl looked across at the hills.

"They're lovely hills," she said. "They don't really look like white elephants. I just meant the coloring of their skin through the trees."

"Should we have another drink?"

"All right."

The warm wind blew the bead curtain against the table.

"The beer's nice and cool," the man said.

"It's lovely," the girl said.

"It's really an awfully simple operation, Jig," the man said. "It's not really an operation at all."

The girl looked at the ground the table legs rested on.

"I know you wouldn't mind it, Jig. It's really not anything. It's just to let the air in."

The girl did not say anything.

"I'll go with you and I'll stay with you all the time. They just let the air in and then it's all perfectly natural."

"Then what will we do afterward?"

"We'll be fine afterward. Just like we were before."

"What makes you think so?"

"That's the only thing that bothers us. It's the only thing that's made us unhappy."

The girl looked at the bead curtain, put her hand out and took hold of two of the strings of beads.

"And you think then we'll be all right and be happy."

"I know we will. You don't have to be afraid. I've known lots of people that have done it."

"So have I," said the girl. "And afterward they were all so happy."

"Well," the man said, "if you don't want to you don't have to. I wouldn't have you do it if you didn't want to. But I know it's perfectly simple."

"And you really want to?"

"I think it's the best thing to do. But I don't want you to do it if you don't really want to."

"And if I do it you'll be happy and things will be like they were and you'll love me?"

"I love you now. You know I love you."

"I know. But if I do it, then it will be nice again if I say things are like white elephants, and you'll like it?"

"I'll love it. I love it now but I just can't think about it. You know how I get when I worry."

"If I do it you won't ever worry?"

"I won't worry about that because it's perfectly simple."

"Then I'll do it. Because I don't care about me."

"What do you mean?"

"I don't care about me."

"Well, I care about you."

"Oh, yes. But I don't care about me. And I'll do it and then everything will be fine."

"I don't want you to do it if you feel that way."

The girl stood up and walked to the end of the station. Across, on the other side, were fields of grain and trees along the banks of the Ebro. Far away, beyond the river, were mountains. The shadow of a cloud moved across the field of grain and she saw the river through the trees.

"And we could have all this," she said. "And we could have everything and every day we make it more impossible."

"What did you say?"

"I said we could have everything."

"We can have everything."

"No, we can't."

"We can have the whole world."

"No, we can't."

"We can go everywhere."

"No, we can't. It isn't ours any more."

"It's ours."

"No, it isn't. And once they take it away, you never get it back."

"But they haven't taken it away."

"We'll wait and see."

"Come on back in the shade," he said. "You mustn't feel that way."

"I don't feel any way," the girl said. "I just know things."

"I don't want you to do anything that you don't want to do—"

"Nor that isn't good for me," she said. "I know. Could we have another beer?"

"All right. But you've got to realize—"

"I realize," the girl said. "Can't we maybe stop talking?"

They sat down at the table and the girl looked across at the hills on the dry side of the valley and the man looked at her and at the table.

"You've got to realize," he said, "that I don't want you to do it if you don't want to. I'm perfectly willing to go through with it if it means anything to you."

"Doesn't it mean anything to you? We could get along."

"Of course it does. But I don't want anybody but you. I don't want anyone else. And I know it's perfectly simple."

"Yes, you know it's perfectly simple."

"It's all right for you to say that, but I do know it."

"Would you do something for me now?"

"I'd do anything for you."

"Would you please please please please please please please stop talking?"

He did not say anything but looked at the bags against the wall of the station. There were labels on them from all the hotels where they had spent nights.

"But I don't want you to," he said, "I don't care anything about it."

"I'll scream," the girl said.

The woman came out through the curtains with two glasses of beer and put them down on the damp felt pads. "The train comes in five minutes," she said.

"What did she say?" asked the girl.

"That the train is coming in five minutes."

The girl smiled brightly at the woman, to thank her.

"I'd better take the bags over to the other side of the station," the man said. She smiled at him.

"All right. Then come back and we'll finish the beer."

He picked up the two heavy bags and carried them around the station to the other tracks. He looked up the tracks but could not see the train. Coming back, he walked through the barroom, where people waiting for the train were drinking. He drank an Anis at the bar and looked at the people. They were all waiting reasonably for the train. He went out through the bead curtain. She was sitting at the table and smiled at him.

"Do you feel better?" he asked.

"I feel fine," she said. "There's nothing wrong with me. I feel fine."

How It Works

1. What is the unspoken conflict between the characters in this story? How does Hemingway reveal the conflict? What lines suggest it?

2. Without looking back at the story, write a description of its setting. Include everything in your mental picture of the place. Then reread the story and compare your description with Hemingway's. How many of your impressions were drawn directly from the story? Trace the source of those that were not. Describe your emotions as

you read Hemingway's descriptions of setting. What do they add to the scene? How would the pacing and the mood change if they were deleted?

3. Hemingway's style can be contagious; its deceptive simplicity often tempts imitators. For instance, this story's tight parameters— its narrowly defined setting and the fact that it is told almost entirely in dialogue— seem to simplify the task of writing, but actually present serious challenges as well. How, within this tightly defined situation, does the author convey past events? List what you believe has occurred before the story's beginning, and then look for what in the story indicated this to you.

4. Pick a few passages of dialogue, and write out the subtext behind each one. How close in meaning are the dialogue and the subtext? What does that tell you about each of the characters?

James Joyce

James Joyce was born to a large Catholic family in Dublin, Ireland, in 1882. Although he lived outside Ireland for most of his life, all of his stories and books were set in Dublin. He was very poor and his writing was unknown until the publication of Ulysses, *which established him as a major literary figure. Joyce revolutionized the writing of fiction with such techniques as interior monologue and stream of consciousness, which give readers direct access to characters' thoughts. His autobiographical novel* A Portrait of the Artist as a Young Man *dramatizes Joyce's conflicts with the Roman Catholic Church, his family, and Irish nationalism. His later work, including the novels* Ulysses *and* Finnegans Wake, *became increasingly complex, allu-*

sive, and poetic. Although many readers find these novels difficult, critics consider Joyce's gifts almost unparalleled. Joyce suffered from an incurable and painful eye disease and eventually became almost completely blind. He died in 1941.

Araby

North Richmond Street, being blind, was a quiet street except at the hour when the Christian Brothers' School set the boys free. An uninhabited house of two stories stood at the blind end, detached from its neighbors in a square ground. The other houses of the street, conscious of decent lives within them, gazed at one another with brown imperturbable faces.

The former tenant of our house, a priest, had died in the back drawing-room. Air, musty from having long been enclosed, hung in all the rooms, and the waste room behind the kitchen was littered with old useless papers. Among these I found a few paper-covered books, the pages of which were curled and damp: *The Abbot*, by Walter Scott, *The Devout Communicant* and *The Memoirs of Vidocq*. I liked the last best because its leaves were yellow. The wild garden behind the house contained a central apple-tree and a few straggling bushes under one of which I found the late tenant's rusty bicycle-pump. He had been a very charitable priest: in his will he had left all his money to institutions and the furniture of his house to his sister.

When the short days of winter came dusk fell before we had well eaten our dinners. When we met in the street the houses had grown somber. The space of sky above us was the color of ever-changing violet and towards it the lamps of the street lifted their feeble lanterns. The cold air stung us and we played till our bodies glowed. Our shouts echoed in the silent street. The career of our play brought us through the dark muddy lanes behind the houses where we ran the gauntlet of the rough tribes from the cottages, to the back doors of the dark dripping gardens where odors arose from the ashpits, to the dark odorous stables where a coachman smoothed and combed the horse or shook music from the buckled harness. When we returned to the street light from the kitchen windows had filled the areas. If my uncle was seen turning the corner we hid in the shadow until we had seen him safely housed. Or if Mangan's sister came out on the doorstep to call her brother in to his tea we watched her from our shadow peer up and down the street. We waited to see whether she would remain or go in and, if she remained, we left our shadow and walked up to Mangan's steps resignedly. She was waiting for us, her figure defined by the light from the half-opened door. Her brother always teased her before he obeyed and I stood by the railings looking at her. Her dress swung as she moved her body and the soft rope of her hair tossed from side to side.

Every morning I lay on the floor in the front parlor watching her door. The blind was pulled down within an inch of the sash so that I could not be seen. When she came out on the doorstep my heart leaped. I ran to the hall, seized my books and followed her. I kept her brown figure always in my eye and, when we came near the point at which our ways diverged, I quickened my pace and passed her. This happened morning after morning. I had never spoken to her, except for a few casual words, and yet her name was like a summons to all my foolish blood.

Her image accompanied me even in places the most hostile to romance. On Saturday evenings when my aunt went marketing I had to go to carry some of the parcels. We walked through the flaring streets, jostled by drunken men and bargaining women, amid the curses of laborers, the shrill litanies of shop-boys who stood on guard by the barrels of pigs' cheeks, the nasal chanting of street singers, who sang a *come-all-you* about O'Donovan Rossa, or a ballad about the troubles in our native land. These noises converged in a single sensation of life for me: I imagined that I bore my chalice safely through a throng of foes. Her name sprang to my lips at moments in strange prayers and praises which I myself did not understand. My eyes were often full of tears (I could not tell why) and at times a flood from my heart seemed to pour itself out into my bosom. I thought little of the future. I did not know whether I would ever speak to her or not or, if I spoke to her, how I could tell her of my confused adoration. But my body was like a harp and her words and gestures were like fingers running upon the wires.

One evening I went into the back drawing-room in which the priest had died. It was a dark rainy evening and there was no sound in the house. Through one of the broken panes I heard the rain impinge upon the earth, the fine incessant needles of water playing in the sodden beds. Some distant lamp or lighted window gleamed below me. I was thankful that I could see so little. All my senses seemed to desire to veil themselves and, feeling that I was about to slip from them, I pressed the palms of my hands together until they trembled, murmuring: *"O love! O love!"* many times.

At last she spoke to me. When she addressed the first words to me I was so confused that I did not know what to answer. She asked me was I going to *Araby*. I forget whether I answered yes or no. It would be a splendid bazaar, she said; she would love to go.

"And why can't you?" I asked.

While she spoke she turned a silver bracelet round and round her wrist. She could not go, she said, because there would be a retreat that week in her convent. Her brother and two other boys were fighting for their caps and I was alone at the railings. She held one of the spikes, bowing her head towards me. The light from the lamp opposite our door caught the white curve of her neck, lit up her hair that rested there and, falling, lit up the hand upon the railing. It fell over one side of her dress and caught the white border of a petticoat, just visible as she stood at ease.

"It's well for you," she said.

"If I go," I said, "I will bring you something."

What innumerable follies laid waste my waking and sleeping thoughts after that evening! I wished to annihilate the tedious intervening days. I chafed against the work of school. At night in my bedroom and by day in the classroom her image came between me and the page I strove to read. The syllables of the word *Araby* were called to me through the silence in which my soul luxuriated and cast an Eastern enchantment over me. I asked for leave to go to the bazaar on Saturday night. My aunt was surprised and hoped it was not some Freemason affair. I answered few questions in class. I watched my master's face pass from amiability to sternness; he hoped I was not beginning to idle. I could not call my wandering thoughts together. I had hardly any patience with the serious work of life which, now that it stood between me and my desire, seemed to me child's play, ugly monotonous child's play.

On Saturday morning I reminded my uncle that I wished to go to the bazaar in the evening. He was fussing at the hall-stand, looking for the hat-brush, and answered me curtly:

"Yes, boy, I know."

As he was in the hall I could not go into the front parlor and lie at the window. I left the house in bad humor and walked slowly towards the school. The air was pitilessly raw and already my heart misgave me.

When I came home to dinner my uncle had not yet been home. Still it was early. I sat staring at the clock for some time and, when its ticking began to irritate me, I left the room. I mounted the staircase and gained the upper part of the house. The high cold empty gloomy rooms liberated me and I went from room to room singing. From the front window I saw my companions playing below in the street. Their cries reached me weakened and indistinct and, leaning my forehead against the cool glass, I looked over at the dark house where she lived. I may have stood there for an hour, seeing nothing but the brown-clad figure cast by my imagination, touched discreetly by the lamplight at the curved neck, at the hand upon the railings and at the border below the dress.

When I came downstairs again I found Mrs. Mercer sitting at the fire. She was an old garrulous woman, a pawnbroker's widow, who collected used stamps for some pious purpose. I had to endure the gossip of the tea-table. The meal was prolonged beyond an hour and still my uncle did not come. Mrs. Mercer stood up to go: she was sorry she couldn't wait any longer, but it was after eight o'clock and she did not like to be out late, as the night air was bad for her. When she had gone I began to walk up and down the room, clenching my fists. My aunt said:

"I'm afraid you may put off your bazaar for this night of Our Lord."

At nine o'clock I heard my uncle's latchkey in the halldoor. I heard him talking to himself and heard the hallstand rocking when it had received the weight of his overcoat. I could interpret these signs. When he was midway through his dinner I asked him to give me the money to go to the bazaar. He had forgotten.

"The people are in bed and after their first sleep now," he said.

I did not smile. My aunt said to him energetically:

"Can't you give him the money and let him go? You've kept him late enough as it is."

My uncle said he was very sorry he had forgotten. He said he believed in the old saying:

"All work and no play makes Jack a dull boy." He asked me where I was going and, when I had told him a second time he asked me did I know *The Arab's Farewell to His Steed*. When I left the kitchen he was about to recite the opening lines of the piece to my aunt.

I held a florin tightly in my hands as I strode down Buckingham Street towards the station. The sight of the streets thronged with buyers and glaring with gas recalled to me the purpose of my journey. I took my seat in a third-class carriage of a deserted train. After an intolerable delay the train moved out of the station slowly. It crept onward among ruinous houses and over the twinkling river. At Westland Row Station a crowd of people pressed to the carriage doors; but the porters moved them back, saying that it was a special train for the bazaar. I remained alone in the bare carriage. In a few minutes the train drew up beside an improvised wooden platform. I passed out on to the road and saw by the lighted dial of a clock that it was ten minutes to ten. In front of me was a large building which displayed the magical name.

I could not find any sixpenny entrance and, fearing that the bazaar would be closed, I passed in quickly through a turnstile, handing a shilling to a weary-looking man. I found myself in a big hall girdled at half its height by a gallery. Nearly all the stalls were closed and the greater part of the hall was in darkness. I recognized a silence like that which pervades a church after a service. I walked into the center of the bazaar timidly. A few people were gathered about the stalls which were still open. Before a curtain, over which the words *Café Chantant* were written in colored lamps, two men were counting money on a salver. I listened to the fall of the coins.

Remembering with difficulty why I had come I went over to one of the stalls and examined porcelain vases and flowered tea-sets. At the door of the stall a young lady was talking and laughing with two young gentlemen. I remarked their English accents and listened vaguely to their conversation.

"O, I never said such a thing!"

"O, but you did!"

"O, but I didn't!"

"Didn't she say that?"

"Yes. I heard her."

"O, there's a . . . fib!"

Observing me the young lady came over and asked me did I wish to buy anything. The tone of her voice was not encouraging; she seemed to have spoken to me out of a sense of duty. I looked humbly at the great jars that stood like eastern guards at either side of the dark entrance to the stall and murmured:

"No, thank you."

The young lady changed the position of one of the vases and went back to the two young men. They began to talk of the same subject. Once or twice the young lady glanced at me over her shoulder.

I lingered before her stall, though I knew my stay was useless, to make my interest in her wares seem the more real. Then I turned away slowly and walked down the middle of the bazaar. I allowed the two pennies to fall against the sixpence in my pocket. I heard a voice call from one end of the gallery that the light was out. The upper part of the hall was now completely dark.

Gazing up into the darkness I saw myself as a creature driven and derided by vanity; and my eyes burned with anguish and anger.

How It Works

1. What does the main character of this story want? How does Joyce convey the boy's desire? Is the boy's wish realistic? If he were to have what he wants, how would his life be different?

2. How would you describe the story's setting? Underline descriptions of the boy's neighborhood. What colors and images does Joyce use to describe it? How does this setting contrast with the boy's fantasy of what the fair will be like? How accurate is that fantasy?

3. Look closely at the descriptions of Mangan's sister. In what ways does she contrast with Joyce's descriptions of the neighborhood, the boy's house, and the fair?

4. Try writing an extended conversation between the boy and Mangan's sister. How would such a conversation change the story's impact?

Michael McFee

Michael McFee was born in Asheville, North Carolina, in 1954, and now teaches poetry writing and contemporary North Carolina literature at The University of Carolina at Chapel Hill. He has published six books of poetry, most recently Earthly *(Carnegie Mellon University Press, 2001), and two anthologies, most recently* This Is Where We Live: Short Stories by 25 Contemporary North Carolina Writers

(University of North Carolina Press, 2000). An eclectic listener, McFee aims in his writing for "an understated but vivid musicality, a plainspoken but charged eloquence, an informal formality."

About "The Halo," McFee writes, "This story probably came from growing up saturated in Jesus stories in our Baptist church, and from years of studying art history (especially religious paintings), and from my reading a lot of prose poetry by Baudelaire or Charles Simic or Zbignew Herbert just before I sat down to write "The Halo"; so when it wouldn't turn into a poem, it quite naturally turned into this strange charged little story that still surprises me when I read it."

The Halo

When Jesus was born, I thought he had a caul; but with his first cry, it began to glow. That was the halo—always in the way, poking my breast when he nursed, nicking Joseph when he'd bend to kiss the boy goodnight. But if we reached to take it off, somehow it wasn't there: it was a mirage, a shadow, a little golden cloud we couldn't quite touch.

Jesus could remove it, though. He'd fly it like a kite, the sun on a string. He'd skip it across the lake and it would always return. He'd even work it into his juggling routine, pieces of fruit landing on a dazzling plate, ta-dah!

Joseph was embarrassed. Maybe the halo reminded him of what he wasn't. So he built it a fine cedar box, and made Jesus take it off and lock it inside and bury it out back under the fig tree and promise not to dig it up. Joseph told him he could have it back one day, when he was a man.

And so Jesus grew up a normal boy, and everybody forgot about the halo.

But last night I dreamed that a couple of thieves dug up the box. And when they opened it, the fig tree burst into golden fruit, hundreds of sweet halos and not a snake in sight.

How It Works

1. How would you describe this story's depiction of Jesus, Mary, and Joseph? In what ways does each character resemble its biblical counterpart, or your impression of him or her? In what ways do these characters depart from their models? What is the effect when the character differentiates from its model?

2. The story's title invokes the image of a circle. In what ways is the story itself circular? How is the concept of a circle appropriate to this story?

3. In ballads and folk stories, Mary has often been characterized as knowing more than those around her. How does McFee convey that idea? What is the emotional implication of this idea for the story?

4. What symbols does this story use? Without trying to attach a specific meaning to them, think about their effect. What feelings does each one evoke? Try doing the dream exercise described on page 23 with them. Describe each symbol in a series of sentences beginning with the words "I am." What meanings emerge?

Brenda Miller

Brenda Miller teaches at Western Washington University. She has received two Pushcart Prizes for her work in creative nonfiction, and her essays have been published in periodicals such as The Sun, Utne Reader, Prairie Schooner, Georgia Review, Seneca Review, *and* Fourth Genre: Explorations in Nonfiction. *Her work appears in the anthologies* The Beacon Best of 1999: Creative Writing by Women and Men of All Colors; Storming Heaven's Gate: An Anthology of Spiritual Writings by Women; *and* In Brief: Short Takes on the Personal. *She is the editor-in-chief of the* Bellingham Review. *A collection of her personal essays,* Season of the Body, *will be published by Sarabande Books in spring, 2002.*

I taught Brenda Miller's "A Thousand Buddhas" in all of my fiction writing classes for several years before the author informed me, as I sought permission to include it in this book, that it is actually a personal essay, not a story. Miller feels strongly about the distinction between fiction and nonfiction: "When I choose to write a personal essay rather than a work of fiction, I am taking a certain stance as a writer. I am saying that the work is rooted in the 'real' world; though it may contain fictional elements, the essay is directly connected to me as the author behind the text. There is a 'truth' to it that I want to claim as my own, a bond of trust between reader and writer. If I present a piece as fiction, I am saying that it is rooted in the world of the imagination; though it may contain autobiographical elements, the reader cannot assume that the story has a direct bearing on the 'truth' of the writer's life. At some point, every writer needs to decide how she wants to situate herself in relationship to the reader; the choice of genre establishes that relationship and the rules of engagement."

I have chosen to include "A Thousand Buddhas" in this anthology because of the beauty of the prose, and because this essay illustrates the skillful ordering of personal experience. Although "A Thousand Buddhas" is nonfiction, it employs a number of techniques described in this book. Writers considering basing their work upon their experience would do well to study this personal essay.

A Thousand Buddhas

My hand's the universe, it can do anything.
—Shinkichi Takahashi

I

I have never been touched by someone blind, but I can imagine what it would be like. She would read me like Braille, her fingertips hovering on the raised points of my flesh, then peel back the sheets of my skin, lay one finger on my quivering heart. We could beat like that, two hummingbirds, and become very still. Her hands might move across my abdomen, flick the scar below my belly button. My eyelids would flutter at her touch, and my skin dissolve into hot streams of tears.

I have never been touched by a blind person, but I have given whole massages with my eyes halfway closed, and the bodies I touched became something else. Their boundaries disappeared, and they spread out on the table—masses of flesh, all the borders gone. I touched them in tender places: between the toes, under the cheekbones, along the high-arching curves of their feet. When I opened my eyes they coalesced into something human, but I walked outside and slipped into the pool, feeling like a primordial fish, all my substance gone. I'd see them afterward, and they leaned toward me, their mouths open, but they hardly spoke. My arms opened and they fell against me; I held my hands on the middle of their backs, holding their hearts in place.

Sometimes they cried. I was too professional, then, to cry, knew that I had to keep some distance in order to make this relationship work. If I had cried, then we might have been lovers, and that would make it wrong somehow when they handed me the check for thirty dollars. Sometimes they pressed the payment into my hands and looked away, and said *I can't even tell you.* I nudged them in the direction of the baths, and they went like obedient children, their naked bodies swaying under their towels as they shuffled across the old, wooden bridge.

II

I have a picture from that time—of myself in the hot tub at Orr Hot Springs. At least, some people claim it is me, pointing out the slope of my breasts, the flare of my hips, the unique circumference of my thighs. Positive identification is impossible since the woman in the picture cradles her face in her hands.

Light streams through a low doorway into the gazebo, and this young woman leans her back against the deck. The sunlight zeroes into a circle on her belly. Jasmine bush and bamboo are reflected in the glass. The woman bends her head and covers her eyes as if she were about to weep. Steam rises and beads on the glass, obscuring detail and memory.

The woman is not weeping. She is scooping up the water from the tub and splashing it to her face. If this woman is me, she is mumbling some kind of grateful prayer, alchemizing the water into a potion that will heal.

It's easy to know what we're doing, once we're not doing it anymore.

III

Before I lived at Orr Hot Springs, I spent a summer baking bread for fifty children on a farm outside Willits. I didn't know I was in practice for becoming a massage therapist, but I knew I mended wounds buried deep inside me as I handled the huge mounds of dough. ("Talking things out" carves paths around and in-between the issues, but the body knows things the mind could never face.) The repetitive motions of grasping and pushing, the bend of my waist, the slow ache in my shoulder—before long, I became automatic and blank. I kept my hands covered in flour, and thought continually of food, of what is nourishing. I dreamed of my mouth always open and filled.

Children clustered around me, tugged at my apron, took little balls of dough and rolled them lightly between their teeth. The bread rose and came out of the oven, broke into tender crumbs, tasted good. I watched the children and gave them small lumps of dough to press. I touched their miniature shoulders and smiled, but I said very little. At the midsummer dance, they braided flowers into my hair and held my hands, as if I were an old person convalescing from a long, wasting illness.

IV

Today I look at my hands. I remember the bodies I've touched, the lives that came through them. Sometimes I trace the edges of my fingers, as children in kindergarten do on newsprint with green tempera paint. Hands become what they have held; our hands shape themselves around what they hold most dear, or what has made an impression, or what we press on others.

My friend Dana once grabbed my hand off the stick shift as I drove through L.A. "These," he said running a fingertip around my palm, "are healing hands."

I drove with my left hand on the wheel, while he examined every finger of my right. I swerved to avoid a dog.

"They're like a sculptor's hands," he said dreamily, dropping my hand and gripping his own.

Dana is a sculptor with a propensity for twisted nude forms, estranged limbs, fingers in a bowl. Once, before he left for Peru, he painted all his walls, the appliances, even his books, a startling white: a "blank canvas," he said, for his friends to spill upon. And we did, troweling up purples and reds, oranges and blues, a cacophony of personalities rolling across his walls.

I pressed my hands in blue paint and handwalked an awkward bridge along the wall above his couch.

V

What follows may, or may not, be true:

"It's been too long," the man said.

My old lover Jon stepped inside, closed the door, and settled himself carefully on the edge of my massage table. "I just came to soak in the baths, decided to get a massage on the spur of the moment," he said. "I didn't know it was you."

We stared at each other. I don't know what he saw in my face—a barrier, perhaps, a careful retreat—but in his face I saw a deep sorrow. My eyes involuntarily shifted into professional gear, scanning his body and making notes: a slump in the left shoulder, a grim tightness in the left arm and fist, chest slightly concave, breathing shallow.

In massage school, before we were lovers, Jon and I had been partners. The teacher insisted on partner rotation, but somehow Jon and I ended up together more times than not. We learned well on each other. We breathed

freely; we allowed each other's hands to cup the muscles and slide, so slowly, down the length of connecting fibers and tissue; we allowed thumbs to probe deep into unyielding spots. It was like a dance—the way our teacher said it always should be: an effortless give and take, back and forth, with the breath as well as the body. Communication—transcendent and absolute.

"Listen," Jon was saying. "I understand if you don't want to do this." His body leaned toward me, and my spine tipped forward in response. A massage room is a very close environment. Intimacy is immediate; truth prevails.

I glanced away and gazed at the far wall, at the painting called *A Thousand Buddhas* he had given me as a graduation present. For the last year, I had looked at that picture every day, and every day it reminded me of Jon less and less. A process of pain, moving ahead on its own momentum. The primary Buddha sat in the center, immovable, surrounded by a helix of buddhas that spun around and around.

My palms relaxed—a good sign. "It might be awkward," I said, "but I'll try." I took a deep breath, and whatever had been prickling at the back of my throat subsided.

What did my body feel when I placed my hands on Jon's back? My palms curved instinctively to the crook of his shoulders; my own shoulders softened when I asked Jon to breathe, and I inhaled with him, stretching my lungs, and on the exhale my hands slid down his back, kneading the muscles on the downward slide, pulling up along the lats, crossing over his spine, and again and again, until he seemed to flatten and there was no distinction between the flesh of his back or the bones in his arms or the curve of his buttocks—no distinction, in fact, between his breath and mine. I felt a small opening in my heart, a valve releasing, and an old love—a love aged and smooth as wine—flowed down my arms and sparked on Jon's skin. I knew, then, that sometime in the night I would remember this gushing, and I would be shattered by a sense of tremendous loss, a grasping ache in my palms, and I would cry, but even this certainty could not stop my hands in their circular route through Jon's familiar and beautiful body. He inhaled and began to sob. The tears shuddered through his back, his arms, his legs, and I felt them empty from him in one bountiful wave. My right hand floated to rest on his sacrum. My left hand brushed the air above his head in long, sweeping arcs.

There is a powder that covers the heart, a sifting of particles fine as talc. It is protection—gauzy and insubstantial, but protection nonetheless. Occasionally, a hand rubs against you and wipes a patch clear. That's when the heart bulges, beating with a raw and healthy ferocity.

VI

I keep another picture hidden in a drawer: me before I moved to Orr Springs—before I even knew such places existed. I am young, young, young.

I am standing barefoot on the porch of a cabin within Prairie Creek State Park on the north coast of California. It is late summer. I am wearing a purple tank top, tight Levis, and a forest ranger's hat. The morning sun is full in my face, and I am smiling a goofy, lopsided grin, my hands at my sides, my feet planted solidly on the wooden planks.

I am pregnant—about three weeks along—and the embryo is curled tightly in a fallopian tube. The pregnancy will end one week later in a long terrifying miscarriage, but in the picture I do not know this. I don't even know I am pregnant. I am twenty-one years old and healthy from a long summer in Wyoming. It is a beautiful morning, and I am happy to be back in California. My world has not yet shifted to include the indifferent hands of nurses, the blind lights of an operating dome, the smell of bandages steeped in antiseptics and blood.

If you look carefully at the belly for some sign of the child, at the face for some indication of motherhood, there is none. The snapshot is flat and ordinary: a young woman on vacation, nothing more. But I look at this photo and sense a swelling in my pelvis, a fullness in my breasts. I feel my skin inviolate and smooth, the substance of everything I've lost and meant to regain.

VII

Someone called them midwife's hands. A midwife's hands cradle and protect, hold a life between them. Recall the classic posture for the hands in photographs: one hand cupped under the baby's emerging head, the other lightly curled on the baby's crown.

There is a polarity position like this: at the client's head, cradling, not pulling but imparting the sense of emergence just the same. If you stay long enough—motionless, breathing little sips out of the air—the head appears to become larger, grows and trembles. The eyelids flutter. Sometimes I have touched the top of my head to the top of my client's head, and we were plugged in; we took deep breaths, heaved long important sighs.

VIII

Sean was born. Not from my body. From Rhea's. I held the mirror at an angle so she could see the crown of his head as it split her body in two.

The midwife placed one hand on the skull and rotated it so the face pointed toward heaven. The eyes were open, glazed with an unearthly shine.

Rhea screamed. The world paused and listened. The body followed, sheathed in cream and wax.

IX

What does the body contain? And how do the hands release it? In the late seventies, "hug clinics" opened on college campuses in California. Distraught people were invited to drop in if they needed to be secured for a moment by a pair of strong encircling arms.

One of the most powerful massage holds I've used has the client on his side, curled into a fetal position. I cupped one hand to the base of the spine, laid the other on the back between the shoulder blades. These are the two places our mother's hands fell when holding us as babies.

Some people cried with little shoulder-shaking sobs. Others fell promptly asleep. Most of them believed my hands were still on them long after I'd walk away.

X

In the hospital, the nurse stuck an IV needle into the back of my hand, over and over. I squinted and clenched my teeth.

"Does that hurt?" the nurse said, looking up, scowling.

I nodded.

"It's not supposed to hurt," she said, setting the needle aside and trying again.

When she was done, I lay on top of the covers, shivering, my eyes halfway closed, my palm flat on the bed. The IV fluid ticked into my blood. Already, I could feel myself forgetting everything.

My body was a container of pain. And then it contained nothing—an absence so absolute I couldn't even cry.

XI

The hand is shaped to touch the different parts of the world. We hurt, and the hand reaches to the chest. A newborn's head fits snugly into the center of a palm. Fertile soil runs through our fingers, or we mold our hands into a cup sealed for a drink of water. We can use our hands like primeval jaws to pluck whatever is ripe.

The midwife had fingers so long I almost asked her if she played the piano. The words were nearly out of my mouth, but then she handed Sean to me, and I forgot about pianos, about that kind of music.

I held him while the midwife and Rhea struggled with the afterbirth. I held him against my shoulder. His eyes were open; he blinked slowly and rarely, like a baby owl. The light in the room was gold, the color of honey. I thought I saw something in his eyes, but I can't be sure. I thought I saw a nod of acceptance, a little man bowing to me, his hands pressed together in an attitude of prayer.

XII

They came to me hot and pink from the baths, most of my work already done. They came naked and slick and gorgeous.

What did I give them? Nothing but myself—and not even that, but rather the benefit of my whole attention, the focus of my hands on them, the focus of my heart. I don't know how long the change lasted. They left the room and lingered in the baths, got out, got dressed, and drove home. I waved goodbye and walked up the steps to my cabin, looked out my window to the luscious woods, and thought about these people more than I probably should have. When the time approached for me to leave Orr Springs, I thought about them with a frantic longing for a life that could be balanced and whole.

I wanted to massage myself before I left. I wanted to send myself off with a stroke of my fingers and a hand along my spine: an affirmation for abundance, a momentary release from every memory that weighed me down. I thought it might help, if only for the drive out on the rutted and dusty road.

XIII

Years after I left Orr Springs, I worked for the Human Resource Council in Missoula, Montana. I didn't massage people anymore. I tried, but I zipped through the parts of the body as if I were taking inventory. I chattered like a barber giving a haircut. I thought about dinner, gas mileage, bills to be paid.

In my job, I interviewed clients and determined their eligibility for a heating-assistance program. Many of the people I saw were elderly and disabled; all of them had stories to tell, stories that could take a lifetime. I had only twenty minutes to spend with each one. I found that when I gave them my whole and complete attention for even five minutes, that was enough. I looked them in the eyes and smiled, laughed with them, murmured consolations. They looked back and told me what they knew. My hands kept very still on my desk.

One seventy-six-year-old woman spoke to me in short, disjointed sentences, her head nodding emphatically with each word, spittle forming at the corners of her mouth. She smelled of cigarettes and bitter lemons. As I walked her to the door of my office, she swirled about and grabbed me around the waist. She was only as tall as my chest, and I settled my arms onto her shoulders. We stood like that for a few seconds under the fluorescent lights, the computers humming around us. Then I slid one hand

down her back and held her there; my hand quivered, near as it was to her old and fragile heart.

XIV

I'm lying on my massage table. It's for sale. I'm lying on it, and I feel utterly relaxed. My breath swirls through my body in a contented daze.

I'm lying on my back. I open my eyes, and I see my face. I see me leaning over the table. My right hand comes to rest on my womb; my left hand hovers over my throat.

Forgive Me. Those are the words that pass between us.

How It Works

1. What elements of fiction does Miller use? What do these add to the text?

2. Although "A Thousand Buddhas" is an essay and although it is not conventionally structured, it does have a plot. What events does the narrator chronicle, and in what order?

3. Transitions and other structural cues are crucial in a nonchronological narrative. How does this author link one scene to the next? How do you know which event happens when? How would the effect be different if the events had been told chronologically?

4. Read any one of this essay's sections aloud. How does your voice sound as you read it? How would you describe this essay's voice? What feelings does it convey? How? Try rewriting the same material in a different voice. How does the narrative change?

Joseph Moser

Joseph Moser grew up in Minnesota and began writing fiction as a student at Emerson College. He is currently at work on a novel, but emphasizes that he also has extensive experience "shoveling and heaving things," and "isn't the kind of bespectacled wus that would never use birch leaves as toilet paper." Finding the right narrative voice was the pivotal factor in writing "Close Enough," Moser says: "a character who is simple without being a dullard, a boy who is perceptive, yet virtually guileless." This story is based in part on a real incident that happened in Minnesota in the early 1990s.

Close Enough

My brother Isaac hated Frank Sinatra. But me, I liked him more than any other singer. I still do. So when I remember everything that happened when I was seventeen, I always think about Frank singing "It Was a Very Good Year." It doesn't make a whole lot of sense, but I just do.

When I was seventeen, my brother Isaac was twenty-two. Maybe it was because he was older, but my dad was always nicer to him. I think he liked him better than me. Mom was nice to both of us. She was nice to everybody. She treated Dad nice even when I thought he was a jerk to me.

Maybe I shouldn't say that my dad was a jerk. He was a preacher and he still is and people look up to him and believe what he says. But a lot of times it seemed like he just got a kick out of getting on my case. He wasn't so tall, but he had big hands and big eyes that were always watery and a big deep voice. Sometimes I would be reading a comic book or maybe even a real book and he would come in and say, "Frederic,

your brother's out splitting wood and you're in here daydreaming. You could get something done once in a while. Now, move your butt and go help your brother."

Then I would go outside and start stacking the wood and setting up the logs for Isaac to split, but sooner or later, I wouldn't be doing things right or fast enough and Isaac would say, "Just forget it, spit sack. You know, I never asked you to help me in the first place. Just go back inside."

I suppose things were like that a lot, except when we went hunting the first couple weekends of November every year. Then I was glad to be with my brother and my dad no matter what. We went with my uncle Raymond and my uncle Pete. It was just us five and nobody else. Some of our cousins who were Pete and Raymond's sons used to hunt with us, too, when I first started, but both of them quit when they got married. Their wives were from the city and they didn't understand.

When we went hunting that November, I had still never shot a deer. I had shot at plenty of them, though. Whenever anybody had a doe permit, he would say, "Freddie go ahead and shoot a doe." So then maybe I'd see one, but I always did something wrong and missed it. I guess I wasn't a very good shot, but a lot of times I'd get up too quick or make a noise in my stand and then the deer would start running which made it about impossible. Another time, I had a doe and a fawn walk about forty yards in front of my stand but when I lined the doe up in the sights and pulled the trigger, the hammer just clicked. The two deer just stood looking at me while I tried to lever another shell in. I even tried banging the stock on the bottom of the stand to loosen up the shell, but pretty soon I gave up and started whooping at the deer so they'd go over to Isaac's stand and he could shoot them.

"Here they come," I yelled to Isaac, "Shoot 'em."

Isaac didn't shoot the doe, though, because he had no interest in shooting does. He figured that wasn't much of a challenge and maybe it wasn't.

My dad chewed me out after that incident because he said I hadn't levered the shell in hard enough when I loaded my gun.

Of course, my dad and Isaac had killed plenty of deer, and so had Raymond and Pete.

Hunting season that year started out like it always had before. Dad and Isaac and I got all the clothes and other stuff out of the basement that we only use when we hunt. We got ready, loaded everything we needed into the truck, and drove over to Uncle Raymond's house. Where we hunted is only a couple miles from Raymond's house and my dad kept his tractor and trailer behind Raymond's shed, so when we got there, we loaded everything into the trailer. It was about seven o'clock by then and the night was cold and clear. Raymond and Pete went up into the woods in Pete's truck, and Dad, Isaac, and I went in the tractor. From Raymond's house, we drove for a while on a nice wide dirt road before we turned off into the woods onto an old trail that was almost always soupy this time of year unless it was frozen over. Isaac and I rode on the front of the trailer behind the big tractor wheels. We tried not to get muddy, but there wasn't much we could do. Dad drove, of course, and Isaac talked to him a little, but he had to pay attention. It usually took us about an hour to get to the shack, depending on how bad the trail was. We got there about nine o'clock, and so it was plenty dark.

I suppose the shack was about twenty feet long and fifteen feet wide. The outside was tar paper, but it had a good roof with shingles. Inside, mainly, it had two gas lights, a gas stove for cooking, a barrel stove for heating, benches and a picnic table with iron pipe for legs, and four bunks big enough to hold two people each.

We brought all of our stuff into the shack and got situated and then we had supper. It was pot roast that Aunt Helen had made. It was pretty tough meat and I could tell that Raymond felt bad for bringing it. We were all polite enough to try and eat it and not say anything, except Pete who said, "You say this is pot roast, Raymond? Tastes more like pup roast to me."

"Helen must've set the timer wrong," Raymond said.

Helen was a nice lady, just not such a good cook. When we'd go over to her house when we were little to play with our cousins and she'd try to give us cookies or pie, Isaac would always say that we both already had too many cavities and our mom wouldn't let us have sweets anymore. He usually stuck to that excuse because it wouldn't work as good if he said we were both sick or we were both allergic to something in the food. We didn't know how our cousins could stand it, or Raymond either. They had to eat Helen's cooking I guess and I suppose they just got so used to it that they didn't know any better, but Isaac and I could wait until we got home and eat something better. The only trouble was that one time we went to visit when I'd just had a dentist appointment and Helen asked me how many cavities I had this time and I said, "None. I've never had a cavity."

She opened her mouth like she was going to say something, but then she just sort of smiled and went back to doing her laundry. Isaac looked at me and said, "Nice job, lame brain," and then I knew what I'd done wrong.

So Aunt Helen wasn't known for her cooking and supper wasn't so good, especially since dessert was one of Aunt Helen's mince meat pies. No one was feeling that great afterwards. We all just went to bed.

Dad set the alarm for five, like usual. He and Raymond got up and cooked breakfast while the rest of us stayed in bed a little longer. Everybody ate a big helping of pancakes and bacon, except for me. I never ate breakfast hunting because I got nervous. The first year I hunted I threw up out of my stand and everybody knows about that because Isaac heard the noise. "I thought I heard a sick coyote this morning, but I guess it was just Freddie because when I came in I saw his breakfast layin' under his stand. Get a little excited, do you, Freddie?"

So, even though everybody knew I didn't like the breakfast, they'd always ask me wouldn't I like some pancakes and bacon and why don't I eat, it's so long until lunch, because they knew it'd get a rise out of me.

This day was Saturday, and after we got dressed and went outside we could see that the sky was clear because there were still a few stars, and so we knew it would be light soon.

Everybody said good luck, then Raymond and Pete went south to their stands and Dad, Isaac, and I walked northeast, then east to ours. It was about a quarter mile to my stand, Isaac's was about two hundred yards east of me, and Dad had to go another quarter-mile or so past Isaac.

My stand was about two feet long and maybe eighteen inches wide. It was up in two poplar trees about fifteen feet off the ground. There was a shooting rail nailed on one side and it was a good thing because there was nothing else to lean on but the trees. You couldn't really sit down up there. I used to when I was younger, I'd just sit on the floor of the stand and put my feet on the first step down, but my dad said if something were to come you'd have a hell of a

time getting up and in position in time to do any kind of shooting. I figured he was right, so I just stood up there until I thought I was as sick of it as I could be, and then I'd stand some more to make sure I was sure I couldn't do it anymore. I had to be careful, too, because at 6:30 in the morning a guy's liable to go to sleep, and up there the waking up can be scary—you forget what you're doing for a second and you think you're standing on top of a big bird house.

The morning lasted a long time hunting, but the sunrise was always pretty. It was like someone had buried the sun and now he was digging himself out from underneath the dirt. There was snow on the ground that day, so everything at first started to glow just a little, and then ever so slightly things brightened up so you could make out the shapes of more and more trees and logs and eventually the big swamp and the beaver dam northeast of me.

I didn't have a watch and I was glad of it. I just would have looked at it every two minutes and the time would have gone by slower than cold molasses. I tried to be patient and think about other things than what I was doing. I tried to wait until I thought I had stood one way long enough before I moved and faced another direction. It was pretty cold and a little windy, so I pulled down my face mask, which made it so I couldn't hear as well. I knew my dad wouldn't have anything over his ears, but I figured my stand was up higher than his and had about no wind protection, so it was all right.

About all the trees and brush anywhere near my stand were poplar, except for a few pines here and there like the ones that Isaac's stand was in. I had a pretty decent view around me— maybe a hundred yards in most directions I could have shot something—but they say now that if I were hunting there today I wouldn't have had a shot at the deer I saw that morning. All the brush is so overgrown now.

It must have been about a half-hour after the sun had come all the way up that I heard something I thought might be a deer. I got pretty lackadaisical pretty quick standing up there, because you would hear a noise, you'd pick up your gun and get all ready, then you didn't hear it again or it was just a squirrel or a partridge, so after a couple times, you got pretty sick of getting all excited, taking off your gloves, and picking up your gun. To tell the truth, I almost would've rather not seen any deer, because then I wouldn't have had to worry about missing them.

But that day I guess I got lucky. I heard a crash in the thick brush northeast of me, and I picked up my .30-30. Then I finally saw the deer step out of the brush and into the open on the near side of the big swamp about seventy-five or a hundred yards from my stand. I pulled back the hammer and it clicked. My dad had showed me a way to squeeze the trigger while you cock the gun so it wouldn't make a noise, but I never did that for fear I'd shoot by accident. That deer didn't hear the click, anyway, and he acted like he didn't hear it when I shot at him the first time. He was facing towards the swamp, and he just stood there looking around kind of confused, so I levered another one in the chamber and had at him again. This time he took off running, sort of west, and I wasn't sure I'd hit him, so I took a third poke at him. He fell down in the brush about pure north of my stand, and I gave kind of a whoop because I was pretty surprised I'd got him and happy, too, I guess.

I say he was a he because I know he was now, but when I shot at him I hadn't noticed any horns. We had two doe permits, so I was supposed to shoot at anything and I didn't bother

to make out whether he had horns or not. I got down from my stand and started walking to about where I thought he was, but I got disoriented a little and it took me about fifteen minutes before I finally found him lying in the poplar brush. The first thing I noticed were the horns. He was an eight-pointer, and it was just pure dumb luck because I hadn't even known the difference. There was a big hole in his back on the left of his spine and on top of his shoulder and that was the only place I had hit him. It had gotten to his vitals and that's why he ran and died so quick. It was a clean kill, and that was lucky too.

I had never gutted a deer before because I had never killed one. I knew Isaac would come over now and he'd have to help me. I wondered what he'd say when he saw this. It was always hard to tell with him, especially then. He could be all right sometimes and mean other times, but since he had gotten cut from the University of Minnesota basketball team after he graduated, he'd been mean more often than not. That was three years before, and I think it still made him mad. He was the best player on the team in high school. He had his pick of all the girls— he brought a lot of them home—and I never heard anybody say they didn't like him. It didn't do me much good, though. When I was younger and he was still in school, everyone would say, "I bet you think you're cool just because your brother's a big star." Then later when he didn't make it with the Gophers, everybody said, "Too bad your brother wasn't good enough to play for the U. Now, he'll have to work at the saw mill the rest of his life." I couldn't win either way, but I wished he would have stayed at college even when he got cut instead of quitting and coming back here. I guess I would have missed him, but now he probably would work at the saw mill the rest of his life, like they said. I think my dad felt sort of the same about it. I'm sure he'd talked about it with everybody in the café in town, saying how his son was going to be a Gopher and how proud he was, so he must have felt a little dumb after everybody found out. He didn't act like it at home, though. When Isaac came back, Dad just shook his hand and said, "It's good to have you back, son," and nobody ever said anything about it again. I sure didn't bring it up.

I whistled at Isaac to make sure he knew to come over and so he wouldn't think I had missed and there was no point. I walked back towards my stand so he'd see me. I could make out the orange of his coveralls about as soon as he got down from his stand. Coming up the little trail, he didn't seem so tall. He walked different, but from forty yards away, maybe even twenty, I thought he looked quite a bit like me. He had real light brown hair that was curly and blue eyes. His nose was small and his ears were a little big. He was still skinny, but not like in high school. Not like I still was.

As he got closer, I saw his whiskers and his Adam's apple and the cleft in his chin.

When he got to where I was, we had to go find the deer again because I hadn't kept good track. He was frustrated that I'd left my stand in the first place and he looked at me funny when I said it was a buck.

"You sure?" he said.

"Yeah, I told you. I saw him."

When we got there, he shook his head for a minute, but then he looked up at me and a smile sort of crept into his face. "Well, I'll be damned," he said. "I'll just hafta be damned. And you say you shot him over there by the crick? Well now, that ain't no easy shot."

"I just kinda let fly, I guess. To tell you the truth, I didn't even see his horns until I found him dead over here."

"Well, that's pretty weird, but it's still a pretty good shot, Freddie. Not too bad, really."

"Thanks."

"But I heard you yell and you shouldn't've done that. That's greenhorn behavior."

"Yeah, I guess so. That was sorta dumb."

Still, I thought maybe he was a little proud of me and maybe even a little jealous. He helped me gut the deer—he pretty much did all the cutting and just had me pull everything out. It took a little while, but it was warm next to the deer's insides. Everything came out fine, except Isaac cut open the stomach a little when he opened up the hide and so some partly digested grass spilled out on the other insides and onto me when I pulled it out.

"How much you figure he weighs, Isaac?" I said, after we'd got him all dressed out.

"Well, he ain't little. Maybe 175-180. No picnic to drag, I'll tell you that."

Isaac had a better rope than mine, so he tied a fancy knot around the horns, slung the rope over his back, and told me to grab on and pull by the horns. I did what he said, and we pulled him out of the brush and through the swamp towards camp. He was plenty heavy. We'd stop every twenty yards or so and take a breather. Isaac was looking pretty tired after a while because he was doing most of the pulling.

Right before the edge of the little swamp, he tripped on something and fell flat in the muck. He had his rifle slung over his right shoulder and I'm sure he still had a shell in the chamber. He lay still for a second, then he pushed himself up with his hands and started spitting the stuff out of his mouth. He and I didn't say anything, but when he turned around I gave him my hand and helped pull him up. He wiped some of the muck off his face and he looked at me.

"You shoulda let me take the heavy job for a while," I said, "you just got too tired."

He took a look at himself for a second—he was full of muck all down his front—and then he just laughed. He rubbed my face with one of his filthy hands and he said, "Naw, even your big brother falls on his face once in a while."

"I guess so," I said, and I must have smiled.

He took his gun off his shoulder and looked at it. "Lucky I didn't get the old girl all dirty."

We dragged the deer the rest of the way back to the shack—it was easier going once we got out of the swamp—and we hung him out on a limb to let the blood drip down. It seemed like an awfully long time since I'd shot him, but right then it was only nine o'clock. We still had to sit another three hours before lunch. Isaac and I went in the shack and had a can of pop, and then we walked back to our stands.

When I got back up there, it was almost 9:30, and I felt pretty good, so the rest of the morning went by faster than before. I hoped my dad would be proud of me and I hoped Isaac wouldn't tell him about my deer and make it sound like just pure dumb luck. I had finally killed something at least, so my dad couldn't just look at me and shake his head a little and not say anything, like he always did after I'd missed one.

It was sunny and it seemed to get a little warmer all morning long. I heard shooting that I thought might be Pete or Raymond at about ten o'clock, and about quarter to twelve I thought I heard my dad shoot. He had the loudest rifle I'd ever heard.

Dad came walking out to Isaac and me at about twenty after twelve. I grabbed my rifle and climbed down.

"Did you get one, Dad?" I said.

"Yep, a little fork-horn. And Isaac tells me you shot a pretty nice buck in spite of yourself."

"Yeah, pretty lucky, I guess."

We went back to the shack and when we got there we saw a nice doe hanging on the limb next to my deer.

"You get that one, Pete?" asked my Dad.

"Yep. She came along with two fawns a little after ten, just kinda creeping along the ridge. I almost didn't get her."

"I thought that must have been you shooting," said my dad.

"You got good ears if you can tell between me and Raymond from way to hell and gone up where you sit."

Dad and Raymond unloaded Raymond's three-wheeler from his truck and Dad drove back to his stand to get his deer. He had to use the old trail, which was a long way around, so he didn't get back until after one. The rest of us cooked hot dogs in the barrel stove and had lunch. Pete and Raymond gave me crap about not seeing the horns on my deer, but they were a little proud, too, I think.

"When I hear three shots like that, it usually doesn't get my hopes up much, particularly when it comes from your direction, Freddie," Pete said, grabbing my shoulder. "So I was just glad you got one."

When Dad got back, we finished lunch and helped him hang up his deer. It was almost two o'clock before I finally got back in my stand, and I didn't mind a bit.

The afternoon goes quicker hunting because, first of all, you're sitting for less time, and second of all, you can look forward to the day being over, a good supper, some sitting around, and some sleep. When the sun starts going down a little after four, you know you're almost finished standing your post, and it feels pretty good.

I didn't see any deer that afternoon, only a couple partridges, which scared me quite a bit when they jumped, but I did hear some more shooting that I thought might be Pete or Raymond.

When the sun went down, pretty soon Dad and Isaac came walking out to me, and we all went back to camp. Raymond had shot another doe, and he'd been in the shack since about 3:30.

"Well, boys, the radio says a blizzard's comin'," Raymond said. "We got four already, I figure we may as well pack up and be gone."

"That fine by me, but Isaac's the one who hasn't gotten his buck yet," said my dad. "I think it's up to him."

"There's always next weekend, old timer," said Pete.

Isaac looked at the ground. "It don't matter to me, I guess. Either way's fine."

But it looked like it did matter and everybody knew it, so nobody said anything, we all just decided to stay and hunt Sunday, too. The sun was down, and it was pretty well dark by six o'clock.

The sun didn't ever come up on Sunday.

When my dad got up in the morning, he went out to use the biffy and then decided that he and Raymond might as well go back to sleep until 5:30.

"How much snow, you figure?" said Raymond.

"Oh, eight or ten inches, I'd guess," my dad said, "And it isn't any more than five above out there."

"And windy as hell, I'll just bet. It's gonna be prime sittin' weather today, boys," said Pete.

"Aw, quit your bitchin'," said Isaac. He still sounded sleepy, so I didn't know if he meant anything by it.

After we got up and everybody had their breakfast, we put on everything we wore Satur-

day and all the extra stuff we had, too. After I got all my stuff on, I remembered that I hadn't gone to the bathroom since I'd gotten up. If I didn't go then, I'd have to wait until lunch. My dad and Isaac were all dressed and ready to go.

"Dad," I said, "I've gotta pee before I go."

"Shit, Freddie. Why didn't you think of that before you got all your stuff on?" said Isaac.

"It's getting late, Frederic," said my dad. "Some of us want to be in our stands before it's light."

"Just go without me," I said. "I know how to get there by myself."

"Remember fellas, if any of you gets one, just fire off three quick ones," said Raymond.

"Then we can be for gettin' the hell outta here before the snow's up to our asses," said Pete.

Isaac didn't say anything. The four of them headed out.

I took everything off except my longjohns and then I went outside and peed. I looked up the trail and I saw my dad and Isaac walking away. I could just see them for a minute. Dad was in front and Isaac was behind him. It was still mostly dark, and pretty soon they were gone in the woods. It's just like there's no color that time in the morning. They were just gray spots moving into all the rest of the gray. They sort of disappeared and it made me remember something. I wasn't really sure why.

I thought about the time I'd been in eighth grade and lost the first baseball game I started in. Isaac and my Dad were there to watch me. I played second base and I was nervous. I batted last and struck out three times. I hit a couple foul balls and that was the best I could do. I didn't have any balls hit to me in the field for most of the game. I only had to cover second sometimes. But then in the seventh inning when the score was still tied and a guy was on first, this big left-handed guy hit a little grounder to me. I was playing far back because I expected him to hit it hard. I took a couple steps forward and put my glove down.

"Frederic!" I heard my dad yell.

I got nervous and stopped paying attention to what I was doing for a second. Then I moved too slow. I put my glove down by the ground, but the ball went right under it and through my legs. Then I just stood there for minute, staring at the dirt.

"What are you lookin' at Jensen?" the first baseman said to me.

"Thanks, shit-for-brains," said the big guy on first. The old runner on first had gone to third.

The next batter hit one over the shortstop's head, and that was it. We lost, and that was the only game I ever started.

I got through the line where we slapped hands with the other team, except that we didn't say "good game" like usual, and then I went right towards the parking lot. I didn't want to talk to anybody and I didn't want to ride home on the bus. I saw my dad and Isaac climbing down from the bleachers and I started to run towards left field to get around the fence that was in front of the bleachers. I figured they must have seen me. But when I got outside the fence, I saw them walking out to the parking lot. Dad was in front and Isaac was behind him. I watched them go. They didn't turn around. Dad let Isaac drive. They just got in the truck and went.

That was a long time ago, but I thought about it when I went back in the shack and put all my clothes on again.

The trail was slower going after all the snow. By the time I got to my stand, it was already light enough that I could see the water in the big swamp. It must have been almost seven o'clock. I climbed up, levered a shell in, put the safety on, and set my gun down against the tree. Then I zipped up my coat and pulled down my face mask. If I got too cold, I had a hood, too. I stood there with my arms on the shooting rail.

The wind was bad and it blew the snow around in big sheets. It wasn't clumpy snowman snow, it was icy blizzard snow and it felt like cold sand when it hit your face. I couldn't tell if it was still snowing anymore or if it was all just the wind. I kept wiggling my toes in my boots to keep them from getting numb, but after a while it didn't matter anymore.

Except for having to wade through the snow, it would have been nicer to shoot my deer on this day. I could have used an excuse to moved around and get warmed up. I don't think anyone knows just what a difference there is in the cold between sitting still and just walking around, until they've gone hunting. Even with all the clothes you have on, it never quite does the trick. And, that day, with the wind blowing like it was, sitting in a stand for five hours wasn't much fun at all. I wanted to be done hunting. I hoped we'd go home at lunch time or maybe earlier if somebody got one. I wondered if my dad had his ear-flaps down.

In a little while, I started to remember more. I thought about the night after that base-ball game. My mom picked me up at the school. When she saw me she just looked at me and said, "Hi, Freddie."

I didn't want to talk I guess and she proba-bly could tell. When I got home I went right to my room. I lay on the floor and I could hear Mom and Dad downstairs in the kitchen. When they talked, they almost always talked loud.

"Richard, he's not the only one on the team," Mom said. "It wasn't all his fault."

"Close enough," said Dad.

"He's your son. If you don't give him the benefit of the doubt, then who will?"

Dad talked louder. I could tell he was getting mad. "Oh, he's so neglected, isn't he? God forbid someone expect something from him. My dad would've kicked my rear end if I'd have ever pitted around the way he does. How does Isaac manage to make something of himself? How do the rest of us?"

Mom said, louder than before, "Then leave him be, Richard. If you won't try and help him, then at least you can leave him alone."

"Fine," he said.

I didn't remember hearing any more after that. I must have ended up falling asleep on the floor. I tried to think about something else.

After a couple hours in the stand, I was chilled pretty much all over. I wanted to get down and walk over to Isaac or maybe even walk back to the shack, but I didn't. I just kept standing and waiting. My dad said that deer didn't like to move around much when the weather was bad, so I figured nobody'd probably see anything and then I wondered why we were still hunting.

Then at maybe around 10:30 or eleven I heard shooting. I knew it was Isaac because it was so close. There were two shots right together. I picked up my gun and faced towards Isaac in case he hadn't gotten it and scared it my way. I thought maybe Isaac would whistle for me to come over if he'd killed one, but he didn't. I waited and nothing happened, so pretty soon I just got down and walked over to Isaac's stand. I needed to move around anyway and get down out of the wind a little.

Isaac wasn't in his stand and I didn't see him walking around anywhere. I looked at the ground and saw his boot tracks going sort of southeast into the poplar brush. It's not too hard to track a person in the snow, so I started

following Isaac's trail. Pretty soon, I started to notice a fresh-looking deer track here and there between Isaac's tracks or next to his tracks. And then there was blood. First just little drops and splatters every few yards in the snow, and after awhile patches of bloody snow, and then a huge bloody place as big as the top of an umbrella where the deer must have laid down for minute.

Even I could tell that this deer was gut shot. It had to have been a hard shot or else Isaac would have gotten him in the neck or front shoulder and that would have been it. I figured Isaac must be pretty upset because he was a good shot like Dad, and a gut shot deer can run and run and you might never catch him.

After the big bloody place, I kept walking for probably a quarter of a mile or so and then I heard another shot. I sort of jumped because it was so loud and close. I ran for a minute through the brush and the snow with my gun out in front of me until I was too tired, and then I just tried to walk as fast as I could. It must have taken me about ten minutes to find Isaac. It had started to really snow again.

I came out of the poplar brush and into a little field. I saw Isaac and then I saw the deer. The deer was down and sort of grunting and moaning. He was dragging himself towards the brush. He was trying to get up, but he couldn't. He was bigger than my buck and had bigger horns and he had two big bloody holes in his side. Isaac was close to him and I was pretty close to them, but Isaac still hadn't seen me. He had the scope flipped down on his .308 and he was walking towards the deer. He stopped trying to move but he still made noise. Isaac was within about ten feet of him and he kept putting his gun up to shoot and then taking it down again. Then pretty soon he just walked right up to him, put the gun barrel behind his head, and shot. He levered out the shell and the deer stopped making noise.

"Are you dead yet, you son of a bitch?" Isaac said.

He sat down next to the deer and put his gun across his knees. Then he looked up and saw me. "Christ, Freddie, you almost scared the shit outta me. What the hell ya doin'?" He turned his head and spat. "Anyway, now you're here you can help me drag this bastard."

"He sure is big," I said.

"Yeah. Almost worth the trouble."

I walked over to him and he got up. The wind was blowing through the field something fierce.

"Go find someplace for our guns." He handed me the .308. "And you fire the three quick ones. I've only got one shell left in mine."

I went and leaned Isaac's gun against a tree with a log in front of it to keep it out of the snow. Then I pulled the hammer back on the .30-30, fired, levered, fired, levered, and fired out above the tree line. I put my gun on the log against the tree and went back to help Isaac with his deer.

Gutting it out was a big fat mess. One bullet can wreck a lot of insides. Isaac let me do some of the cutting. He'd yank on stuff and then tell me where to cut. I got out the stomach and all the intestines and kept everything together. I was getting half-decent at it.

I put the knife in my pocket for a second and wiped my hands on my coveralls. "Isaac," I said, "Do you think you like hunting so much that you don't ever want to move away?"

He looked up from the deer. "Hell, I guess I never thought about it much." He wiped his nose with his hand. "'Course, even if I lived in the cities, I'd still come up and hunt."

"I mean, what if you moved farther away? Like Arizona or something?"

He laughed. "What the hell's in Arizona?"

"I don't know," I said. "I've heard people say it's nice."

Isaac shook his head and spat over his shoulder. "Don't worry about me, Freddie. Until further notice, I'm pretty much stuck here." He looked back at me. "Why, you wanna move away?"

"Sometimes."

"Yeah, me too sometimes. Me too a hell of a lot of the time."

He grabbed some snow and wiped off his hands. "Get cuttin', Freddie, so we can get outta here. This storm looks like serious shit."

I started in again, but when we got to the bunghole, which is hard to cut around, I slipped and got Isaac with the knife.

He pulled his hand away, held it with his other one, and looked at the cut in his palm. "Shit, Freddie! Be more careful," he said. "Here, just let me do it by myself." He took the knife. It was lucky it was only a Swiss Army knife and not a real buck knife.

When he got done, the arms on his coat were bloody all the way up to the elbows. He tied his rope to the buck's horns, and he said, "Freddie, grab the guns and let's get goin'. We get this bastard to the old trail and we can get the three-wheeler."

I could tell the blizzard really was worse now. I was glad we'd be on our way home pretty soon.

I went to get the guns, but they had gotten blown off the log. Or maybe I had set them there wrong. Anyhow, they were lying in the snow.

"Isaac," I said, "I—"

"What's the story now?" He came over and he was mad.

"I don't know," I said. I reached down to pick up the .308.

"Don't touch it! You wreck everything you touch. Just stay outta my hair for once, goddamit!"

I felt bad. I didn't even pick up my gun. I just started walking back to the deer. I felt cold. I wanted to be at home. It wasn't even noon and already it was all shadowy in the poplars and pines. I came to the deer. He was frosty-looking now from the blowing snow and his bloody places were frozen. I stood there for a second, looking at his head and at the side of him.

Then I heard that shot. I whipped around and fell back on my butt.

I looked over and I saw Isaac just standing still with his gun in his hands. His mouth was wide open and there was some blood on his forehead. He looked like he was going to fall forward. I ran over to him, and then he looked at me. I remember how his face was. He just looked so confused. I'd never seen him look that way before. His eyes and mouth open so wide. He couldn't talk and he couldn't breathe. He made a noise like a raspy hiss. His eyes started to wander all around. I wanted to say something, but I didn't know what.

Isaac dropped his gun and he fell and I grabbed onto his hand. He landed on his side. His chest wasn't moving. His hand was warm and didn't let go. I waited a minute, then I ran my fingers over his face and closed his eyes. You always see people do that in movies.

I didn't know for sure how it happened, but it must have been an accident. Even Isaac made mistakes. Maybe he forgot to put the gun back on safe after he shot the deer. I probably should have checked when I moved it to the log.

I knew my dad would have heard all the shooting and found the trail, so he'd be there before long. I knelt down in the snow by Isaac and prayed that he wouldn't catch up to us now. Then I changed my mind and prayed that he would.

I left the deer and the guns alone. I got Isaac up and leaned him on a poplar tree. Then I picked him up on my shoulder. I'd never carried anyone like that before, but it wasn't bad. He wasn't that much heavier than me.

"I've got you," I said.

I walked toward where I was pretty sure the old trail was. It was hard to walk that way. The brush and the snow and the weight made it hard. But I had to keep going.

Pretty soon, I started hearing brush cracking back behind me. I looked and saw my dad about a hundred yards away.

"Isaac! Isaac!" he called.

He must have seen the big buck and wondered why Isaac had left him there. He would want to keep the deer, I figured.

"Isaac!" he kept calling.

When he got up to where I was, I turned around. "It's Freddie."

"What have—oh my Christ!" he said.

"He—"

"Merciful God! Oh God, oh God, oh God."

Dad came beside me and looked at Isaac. He ran his hand through Isaac's hair, over the hole and the blood. Then he picked up one of Isaac's blood-stained hands and squeezed it with his big fingers.

I could hear my Dad sniffling and breathing hard next to me. He waited, but he still had trouble talking. "Freddie, what did you do?"

He stepped in front of me and I looked away from him. "His gun fell in the snow and that was kinda my fault, but then he picked it up and looked to see if there was any snow in it," I said. "It just—went off—right in his face."

"You saw him do it?"

"Yes."

"Why didn't you yell at me?" His eyes were really watery and his face was red.

"I don't know," I said.

He sighed slow and hard, and cleared his throat. "Give him to me now."

"No."

I walked away from him. I thought we were getting close to the old trail. When we got there, it would only be another half-mile or so.

"Freddie, you hang on a minute," Dad said behind me. "Are you sure that's what happened? Are you sure you weren't horsing around?"

"Just like I said. It was just like I already said."

"You're sure now? This is as serious as it gets, Freddie."

"I'm sure," I said. "I'm sure.

When I walked, my boots went all the way down into the snow. I walked under a pine tree and a bunch of snow came off a branch and some of it fell on Isaac.

"Put him down, Freddie," Dad said, when we got to the trail.

"I'm gonna keep going," I said.

"Just put him down and stay here while I go for the three-wheeler," he said.

I held up for a second, and I moved Isaac up higher on my shoulder. I looked up the trail. "No," I said. My brother didn't feel like a deer. I had to keep going.

"Freddie, just knock it off. You don't know what you're doing. I'm handling this."

I didn't know what to say, so I started walking again. The wind was bad and I pulled down my face mask.

"Frederic, you'd better stop and do as I say, or you're going to wish you had."

"I'm not scared," I said. Isaac was starting to feel heavier on my shoulder.

"Frederic!"

I just kept going.

"Frederic, I said stop it, goddamn it!"

I turned around.

"Goddamn you," I said. It just came out.

I heard him go back. He went to get the guns. In a while he passed by me on the trail and didn't look at me. He just left me alone. After a few minutes, I couldn't see him anymore.

How It Works

1. Joseph Moser drew from his own experience growing up in Minnesota to describe this story's setting. The Minnesota woods and the hunting trip described in the story will be unfamiliar to many readers. Underline places where the writer uses concrete physical detail to make these elements real. What does he show about the place that you haven't seen or thought of before?

2. Similarly, what kind of detail does he provide about the hunt itself? Underline detail that convinced you that the narrator knew what he was talking about.

3. How does the main character change over the course of the story? How has he been affected by his brother's death? What, in terms of this change, is gained by the decision to tell the story in retrospect rather than in strict chronological order?

4. Try rewriting the scene so that Isaac does not die. What other changes in the story would this change require?

Alice Munro

Alice Munro was born in 1931, in Wingham, Ontario, and attended the University of Western Ontario. In 1952 she moved to Vancouver, British Columbia. By exploring the ordinary lives and emotions of women and men, Munro's fiction, always set in rural Canada, touches on the complexity of emotion and human relationships. Her stories, which have appeared in The New Yorker, Atlantic Monthly, *and* Paris Review, *among other journals, are characterized by their humor, political awareness, and careful attention to detail.*

Munro has won the Governor General's Literary Award, Canada's highest literary honor, three times, for the collections of short stories Dance of the Happy Shades *(1968),* Who Do You Think You Are? *(1978; published as* The Beggar Maid *in the United States, 1979), and* The Progress of Love *(1986). She has also won the Lannan Literary Award, the W. H. Smith Award, and the National Book Critics Circle Award. Her other works include the novel* Lives of Girls and Women *(1971) and the short story collections* Something I've Been Meaning to Tell You *(1974),* The Moons of Jupiter *(1982),* Friend of My Youth *(1990),* Open Secrets *(1994), and* The Love of a Good Woman *(1998). Munro is Writer in Residence at the University of Western Ontario.*

Lichen

Stella's father built the place as a summer house, on the clay bluffs overlooking Lake Huron. Her family always called it "the summer cottage." David was surprised when he first saw it, because it had none of the knotty-pine charm, the battened-down coziness, that those words suggested. A city boy, from what Stella's family called "a different background," he had no experience of summer places. It was and is a high, bare wooden house, painted gray—a copy of the old farmhouses nearby, though perhaps less substantial. In front of it are the steep bluffs—they are not so substantial, either, but have held so far—and a long flight of steps down to the beach. Behind it is a small fenced garden, where Stella grows vegetables with considerable skill and coaxing, a short sandy lane, and a jungle of wild blackberry bushes.

As David turns the car in to the lane, Stella steps out of these bushes, holding a colander full of berries. She is a short, fat, white-haired woman, wearing jeans and a dirty T-shirt. there is nothing underneath these clothes, as far as he can see, to support or restrain any part of her.

"Look what's happened to Stella," says David, fuming. "She's turned into a troll."

Catherine, who has never met Stella before, says decently, "Well. She's older."

"Older than what, Catherine? Older than the house? Older than Lake Huron? Older than the cat?"

There is a cat asleep on the path beside the vegetable garden. A large ginger tom with ears mutilated in battle, and one grayed-over eye. His name is Hercules and he dates from David's time.

"She's an older woman," says Catherine in a flutter of defiance. Even defiant, she's meek. "You know what I mean."

David thinks that Stella has done this on purpose. It isn't just an acceptance of natural deterioration—oh, no, it's much more. Stella would always dramatize. But it isn't just Stella.

There's the sort of woman who has to come bursting out of the female envelope at this age, flaunting fat or an indecent scrawniness, sprouting warts and facial hair, refusing to cover pasty veined legs, almost gleeful about it, as if this was what she'd wanted to do all along. Man-haters, from the start. You can't say a thing like that out loud nowadays.

He has parked too close to the berry bushes—too close for Catherine, who slides out of the car on the passenger side and is immediately in trouble. Catherine is slim enough, but her dress has a full skirt and long, billowy sleeves. It's a dress of cobwebby cotton, shading from pink to rose, with scores of tiny, irregular pleats that look like wrinkles. A pretty dress but hardly a good choice for Stella's domain. The blackberry bushes catch it everywhere, and Catherine has to keep picking herself loose.

"David, really, you could have left her some room," says Stella.

Catherine laughs at her predicament. "I'm all right, I'm okay, really."

"Stella, Catherine," says David, introducing.

"Have some berries, Catherine," says Stella sympathetically. "David?"

David shakes his head, but Catherine takes a couple. "Lovely," she says. "Warm from the sun."

"I'm sick of the sight of them," says Stella.

Close up, Stella looks a bit better—with her smooth, tanned skin, childishly cropped hair, wide brown eyes. Catherine, drooping over her, is a tall, frail, bony woman with fair hair and sensitive skin. Her skin is so sensitive it won't stand any makeup at all, and is easily inflamed by colds, foods, emotions. Lately she has taken to wearing blue eye shadow and black mascara, which David thinks is a mistake. Blackening those sparse wisps of lashes emphasizes the watery blue of her eyes, which look as if

they couldn't stand daylight, and the dryness of the skin underneath. When David first met Catherine, about eighteen months ago, he thought she was a little over thirty. He saw many remnants of girlishness; he loved her fairness and tall fragility. She has aged since then. And she was older than he thought to start with—she is nearing forty.

"But what will you do with them?" Catherine says to Stella. "Make jam?"

"I've made about five million jars of jam already," Stella says. "I put them in little jars with those artsy-fartsy gingham tops on them and I give them away to all my neighbors who are too lazy or too smart to pick their own. Sometimes I don't know why I don't just let Nature's bounty rot on the vine."

"It isn't on the vine," says David. "It's on those god-awful thorn bushes, which ought to be cleaned out and burned. Then there'd be room to park a car."

Stella says to Catherine, "Listen to him, still sounding like a husband."

Stella and David were married for twenty-one years. They have been separated for eight.

"It's true, David," says Stella contritely. "I should clean them out. There's a long list of things I never get around to doing. Come on in and I'll get changed."

"We'll have to stop at the liquor store," says David. "I didn't get a chance."

Once every summer, he makes this visit, timing it as nearly as he can to Stella's father's birthday. He always brings the same present—a bottle of Scotch whisky. This birthday is his father-in-law's ninety-third. He is in a nursing home a few miles away, where Stella can visit him two or three times a week.

"I just have to wash," Stella says. "And put on something bright. Not for Daddy, he's completely blind now. But I think the others like it, the sight of me dressed in pink or blue or something cheers them up the way a balloon would. You two have time for a quick drink. Actually, you can make me one too."

She leads them, single file, up the path to the house. Hercules doesn't move.

"Lazy beast," says Stella. "He's getting about as bad as Daddy. You think the house needs painting, David?"

"Yes."

"Daddy always said every seven years. I don't know—I'm considering putting on siding. I'd get more protection from the wind. Even since I winterized, it sometimes feels as if I'm living in an open crate."

Stella lives here all year round. In the beginning, one or the other of the children would often be with her. But now Paul is studying forestry in Oregon and Deirdre is teaching at an English-language school in Brazil.

"But could you get anything like that color in siding?" says Catherine. "It's so nice, that lovely weather-beaten color."

"I was thinking of cream," says Stella.

Alone in this house, in this community, Stella leads a busy and sometimes chaotic life. Evidence of this is all around them as they progress through the back porch and the kitchen to the living room. Here are some plants she has been potting, and the jam she mentioned—not all given away but waiting, she explains, for bake sales and the fall fair. Here is her winemaking apparatus; then, in the long living room, overlooking the lake, her typewriter, surrounded by stacks of books and papers.

"I'm writing my memoirs," says Stella. She rolls her eyes at Catherine. "I'll stop for a cash payment. No, it's okay, David, I'm writing an article on the old lighthouse." She points the lighthouse out to Catherine. "You can see it from this window if you squeeze right down to the end. I'm doing a piece for the historical society and the local paper. Quite the budding authoress."

Besides the historical society, she says, she belongs to a play-reading group, a church choir, the winemakers' club, and an informal group in which the members entertain one another weekly at dinner parties that have a fixed (low) cost.

"To test our ingenuity," she says. "Always testing something."

And that is only the more or less organized part of it. Her friends are a mixed bag. People who have retired here, who live in remodelled farmhouses or winterized summer cottages; younger people of diverse background who have settled on the land, taking over rocky old farms that born-and-bred farmers won't bother about anymore. And a local dentist and his friend, who are gay.

"We're marvellously tolerant around here now," shouts Stella, who has gone into the bathroom and is conveying her information over the sound of running water. "We don't insist on matching up the sexes. It's nice for us pensioned-off wives. There are about half a dozen of us. One's a weaver."

"I can't find the tonic," yells David from the kitchen.

"It's in cans. The box on the floor by the fridge. This woman has her own sheep. The weaver woman. She has her own spinning wheel. She spins the wool and then she weaves it into cloth."

"Holy shit," says David thoughtfully.

Stella has turned the tap off, and is splashing.

"I thought you'd like that. See, I'm not so far gone. I just make jam."

In a moment, she comes out with a towel wrapped around her, saying, "Where's my drink?" The top corners of the towel are tucked together under one arm, the bottom corners are flapping dangerously free. She accepts a gin-and-tonic.

"I'll drink it while I dress. I have two new summer outfits. One is flamingo and one is turquoise. I can mix and match. Either way, I look stupendous."

Catherine comes from the living room to get her drink, and takes the first two gulps as if it were a glass of water.

"I love this house," she says with a soft vehemence. "I really do. It's so primitive and unpretentious. It's full of light. I've been trying to think what it reminds me of, and now I know. Did you ever see that old Ingmar Bergman movie where there is a family living in a summer house on an island? A lovely shabby house. The girl was going crazy. I remember thinking at the time, That's what summer houses should be like, and they never are."

"That was the one where God was a helicopter," David says. "And the girl fooled around with her brother in the bottom of a boat."

"We never had anything quite so interesting going on around here, I'm afraid," says Stella over the bedroom wall. "I can't say I ever really appreciated Bergman movies. I always thought they were sort of bleak and neurotic."

"Conversations tend to be widespread around here," says David to Catherine. "Notice how none of the partitions go up to the ceiling? Except the bathroom, thank God. It makes for a lot of family life."

"Whenever David and I wanted to say something private, we had to put our heads under the covers," Stella says. She comes out of the bedroom wearing a pair of turquoise stretch pants and a sleeveless top. The top has turquoise flowers and fronds on a white background. At least, she seems to have put on a brassiere. A light-colored strap is visible, biting the flesh of her shoulder.

"Remember one night we were in bed," she says, "and we were talking about getting a new car, saying we wondered what kind of mileage you got with a such-and-such, I forget what. Well, Daddy was always mad about cars, he knew everything, and all of a sudden we heard him say, 'Twenty-eight miles to the gallon,' or whatever, just as if he were right there on the other side of the bed. Of course, he wasn't—he was lying in bed in his own room. David was quite blasé about it; he just said, 'Oh, thank you, sir', as if we'd been including Daddy all along!"

When David comes out of the liquor store, in the village, Stella has rolled down the car window and is talking to a couple she introduces as Ron and Mary. They are in their mid-sixties probably, but very tanned and trim. They wear matching plaid pants and white sweatshirts and plaid caps.

"Glad to meet you," says Ron. "So you're up here seeing how the smart folks live!" He has the sort of jolly voice that suggests boxing feints, playful punches. "When are you going to retire and come up here and join us?"

That makes David wonder what Stella has been telling them about the separation.

"It's not my turn to retire yet."

"Retire early! That's what a lot of us up here did! We got ourselves out of the whole routine. Toiling and moiling and earning and spending."

"Well, I'm not in that," says David. "I'm just a civil servant. We take the taxpayers' money and try not to do any work at all."

"That's not true," says Stella, scolding—wifely. "He works in the Department of Education and he works hard. He just will never admit it."

"A simple serpent!" says Mary, with a crow of pleasure. "I used to work in Ottawa—that was eons ago——and we used to call ourselves simple serpents! Civil serpents. Servants."

Mary is not in the least fat, but something has happened to her chin that usually happens to the chins of fat women. It has collapsed into a series of terraces flowing into her neck.

"Kidding aside," says Ron. "This is a wonderful life. You wouldn't believe how much we find to do. The day is never long enough."

"You have a lot of interests?" says David. He is perfectly serious now, respectful and attentive.

This is a tone that warns Stella, and she tries to deflect Mary. "What are you going to do with the material you brought back from Morocco?"

"I can't decide. It would make a gorgeous dress but it's hardly me. I might just end up putting it on a bed."

"There's so many activities, you can just keep up forever," Ron says. "For instance, skiing. Cross-country. We were out nineteen days in the month of February. Beautiful weather this year. We don't have to drive anywhere. We just go down the back lane—"

"I try to keep up my interests too," says David. "I think it keeps you young."

"There is no doubt it does!"

David has one hand in the inner pocket of his jacket. He brings out something he keeps cupped in his palm, shows it to Ron with a deprecating smile.

"One of my interests," he says.

"Want to see what I showed Ron?" David says later. They are driving along the bluffs to the nursing home.

"No, thank you."

"I hope Ron liked it," David says pleasantly.

He starts to sing. He and Stella met while singing madrigals at university. Or that's what Stella tells people. They sang other things too, not just madrigals. "David was a skinny innocent bit of a lad with a pure sweet tenor and I was a stocky little brute of a girl with a big deep alto," Stella likes to say. "There was nothing he could do about it. Destiny."

"O, Mistress mine, where are you roaming?" sings David, who has a fine tenor voice to this day:

"O, Mistress mine, where are you roaming?
O, Mistress mine, where are you roaming?
O, stay and hear, your true love's coming,
O, stay and hear, your true love's coming,
Who can sing, both High and Low."

Down on the beach, at either end of Stella's property, there are long, low walls of rocks that have been stacked in baskets of wire, stretching out into the water. They are there to protect the beach from erosion. On one of these walls, Catherine is sitting, looking out at the water, with the lake breeze blowing her filmy dress and her long hair. She could be posed for a picture. She might be advertising something, Stella thinks—either something very intimate, and potentially disgusting, or something truly respectable and rather splendid, like life insurance.

"I've been meaning to ask you," says Stella. "Is there anything the matter with her eyes?"

"Eyes?" says David.

"Her eyesight. It's just that she doesn't seem to be quite focusing close up. I don't know how to describe it."

Stella and David are standing at the living-room window. Returned from the nursing home, they each hold a fresh, restorative drink.

They have hardly spoken on the way home, but the silence has not been hostile. They are feeling chastened and reasonably companionable.

"There isn't anything wrong with her eyesight that I know of."

Stella goes into the kitchen, gets out the roasting pan, rubs the roast of pork with cloves of garlic and fresh sage leaves.

"You know, there's a smell women get," says David, standing in the living-room doorway. "It's when they know you don't want them anymore. Stale."

Stella slaps the meat over.

"Those groins are going to have to be rewired entirely," she says. "The wire is just worn to cobwebs in some places. You should see. The power of water. It can wear out tough wire. I'll have to have a work party this fall. Just make a lot of food and ask some people over and make sure enough of them are able-bodied. That's what we all do."

She puts the roast in the oven and rinses her hands.

"It was Catherine you were telling me about last summer, wasn't it? She was the one you said was inclined to be fey."

David groans. "I said what?"

"Inclined to be fey." Stella bangs around, getting out apples, potatoes, onions.

"All right, tell me," says David, coming into the kitchen to stand close to her. "Tell me what I said?"

"That's all, really. I don't remember anything else."

"Stella. Tell me all I said about her."

"I don't, really. I don't remember."

Of course she remembers. She remembers the exact tone in which he said "inclined to be fey." The pride and irony in his voice. In the throes of love, he can be counted on to speak of the woman with tender disparagement—with

amazement, even. He likes to say that it's crazy, he does not understand it, he can plainly see that this person isn't his kind of person at all. And yet, and yet, and yet. And yet it's beyond him, irresistible. He told Stella that Catherine believed in horoscopes, was a vegetarian, and painted weird pictures in which tiny figures were enclosed in plastic bubbles.

"The roast," says Stella, suddenly alarmed. "Will she eat meat?"

"What?"

"Will Catherine eat meat?"

"She may not eat anything. She may be too spaced out."

"I'm making an apple-and-onion casserole. It'll be quite substantial. Maybe she'll eat that."

Last summer he said, "She's a hippie survivor, really. She doesn't even know those times are gone. I don't think she's ever read a newspaper. She hasn't the remotest idea of what's going on in the world. Unless she's heard it from a fortune-teller. That's her idea of reality. I don't think she can read a map. She's all instinct. Do you know what she did? She went to Ireland to see the Book of Kells. She'd heard the Book of Kells was in Ireland. So she just got off the plane at Shannon Airport, and asked somebody the way to the Book of Kells. And you know what, she found it!"

Stella asked how this fey creature earned the money for trips to Ireland.

"Oh, she has a job," David said. "Sort of a job. She teaches art, part time. God knows what she teaches them. To paint by their horoscopes, I think."

Now he says, "There's somebody else. I haven't told Catherine. Do you think she senses it? I think she does. I think she senses it."

He is leaning against the counter, watching Stella peel apples. He reaches quickly into his inside pocket, and before Stella can turn her head away he is holding a Polaroid snapshot in front of her eyes.

"That's my new girl," he says.

"It looks like lichen," says Stella, her paring knife halting. "Except it's rather dark. It looks to me like moss on a rock."

"Don't be dumb, Stella, Don't be cute. You can see her. See her legs?"

Stella puts the paring knife down and squints obediently. There is a flattened-out breast far away on the horizon. And the legs spreading into the foreground. The legs are spread wide—smooth, golden, monumental: fallen columns. Between them is the dark blot she called moss, or lichen. But it's really more like the dark pelt of an animal, with the head and tail and feet chopped off. Dark silky pelt of some unlucky rodent.

"Well, I can see now," she says, in a sensible voice.

"Her name is Dina. Dina without an 'h.' She's twenty-two years old."

Stella won't ask him to put the picture away, or even to stop holding it in front of her face.

"She's a bad girl," says David. "Oh, she's a bad girl! She went to school to the nuns. There are no bad girls like those convent-school girls, once they decide to go wild! She was a student at the art college where Catherine teaches. She quit. Now she's a cocktail waitress."

"That doesn't sound so terribly depraved to me. Deirdre was a cocktail waitress for a while when she was at college."

"Dina's not like Deirdre."

At last, the hand holding the picture drops, and Stella picks up her knife and resumes peeling the apples. But David doesn't put the picture away. He starts to, then changes his mind.

"The little witch," he says. "She torments my soul."

His voice when he talks about this girl seems to Stella peculiarly artificial. But who is she to say, with David, what is artificial and what is not? This special voice of his is rather high-pitched, monotonous, insistent, with a deliberate, cruel sweetness. Whom does he want to be cruel to—Stella, Catherine, the girl, himself? Stella gives a sigh that is noisier and more exasperated than she meant it to be and puts down an apple half-peeled. She goes into the living room and looks out the window.

Catherine is climbing off the wall. Or she's trying to. Her dress is caught in the wire.

"That pretty li'l old dress is giving her all sorts of trouble today," Stella says, surprising herself with the bad accent and a certain viciousness of tone.

"Stella. I wish you'd keep this picture for me."

"Me keep it?"

"I'm afraid I'll show it to Catherine. I keep wanting to. I'm afraid I will."

Catherine has disengaged herself, and has spotted them at the window. She waves, and Stella waves back.

"I'm sure you have others," says Stella. "Pictures."

"Not with me. It's not that I want to hurt her."

"Then don't."

"She makes me want to hurt her. She hangs on me with her weepy looks. She takes pills. Mood elevators. She drinks. Sometimes I think the best thing to do would be to give her the big chop. *Coup de grâce. Coup de grâce,* Catherine. Here you are. Big chop. But I worry about what she'll do."

"Mood elevator," says Stella. "Mood elevator, going up!"

"I'm serious, Stella. Those pills are deadly."

"That's your affair."

"Very funny."

"I didn't even mean it to be. Whenever something slips out like that, I always pretend I meant it, though. I'll take all the credit I can get!"

These three people feel better at dinnertime than any of them might have expected. David feels better because he has remembered that there is a telephone booth across from the liquor store. Stella always feels better when she has cooked a meal and it has turned out so well. Catherine's reasons for feeling better are chemical.

Conversation is not difficult. Stella tells stories that she has come across in doing research for her article, about wrecks on the Great Lakes. Catherine knows something about wrecks. She has a boyfriend—a former boyfriend—who is a diver. David is gallant enough to assert that he is jealous of this fellow, does not care to hear about his deep-water prowess. Perhaps this is the truth.

After dinner, David says he needs to go for a walk. Catherine tells him to go ahead. "Go on," she says merrily. "We don't need you here. Stella and I will get along fine without you!"

Stella wonders where this new voice of Catherine's comes from, this pert and rather foolish and flirtatious voice. Drink wouldn't do it. Whatever Catherine has taken has made her sharper, not blunter. Several layers of wispy apology, tentative flattery, fearfulness, or hopefulness have simply blown away in this brisk chemical breeze.

But when Catherine gets up and tries to clear the table it becomes apparent that the sharpening is not physical. Catherine bumps into a corner of the counter. She makes Stella think of an amputee. Not much cut off, just the tips of her fingers and maybe her toes. Stella has to keep an eye on her, relieving her of the dishes before they slide away.

"Did you notice the hair?" says Catherine. Her voice goes up and down like a Ferris wheel; it dips and sparkles. "He's dyeing it!"

"David is?" says Stella, in genuine surprise.

"Every time he'd think of it, he'd tilt his head back, so you couldn't get too close a look. I think he was afraid you'd say something. He's slightly afraid of you. Actually, it looks very natural."

"I really didn't notice."

"He started a couple of months ago. I said, 'David, what does it matter—your hair was getting gray when I fell in love with you, do you think it's going to bother me now?' Love is strange, it does strange things. David is actually a sensitive person—he's a vulnerable person." Stella rescues a wineglass that is drooping from Catherine's fingers. "It can make you mean. Love can make you mean. If you feel dependent on somebody, then you can be mean to them. I understand that in David."

They drink mead at dinner. This is the first time Stella has tried this batch of homemade mead and she thinks now how good it was, dry and sparkling. It looked like champagne. She checks to see if there is any left in the bottle. About half a glass. She pours it out for herself, sets her glass behind the blender, rinses the bottle.

"You have a good life here," Catherine says.

"I have a fine life. Yes."

"I feel a change coming in my life. I love David, but I've been submerged in this love for so long. Too long. Do you know what I mean? I was down looking at the waves and I started saying, 'He loves me, he loves me not.' I do that often. Then I thought, Well, there isn't any end to the waves, not like there is to a daisy. Or even like there is to my footsteps, if I start counting them to the end of the block. I thought, The waves never, ever come to an end. So then I know, this is a message for me."

"Just leave the pots, Catherine. I'll deal with them later."

Why doesn't Stella say, "Sit down, I can manage better by myself"? It's a thing she has said often to helpers less inept than Catherine. She doesn't say it because she's wary of something. Catherine's state seems so brittle and delicate. Tripping her up could have consequences.

"He loves me, he loves me not," says Catherine. "That's the way it goes. It goes forever. That's what the waves were trying to tell me."

"Just out of curiosity," says Stella, "do you believe in horoscopes?"

"You mean have I had mine done? No, not really. I know people who have. I've thought about it. I guess I don't quite believe in it enough to spend the money. I look at those things in the newspapers sometimes."

"You read the newspapers?"

"I read parts. I get one delivered. I don't read it all."

"And you eat meat? You ate pork for dinner."

Catherine doesn't seem to mind being interrogated, or even to notice that this is an interrogation.

"Well, I can live on salads, particularly at this time of year. But I do eat meat from time to time. I'm a sort of very lackadaisical vegetarian. It was fantastic, the roast. Did you put garlic on it?"

"Garlic and sage and rosemary."

"It was delicious."

"I'm glad."

Catherine sits down suddenly, and spreads out her long legs in a tomboyish way, letting her dress droop between them. Hercules, who has slept all through dinner on the fourth chair, at the other side of the table, takes a determined leap and lands on what there is of her lap.

Catherine laughs, "Crazy cat."

"If he bothers you, just bat him off."

Freed now of the need to watch Catherine, Stella gets busy scraping and stacking the plates, rinsing glasses, cleaning off the table, shaking the cloth, wiping the counters. She feels well satisfied and full of energy. She takes a sip of the mead. Lines of a song are going through her head, and she doesn't realize until a few words of this song reach the surface that it's the same one David was singing, earlier in the day. "What's to come is still unsure!"

Catherine gives a light snore, and jerks her head up. Hercules doesn't take fright, but tries to settle himself more permanently, getting his claws into her dress.

"Was that me?" says Catherine.

"You need some coffee," Stella says. "Hang on. You probably shouldn't go to sleep right now."

"I'm tired," says Catherine stubbornly.

"I know. But you shouldn't go to sleep right now. Hang on, and we'll get some coffee into you."

Stella takes a hand towel from the drawer, soaks it in cold water, holds it to Catherine's face.

"There, now," says Stella. "You hold it, I'll start the coffee. We're not going to have you passing out here, are we? David would carry on about it. He'd say it was my mead or my cooking or my company, or something. Hang on, Catherine."

David, in the phone booth, begins to dial Dina's number. Then he remembers that it's long distance. He must dial the operator. He dials the operator, asks how much the call will cost, empties his pockets of change. He picks out a dollar and thirty-five cents in quarters and dimes, stacks it ready on the shelf. He starts dialing again. His fingers are shaky, his palms sweaty. His legs, gut, and chest are filled with rising commotion. The first ring of the phone, in Dina's cramped apartment, sets his innards bubbling. This is craziness. He starts to feed in quarters.

"I will tell you when to deposit your money," says the operator. "Sir? I will tell you when to deposit it." His quarters clank down into the change return and he has trouble scooping them out. The phone rings again, on Dina's dresser, in the jumble of makeup, panty hose, beads and chains, long feathered earrings, a silly cigarette holder, an assortment of windup toys. He can see them: the green frog, the yellow duck, the brown bear—all the same size. Frogs and bears are equal. Also some space monsters, based on characters in a movie. When set going, these toys will lurch and clatter across Dina's floor or table, spitting sparks out of their mouths. She likes to set up races, or put a couple of them on a collision course. Then she squeals, and even screams with excitement, as they go their unpredictable ways.

"There doesn't seem to be any answer, sir."

"Let it ring a few more times."

Dina's bathroom is across the hall. She shares it with another girl. If she is in the bathroom, even in the bathtub, how long will it take her to decide whether to answer it at all? He decides to count ten rings more, starting now.

"Still no answer, sir."

Ten more.

"Sir, would you like to try again later?"

He hangs up, having thought of something. Immediately, energetically, he dials information.

"For what place, sir?"

"Toronto."

"Go ahead, sir."

He asks for the phone number of a Michael Read. No, he does not have a street address. All he has is the name—the name of her last, and perhaps not quite finished with, boyfriend.

"I have no listing for a Michael Read."

"All right. Try Reade, R-E-A-D-E."

There is indeed an M. Reade, on Davenport Road. Not a Michael but at least an M. Check back and see, then. Is there an M. Read? Read? Yes. Yes, there is an M. Read, living on Simcoe Street. And another M. Read, R-E-A-D, living on Harbord. Why didn't she say that sooner?

He picks Harbord on a hunch. That's not too far from Dina's apartment. The operator tells him the number. He tries to memorize it. He has nothing to write with. He feels it's important not to ask the operator to repeat the number more than once. He should not reveal that he is here in a phone booth without a pen or pencil. It seems to him that the desperate, furtive nature of his quest is apparent, and that at any moment he may be shut off, not permitted to acquire any further information about M. Read, or M. Reade, on Harbord or Simcoe or Davenport, or wherever.

Now he must start all over again. The Toronto area code. No, the operator. The memorized number. Quick, before he loses his nerve or loses the number. If she should answer, what is he going to say? But it isn't likely that she will answer, even if she is there. M. Read would answer. Then David must ask for Dina. But perhaps not in his own voice. Perhaps not in a man's voice at all. He used to be able to do different voices on the phone. He could even fool Stella at one time.

Perhaps he could do a woman's voice, squeaky. Or a child's voice, a little-sister voice. *Is Dina there?*

"I beg your pardon, sir?"

"Nothing. Sorry."

"It's ringing now. I will let you know when to deposit your money."

What if M. Read is a woman? Not Michael Read at all. Mary Read. Old-age pensioner. Career girl. What are you phoning me for? Sexual harassment. Back to information, then. Try M. Read on Simcoe. Try M. Read on Davenport. Keep trying.

"I'm sorry. I can't seem to get an answer."

The phone rings again and again in M. Read's apartment, or house, or room. David leans against the metal shelf, where his change is waiting. A car has parked in the liquor-store lot. The couple in it are watching him. Obviously waiting to use the phone. With any luck, Ron and Mary will drive up next.

Dina lives above an Indian-import shop. Her clothing and hair always have a smell of curry powder, nutmeg, incense, added to what David thinks of as her natural smell, of cigarettes and dope and sex. Her hair is dyed dead black. Her cheeks bear a slash of crude color and her eyelids are sometimes brick red. She tried out once for a part in a movie some people she knew about were making. She failed to get the part because of some squeamishness about holding a tame rat between her legs. This failure humiliated her.

David sweats now, trying not to catch her out but to catch her any way at all, to hear her harsh young voice, with its involuntary tremor and insistent obscenities. Even if hearing it, at this moment, means that she has betrayed him. Of course she has betrayed him. She betrays him all the time. If only she would answer (he

has almost forgotten it's M. Read who is supposed to answer), he could howl at her, berate her, and if he felt low enough—he *would* feel low enough—he could plead with her. He would welcome the chance. Any chance. At dinner, talking in a lively way to Stella and Catherine, he kept writing the name Dina with his finger on the underside of the wooden table.

People don't have any patience with this sort of suffering, and why should they? The sufferer must forgo sympathy, give up on dignity, cope with the ravages. And on top of that, people will take time out to tell you that this isn't real love. These bouts of desire and dependence and worship and perversity, willed but terrible transformations—they aren't real love.

Stella used to tell him he wasn't interested in love. "Or sex, even. I don't think you're even interested in sex, David. I think all you're interested in is being a big bad boy."

Real love—that would be going on living with Stella, or taking on Catherine. A person presumed to know all about Real Love might be Ron, of Ron-and-Mary.

David knows what he's doing. This is the interesting part of it, he thinks, and has said. He knows that Dina is not really so wild, or so avid, or doomed, as he pretends she is, or as she sometimes pretends she is. In ten years' time, she won't be wrecked by her crazy life, she won't be a glamorous whore. She'll be a woman tagged by little children in the laundromat. The delicious, old-fashioned word *trollop*, which he used to describe her, doesn't apply to her, really—has no more to do with her than *hippie* had to do with Catherine, a person he cannot now bear to think about. He knows that sooner or later, if Dina allows her disguise to crack, as Catherine did, he will have to move on. He will have to do that anyway—move on.

He knows all this and observes himself, and such knowledge and observation has no effect at all on his quaking gut, zealous sweat glands, fierce prayers.

"Sir? Do you want to keep on trying?"

The nursing home that they visited, earlier in the day, is called the Balm of Gilead Home. It is named after the balm-of-Gilead trees, a kind of poplar, that grow plentifully near the lake. A large stone mansion built by a nineteenth-century millionaire, it is now disfigured by ramps and fire escapes.

Voices summoned Stella, from the clusters of wheelchairs on the front lawn. She called out various names in answer, detoured to press hands and drop kisses. Vibrating here and there like a fat hummingbird.

She sang when she rejoined David:

"I'm your little sunbeam, short and stout,
Turn me over, pour me out!"

Out of breath, she said, "Actually it's *teapot.* I don't think you'll see much change in Daddy. Except the blindness is total now."

She led him through the green-painted corridors, with their low false ceilings (cutting the heating costs), their paint-by-number pictures, their disinfectant—and other—smells. Out on a back porch, alone, her father sat wrapped in blankets, strapped into his wheelchair so that he wouldn't fall out.

Her father said, "David?"

The sound seemed to come from a wet cave deep inside him, to be unshaped by lips or jaws or tongue. These could not be seen to move. Nor did he move his head.

Stella went behind the chair and put her arms around his neck. She touched him very lightly.

"Yes, it's David, Daddy," she said. "You knew his step!"

Her father didn't answer. David bent to touch the old man's hands, which were not cold, as he expected, but warm and very dry. He laid the whisky bottle in them.

"Careful. He can't hold it," said Stella softly. David kept his own hands on the bottle while Stella pushed up a chair, so that he could sit down opposite her father.

"Same old present," David said.

His father-in-law made an acknowledging sound.

"I'm going to get some glasses," Stella said. "It's against the rules to drink outside, but I can generally get them to bend the rules a bit. I'll tell them it's a celebration."

To get used to looking at his father-in-law, David tried to think of him as a post-human development, something new in the species. Survival hadn't just preserved, it had transformed him. Bluish-gray skin, with dark-blue spots, whitened eyes, a ribbed neck with delicate deep hollows, like a smoked-glass vase. Up through this neck came further sounds, a conversational offering. It was the core of each syllable that was presented, a damp vowel barely held in shape by surrounding consonants.

"Traffic—bad?"

David described conditions on the freeway and on the secondary highways. He told his father-in-law that he had recently bought a car, a Japanese car. He told how he had not, at first, been able to get anything close to the advertised mileage. But he had complained, he had persisted, had taken the car back to the dealer. Various adjustments had been tried, and now the situation had improved and the figure was satisfactory, if not quite what had been promised.

This conversation seemed welcome. His father-in-law appeared to follow it. He nodded, and on his narrow, elongated, bluish, post-human face there were traces of old expressions. An expression of shrewd and dignified concern, suspicion of advertising and of foreign cars and car dealers. There was even a suggestion of doubt—as in the old days—that David could be trusted to handle such things well. And relief that he had done so. In his father-in-law's eyes David would always be somebody learning how to be a man, somebody who might never learn, might never achieve the steadfastness and control, the decent narrowness of range. David, who preferred gin to whisky, read novels, didn't understand the stock market, talked to women, and had started out as a teacher. David, who had always driven small cars, foreign cars. But that was all right now. Small cars were not a sign of any of the things they used to be a sign of. Even here on the bluffs above Lake Huron at the very end of life, certain shifts had registered, certain changes had been understood, by a man who couldn't grasp or see.

"Hear anything about—Lada?"

It happens luckily that David has a colleague who drives a Lada, and many boring lunch and coffee breaks have been taken up with the discussion of this car's strengths and failings and the difficulty of getting parts. David recounted these, and his father-in-law seemed satisfied.

"Gray. Dort. Gray-Dort. First car—ever drove. Yonge Street. Sixty miles. Sixty miles. Uh. Uh. Hour."

"He certainly never drove a Gray-Dort down Yonge Street at sixty miles an hour," said Stella when they had got her father and his bottle back to his room, had said goodbye, and were walking back through the green corridors. "Never. Whose Gray-Dort? They were out of production long before he had the money to buy a car. And he'd never have taken the risk with anybody else's. It's his fantasy. He's reached the stage where that's his big recreation—fixing up the past so anything he wishes had happened did happen. Wonder if we'll get to that stage? What would your fantasy be, David? No. Don't tell me!"

"What would yours be?" said David.

"That you didn't leave? That you didn't want to leave? I bet that's what you think mine would be, but I'm not so sure! Daddy was so pleased to see you, David. A man just means more, for Daddy. I suppose if he thought about you and me he'd have to be on my side, but that's all right, he doesn't have to think about it."

Stella, at the nursing home, seemed to have regained some sleekness and suppleness of former times. Her attentions to her father, and even to the wheelchair contingent, brought back a trace of deferential grace to her movements, a wistfulness to her voice. David had a picture of her as she had been twelve or fifteen years before. He saw her coming across the lawn at a suburban party, carrying a casserole. She was wearing a sundress. She always claimed in those days that she was too fat for pants, though she was not half so fat as now. Why did this picture please him so much? Stella coming across the lawn, with her sunlit hair—the gray in it then merely made it ash blond—and her bare toasted shoulders, crying out greetings to her neighbors, laughing, protesting about some cooking misadventure. Of course the food she brought would be wonderful, and she brought not only food but the whole longed-for spirit of the neighborhood party. With her over-whelming sociability, she gathered everybody in. And David felt quite free of irritation, though there were times, certainly, when these gifts of Stella's had irritated him. Her vivacious exasperation, her exaggeration, her wide-eyed humorous appeals for sympathy had irritated him. For others' entertainment he had heard her shaping stories out of their life—the children's daily mishaps and provocations, the cat's visit to the vet, her son's first hangover, the perversity of the power lawnmower, the papering of the upstairs hall. A charming wife, a wonderful person at a party, she has such a funny way of looking at things. Sometimes she was a riot. *Your wife's a riot.*

Well, he forgave her—he loved her—as she walked across the lawn. At that moment, with his bare foot, he was stroking the cold, brown, shaved, and prickly calf of another neighborhood wife, who had just come out of the pool and had thrown on a long, concealing scarlet robe. A dark-haired, childless, chain-smoking woman, given—at least at that stage in their relationship—to tantalizing silences. (His first, that one, the first while married to Stella. Rosemary. A sweet dark name, though finally a shrill trite woman.)

It wasn't just that. The unexpected delight in Stella just as she was, the unusual feeling of being at peace with her, didn't come from just that—the illicit activity of his big toe. This seemed profound, this revelation about himself and Stella—how they were bound together after all, and how as long as he could feel such benevolence toward her, what he did secretly and separately was somehow done with her blessing.

That did not turn out to be a notion Stella shared at all. And they weren't so bound, or if they were it was a bond he had to break.

We've been together so long, couldn't we just tough it out, said Stella at the time, trying to make it a joke. She didn't understand, probably didn't understand yet, how that was one of the things that made it impossible. This white-haired woman walking beside him through the nursing home dragged so much weight with her—a weight not just of his sexual secrets but of his middle-of-the-night speculations about God, his psychosomatic chest pains, his digestive sensitivity, his escape plans, which once included her and involved Africa or Indonesia. All his ordinary and extraordinary life—even some things it was unlikely she knew about—seemed stored up in her. He could never feel any lightness, any secret and victorious expansion, with a woman who knew so much. She was bloated with all she knew. Nevertheless he put his arms around Stella. They embraced, both willingly.

A young girl, a Chinese or Vietnamese girl, slight as a child in her pale-green uniform, but with painted lips and cheeks, was coming along the corridor, pushing a cart. On the cart were paper cups and plastic containers of orange and grape juice.

"Juice time," the girl was calling, in her pleasant and indifferent singsong. "Juice time. Orange. Grape. Juice." She took no notice of David and Stella, but they let go of each other and resumed walking. David did feel a slight, very slight, discomfort at being seen by such a young and pretty girl in the embrace of Stella. It was not an important feeling—it simply brushed him and passed—but Stella, as he held the door open for her, said, "Never mind, David. I could be your sister. You could be comforting your sister. *Older* sister."

"Madam Stella, the celebrated mind reader."

It was strange, the way they said these things. They used to say bitter and wounding things, and pretend, when they said them, to be mildly amused, dispassionate, even kindly. Now this tone that was once a pretense had soaked down, deep down, through all their sharp feelings, and the bitterness, though not transformed, seemed stale, useless and formal.

A week or so later, when she is tidying up the living room, getting ready for a meeting of the historical society that is to take place at her house, Stella finds the picture, a Polaroid snapshot. David has left it with her after all—hiding it, but not hiding it very well, behind the curtains at one end of the living-room window, at the spot where you stand to get a view of the lighthouse.

Lying in the sun had faded it, of course. Stella stands looking at it, with a dust cloth in her hand. The day is perfect. The windows are open, her house is pleasantly in order, and a good fish soup is simmering on the stove. She sees that the black pelt in the picture has changed to gray. It's a bluish or greenish gray now. She remembers what she said when she first saw it. She said it was lichen. No, she said it looked like lichen. But she knew what it was at once. It seems to her now that she knew what it was even when David put his hand to his pocket. She felt the old cavity opening up in her. But she held on. She said, "Lichen." and now, look, her words have come true. The outline of the breast has disappeared. You would never know that the legs were legs. The black has turned to gray, to the soft, dry color of a plant mysteriously nourished on the rocks.

This is David's doing. He left it there, in the sun.

Stella's words have come true. This thought will keep coming back to her—a pause, a lost heartbeat, a harsh little break in the flow of the days and nights as she keeps them going.

How It Works

1. How would you describe the relationships between these characters, particularly between the two women? Underline sentences in the story that created these impressions.

2. Underline descriptions of the characters in the story. From whose point of view is each description written? What does each description suggest about the attitude of the point-of-view character toward the one being described? How does Munro use point of view to suggest the tensions within this triangle?

3. Do these characters ever behave in ways that surprise you? How might other people have responded differently to the same situations? How would the story be different if the three characters formed a more typical love triangle?

4. "Lichen" is not a story about wild or extreme characters; no one gets killed or commits crimes. The people and the events are relatively ordinary, yet they combine at this particular time and place to create an emotionally compelling narrative. What details does the author use to bring them to life? How does drama arise out of the intersection of character and event? Experiment with this story; rewrite a scene or two, intensifying the characters' actions or changing their descriptions to make them more extreme. How is the story affected?

Flannery O'Connor

Flannery O'Connor was born in 1925, in Savannah, Georgia. She attended the Iowa Writers' Workshop and began publishing shortly after she graduated. Her career suffered a blow when she became ill with lupus erythematosus, an inflammatory disease that was at the time fatal. In order to conserve her strength, she moved home to her mother's farm in Milledgeville, Georgia. O'Connor's letters (collected by Sally Fitzgerald in a volume called The Habit of Being*) convey her daily life as well as her thought on a variety of subjects from writing to religion. O'Connor's fiction combines her often cutting wit, her sense of the grotesque, and her strong, unsentimental religious conviction. Her writing was often misunderstood by religious people around her and by the literary establishment. Flannery O'Connor wrote two novels, a collection of essays about writing (*Mysteries and Manners*), and a number of short stories, for which she is best known. The posthumous collection* Flannery O'Connor: The Complete Stories *won the 1972 National Book Award for fiction.*

A Good Man Is Hard to Find

The grandmother didn't want to go to Florida. She wanted to visit some of her connections in east Tennessee and she was seizing at every chance to change Bailey's mind. Bailey was the son she lived with, her only boy. He was sitting on the edge of his chair at the table, bent over the orange sports section of the *Journal*. "Now look here, Bailey," she said, "see here, read this," and she stood with one hand on her thin hip and the other rattling the newspaper at his bald head. "Here this fellow that calls himself The Misfit is aloose from the Federal Pen and headed toward Florida and you read here what it says he did to these people. Just you read it. I wouldn't take my children in any direction with a criminal like that aloose in it. I couldn't answer to my conscience if I did."

Bailey didn't look up from his reading so she wheeled around then and faced the children's mother, a young woman in slacks, whose face was as broad and innocent as a cabbage and was tied around with a green head-kerchief that had two points on the top like rabbit's ears. She was sitting on the sofa, feeding the baby his apricots out of a jar. "The children have been to Florida before," the old lady said. "You all ought to take them somewhere else for a change so they would see different parts of the world and be broad. They never have been to east Tennessee."

The children's mother didn't seem to hear her but the eight-year-old boy, John Wesley, a stocky child with glasses, said, "If you don't want to go to Florida, why dontcha stay at home?" He and the little girl, June Star, were reading the funny papers on the floor.

"She wouldn't stay at home to be queen for a day," June Star said without raising her yellow head.

"Yes and what would you do if this fellow, The Misfit, caught you?" the grandmother said.

"I'd smack his face," John Wesley said.

"She wouldn't stay at home for a million bucks," June Star said. "Afraid she'd miss something. She has to go everywhere we go."

"All right, Miss," the grandmother said. "Just remember that the next time you want me to curl your hair."

June Star said her hair was naturally curly.

The next morning the grandmother was the first one in the car, ready to go. She had her big black valise that looked like the head of a hippopotamus in one corner, and underneath it she was hiding a basket with Pitty Sing, the cat, in it. She didn't intend for the cat to be left alone in the house for three days because he would miss her too much and she was afraid he might brush against one of the gas burners and accidentally asphyxiate himself. Her son, Bailey, didn't like to arrive at a motel with a cat.

She sat in the middle of the back seat with John Wesley and June Star on either side of her. Bailey and the children's mother and the baby sat in front and they left Atlanta at eight forty-five with the mileage on the car at 55890. The grandmother wrote this down because she thought it would be interesting to say how many miles they had been when they got back. It took them twenty minutes to reach the outskirts of the city.

The old lady settled herself comfortably, removing her white cotton gloves and putting them up with her purse on the shelf in front of the back window. The children's mother still had on slacks and still had her hair tied up in a green kerchief, but the grandmother had on a navy blue straw sailor hat with a bunch of white violets on the brim and a navy blue dress with a small white dot in the print. Her collars and cuffs were white organdy trimmed with lace and at her neckline she had pinned a purple spray of cloth violets containing a sachet. In case of an accident, anyone seeing her dead on the highway would know at once that she was a lady.

She said she thought it was going to be a good day for driving, neither too hot nor too cold, and she cautioned Bailey that the speed limit was fifty-five miles an hour and that the

patrolmen hid themselves behind billboards and small clumps of trees and sped out after you before you had a chance to slow down. She pointed out interesting details of the scenery: Stone Mountain; the blue granite that in some places came up to both sides of the highway; the brilliant red clay banks slightly streaked with purple; and the various crops that made rows of green lace-work on the ground. The trees were full of silver-white sunlight and the meanest of them sparkled. The children were reading comic magazines and their mother had gone back to sleep.

"Let's go through Georgia fast so we won't have to look at it much," John Wesley said.

"If I were a little boy," said the grandmother, "I wouldn't talk about my native state that way. Tennessee has the mountains and Georgia has the hills."

"Tennessee is just a hillbilly dumping ground," John Wesley said, "and Georgia is a lousy state too."

"You said it," June Star said.

"In my time," said the grandmother, folding her thin veined fingers, "children were more respectful of their native states and their parents and everything else. People did right then. Oh look at the cute little pickaninny!" she said and pointed to a Negro child standing in the door of a shack. "Wouldn't that make a picture, now?" she asked and they all turned and looked at the little Negro out of the back window. He waved.

"He didn't have any britches on," June Star said.

"He probably didn't have any," the grandmother explained. "Little niggers in the country don't have things like we do. If I could paint, I'd paint that picture," she said.

The children exchanged comic books.

The grandmother offered to hold the baby and the children's mother passed him over the front seat to her. She set him on her knee and bounced him and told him about the things they were passing. She rolled her eyes and screwed up her mouth and stuck her leathery thin face into his smooth bland one. Occasionally he gave her a faraway smile. They passed a large cotton field with five or six graves fenced in the middle of it, like a small island. "Look at the graveyard!" the grandmother said, pointing it out. "That was the old family burying ground. That belonged to the plantation."

"Where's the plantation?" John Wesley asked.

"Gone With the Wind," said the grandmother. "Ha. Ha."

When the children finished all the comic books they had brought, they opened the lunch and ate it. The grandmother ate a peanut butter sandwich and an olive and would not let the children throw the box and the paper napkins out the window. When there was nothing else to do they played a game by choosing a cloud and making the other two guess what shape it suggested. John Wesley took one the shape of a cow and June Star guessed a cow and John Wesley said, no, an automobile, and June Star said he didn't play fair, and they began to slap each other over the grandmother.

The grandmother said she would tell them a story if they would keep quiet. When she told a story, she rolled her eyes and waved her head and was very dramatic. She said once when she was a maiden lady she had been courted by a Mr. Edgar Atkins Teagarden from Jasper, Georgia. She said he was a very good-looking man and a gentleman and that he brought her a watermelon every Saturday afternoon with his initials cut in it, E. A. T. Well, one Saturday, she said, Mr. Teagarden brought the watermelon and there was nobody at home and he left it on the front porch and returned in his buggy to Jasper, but she never got the watermelon, she said, because a nigger boy ate it when he saw the initials, E. A. T.!

This story tickled John Wesley's funny bone and he giggled and giggled but June Star didn't think it was any good. She said she wouldn't marry a man that just brought her a watermelon on Saturday. The grandmother said she would have done well to marry Mr. Teagarden because he was a gentleman and had bought Coca-Cola stock when it first came out and that he had died only a few years ago, a very wealthy man.

They stopped at The Tower for barbecued sandwiches. The Tower was a part stucco and part wood filling station and dance hall set in a clearing outside of Timothy. A fat man named Red Sammy Butts ran it and there were signs stuck here and there on the building and for miles up and down the highway saying, TRY RED SAMMY'S FAMOUS BARBECUE. NONE LIKE FAMOUS RED SAMMY'S! RED SAM! THE FAT BOY WITH THE HAPPY LAUGH. A VETERAN! RED SAMMY'S YOUR MAN!

Red Sammy was lying on the bare ground outside The Tower with his head under a truck while a gray monkey about a foot high, chained to a small chinaberry tree, chattered nearby. The monkey sprang back into the tree and got on the highest limb as soon as he saw the children jump out of the car and run toward him.

Inside, The Tower was a long dark room with a counter at one end and tables at the other and dancing space in the middle. They all sat down at a board table next to the nickelodeon and Red Sam's wife, a tall burnt-brown woman with hair and eyes lighter than her skin, came and took their order. The children's mother put a dime in the machine and played "The

Tennessee Waltz," and the grandmother said that tune always made her want to dance. She asked Bailey if he would like to dance but he only glared at her. He didn't have a naturally sunny disposition like she did and trips made him nervous. The grandmother's brown eyes were very bright. She swayed her head from side to side and pretended she was dancing in her chair. June Star said play something she could tap to so the children's mother put in another dime and played a fast number and June Star stepped out onto the dance floor and did her tap routine.

"Ain't she cute?" Red Sam's wife said, leaning over the counter. "Would you like to come be my little girl?"

"No I certainly wouldn't," June Star said. "I wouldn't live in a broken-down place like this for a million bucks!" and she ran back to the table.

"Ain't she cute?" the woman repeated, stretching her mouth politely.

"Ain't you ashamed?" hissed the grandmother.

Red Sam came in and told his wife to quit lounging on the counter and hurry up with these people's order. His khaki trousers reached just to his hip bones and his stomach hung over them like a sack of meal swaying under his shirt. He came over and sat down at a table nearby and let out a combination sigh and yodel. "You can't win," he said. "You can't win," and he wiped his sweating red face off with a gray handkerchief. "These days you don't know who to trust," he said. "Ain't that the truth?"

"People are certainly not nice like they used to be," said the grandmother.

"Two fellers come in here last week," Red Sammy said, "driving a Chrysler. It was a old beat-up car but it was a good one and these boys looked all right to me. Said they worked at the mill and you know I let them fellers charge the gas they bought? Now why did I do that?"

"Because you're a good man!" the grandmother said at once.

"Yes'm, I suppose so," Red Sam said as if he were struck with this answer.

His wife brought the orders, carrying the five plates all at once without a tray, two in each hand and one balanced on her arm. "It isn't a soul in this green world of God's that you can trust," she said. "And I don't count nobody out of that, not nobody," she repeated, looking at Red Sammy.

"Did you read about that criminal, The Misfit, that's escaped?" asked the grandmother.

"I wouldn't be a bit surprised if he didn't attact this place right here," said the woman. "If he hears about it being here, I wouldn't be none surprised to see him. If he hears it's two cent in the cash register, I wouldn't be a-tall surprised if he . . ."

"That'll do," Red Sam said. "Go bring these people their Co'-Colas," and the woman went off to get the rest of the order.

"A good man is hard to find," Red Sammy said. "Everything is getting terrible. I remember the day you could go off and leave your screen door unlatched. Not no more."

He and the grandmother discussed better times. The old lady said that in her opinion Europe was entirely to blame for the way things were now. She said the way Europe acted you would think we were made of money and Red Sam said it was no use talking about it, she was exactly right. The children ran outside into the white sunlight and looked at the monkey in the lacy chinaberry tree. He was busy catching fleas on himself and biting each one carefully between his teeth as if it were a delicacy.

They drove off again into the hot afternoon. The grandmother took cat naps and woke up every five minutes with her own snoring. Outside of Toombsboro she woke up and recalled an old plantation that she had visited in this neighborhood once when she was a young lady. She said the house had six white columns across the front and that there was an avenue of oaks leading up to it and two little wooden trellis arbors on either side in front where you sat down with your suitor after a stroll in the garden. She recalled exactly which road to turn off to get to it. She knew that Bailey would not be willing to lose any time looking at an old house, but the more she talked about it, the more she wanted to see it once again and find out if the little twin arbors were still standing. "There was a secret panel in this house," she said craftily, not telling the truth but wishing that she were, "and the story went that all the family silver was hidden in it when Sherman came through but it was never found . . ."

"Hey!" John Wesley said. "Let's go see it! We'll find it! We'll poke all the woodwork and find it! Who lives there? Where do you turn off at? Hey, Pop, can't we turn off there?"

"We never have seen a house with a secret panel!" June Star shrieked. "Let's go to the house with the secret panel! Hey Pop, can't we go see the house with the secret panel!"

"It's not far from here, I know," the grandmother said. "It wouldn't take over twenty minutes."

Bailey was looking straight ahead. His jaw was as rigid as a horseshoe. "No," he said.

The children began to yell and scream that they wanted to see the house with the secret panel. John Wesley kicked the back of the front seat and June Star hung over her mother's shoulder and whined desperately into her ear that they never had any fun even on their vacation, that they could never do what THEY wanted to do. The baby began to scream and John Wesley

kicked the back of the seat so hard that his father could feel the blows in his kidney.

"All right!" he shouted and drew the car to a stop at the side of the road. "Will you all shut up? Will you all just shut up for one second? If you don't shut up, we won't go anywhere."

"It would be very educational for them," the grandmother murmured.

"All right," Bailey said, "but get this: this is the only time we're going to stop for anything like this. This is the one and only time."

"The dirt road that you have to turn down is about a mile back," the grandmother directed. "I marked it when we passed."

"A dirt road," Bailey groaned.

After they had turned around and were headed toward the dirt road, the grandmother recalled other points about the house, the beautiful glass over the front doorway and the candle-lamp in the hall. John Wesley said that the secret panel was probably in the fireplace.

"You can't go inside this house," Bailey said. "You don't know who lives there."

"While you all talk to the people in front, I'll run around behind and get in a window," John Wesley suggested.

"We'll all stay in the car," his mother said.

They turned onto the dirt road and the car raced roughly along in a swirl of pink dust. The grandmother recalled the times when there were no paved roads and thirty miles was a day's journey. The dirt road was hilly and there were sudden washes in it and sharp curves on dangerous embankments. All at once they would be on a hill, looking down over the blue tops of trees for miles around, then the next minute, they would be in a red depression with the dust-coated trees looking down on them.

"This place had better turn up in a minute," Bailey said, "or I'm going to turn around."

The road looked as if no one had traveled on it for months.

"It's not much farther," the grandmother said and just as she said it, a horrible thought came to her. The thought was so embarrassing that she turned red in the face and her eyes dilated and her feet jumped up, upsetting her valise in the corner. The instant the valise moved, the newspaper top she had over the basket under it rose with a snarl and Pitty Sing, the cat, sprang onto Bailey's shoulder.

The children were thrown to the floor and their mother, clutching the baby, was thrown out the door onto the ground; the old lady was thrown into the front seat. The car turned over once and landed right-side-up in a gulch off the side of the road. Bailey remained in the driver's seat with the cat—gray-striped with a broad white face and an orange nose—clinging to his neck like a caterpillar.

As soon as the children saw they could move their arms and legs, they scrambled out of the car, shouting, "We've had an ACCIDENT!" The grandmother was curled up under the dashboard, hoping she was injured so that Bailey's wrath would not come down on her all at once. The horrible thought she had had before the accident was that the house she had remembered so vividly was not in Georgia but in Tennessee.

Bailey removed the cat from his neck with both hands and flung it out the window against the side of a pine tree. Then he got out of the car and started looking for the children's mother. She was sitting against the side of the red gutted ditch, holding the screaming baby, but she only had a cut down her face and a broken shoulder. "We've had an ACCIDENT!" the children screamed in a frenzy of delight.

"But nobody's killed," June Star said with disappointment as the grandmother limped out of the car, her hat still pinned to her head but the broken front brim standing up at a jaunty angle and the violet spray hanging off the side. They all sat down in the ditch, except the children, to recover from the shock. They were all shaking.

"Maybe a car will come along," said the children's mother hoarsely.

"I believe I have injured an organ," said the grandmother, pressing her side, but no one answered her. Bailey's teeth were clattering. He had on a yellow sport shirt with bright blue parrots designed in it and his face was as yellow as the shirt. The grandmother decided that she would not mention that the house was in Tennessee.

The road was about ten feet above and they could see only the tops of the trees on the other side of it. Behind the ditch they were sitting in there were more woods, tall and dark and deep. In a few minutes they saw a car some distance away on top of a hill, coming slowly as if the occupants were watching them. The grandmother stood up and waved both her arms dramatically to attract their attention. The car continued to come on slowly, disappeared around a bend and appeared again, moving even slower, on top of the hill they had gone over. It was a big black battered hearse-like automobile. There were three men in it.

It came to a stop just over them and for some minutes, the driver looked down with a steady expressionless gaze to where they were sitting, and didn't speak. Then he turned his head and muttered something to the other two and they got out. One was a fat boy in black trousers and a red sweat shirt with a silver stallion embossed on the front of it. He moved around on the right side of them and stood staring, his mouth partly open in a kind of loose grin. The other had on khaki pants and a blue striped coat and a gray hat pulled down very low, hiding most of his face. He came around slowly on the left side. Neither spoke.

The driver got out of the car and stood by the side of it, looking down at them. He was an older man than the other two. His hair was just beginning to gray and he wore silver-rimmed spectacles that gave him a scholarly look. He had a long creased face and didn't have on any shirt or undershirt. He had on blue jeans that were too tight for him and was holding a black hat and a gun. The two boys also had guns.

"We've had an ACCIDENT!" the children screamed.

The grandmother had the peculiar feeling that the bespectacled man was someone she knew. His face was as familiar to her as if she had known him all her life but she could not recall who he was. He moved away from the car and began to come down the embankment, placing his feet carefully so that he wouldn't slip. He had on tan and white shoes and no socks, and his ankles were red and thin. "Good afternoon," he said. "I see you all had you a little spill?"

"We turned over twice!" said the grandmother.

"Oncet," he corrected. "We seen it happen. Try their car and see will it run, Hiram," he said quietly to the boy with the gray hat.

"What you got that gun for?" John Wesley asked. "Whatcha gonna do with that gun?"

"Lady," the man said to the children's mother, "would you mind calling them children to sit down by you? Children make me nervous. I want all you all to sit down right together there where you're at."

"What are you telling US what to do for?" June Star asked.

Behind them the line of woods gaped like a dark open mouth. "Come here," said their mother.

"Look here now," Bailey began suddenly, "we're in a predicament! We're in . . ."

The grandmother shrieked. She scrambled to her feet and stood staring. "You're The Misfit!" she said. "I recognized you at once!"

"Yes'm," the man said, smiling slightly as if he were pleased in spite of himself to be known, "but it would have been better for all of you, lady, if you hadn't of reckernized me."

Bailey turned his head sharply and said something to his mother that shocked even the children. The old lady began to cry and The Misfit reddened.

"Lady," he said, "don't you get upset. Sometimes a man says things he don't mean. I don't reckon he meant to talk to you thataway."

"You wouldn't shoot a lady, would you?" the grandmother said and removed a clean handkerchief from her cuff and began to slap at her eyes with it.

The Misfit pointed the toe of his shoe into the ground and made a little hole and then covered it up again. "I would hate to have to," he said.

"Listen," the grandmother almost screamed, "I know you're a good man. You don't look a bit like you have common blood. I know you must come from nice people!"

"Yes ma'am," he said, "finest people in the world." When he smiled he showed a row of strong white teeth. "God never made a finer woman than my mother and my daddy's heart was pure gold," he said. The boy with the red sweat shirt had come around behind them and was standing with his gun at his hip. The Misfit squatted down on the ground. "Watch them children, Bobby Lee," he said. "You know they make me nervous." He looked at the six of them huddled together in front of him and he seemed to be embarrassed as if he couldn't think of anything to say. "Ain't a cloud in the sky," he remarked, looking up at it. "Don't see no sun but don't see no cloud neither."

"Yes, it's a beautiful day," said the grandmother. "Listen," she said, "you shouldn't call yourself The Misfit because I know you're a good man at heart. I can just look at you and tell."

"Hush!" Bailey yelled. "Hush! Everybody shut up and let me handle this!" He was squatting in the position of a runner about to sprint forward but he didn't move.

"I pre-chate that, lady," The Misfit said and drew a little circle in the ground with the butt of his gun.

"It'll take a half a hour to fix this here car," Hiram called, looking over the raised hood of it.

"Well, first you and Bobby Lee get him and that little boy to step over yonder with you," The Misfit said, pointing to Bailey and John Wesley. "The boys want to ast you something," he said to Bailey. "Would you mind stepping back in them woods there with them?"

"Listen," Bailey began, "we're in a terrible predicament! Nobody realizes what this is," and his voice cracked. His eyes were as blue and intense as the parrots in his shirt and he remained perfectly still.

The grandmother reached up to adjust her hat brim as if she were going to the woods with him but it came off in her hand. She stood staring at it and after a second she let it fall on the ground. Hiram pulled Bailey up by the arm as if he were assisting an old man. John Wesley caught hold of his father's hand and Bobby Lee followed. They went off toward the woods and just as they reached the dark edge, Bailey turned and supporting himself against a gray naked pine trunk, he shouted, "I'll be back in a minute, Mamma, wait on me!"

"Come back this instant!" his mother shrilled but they all disappeared into the woods.

"Bailey Boy!" the grandmother called in a tragic voice but she found she was looking at The Misfit squatting on the ground in front of her. "I just know you're a good man," she said desperately. "You're not a bit common!"

"Nome, I ain't a good man," The Misfit said after a second as if he had considered her statement carefully, "but I ain't the worst in the world neither. My daddy said I was a different breed of dog from my brothers and sisters. 'You know,' Daddy said, 'it's some that can live their whole life out without asking about it and it's others has to know why it is, and this boy is one of the latters. He's going to be into everything!'" He put on his black hat and looked up suddenly and then away deep into the woods as if he were embarrassed again. "I'm sorry I don't have on a shirt before you ladies," he said, hunching his shoulders slightly. "We buried our clothes that we had on when we escaped and we're just making do until we can get better. We borrowed these from some folks we met," he explained.

"That's perfectly all right," the grandmother said. "Maybe Bailey has an extra shirt in his suitcase."

"I'll look and see terrectly," The Misfit said.

"Where are they taking him?" the children's mother screamed.

"Daddy was a card himself," The Misfit said. "You couldn't put anything over on him. He never got in trouble with the Authorities though. Just had the knack of handling them."

"You could be honest too if you'd only try," said the grandmother. "Think how wonderful it would be to settle down and live a comfortable life and not have to think about somebody chasing you all the time."

The Misfit kept scratching in the ground with the butt of his gun as if he were thinking about it. "Yes'm, somebody is always after you," he murmured.

The grandmother noticed how thin his shoulder blades were just behind his hat because she was standing up looking down on him. "Do you ever pray?" she asked.

He shook his head. All she saw was the black hat wiggle between his shoulder blades. "Nome," he said.

There was a pistol shot from the woods, followed closely by another. Then silence. The old lady's head jerked around. She could hear the wind move through the tree tops like a long satisfied insuck of breath. "Bailey Boy!" she called.

"I was a gospel singer for a while," The Misfit said. "I been most everything. Been in the arm service, both land and sea, at home and abroad, been twict married, been an undertaker, been with the railroads, plowed Mother Earth, been in a tornado, seen a man burnt alive oncet," and he looked up at the children's mother and the little girl who were sitting close together, their faces white and their eyes glassy; "I even seen a woman flogged," he said.

"Pray, pray," the grandmother began, "pray, pray . . ."

"I never was a bad boy that I remember of," The Misfit said in an almost dreamy voice, "but somewheres along the line I done something wrong and got sent to the penitentiary. I was buried alive," and he looked up and held her attention to him by a steady stare. "That's when you should have started to pray," she said. "What did you do to get sent up to the penitentiary that first time?"

"Turn to the right, it was a wall," The Misfit said, looking up again at the cloudless sky.

"Turn to the left, it was a wall. Look up it was a ceiling, look down it was a floor. I forget what I done, lady. I set there and set there, trying to remember what it was I done and I ain't recalled it to this day. Oncet in a while, I would think it was coming to me, but it never come."

"Maybe they put you in by mistake," the old lady said vaguely.

"Nome," he said. "It wasn't no mistake. They had the papers on me."

"You must have stolen something," she said.

The Misfit sneered slightly. "Nobody had nothing I wanted," he said. "It was a head-doctor at the penitentiary said what I had done was kill my daddy but I known that for a lie. My daddy died in nineteen ought nineteen of the epidemic flu and I never had a thing to do with it. He was buried in the Mount Hopewell Baptist churchyard and you can go there and see for yourself."

"If you would pray," the old lady said, "Jesus would help you."

"That's right," The Misfit said.

"Well then, why don't you pray?" she asked trembling with delight suddenly.

"I don't want no hep," he said. "I'm doing all right by myself."

Bobby Lee and Hiram came ambling back from the woods. Bobby Lee was dragging a yellow shirt with bright blue parrots in it.

"Thow me that shirt, Bobby Lee," The Misfit said. The shirt came flying at him and landed on his shoulder and he put it on. The grandmother couldn't name what the shirt reminded her of. "No, lady," The Misfit said while he was buttoning it up, "I found out the crime don't matter. You can do one thing or you can do another, kill a man or take a tire off his car, because sooner or later you're going to forget what it was you done and just be punished for it."

The children's mother had begun to make heaving noises as if she couldn't get her breath. "Lady," he asked, "would you and that little girl like to step off yonder with Bobby Lee and Hiram and join your husband?"

"Yes, thank you," the mother said faintly. Her left arm dangled helplessly and she was holding the baby, who had gone to sleep, in the other. "Hep that lady up, Hiram," The Misfit said as she struggled to climb out of the ditch, "and Bobby Lee, you hold onto that little girl's hand."

"I don't want to hold hands with him," June Star said. "He reminds me of a pig."

The fat boy blushed and laughed and caught her by the arm and pulled her off into the woods after Hiram and her mother.

Alone with The Misfit, the grandmother found that she had lost her voice. There was not a cloud in the sky nor any sun. There was nothing around her but woods. She wanted to tell him that he must pray. She opened and closed her mouth several times before anything came out. Finally she found herself saying, "Jesus. Jesus," meaning, Jesus will help you, but the way she was saying it, it sounded as if she might be cursing.

"Yes'm," The Misfit said as if he agreed. "Jesus thown everything off balance. It was the same case with Him as with me except He hadn't committed any crime and they could prove I had committed one because they had the papers on me. Of course," he said, "they never shown me my papers. That's why I sign myself now. I said long ago, you get you a signature and sign everything you do and keep a copy of it. Then you'll know what you done and you can hold up the crime to the punishment and see do they match and in the end you'll have something to prove you ain't been treated right. I call myself The Misfit," he said, "because I can't make

what all I done wrong fit what all I gone through in punishment."

There was a piercing scream from the woods, followed closely by a pistol report. "Does it seem right to you, lady, that one is punished a heap and another ain't punished at all?"

"Jesus!" the old lady cried. "You've got good blood! I know you wouldn't shoot a lady! I know you come from nice people! Pray! Jesus, you ought not to shoot a lady. I'll give you all the money I've got!"

"Lady," The Misfit said, looking beyond her far into the woods, "there never was a body that give the undertaker a tip."

There were two more pistol reports and the grandmother raised her head like a parched old turkey hen crying for water and called, "Bailey Boy, Bailey Boy!" as if her heart would break.

"Jesus was the only One that ever raised the dead," The Misfit continued, "and He shouldn't have done it. He thown everything off balance. If He did what He said, then it's nothing for you to do but thow away everything and follow Him, and if He didn't, then it's nothing for you to do but enjoy the few minutes you got left the best way you can—by killing somebody or burning down his house or doing some other meanness to him. No pleasure but meanness," he said and his voice had become almost a snarl.

"Maybe He didn't raise the dead," the old lady mumbled, not knowing what she was saying and feeling so dizzy that she sank down in the ditch with her legs twisted under her.

"I wasn't there so I can't say He didn't," The Misfit said. "I wisht I had of been there," he said, hitting the ground with his fist. "It ain't right I wasn't there because if I had of been there I would of known. Listen lady," he said in a high voice, "if I had of been there I would of known and I wouldn't be like I am now." His voice seemed about to crack and the grand-mother's head cleared for an instant. She saw the man's face twisted close to her own as if he were going to cry and she murmured, "Why you're one of my babies. You're one of my own children!" She reached out and touched him on the shoulder. The Misfit sprang back as if a snake had bitten him and shot her three times through the chest. Then he put his gun down on the ground and took off his glasses and began to clean them.

Hiram and Bobby Lee returned from the woods and stood over the ditch, looking down at the grandmother who half sat and half lay in a puddle of blood with her legs crossed under her like a child's and her face smiling up at the cloudless sky.

Without his glasses, The Misfit's eyes were red-rimmed and pale and defenseless-looking. "Take her off and thow her where you thown the others," he said, picking up the cat that was rubbing itself against his leg.

"She was a talker, wasn't she?" Bobby Lee said, sliding down the ditch with a yodel.

"She would of been a good woman," The Misfit said, "if it had been somebody there to shoot her every minute of her life."

"Some fun!" Bobby Lee said.

"Shut up, Bobby Lee," The Misfit said. "It's no real pleasure in life."

How It Works

1. Reread the story, marking down your emotional reactions as you go. What phrases or descriptions made you feel particularly tense or apprehensive? What techniques does O'Connor use to build the tension in the course of the trip?

2. How would you describe Bailey and his family? Do you think you'd like them if you knew them? How does O'Connor's choice to make them less than ideally admirable affect the emotional impact of the story's ending? How does she avoid sentimentality when rendering their deaths?

3. How does the grandmother change in the course of the story? When, exactly, does the change occur? How does the author suggest its meaning? Underline symbols in the narration and in the dialogue.

4. O'Connor described The Misfit as the devil. What evidence of that do you find in the story? Initially, many readers missed the connection entirely and thought of the story as a sympathetic portrait of a killer. Underline descriptions of the Misfit and things he says. Rewrite these details to make The Misfit seem more sympathetic. Now reread your altered version of the story. How is its emotional impact affected?

Seth Pase

Seth Christian Pase was born in Castleton, New York, in 1973. During his adolescence, he turned to writing as a way of avoiding exercise, yard work, and human contact. Since graduating with honors from Emerson College, where he wrote "The Father," he has been working as an editor and copywriter, with occasional extended visits home to his parents' house, where he lives in the attic and writes, occasionally venturing out to rake leaves or shovel out the driveway.

Pase has said that he was thinking about three things when he wrote "The Father": the cyclical repetition of action over the course of generations, the influence parents have on their children, and postfeminist backlash against the "gendering" of issues that affect everyone. "I didn't want to make the story of this young woman's abortion all about the male's grief, but I wanted to write a story that didn't leave the male emotionally disconnected from the event, present him as a mere appendage, or turn him into a stereotype. This story shows how everybody suffers, and where that suffering can come from, where it can lead. I wanted to show the humanity in the situation, and that all gender issues are really human issues."

The Father

He pulls the car up slowly and puts his blinker on before turning into the driveway. Her father is watching from behind the curtains in the living room with a long cigar hanging from his mouth, unlit. He considers simply honking the horn and waiting in the car, but thinks better of it. He kills the engine, gets out of the car, and taking a deep breath, climbs the steps to the back door.

The door swings open and he stands there a moment, his fist poised to knock. Her father blocks the doorway, his thin cigar sending out thick puffs of smoke. His face is drawn and haggard, hardened by a few deep wrinkles around his mouth and eyes. Most of the hair on top of his head is gone; long pieces have been grown on one side and carefully combed across the crown and forehead to create the illusion of a full head of hair, parted to the side. A faded red plaid bathrobe covers his dirty undershirt and a pair of brown polyester pants that don't quite reach his slippers. He crosses his arms and chews his cigar to the other corner of his mouth, rubs the scruff on his chin and sighs.

"You're here for Mary I assume?" He raises an eyebrow and looks at the young man over the rims of his bifocals.

"Uh, yes. I called earlier. My name's Leo." He sticks out his hand and forces what he hopes is a fairly congenial smile.

Inside, the crowd on the television hisses and boos. The father glances over his shoulder and frowns.

"Well, hurry up and come in before you let all the heat out, and don't forget to take off those shoes," he grumbles, and pads back along a faded trail in the carpet to a reclining chair positioned directly in front of the television.

Leo pushes the door closed with his back, slips out of his moccasins, and steps into the living room. All the curtains in the house have been drawn, shutting out the bright winter sun. The television's glare illuminates the room as shadows flicker across the old man's face. He looks younger in this light, Leo observes. From across the room, he barely looks older than me.

"Mary!" the father bawls suddenly. He shifts his weight from side to side, settling back into his nest. "Somebody here for you! Mary!" He grabs a beer out of the box by his chair and cracks the tab.

Leo leans his shoulder against the wall and checks his watch. It is almost 3:30; she is running late. He idly wonders what will happen if they are late, if they can be late.

On the screen, men in tights and helmets line up, bounce off each other, and line up again. Leo fixes his eyes on them and tries to look interested.

"Who's winning here?" he asks. His voice sounds loud and over-friendly to him.

The father flicks his wrist and the television goes mute. He stares at the side of Leo's head, forcing him to look away from the screen.

"Wanna beer?" The old man smiles and drops a hand into the box beside him, bringing up a fresh can with a smooth and practiced motion. Leo shakes his head and tries to focus on the television again. "No thanks," he says, concentrating on the screen.

"Ha! Good! Good for you, Leon!" The father mockingly tips the can of beer toward Leo. He chuckles to himself, hitches, and wheezes into a fit of thick coughs and sputters. Leo keeps his eyes on the screen and tries not to notice. With a tremendous hack, the old man stops and, wiping his nose with the back of his hand, shifts his attention back to Leo. After a moment of study, he leans forward and asks, "Howsa game? You like TV with no sound?"

Leo's eyes do not move from the screen as he considers his reply. Do not be wise, do not play games, do not give a stupid answer. The father, grinning, leans farther out of his chair, his face red with anticipation. Leo blinks and takes a deep breath.

"You don't need sound for sports. They flash up enough statistics for anyone to know what's going on without the babble of the commentators. Plus the game speaks for itself. It *is* kind of awkward to just watch it in complete silence, though. If you're going to turn the sound off on the TV, at least put some music on to fill that void, you know what I mean?" Leo watches the helmets bounce and huddle as the ball sails between the open goal posts and wonders if he can babble like this until Mary decides to make an entrance.

"Shut up," her father says, flicking the sound on again and saving Leo any further trouble. "Mary! Today!" He belches lightly, returning to his beer and his television.

"OK! I'm right here." She is walking down the stairs with her head down and her hair is in her face. She grabs her purse, stuffs a gray woollen cap on her head, and slips into her pea coat. Passing Leo, she walks quickly behind her father, heading for the door.

"Let's go. See you later, Dad, we have to go, I think we're late. Are we running a little late?" She pauses with her hand on the doorknob, waiting for Leo to cross the room and put on his shoes.

"Wait a second." The father flicks off the sound but does not shift his gaze from the glow of the television. Leo and Mary, half out the door, look at the back of his chair. "I have a right to know where you're going in such a hurry, and maybe if you'll be back to cook dinner."

"We're going to a movie at the library and I'll be back at around seven. I made you a turkey sub. It's in the fridge, and don't forget your pill." Mary speaks quickly but waits for a reply; her father drums his fingers lightly on the remote for a moment, considering, before flicking the sound back on and dropping his empty can on the floor.

Leo starts the car while Mary puts on her sunglasses and searches through her purse for some cigarettes. In less than a minute they are driving through the outskirts of town, past the wharf and down the river road toward the city. Mary stares blankly out the window, smoking her cigarette in complete silence. Leo turns down the heater and cracks his window, uncomfortable in the heat and the silence.

He can feel the wad of cash bulging in his pocket. Three hundred dollars, and there was another fifty in a bank envelope in the glove box. He had no idea if there would be tax or what to expect, really, but he was at least financially prepared.

"If there's anything else I can do, just let me know," he finally manages. "If you need to stay some place, if you need some money . . ."

"Listen, all I want from you is a ride. I don't want money, I don't even want to see you. They just won't let me leave without a ride. I'd rather've driven myself, but they won't let you do that. You have to relax and sit still afterwards. I shouldn't even leave right away. They want you to stay for at least a little while afterwards. Everyone reacts differently and they like to make sure everything is OK before they let you just waltz out of there, so they don't get anymore bad press, I suppose." She looks down at her hands, out the window, anywhere away from him. "I just need a ride."

Leo drives on, his hands tensing and relaxing on the wheel. After a moment of deliberation he says, "Are you sure about the money? I've got it, it's no big deal, really. Let me at least give you half." He tries to take her hand.

Mary does not move. She continues to look out the window as the river goes by. She does not take his hand. Finally she says, "Half. Fine, OK. Half and a ride back next week if they want me to come, OK? They probably won't need to see me, but . . ."

"OK," he says. "Whatever you need. I'm there. I mean I'm here."

With this, Leo drives into the city. He takes a breath, drawing the frigid air deep into his lungs. He tightens his grip on the steering wheel and squints at the gray half-light of the afternoon.

How It Works

1. In all of his stories, Seth Pase prefers understatement. How does he get his point across? Where are Leo and Mary driving? When does their destination become clear? Which details hint at what is going on?

2. At what point during the drive does Leo change? How would you describe his change? Underline the gestures and dialogue that convey the change.

3. What is the effect of starting out the story with Mary's father, who does not then reappear? Is anything gained through the use of this technique?

4. Rewrite one of your own scenes so that, as in "The Father," two characters are confined in a small space together. How does the change in setting affect the scene's emotional nuances and subtext?

Jayne Anne Phillips

Jayne Anne Phillips was born in West Virginia. She is the author of three novels, Motherkind *(2000),* Shelter *(1994), and* Machine Dreams *(1984), and two widely anthologized collections of stories,* Fast Lanes *(1987) and* Black Tickets *(1979). Her works have been translated and published in nine languages. She is the recipient of a Guggenheim Fellowship, two National Endowment for the Arts fellowships, a Bunting Fellowship from the Bunting Institute of Radcliffe College, and a National Book Critics Circle Award nomination. She was awarded the Sue Kaufman Prize (1980) and an Academy Award in Literature (1997) by the American Academy and Institute of Arts and Letters. Her work has appeared most recently in* Harper's Magazine, Granta, *and* Doubletake, *and in the* Norton Anthology of Contemporary Fiction. *She has taught at Harvard University, Williams College, and Boston University and is currently Writer in Residence at Brandeis University.*

Souvenir

Kate always sent her mother a card on Valentine's Day. She timed the mails from wherever she was so that the cards arrived on February 14th. Her parents had celebrated the day in some small fashion, and since her father's death six years before, Kate made a gesture of compensatory remembrance. At first, she made the cards herself: collage and pressed grasses on construction paper sewn in fabric. Now she settled for art reproductions, glossy cards with blank insides. Kate wrote in them with colored inks. "You have always been my Valentine," or simply "Hey, take care of yourself." She might enclose a present as well, something small enough to fit into an envelope; a sachet, a perfumed soap, a funny tintype of a prune-faced man in a bowler hat.

This time, she forgot. Despite the garish displays of paper cupids and heart-shaped boxes in drugstore windows, she let the day nearly approach before remembering. It was too late to send anything in the mail. She called her mother long-distance at night when the rates were low.

"Mom? How are you?"

"It's you! How are *you?*" Her mother's voice grew suddenly brighter; Kate recognized a tone reserved for welcome company. Sometimes it took a while to warm up.

"I'm fine," answered Kate. "What have you been doing?"

"Well, actually I was trying to sleep."

"Sleep? You should be out setting the old hometown on fire."

"The old hometown can burn up without me tonight."

"Really? What's going on?"

"I'm running in-service training sessions for the primary teachers." Kate's mother was a school superintendent. "They're driving me batty. You'd think their brains were rubber."

"They are," Kate said. "Or you wouldn't have to train them. Think of them as a salvation, they create a need for your job."

"Some salvation. Besides, your logic is ridiculous. Just because someone needs training doesn't mean they're stupid."

"I'm just kidding. But *I'm* stupid. I forgot to send you a Valentine's card."

"You did? That's bad. I'm trained to receive one. They bring me luck."

"You're receiving a phone call instead," Kate said. "Won't that do?"

"Of course," said her mother, "but this is costing you money. Tell me quick, how are you?"

"Oh, you know. Doctoral pursuits. Doing my student trip, grooving with the professors."

"The professors? You'd better watch yourself."

"It's a joke, Mom, a joke. But what about you? Any men on the horizon?"

"No, not really. A married salesman or two asking me to dinner when they come through the office. Thank heavens I never let those things get started."

"You should do what you want to," Kate said.

"Sure," said her mother. "And where would I be then?"

"I don't know. Maybe Venezuela."

"They don't even have plumbing in Venezuela."

"Yes, but their sunsets are perfect, and the villages are full of dark passionate men in blousy shirts."

"That's your department, not mine."

"Ha," Kate said, "I wish it were my department. Sounds a lot more exciting than teaching undergraduates."

Her mother laughed. "Be careful," she said. "You'll get what you want. End up sweeping a dirt floor with a squawling baby around your neck."

"A dark baby," Kate said, "to stir up the family blood."

"Nothing would surprise me," her mother said as the line went fuzzy. Her voice was submerged in static, then surfaced. "Listen," she was saying. "Write to me. You seem so far away."

They hung up and Kate sat watching the windows of the neighboring house. The curtains were transparent and flowered and none of them matched. Silhouettes of the window frames spread across them like single dark bars. Her mother's curtains were all the same, white cotton hemmed with a ruffle, tiebacks blousing the cloth into identical shapes. From the street it looked as if the house was always in order.

Kate made a cup of strong Chinese tea, turned the lights off, and sat holding the warm cup in the dark. Her mother kept no real tea in the house, just packets of instant diabetic mixture which tasted of chemical sweetener and had a bitter aftertaste. The packets sat on the shelf next to her mother's miniature scales. The scales were white. Kate saw clearly the face of the metal dial on the front, its markings and trembling needle. Her mother weighed portions of food for meals: frozen broccoli, slices of plastic-wrapped Kraft cheese, careful chunks of roast beef. A dog-eared copy of *The Diabetic Diet* had remained propped against the salt shaker for the last two years.

Kate rubbed her forehead. Often at night she had headaches. Sometimes she wondered if there were an agent in her body, a secret in her blood making ready to work against her.

The phone blared repeatedly, careening into her sleep. Kate scrambled out of bed, naked and cold, stumbling, before she recognized the striped wallpaper of her bedroom and realized the phone was right there on the bedside table, as always. She picked up the receiver.

"Kate?" said her brother's voice. "It's Robert. Mom is in the hospital. They don't know what's wrong but she's in for tests."

"Tests? What's happened? I just talked to her last night."

"I'm not sure. She called the neighbors and they took her to the emergency room around dawn." Robert's voice still had that slight twang Kate knew was disappearing from her own. He would be calling from his insurance office, nine o'clock their time, in his thick glasses and wide, perfectly knotted tie. He was a member of the million-dollar club and his picture, tiny, the size of a postage stamp, appeared in the Mutual of Omaha magazine. His voice seemed small too over the distance. Kate felt heavy and dulled. She would never make much money, and recently she had begun wearing make-up again, waking in smeared mascara as she had in high school.

"Is Mom all right?" she managed now. "How serious is it?"

"They're not sure," Robert said. "Her doctor thinks it could have been any of several things, but they're doing X rays."

"Her doctor *thinks?* Doesn't he know? Get her to someone else. There aren't any doctors in that one-horse town."

"I don't know about that," Robert said defensively. "Anyway, I can't force her. You know how she is about money."

"Money? She could have a stroke and drop dead while her doctor wonders what's wrong."

"Doesn't matter. You know you can't tell her what to do."

"Could I call her somehow?"

"No, not yet. And don't get her all worried. She's been scared enough as it is. I'll tell her what you said about getting another opinion, and I'll call you back in a few hours when I have some news. Meanwhile, she's all right, do you hear?"

The line went dead with a click and Kate walked to the bathroom to wash her face. She splashed her eyes and felt guilty about the Valentine's card. Slogans danced in her head like reprimands. *For A Special One. Dearest Mother. My Best Friend.* Despite Robert, after breakfast she would call the hospital.

She sat a long time with her coffee, waiting for minutes to pass, considering how many meals she and her mother ate alone. Similar times of day, hundreds of miles apart. Women by themselves. The last person Kate had eaten breakfast with had been someone she'd met in a bar. He was passing through town. He liked his fried eggs gelatinized in the center, only slightly runny, and Kate had studiously looked away as he ate. The night before he'd looked down from above her as he finished and she still moved under him. "You're still wanting," he'd said. "That's nice." Mornings now, Kate saw her own face in the mirror and was glad she'd forgotten his name. When she looked at her reflection from the side, she saw a faint etching of lines beside her mouth. She hadn't slept with anyone for five weeks, and the skin beneath her eyes had taken on a creamy darkness.

She reached for the phone but drew back. It seemed bad luck to ask for news, to push toward whatever was coming as though she had no respect for it.

Standing in the kitchen last summer, her mother had stirred gravy and argued with her.

"I'm thinking of your own good, not mine," she'd said. "Think of what you put yourself through. And how can you feel right about it? You were born here, I don't care what you

say." Her voice broke and she looked, perplexed, at the broth in the pan.

"But, hypothetically," Kate continued, her own voice unaccountably shaking, "if I'm willing to endure whatever I have to, do you have a right to object? You're my mother. You're supposed to defend my choices."

"You'll have enough trouble without choosing more for yourself. Using birth control that'll ruin your insides, moving from one place to another. I can't defend your choices. I can't even defend myself against you." She wiped her eyes on a napkin.

"Why do you have to make me feel so guilty?" Kate said, fighting tears of frustration. "I'm not attacking you."

"You're not? Then who are you talking to?"

"Oh Mom, give me a break."

"I've tried to give you more than that," her mother said. "I know what your choices are saying to me." She set the steaming gravy off the stove. "You may feel very differently later on. It's just a shame I won't be around to see it."

"Oh? Where will you be?"

"Floating around on a fleecy cloud."

Kate got up to set the table before she realized her mother had already done it.

The days went by. They'd gone shopping before Kate left. Standing at the cash register in an antique shop on Main Street, they bought each other pewter candle holders. "A souvenir," her mother said. "A reminder to always be nice to yourself. If you live alone you should eat by candlelight."

"Listen," Kate said, "I eat in a heart-shaped tub with bubbles to my chin. I sleep on satin sheets and my mattress has a built-in massage engine. My overnight guests are impressed. You don't have to tell me about the solitary pleasures."

They laughed and touched hands.

"Well," her mother said. "If you like your-self, I must have done something right."

Robert didn't phone until evening. His voice was fatigued and thin. "I've moved her to the university hospital," he said. "They can't deal with it at home."

Kate waited, saying nothing. She concentrated on the toes of her shoes. They needed shining. *You never take care of anything,* her mother would say.

"She has a tumor in her head." He said it firmly, as though Kate might challenge him.

"I'll take a plane tomorrow morning," Kate answered, "I'll be there by noon."

Robert exhaled. "Look," he said, "don't even come back here unless you can keep your mouth shut and do it my way."

"Get to the point."

"The point is they believe she has a malignancy and we're not going to tell her. I almost didn't tell you." His voice faltered. "They're going to operate but if they find what they're expecting, they don't think they can stop it."

For a moment there was no sound except an oceanic vibration of distance on the wire. Even that sound grew still. Robert breathed. Kate could almost see him, in a booth at the hospital, staring straight ahead at the plastic instructions screwed to the narrow rectangular body of the telephone. It seemed to her that she was hurtling toward him.

"I'll do it your way," she said.

The hospital cafeteria was a large room full of orange Formica tables. Its southern wall was glass. Across the highway, Kate saw a small park modestly dotted with amusement rides and bordered by a narrow band of river. How odd, to build a children's park across from a medical center. The sight was pleasant in a cruel way. The rolling lawn of the little park was perfectly, relentlessly green.

Robert sat down. Their mother was to have surgery in two days.

"After it's over," he said, "they're not certain what will happen. The tumor is in a bad place. There may be some paralysis."

"What kind of paralysis?" Kate said. She watched him twist the green-edged coffee cup around and around on its saucer.

"Facial. And maybe worse."

"You've told her this?"

He didn't answer.

"Robert, what is she going to think if she wakes up and—"

He leaned forward, grasping the cup and speaking through clenched teeth. "Don't you think I thought of that?" He gripped the sides of the table and the cup rolled onto the carpeted floor with a dull thud. He seemed ready to throw the table after it, then grabbed Kate's wrists and squeezed them hard.

"You didn't drive her here," he said. "She was so scared she couldn't talk. How much do you want to hand her at once?"

Kate watched the cup sitting solidly on the nubby carpet.

"We've told her it's benign," Robert said, "that the surgery will cause complications, but she can learn back whatever is lost."

Kate looked at him. "Is that true?"

"They hope so."

"We're lying to her, all of us, more and more." Kate pulled her hands away and Robert touched her shoulder.

"What do *you* want to tell her, Kate? 'You're fifty-five and you're done for'?"

She stiffened. "Why put her through the operation at all?"

He sat back and dropped his arms, lowering his head. "Because without it she'd be in bad pain. Soon." They were silent, then he looked up. "And anyway," he said softly, "we don't *know* do we? She may have a better chance than they think."

Kate put her hands on her face. Behind her closed eyes she saw a succession of blocks tumbling over.

They took the elevator up to the hospital room. They were alone and they stood close together. Above the door red numerals lit up, flashing. Behind the illuminated shapes droned an impersonal hum of machinery.

Then the doors opened with a sucking sound. Three nurses stood waiting with a lunch cart, identical covered trays stacked in tiers. There was a hot bland smell, like warm cardboard. One of the women caught the thick steel door with her arm and smiled. Kate looked quickly at their rubber-soled shoes. White polish, the kind that rubs off. And their legs seemed only white shapes, boneless and two-dimensional, stepping silently into the metal cage.

She looked smaller in the white bed. The chrome side rails were pulled up and she seemed powerless behind them, her dark hair pushed back from her face and her forearms delicate in the baggy hospital gown. Her eyes were different in some nearly imperceptible way; she held them wider, they were shiny with a veiled wetness. For a moment the room seemed empty of all else; there were only her eyes and the dark blossoms of the flowers on the table beside her. Red roses with pine. Everyone had sent the same thing.

Robert walked close to the bed with his hands clasped behind his back, as though afraid to touch. "Where did all the flowers come from?" he asked.

"From school, and the neighbors. And Katie." She smiled.

"FTD," Kate said. "Before I left home. I felt so bad for not being here all along."

"That's silly," said their mother. "You can hardly sit at home and wait for some problem to arise."

"Speaking of problems," Robert said, "the doctor tells me you're not eating. Do I have to urge you a little?" He sat down on the edge of the bed and shook the silverware from its paper sleeve.

Kate touched the plastic tray. "Jell-O and canned cream of chicken soup. Looks great. We should have brought you something."

"They don't *want* us to bring her anything," Robert said. "This is a hospital. And I'm sure your comments make her lunch seem even more appetizing."

"I'll eat it!" said their mother in mock dismay. "Admit they sent you in here to stage a battle until I gave in."

"I'm sorry," Kate said. "He's right."

Robert grinned. "Did you hear that? She says I'm right. I don't believe it." He pushed the tray closer to his mother's chest and made a show of tucking a napkin under her chin.

"Of course you're right, dear." She smiled and gave Kate an obvious wink.

"Yeah," Robert said, "I know you two. But seriously, you eat this. I have to go make some business calls from the motel room."

Their mother frowned. "That motel must be costing you a fortune."

"No. It's reasonable," he said. "Kate can stay for a week or two and I'll drive back and forth from home. If you think this food is bad, you should see the meals in that motel restaurant." He got up to go, flashing Kate a glance of collusion. "I'll be back after supper."

His footsteps echoed down the hallway. Kate and her mother looked wordlessly at each other, relieved. Kate looked away guiltily. Then her mother spoke, apologetic. "He's so tired," she said. "He's been with me since yesterday."

She looked at Kate, then into the air of the room. "I'm in a fix," she said. "Except for when the pain comes, it's all a show that goes on without me. I'm like an invalid, or a lunatic."

Kate moved close and touched her mother's arms. "That's all right, we're going to get you through it. Someone's covering for you at work?"

"I had to take a leave of absence. It's going to take a while afterward—"

"I know. But it's the last thing to worry about, it can't be helped."

"Like spilt milk. Isn't that what they say?"

"I don't know what they say. But why didn't you tell me? Didn't you know something was wrong?"

"Yes . . . bad headaches. Migraines, I thought, or the diabetes getting worse. I was afraid they'd start me on insulin." She tightened the corner of her mouth. "Little did I know . . ."

They heard the shuffle of slippers. An old woman stood at the open door of the room, looking in confusedly. She seemed about to speak, then moved on.

"Oh," said Kate's mother in exasperation, "shut that door, please? They let these old women wander around like refugees." She sat up, reaching for a robe. "And let's get me out of this bed."

They sat near the window while she finished eating. Bars of moted yellow banded the floor of the room. The light held a tinge of spring which seemed painful because it might vanish. They heard the rattle of the meal cart outside the closed door, and the clunk-slide of patients with aluminum walkers. Kate's mother sighed and pushed away the half-empty soup bowl.

"They'll be here after me any minute. More tests. I just want to stay with you." Her face was warm and smooth in the slanted light, lines in her skin delicate, unreal; as though a face behind her face was now apparent after many years. She sat looking at Kate and smiled.

"One day when you were about four you were dragging a broom around the kitchen. I asked what you were doing and you told me that when you got old you were going to be an angel and sweep the rotten rain off the clouds."

"What did you say to that?"

"I said that when you were old I was sure God would see to it." Her mother laughed. "I'm glad you weren't such a smart aleck then," she said. "You would have told me my view of God was paternalistic."

"Ah yes," sighed Kate. "God, that famous dude. Here I am, getting old, facing unemployment, alone, and where is He?"

"You're not alone," her mother said. "I'm right here."

Kate didn't answer. She sat motionless and felt her heart begin to open like a box with a hinged lid. The fullness had no edges.

Her mother stood. She rubbed her hands slowly, twisting her wedding rings. "My hands are so dry in the winter," she said softly, "I brought some hand cream with me but I can't find it anywhere, my suitcase is so jumbled. Thank heavens spring is early this year. . . . They told me that little park over there doesn't usually open till the end of March . . ."

She's helping me, thought Kate, I'm not supposed to let her down.

". . . but they're already running it on weekends. Even past dusk. We'll see the lights tonight. You can't see the shapes this far away, just the motion . . ."

A nurse came in with a wheelchair. Kate's mother pulled a wry face. "This wheelchair is a bit much," she said.

"We don't want to tire you out," said the nurse.

The chair took her weight quietly. At the door she put out her hand to stop, turned, and said anxiously. "Kate, see if you can find that hand cream?"

It was the blue suitcase from years ago, still almost new. She'd brought things she never used for everyday; a cashmere sweater, lace slips, silk underpants wrapped in tissue. Folded beneath was a stack of postmarked envelopes, slightly ragged, tied with twine. Kate opened one and realized that all the cards were there, beginning with the first of the marriage. There were a few photographs of her and Robert, baby pictures almost indistinguishable from each other, and then Kate's homemade Valentines, fastened together with rubber bands. *What will I do with these things?* She wanted air; she needed to breathe. She walked to the window and put the bundled papers on the sill. She'd raised the glass and pushed back the screen when suddenly, her mother's clock radio went off with a flat buzz. Kate moved to switch it off and brushed the cards with her arm. Envelopes shifted and slid, scattering on the floor of the room. A few snapshots wafted silently out the window. They dipped and turned, twirling. Kate didn't try to reach them. They seemed only scraps, buoyant and yellowed, blown away, the faces small as pennies. Somewhere far-off there were sirens, almost musical, drawn out and carefully approaching.

The nurse came in with evening medication. Kate's mother lay in bed. "I hope this is strong enough," she said. "Last night I couldn't sleep at all. So many sounds in a hospital . . ."

"You'll sleep tonight," the nurse assured her.

Kate winked at her mother. "That's right," she said, "I'll help you out if I have to."

They stayed up for an hour, watching the moving lights outside and the stationary glows of houses across the distant river. The halls grew darker, were lit with night lights, and the hospital dimmed. Kate waited. Her mother's eyes fluttered and finally she slept. Her breathing was low and regular.

Kate didn't move. Robert had said he'd be back; where was he? She felt a sunken anger and shook her head. She'd been on the point of telling her mother everything. The secrets were a travesty. What if there were things her mother wanted done, people she needed to see? Kate wanted to wake her before these hours passed in the dark and confess that she had lied. Between them, through the tension, there had always been a trusted clarity. Now it was twisted. Kate sat leaning forward, nearly touching the hospital bed.

Suddenly her mother sat bolt upright, her eyes open and her face transfixed. She looked blindly toward Kate but seemed to see nothing. "Who are you?" she whispered. Kate stood, at first unable to move. The woman in the bed opened and closed her mouth several times, as though she were gasping. Then she said loudly, "Stop moving the table. Stop it this instant!" Her eyes were wide with fright and her body was vibrating.

Kate reached her. "Mama, wake up, you're dreaming." Her mother jerked, flinging her arms out. Kate held her tightly.

"I can hear the wheels," she moaned.

"No, no," Kate said. "You're here with me."

"It's not so?"

"No," Kate said. "It's not so."

She went limp. Kate felt for her pulse and found it rapid, then regular. She sat rocking her mother. In a few minutes she lay her back on the pillows and smoothed the damp hair at her temples, smoothed the sheets of the bed. Later she slept fitfully in a chair, waking repeatedly to assure herself that her mother was breathing.

Near dawn she got up, exhausted, and left the room to walk in the corridor. In front of the window at the end of the hallway she saw a man slumped on a couch; the man slowly stood and wavered before her like a specter. It was Robert.

"Kate?" he said.

Years ago he had flunked out of a small junior college and their mother sat in her bedroom rocker, crying hard for over an hour while Kate tried in vain to comfort her. Kate went to the university the next fall, so anxious that she studied frantically, outlining whole textbooks in yellow ink. She sat in the front rows of large classrooms to take voluminous notes, writing quickly in her thick notebook. Robert had gone home, held a job in a plant that manufactured business forms and worked his way through the hometown college. By that time their father was dead, and Robert became, always and forever, the man of the house.

"Robert," Kate said, "I'll stay. Go home."

After breakfast they sat waiting for Robert, who had called and said he'd arrive soon. Kate's fatigue had given way to an intense awareness of every sound, every gesture. How would they get through the day? Her mother had awakened from the drugged sleep still groggy, unable to eat. The meal was sent away untouched and she watched the window as though she feared the walls of the room.

"I'm glad your father isn't here to see this," she said. There was a silence and Kate opened her mouth to speak. "I mean," said her mother quickly, "I'm going to look horrible for a few weeks, with my head all shaved." She pulled an afghan up around her lap and straightened the magazines on the table beside her chair.

"Mom," Kate said, "your hair will grow back."

Her mother pulled the afghan closer. "I've been thinking of your father," she said. "It's not that I'd have wanted him to suffer. But if he had to die, sometimes I wish he'd done it more gently. That heart attack, so finished; never a warning. I wish I'd had some time to nurse him. In a way, it's a chance to settle things."

"Did things need settling?"

"They always do, don't they?" She sat looking out the window, then said softly, "I wonder where I'm headed."

"You're not headed anywhere," Kate said. "I want you right here to see me settle down into normal American womanhood."

Her mother smiled reassuringly. "Where are my grandchildren?" she said. "That's what I'd like to know."

"You stick around," said Kate, "and I promise to start working on it." She moved her chair closer, so that their knees were touching and they could both see out the window. Below them cars moved on the highway and the Ferris wheel in the little park was turning.

"I remember when you were one of the little girls in the parade at the county fair. You weren't even in school yet; you were beautiful in that white organdy dress and pinafore. You wore those shiny black patent shoes and a crown of real apple blossoms. Do you remember?"

"Yes," Kate said. "That long parade. They told me not to move and I sat so still my legs went to sleep. When they lifted me off the float I couldn't stand up. They put me under a tree to wait for you, and you came, in a full white skirt and white sandals, your hair tied back in a red scarf. I can see you yet."

Her mother laughed. "Sounds like a pretty exaggerated picture."

Kate nodded. "I was little. You were big."

"You loved the county fair. You were wild about the carnivals." They looked down at the little park. "Magic, isn't it?" her mother said.

"Maybe we could go see it," said Kate. "I'll ask the doctor."

They walked across a pedestrian footbridge spanning the highway. Kate had bundled her mother into a winter coat and gloves despite the sunny weather. The day was sharp, nearly still, holding its bright air like illusion. Kate tasted the brittle water of her breath, felt for the cool handrail and thin steel of the webbed fencing. Cars moved steadily under the bridge. Beyond a muted roar of motors the park spread green and wooded, its limits clearly visible.

Kate's mother had combed her hair and put on lipstick. Her mouth was defined and brilliant; she linked arms with Kate like an escort. "I was afraid they'd tell us no," she said. "I was ready to run away!"

"I promised I wouldn't let you. And we only have ten minutes, long enough for the Ferris wheel." Kate grinned.

"I haven't ridden one in years. I wonder if I still know how."

"Of course you do. Ferris wheels are genetic knowledge."

"All right, whatever you say." She smiled. "We'll just hold on."

They drew closer and walked quickly through the sounds of the highway. When they reached the grass it was ankle-high and thick, longer and more ragged than it appeared from a distance. The Ferris wheel sat squarely near a grove of swaying elms, squat and laboring, taller than trees. Its neon lights still burned, pale in the sun, spiraling from inside like an imagined bloom. The naked elms surrounded it, their topmost branches tapping. Steel ribs of the machine were graceful and slightly rusted, squeaking faintly above a tinkling music. Only a few people were riding.

"Looks a little rickety," Kate said.

"Oh, don't worry," said her mother.

Kate tried to buy tickets but the ride was free. The old man running the motor wore an engineer's cap and patched overalls. He stopped the wheel and led them on a short ramp to an open car. It dipped gently, padded with black cushions. An orderly and his children rode in the car above. Kate saw their dangling feet, the girl's dusty sandals and gray socks beside their father's shoes and the hem of his white pants. The youngest one swung her feet absently, so it seemed the breeze blew her legs like fabric hung on a line.

Kate looked at her mother. "Are you ready for the big sky?" They laughed. Beyond them the river moved lazily. Houses on the opposite bank seemed empty, but a few rowboats bobbed at the docks. The surface of the water lapped and reflected clouds, and as Kate watched, searching for a definition of line, the Ferris wheel jerked into motion. The car rocked. They looked into the distance and Kate caught her mother's hand as they ascended.

Far away the hospital rose up white and glistening, its windows catching the glint of the sun. Directly below, the park was nearly deserted. There were a few cars in the parking lot and several dogs chasing each other across the grass. Two or three lone women held children on the teeter-totters and a wind was coming up. The forlorn swings moved on their chains. Kate had a vision of the park at night, totally empty, wind weaving heavily through the trees and children's playthings like a great black fish about to surface. She felt a chill on her arms. The light had gone darker, quietly, like a minor chord.

"Mom," Kate said. "It's going to storm." Her own voice seemed distant, the sound strained through layers of screen or gauze.

"No," said her mother, "it's going to pass over." She moved her hand to Kate's knee and touched the cloth of her daughter's skirt.

Kate gripped the metal bar at their waists and looked straight ahead. They were rising again and she felt she would scream. She tried to breathe rhythmically, steadily. She felt the immense weight of the air as they moved through it.

They came almost to the top and stopped. The little car swayed back and forth.

"You're sick, aren't you," her mother said.

Kate shook her head. Below them the grass seemed to glitter coldly, like a sea. Kate sat wordless, feeling the touch of her mother's hand. The hand moved away and Kate felt the absence of the warmth.

They looked at each other levelly.

"I know all about it," her mother said. "I know what you haven't told me."

The sky circled around them, a sure gray movement. Kate swallowed calmly and let their gaze grow endless. She saw herself in her mother's wide brown eyes and felt she was falling slowly into them.

How It Works

1. Outline this story's events in chronological order. Now try reordering them into another structure—say, as a frame story, or a nonlinear narrative such as Brenda Miller's "A Thousand Buddhas." How does each different organization affect the story's emotional impact?

2. Imagine this story without the Ferris wheel at the end. What would be different? How does Phillips prepare readers for this significant shift in setting?

3. What souvenir does the title refer to? How many and what kinds of souvenirs does the story contain? How does the author use these objects to develop the story's emotional and thematic content?

4. This story employs both concrete and abstract description. Underline places where emotions are conveyed either concretely or abstractly. In each case, what is the emotion? Are all of these feelings easy to name? In each case, what would be the effect of choosing the opposite approach? Try a few examples: write out the feelings where Phillips conveys them concretely; and look for abstract ways of conveying what she has explained directly. Can you see reasons for her decisions?

Lisa Usani Phillips

Born in 1970, Lisa Usani Phillips was raised in Connecticut by her father, a psychiatrist, and her mother, "the best cook in the world." Writing has been important to Phillips since the age of nine, when she *began to keep a journal and compose poems. She has studied writing at the Center for Creative Youth, Connecticut College, the Salt Center for Documentary Field Studies, and Emerson College where, as an MFA candidate, she was granted an Emerging Writer scholarship in 1995. Phillips currently lives and writes in Boston, Massachusetts.*

"City of Dreams" originally appeared in the Beacon Street Review *and is Phillips's first published short-short story.*

City of Dreams

Now I'm Freud, out for a stomp around the Ringstrasse. My fellow Fussgangers hurry past, towards this café and that, towards sumptuous leather booths, strong black coffee, shelter from the drizzle and spit. Though I am in little danger of being interrupted, my pace is brisk. My thoughts have legs and I must maintain a certain speed if I wish to catch them. Here is what I do not see: trees, the magnolias and limes whose pubescent buds taste, I imagine, like Turkish delight. The truffles of which I am so fond, the tangy, voluptuous Herrenpilze, hidden between gnarled tree roots and piles of poodle shit. The steeples and domes, turrets and cornices, buttresses and parapets, which jut out like genitalia over the city. Through practice and discipline, I have become blind to all distraction.

Or so I thought.

Under a nearby awning, a profusion of scarlet and chartreuse wings flutters in a brass cage, compelling me to gaze upon it. The gentleman adjacent to the cage sweeps aside his purple cape and, with a flourish, tips the spangled tin crown from his temples. He bows low to greet me and I return the favor, for it is a genuine pleasure to meet my itinerant colleague, the King of the Birds, Sovereign of Sidewalks, Avian Librettist, Dramaturge, and Psychic. The King's parrots do as the King does, each in turn.

I return the courtesy, but say nothing; the birds, though well-trained, are known to be insatiable gossips.

The King motions to his parrots. One of the larger birds plucks an envelope from the cage floor and flies it right into the King's fingers. "Your fortune, Herr Doktor," the King says.

I nod.

"You have sexual fantasies about your mother and other tangy, voluptuous women."

Stunned by the King's penetrating insight, I demand my fortune—literally, for just imagine the paper one could write on this subject! Any such desire on my part, however is frustrated instantly by an eruption from the cage.

"Figaro," the parrots sing, in chorus. "Where art thou, Figaro?" The birds are agitated. Stray feathers rain from the cage. A black fiacre with golden wheels, drawn by two Imperial Lippizaner stallions, pulls up to the curb.

Inside, a cortege of enormous corseted cats blinks and stares. The birds' shrieks hush to a querulous murmur. The cats are from the Emperor's court at Hofburg. I have seen the Emperor, a walrus in a medallion-studded white uniform. And I have seen these cats in ballrooms, mincing and waltzing, paying homage to the Emperor's long, almost prehensile whiskers. The King of the Birds wrings his leathery hands and cringes as a cat, a white Persian, descends.

"His Imperial Highness wishes to present to your Majesty this small, edible token of His inestimable esteem," says the Persian, in a lisping falsetto. The Persian taps a beautifully wrapped box towards the King of the Birds, who takes it slowly, as if it might explode. On the Persian's signal, the other cats whisk out of the carriage and take the cage back into the fiacre, which races away before the King can utter a single word.

"My birds," he says.

"Open the box," I say. The King is clearly inconsolable, and needs explicit directions for the simplest task. The seal bears the name of Demel's, confectioner by favor to his Imperial Highness, and I can hardly refrain from slitting the wax myself.

Inside, an exact replica of Vienna nestles within little clouds of silvery tissue paper. First the meringue palaces, the Hofburg, the Schonbrunn, the Belvedere, and countless others, resting on chestnut cobblestones. Then St. Stephen's Cathedral, rendered in marzipan, accurate down to the tile, to statue after sugary statue. Followed by the strudel Bergtheater, the Sachertorte Opera House, and the pancake Plague Memorial, all drizzled in the finest dark chocolate and garnished with tiny white doves chiseled out of almonds.

The King of Birds and I stare and blink for several moments at the miracle in the box. Then he holds it out to me.

"Please," the King says.

"No," I say. "I couldn't."

"It would be my pleasure," he says. "My honor."

"After you then, your Majesty."

We take turns dipping into the city, breaking off a taffy spire here, a fence of licorice filigree there, until we have eaten every last crumb.

How It Works

1. How would you describe this story's voice? Look closely at the author's vocabulary, syntax, and rhetorical devices, and break the voice down. How has the author achieved it?

2. Writers are usually advised to use adjectives and adverbs sparingly. Underline all of the modifiers you can find in this story. If you were discussing it in a workshop and someone suggested deleting them, how would you respond?

3. Another "rule" of writing is to avoid metaphors and similes. Look closely at the metaphoric language in this story. What purposes does it serve? Do you see any places where it does not serve a purpose?

4. Look again at the preceding two questions. Try rewriting some sentences in this story, removing modifiers and metaphors. How do these changes affect the story? What is lost or gained?

Juan Rulfo

Juan Rulfo was born in Mexico in 1918. His well-to-do family lost everything during the revolution of 1910, which was particularly violent in his home state of Jalisco. His short-story collection The Burning Plain and Other Stories *(El Llano en Llamas, 1953), starkly depicts the lives of rural Mexicans. His novel* Pedro Paramo *(1955) chronicles a son's search for his father. During his lifetime, Rulfo contributed to and worked with a number of prestigious Mexican publications and headed the editorial department of the National Indigenous Institute. In addition to writing fiction, Rulfo painted and took photographs. He won the Premio [prize] Xavier Villaurrutia in 1956, the Premio Nacional Letras in 1970, the Premio Jalisco in 1981, and the Premio Principe de Asturias in 1983. Juan Rulfo died in 1986.*

Macario

translated by George D. Schade

I am sitting by the sewer waiting for the frogs to come out. While we were having supper last night they started making a great racket and they didn't stop singing till dawn. Godmother says so too—the cries of the frogs scared her sleep away. And now she would really like to sleep. That's why she ordered me to sit here, by the sewer, with a board in my hand to whack to smithereens every frog that may come hopping out— Frogs are green all over except on the belly. Toads are black. Godmother's eyes are also black. Frogs make good eating. Toads don't. People just don't eat toads. People don't, but I do, and they taste just like frogs. Felipa is the one who says it's bad to eat toads. Felipa has green eyes like a cat's eyes. She feeds me in the kitchen whenever I get to eat. She doesn't want me to hurt frogs. But then Godmother is the one who orders me to do things— I love Felipa more than Godmother. But Godmother is the one who takes money out of her purse so Felipa can buy all the food. Felipa stays alone in the kitchen cooking food for the three of us. Since I've known her, that's all she does. Washing the dishes is up to me. Carrying in wood for the stove is my job too. Then Godmother is the one who dishes out food to us. After she has eaten, she makes two little piles with her hands, one for Felipa, the other for me. But sometimes Felipa doesn't feel like eating and then the two little piles are for me. That's why I love Felipa, because I'm always hungry and I never get filled up—never, not even when I eat up her food. They say a person does get filled up eating, but I know very well that I don't

even though I eat all they give me. And Felipa knows it too— They say in the street that I'm crazy because I never stop being hungry. Godmother has heard them say that. I haven't. Godmother won't let me go out alone on the street. When she takes me out, it's to go to church to hear Mass. There she sets me down next to her and ties my hands with the fringe of her shawl. I don't know why she ties my hands, but she says it's because they say I do crazy things. One day they found me hanging somebody; I was hanging a lady just to be doing it. I don't remember. But then Godmother is the one who says what I do and she never goes about telling lies. When she calls me to eat, it's to give me my part of the food. She's not like other people who invite me to eat with them and then when I get close throw rocks at me until I run away without eating anything. No, Godmother is good to me. That's why I'm content in her house. Besides, Felipa lives here. Felipa is very good to me. That's why I love her— Felipa's milk is as sweet as hibiscus flowers. I've drunk goat's milk and also the milk of a sow that had recently had pigs. But no, it isn't as good as Felipa's milk— Now it's been a long time since she has let me nurse the breasts that she has where we just have ribs, and where there comes out, if you know how to get it, a better milk than the one Godmother gives us for lunch on Sundays— Felipa used to come every night to the room where I sleep, and snuggle up to me, leaning over me or a little to one side. Then she would fix her breasts so that I could suck the sweet, hot milk that came out in streams on my tongue— Many times I've eaten hibiscus flowers to try to forget my hunger. And Felipa's milk had the same flavor, except that I liked it better because, at the same time that she let me nurse,

Felipa would tickle me all over. Then almost always she would stay there sleeping by me until dawn. And that was very good for me, because I didn't worry about the cold and I wasn't afraid of being damned to hell if I died there alone some night— Sometimes I'm not so afraid of hell. But sometimes I am. And then I like to scare myself about going to hell any day now, because my head is so hard and I like to bang it against the first thing I come across. But Felipa comes and scares away my fears. She tickles me with her hands like she knows how to do and she stops that fear of mine that I have of dying. And for a little while I even forget it— Felipa says, when she feels like being with me, that she will tell the Lord all my sins. She will go to heaven very soon and will talk with Him, asking Him to pardon me for all the great wickedness that fills my body from head to toe. She will tell Him to pardon me so I won't worry about it any more. That's why she goes to confession every day. Not because she's bad, but because I'm full of devils inside, and she has to drive them out of my body by confessing for me. Every single day. Every single afternoon of every single day. She will do that favor for me her whole life. That's what Felipa says. That's why I love her so much— Still, having a head so hard is the great thing. I bang it against the pillars of the corridor hours on end and nothing happens to it. It stands banging and doesn't crack. I bang it against the floor—first slowly, then harder—and that sounds like a drum. Just like the drum that goes with the wood flute when I hear them through the window of the church, tied to Godmother, and hearing outside the boom boom of the drum— And Godmother says that if there are chinches and cockroaches and scorpions in my room it's because I'm going to burn in hell if I keep on with this business of banging my head on the floor. But what I like is to hear the drum. She should know that. Even when I'm in church, waiting to go out soon into the street to see why the drum is heard from so far away, deep inside the church and above the damning of the priest— "The road of good things is filled with light. The road of bad things is dark." That's what the priest says— I get up and go out of my room while it's still dark. I sweep the street and I go back in my room before daylight grabs me. On the street things happen. There are lots of people who will hit me on the head with rocks as soon as they see me. Big sharp rocks rain from every side. And then my shirt has to be mended and I have to wait many days for the scabs on my face or knees to heal. And go through having my hands tied again, because if I don't they'll hurry to scratch off the scabs and a stream of blood will come out again. Blood has a good flavor too, although it isn't really like the flavor of Felipa's milk— That's why I always live shut up in my house—so they won't throw rocks at me. As soon as they feed me I lock myself in my room and bar the door so my sins won't find me out, because it's dark. And I don't even light the torch to see where the cockroaches are climbing on me. Now I keep quiet. I go to bed on my sacks, and as soon as I feel a cockroach walking along my neck with its scratchy feet I give it a slap with my hand and squash it. But I don't light the torch. I'm not going to let my sins catch me off guard with my torch lit looking for cockroaches under my blanket— Cockroaches pop like firecrackers when you mash them. I don't know whether crickets pop. I never kill crickets. Felipa says that crickets always make noise so you can't hear the cries of souls suffering in purgatory. The day there are no more crickets the world will be filled with the screams of holy souls and we'll all start running scared out of our wits. Besides, I like very much to prick my ears up and listen to the noise of the crickets. There are lots of them in my room. Maybe there are more crickets than cockroaches among the folds of the sacks where I sleep. There are scorpions too. Every once in a while they fall from the ceiling and I have to hold my breath until they've made their way across me to reach the floor. Because if an arm moves or one of my bones begins to tremble, I feel the burn of the sting right away. That hurts. Once Felipa got stung on the behind by one of them. She started moaning and making soft little cries to the Holy Virgin that her behind wouldn't be ruined. I rubbed spit on her. All night I spent rubbing spit on her and praying with her, and after a while, when I saw that my spit wasn't making her any better, I also helped her to cry with my eyes all that I could— Anyway, I like it better in my room than out on the street, attracting the attention of those who love to throw rocks at people. Here nobody does anything to me. Godmother doesn't even scold me when she sees me eating up her hibiscus flowers, or her myrtles, or her pomegranates. She knows how awfully hungry I am all the time. She knows that I'm always hungry. She knows that no meal is enough to fill up my insides, even though I go about snitching things to eat here and there all the time. She knows that I gobble up the chick-pea slop I give to the fat pigs and the dry-corn slop I give to the skinny pigs. So she knows how hungry I go around from the time I get up until the time I go to bed. And as long as I find something to eat here in this house I'll stay here. Because I think that the day I quit eating I'm going to die, and then I'll surely go straight to hell. And nobody will get me out of there, not even Felipa, who is so good to me, or the scapular that Godmother gave to me and that I wear hung around my neck— Now I'm by the sewer waiting for the frogs to come out. And not one has come out all this while I've been talking. If they take much longer to come out I may go to sleep and then there won't be any way to kill them and Godmother won't be able to sleep at all if she hears them singing and she'll get very angry. And then she'll ask one of that string of saints she has in her room to send the devils after me, to take me off to eternal damnation, right now, without even passing through purgatory, and then I won't be able to see my papa or mamma, because that's where they are— So I just better keep on talking— What I would really like to do is take a few swallows of Felipa's milk, that good milk as sweet as honey that comes from under the hibiscus flowers—

How It Works

1. Reread the story, underlining sentences and phrases that tell you about the narrator's age, life circumstances, emotional and mental state. What techniques has the author used to create these impressions? How does the story's structure (the entire story told in one paragraph) contribute to this characterization?

2. Underline descriptions of the story's setting. How does the author convey the narrator's living conditions? Does he offer an overview at the beginning of the story, or does he depend on details as he goes along?

3. How does this narrator survive? What hardships does he endure, and what comforts? How does the author convey these things?

4. Underline the passages that refer to Felipa. How would you describe the narrator's feelings for her? What specific words convey

these feelings? What happens if you substitute other words—how is the story's emotion affected? Try writing out the feelings in more detail than Rulfo has. What does that approach add to the story? Does it take anything away?

Akhil Sharma

Akhil Sharma was born in Delhi, India, and moved to the United States when he was eight years old. He graduated from Princeton University and Harvard Law School and was also a Stegner Writing Fellow at Stanford University. He worked for a time as a screenwriter in Los Angeles and is currently an investment banker in New York. "I need to earn a living, and neither the writing nor the other careers I attempted panned out," he explains. "Cosmopolitan" was written when he was twenty, a period when he believed that "sad stories were better than happy ones." Around that time, Sharma was reading John Cheever, whose style and sensibility influenced him deeply. In the first draft of "Cosmopolitan," the main character Gopal was a wife-beater. "That draft was lifeless," Sharma writes. "All sorts of dramatic things happened (fights, somebody running naked out of a house into a snowstorm), but the story felt schematic and boring." The second draft had almost nothing in common with the first "except for such details as the layout of Gopal's house and him eating dinner standing up." However, Sharma was still dissatisfied with the story. "Gopal's guilt was too real. His development as a character did not feel credible, because the way he developed did not take into account whatever might have been the real source of his guilt." In the third draft, Sharma removed everything that could have suggested that Gopal was justified in his guilt. Once this was done, he writes,

"'Cosmopolitan' became what it is now: a story about a man discovering who he is and that he is capable of fighting for his own happiness."

Cosmopolitan

A little after ten in the morning Mrs. Shaw walked across Gopal Maurya's lawn to his house. It was Saturday, and Gopal was asleep on the couch. The house was dark. When he first heard the doorbell, the ringing became part of a dream. Only he had been in the house during the four months since his wife had followed his daughter out of his life, and the sound of the bell joined somehow with his dream to make him feel ridiculous. Mrs. Shaw rang the bell again. Gopal woke confused and anxious, the state he was in most mornings. He was wearing only underwear and socks, but his blanket was cold from sweat.

He stood up and hurried to the door. He looked through the peephole. The sky was bright and clear. Mrs. Shaw was standing sideways about a foot from the door, and appeared to be staring out over his lawn at her house. She was short and red-haired and wore a pink sweatshirt and gray jogging pants.

"Hold on! Hold on, Mrs. Shaw!" he shouted, and ran back into the living room to search for a pair of pants and a shirt. The light was dim, and he had difficulty finding them. As he groped under and behind the couch and looked among the clothes crumpled on the floor, he worried that Mrs. Shaw would not wait and was already walking down the steps. He wondered if he had time to turn on the light to make his search easier. This was typical of the details that could baffle him in the morning.

Mrs. Shaw and Gopal had been neighbors for about two years, but Gopal had met her only three or four times in passing. From his wife he had learned that Mrs. Shaw was a guidance counselor at the high school his daughter had attended. He also learned that she had been divorced for a decade. Her husband, a successful orthodontist, had left her. Since then Mrs. Shaw had moved five or six times, though rarely more than a few miles from where she had last lived. She had bought the small mustard-colored house next to Gopal's as part of this restlessness. Although he did not dislike Mrs. Shaw, Gopal was irritated by the peeling paint on her house and the weeds sprouting out of her broken asphalt driveway, as if by association his house were becoming shabbier. The various cars that left her house late at night made him see her as dissolute. But all this Gopal was willing to forget that morning, in exchange for even a minor friendship.

Gopal found the pants and shirt and tugged them on as he returned to open the door. The light and cold air swept in, reminding him of what he must look like. Gopal was a small man, with delicate high cheekbones and long eyelashes. He had always been proud of his looks and had dressed well. Now he feared that the gray stubble and long hair made him appear bereft.

"Hello, Mr. Maurya," Mrs. Shaw said, looking at him and through him into the darkened house and then again at him. The sun shone behind her. The sky was blue dissolving into white. "How are you?" she asked gently.

"Oh, Mrs. Shaw," Gopal said, his voice pitted and rough, "some bad things have happened to me." He had not meant to speak so directly. He stepped out of the doorway.

The front door opened into a vestibule, and one had a clear view from there of the living room and the couch where Gopal slept. He switched on the lights. To the right was the kitchen. The round Formica table and the counters were dusty. Mrs. Shaw appeared startled by this detail. After a moment she said, "I heard." She paused and then quickly added, "I am sorry, Mr. Maurya. It must be hard. You must not feel ashamed; it's no fault of yours."

"Please, sit," Gopal said, motioning to a chair next to the kitchen table. He wanted to tangle her in conversation and keep her there for hours. He wanted to tell her how the loneliness had made him fantasize about calling an ambulance so that he could be touched and prodded, or how for a while he had begun loitering at the Indian grocery store like the old men who have not learned English. What a pretty, good woman, he thought.

Mrs. Shaw stood in the center of the room and looked around her. She was slightly overweight, and her nostrils appeared to be perfect circles, but her small white Reebok sneakers made Gopal see her as fleet with youth and innocence. "I've been thinking of coming over. I'm sorry I didn't."

"That's fine, Mrs. Shaw," Gopal said, standing near the phone on the kitchen wall. "What could anyone do? I am glad, though, that you are visiting." He searched for something else to say. To extend their time together, Gopal walked to the refrigerator and asked her if she wanted anything to drink.

"No, thank you," she said.

"Orange juice, apple juice, or grape, pineapple, guava. I also have some tropical punch," he continued, opening the refrigerator door wide, as if to show he was not lying.

"That's all right," Mrs. Shaw said, and they both became quiet. The sunlight pressed through windows that were laminated with dirt. "You must remember, everybody plays a part in these things, not just the one who is left," she said, and then they were silent again. "Do you need anything?"

"No. Thank you." They stared at each other. "Did you come for something?" Gopal asked, although he did not want to imply that he was trying to end the conversation.

"I wanted to borrow your lawn mower."

"Already?" April was just starting, and the dew did not evaporate until midday.

"Spring fever," she said.

Gopal's mind refused to provide a response to this. "Let me get you the mower."

They went to the garage. The warm sun on the back of his neck made Gopal hopeful. He believed that something would soon be said or done to delay Mrs. Shaw's departure, for certainly God could not leave him alone again. The garage smelled of must and gasoline. The lawn mower was in a shadowy corner with an aluminum ladder resting on it. "I haven't used it in a while," Gopal said, placing the ladder on the ground and smiling at Mrs. Shaw beside him. "But it should be fine." As he stood up, he suddenly felt aroused by Mrs. Shaw's large breasts, boy's haircut, and little-girl sneakers. Even her

nostrils suggested a frank sexuality. Gopal wanted to put his hands on her waist and pull her toward him. And then he realized that he had.

"No. No," Mrs. Shaw said, laughing and putting her palms flat against his chest. "Not now." She pushed him away gently.

Gopal did not try kissing her again, but he was excited. *Not now* he thought. He carefully poured gasoline into the lawn mower, wanting to appear calm, as if the two of them had already made some commitment and there was no need for nervousness. He pushed the lawn mower out onto the gravel driveway and jerked the cord to test the engine. *Not now, not now,* he thought, each time he tugged. He let the engine run for a minute. Mrs. Shaw stood silent beside him. Gopal felt like smiling, but wanted to make everything appear casual. "You can have it for as long as you need," he said.

"Thank you," Mrs. Shaw replied, and smiled. They looked at each other for a moment without saying anything. Then she rolled the lawn mower down the driveway and onto the road. She stopped, turned to look at him, and said, "I'll call."

"Good," Gopal answered, and watched her push the lawn mower down the road and up her driveway into the tin shack that huddled at its end. The driveway was separated from her ranch-style house by ten or fifteen feet of grass, and they were connected by a trampled path. Before she entered her house, Mrs. Shaw turned and looked at him as he stood at the top of his driveway. She smiled and waved.

When he went back into his house, Gopal was too excited to sleep. Before Mrs. Shaw, the only woman he had ever embraced was his wife, and a part of him assumed that it was now only a matter of time before he and Mrs. Shaw fell in love and his life resumed its normalcy. Oh, to live again as he had for nearly thirty years! Gopal thought, with such force that he shocked himself. Unable to sit, unable even to think coherently, he walked around his house.

His daughter's departure had made Gopal sick at his heart for two or three weeks, but then she sank so completely from his thoughts that he questioned whether his pain had been hurt pride rather than grief. Gitu had been a graduate student and spent only a few weeks with them each year, so it was understandable that he would not miss her for long. But the swiftness with which the dense absence on the other side of his bed unknotted and evaporated made him wonder whether he had ever loved his wife. It made him think that his wife's abrupt decision never to return from her visit to India was as much his fault as God's. Anita, he thought, must have decided upon seeing Gitu leave that there was no more reason to stay, and that perhaps, after all, it was not too late to start again. Anita had gone to India at the end of November—a month after Gitu got on a Lufthansa flight to go live with her boyfriend in Germany—and a week later, over an echoing phone line, she told him of the guru and her enlightenment.

Perhaps if Gopal had not retired early from AT&T, he could have worked long hours and his wife's and daughter's slipping from his thoughts might have been mistaken for healing. But he had nothing to do. Most of his acquaintances had come by way of his wife, and when she left, Gopal did not call them, both because they had always been more Anita's friends than his and because he felt ashamed, as if his wife's departure revealed his inability to love her. At one point, around Christmas, he went to a dinner party, but he did not enjoy it. He found that he was not curious about other people's lives and did not want to talk about his own.

A month after Anita's departure a letter from her arrived—a blue aerogram, telling of the ashram, and of sweeping the courtyard, and of the daily prayers. Gopal responded immediately, but she never wrote again. His pride prevented him from trying to continue the correspondence, though he read her one letter so many times that he inadvertently memorized the Pune address. His brothers sent a flurry of long missives from India, on paper so thin that it was almost translucent, but his contact with them over the decades had been minimal, and the tragedy pushed them apart instead of pulling them closer.

Gitu sent a picture of herself wearing a yellow-and-blue ski jacket in the Swiss Alps. Gopal wrote her back in a stiff, formal way, and she responded with a breezy postcard to which he replied only after a long wait.

Other than this, Gopal had had little personal contact with the world. He was accustomed to getting up early and going to bed late, but now, since he had no work and no friends, after he spent the morning reading *The New York Times* and *The Home News & Tribune* front to back, Gopal felt adrift through the afternoon and evening. For a few weeks he tried to fill his days by showering and shaving twice daily, brushing his teeth after every snack and meal. But the purposelessness of this made him despair, and he stopped bathing altogether and instead began sleeping more and more, sometimes sixteen hours a day. He slept in the living room, long and narrow with high rectangular windows blocked by trees. At some point, in a burst of self-hate, Gopal moved his clothes from the bedroom closet to a corner of the living room, wanting to avoid comforting himself with any illusions that his life was normal.

But he yearned for his old life, the life of a clean kitchen, of a bedroom, of going out into the sun, and on a half-conscious level that morning Gopal decided to use the excitement of clasping Mrs. Shaw to change himself back to the man he had been. She might be spending time at his house, he thought, so he mopped the kitchen floor, moved back into his bedroom, vacuumed and dusted all the rooms. He spent most of the afternoon doing this, aware always of his humming lawn mower in the background. He had only to focus on it to make his heart race. Every now and then he would stop working and go to his bedroom window, where, from behind the curtains, he would stare at Mrs. Shaw. She had a red bandanna tied around her forehead and he somehow found this appealing. That night he made himself an elaborate dinner with three dishes and a mango shake. For the first time in months Gopal watched the eleven o'clock news. He had the lights off and his feet up on a low table. Lebanon was being bombed again, and Gopal kept bursting into giggles for no reason. He tried to think of what he would do tomorrow. Gopal knew that he was happy and that to avoid depression he must keep himself busy until Mrs. Shaw called. He suddenly realized that he did not know Mrs. Shaw's first name. He padded into the darkened kitchen and looked at the phone diary. "Helen Shaw" was written in the big, loopy handwriting of his wife. Having his wife help him in this way did not bother him at all, and then he felt ashamed that it didn't.

The next day was Sunday, and Gopal anticipated it cheerfully, for the Sunday *Times* was frequently so thick that he could spend the whole day reading it. But this time he did not read it all the way through. He left the book review and the other features sections to fill time over the next few days. After eating a large breakfast—the idea of preparing elaborate meals had begun to appeal to him—he went for a haircut. Gopal had not left his house in several days. He rolled down the window of his blue Honda Civic and took the long way, past the lake, to the mall. Instead of going to his usual barber, he went to a hair stylist, where a woman with long nails and large, contented breasts shampooed his hair before cutting it. Then Gopal wandered around the mall, savoring its buttered-popcorn smell and enjoying the sight of the girls with their sometimes odd-colored hair. He went into some of the small shops and looked at clothes, and considered buying a half pound of cocoa amaretto coffee beans, although he had never cared much for coffee. After walking for nearly two hours, Gopal sat on a bench and ate an ice cream cone while reading an article in *Cosmopolitan* about what makes a good lover. He had seen the magazine in CVS and, noting the article mentioned on the cover, had been reminded how easily one can learn anything in America. Because Mrs. Shaw was an American, Gopal thought, he needed to do research into what might be expected of him. Although the article was about what makes a woman a good lover, it offered clues for men as well. Gopal felt confident that given time, Mrs. Shaw would love him. The article made attachment appear effortless. All you had to do was listen closely and speak honestly.

He returned home around five, and Mrs. Shaw called soon after. "If you want, you can come over now."

"All right," Gopal answered. He was calm. He showered and put on a blue cotton shirt and khaki slacks. When he stepped outside, the sky was turning pink, and the air smelled of wet earth. He felt young, as if he had just arrived in America and the huge scale of things had made him a giant as well.

But when he rang Mrs. Shaw's doorbell, Gopal became nervous. He turned around and looked at the white clouds against the enormous sky. He heard footsteps and then the door swishing open and Mrs. Shaw's voice. "You look handsome," she said. Gopal faced her, smiling and uncomfortable. She wore a different sweatshirt, but still had on yesterday's jogging pants. She was barefoot. A yellow light shone behind her.

"Thank you," Gopal said, and then nervously added "Helen," to confirm their new relationship. "You look nice too." She did look pretty to him. Mrs. Shaw stepped aside to let him in. They were in a large room. In the center were two pale couches forming an L, with a television in front of them. Off to the side was a kitchenette—a stove, a refrigerator, and some cabinets over a sink and counter.

Seeing Gopal looking around, Mrs. Shaw said, "There are two bedrooms in the back, and a bathroom. Would you like anything to drink? I have juice, if you want." She walked to the kitchen.

"What are you going to have?" Gopal asked, following her. "If you have something, I'll have something." Then he felt embarrassed. Mrs. Shaw had not dressed up; obviously, "Not now" had been a polite rebuff.

"I was going to have a gin and tonic," she said, opening the refrigerator and standing before it with one hand on her hip.

"I would like that too." Gopal came close to her and with a dart kissed her on the lips. She did not resist, but neither did she respond. Her lips were chapped. Gopal pulled away and let her make the drinks. He had hoped the kiss would tell him something of what to expect.

They sat side by side on a couch and sipped their drinks. A table lamp cast a diffused light over them.

"Thank you for letting me borrow the lawn mower."

"It's nothing." There was a long pause. Gopal could not think of anything to say. *Cosmopolitan* had suggested trying to learn as much as possible about your lover, so he asked, "What's your favorite color?"

"Why?"

"I want to know everything about you."

"That's sweet," Mrs. Shaw said, and patted his hand. Gopal felt embarrassed and looked down. He did not know whether he should have spoken so frankly, but part of his intention had been to flatter her with his interest. "I don't have one," she said. She kept her hand on his.

Gopal suddenly thought that they might make love tonight, and he felt his heart kick. "Tell me all about yourself," he said with a voice full of feeling. "Where were you born?"

"I was born in Jersey City on May fifth, but I won't tell you the year." Gopal tried to grin gamely and memorize the date. A part of him was disturbed that she did not feel comfortable enough with him to reveal her age.

"Did you grow up there?" he asked, taking a sip of the gin and tonic. Gopal drank slowly, because he knew that he could not hold his alcohol. He saw that Mrs. Shaw's toes were painted bright red. Anita had never used nail polish, and Gopal wondered what a woman who would paint her toenails might do.

"I moved to Newark when I was three. My parents ran a newspaper-and-candy shop. We sold greeting cards, stamps." Mrs. Shaw had nearly finished her drink. "They opened at eight in the morning and closed at seven-thirty at night. Six days a week." When she paused between swallows, she rested the glass on her knee.

Gopal had never known anyone who worked in such a shop, and he became genuinely interested in what she was saying. He remembered his lack of interest at the Christmas party and wondered whether it was the possibility of sex that made him fascinated with Mrs. Shaw's story. "Were you a happy child?" he asked, grinning broadly and then bringing the grin to a quick end, because he did not want to appear ironic. The half glass that Gopal had drunk had already begun to make him feel light-headed and gay.

"Oh, pretty happy," she said, "although I liked to think of myself as serious. I would look at the evening sky and think that no one else had felt what I was feeling." Mrs. Shaw's understanding of her own feelings disconcerted Gopal and made him momentarily think that he wasn't learning anything important, or that she was in some way independent of her past and thus incapable of the sentimental attachments through which he expected her love for him to grow.

Cosmopolitan had recommended that both partners reveal themselves, so Gopal decided to tell a story about himself. He did not believe that being honest about himself would actually change him. Rather, he thought the deliberateness of telling the story would rob it of the power to make him vulnerable. He started to say something, but the words twisted in his mouth, and he said, "You know, I don't really drink much." Gopal felt embarrassed by the non sequitur. He thought he sounded foolish, though he had hoped that the story he would tell would make him appear sensitive.

"I kind of guessed that from the juices," she said, smiling. Gopal laughed.

He tried to say what he had wanted to confess earlier. "I associate drinking with being American, and I haven't been able to truly Americanize. On my daughter's nineteenth birthday we took her to dinner and a movie, but we didn't talk much, and the dinner finished earlier than we had expected it would. The restaurant was in a mall, and we had nothing to do until the movie started, so we wandered around Foodtown." Gopal thought he sounded pathetic, so he tried to shift the story. "After all my years in America, I am still astonished by those huge grocery stores and enjoy walking in them. But my daughter is an American, so our wandering around in Foodtown must have been very strange for her. She doesn't know Hindi, and her parents must seem very strange." Gopal noticed that his heart was racing. He wondered if he was sadder than he knew.

"That's sweet," Mrs. Shaw said. The brevity of her response made Gopal nervous.

Mrs. Shaw kissed his cheek. Her lips were dry, Gopal noticed. He turned slightly so that their lips could touch. They kissed again. Mrs. Shaw opened her lips and closed her eyes. They kissed for a long time. When they pulled apart, they continued their conversation calmly, as if they were accustomed to each other. "I didn't go into a big grocery store until I was in college," she said. "We always went to the small shops around us. When I first saw those long aisles, I wondered what happens to the food if no one buys it. I was living then with a man who was seven or eight years older than I, and when I told him, he laughed at me, and I felt so young." She stopped and then added, "I ended up leaving him because he always made me feel young." Her face was only an inch or two from Gopal's.

"Now I'd marry someone who could make me feel that way." Gopal felt his romantic feelings drain away at the idea of how many men she had slept with. But the fact that Mrs. Shaw and he had experienced something removed some of the loneliness he was feeling, and Mrs. Shaw had large breasts. They began kissing again. Soon they were tussling and groping on the floor.

Her bed was large and low to the ground. Behind it was a window, and although the shade was drawn, the lights of passing cars cast patterns on the opposing wall. Gopal lay next to Mrs. Shaw and watched the shadows change. He felt his head and found that his hair was standing up on either side like horns. The shock of seeing a new naked body, so different in its amplitude from his wife's, had been exciting. A part of him was giddy with this, as if he had checked his bank balance and discovered that he had thousands more than he expected. "You are very beautiful," he said, for *Cosmopolitan* had advised saying this after making love. Mrs. Shaw rolled over and kissed his shoulder.

"No, I'm not. I'm kind of fat, and my nose is strange. But thank you," she said. Gopal looked at her and saw that even when her mouth was slack, the lines around it were deep. "You look like you've been rolled around in a dryer," she said, and laughed. Her laughter was sudden and confident. He had noticed it before, and it made him laugh as well.

They became silent and lay quietly for several minutes, and when Gopal began feeling self-conscious, he said, "Describe the first house you lived in."

Mrs. Shaw sat up. Her stomach bulged, and her breasts drooped. She saw him looking and pulled her knees to her chest. "You're very thoughtful," she said.

Gopal felt flattered. "Oh, it's not thoughtfulness."

"I guess if it weren't for your accent, the questions would sound artificial," she said. Gopal felt his stomach clench. "I lived in a block of small houses that the Army built for returning GIs. They were all drab, and the lawns ran into each other. They were near Newark airport. I liked to sit at my window and watch the planes land. That was when Newark was a local airport."

"Your house was two stories?"

"Yes. And my room was on the second floor. Tell me about yourself."

"I am the third of five brothers. We grew up in a small, poor village. I got my first pair of shoes when I left high school." As Gopal was telling her the story, he remembered how he used to make Gitu feel lazy with stories of his childhood, and his voice fell. "Everybody was like us, so I never thought of myself as poor."

They talked this way for half an hour, with Gopal asking most of the questions and trying to discover where Mrs. Shaw was vulnerable and how this vulnerability made him attractive to her. Although she answered his questions candidly, Gopal could not find the unhappy childhood or the trauma of an abandoned wife that might explain the urgency of this moment in bed. "I was planning to leave my husband," she explained casually. "He was crazy. Almost literally. He thought he was going to be a captain of industry or a senator. He wasn't registered to vote. He knew nothing about business. Once, he invested almost everything we had in a hydroponic farm in Southampton. With him I was always scared of being poor. He used to spend two hundred dollars a week on lottery tickets, and he would save the old tickets in shoe boxes in the garage." Gopal did not personally know any Indian who was divorced, and he had never been intimate enough with an American to learn what a divorce was like, but he had expected something more painful—tears and recriminations. The details she gave made the story sound practiced, and he began to think that he would never have a hold over Mrs. Shaw.

Around eight Mrs. Shaw said, "I am going to do my bills tonight." Gopal had been wondering whether she wanted him to have dinner with her and spent the night. He would have liked to, but he did not protest.

As she closed the door behind him, Mrs. Shaw said, "The lawn mower's in the back. If you want it." Night had come, and the stars were out. As Gopal pushed the lawn mower down the road, he wished that he loved Mrs. Shaw and that she loved him.

He had left the kitchen light on by mistake, and its glow was comforting. "Come, come, cheer up," he said aloud, pacing in the kitchen. "You have a lover." He tried to smile and grimaced instead. "You can make love as often as you want. Be happy." He started preparing dinner. He fried okra and steam-cooked lentils. He made both rice and bread.

As he ate, Gopal watched a television movie about a woman who had been in a coma for twenty years and suddenly woke up one day; adding to her confusion, she was pregnant. After washing the dishes he finished the article in *Cosmopolitan* that he had begun reading in the mall. The article was the second of two parts, and it mentioned that when leaving after making love for the first time, one should always arrange the next meeting. Gopal had not done this, and he phoned Mrs. Shaw.

He used the phone in the kitchen, and as he waited for her to pick up, he wondered whether he should introduce himself or assume that she would recognize his voice. "Hi, Helen," he blurted out as soon as she said "Hello." "I was just thinking of you and thought I'd call." He felt more nervous now than he had while he was with her.

"That's sweet," she said, with what Gopal thought was tenderness. "How are you?"

"I just had dinner. Did you eat?" He imagined her sitting on the floor between the couches with a pile of receipts before her. She would have a small pencil in her hand.

"I'm not hungry. I normally make myself an omelet for dinner, but I didn't want to tonight. I'm having another drink." Then, self-conscious, she added, "Otherwise I grind my teeth. I started after my divorce and I didn't have health insurance or enough money to go to a dentist." Gopal wanted to ask if she still ground her teeth, but he did not want to imply anything.

"Would you like to have dinner tomorrow? I'll cook." They agreed to meet at six. The conversation continued for a few minutes longer, and when Gopal hung up, he was pleased at how well he had handled things.

While lying in bed, waiting for sleep, Gopal read another article in *Cosmopolitan*, about job pressure's effects on one's sex life. He had enjoyed both articles and was happy with himself for his efforts at understanding Mrs. Shaw. He fell asleep smiling.

The next day, after reading the papers, Gopal went to the library to read the first part of the *Cosmopolitan* article. He ended up reading articles from *Elle, Redbook, Glamour, Mademoiselle*, and *Family Circle*, and one from *Reader's Digest*—"How to Tell If Your Marriage Is on the Rocks." He tried to memorize jokes from the "Laughter Is the Best Medicine" section, so that he would never be at a loss for conversation.

Gopal arrived at home by four and began cooking. Dinner was pleasant though, they ate in the kitchen, which was lit with buzzing fluorescent tubes. Gopal worried that yesterday's lovemaking might have been a fluke. Soon after they finished the meal, however, they were on the couch, struggling with each other's clothing.

Gopal wanted Mrs. Shaw to spend the night, but she refused, saying that she had not slept a full night with anyone since her divorce. At first Gopal was touched by this. They lay on his bed in the dark. The alarm clock on the lampstand said 9:12 in big red figures. "Why?" Gopal asked, rolling over and resting his cheek on her cool shoulder. He wanted to reassure her that he was eager to listen.

"I think I'm a serial monogamist and I don't want to make things too complicated." She twisted a lock of his hair around her middle finger. "It isn't because of you sweetie. It's with every man."

"Oh," Gopal said, hurt by the idea of other men and disillusioned about her motives. He continued believing, however, that now that they were lovers, the power of his concern would make her love him back. One of the articles he had read that day had suggested that people become dependent in spite of themselves when they are constantly cared for. So he made himself relax and act understanding.

Gopal went to bed an hour after Mrs. Shaw left. Before going to sleep he called her and wished her good night. He began calling her frequently after that, two or three times a day. Over the next few weeks Gopal found himself becoming coy and playful with her. When Mrs. Shaw picked up the phone, he made panting noises, and she laughed at him. She liked his being childlike with her. Sometimes she would point to a spot on his chest, and he would look down, even though he knew nothing was there, so that she could tap his nose. When they made love, she was thoughtful about asking what pleased him, and Gopal learned from this and began asking her the same. They saw each other nearly every day, though sometimes only briefly, for a few minutes in the evening or at night. But Gopal continued to feel nervous around her, as if he were somehow imposing. If she phoned him and invited him over, he was always flattered. As Gopal learned more about Mrs. Shaw, he began thinking she was very smart. She read constantly, primarily history and economics. He was always surprised, therefore, when she became moody and sentimental and talked about how loneliness is incurable. Gopal liked Mrs. Shaw in this mood, because it made him feel needed, but he felt ashamed that he was so insecure. When she did not laugh at a joke, Gopal doubted that she would ever love him. When they were in bed together and he thought she might be looking at him, he kept his stomach sucked in.

This sense of precariousness made Gopal try developing other supports for himself. One morning early in his involvement with Mrs. Shaw he phoned an Indian engineer with whom he had worked on a project about corrosion of copper wires and who had also taken early retirement from AT&T. They had met briefly several times since then and had agreed each time to get together again, but neither had made the effort. Gopal waited until eleven before calling, because he felt that any earlier would make him sound needy. A woman picked up the phone. She told him to wait a minute as she called for Rishi. Gopal felt vaguely deceitful, as if he were trying to pass himself off as just like everyone else, although his wife and child had left him.

"I haven't been doing much," he confessed immediately to Rishi. "I read a lot." When Rishi asked what, Gopal answered "Magazines," with embarrassment. They were silent then. Gopal did not want to ask Rishi immediately if he would like to meet for dinner, so he hunted desperately for a conversational opening. He was sitting in the kitchen. He looked at the sunlight on the newspaper before him and remembered that he could ask Rishi questions. "How are *you* doing?"

"It isn't like India," Rishi responded, complaining. "In India the older you are, the closer you are to the center of attention. Here you have to keep going. Your children are away and you have nothing to do. I would go back, but Ratha doesn't want to. America is much better for women."

Gopal felt a rush of relief that Rishi had spoken so much. "Are you just at home or are you doing something part time?"

"I am the president of the Indian Cultural Association," Rishi said boastfully.

"That's wonderful," Gopal said, and with a leap added, "I want to get involved in that more, now that I have time."

"We always need help. We are going to have a fair," Rishi said. "It's on the twenty-fourth, next month. We need help coordinating things, arranging food, putting up flyers."

"I can help," Gopal said. They decided that he should come to Rishi's house on Wednesday, two days later.

Gopal was about to hang up when Rishi added, "I heard about your family." Gopal felt as if he had been caught in a lie. "I am sorry," Rishi said.

Gopal was quiet for a moment and then said, "Thank you." He did not know whether he should pretend to be sad. "It takes some getting used to," he said, "but you can go on from nearly anything."

Gopal went to see Rishi that Wednesday, and on Sunday he attended a board meeting to plan for the fair. He told jokes about a near-sighted snake and a water hose, and about a golf instructor and God. One of the men he met there invited him to dinner.

Mrs. Shaw, however, continued to dominate his thoughts. The more they made love, the more absorbed Gopal became in the texture of her nipples in his mouth and the heft of her hips in his hands. He thought of this in the shower, while driving, while stirring his cereal. Two or three times over the next month Gopal picked her up during her lunch hour and they hurried home to make love. They would make love and then talk. Mrs. Shaw had once worked at a dry cleaner, and Gopal found this fascinating. He had met only one person in his life before Mrs. Shaw who had worked in a dry-cleaning business, and that was different, because it was in India, where dry cleaning still had the glamour of advancing technology. Being the lover of someone who had worked in a dry-cleaning business made Gopal feel strange. It made him think that the world was huge beyond comprehension, and to spend his time trying to control his own small world was inefficient. Gopal began thinking that he loved Mrs. Shaw. He started listening to the golden-oldies station in the car, so that he could hear what she had heard in her youth.

Mrs. Shaw would ask about his life, and Gopal tried to tell her everything she wanted to know in as much detail as possible. Once, he told her of how he had begun worrying when his daughter was finishing high school that she was going to slip from his life. To show that he loved her, he had arbitrarily forbidden her to ski, claiming that skiing was dangerous. He had hoped that she would find this quaintly immigrant, but she was just angry. At first the words twisted in his mouth, and he spoke to Mrs. Shaw about skiing in general. Only with an effort could he tell her about his fight with Gitu. Mrs. Shaw did not say anything at first. Then she said, "It's all right if you were that way once, as long as you aren't that way now." Listening to her, Gopal suddenly felt angry.

"Why do you talk like this?" he asked.

"What?"

"When you talk about how your breasts fall or how your behind is too wide, I always say that's not true. I always see you with eyes that make you beautiful."

"Because I want the truth," she said, also angry.

Gopal became quiet. Her desire for honesty appeared to refute all his delicate and constant manipulations. Was he actually in love with her, he wondered, or was this love just a way to avoid loneliness? And did it matter that so much of what he did was conscious?

He questioned his love more and more as the day of the Indian festival approached and Gopal realized that he was delaying asking Mrs. Shaw to come with him. She knew about the fair but had not mentioned her feelings. Gopal told himself that she would feel uncomfortable among so many Indians, but he knew that he hadn't asked her because bringing her would make him feel awkward. For some reason he was nervous that word of Mrs. Shaw might get to his wife and daughter. He was also anxious about what the Indians with whom he had recently become friendly would think. He had met mixed couples at Indian parties before, and they were always treated with the deference usually reserved for cripples. If Mrs. Shaw had been of any sort of marginalized ethnic group—a first-genera-

tion immigrant, for instance—then things might have been easier.

The festival was held in the Edison First Aid Squad's square blue-and-white building. A children's dance troupe performed in red dresses so stiff with gold thread that the girls appeared to hobble as they moved about the center of the concrete floor. A balding comedian in oxblood shoes and a white suit performed. Light folding tables along one wall were precariously laden with large pots, pans, and trays of food. Gopal stood in a corner with several men who had retired from AT&T and, slightly drunk, improvised on jokes he had read in *1,001 Polish Jokes.* The Poles became Sikhs, but he kept most of the rest. He was laughing and feeling proud that he could so easily become the center of attention, but he felt lonely at the thought that when the food was served, the men at his side would drift away to join their families and he would stand alone in line. After listening to talk of someone's marriage, he began thinking about Mrs. Shaw. The men were clustered together, and the women conversed separately. They will go home and make love and not talk, Gopal thought. Then he felt sad and frightened. To make amends for his guilt at not bringing Mrs. Shaw along, he told a bearded man with yellow teeth, "These Sikhs aren't so bad. They are the smartest ones in India, and no one can match a Sikh for courage." Then Gopal felt dazed and ready to leave.

When Gopal pulled into his driveway, it was late afternoon. His head felt oddly still, as it always did when alcohol started wearing off, but Gopal knew that he was drunk enough to do something foolish. He parked and walked down the road to Mrs. Shaw's. He wondered if she would be in. Pale tulips bloomed in a thin, uneven row in front of her house. The sight of them made him hopeful.

Mrs. Shaw opened the door before he could knock. For a moment Gopal did not say anything. She was wearing a denim skirt and a sleeveless white shirt. She smiled at him. Gopal spoke solemnly and from far off. "I love you," he said to her for the first time. "I am sorry I didn't invite you to the fair." He waited a moment for his statement to sink in and for her to respond with a similar endearment. When she did not, he repeated, "I love you."

Then she said, "Thank you," and told him not to worry about the fair. She invited him in. Gopal was confused and flustered by her reticence. He began feeling awkward about his confession. They kissed briefly, and then Gopal went home.

The next night, as they sat together watching TV in his living room, Mrs. Shaw suddenly turned to Gopal and said, "You really do love me, don't you?" Although Gopal had expected the question, he was momentarily disconcerted by it, because it made him wonder what love was and whether he was capable of it. But he did not think that this was the time to quibble over semantics. After being silent long enough to suggest that he was struggling with his vulnerability, Gopal said yes and waited for Mrs. Shaw's response. Again she did not confess her love. She kissed his forehead tenderly. This show of sentiment made Gopal angry, but he said nothing. He was glad though, when Mrs. Shaw left that night.

The next day Gopal waited for Mrs. Shaw to return home from work. He had decided that the time had come for the next step in their relationship. As soon as he saw her struggle through her doorway, hugging sacks of groceries, Gopal phoned. He stood on the steps to his house, with the extension cord trailing over

one shoulder, and looked at her house and at her rusted and exhausted-looking station wagon, which he had begun to associate strongly and warmly with the broad sweep of Mrs. Shaw's life. Gopal nearly said, "I missed you" when she picked up the phone, but he became embarrassed and asked, "How was your day?"

"Fine," she said, and Gopal imagined her moving about the kitchen, putting away whatever she had bought, placing the tea kettle on the stove, and sorting her mail on the kitchen table. This image of domesticity and independence moved him deeply. "There's a guidance counselor who is dying of cancer," she said, "and his friends are having a party for him, and they put up a sign saying 'RSVP with your money now! Henry can't wait for the party!'" Gopal and Mrs. Shaw laughed.

"Let's do something," he said.

"What?"

Gopal had not thought this part out. He wanted to do something romantic that would last until bedtime, so that he could pressure her to spend the night. "Would you like to have dinner?"

"Sure," she said. Gopal was pleased. He had gone to a liquor store a few days earlier and bought wine, just in case he had an opportunity to get Mrs. Shaw drunk and get her to fall asleep beside him.

Gopal plied Mrs. Shaw with wine as they ate the linguine he had cooked. They sat in the kitchen, but he had turned off the fluorescent lights and lit a candle. By the third glass Gopal was feeling very brave; he placed his hand on her inner thigh.

"My mother and father," Mrs. Shaw said halfway through the meal, pointing at him with her fork and speaking with the deliberateness of the drunk, "convinced me that people are not meant to live together for long periods of time." She was speaking in response to Gopal's hint earlier that only over time and through living together could people get to know each other properly. "If you know someone that well, you are bound to be disappointed."

"Maybe that's because you haven't met the right person," Gopal answered, feeling awkward for saying something that could be considered arrogant when he was trying to appear vulnerable.

"I don't think there is a right person. Not for me. To fall in love I think you need a certain suspension of disbelief, which I don't think I am capable of."

Gopal wondered whether Mrs. Shaw believed what she was saying or was trying not to hurt his feelings by revealing that she couldn't love him. He stopped eating.

Mrs. Shaw stared at him. She put her fork down and said, "I love you. I love how you care for me and how gentle you are."

Gopal smiled. Perhaps, he thought, the first part of her statement had been a preface to a confession that he mattered so much that she was willing to make an exception for him. "I love you too," Gopal said. "I love how funny and smart and honest you are. You are very beautiful." He leaned over slightly to suggest that he wanted to kiss her, but Mrs. Shaw did not respond.

Her face was stiff. "I love you," she said again, and Gopal became nervous. "But I am not *in* love with you." She stopped and stared at Gopal.

Gopal felt confused. "What's the difference?"

"When you are *in* love, you never think about yourself, because you love the other person so completely. I've lived too long to think anyone is that perfect." Gopal still didn't understand the distinction, but he was too embarrassed to ask more. It was only fair, a part of

him thought, that God would punish him this way for driving away his wife and child. How could anyone love him?

Mrs. Shaw took his hands in hers. "I think we should take a little break from each other, so we don't get confused. Being with you, I'm getting confused too. We should see other people."

"Oh." Gopal's chest hurt despite his understanding of the justice of what was happening.

"I don't want to hide anything. I love you. I truly love you. You are the kindest lover I've ever had."

"Oh."

For a week after this Gopal observed that Mrs. Shaw did not bring another man to her house. He went to the Sunday board meeting of the cultural association, where he regaled the members with jokes from *Reader's Digest.* He taught his first Hindi class to children at the temple. He took his car to be serviced. Gopal did all these things. He ate. He slept. He even made love to Mrs. Shaw once, and until she asked him to leave, he thought everything was all right again.

Then, one night, Gopal was awakened at a little after three by a car pulling out of Mrs. Shaw's driveway. It is just a friend, he thought, standing by his bedroom window and watching the Toyota move down the road. Gopal tried falling asleep again, but he could not, though he was not thinking of anything in particular. His mind was blank, but sleep did not come.

I will not call her, Gopal thought in the morning. And as he was dialing her, he thought he would hang up before all the numbers had been pressed. He heard the receiver being lifted on the other side and Mrs. Shaw saying "Hello." He did not say anything. "Don't do this Gopal," she said softly. "Don't hurt me."

"Hi," Gopal whispered, wanting very much to hurt her. He leaned his head against the kitchen wall. His face twitched as he whispered, "I'm sorry."

"Don't be that way. I love you. I didn't want to hurt you. That's why I told you."

"I know."

"All right?"

"Yes." They were silent for a long time. Then Gopal hung up. He wondered if she would call back. He waited, and when she didn't, he began jumping up and down in place.

For the next few weeks Gopal tried to spend as little time as possible in his house. He read the morning papers in the library, and then had lunch at a diner, and then went back to the library. On Sundays he spent all day at the mall. His anger at Mrs. Shaw soon disappeared, because he thought that the blame for her leaving lay with him. Gopal continued, however, to avoid home, because he did not want to experience the jealousy that would keep him awake all night. Only if he arrived late enough and tired enough could he fall asleep. In the evening Gopal either went to the temple and helped at the seven o'clock service or visited one of his new acquaintances. But over the weeks he exhausted the kindheartedness of his acquaintances and had a disagreement with one man's wife, and he was forced to return home.

The first few evenings he spent at home Gopal thought he would have to flee his house in despair. He slept awkwardly, waking at the barest rustle outside his window, thinking that a car was pulling out of Mrs. Shaw's driveway. The days were easier than the nights, especially when Mrs. Shaw was away at work. Gopal would sleep a few hours at night and then nap during the day, but this left him exhausted and dizzy. In the afternoon he liked to sit on the steps and read the paper, pausing occasionally to look at her house. He liked the sun sliding up its walls. Sometimes he was sitting outside when she drove home from work. Mrs. Shaw waved to him once or twice, but he did not respond, not because he was angry but because he felt himself become so still at the sight of her that he could neither wave nor smile.

A month and a half after they separated, Gopal still could not sleep at night if he thought there were two cars in Mrs. Shaw's driveway. Once, after a series of sleepless nights, he was up until three watching a dark shape behind Mrs. Shaw's station wagon. He waited by his bedroom window, paralyzed with fear and hope, for a car to pass in front of her house and strike the shape with its headlights. After a long time in which no car went by, Gopal decided to check for himself.

He started across his lawn crouched over and running. The air was warm and smelled of jasmine, and Gopal was so tired that he thought he might spill to the ground. After a few steps he stopped and straightened up. The sky was clear, and there were so many stars that Gopal felt as if he were in his village in India. The houses along the street were dark and drawn in on themselves. Even in India, he thought, late at night the houses look like sleeping faces. He remembered how surprised he had been by the pitched roofs of American houses when he had first come here, and how this had made him yearn to return to India, where he could sleep on the roof. He started across the lawn again. Gopal walked slowly, and he felt as if he were crossing a great distance.

The station wagon stood battered and alone, smelling faintly of gasoline and the day's heat. Gopal leaned against its hood. The station wagon was so old that the odometer had gone all the way around. Like me, he thought, and like Helen, too. This is who we are, he thought—dusty, corroded, and dented from our voyages, with our unflagging hearts rattling on inside. We are made who we are by the dust and corrosion and dents and unflagging hearts. Why should we need anything else to fall in love? he wondered. We learn and change and get better. He leaned against the car for a minute or two. Fireflies swung flickering in the breeze. Then he walked home.

Gopal woke early and showered and shaved and made breakfast. He brushed his teeth after eating and felt his cheeks to see whether he should shave again, this time against the grain. At nine he crossed his lawn and rang Mrs. Shaw's doorbell. He had to ring it several times before he heard her footsteps. When she opened the door and saw him, Mrs. Shaw drew back as if she were afraid. Gopal felt sad that she could think he might hurt her. "May I come in?" he asked. She stared at him. He saw mascara stains beneath her eyes and silver strands mingled with her red hair. He thought he had never seen a woman as beautiful or as gallant.

How It Works

1. Underline Gopal's interpretations of his lover Mrs. Shaw's behavior. How accurate do you think these interpretations are? How does the author suggest the degrees of his narrator's reliability throughout the story?

2. Underline the descriptions of setting in the scenes between Gopal and Mrs. Shaw. Now read the scenes without them. What is lost? How does the author use setting to pace the scenes and heighten emotion?

3. How does Gopal change in the course of the story? Does Mrs. Shaw also change? How does the author use point of view and descriptive detail to keep the story's focus on its main character without losing sight of the secondary character?

4. Try writing out the subtext of the story's first scene between Gopal and Mrs. Shaw. What are these characters' unspoken feelings? How does the author convey them? What are some other ways such feelings might be conveyed?

Leslie Marmon Silko

Leslie Marmon Silko was born in 1948 in Albuquerque, New Mexico. She is of Pueblo, Laguna, Mexican, and Caucasian descent, and grew up on the Laguna Pueblo Reservation. Silko graduated with honors from the University of New Mexico in 1969. Her novels, Ceremony *and* Storyteller, *emphasize the Pueblo culture and the role of storytelling within it.* Delicacy and the Strength of Lace: Letters, *published in 1986, is an edited version of her correspondence with poet James Wright. Silko has taught at the University of New Mexico, Albuquerque; Navajo Community College in Tsaile, Arizona; and the University of Arizona, Tucson, where she is currently a professor of English.*

Yellow Woman

What Whirlwind Man Told Kochininako, Yellow Woman
 I myself belong to the wind
 and so it is we will travel swiftly
 this whole world
 with dust and with windstorms.

My thigh clung to his with dampness, and I watched the sun rising up through the tamaracks and willows. The small brown water birds came to the river and hopped across the mud, leaving brown scratches in the alkali-white crust. They bathed in the river silently. I could hear the water, almost at our feet where the narrow fast channel bubbled and washed green ragged moss and fern leaves. I looked at him beside me, rolled in the red blanket on the white river sand. I cleaned the sand out of the cracks between my toes, squinting because the sun was above the willow trees. I looked at him for the last time, sleeping on the white river sand.

I felt hungry and followed the river south the way we had come the afternoon before, following our footprints that were already blurred by lizard tracks and bug trails. The horses were still lying down, and the black one whinnied when he saw me but he did not get up—maybe it was because the corral was made out of thick cedar branches and the horses had not yet felt the sun like I had. I tried to look beyond the pale red mesas to the pueblo. I knew it was there, even if I could not see it, on the sandrock hill above the river, the same river that moved past me now and had reflected the moon last night.

The horse felt warm underneath me. He shook his head and pawed the sand. The bay whinnied and leaned against the gate trying to follow, and I remembered him asleep in the red blanket beside the river. I slid off the horse and tied him close to the other horse, I walked north with the river again, and the white sand broke loose in footprints over footprints.

"Wake up."

He moved in the blanket and turned his face to me with his eyes still closed. I knelt down to touch him.

"I'm leaving."

He smiled now, eyes still closed. "You are coming with me, remember?" He sat up now with his bare dark chest and belly in the sun.

"Where?"

"To my place."

"And will I come back?"

He pulled his pants on. I walked away from him, feeling him behind me and smelling the willows.

"Yellow Woman," he said.

I turned to face him. "Who are you?" I asked.

He laughed and knelt on the low, sandy bank, washing his face in the river. "Last night you guessed my name, and you knew why I had come."

I stared past him at the shallow moving water and tried to remember the night, but I could only see the moon in the water and remember his warmth around me.

"But I only said that you were him and that I was Yellow Woman—I'm not really her—I have my own name and I come from the pueblo on the other side of the mesa. Your name is Silva and you are a stranger I met by the river yesterday afternoon."

He laughed softly. "What happened yesterday has nothing to do with what you will do today, Yellow Woman."

"I know—that's what I'm saying—the old stories about the ka'tsina spirit and Yellow Woman can't mean us."

My old grandpa liked to tell these stories best. There is one about Badger and Coyote who went hunting and were gone all day, and when the sun was going down they found a house. There was a girl living there alone, and she had light hair and eyes and she told them that they could sleep with her. Coyote wanted to be with her all night so he sent Badger into a prairie-dog hole, telling him he thought he saw something in it. As soon as Badger crawled in, Coyote blocked up the entrance with rocks and hurried back to Yellow Woman.

"Come here," he said gently.

He touched my neck and I moved close to him to feel his breathing and to hear his heart. I was wondering if Yellow Woman had known who she was—if she knew that she would become part of the stories. Maybe she'd had another name that her husband and relatives called her so that only the ka'tsina from the north and the storytellers would know her as Yellow Woman. But I didn't go on; I felt him all around me, pushing me down into the white river sand.

Yellow Woman went away with the spirit from the north and lived with him and his relatives. She was gone for a long time, but then one day she came back and she brought twin boys.

"Do you know the story?"

"What story?" He smiled and pulled me close to him as he said this. I was afraid lying there on the red blanket. All I could know was the way he felt, warm, damp, his body beside me. This is the way it happens in the stories, I was thinking, with no thought beyond the moment she meets the ka'tsina spirit and they go.

"I don't have to go. What they tell in stories was real only then, back in time immemorial, like they say."

He stood up and pointed at my clothes tangled in the blanket. "Let's go," he said.

I walked beside him, breathing hard because he walked fast, his hand around my wrist. I had stopped trying to pull away from him, because his hand felt cool and the sun was high, drying the river bed into alkali. I will see someone, eventually I will see someone, and then I will be certain that he is only a man—some man from nearby—and I will be sure that I am not Yellow Woman. Because she is from out of time past and I live now and I've been to school and there are highways and pickup trucks that Yellow Woman never saw.

It was an easy ride north on horseback. I watched the change from the cottonwood trees along the river to the junipers that brushed past us in the foothills, and finally there were only piñons, and when I looked up at the rim of the mountain plateau I could see pine trees growing on the edge. Once I stopped to look down, but the pale sandstone had disappeared and the river was gone and the dark lava hills were all around. He touched my hand, not speaking, but always singing softly a mountain song and looking into my eyes.

I felt hungry and wondered what they were doing at home now—my mother, my grandmother, my husband, and the baby. Cooking breakfast, saying, "Where did she go?—maybe kidnaped." And Al going to the tribal police with the details: "She went walking along the river."

The house was made with black lava rock and red mud. It was high above the spreading miles of arroyos and long mesas. I smelled a mountain smell of pitch and buck brush. I stood there beside the black horse, looking down on the small, dim country we had passed, and I shivered.

"Yellow Woman, come inside where it's warm."

He lit a fire in the stove. It was an old stove with a round belly and an enamel coffeepot on top. There was only the stove, some faded Navajo blankets, and a bedroll and cardboard box. The floor was made of smooth adobe plaster, and there was one small window facing east. He pointed at the box.

"There's some potatoes and the frying pan." He sat on the floor with his arms around his knees pulling them close to his chest and he watched me fry the potatoes. I didn't mind him watching me because he was always watching me—he had been watching me since I came upon him sitting on the river bank trimming leaves from a willow twig with his knife. We ate from the pan and he wiped the grease from his fingers on his Levi's.

"Have you brought women here before?" He smiled and kept chewing, so I said, "Do you always use the same tricks?"

"What tricks?" He looked at me like he didn't understand.

"The story about being a ka'tsina from the mountains. The story about Yellow Woman."

Silva was silent; his face was calm.

"I don't believe it. Those stories couldn't happen now," I said.

He shook his head and said softly, "But someday they will talk about us, and they will say 'Those two lived long ago when things like that happened.'"

He stood up and went out. I ate the rest of the potatoes and thought about things—about the noise the stove was making and the sound of the mountain wind outside. I remembered yesterday and the day before, and then I went outside.

I walked past the corral to the edge where the narrow trail cut through the black rim rock. I was standing in the sky with nothing around me but the wind that came down from the blue mountain peak behind me. I could see faint mountain images in the distance miles across the vast spread of mesas and valleys and plains. I wondered who was over there to feel the moun-

tain wind on those sheer blue edges—who walks on the pine needles in those blue mountains.

"Can you see the pueblo?" Silva was standing behind me.

I shook my head. "We're too far away."

"From here I can see the world." He stepped out on the edge. "The Navajo reservation begins over there." He pointed to the east. "The Pueblo boundaries are over here." He looked below us to the south, where the narrow trail seemed to come from. "The Texans have their ranches over there, starting with that valley, the Concho Valley. The Mexicans run some cattle over there too."

"Do you ever work for them?"

"I steal from them," Silva answered. The sun was dropping behind us and the shadows were filling the land below. I turned away from the edge that dropped forever into the valleys below.

"I'm cold," I said, "I'm going inside." I started wondering about this man who could speak the Pueblo language so well but who lived on a mountain and rustled cattle. I decided that this man Silva must be Navajo, because Pueblo men didn't do things like that.

"You must be a Navajo."

Silva shook his head gently. "Little Yellow Woman," he said, "you never give up, do you? I have told you who I am. The Navajo people know me, too." He knelt down and unrolled the bedroll and spread the extra blankets out on a piece of canvas. The sun was down, and the only light in the house came from outside—the dim orange light from sundown.

I stood there and waited for him to crawl under the blankets.

"What are you waiting for?" he said, and I lay down beside him. He undressed me slowly like the night before beside the river—kissing my face gently and running his hands up and down my belly and legs. He took off my pants and then he laughed.

"Why are you laughing?"

"You are breathing so hard."

I pulled away from him and turned my back to him.

He pulled me around and pinned me down with his arms and chest. "You don't understand, do you, little Yellow Woman? You will do what I want."

And again he was all around me with his skin slippery against mine, and I was afraid because I understood that his strength could hurt me. I lay underneath him and I knew that he could destroy me. But later, while he slept beside me, I touched his face and I had a feeling— the kind of feeling for him that overcame me that morning along the river. I kissed him on the forehead and he reached out for me.

When I woke up in the morning he was gone. It gave me a strange feeling because for a long time I sat there on the blankets and looked around the little house for some object of his— some proof that he had been there or maybe that he was coming back. Only the blankets and the cardboard box remained. The .30-30 that had been leaning in the corner was gone, and so was the knife I had used the night before. He was gone, and I had my chance to go now. But first I had to eat, because I knew it would be a long walk home.

I found some dried apricots in the cardboard box, and I sat down on a rock at the edge of the plateau rim. There was no wind and the sun warmed me. I was surrounded by silence. I drowsed with apricots in my mouth, and I didn't believe that there were highways or railroads or cattle to steal.

When I woke up, I stared down at my feet in the black mountain dirt. Little black ants were swarming over the pine needles around my foot. They must have smelled the apricots. I thought about my family far below me. They would be wondering about me, because this had never happened to me before. The tribal police would file a report. But if old Grandpa weren't dead he would tell them what happened—he would laugh and say, "Stolen by a ka'tsina, a mountain spirit. She'll come home—they usually do." There are enough of them to handle things. My mother and grandmother will raise the baby like they raised me. Al will find someone else, and they will go on like before, except that there will be a story about the day I disappeared while I was walking along the river. Silva had come for me; he said he had. I did not decide to go. I just went. Moonflowers blossom in the sand hills before dawn, just as I followed him. That's what I was thinking as I wandered along the trail through the pine trees.

It was noon when I got back. When I saw the stone house I remembered that I had meant to go home. But that didn't seem important any more, maybe because there were little blue flowers growing in the meadow behind the stone house and the gray squirrels were playing in the pines next to the house. The horses were standing in the corral, and there was a beef carcass hanging on the shady side of a big pine in front of the house. Flies buzzed around the clotted blood that hung from the carcass. Silva was washing his hands in a bucket full of water. He must have heard me coming because he spoke to me without turning to face me.

"I've been waiting for you."

"I went walking in the big pine trees."

I looked into the bucket full of bloody water with brown-and-white animal hairs floating in it. Silva stood there letting his hand drip, examining me intently.

"Are you coming with me?"

"Where?" I asked him.

"To sell the meat in Marquez."

"If you're sure it's O.K."

"I wouldn't ask you if it wasn't," he answered.

He sloshed the water around in the bucket before he dumped it out and set the bucket upside down near the door. I followed him to the corral and watched him saddle the horses. Even beside the horses he looked tall, and I asked him again if he wasn't Navajo. He didn't say anything; he just shook his head and kept cinching up the saddle.

"But Navajos are tall."

"Get on the horse," he said, "and let's go."

The last thing he did before we started down the steep trail was to grab the .30-30 from the corner. He slid the rifle into the scabbard that hung from his saddle.

"Do they ever try to catch you?" I asked.

"They don't know who I am."

"Then why did you bring the rifle?"

"Because we are going to Marquez where the Mexicans live."

The trail leveled out on a narrow ridge that was steep on both sides like an animal spine. On one side I could see where the trail went around the rocky gray hills and disappeared into the southeast where the pale sandrock mesas stood in the distance near my home. On the other side was a trail that went west, and as I looked far into the distance I thought I saw the little town. But Silva said no, that I was looking in the wrong place, that I just thought I saw houses. After that I quit looking off into the distance; it was hot and the wildflowers were closing up their deep-yellow petals. Only the waxy cactus flowers bloomed in the bright sun, and I saw every color that a cactus blossom can be; the white ones and the red ones were still buds, but the purple and the yellow were blossoms, open full and the most beautiful of all.

Silva saw him before I did. The white man was riding a big gray horse, coming up the trail towards us. He was traveling fast and the gray horse's feet sent rocks rolling off the trail into the dry tumbleweeds. Silva motioned for me to stop and we watched the white man. He didn't see us right away, but finally his horse whinnied at our horses and he stopped. He looked at us briefly before he lapped the gray horse across the three hundred yards that separated us. He stopped his horse in front of Silva, and his young fat face was shadowed by the brim of his hat. He didn't look mad, but his small, pale eyes moved from the blood-soaked gunny sacks hanging from my saddle to Silva's face and then back to my face.

"Where did you get the fresh meat?" the white man asked.

"I've been hunting," Silva said, and when he shifted his weight in the saddle the leather creaked.

"The hell you have, Indian. You've been rustling cattle. We've been looking for the thief for a long time."

The rancher was fat, and sweat began to soak through his white cowboy shirt and the wet cloth stuck to the thick rolls of belly fat. He almost seemed to be panting from the exertion of talking, and he smelled rancid, maybe because Silva scared him.

Silva turned to me and smiled. "Go back up the mountain, Yellow Woman."

The white man got angry when he heard Silva speak in a language he couldn't understand. "Don't try anything, Indian. Just keep riding to Marquez. We'll call the state police from there."

The rancher must have been unarmed because he was very frightened and if he had a gun he would have pulled it out then. I turned my horse around and the rancher yelled, "Stop!" I looked at Silva for an instant and there was something ancient and dark—something I could feel in my stomach—in his eyes, and when I glanced at his hand I saw his finger on the trigger of the .30-30 that was still in the saddle scabbard. I slapped my horse across the flank and the sacks of raw meat swung against my knees as the horse leaped up the trail. It was hard to keep my balance, and once I thought I felt the saddle slipping backward; it was because of this that I could not look back.

I didn't stop until I reached the ridge where the trail forked. The horse was breathing deep gasps and there was a dark film of sweat on its neck. I looked down in the direction I had come from, but I couldn't see the place. I waited. The wind came up and pushed warm air past me. I looked up at the sky, pale blue and full of thin clouds and fading vapor trails left by jets.

I think four shots were fired—I remember hearing four hollow explosions that reminded me of deer hunting. There could have been more shots after that, but I couldn't have heard them because my horse was running again and the loose rocks were making too much noise as they scattered around his feet.

Horses have a hard time running downhill, but I went that way instead of uphill to the mountain because I thought it was safer. I felt better with the horse running southeast past the round gray hills that were covered with cedar trees and black lava rock. When I got to the plain in the distance I could see the dark green patches of tamaracks that grew along the river; and beyond the river I could see the beginning of the pale sandrock mesas. I stopped the horse and looked back to see if anyone was coming; then I got off the horse and turned the horse around, wondering if it would go back to its corral under the pines on the mountain. It looked back at me for a moment and then plucked a mouthful of green tumbleweeds before it trotted back up the trail with its ears pointed forward, carrying its head daintily to one side to avoid stepping on the dragging reins. When the horse disappeared over the last hill, the gunny sacks full of meat were still swinging and bouncing.

I walked toward the river on a wood-hauler's road that I knew would eventually lead to the paved road. I was thinking about waiting beside the road for someone to drive by, but by the time I got to the pavement I had decided it wasn't very far to walk if I followed the river back the way Silva and I had come.

The river water tasted good, and I sat in the shade under a cluster of silvery willows. I thought about Silva, and I felt sad at leaving him; still, there was something strange about him, and I tried to figure it out all the way back home.

I came back to the place on the river bank where he had been sitting the first time I saw him. The green willow leaves that he had trimmed from the branch were still lying there, wilted in the sand. I saw the leaves and I wanted to go back to him—to kiss him and to touch him—but the mountains were too far away now. And I told myself, because I believe it, he will come back sometime and be waiting again by the river.

I followed the path up from the river into the village. The sun was getting low, and I could smell supper cooking when I got to the screen door of my house. I could hear their voices inside—my mother was telling my grandmother how to fix the Jell-O and my husband, Al, was playing with the baby. I decided to tell them that some Navajo had kidnaped me, but I was sorry that old Grandpa wasn't alive to hear my story because it was the Yellow Woman stories he liked to tell best.

How It Works

1. Underline the descriptions of setting in this story. Notice the choice of details, the placement of the description, and how the characters interact with the land. What techniques does the author use to evoke emotion and develop theme and conflict through the setting?

2. At the end of the story, the main character returns home. How do you think her life will be different after this day? What information has the author provided that led you to your conclusion?

3. How would you describe the character of Silva? What details does the author use to convey his personality traits? What details does she use to characterize the relationship between the two main characters? What would have been the effect if, instead, she had described it using adjectives? Pick a passage and rewrite it, using more adjectives and adverbs to clarify the characters' emotions. What is the effect?

4. How does the author use the Yellow Woman legend to enhance the story? What would have been lost if she had decided not to include it? Underline places in the story that refer to this legend. Notice that Silko doesn't explain it in detail. How does she introduce and develop it? How does she relate it to the characters? Can you think of a legend or tradition that relates to a story you're working on? Try using some of Silko's techniques to introduce it into your story. How is the story enhanced? What difficulties do you encounter?

Mary Austin Speaker

Mary Austin Speaker received her BFA from Emerson College in 1999, where she received the undergraduate Senior Writing Award for her poetry thesis, A Human Admission. Her work has appeared in The Boston Poet *and in* Timeless, *an anthology (Thoughts Falling Press, 1997), and on bothmagazine.com. She explains that "The Day the Flames Would Stop" came from a scene from a much longer as-yet-to-be-written work. "It began as a twenty-five-page novel outline, and was eventually whittled down to the wedding scene and the creation of an atmosphere surrounding the characters, which helped in my discovery of their foreground and background. The workshop in which I wrote this story was invaluable in helping me to hone its direction and point out the characters' most striking aspects." Speaker lives in Brooklyn, designing books for a living, writing poems and the beginnings of many stories. Someday she plans to finish another one.*

The Day the Flames Would Stop

On a Thursday in May of 1992, at eight o'clock in the morning, Alice and Jim were just past Flagstaff on U.S. 40. They had stopped speaking somewhere around Tucumcari in New Mexico, the silence between them comfortable and expected. Alice watched the road, or she watched Jim watching the road while the Chevy truck's engine buzzed dully and Johnny Cash sang a droll "Ring of Fire." Jim was driving as he always did, hunched over the steering wheel and staring forward at the road, his brow furrowed and raised at once. With her eyes, Alice traced the lines of his forehead, the long slope of his nose, his slightly crooked lips, the small round chin, and the slope toward his neck. This was what she would see every morning for the rest of her life. Jim's neck, Jim's face, Jim's shoulder, all turned away to the window, would be the first thing she'd see every day. Jim's profile before breakfast, and at dinner when he came home from work. She saw more of his profile than any other part of him. He was always occupied in his thoughts, or in his books. She liked this about him; he wasn't like the rest, the ones that she could read like an open book before a month was up. It had been seven months, and she still hadn't been able to read him.

The baby was another puzzle. She passed a hand over her stomach and felt the growing bulge. When she went to sleep she could think nothing but, This must be how dark it is. She would curl into fetal position and imagine herself in a vast dark womb, alone, surrounded by warm liquids. Her own body seemed too poor a place to grow a child, but she'd gained four pounds since she'd found out at six weeks. Already she was becoming consumed with mothersome thoughts: picturing the birth, the cry, the gurgle and clasping of hands, the feeding. Jim talked about it all the time, and whispered things to the growing small child in her womb when they lay awake in bed at night. It might seal their bond, she thought. It might seal her own gaps.

The highway sprawled out before them, long and grey and wandering off into the distance. She had no idea what would be on the other side of the desert. Vegas was a mecca for those who were looking to strike something, anything. People looked for the rest of their lives there. Some kind of luck, she thought. Maybe it really was there, a great mound of it in the sand, waiting to be tooled down and doled out to the poor unfortunates that wandered in with their shovels and empty bags. As they passed through the desert she felt a movement in her belly. She soothed it with a caress, and closed her eyes. This must be how dark it is. Her eyes opened and she looked out at the endless flat horizon. She wondered what it would be like to see light for the first time.

Jim's eyes were fixed on the road, the arrow-straight highway that sliced through the middle of the dry land. The horizon floated before them for hours on end, never-ending, dwarfing and flat everywhere. He couldn't help but feel like an ant marching across the desert, driven by something bigger than himself. They were all ants anyway, all little drones put here for a purpose of building something huge and intricate. Alice was pregnant, must be a sign he should stay around for a while.

They were driving to Las Vegas, and even though he'd been there before he got the feeling they were heading somewhere he couldn't even imagine, that the highway would continue forever until they both died. The sun would take care of that, he thought. Living in Texas his whole life had shown him how nature could rule a person. How the weather could darken your mood, how the sun could make you happy. Women could do the same thing, take over your whole train of thought until it lurched right off its tracks. Alice was nestled deep within him and surrounded him at once, and he reveled in the way she encompassed him. The first time he realized it they were in his truck, she was on her back with her hair spread out. Her eyes played over him like small searchlights, focusing here, there. She told him to shut up when he said that he loved her. He'd only known her for two weeks; she wouldn't jump the gun like he would. He had to work on her for a few weeks until she agreed to go to Vegas.

His life as a bachelor passed before his eyes as he stared at the highway. Every mile marker was another memory that would never happen again. He passed mile number four hundred and ninety: Mexico, peyote, the mountain. Another ten miles, the cheap girl he picked up on Main Street at the Bone. Five hundred and ten: Boystown, the nickel show with the girl and the donkey. Five hundred and twenty: parking cars at the symphony center to get enough money for a few beers at Pete's Grill. He wasn't sad to see them go. He looked at Alice again, the way her dark lips jutted out from her fair skin made all the mile markers fade into some far-off deep darkness within him. He smiled to himself and drew in her presence beside him like a clean breath; this was why she was here. She would save him. She would pour over him like white light and find the parts of him he thought had been killed. He could feel them waking up as the sun was setting. Everything seemed ridiculously symbolic—the mile markers, the sunset—he knew by the time dawn came they would be in Las Vegas pledging their lives to one another. He felt good.

Marriage, she thought. What a fucked up concept. Even though there was a part of her that thought of Jim as *the one*, her doubts were beginning to well up. She was twenty. She was pregnant. But they were all going down in flames soon, anyway, like Jim said. No reason not to do what they could while they were here. This was kind of an exploration, a search to see if they could make something no one else ever had. They already had something, and beyond the singular fire that crept up all around them they had *someone*. Her mind swam with curiosity when she imagined what a combination of herself and Jim would be like. She half-hoped it would be quiet like Jim. She put their features together like a jigsaw puzzle, his confused brow, her fair skin, his small chin, her thin fingers. It would be beautiful. She rolled down the window and stared into the small rounded mirror on the side of the Chevy at her own reflection. Her reflection squinted back at her as though saying, "Don't look at me." She stared into it. She did this compulsively, even when she was driving, watching her eyes in the rearview mirror. It wasn't out of vanity, but curiosity. Could she read her own thoughts on her face? Yes. Just like she could on everyone else's. Except Jim's. One of the main reasons they were together, she thought, was that she didn't know why he loved her, and he didn't know why she loved him. It was better that way. If he knew it was the way he kept escaping her, like the answer to a riddle she'd *almost* figured out, he'd get a big head. He considered himself quite the enigma, but believed, for some reason, that she understood him. Or that she was like him, and that put them right up there together. She didn't exactly agree with that either. If she knew why he loved her, she might actually figure him out.

They reached Las Vegas just as dawn was breaking over the hills. The city loomed up in front of them and she curled into his arm as they watched the new sunlight gleaming off the smooth planes of the skyscraping hotels. They drove into town slowly, passing the Monte Carlo, the Carriage House, the infamous Caesar's Palace. Glittery golddiggers wandered the streets, still in their evening wear, still in their evening stupor.

"Hey, how about some breakfast before we sign our lives away?" she asked.

"I'm not hungry, but okay." His eyes drifted closed for a second. "Actually I could use some coffee."

They pulled into the parking lot of an orange-rimmed shack called the Metro Diner and ordered coffee, coffee, hashbrowns, toast, an egg.

He shifted his position in the booth three times, drummed his fingers on the table, and looked around at the identical orange plastic booths.

Alice looked at his profile. She stayed his hand. "You're so fidgety. Nervous?"

"What? Naw, I'm not nervous." He ran his free hand through his hair and sat hunched, scratching the back of his neck. He looked up at her. "What are you looking at? Do I look that nervous?"

"Um, yeah. You look like you did something stupid and I found out about it." She released his clammy hand. "Did you do something stupid I should know about?" she questioned.

He laughed, nervously. "No. I'm not nervous." He took a cigarette from his pack and lit it, inhaling for too long. He glanced around the restaurant. "What's to be nervous about? Getting married?"

"Don't act like it's no big deal. It is a big deal." She took his hand again and twined her fingers through his.

"People do this every day. Especially here. Look over there." He pointed to a couple across the restaurant. "Newlyweds. Look at those grins. Happiness in fifteen minutes. Didn't you see the billboard for Annie's Quickie-Wed on the way into town?" He put his hand on hers. "We've got nothing to lose."

Nothing to lose. Hell of a thing to say in Vegas. Only hope, she thought. The waitress showed up with their food and gave them a knowing smile as she arranged the place settings on the table. "I feel like everyone knows what we're about to do. I don't know. Getting married doesn't seem that romantic here. It's like going to get a burger, just something people do."

"That's exactly what it is. We're just doing it. No forethought." He sipped his coffee, winced, and began putting cream in it.

"See what happens with no forethought? You get burned." she said with a smirk. "Besides, it's kind of hard not to have forethought when you have about eight hours of highway to contemplate before you do a thing. It's not like we just sort of appeared here. Everything takes time. But people here don't even know about time. Nothing's real here. It's all glitz and plastic and paint covering up the shitty insides. I don't want to end up like that." She blew on her coffee.

"You worry too much. It'll be fine." Jim began spreading jelly on his toast.

"I suppose . . . ask me again, would you? Just to get me in the mood."

"You're incurable, you know that?" He pushed himself out of the booth and got down on one knee and took her hand again. "Alice, darling . . . will you marry me?"

"Yeah." She smiled. She breathed a sigh of relief. It would be fine. Just like he said.

"So how about the Holy House of Elvis?" Jim suggested.

"*No.* I don't even like Elvis. There's gotta be something at least *pretty* around here." Alice folded her arms in front of her. They finished their breakfast and began searching for a place to get married.

"The Original Chapel of Love?"

"Uh-uh." she shook her head. "Let's try down Flamingo Road."

Jim made a U-turn on Las Vegas Boulevard and turned right onto Flamingo. A few neon-lit chapels appeared, a spangled showgirl and a fat man in a suit stumbled laughing out of the The Golden House of Marriage. A nervous frail woman and a tall thin man were entering Annie's Quick-Wed. The white picket fence made Jim laugh.

"What?" she smiled, glancing at him.

"Nothing. How about this one? Looks barely respectable." They neared the Chapel of the Holy Sorrows, and Alice nodded.

"This is it."

They parked next to the chapel, and stood observing it for a moment. It was white, wooden, neat. Rows of red Gerber daisies snaked along the front walk, leading to a small porch with white iron railings. They walked to the front door, where a small electric candle burned under an ornate etched glass shell. They knocked. A tall woman appeared, and spoke in a low serious tone. "You wish to wed?"

"Yes. Yes, we do," Jim said, bracing himself on the rail with one hand and on Alice's shoulder with the other. This was the beginning of the rest of his life. No reason not to, he thought.

"Come in." She swept her hand out to welcome them, and they entered the dim parlor. An old couple dressed in Sunday clothing sat reading newspapers on a flowered couch. They looked up as Jim and Alice stood awkwardly before them.

"Oh, Ned, look. They'll make a lovely couple. We'll be your witnesses today, dears. I'm Nora Keene and this is my husband Ned. We were married here ourselves. Isn't it lovely?" The old woman smiled thinly at them and smoothed her lace collar.

Alice said nothing. Jim stood wondering where the tall woman had gone. She reappeared in another doorway and beckoned them into a room.

A man with a white priest's collar sat behind a large desk. His hands were folded, and he grinned at them over a pair of thick glasses. "You all sure about this? People often jump the gun here in Las Vegas." He smiled.

"Sure as sure can be, Father. We've come a long way for this," Jim said, his voice wavering a little.

"And you, Miss? Are you ready?" He peered at Alice.

"Yes, Father." She took Jim's hand and looked at his profile. Jim looked back at her. He leaned and kissed her.

"Well, I can see the two of you mean it. We'll get this done quicker than water off a duck's back. Just fill out these forms, and we'll have you two husband and wife in a jiffy."

They sat at the desk and began filling out the forms. Alice felt her face begin to grow warm as she penned in her name, place of birth, all the necessary information. This was not how she thought she would be married. She had planned her whole marriage out when she was a little girl, and a chapel in Las Vegas was not it. There were no white weddings here, just short, squat men in white collars performing ceremonies they'd learned for fifty bucks in a correspondence course.

But it would be fine. She signed her name at the bottom. Jim was signing his name. "All finished." He took hers and passed their forms to the priest.

"Very good. Just through the yellow door you'll find the chapel; that's where the service will be conducted. Jim, you go on in, and Alice, follow Miss Liza. She'll take care of you." the priest hefted himself up from his chair with his short stubby arms, and followed Jim into the

Chapel. "Quicker than water off a duck's back," Alice heard him say to Jim as she followed the tall woman into the bridal room.

She chose a light blue veil, and a nice bunch of white daisies from the cooler in the bridal room. She looked at her reflection in the mirror. "Only happens once," she thought.

As she walked into the chapel, Nora Keene began playing "Here Comes the Bride" a little too jauntily. She felt a small kick in her stomach. The baby. It knew, too, what they were doing. Was it a soft, approving kick? A warning? Jim gazed at her as she walked; she could see the hope in his eyes. She cast her own down, thinking that she would never tell him that this felt very wrong. In an instant she knew why he loved her, and why she wanted the baby. He thought the flames would stop—she would save him, the baby would save him. She could read it on his face.

How It Works

1. Why this day? How would the story be different if the author had chosen to set it on the day after the wedding, or at some later date? What does this particular choice add to the story? Suppose you were discussing the story in class and someone suggested developing the events that precede this day into scenes? How would you respond?

2. What does the location of the story in Las Vegas add to it? How would it be different if it took place in Salt Lake City, in Miami, or in New York? Underline places where the author's description of the setting adds to your understanding of the characters or the conflict.

3. Mary Austin Speaker is primarily a poet, and her sensitivity to language is evident in the way this story shifts skillfully between two points of view. Underline the transitions. Exactly how does the author accomplish these moves from character to character?

4. What does the main character realize on her wedding day? How does the author set up that realization? What problem or problems does she pose early in the story, and how does she intensify and develop those as the story progresses? Try plotting this story's narrative arc. Place all of the major events where they belong on the arc.

Darrell Spencer

Darrell Spencer grew up in Las Vegas, Nevada. He now teaches at Ohio University in Athens, Ohio. Spencer has published three collections of stories: A Woman Packing a Pistol, Our Secret's Out *and* Caution: Men in Trees. *"I am above all interested in telling a good story, which, for me, means finding the voice that feels genuine," he says. "That voice is somehow honest to the tale it is inventing." He is interested in language— "the demotic, slang, argot, shop talk. My work is driven by an aesthetic that novelist Stanley Elkin identified as the 'the great gift of fiction: that it gives language an opportunity to happen.'"*

Park Host

So Rose and Red Cogsby, they get into these one-on-ones where they lock horns, do these everyday equivalents of Piper Cub open-cockpit wingovers (years back when his wits were quicker and his feet still good, Red flew supply drops and the U.S. mail into Nevada mountains and deserts, was expert in the Great Basin the way you are master of and have down cold the streets you drive to and from work). So anyway, Rose and Red, they get into these give-and-takes, push-and-shoves, these climb-and-stall-and-reverse-your-directions until Red says, "You forget, I have my hat on," and she says, "Meaning what, that I'm under arrest?" Borrowed lines from one of the Frankenstein sequels, the movie where Dr. Frankenstein's son returns to his ancestral castle and he's determined he's not going to repeat his father's mistakes, but of course he does.

Krogh, the police inspector, the one whose arm the monster tore from its roots and tossed aside in the landmark original film, has come to arrest Herr Dr. Frankenstein—the son, that is. Ygor's goaded the monster into revenge and a murder spree, and the Inspector is here to accuse young Dr. Frankenstein of knowing, at the very least, who's to blame. It's clear Krogh thinks Ygor and Dr. Frankenstein are in cahoots. Basil Rathbone plays the son. His pencil-line mustache is jittery. He snarls, "Is it the legendary monster of my father's time, or am I supposed to have whipped one up as a housewife whips up an omelet? I've been here a month, you know."

The Inspector confronts Frankenstein, irks him. All the time Basil's pitching darts at a dartboard, throwing bull's-eyes and retrieving them. "There's a monster afoot," Inspector Krogh says. "And you know it."

Basil flings darts, baits the Inspector toss after toss, needles the hell out of him, until the Inspector says, "You forget, I have my hat on."

The hat's a matter of form. Signifies official business.

"Meaning what," Basil says, "that I'm under arrest?"

The Inspector clicks his heels together and resets his wooden arm. Basil *is* under arrest.

So, on his way out of their camper this afternoon, Red says to Rose, "You forget. I have my hat on," and she, huddled close to the 13-inch Sony, which is jacked up loud, *Talk Back Live* on, says, "Then take it off." She's supposed to feed him Frankenstein's line.

Or ad-lib something equally droll.

Repartee.

Quid pro quo.

Quip for quip. Dart, as the movie would have it, for dart. Zinger for zinger.

One time she said, "What, you've got a monster up your butt?" She can be salty. She's said, "Hat, smat." And once, "Go tell it to the villagers."

Only a gooseneck lamp is on in the camper when Red says, "You forget, I have my hat on," and Rose says, "Then take it off." The lamp's at Rose's side, on a tilt-top table, bent so it could be flesh-eating plant life sizing up her face.

These days, Rose keeps every rectangle of curtain shut. *Talk Back Live*, taking a break from the O. J. Simpson trial, is about the South Carolina woman who drowned her boys and then told the world a black man kidnapped them. Just babies, they were. Michael, three. Alex, a little over a year. The studio audience is forgiving her, saying what she did was not her doing, arguing it was not really the woman who strapped her boys in and let the car roll into the lake. It was the devil incarnate. They're claiming you have to distinguish act from person. Some lamebrain dressed head-to-toe in denim, a 9-inch daisy embroidered smack-dead-center on her chest, another daisy sewn to the crown of her floppy hat, this fool is saying, "Jesus can forgive. If Jesus can forgive her, where would I be with Jesus if I didn't forgive?"

As if she is Christ's personal friend.

Red hesitates on his way out the camper's door long enough to say, "Who died and made her our redeemer?"

Not a peep from Rose. She's been mopey and has wasted no words for weeks. Red and Rose, their talk's turned basic. You up. I'm up. Good. Do this. Do that. Curt and fundamental, that's Red and Rose Cogsby. Red misses their pillow talk, their comparing of notes. He's a man who relishes the bones they pick. Daily, Red fills the Prowler with the noise of his being, trusting against logic she'll take notice, and she's steadfastly aloof, sometimes icy. End result is Red feels like a beggar, like a clod wagging the dog's tail, hoping for a grin.

On the TV, a man gets to his feet and the woman who runs this show skips over and puts a mike in his face. He says, "God just borrowed to her the children. They back now with God."

Square his IQ and the man'd still be in trouble.

Red says to Rose, "Someone ought to check to see how much of that guy's brain is actually missing in action." He resets his cap, tugging at its bill, fitting it solidly to his head. Is about to repeat his line, to say, "You forget, I have my hat on," when the savvy part of his brain, that seat of common sense and wisdom that got him through wind shear and dust storm back when he was flying the mail, warns him now is not the time.

Rose, glued to the TV, waves Red out of the camper, tells him she draped the kitchen throw rug over the picnic table to dry and if he brings it in now or later he's to shake it in case there are earwigs. "Look it up and down, front and back. Flap it good," she says. "And take out the birds." Used to be, before she took the blues to her heart, Rose'd have the budgies out by 7 A.M. Now they're still in their cage in a dark corner of the camper. One, Kathie Lee, is sour-apple green, and the other one, Regis, is sky-blue.

Rose and Red, they're here in Canyon Glen Park east of Provo, Utah. He's the park host, has been every summer for twenty-three years, and this afternoon he does have official business, it being July 6th, the day after the 5th, which was the day everyone celebrated the 4th because it fell on a Sunday and Utah shuts down for the Sabbath. Yesterday was, as Red's grandkids put things, the holiday from hell. Someone reported a man carrying a gun, and five sheriffs in five 4-Runners showed up, ex-football types carrying shotguns, nervous sullen men who concentrated on the ground and their own feet. One had a Remington sniper rifle. Turned out the man with a gun was a man with a camera. Must have been three hundred people in campgrounds fit for one-third that number. The Utah Boys Ranch delivered carloads full of juvenile delinquents. One ran away and wasn't located until dark. Another one lost his temper and, given his limited and crude perspective on the world, didn't know what the civilized thing to do was, so he tore his clothes off and sat naked on a picnic table. Red kept chasing after kids and their firecrackers, but caught no one.

So, on his way out, Red collects the budgies, and, hiking their cage onto a shoulder, uses his foot to nudge the Prowler's door open, which is so narrow and otherwise dinky and flimsy it always reminds him of the door to the pisser on an airplane. He juggles the budgies' cage, gets leverage and a firmer grip, eases it through the door, stands on the footstool they use as a step, and says to Rose, "If you look in the local section of last night's paper you'll find an article that tells you how to keep earwigs out of your garden."

"A duck is how," she says.

Damn, but she knows stuff. Red's taken again by the miscellany Rose has up her sleeve. "That sounds good to me," he says. "I didn't read it," and he leans in for a final look, anticipation in his left eye and optimism in his right. Shows no fear of her wretched melancholy. Hope is the horse he rides.

And she speaks to him.

"Hate those things," Rose says. She means the earwigs.

"They are one of God's ugliest creatures," Red says. He shifts the budgies' cage around and resets his legs for balance.

She says, "They're like something big made small, so out of spite they end up ugly and underfoot, like a dinosaur brought to its knees, made to say uncle." She puts her hand to her mouth as if she's checking it for puffiness.

"You got that right," he says.

Smart as an encyclopedia, Rose is, and she used to rise early and whistle tunes. Now she's a killjoy. The overriding problem seems to be the dark cloud called the O. J. Simpson trial. She's up to her elbows in it. Is angry. Is getting peeved about what she sees as justice going down the tubes. All day she watches the trial, bouncing from CNN to OJE, and most of the night, into the A.M., she hunts talk shows—*Larry King Live, Geraldo, Leno*—for the jokes and the dancing Itos. Lots of ire on her part. Indignation. Rose won't miss *Dateline.* She sends Red into Provo to pick up the *L.A. Times* at Barnes & Noble, and she reads the tabloids, but only the O. J. news.

Red transfers the budgies to their large outside cage. It's full of ladders, bells, monkey bars, and spinning wheels. He settles the birds, then fills their feeders. Grass seeds, millet, groats. He slices up an apple and a banana. Regis, the sky-blue budgie, nips at a triangular music box and it plays "You Are My Sunshine." A second box can play "Take Me Out to the Ball Game." Red

sets up this cage as far from where he and Rose eat as their campsite allows. The budgies are messy. There is a redwood table centered on the 10-by-15-foot slab of cement that serves as their patio. First thing he does when they pull the Prowler in each spring is to hook up the cable TV. Then he covers the cement pad with Astroturf. A cloth awning attached to the top of the trailer unrolls and stretches over the patio. Their camp is ten yards from the river and is surrounded by trees, is shaded all day long, never gets hotter than eighty, even in July and August. Nights, it's cool enough for cloth jackets. Red wipes the nozzle of a used Windex sprayer he's filled with water and mists Kathie Lee and Regis. They preen and chat. Join the day's bird songs.

"Beautiful afternoon," Red says to the budgies.

Regis says, "Pretty neat."

Kathie Lee says, "Get a fix on it. Get a fix on it." It's something Rose taught her.

Two hours later, Red's filled the bed of a city pickup with bags of trash from the park cans, and he's taking a break, loitering here halfway across the wooden footbridge just south of their camper. He rests his arms on its railing. The Provo River, brown and green, is high and fast, meaner than it was last year or the year before. Below him, on its bank, a man and a woman are sitting on boulders. Their black Lab paws at leaves caught in an eddy. The man's got hair thick as a bobcat's. Like everyone these days, he's wearing a goatee. He's smoking. On the other bank are the remains of a fire. Shouldn't be. You can't get into the park and not run headlong into a sign that lists the park rules and hours. 8 A.M. – 10:30 P.M. NO ALCOHOL / PETS ON LEASH ONLY / NO MOTORIZED VEHICLES / FIRES IN FIRERINGS ONLY / NO LOUD MUSIC. The signs tell you to

SEE THE PARK HOST ABOUT FEE SCHEDULES.

That's Red, the park host, only he'll admit he doesn't know the fees, will tell you he ought to after all these years, but they change and he misplaces the sheet the state gives him every spring, so charges overnighters a couple of bucks is all.

He digs a pack of Camels from his shirt pocket and smacks the box against his palm, rotating the pack, side, bottom, side, top, the way his family does, so loud he could be striking someone. He pulls the pack's thread, pockets its cellophane, flicks open the lid, and taps one free. Stewing is what he's at. Thinking on Rose and on her short fuse. Is pondering how touchy she is. Not a Rose he's dealt with until now in all their years together. He pictures her long face, her eyelids heavy as a hound dog's. He chews on what accounts for it all. The trail? Okay, but only as contributing factor. The canyon? Age? No one thing he can pin down. Rose has hit rock bottom.

Red locates his matches. He smokes twenty cigarettes a day, no more, no less, Camel filters, one pack. That's it.

A tree limb floats under the bridge, and the dog locks on it, trembles like he's spotted waterfowl, takes two doubtful steps off the shore, then his legs wobble. The Provo runs cold enough for a wet suit through most of the summer. Lab's going to end up drowned if someone doesn't stop him. TV is warning the state that kids and dogs are dying like flies in the rivers of Utah this year. You blink, they're gone.

The man notices Red, who's ducking into himself and striking a match. "You want something?" the man says. He has to raise his voice. The water's loud.

Red relaxes. Inhales slow and lost in thought. Wool-gathers, then blows smoke. He's the stranger who's come to town in every movie you've seen, the man you can't rattle. Red wrote the protocol. He made up the riddles and holds the answers. The woman duckwalks over and reaches for the dog. Bobcat Hair is manufacturing a scowl. It seems it's important to him that he express his resentment at Red's being here. Guy's taken umbrage. Behind Red, bouncing the bridge's planks, two runners jog by.

"Just peace of mind," Red says. Like you and your dog and that woman, he thinks, but keeps this theory to himself.

She grabs the dog's collar and hunkers by its side. She whispers in its ear and points at the tree limb. The woman's getting the toes of her sandals wet.

"How about finding it somewhere else?" Bobcat Hair says.

It's no way to talk to the park host.

The man's dumb around the eyes. Got X's for pupils. He's the type whose life work is piling mistake on top of mistake in the name of high jinks and free will. Give him enough rope, and you've heard that story.

Red sucks on his Camel, not looking at Bobcat Hair, acting like he didn't really hear or more like he's going to let Bobcat Hair off by acting like he didn't hear. Acting like the water's too loud, like you'll have to speak up, make an effort, if you want to insult Red Cogsby. Bobcat Hair doesn't realize Red could take him out. Back in the camper Red's got an arsenal, mostly handguns, and one Mossberg, 9-shot capacity, a shotgun Bobcat Hair doesn't want to be asking forgiveness of. Everything is legal, his Rugers, his two Smith & Wesson .38-.44s, his original single-action Schofield, even his ammo. Everything legal, except a box of Black Knight bullets Red bought a year ago off Earl Tall, who's most likely right now camped at Nunn's Park, half a mile to the east. Bobcat Hair doesn't seem to understand what kind of world this one has backslid into. More often than you'd like, you're dead before you figure it out. Say you're sitting on your porch, enjoying a full moon, your girl or your beau at your side. It's a honey of a night, and then one or both of you has a bullet in your head. It's come from God knows where. Or let's say you flip off a tailgater, or you make a wrong turn in an unfamiliar city. Bing, bam, you're dead. Just read the news. No Mayberrys left. The kids in Pleasantville gang bang.

Red leans into the railing until he finishes his cigarette. He can't hear what the man and woman are saying, but the woman seems to be urging Bobcat Hair to relax. Chill, Red's grandkids say. Hey, we're out in nature, the woman is suggesting. Supposed to calm you down, take your mind off your troubles. Unwind. Count to ten. Red drops his cigarette, pivots on the butt, retrieves it from the bridge, and stubs what's left into a Copenhagen tin he carries. He lives and enforces the park rules, is Red Cogsby your basic shining example. It rained buckets in the spring, then not a drop for two months, and the hills are crackling, are ready to go up like brittle paper.

Back at the Prowler, Red sweeps the Astroturf clean, then mists the budgies. They're not talking, aren't mimicking the park's birds. They're not wisecracking Red. Too many hours inside, curtains tight, TV on, Rose unapproachable. Her mood's disheartening them, too. She's the one who spent two years teaching them to talk, and now she can't be bothered. She's either crept into a corner or is disgusted. Red can hear the TV. "Rose speak to you?" he says to Regis. The bird scrambles up a ladder, gets beak to nose with him. Red says, "Do you know what the problem is?"

Kathie Lee says, "What's up?"

"Your guess," Red says, "is as good as mine." He sprays the misty water above the cage,

and it falls like the gentlest of rains. Kathie Lee pulls a feather loose, says, "Good show."

Inside, Red locates his Colt and wrangles himself into a shoulder holster. He looks like a gangster. Rose has asked him not to wear the getup in the park. Someone always calls the cops. The TV's so loud Red doesn't say a word to her. He cuts up another apple and takes it to the budgies, then ties a rope around a hitch on a pump and drags the outfit down to the river, where he attaches fifty feet of leaky fire hose. The pump generates enough pressure that he can spray down the park's central pavilion. He'll clean it twice today. A family named Johannson reserved it from noon to six. Then a Scout troop's scheduled it from seven to ten. Done, Red waters a couple of dry spots in the grass, then hauls the pump to the other side of the river, couples another twenty-five feet of hose to the hose he's already laid out, and angles the nozzle so it will flood the clearing north of his and Rose's campsite. He's got three hours before the water reaches the rest rooms near the Prowler.

Some jerk let domestic rabbits loose in the park, and one sits on a knoll watching Red. It's the brown of milk chocolates. Rose feeds them. Or she did. Lately she's left her chores to Red. She's also abandoned the rest rooms. It's Red who sprinkles Comet and scrubs the sinks and toilets. For the rabbits, he buys pellets at the Petsmart in town. Rose counted five, two lop-ears and three she didn't recognize. They don't have a chance in the park. Can't fend for themselves. They're pets, for God's sake, Rose says.

Up the river, Red stops for another smoke. Nine left in his pack. Rate he's going this afternoon he'll be borrowing on tomorrow's allotment before he climbs into bed. He stands on a concrete bridge that crosses a steep bend in the river. There's serious white water here. The canyon's asphalt trail passes behind him. It begins fifteen miles away at Utah Lake, curves alongside the river through two cities to this point, then continues for another four miles, weaving through Nunn's Park, before it reaches Bridal Veil Falls. There's also a grid of trails in the glen below Red. He can see the pavilion to his right. To his left is a larger clearing where two summers ago he built a backstop for baseball. The diamond amounts to bare spots kids have worn in the grass, dirt marking the base pads. There's a half-assed game going on, two girls at bat, and three more in the outfield. Softball.

Bobcat Hair and the woman cross the clearing, their dog, not on a leash, sniffing at the girls. The pitcher twists her cap around backward and frowns at the dog. Red stubs out his cigarette, adds it to his tin. Checks his pack. He miscounted. Only seven left. He follows the trail until it meets a gravel road that borders the clearing. He drops through a grove of cottonwoods and can see Bobcat Hair, the woman, and their dog. She's carrying her sandals. Bobcat Hair is wearing black harness boots, and he's taken his shirt off. The number nine is tattooed on both his arms near his wrists. The dog's only a puppy. Red retrieves a plastic bag from where it's stuck itself to a bench leg and tosses it in the trash, lights a Camel and walks toward them.

The woman tries to catch hold of Bobcat Hair's arm. Most likely she wants him to take stock of the fact that this man smoking the Camel is armed, but Bobcat Hair, he pulls away, says to Red, "What's your problem?"

Red sucks hard on his cigarette. The Colt rests against his ribs, comfortable, offering a glimpse of itself.

"You work here?" Bobcat Hair says. "You're on us like a cop."

Red says, "I do work here," smoke trailing the words.

"Did someone assign you to us?" Bobcat Hair says. The woman tugs at him. All of her now saying, *The man's got a gun.* Bobcat Hair says, "Why are you busting our balls?" He's steamed because it's his habit. He says, "Quit following us."

"Exactly what I'm doing," Red says. "Not following you, I mean. My camper's over there." He nods toward the Prowler and says, "I thought I'd let you people know that I'm flooding the clearing." He flicks ash into his tin, aims his cig toward the fire hose, and says, "It takes a few hours."

"You see us as your duty, is that it?" Bobcat Hair says.

"I'm the park host," Red says. "I'm Red Cogsby."

Bobcat Hair says, "We're real proud for you."

Red says, "Thought I'd also remind you that your dog needs to be on a leash. There's a city ordinance, and there's a park rule."

"It's no problem," Bobcat Hair says. "Our dog's friendly."

The woman slips into her sandals and calls the dog. "Hero," she says. "Here, boy." Hero wanders farther away. She whistles, and Hero glances over his shoulder, keeps drifting.

"I'm thinking of your good," Red says. "I'm not trying to be a hard-ass."

"Be a hard-ass," Bobcat Hair says. "Me and my wife don't give a shit. The dog don't care either. You can be this country's number one hard-ass, and it don't mean two cents to us." His wife's gotten hold of Hero's collar and is lopsided walking him toward Red and Bobcat Hair. She says, "We were driving through from New Mexico and stopped. We don't know the rules."

Bobcat Hair says to her, "You don't need to tell this man our business."

"Babe," she says.

"It's no problem," Red says. Red stubs his Camel into his tin.

"You got that right," Bobcat Hair says.

"I'm thinking mostly about your puppy," Red says. He hunkers down and extends an open hand to Hero. The dog ignores him. He says, "The dogs, they get hit on the trail. We get a lot of people on bikes, and they fly up and down, no concern for anyone. You don't hear them until they're right on top of you."

The wife says, "There might be something in the trunk we can use. Maybe some rope."

"It's for your good," Red says.

"We appreciate you telling us," she says. She's bent over, hanging onto Hero.

"One more thing, I ought also let you know we've got more than our share of diamondbacks this year," Red says. "I've killed fifteen already. It's usually one or two a summer."

"Rattlesnakes?" she says.

"You'll recognize them," Red says. "We got our blow snakes and greens, and they don't do harm. But you can't miss a rattler. They got their fat heads, and the diamonds. The rattles are a lighter brown in the tail."

Bobcat Hair has walked off. He's headed for a redwood table and picnic area across the gravel road.

Red touches his cap park-host like and says, "Be careful, ma'am." On his way to the Prowler, he warns the softballers that the water will reach the outfield in about half an hour. He can see they're scared—the gun, the shoulder holster.

Between six and seven, Red hoses down the pavilion. The Boy Scout leaders have already arrived and are setting up. Looks like they might show videos or slides. There's a portable screen. At the Prowler, he freshens the budgies' water. Regis is spinning one of the wheels, and Kathie Lee says, "Keep your eye on the ball." Red taught her that one.

He says, "Has Rose been out?" The birds tilt their heads, puzzled. He checks the throw rug for earwigs, then tucks it under his arm. Regis flies to the ladder and, upside down, climbs its rungs. Red sprays mist above the cage, and Kathie Lee says, "We wish you a Merry Christmas. We wish you a Merry Christmas."

Red knocks sharply on the Prowler's door before he steps inside. It's one of Rose's most recent requests. Doesn't Red know why they invented doors? she wants to know. He doesn't have to wait for *come in.* Just knock. That's all she's asking for. Rose is yelling at the TV. "DNA can't fly," she says. She calls someone a horse's ass. O. J.'s back on.

"Did you eat yet?" Red says.

There's an empty cereal bowl sitting in the light of the gooseneck on the tilt-top table. Looks like she's had Wheaties. The bowl ought to be soaking.

He says, "Rug's fine. No earwigs," and he flattens it to the floor in the kitchen area.

"Justice takes a holiday," Rose says, and she jabs the remote at the Sony, kills the sound. "Earl Tall sent you a note," she says. She points at the kitchen counter. "Some kid brought it to the door, one of those lunatics on skates. Starts banging on the door so the birds are screaming, and I'm not going to bother, but then he's hollering. Tall must've told him our name. He's saying, 'Mr. Cogsby. Mrs. Cogsby.' So I went so he'd shut up." She punches up the sound, catches Larry King saying, "Hold that thought. We'll be right back."

The note's folded in half. Earl Tall is asking Red to come see him at his campsite. *It's important,* Earl writes. Red says to Rose, "I think I'll go for chicken. You want to come?" He's thinking he'll bring some to Earl, and he's wondering if important means urgent or worth his while.

Rose waves Red off, says, "Already eaten."

Piss-poor idea of eating, he thinks.

It'll be dark if he drives into town, runs errands, and buys the chicken, so he puts together a peanut-butter-and-jelly sandwich and starts for the door.

"Your gun," Rose says.

Red says, "I got some questions for Earl. About the trigger and loading it."

"In the abstract," she says. "Ask him in the abstract. You don't need to do show-and-tell. You scare people, and I don't want cops disrupting my evening. Draw pictures for him."

Red gulps his sandwich. In their bedroom, he gets free of the holster and sneaks the pistol into his back pocket. His windbreaker covers it. Earl Tall and Red, they've known each other something over ten years. They met here in the canyon, only to learn they both live in Bountiful, Utah. Every summer Earl reserves a space in Nunn's the first two weeks of July. He camps alone, gets away from the wife, Eva, and their boys, who've got their own families but who built houses only half a block away from Eva and Earl. Red and Earl have guns in common. Earl worked as a pistol smith when he was younger. Back in the city, the two of them volunteer as Santa Clauses every year—even, for the hell of it, went to Tom Valent's famous Santa Claus school, drove themselves to Midland, Michigan, where they learned the basics, which are Never Flirt, Never Drink, Never Smoke. The biggest mistake you can make is too much *yo* and not enough *ho*. Still, theirs is one of those nonpersonal, now-and-then friendships. Except for the Santa Clausing, they don't see each other in Bountiful. No get-together with the wives. It's like they keep the good footing they offer each other separate from family.

The evening's hot, so once Red hits the trail to Nunn's he folds up the windbreaker and carries it. It's a twenty-minute walk. He hugs the shade to the south side of the trail. There are a few joggers, but mostly couples strolling. He sees one of the pet rabbits down by the river. It's brown and white, spotted the way pintos are and lop-eared. It looks worried.

A small hill lowers the trail into Nunn's. The river borders the park on its north side, and an asphalt road circles through it. There are twenty-two campsites. Red plans to check permits before he leaves. Most of the families are picnicking and will be done before ten, but there are four places booked for the night. He can see some pup tents. Near one, a husky is tethered to a tree, and in the clearing next to it a young couple are eating dinner, sitting on blankets. They're both wearing baseball caps. Red's about to cross to the other side of the trail when he hears "Passing" and a bike rider whips by his shoulder. They come out of nowhere. You look behind you. Nothing there. All's clear. You're safe. Then you take a step toward the other side, and a bike's on top of you.

Earl's in site twelve, the first one off the trail at this end of the park. It's back in the trees. He drives an old VW van he's cut down and welded a camper shell to. You can stand full height inside. He's added bunk beds, and there's a refrigerator and a stove. His mountain bike bolts on above the front bumper.

Red finds Earl down by the river where he's shaking leaves from a tarp. Earl's wearing bushwhacker shorts and no shirt. He's barefoot, his boots and socks on the site's redwood table. He's kept the white beard he grew last Christmas.

"Too much *yo*, not enough *ho*," Red says before Earl sees him.

Earl whacks the tarp like he hates it, then spreads it across one end of the table and grabs

Red's hand. He tugs Red in and claps his back. He says, "Don't smoke."

Red says, "Don't drink."

"Don't flirt."

"No neck jewelry."

Earl steps aside. "You came," he says.

Red says, "Was there a question that Red Cogsby would?"

"Only in my head," Earl says.

Red unwedges the pistol from his back pocket and says, "Can you take a look at this?" It's a Gold Cup, Series 70. Red tells Earl he plans to replace the sear and hammer, maybe the trigger. He heard that you can, but he's not sure he trusts the source of that information, an ex-cop.

Earl says, "Let's go take a load off. Coffee's on." He checks his tarp, straightens one end. He takes the Colt from Red, saying, "You do the sear and hammer and you'll want to replace the slide, too." At the front of the VW, Earl collects a dead rattlesnake he's hooked over his mountain bike's handlebars. He dangles it between them. Earl chopped its head off. It's probably four feet long and as thick as his forearm. "That's my third one already," he says.

"They're bad as insects this year," Red says.

Earl says, "I wouldn't mind if they bit a few of these idiots on bicycles, would you?" He tosses the snake into some cottonwoods.

"Not on your life."

Inside, Red and Earl sit in canvas tent chairs and talk guns. Earl's coffee's thick as tar. He spikes it, though, Johnnie Walker scotch whiskey. Earl shows Red the Colt revolver he bought in North Carolina. It's one of the famous Peacemakers. He digs in a drawer, comes up with cartridges, and loads the revolver. Like he's holding a tray, he displays it for Red, says, "You want it?"

Red's comfortable around guns, only he doesn't like this one being loaded. Doesn't know why Earl did that, why he'd bother. His Colt, unloaded, sits in his lap on his windbreaker. Red says, "How much are you asking?"

"I'm not asking, except for the biggest favor you've ever done a man," Earl says.

"What's that?"

Earl gestures for Red to heft the gun, to get a feel for its weight and balance. Red takes it, and Earl says, "Alzheimer's runs in families." Earl sits back, says, "You can have your genotype done, and you'll know the sorry or good news. Some people know that's possible. That you can find out, if you want. Did you?"

Red offers him the revolver. He won't take it, so Red sets it on the floor between his feet. Red says, "Rose'd know."

"Of course she would."

"She could tell you the details."

"I got two brothers, both dead from it," Earl says. "My sister needs twenty-four-hour-a-day care. She doesn't remember how to button her own clothes. She believes her teeth are tombstones. Wicked people are buried in her mouth."

"All this is terrible news," Red says.

"The terrible news is I have it," Earl says.

Red looks at his feet, one foot on each side of the revolver. He looks at Earl's bare feet.

"Twice now I've started for one place and ended up states and days away from where I was going," Earl says. "It's happened months apart, but it's happened."

"You're exaggerating."

"Only a little."

"Could be our age, Earl," Red says. "What you're describing sounds like something I do every day."

"You've found yourself a thousand miles from where you meant to be?"

"Not quite."

"Forgetting to take out the garbage isn't the same."

"Don't they say, 'If you think you've got it, you don't?'"

"The day I came here, I was about settled in, when my son drives up," Earl says. "I'm thinking, what's he doing here? He's never come down before. Not once, in—what?—ten years. He tells me—he says, 'Dad, I was visiting a buddy in Provo and stopped to say hello.' I say right to his face, 'Bullshit,' and he acts like I slugged him. I say, 'Your mother sent you because all of you think I might have driven to Nebraska.'"

Earl gets out of his chair. He's talking, and he starts knocking books and tools from the shelves. He turns over a chair. He doesn't look angry, and he doesn't sound angry. It's like he's practiced what he's doing. Like he's in a play. He's pictured in his head how he'll do it. He says, "I told my boy that if he was going to look after his father he'd need to know how to change diapers because that's what it's going to come to." Earl opens a drawer in the one chest he has and dumps out cards, screws, pens, paper. He yanks clothes from two other drawers. He's ransacking his place. "I read in a magazine," he says, "where one man forgot how to use his utensils. His knife, his fork and spoon, could have been rocks. When he did get food in, it sat in his mouth. He'd forgotten how to chew."

Earl kicks a throw rug to the side of his chair, and Red scoots back. The revolver's there on the floor. "That's a true story," Earl says. "I can show you the magazine." He stands in front of Red and says, "A month ago I woke up, peed okay, but looked in the bathroom mirror and had no idea how to shave. I knew I needed to shave, understood the obligation I had, but I couldn't have done it if you'd have given me the Chinese torture." He squats and picks up the re-

volver, checks the chamber, and offers it to Red, says, "Which is what I want you to do, my friend."

Red won't take the gun.

"But right here," Earl says, and he touches his chest where his heart is. "Three bullets."

His sadness cuts up Red.

Red says, "I won't do that no matter what you say you have, even if you prove it."

"It's a robbery," Earl says and he gestures toward the mess he's made. "I worked it out," Earl says. "Come back tonight and take whatever you want. I'll help you." He finds a pillowcase and opens it. "We'll fill this with stuff," he says. "I own a coin collection I brought along. Take all the guns." He drops the pillowcase, says, "Who would ever know?"

Red gets up and stuffs his Colt into his back pocket. He climbs into his windbreaker.

Earl pokes the revolver at Red. Earl's got his white beard and his white chest hair. He's tan. "I need you to do this," Earl says. "The time's coming when I won't exist anymore. Who am I if I don't recognize myself? Can you understand that?"

"We're just who we are," Red says.

"No," Earl says. He turns the handle of the revolver toward Red and says, "Take it."

Red does. This is the Colt that won the West. Its balance is a thing you can't match.

"It's a wonderful shooting iron," Earl says. "All you have to do is come back after dark. There's no moon tonight. I checked. You can see on the calendar. No one will see you."

Red says, "I couldn't for any reason."

"The man forgot how to chew," Earl says. He chomps his teeth together. "I read about it in that magazine. He thought his grandson was an owl. He talked to bushes."

Red backs out the door like he's the one who's about to be shot, and he places the revolver on the camper steps. Earl's crying. Last thing Red says to him is "Sorry." Earl doesn't need Red's advice, which is, Let the bad news settle. He doesn't want Red to tell him how stupid he's acting, how sorry he'd be.

The sky above the mountains to the west is white. It'll be dark in half an hour. Red notices Bobcat Hair's wife outside a tent they've put up. They've started a fire, circled it with rocks. There's no camping here, not in this area. Hero the dog is roaming in the clearing. Red gets a piece of rope from his truck and brings it to the wife. "I think this will work on the dog," he says, and he hands the rope to her.

"That's nice of you," she says. "We're sort of between good times."

Red shows her how to tie a clove hitch. There's a tree close to the tent and they hook the dog to it. "If he'll allow," Red says, "you'd be better off keeping the dog inside with you."

"The dog?" she says.

Red says, "Your husband, if your husband will let you."

She says, "He won't."

Red says, "Have you got something to eat?"

"We do."

"Because we've got plenty," Red says.

"We're just fine. Thank you."

"If you need anything," Red says, "let me know," and he heads for the Prowler.

Two weeks later it's Rose who points out Earl's obituary in the *Tribune.* She mutes the television and reads out loud to Red. "Seventeen grand-kids, if you can believe that," she says. "He's got family spread all over the place." Red wonders how he died, and she tells him the paper didn't say. He puts in a few phone calls. Accidental, he is told. While Earl was cleaning his guns.

My foot, Red thinks.

The day of the funeral the O. J. Simpson trial is in recess, and Red talks Rose into driving up to Bountiful with him. It rained seriously all night, then quit at sunrise. They'll be gone most of the day so they leave the budgies in the trailer. Red opens the curtains, notices furniture he hasn't seen for weeks. Everything's dusty. In the sunlight, Kathie Lee says, "Life in the fast lane." Regis pecks at the music box in his cage, and it begins *Love Me Tender.* Regis sings along, sounds a lot like Elvis himself. Kathie Lee butts in, adds, "Love me sweet."

Rose and Red take their new GM truck. The drive is two hours, and Rose, she studies the Wasatch Mountains like they contain the hallelujah of all creation, as if they stand for all that is trustworthy, are truly God's handi-work. Red mentions the budgies and their distress. She doesn't blink. He tries the weather as an icebreaker. "They say this is the leading edge of a rain train," he says. She gives him her coldest shoulder. He shuts up. Once bitten, twice shy.

Rose stares at the heavens washed clean by the rain, or she reads, a book on DNA. Red knits together the bits and pieces of his life up to this minute here in this truck on I-15 driving to the funeral of Earl Tall. Wonders what turns he took he shouldn't have. Wonders if he could have jumped up and down more. Rose taught the budgies that Robert Frost poem everyone learns in school, the one about the fork in the road, and how you regret you can't travel both of them and experience wherever it is they take you, the point being that you have to make choices. It took her a year, and the birds, they've got it down pat.

What if Red'd shot Earl Tall?

What if he'd done his pal that favor?

He calculates the cost, adds pro to con, weighs debt against request. Plus or minus, Red can't decide. Even in the abstract.

Rose videotaped Kathie Lee and Regis reciting the Frost poem. They do it word for word. No mistakes. On film, they sway like '50s rock and roll singers.

The cemetery's soaked, water puddles on the grass, and the mortuary laid down plywood for the mourners to walk across. Earl Tall is buried with full military honors. Nine old duffers, potbellied, all wearing army-green shirts and army-brown trousers, aviator glasses, and bolo ties and standing like clothespins, present arms and fire three rounds, their rifles dropping lower with each shot. They stand in a street that enters the cemetery, and their spent cartridges ping when they hit the pavement. A little girl begins crying. One of the veterans steps forward and plays taps. Two others remove the American flag from the casket, fold it military fashion, and present it to Eva Tall.

Red catches up to her when she's leaving. Her sons, bulky men, stand at her side. Grandkids blast in and out, mud on their shoes, mud spotting their trousers. Eva wears a pillbox hat. It has a veil. "I served with Earl in Korea," Red says to her. It's a lie. As baldfaced as a lie can be. He's betting Earl didn't talk much to Eva about him. Eva tucks her handkerchief up her sleeve and gathers in the handshake Red offers, her grip soft as a daylily's would be.

"I'm sorry. We've met," she says. "You're from the canyon, but I don't know your name."

"I'm Red Cogsby," Red says. "I was an orderly in the war, like on the TV show, and your husband was the best surgeon they had. Under those conditions, no one could hold a candle to him."

"I appreciate your telling me that," she says.

Red says, "He was one of the great doctors."

Eva shakes her head sadly.

Rose, who's come up beside Red, says, "He's lying. That's a fat lie."

Eva lets go of Red's hand and steps away. Her sons move in, catch hold of her arms. They act like FBI. One of them says, "What is this? What are you doing?" The other one says, "Who are you?" Their mother stumbles. A son says, "Get his name."

"He thinks he's making you feel better by lying to you," Rose says. "He wasn't in Korea, and he certainly wasn't an orderly. He didn't know your husband in the war."

Eva's sons support her, begin to escort her away.

"There's too much lying going on," Rose says to Eva's back. "Too much cock-and-bull."

Red follows Eva and her boys a few steps, then turns and says, "Rose."

But she's gone. Rose is briskly walking across the wet grass. She's headed for a cemetery exit.

It's an eighty-mile walk if that's her plan.

Eva's sons guide their mother along a slope toward the hearse. One stands guard, glowers at Red. Red says, "Did you get someone to watch your house?" He's close enough they all hear him. One even lets go of his mother and starts back toward Red, and Red says, "No harm meant." He holds up his hands and says, "It's just a good idea in these times."

Eva's boy, the one closest to Red, says, "Get the hell out of here."

Mourners group at their cars, and Red, a little disoriented, hunts for the truck, thinking there's got to be more than one exit to this place. He'll take his. Rose can take hers. He stops at the casket, stands on the Astroturf that surrounds it. There's a short brass guardrail.

He could have shot Earl Tall. He could have done that favor for his friend.

He can't see Rose anywhere.

Maybe he'll get in the truck and just drive. Let Rose walk. Get a lift. Do whatever she can.

But he won't.

Standing here by Earl Tall's casket, Red sees himself ten minutes from now on a side street, the truck in low gear, the engine lugging Red alongside Rose, who's walking like her pants are on fire. No sidewalks here, just gravel that edges the yards. She's kicking up dust. Red sees himself talking a mile a minute. He reasons with her, lays down a ladder of logic, rung after rung.

Rung one, the O. J. trial will end, sooner or later.

Rung two, love never dies.

Rung three, a lie isn't a half-bad thing.

Rung four, Red is, after all is said and done, the park host. The title obligates Red.

She'll trudge on, and Red'll beg. Red'll court her.

She could be wearing blinders.

Maybe, when Red locates the truck, he'll head east. Or west. Maybe Red'll just go where the road takes him. America was built on the concept that this is a big country. There are places where no one knows Red and he can stop, pull up a chair, pay for a round of drinks, and tell any story he wants. He can tell the one about how Red Cogsby shot a man as a favor simply because the man asked him to.

How It Works

1. Who is telling this story? Is the narrator a character? See Spencer's description of how he developed the story's point of view (p. 98). What does the decision to use free indirect discourse contribute to the story?

2. Anton Chekhov wrote that if a loaded gun is present in the first act of a play it must go off in the third. How does the gun function in this story?

3. "Park Host" includes nonhuman characters such as birds, snakes, and dogs. How do the animals in the story contribute to its narrative tension? To its thematic development? How would the story be different without them?

4. In a number of ways, Spencer creates a sense of disorientation. Underline passages where you felt some confusion or uncertainty, or where the characters seemed to. How does your own confusion as you read this story contribute to its impact? Try rewriting these passages so that everything is very clear. What is lost in your rewriting?

James Leon Suffern

James Leon Suffern graduated from Emerson College in 2000 and he remains at large in Boston. "When the Summer Ends" is the third story in an unnamed trilogy James wrote during his senior year of college. The characters and their world, however, were born a year beforehand in a fiction writing workshop. James wanted to suggest supernatural phenomona in this story yet remain in the characters' ordinary world.

When the Summer Ends

Jackson was telling them about this kid he knew who made a drawing of a tornado during homeroom one morning. "That same afternoon," he said, "the sirens went off."

He looked around the table, gauging their reactions. Scott and Alan and Chad sat around Alan's kitchen table with him. They were riding out a thunderstorm. They all looked like they might not have heard him. "You know, the sirens," Jackson said.

"Yeah? So did it tear up your school or what?" Chad asked. Alan stopped tapping his finger and listened. They were all looking at Jackson now for the awful, incredible climax. He held his face steady, building up the tension. Jackson knew he was a good storyteller. Sometimes the guys even told him so. This particular story, though, had a lousy ending, and after a few seconds Jackson exhaled and came clean.

"It touched down a few miles across town. The point is, the kid drew the tornado on a little piece of scrap paper, and then it came to life. I could hear it from inside the school."

"Yeah?" Alan rolled four fingertips against the table again. His mom wouldn't like them being inside the house when she wasn't there, but they'd been on his porch when the rain started. Thunderstorms were hitting almost every day now that August had begun. The sky was threatening to open up each morning and afternoon.

"You can't hear a tornado from a few miles away," Scott said and got up from his chair to look out the window. Scott's voice had changed so quickly in the last few months that it still surprised them when he spoke. Sometimes it seemed weird and made them want to giggle, and sometimes it made them jealous.

Jackson ignored him and spoke to Alan and Chad. "Did you know an F-5 produces winds over 260 miles per hour?" Even though he talked a lot of shit, it was hard not believing him about tornadoes. They had all seen picture books and case studies in Jackson's room. He owned three natural disaster videotapes and he made them all watch his favorite one a few times each summer. He'd point, touching the television screen when a lady in Oklahoma fell off her roof holding a camcorder just as the tornado lifts her neighbor's house in the air. They could ask him, How many touchdowns in Kentucky last year? How many fatalities? He would know. Jackson was obsessed.

This storm was passing already. Lightning came four or five seconds after each thunderclap and the wind didn't howl anymore.

"It's moving northeast," Jackson said. He knew a lot of facts about storms, but Alan was more impressed by his nose for them. He sniffed them out, it seemed, watched the sky, saw and heard things that the rest of them missed. "What did it sound like, when it hit your house?" Alan asked.

Jackson spoke to Scott. "Better get away from that window. It's not safe yet."

Without facing him, Scott quietly said, "Shut up."

Alan smiled and tried to hide it. They were always telling him to shut up, but no one ever said that to Jackson. Alan repeated the question.

"I'll tell you what it sounds like," Jackson said and waited until they all listened. "It sounds like a two-train wreck." His eyes widened for dramatic effect and a loud thunderclap hit, like he had struck a deal with the heavens. It was probably the final great thunder of the dying storm, and he'd timed it perfectly.

"A two-train wreck, huh?" Scott said, sitting down again. Jackson nodded. "What the hell is that?"

"It's a wreck involving two trains," Jackson explained. "It sounds like a regular train wreck, but worse than that."

"What's a train wreck sound like?" Chad asked.

"It's very, very loud." They kept looking at him. "I can't just describe it to you."

"That's what everyone says," Chad said loudly, snapping out of something. "I heard lots of people say it sounds like a train or a train wreck or a train rolling in the sky. I think anyone who says that is just hearing it from someone else." Jackson snuck a glance at Scott and thought he was nodding.

"Well, I heard it with my own ears! And I saw it, too. It came down from where I spotted it in the sky, less than a minute, and it sounded like a damn coal train tipping over on my roof." Jackson had stood up and spoken to the tops of their heads and now didn't know what to do. "Alan," he said, "I'm getting more Kool-Aid."

Alan said, "No." He was saying that more often now, after punching Jackson's dog last week. Jackson opened the refrigerator anyway, and Alan told him, "Save some for my sister, please."

"Don't get him excited," Chad told Jackson. "I don't want him beating up Brimestone again." They began to laugh, and when Jackson turned around smiling, Alan knew he could laugh a little, too.

"That's right," Jackson said, looking dead at Alan now. "He's out of control. We'd all best watch out."

Jackson thought the conversation was done, but Scott shifted his weight and kept his eyes on the table.

"My dad told me it sounded like the bowling alley," he said. Scott was the only other person any of them knew who'd been in a tornado. He was three when it happened, and his only memory of it was his mother waking him up during the night. Alan and Chad had known Scott since then, and had always hung out. Jackson moved to Valtone six years later, after a tornado tore through his old house in Trimble County; he was nine years old then. It never really happened, but Jackson was constantly talking and thinking about tornadoes, especially during summers. It wouldn't be right if they all knew he'd never been in one, or seen one. They'd think it was all fear. Now Jackson had mentioned his tornado so many times that he could talk about it and forget he'd invented the whole thing.

He sat down hard in his chair; the pitcher hit the table and a few drops of the purple water spilled over. "It doesn't sound like a bowling alley," he said.

"I don't know, man, I've heard that before," Chad said, pushing his cup towards the pitcher.

"My god," Jackson muttered. He pointed his whole hand at Scott. "He was only three."

"I didn't say it, my dad did."

The thunder rolled gently now, but Jackson told Alan to turn his TV on anyhow. "See if there's any storm warnings."

"No." Alan said.

"Fine, suit yourself."

"He's right," Chad said. "It's cleared up."

"Yeah, let's get out of here."

When the rain finally did let up it was almost one and they were all pretty hungry, except for Alan. "You're never hungry, Alan. You eat like a bird. Like a girl bird."

Alan giggled. "Yeah, I do. Yeah, yeah, yeah, I do, do, do." The thunderstorm had made them all a little punch-drunk, and when Alan did a little jig and called it the girl bird dance, everyone laughed, even Jackson had to.

"Well, girl bird, you can do what you want, but I'm getting lunch." The rest agreed, they might as well. The driveways wouldn't be dry for another hour at least, and you couldn't play a game with three guys. They split up, saying they'd meet back at one-thirty.

Jackson walked home swinging his arms and half-running. It only sprinkled now, and it relieved him that the storm had passed and no one had figured on his fear. Once, a couple years ago, Scott had called Jackson chickenshit during a tornado watch. Jackson wouldn't go outside until the National Weather Service officially canceled it. Come on, man, they said, the sky is fucking blue. When Alan teased him too, that was enough. Jackson grabbed his tennis ball from the floor and said, "Let's go. I don't care about a tornado watch. What's gonna happen, anyway?" That was before Scott had got his growth spurt. As Jackson thought about it, he realized the Scott he imagined was the older one, the one with stretched-out arms and legs, a harder chin. He tried to picture his friend as he really had looked then, but it wouldn't come.

A week later that summer he'd made up the story of the tornado he'd seen. He'd told them all after a game of 21 down at his house. Matthews was there that day, showing off his dumb new pocketknife with the eagle on it.

"It tore up our whole house, and five houses after ours," Jackson said. "That's why we had to move to Valtone." Chad and Scott looked at each other. Alan picked up a free ball and shot a lay-up. "It was bigger than the sky itself." Alan stopped shooting for a second and seemed about to ask something, but then he turned back to the basket. Then Jackson knew he was safe. No one would say anything with Matthews

there. Jackson said, "Didn't I ever tell you guys before?" He cleared his throat. Every time he made up something new he spoke louder than before. He said, "I can't even begin to describe it to you."

Without stopping his lay-ups again Alan said, "It must have been scary." It sounded like he might have even meant it. Chad said, "Yeah, Jackson. I wish you had told us that story before." Jackson looked quick at Matthews. He was opening the blade, pointing it down, and closing it. He said, "What, man?" when he saw Jackson studying him.

The rest of the summer, Jackson would bring up the tornado that ran over his house every few days, adding new flourishes if anyone would let him start talking. One time he called it the strongest tornado in Kentucky history. Hadn't you heard of it? I can't believe you guys don't remember that. Another time, Jackson remembered that he'd run outside and picked up Brimstone while the storm was coming up his street. Sometimes he changed things so they were smaller. It wrecked three houses, not five. It was the strongest one in Kentucky that year.

Still, as much as Jackson worried that his tornado never sounded the same, he talked about it so much, the guys began to forget that they never believed him. His tornado didn't quite become real, it just was something they'd grown tired of doubting. Jackson figured that meant he'd convinced them of something.

He walked through the front door and his mother called to him, "Wash your hands." In his house there were rules and if you didn't like them, tough. Jackson was the youngest and the only kid left, so all the rules and chores fell on him now.

He had two brothers. William was ten years older, and he'd always acted like an uncle, Jackson thought. Friendly enough, but not really around too much. He'd gone away to Eastern Kentucky University to study farming six years ago and no one heard much from him since.

Danny was different. Danny was a fuck-up. He'd been arrested seven times before he was sixteen. Grand theft auto for taking Mr. Diebel's tractor, breaking and entering his own house.

Danny was a joke to everyone in Valtone, but they were still brothers, and Jackson loved him. Last year a guy at school told Jackson that Danny'd been arrested the night before for killing cows along U.S. Highway 53. Jackson punched him in the eye and yelled, "You're the goddamn devil. You don't even know Danny." When he got home that day Jackson found his mother in the living room with two officers. Her eyes were washed out and tissues were scattered around her feet.

Now Jackson walked into the kitchen and sat down with a thud. His mother eyed him from the counter. Her first son was gone, and she wished the second would leave. They'd made her harder, and though she liked Jackson enough, she took no crap and no lies from him. She asked him where he'd been for the storm.

"We were up at Alan's. And Chad's."

"Both?"

"Uh-huh." Jackson sat up straighter now in his chair and smiled. "We walked to Chad's in the middle of it."

"That was awfully brave. And dumb. Did you know that there was a thunderstorm warning for Bennelle?" That was the name of their county.

"No, ma'am."

"Well, it was." She brought over a plate of leftover casserole with tuna fish and yellow noo-

dles, and walked back to the counter. Jackson chewed a few bites. He could feel her watching him. Her arms were crossed. She would say something else real soon.

"Were you scared, Jackson?"

He tried to look into her eyes and say no, but he couldn't, so he said it to his plate.

"Of another thunderstorm?"

When she stayed silent he added, "Alan was, as usual." Jackson swallowed some milk. "Do you know what he said? He said he'd rather die once than live through a tornado twice."

Jackson waited for her answer.

After some time she grunted and said, "Alan's a smart guy, huh?"

"I guess." She wandered to the table and looked down at him, but waited for him to speak. "So, Mom," Jackson said, trying to make it sound like a joke, "were you scared?"

"No, I wasn't." Her words sounded triumphant to Jackson, like she had scored some victory, and scored it long ago. He turned his head to her; there was lightning in her eyes, across her smile. It made him mad as hell. He knew she used to be scared by them too. They used to talk about it, it was something they shared when Jackson's father and brothers were unfazed by any storm. Now Jackson knew it was only him. Why would a woman grow out of that fear before a guy, he wondered. It seemed off somehow, or at least not fair.

"Well," he said, "Alan was scared."

His mom said, "Alan was," and nodded. Then she left the room. Her soaps were starting, first *All My Children*, then the other one. Jackson turned back to his lunch. The tuna and celery looked boiled gray and sick-green. He got up and silently shoveled the rest into the trash. He placed the dishes in the rack and walked outdoors, trying not to make a sound going out.

There was a breeze, cold on Jackson's arms, but already the air was turning thicker again, and hotter. It'd get so hot you didn't want to move and then it would storm hard again. On his front steps he heard the echo of a ball bouncing on asphalt, leading him to Chad's. On the way there Jackson realized playing basketball was the last thing he wanted to do. It was either gonna be thick-hot or storming all day, you could tell. Better to stay indoors.

The three of them were shooting on Chad's goal when Jackson stepped onto the driveway. Scott had finally missed a shot, and Alan let the ball fall into his hands. "Here," Jackson said, and held his hands at his chest. Alan hesitated. It was hard getting rebounds. Alan was three inches shorter than anyone else, and couldn't jump a lick.

"Here!" Jackson yelled.

"Fine!" Alan threw it to him; he threw the ball about as hard as he could, thinking it'd be tough to hold on to. Jackson caught it easily and dribbled a few times. He looked up at the others. Alan said, "What are teams?"

"Let's play 3-on-1. Alan versus all." Scott smiled wide and Chad said it sounded fair to him. "Yeah," Jackson said, "the girl bird versus everyone." Alan didn't dance now, he just walked underneath the basket and looked up at the rim, waiting for another rebound, but they weren't coming. Jackson held onto the other ball, refusing to shoot.

"Put the ball up, damn it," Chad told him.

"Yeah," Alan said, "while we're still young. Come on."

"What's the point?" Jackson said.

Alan walked up to Jackson and slapped the ball out of his hands. "You idiot. There's no point. Let's play." Alan shot from a few feet out and the ball bounced twice on the rim.

At the same moment Jackson said, "It's only gonna storm again," and as the ball was falling off the rim thunder began rolling a little ways off.

"How the hell did you do that?" Chad asked.

"It's inside him," someone said, and they all nodded together.

During the next few days thunderstorms and tornadoes tore across the Southeast. The storm cells traveled as far north as Indianapolis and all the way down to Florida. On Wednesday, a funnel cloud landed in the center of downtown Miami near rush hour, but no one was injured. The day before, two twisters—one in the morning and one in the afternoon—struck the same small town sixty miles west of Atlanta. Fifteen people were dead.

At first, Jackson tried to forget about the storms. He wouldn't be alone. One day he asked his mom if they could all come over and play Nintendo, but she said no. "Why not?" he asked.

"That boy will never come inside my house or my property or within a mile of Brimstone," she said. "He's lucky I don't beat on his head."

So when he was left isolated, Jackson read the papers, usually in the morning. He used to only skim the *Courier's* sports section, but now when he woke up the first thing he thought was, time to walk across the street. The twenty or so feet to his mailbox was a walk of dread; he didn't want to read about more destruction and fatalities, but each morning he sensed that the fatalities were there, waiting for him. Ignoring the newspaper wasn't going to make those storms any less deadly.

On Friday morning Jackson woke and sat right up without any slow drowsiness. His feet slid into slippers and he stood like a zombie, walking out his front door. He did not consider what he was doing. He already knew how many were dead.

He wasn't surprised, then, that the storms had finally made the front page. He stood on his street next to the mailbox, staring at the photo. It was of a house in Trimble County, two counties over, less than an hour's drive. It was lifted into the air, and tilted. The roof was slanted too, but disconnected from the house and flying off in the other direction. To Jackson it looked too much like *The Wizard of Oz.* It must be that, he thought, or some movie, because I've seen this picture before. Something exactly like it. He shook his head deliberately, trying to form a snicker or an appropriate response, but nothing. A choked feeling tied up his throat, the kind you get when you eat too many tart candies too fast. He couldn't speak. Every day now, a bigger one landed, always closer to Valtone. Florida was almost a whole country away. Even the day before, when six tornadoes landed in the same hour in eastern Texas, that seemed like news. Not real. But now they'd gotten to Kentucky, to Trimble County, and it made Jackson fear them more secretly. And still, he wanted them to get closer.

A warm breeze ruffled the newspaper and then cooler wind blew from the other direction. Jackson looked up at the sky. It wasn't black, it didn't seem menacing. The whole sky had a greenish tint lingering over the gray, and even as thin gray clouds crisscrossed quickly above him, the main impression the sky gave was one of immense and awful stillness. Jackson said, "Oh, shit," and spat on the grass, walking inside.

He sat on the couch and spread the front section on his lap. He knew his mom would be back from the store soon, so he scanned the pages, trying to absorb it all at once. But what he found was, he already knew all the information.

He read a headline: TWO IF BY LAND, his head shot up, he closed his eyes, a little yelp escaped from his mouth. The headline sparked something inside him, and with his eyes still closed Jackson watched a scene unfold, like a movie projector was rolling in his head. Two funnel clouds cross in the sky and then come down separately within minutes of each other. He watched as the first one dips, travels across some fields, lifts an old hay barn to the sky. It tears a fence out of the earth and then quickly goes back up with no more mischief. The other one lands near a trailer park. It doesn't directly run over anything, but still the homes topple into one another, leaving gaping holes where kitchens and living rooms were. Jackson saw all this from his couch, sort of like a video game, and whenever the tornado got close to buildings or people, he would shift his weight to one side slightly, as if his leaning could control the path.

When Jackson opened his eyes he looked again at the headline: TWO IF BY LAND.

It said no more, but it'd been enough to show him the whole story. Jackson tried to read the article, but the words describing the town and the storms there from the previous night felt like a thin copy of what he'd imagined.

A high-pitched scratching sound made Jackson look up. Brimstone was pawing at the door. "You're not allowed to come inside, buddy," Jackson said out loud. A few seconds later the dog cocked its head and seemed to ask, why not? Jackson just stared at him until he walked away, sulking, and lay down a few feet off their flat back porch. He flipped another page and saw the continuation of the cover story. The new headline read: NIGHTMARE TIMES TWO IN GALKSBORO. Near the end of the article was a quote from a guy who saw the first twister. Jackson's finger followed underneath the words as he read, "I couldn't look away. I knew I should get downstairs but I couldn't not watch it. It torn up nothing but then it lifted and where it'd been was like a field that nobody'd ever stepped on before."

By the time Jackson got to the end of the paragraph he'd watched the whole thing happen in his head. The man, the warm gushing wind, the stink of black dirt flying by. Where were these sensations coming from, he wondered. Just a few words from the article made the storm come alive inside him; he felt everything it created and destroyed, except for the sound. The memory, for that's what Jackson was calling it now, was full except for its silence.

Beside the text was a gray shaded box listing the eleven people already pronounced dead or missing. Four fatalities were listed Anonymous, but for the others a name and age was printed. Tyler Andersson, 18. Regina Burris, 54. Paul Hallowell, 28. Kenneth Hutchinson, 45.

Jackson whispered the first name and a still photograph of Regina Burris came to his mind. A head shot, black and white, like a school picture in the yearbook. He spoke the next name, and then another, and the same still photo appeared: a neutral, calm face. They all looked familiar like an old classmate, but Jackson knew they were no classmates. Most of them were older people, his parents' age or more. Yet, every name generated a face Jackson could hold onto in his mind. In the newspaper the names were thick and black, and when Jackson saw their face the letters appeared in front, floating now. That's how Jackson knew they were dead, not from the newspaper or even the ashen cheeks and foreheads, one after the other like a sort of just-departed roll call. But when the letters and numbers lingered just beneath someone's chin, Jackson would nod gravely.

The faces felt close and distant at the same time. Jackson told himself, I'm matching these names up with old relatives. People I've met once or twice, or only seen in photographs. He looked down at the list of names again and read the first one: Tyler Andersson, 18. Immediately Jackson could see his face: dark eyes, mouth slightly open and smiling, small ears. He saw this Tyler Andersson as clear as an image on TV. It wasn't the first time he'd seen him, neither. And now Tyler Andersson was dead. But he didn't look dead to Jackson, or feel dead. How was it he looked so familiar?

Jackson said out loud, "Who cares." I'm making up people, he thought. So what? They're dead. Their time is done. It felt good, thinking that way. They had time, and now it's over. A tornado had touched down last night on a sleeping town two counties over and killed them. So what? It wasn't Valtone. If eleven people had to die, Jackson told himself, that was too bad, but better there than here. No, he'd never actually been in a tornado, but they'd come close enough all his life, and it felt like dumb luck every time a town two counties over got nailed instead of his. Luck like a board game, luck like drawing a map. It was better that way. He could have his own fake tornado and still be alive. He could make his tornado bigger now, and blacker, and wider. He'd make it an F-5 from now on. He'd been outside, corralling wild horses into a barn when it came and picked him up. Jackson flew ten miles across to the other side of town and landed in a ditch, heart beating. Jackson's tornado sounded like a hundred trains wrecking. His tornado was the size of God, never-ending. And he lived to talk about it. And it didn't matter that it hadn't really happened because no one he knew had really been in a tornado. Well, Scott had, but he was a little kid then, and he couldn't even re-member it. That was like not being there at all.

Jackson had broken away from the newspa-per's spell. He wanted to tell someone, he wasn't scared of tornadoes. No, it had never been that, it was a fascination, an obsession. It felt like he had to pay strict attention to them, like the more violent a storm got, the more he had to be there, watching. And the more he watched, the stronger it grew. It wasn't fear, no, it was an al-liance, a give-and-take.

Jackson stood up from the couch feeling empowered. He walked to the kitchen deciding who to call. Not to brag or nothing, just to see what was up, when the day would finally start. Not Alan, screw him. He's lucky one of us doesn't kill him after what he's done. Chad slept late usually, so that left Scott. Jackson's hand was a half-inch from picking up the phone when it rang; his fingers fell on the receiver but the rest of him jumped back. Like a question, he said hello.

At first there was only a loud whir, like a re-frigerator going.

Jackson said hello louder.

A woman's voice spoke, trying to outdo the hum. "Hello, hon," it said. The voice sounded like it was broken into little pieces and glued back together.

"Mom? Where are you? I can barely hear you."

"Jackson, I was just calling because." She stopped. The hum grew. Barely, he heard her say, "To see if you ever got up this morning."

He was going to tell her he wasn't afraid anymore. "Mom, the tornadoes—"

"I know, hon, I know." The hum became scratchier, and now it was hard to tell between it and her voice.

"How long will you be out?" he asked her.

The connection was quickly getting worse. It sounded like lots of rusty window fans, like little metallic laughs. When she spoke again, she was far away, and Jackson could only guess at the words. "Out. You am, not I is."

"What?" Jackson yelled into the receiver. "Mom?" Only the window fans answered, a harsh buzz now. That's not even Mom anymore, he thought, and then a sucking sound emptied all the noise from the other end and the line went dead.

That was fucked up, Jackson thought, turned off to calling someone now. Scott was probably still sleeping, too. People got older and liked staying in bed later. It wasn't hard imagin-ing Scott dozing the morning away. Jackson saw it, his friend's feet running over the edge of the bed; maybe he had to bend awkwardly at the waist to fit on the mattress. But when Jackson tried to imagine Scott's pillow, he saw no head.

Then something awful happened: Jackson couldn't picture Scott's face at all. When he tried, he saw Tyler Andersson's dark eyes and open mouth. He shut his eyes tight to see Scott's, trying to put his face in familiar places: Chad's court, Alan's porch, his own living room. But each time, a general haziness would soon solidify into a single face. Tyler Andersson's. It occurred to him that the only difference be-tween Scott's face and this Tyler's was a few years, a deeper fullness.

Jackson stood up, took a few steps around the room and sat down again. "Screw this," he said out loud, and swatted the newspaper to the floor. He looked at the folded newspaper there and murmured, "I know what my friends look like." He tried Alan. At first, nothing. Then, the more Alan he added—his voice, the way he walked, his cat—the clearer a face came to him. But it wasn't Alan at all.

It was a man his father's age. He had huge eyebrows and a wide nose and underneath his face a name appeared in black letters, Anthony Lewis, 44. A dead man.

Jackson tried anyone. He thought of lots of people at once, his brother Danny, Chad, his brother William, a kid named Keith, his mom. He focused on one to make it easier. Danny, his brother. At first he thought he had him, and a brief breezelike relief washed over Jackson. He saw a chin just a shade softer than his brother's, and his nose, just more narrow, and those eyes, those were Danny's eyes.

Just when he thought he'd finished the puzzle, his relief turned over to a fast panic. It wasn't Danny's face he'd pictured, it was his own, and over his neck he read, Jackson Sanville, 13. The letters floated the same way, flashing from black to white to black. Things kind of started happening too fast for him. The dog scraped its paw against the door again, the phone rang once and then stopped, a crack of thunder sounded, like glass shattering. Then rain fell, hard and fast. A cloudburst.

Jackson went to turn on the TV for storm warnings, but as he grabbed the remote control, two flashes of lightning lit up the dark living room. Bad idea, he told himself, and ran upstairs. He grabbed an oversized sweatshirt and corduroy pants, and they made him begin feeling a bit safer.

Then, the phone rang again. He didn't want to answer it. But on its second ring, he ran into the kitchen and grabbed the phone, startling himself. It was Chad. "Wanna play ball, man?" he said.

"Very funny. Hey, is there a tornado warning or anything?" Chad had a weather radio, and his mom kept it on all summer.

"Not yet, just a watch. You scared, boy?"

Jackson had heard this a hundred times, and he'd always lied and said he wasn't afraid, but now it was different. Now he really wasn't. No, it's not that I'm scared, Chad. I just know about this time. This is the one. He looked at the tiny holes on the phone's mouthpiece. A mammoth thunderclap hit right over Jackson's house and he turned his back to the window, pretending it was a game.

"Chad?"

"Yeah, man?"

"Why did you call me?"

"Just wanted to let you know about this beautiful storm we're having."

"Shut up," Jackson said. The lightning was coming one-Mississippi after the thunder now. "This is too dangerous. I'm hanging up."

"That's right. Now, come on over here," Chad said. Something told Jackson he was serious now.

"What! I'm not running to your house in this!"

"Yeah, you are. We all want to talk to you. It can't wait."

"We?"

"Scott spent the night and Alan just ran down." There was a pause during which Jackson could tell something within himself was making a decision. Say no, he tried to tell himself. Chad said, "Just fucking do it, Jackson. You have to."

"I have to? What the hell do you mean, I have to?" Jackson was shouting now, but Chad was right and he knew it.

"We're all gonna play 2-on-2, man."

"Shut the fuck up," Jackson said and slammed the phone down. Then he put his windbreaker on and starting convincing himself it wasn't such a long run to Chad's. Thirty seconds, maybe twenty. Lightning doesn't just strike people down. It's only a tornado watch.

Downstairs, Brimstone was standing on two paws, leaning on the door. Jackson considered picking him up and carrying him over to Chad's, but he thought about Alan. Apologies and jokes aside, it was too damn weird what he'd done.

He slid the door open for Brimstone. The dog ran a few steps, stopped, and shook its whole body, making a sneezing sound. Then it peered up at Jackson, cocking its head at him with a look of total unfamiliarity. He began barking madly with the thunder. Jackson told him to shut up and swore to himself to lay out Alan for making his dog crazy.

Jackson stood as close to the glass of the back door as he dared, ignoring Brimstone's barking. He tried to imagine getting over there was a contest, like the 100-meter dash at school, and for a few seconds he clutched the door handle, thinking he would go for it. Then he backed off again.

What he needed was the right moment, when his mind would go blank, no more newspaper names or tornado stories or nothing; when the distance between him and Chad's basement door become just a quick hard sprint. The moment came, and he tore the door open without looking back at the dog. Jackson ran. He muttered, shit shit shit shit to the rhythm of his feet, making record time.

When Jackson got to Chad's, the basement door was open for him. He was drenched, but exhaled deeply a few times, happy to have made it across. They were all there sure enough, Chad behind him closing the door, Scott swinging his legs off the dryer, and Alan, over by the table, listening to the radio.

Jackson slowed his breathing down and looked at all of them. "Guys, this is just like the morning the last time I was in a tornado. It's—"

"Oh, shut up!" Alan yelled. "We're about to fucking die and you can't stop this." He broke into sobs, gurgling noises coming from him like his insides had filled up with water. Jackson forgot what he'd been saying. We're about to what? He'd seen it himself, but hearing someone else say it made Jackson's throat tighten up.

"Does somebody want to explain this to me?" he said.

"We are all going to die, man," Chad said. Jackson couldn't detect any fear in his voice. He sounded certain of his words.

Jackson searched for something to say but Scott took a couple of steps towards him and put a hand on his shoulder. He looked down into Jackson's eyes. "Hey, man. Don't, uh, don't talk about that twister you were in. I know you weren't."

"Shut up!" Jackson said, and spun around to Alan. "What the hell are you looking at?" He shoved Alan in the chest. Alan fell into the side of a chair. Outside a tree branch snapped off the trunk like a bone breaking at the joint.

Scott grabbed Jackson by both shoulders and held him tight. "Hey! We know. I know."

Chad explained. "Scott had a dream this morning."

"Not a dream," Scott said. "A vision? It happened very quickly."

Chad continued. "And he saw himself as a little boy and his parents were there and a big fucking tornado landed on top of their house and they all died." Chad looked at Scott, who nodded once.

"What?" Jackson said. "What the hell do you and your parents have to do with us?"

"My mom and dad and me were thrown against the wall," Scott said. Alan wiped at his eyes with a shirtsleeve. "But then, the dream started over and we were sitting on the couch again but it wasn't my family, it was us."

"You, me, Alan, and Chad?" Jackson's eyes danced everywhere. "But there's four of us!"

Scott leaned in closer to Jackson. He smiled warmly and shrugged his shoulders a bit. "That's what happened, man."

The radio's siren went off three times, like a broken ambulance. All the boys looked at it, just a cheap plastic thing from Radio Shack. It almost looked like a child's toy, and Jackson went to pick it up, but then it spoke.

"The latest word from the National Weather Service: there is now a Tornado Warning for Benelle County. Again, that's a Tornado Warning. A funnel cloud has been spotted in Remmingston and is traveling northeast at approximately ninety miles an hour. Anyone in Remmingston, Valtone, and Goshen should take shelter immediately. Again, the National Weather Service has—" Alan turned the volume all the way down. Suddenly his crying had stopped. He put his hands together in the air like a church. "Here it comes."

Now it was Jackson with tears running down his cheeks, but still he managed to ask Chad, "Why did you tell me to come here if you knew? What's the point of this?"

"Did somebody call you before me, Jackson?" He tried to answer; he couldn't.

Alan said, "The point of this?"

"Did somebody call you, Jackson!" Chad said.

"Yeah, my mom called!" The tears were gushing now, mixing with the rain on his face. "So what, man?"

"So what? So all of our moms called. And they all sounded like they were a million miles away."

Scott was looking out the window, half-listening to Chad speak, but too transfixed by the weather to look away. This was not just another thunderstorm, it was the thunderstorm they had spent their lives fearing and wanting, hating and wishing for. Blow the candles, the lights go out.

Jackson watched as the storm held Scott's face in place. His eyes and lips moved, contracted, kept time with the wind and thunder. His face was a warrior, crumbling; brave, and going down.

Chad was saying, "Nobody's anywhere today. My mom's visiting some friend, Alan's sister is out, no one is around, Jackson. Do you understand? Ghost town, man."

Scott sat down in the chair by Alan. He talked with his hands. "We all saw this happen already, one way or another. You can run back home if you want, but."

Jackson opened his mouth and tried to explain. "The newspaper."

"What?" Alan said.

"I saw my name in the newspaper." The lights snapped off, but Jackson thought Alan was nodding at him. Two lightning flashes lit up the room, not long enough for Jackson to look at his three friends. The rain fell softer momentarily. The sheer noise lessened by degrees and they all noticed it, glancing hopefully out the window. Only Scott knew it meant the end.

"Well," he said. "It's been nice knowing all of ya."

"Wait!" Chad screamed. "What happens after it. When we."

"I don't know, man," Scott said. "Nothing?"

"What do you mean, you don't know?" Jackson punched him over and over on the shoulder. "You've been through this before!"

"I've been through nothing like this before. Stop asking me questions."

Jackson looked over. Alan and Chad were holding on to each other, hugging. He looked back at Scott. The storm slowed to an almost-silence. He was hugging them now, and Scott too, all four of them, holding on, hands and waists and goodbyes. Their shoulders rubbed together, and their foreheads touched, leaving the slightest hole in the middle where a little air passed through.

How It Works

1. How would you describe Jackson's feelings toward each of his three friends? What evidence in the story supports your conclusions?

2. How does this story's point of view contribute to its impact? What would the story lose if the author had decided to tell it from the perspective of one of the other characters?

3. This story describes a number of tornadoes, real and imagined. What details does the author include to make these descriptions feel real? What about the unreal tornadoes—are they convincing too? Should they be?

4. Write out several lines of dialogue from this story. Next to each line, write the character's feelings at that moment, as you perceive them. How directly are these feelings expressed in the dialogue? What techniques has the author used to convey them?

Jeannine Thibodeau

Jeannine Thibodeau was born on September 8, 1970, in Harvey, Illinois, and grew up in Long Island, New York. She began writing "Close" during her sophomore year at Emerson College, revising and rewriting it many times before finishing it during her junior year. Today, Jeannine lives in Brooklyn, New York, where she is at work on her as-yet unnamed novel based on "Close" and related stories. She works as an editor in communication theory, journalism, film, and public speaking at Bedford/St. Martin's, a college textbook publisher.

Close

The coffee shop is empty. A year or so ago, it was popular for its Euro-sleekness, but eventually it died out like these places do. Most close; this one decided to fight it out until the end. Sunlight pours in from a nearby window and offers a view of Third Avenue while warming my face. With my sister Lenore fifteen minutes late already, I know I have another fifteen to wait.

I don't know which direction she's coming from, so my eye wanders up and down the street. As always, my gaze finds them. Every size and every shape, from a firm little lump under a loose blouse to belly bulging, ready to pop. It's not like I seek them out, like I try to spot these pregnant women. I do not try to target them. They're simply everywhere.

I see a flash by the door and look up in time to see Lenore in front of me. "Oh, you cut off all your hair," I say before I can stop myself. Lenore is younger than I, six years, and is beautiful. Today she looks like hell. Her eyes are dark with rings underneath and her cheekbones seem sharper than the last time I saw her, three months ago. Ever since she moved in with Manny, a slouchy guy with long glossy hair and no personality, all she does is party. She says she dropped out of NYU to work on her music. I don't know if she ever picks up her bass anymore.

"Hi, Angie." Lenore air-kisses my cheek. "Do you like it?"

I study her. For years now, her waist-length hair has been her pride. It's been cut off randomly, like a boy's, curls springing in all directions. Her short skirt reveals bony legs.

I nod enthusiastically. "Yeah, it's great." Then, lower, "Are you eating okay? You're so thin."

Lenore rolls her eyes. "Of *course* I'm eating." But when she looks at me, I know she's lying; she doesn't eat enough.

"Are you still living with Manny?" Once it's out of my mouth, I know it's a stupid thing to say. Lenore narrows her eyes at me, to reinforce this.

"Are *you* still living with Paul?" she asks.

Paul and I have been married for four years. I laugh, a nervous giggle, and feel better when Lenore joins in. Nodding to the waitress who hovers like a small bird, Lenore orders a latte with a "Do you mind?" to me. It's always assumed that I'll pay.

"So what's up?" Lenore asks when the waitress goes away.

I know that she wants to know why I've invited her here. Instead, I answer, "Oh, not too much. Paul just got another big job, and I'm still doing the jewelry thing. Two little shops have picked up some of my rings." I don't tell her that the rings are selling well, and that a place in SoHo is interested, too. I don't want her to think I'm bragging.

I hope she'll go along with it, talk to me breezily, two sisters enjoying coffee together. Lenore looks me up and down, like she's trying to figure me out. I try again. "What about you—what are you doing for work?"

"I'm still waiting tables," she says with a sigh. "Manny's doing his comic book thing, waiting for it to pick up." This is the same thing, word for word, that she told me the last time I saw her.

The latte is placed in front of her. Lenore doesn't look up, so I smile at the waitress for her. "How's your music?"

Lenore shrugs. "It's really hard to find the time. You know, to get together with a bunch of people." She seems to take extra care to ignore my encouraging smile—carefully pouring sugar into her coffee, stirring it around and around so that her spoon clinks against the side, over and over.

Finally, Lenore looks up and offers me a smile, a huge Cheshire cat smile. "Well, I have some news for you," she says. I lean towards her, ready to applaud her for any news she tells me at all. She opens her mouth and then closes it, leaning back in her chair. "I've, uh, I've been in touch with Mom," she says. "Isn't that great?" Her eyes dart around, looking for a place to rest—anywhere but on me would do.

My mind races and my heart pounds wildly. In rapid succession, questions fire off in my brain: how did you find her? Where is she? What is she doing? What is her life like? What does she look like? What has she become? And a very small voice pipes in stubbornly: did she ask about me?

"How is she?" is what I ask, my voice cold, aloof.

"Oh, she's great," Lenore says enthusiastically. "She's still in California, living near a beach. She says she's really found peace."

Lenore's cheeks are flushed, her eyes bright. The last time I saw my mother, she insisted on driving me to school, much to my annoyance. Nobody's mother drove a senior to school. She hugged me so closely that day, squeezed me until it hurt, and I could smell the smoke in her hair from the Marlboros she'd recently taken to chain-smoking. "Geez, Mom, I'll be home in a couple of hours," I said. But she was gone by then.

"She left us," I say, my voice low. "Why would you even want to talk to her?"

Lenore scowls at me. "Because no one ever asked for *her* side of the story. It was always— Mom's so terrible, she left us. I wanted to hear what she had to say."

I snort derisively.

"Pop made you see me, didn't he?" Lenore asks suddenly.

"No," I lie, shifting a little. It was the question in his voice that made me call her. Why don't you check on your sister? Don't you love her? "We're worried about you."

"You and Paul?" Lenore asks, all wide-eyed innocence.

"No—I mean yes, he worries, too. But I meant me and Pop."

"I guess I haven't gotten around to returning his phone calls," Lenore says. She plays with the chain around her neck. "I figured he wouldn't care. He's busy with his new family now."

"You're still his daughter," I point out. I try to keep the exasperation out of my voice. I succeed partially. I wasn't thrilled when my father decided to remarry, either, but I manage to stay on friendly terms with him. Lenore decided to pretend he no longer exists.

"How many new kids does he have by now?" she wonders out loud, although she knows very well. She continues to stir her latte.

"Two," I say through gritted teeth.

"In only two years of marriage," Lenore says in seeming wonder. She flicks her chin towards me. "Who would've thought—Pop, a stud, right? I would've placed my money on Pauly."

I can feel my pulse racing, the blood pounding in my temples. I have to hold my hand back from reaching out to smack her. I imagine leaving a hand print on her cheek. Smirking, Lenore lifts her mug halfway to her mouth. In that instant, the color drains from her face. She is paler than I've ever seen her. I ask her if she's okay, and she stands. "Be right back," she says in no more than a whisper.

I know I should go after her, or at least check in to see that she's all right, but I can't make myself do it. I hope she had so much to drink last night that she spends the entire day over the toilet. I want to grab her by her bony shoulders and shake her until her teeth rattle. But then, she doesn't know that it is my problem, and not Paul's, that keeps us from having children. So she makes her catty comments about Paul's virility and I say nothing. I never let on one way or the other. I don't think she would be so cruel if she knew.

Just as I stand to walk towards the bathroom, Lenore returns with streaks of color on her cheeks. "I don't know what *that* was all about," she says, and sits.

"You're okay?"

"Yeah—but maybe this isn't the best time for me." Lenore's eyes avoid mine as she folds and refolds her napkin. "I'm feeling kind of sick," she says, "and I've got a headache."

I wait for the list to continue, but it doesn't. "Then let me walk you home."

Lenore's head snaps up. She's been in this apartment for eight months now, and has never invited me over. Her eyes move back and forth as if she's scanning a mental list of excuses to find the best one without actually saying, I don't want you there. "You don't have to," she says in a flat voice. "Really. I know how you feel about the East Village."

"I'm fine with it," I say. I don't think anyone should have to live there, however. My voice is firm.

Lenore sighs. "Let me call Manny," she says, resigned. "He likes to know when guests are coming."

So he can hide the bong, I think. "Great," I say with a smile. I pay the bill while she's gone.

We walk down Second Avenue, the sun glaring rudely off the buildings and directly onto our faces. Lenore squints at the sidewalk, looking so pained that I hand her my sunglasses. She frowns at them before she puts them on.

"My apartment isn't the immaculate palace yours is," she says. Her smile is sarcastic.

"You didn't see all the places I had before the one on Gramercy," I say. "Half the time I lived in someone's closet and thought it was great."

"Yeah?" Lenore turns a smile on me. "We'll get a bigger place eventually."

"Sure," I say. "That's the way it goes."

We are at St. Mark's Place, and Lenore visibly relaxes. Her pace quickens and she smiles and nods to people along the way, other dropouts like her, with their piercings and tattoos, pale and angry.

I walk a few steps behind her, and she introduces me to no one, even when the bald girl sweating under her leather jacket and dog collar stops to say hi.

"Thanks for the introduction," I say when she moves on.

"Oh, she's nobody," Lenore says with a shrug. "You don't need to know her."

"That's a charming way of looking at your friends."

Lenore laughs. "You know what I mean."

Just before Tompkins Square Park, we see five men lined up in front of the park, their belongings—or someone else's—spread along blankets. Books, plastic toys, shoes and dresses lie in dirty stacks with a few glazed loners stooped over them.

Lenore looks at me from the corner of her eye. "Almost there," she says cheerfully.

Her building is one in a row of tenements, each one the same brown as the one before it, all windows barred. She unlocks the front door and then the two indoor locks. Dim fluorescent light bounces off flat gray walls and casts a jaundiced glow.

"Hope you're in shape." Lenore's smile is fixed.

Her apartment is on the sixth floor, the steps worn slick from years of use. We are both short of breath in front of her door. My calf muscles are cramped.

"Stand back," she pants. She flings open the door and five or six roaches rain down from the door frame. They run, confused, from under Lenore's combat boots and back into the apartment. "Bastards," she mutters.

Manny appears at the door. "It's those damn Buddhists downstairs," he says in greeting. "It's against their religion to kill any living thing." He grins at us like the village idiot.

"Hi," I say, and follow Lenore into their home, the most miserable box of an apartment I've ever seen. Maybe I did live in spaces the size of a closet, but at least they were clean closets. I tried to brighten up the spaces I'd had. Lenore and Manny seem comfortable with their cracked plaster and bare bulbs.

Lighting a cigarette, Manny says, "Mind if I smoke?" The apartment is already thick with the combination smell of pot and incense.

"Well, here's the grand tour," Lenore says, spreading her arms wide. "To your right, the master bedroom." She waves toward the futon. "To your left, the kitchen/bath suite." She gestures toward the shower next to the fridge. "And center stage, the living and dining area." She finishes with her hands on her hips, her voice tight. A fraying couch and a tabletop on milk crates are before us. Lenore's bass and amp are in the corner next to the television.

I look around desperately for something to like. "Nice wardrobe," I say, stepping over piles of clothing to the huge block of wood next to the futon.

"I guess the people who lived here before us didn't want it." Lenore shrugs. "Drink?"

"I made some Kool-Aid," Manny says helpfully. "It's in the fridge."

"I'd love some," I say. I join Lenore on the couch. It smells musty, like a basement. I try not to think of where it came from. Manny hands out smudged glasses filled with red liquid. He and Lenore share.

"We only have two glasses," he explains. Lenore glares at him, but he's oblivious. "Two plates, two pots, two mugs. Usually we don't even eat here, though."

"Oh?" I say politely.

He plows on. "You saw the roaches when you came in. You should see them pour out of the oven when we turn it on. Remember that dream you had, Lenore?"

"No," she says sharply. She looks ready to pounce on him, to clap her hand over his mouth.

"Man," he says, looking at me. "She had this dream once, that these repairmen-type guys came and she thought they were coming to get rid of the roaches. But what they did was replace the walls with some kind of plexi-glass stuff, so you could see *inside* the walls. And there were all these roaches crawling—"

"I think she gets the idea," Lenore snaps.

Manny looks at her, surprised. "More Kool-Aid?" he asks me.

"No thanks," I say. "I should go. I just wanted to make sure you're okay, Lenore."

"I'll walk you downstairs," Lenore says and I follow her out the door. Manny locks it behind us.

Outside, Lenore stands in the doorway, arms folded across her chest. "So what are you going to tell Pop?" Her voice is carefully neutral.

"I'll say you're doing just fine." A relieved smile spreads across Lenore's face. What else could I say to my father, sitting in his new home with his two kids? "Call us, okay?" I add, almost an afterthought.

"I will. Just one more thing, though. Normally I wouldn't ask this . . ." She trails off, waiting for me to prompt her. I don't. She twists a curl around her finger. "Can I borrow some money? Just a little. I get paid next week."

I pull a twenty from my wallet. "Enough?" Lenore's face burns as she takes it. She hugs me, stiffly at first, as if she's not sure how to do it. Then she squeezes me so closely that I can feel her hip bone sharp against my side. My eye follows the slashes her cheekbones make across her face. There is no trace of her more familiar, full face, like mine.

"This money," I say carefully, "won't be used for anything . . . illegal?"

Lenore looks shocked. It's the same look she had as a child, when she got blamed for something she didn't do. "Is that what you think?" she asks, incredulous. Her voice rises. "Does Paul think so, too? And Pop?" I don't say anything. "You do," she says. She shakes her head.

"Well, what then? There's the weight loss, and you get sick during coffee, and you live . . . here—"

"I guess I haven't found a rich man to take care of me just yet," she snaps. "But that doesn't mean I'm a heroin addict."

"I didn't say you were."

"You implied it, though." Lenore looks at me resentfully. "It's nothing like that." She struggles to gain control as her voice begins to break.

"What then?" My voice is as gentle as I can make it.

"I can't say," she chokes out. She angrily wipes away a stray tear.

"You can tell me." I reach out to touch her, but she draws back. "How many times have I bailed you out? Maybe I can help."

Lenore considers this for a moment. We were close at one time, years ago. After our mother took off, I was the one who cried with her, who explained it all to her, who let her sleep in my bed until her nightmares stopped. I still can't let her completely alone, resist stepping in if I can.

She makes a small whimpering noise. "I think—" She stops and takes a gulp of air. "I need to buy a pregnancy test. That's what the money's for. I think I'm pregnant." She bites her lip and shifts her weight from side to side. She's shivering as the July sun burns into me.

I blink at her a few times, unsure of what to say. "Do you want me to go with you?" I hear my voice say, far away from my mind.

Lenore shakes her head no. Would she sneak the pregnancy test into her home in a brown paper bag, and dispose of the evidence as soon as she could? Or would she want Manny there, to stand by her side, to hold her hand?

"Should I call you?"

Again, she shakes her head. "I'll call you. I don't know what I'm going to do." She smiles shakily at me. "You should go." She gives me a gentle push.

Everything shifts, and there's a new person before me. Not my skinny, messed up sister, but a woman, capable of bearing a child. Then she turns, flutters her fingers at me and goes inside. I'm left staring at the door.

From the foyer, I can see Paul in his studio at the other end of our apartment. By New York standards, our five-room apartment is large, but not quite the palace Lenore thinks it is. It was Paul's great aunt Grace's for most of her life, until she became too frail for New York winters and left for Florida. Paul moved in immediately afterwards.

He's hunched over his desk, his red-brown hair falling like a curtain in front of his face. "Hey," he calls, without looking up. "How's it going?"

"Okay," I say. I sound miserable. I leave my shoes by the door and walk through the kitchen into the living room. Great Aunt Grace was hip enough in her day to set up a bar under the stairs that lead to our bedroom loft. Paul wanted to get rid of it because it takes up too much space, but my vote for kitsch eventually won out. "Want a drink?"

"Sure," Paul says. He joins me behind the bar and touches my back lightly. "Went that well?" Watching me pour vodka into my glass, he says, "Go easy on mine. I have to go downtown later to meet people from *Gourmet*, remember? They want to discuss my cake shots." Paul is a professional food photographer. He's in great demand these days, not only for his photographs but also for his skill at shellacking foods. "Then there's that SoHo reception, if you're up for it."

I nod automatically and raise my glass to his. "Here's to your fabulous career." I twist my lips into a smile and he clinks his glass against mine. "And to my fabulous sister," I add before taking a sip.

"Anything in particular, or just the same old?" Paul asks carefully. His eyes are warm brown, flecked with gold, the kindest eyes I've ever seen. I don't want to look into those eyes. I want to keep it to myself, to hold the hurt a little longer.

"I guess the same old—she lives in a horrible pit in Alphabet City and she's not doing a thing."

I picture Lenore in that apartment, living on Kool-Aid and Little Debbies. Lenore was only eleven when our mother took off on that clichéd trip to California "to really get to know herself," as she later wrote us in one of her few letters. Our father became a born-again bachelor and I was left to deal with Lenore. While my friends were picking out prom dresses, I made sure she ate and had clean clothing and went to school.

Paul shrugs. "She's also twenty-one, Angie. Let her figure it out herself. You pulled through okay and God knows you didn't have much help."

I didn't have anyone to help out—it was either pick myself up and do something or get stuck working at a mall in the suburbs. I escaped to the city and lived on tip money from waiting tables while in school. While my roommate planned spring break in Cancun, I planned

to work as many double shifts as I could. Lenore has no ambition. She's aimless. And quite possibly pregnant.

"But she's not me. She's used to everyone picking up after her," I say finally. I roll the ice around my glass.

"Maybe it's time she learns."

"I guess," I say with a sigh. I suck the remaining liquid from the bottom of the glass. "Plus, she thinks she's pregnant," I blurt out. Instantly, I wish I could reach out and grab those words, cram them back down my throat where they belong.

Paul lets out a low whistle. "Shit," he says.

"Yeah." I start to laugh but it comes out as a weird hiccup and then I know it won't work like that. I bury my head in Paul's chest instead.

He pats me awkwardly, unsure of what to do. He never knows, never lets me cry until I can't anymore. He just wants it to stop.

"Maybe she's not. Maybe it's a mistake, like all her partying has made her late or something." He nods to himself, satisfied with his explanation. He looks to me, wanting me to believe that easily, too.

"Maybe." My voice carries no conviction.

While he's gone, I clean. I try to clean the image of Lenore's sad, scared face out of my head, but it won't go away. In my head, I hear a voice—my voice—high and whiny and insistent, saying over and over, *It should be me.*

Don't I deserve it? Haven't I wanted for so long? It was a Sunday, almost two years ago, when Paul looked across the room at me, sitting on the couch petting his ancient cat, Weasel. When I looked up at him, he said, "You'd make a good mother." Just like that.

I scrub each tile in the kitchen until I can see my reflection. Until my arm aches.

"So you want kids someday?" I asked, like I was just making conversation. I was sure Paul could hear my heart pounding across the room.

"Oh yeah," Paul said, and went back to reading the travel section of the paper.

Next I polish the fixtures until the chrome gleams with my bitter reflection. There was no specific moment for me, really, that made me want a baby. It came gradually. I'd see a man smile at his baby and a strange ache would rise in my chest. I'd hear a child, laughing uncontrollably and I'd find myself choking back tears.

Sometimes I can almost feel the weight of a child on my hip, feel our breathing, synchronized. I want that closeness more than I could ever admit out loud, to anyone. Inside, it's different.

We just thought we were unlucky at first. Sometimes couples are, when they're starting out, we'd heard. It wasn't until after the operation that I began to feel the pressure, subtle, but there.

The silence in the apartment is shattered by the phone ringing. I know it's Lenore and I think about letting the machine pick up. I stand in front of the phone, unsure.

"Angie," Lenore's voice says into my ear. "Look—I did it." She starts to cry. "I did it twice. And it said positive both times."

"Listen," I speak slowly, as if Lenore is unable to understand me otherwise. I grip the phone with both hands, knuckles white, back against the wall. "I'm going to take you to my doctor. We'll find out for sure." I can feel this in my stomach, sinking down.

"We already know for sure," Lenore says miserably.

I close my eyes. "I'm taking you to a professional." Why her, and why not me? I picture Lenore with a very pregnant belly, unable to stand on those scrawny legs.

"Do you think I messed it up?" Lenore's voice is small. "Will you wait with me?"

"Of course." I tell myself to focus on Lenore, to try to think about how she must feel, but no thoughts come to me but how I feel. Small and alone, ready to break.

How many times have I been a week late, or even a couple of days late, and practically run to the drugstore, stood in the aisle, carefully considering which test was the best, which one could be done at any time during the day, which one had the highest accuracy percentage?

Then the race home, to tear open the package, read the instructions, and wait until I could use it. Every time—every single time—the results were clear, within seconds. Negative. The sign was always there, without doubt. Not pregnant. Lenore's said positive twice.

It is after eleven when we arrive home from the gallery. The reception brought a big crowd and we were caught up in the free wine and the conversation with others we'd met at other gallery receptions.

I'm in the bedroom loft hanging up my sea-green dress, Paul's favorite, when he peeks his head over the top of the stairs. He whistles at me and I make a face at him.

"That was fun," he says, throwing himself on the bed.

"Yeah, great," I say, and roll my eyes, only half-kidding. He laughs and flings a pillow at me, missing completely. He knows that I hate any kind of artists' gathering. All the attitude and unnecessary frills.

"It wasn't so bad," he says. "I made a lot of connections tonight." He stretches. "Things are really looking up."

My back is to him as I step into my cotton slip. "Not for everyone," I say. My voice is so low I wonder if he hears me.

"What do you mean?" he asks, suddenly alert. "You're doing great. You could do more with your jewelry if you wanted to . . ."

I curl up next to him on the bed, breathing in his skin. "I meant Lenore." I had tried to bring her up all night, but it never seemed right.

"God, Angie," he says, smacking his forehead with his palm. "I'm sorry, I forgot, with *Gourmet* and the reception. Is everything okay? Does she know?"

"She's pregnant," I say simply. My voice is calm, even. "I'm taking her to the doctor tomorrow, but I'm pretty sure."

"What's she going to do?" Paul asks. He combs his fingers through my hair, winding curls around his fingers. "Does she even know?"

"With Lenore, who knows?" I trace the blue-green veins running up and down Paul's inner arm. "She can hardly take care of herself, let alone a baby."

Paul nods, then sighs. "She must be kind of desperate, Angie."

"I think I'm her last resort, you know? You know—" I start to say it, just to come out and say it, but I can't. Paul pokes my side. "It's just so hard that it's not us."

He nods again. "How are you with this?" His face, above mine, searches for clues. I try to keep my face blank, impassive, but I know that Paul can feel me tremble. He accepts my silence as my answer, wraps an arm around me and waits.

I try to close my eyes and sleep, to make it go away, if only for a little bit. I did that when I found out about my trouble getting pregnant, sleep for fourteen hours at a time, until I couldn't sleep anymore. Until the nameless, faceless, sex-less baby I couldn't have invaded my dreams too. Until Paul became distant, a stranger, threatening to leave if I didn't come back.

Beside me, he sighs, on the edge of falling asleep. I trace his jawline with the tip of my finger, barely touching it, and he smiles.

What would they do with a baby? I thought about it all night, through the introductions to other artists, photographers, gallery people. A baby would need a place for its bottle to be warmed, a stove that didn't spew out cockroaches.

I nodded and smiled and laughed in the right places tonight, sipped wine and talked about art. A baby needed a place to crawl around, a place to sleep. Where would the baby sleep, in the middle of the futon?

I twist around to Paul, kicking sheets away. He smiles and opens his eyes halfway, the way cats do. "What's up?" he asks, his voice groggy. I shake him to make sure that he's awake.

The urgency has hit. If I don't speak now, I don't know if I will, ever. "Paul," I say. The words tumble out quickly. "I want us to adopt Lenore's baby. It's the only way it can work. I mean, for all of us."

Paul blinks and looks at me, confused. He sits up, his arms circled around his knees, but doesn't say anything. He stares out of the tiny diamond-shaped window to the left of the bed. Its view is a small patch of sky and a brick wall.

The cab is waiting outside Lenore's apartment. "You know," she says, "I don't think I'm going." She stands in her bra and a pair of shorts, sleep still heavy in her eyes.

"Oh, you're going," I say. "Put on a shirt. The cab's outside."

Lenore digs through a pile of clothing next to the wardrobe. She chooses a rumpled orange shirt and takes her time buttoning it.

"I hate cabs," she says. "Can't we walk?"

"If we had an extra hour we could. We can walk back."

"This doctor is a man?" This is the third time she's asked. When I nod yes again, she says, "I feel uncomfortable going to a male doctor. Maybe we should cancel and find a woman."

"Come on," I say and hold the door open.

She follows me outside slowly, her head hanging down. She's silent during the ride uptown. She watches buildings whizzing by and answers my space-filling questions in a monotone. She focuses on the back of the cabbie's head.

I sneak looks at Lenore from the corner of my eye. She taps her foot to some melody in her head. I clear my throat. Lenore glares at me. I lose my nerve. Not now.

Lenore takes in the Madison Avenue lobby with wide eyes. I follow her gaze to the indoor fountain, the reflective glass that covers the walls, the potted palms. My stomach does a familiar flip-flop, like this is my appointment, like the doctor's news is for me.

"I'm sorry, Angie," Lenore says finally. "This isn't my scene at all." She gestures to the people hurrying about in their pinstriped suits, carrying briefcases. "Thanks for taking me, but I'm going home. I can't deal."

I grab her arm, careful not to squeeze too hard. "You're nervous, and that's understandable. But this is something that doesn't go away, Lenore. You have to deal."

We step into the elevator alone. "I know it doesn't go away," she says, annoyed. "But you don't have to take over for me."

I don't say anything. When the elevator stops, I lead Lenore to Dr. Green's office. It is new, sleek, and sterile-looking. I admire the blond wood and the peace lily on the table.

The waiting room is half full, some women alone, some with partners, anxious, bored or embarrassed. Paul used to come to every appointment with me. He would whisper things about the other waiting patients to try to make me laugh.

"This is nothing like Dr. Kenwood's," Lenore whispers. Beads of perspiration line her pale forehead even though the office is air-conditioned.

I hand her a clipboard full of forms. "Dr. Kenwood is a pediatrician." I wonder if he was the last doctor Lenore has seen, and how many years ago that was.

Lenore flips through the forms quickly and leaves half of them blank. She shrugs at me before returning the clipboard. I glance around the room and wonder what the other women make of Lenore and me.

Lenore looks intently at a magazine and at no one else. I discreetly check out the others waiting. I wonder what each one is here for, if the woman carrying high is having a sonogram done, if she already knows whether her baby will be a boy or a girl. I wonder if the older-looking woman is carrying twins and is excited about this pregnancy.

We jump when Lenore's name is called. "That's me," she says. She smiles weakly at me and walks stiffly behind the nurse. She doesn't look back.

I pick up Lenore's discarded magazine and pretend to read. There's a sudden, stupid lump in my throat when I think of how different Lenore's visit is from my last visit. I think of Doctor Green's voice, low and soothing, and his gentle hands. I think of Lenore, sitting on the table, scared, maybe as scared as I was.

It's not hopeless, he'd said to me. But in all likelihood, it will be difficult for you to become pregnant. Even after the growths are removed, there's a good chance that more will grow.

I could feel the beginnings of tears burn behind my eyes, but I refused to let even one slide out. I took in a sharp breath and made myself speak.

How difficult?

Well. Dr. Green tapped his pen on the desk. It's hard to say, really. About thirty to forty percent of women with endometriosis are infertile. But you may not be one of them.

I did not return his smile, which seemed so fake to me, or Paul's, which seemed so full of pity. "There's still hope," he whispered to me. I shrugged him away.

The office is silent. The surgery was almost a year ago, and now I sit in the same office, alone, waiting to hear about Lenore's pregnancy.

Lenore finally walks back into the waiting room. I stand and meet her halfway across the room, to read the expression on her face. Her eyes dart around the room. She looks at the other women as I did. She rests her hands on her stomach and then I know for sure. She is one of them.

Outside, Lenore's smirk crumbles quickly. I pull her to me, and she lets me. I wrap my arms around her, way too late to shield her. She cries great big heaving sobs, her tears landing on my shoulder and dress. I rub her back and my own tears slide down my face into her hair.

"Why are *you* crying?" she asks. Her voice is ragged. "Oh, God, just get me out of here." As if, once out of the Upper East Side, she'll no longer be pregnant.

I hail a cab, and when the driver asks where we're going, I look to Lenore. She says, "Gramercy Park, please," in a small voice. My neighborhood. "Please don't make me go home yet," she says and bites her lip.

Inside my apartment, she paces. She begins in the kitchen, her boots squeaking on the tile floor. She rearranges magnets on the refrigerator and moves on to the living room, careful to avoid me.

"Can I get you anything?" I ask her finally. It seems as though she's forgotten that I'm there. She sits on the sofa tracing the geometric patterns over and over.

My voice startles her; she jumps. When she looks at me, her eyes are rapidly blinking back tears. "No," she says. Then she laughs, a short bark, running her fingers through her hair. "Well, you could get me out of this mess." She's rolled herself into a ball on the sofa, making herself as small as she can, and she looks bewildered.

I sit down next to her and touch her shoulders. She hunches them forward defensively. The tension is unbelievable. I twist the knots, working them over and over. Her shoulder blades are sharp and unyielding, but Lenore sighs and leans back into my hands.

"What are you going to do?" I ask, barely above a whisper.

She shrugs. "What can I do, Angie? I guess I'll get it taken care of next week."

I feel like I'm in one of those dreams where you run and run but go nowhere. I continue to knead Lenore's shoulders. I try to keep my voice even, normal. "Taken care of? As in—not having it, right?"

"I've been talking to Mom about this," Lenore says slowly. "And we think that it's the best option for me." She moves away from my hands and turns to face me. "I mean, I'm young, I can't afford to have a baby, and Manny would just freak out . . ." She trails off, searching my face for the disapproval she can sense. "What else can I do?" She swallows hard and stands. "Just look at me." She makes a sweeping gesture, head to toe. "I don't really think that I'm in a position to bring up a child, do you?"

But I am, I am, a voice inside my head says. I can't force the words out. I clear my throat to try. "There's adoption," I say. "It's another option, Lenore." My face is hot and I can feel perspiration on my upper lip. "I mean, have you even spoken to Manny about this? Does he even know you're pregnant?"

Lenore cringes at the word, then offers me a half-smile. "There was the time before this, when I thought I was pregnant. Manny thought we should keep it. It was a product of our love, he said." She sniffles and shakes her head. "Poor Manny. But talking to Mom—"

I cut her off. "Why would you even ask for her advice? Of course she's going to tell you to get rid of it. Isn't that basically what she did with us?" My voice is harsher than I intended and surprises even me. Blood rushes to my cheeks and I look down at my hands. "Have you even thought about adoption?"

"Just giving it away after carrying it around with me for so long? Yeah, I've thought of it. And I think of walking down a street and searching every kid's face that goes by to see if I could find myself." She shakes her head. "It would drive me crazy. I couldn't do it."

"Well, how about if someone you knew adopted it?" I ask. "Someone who, right now, is in a better position?" I force my gaze up from the floor and onto Lenore's face. "Someone who might be able to take care of you and a baby? Maybe someone who couldn't have a baby?"

Lenore's mouth is a round circle of surprise. "You," she says, piecing it all together. Her mouth remains open, making little sucking noises. Her eyes leave me, briefly, to flit around the room, but come back to rest on me. "You," she says sadly.

I force my eyes to meet hers. I can see, things are different. Suddenly, she is the older sister, the one with all of the advantages: faster, smarter, better. All the things that I was. Her face, staring back at me, is a mixture of pity and wrath. I hold my breath until she speaks.

"Well, that just figures," she says. She moves away from me and her dark eyes narrow. She looks away, taking in the room—the built-in cherry bookcases, the glass and chrome coffee table, the arched windows and the hanging plants—as if she can't stand the sight of any of it.

Lenore's voice shakes as she speaks. "You couldn't just want to help me, could you? Here I was, thinking, none of my friends want to help because babies freak them out, and they're all suddenly very busy. But my sister, my wonderful sister, steps right up for me." Her eyes return to me, drill into me. Her laugh is short and harsh. "And it's only because you want something from me. Good God, I can't stand you."

"That's not true," I say, my voice pleading. I can feel the hotness on my cheeks, my forehead, my neck. "I would do anything to help you, Lenore, I would." Even as I say the words, in the back of my head I wonder if that's the truth.

"Get over yourself," Lenore says and stands. "I'm leaving. I can deal with this one myself." She throws me a disgusted look. "Giving my baby to you," she spits out, "is just about the last thing I'd ever do."

I try to say something, anything, but my mind is completely blank. Lenore has never looked at me with such complete contempt. A strangled whimper is caught in my throat.

"I'll show myself out, thanks." Lenore walks towards the door. I make no move to get up.

"What's taking so long?" I ask.

I'm in the back of a cab, trying to get to the clinic as fast as possible. Paul is next to me, our fingers entwined. My other hand is balled into a fist, my nails cutting half-moons into my palm.

Paul raps on the plexiglass divider. "Hey pal, can you go any faster?"

When the cab stops at the curb, I nod to Paul and jump out. The clinic is in an old building, sandwiched between a Korean deli and a restaurant supply store. Manny is outside, smoking. "Where is she?" I ask before he can speak.

"Thank God you're here," he says, hugging me. I squirm out of his arms. "She's been yelling for you since she got here—they only let family in. I mean, she's been screaming at the top of her lungs. I think they hooked her up with Valium or something."

Inside, the clinic gets little light. Everything is beige—walls, sofas, floor. My heels click against the tile. I wonder whether or not they clean this place daily.

"Let's sit and wait," Paul suggests. The couches are made of Naugahyde and stick to my skin. I look around at others waiting. There are hardly any men here besides Paul and Manny. There are women with glazed eyes, disheveled hair, bitten-down fingernails. There are women with marks on their arms, bruises or needle marks.

I turn to Manny, and my voice shakes as I speak. "Why here? Why this place?" Manny's face, already pale, twists up like he's a young boy, ready to cry. "Why not a clean hospital?" Paul's arm, already around me, tenses, as if to hold me back.

"She started bleeding," Manny says, "and freaking out. I mean, she lost it completely. And this place—this place was closest." He swallows hard and looks away.

Paul nods to Manny. "It's okay," he says, "You did okay." He reaches for his wallet.

"Manny, would you get us some coffee? Get some for yourself, too."

We watch Manny trot off obediently. "Go easy on him, Angie," Paul says in a quiet voice. "You're not the only one this is affecting."

I can feel a flush creeping slowly onto my face. I glare at Paul. He's looking at me with those eyes, steady and kind, meaning no harm. I want to snap at him, but I can't. Instead I focus my attention on the desk across the room.

"Isn't there more than one nurse here? In the whole freaking place?" I say this out loud, but don't expect an answer. I zero in on the woman behind the desk. She's already helping two women at the same time. Another woman stares into the air and waits. So many defeated faces. I think of Lenore, alone, somewhere in this place. I lean against Paul, close my eyes and breathe in his clean soap smell.

Manny returns and hands a cup to each of us. I don't want coffee, but I take one, just to have something to hold. The coffee is weak and tastes like it's been run through a filter twice. I smile at Manny, sitting there like a lost puppy, and he returns it gratefully.

He leans forward. "See that woman there?" The fat one with the big hair? She's the one you should talk to. She was taking care of Lenore." He points to a second woman behind the desk, leaning over the first.

Paul stands with me, but I shake my head at him. "Be right back," I say.

The woman looks like she hasn't had a good night's sleep in a long time. "Yes," she says impatiently, "what can I do for you?" She doesn't smile.

"My sister," I say. My voice is on the edge of breaking, so I swallow and try again. "My sister is here. Lenore Pallas. How is she?"

"Pallas, Pallas," the woman repeats. She flips through pages on a clipboard, picking at her cuticles as she reads. "Oh yes." She looks up at me. "Lenore. She's been hollering for you since she got here. You can see her." She doesn't wait for my reply.

I follow her through a swinging door and down another beige hallway. Paul's voice comes back to me. I'm not the only one this is affecting. The hallway smells like a mixture of rubbing alcohol and vomit. There are fingerprints smudged into the walls.

The nurse stops in front of a door. "She's in here, but she might be asleep." I start to twist the knob, and she puts her hand over mine. For the first time, I hear a gentleness in her voice. "She's really in shock," she says. She pauses and shrugs, and the gentleness is gone. "You know. Miscarriage." I look at the woman and want to explain. It's my sister in there, not some girl's miscarriage.

Instead, I turn the knob and the door squeals open to a tiny windowless room, barely bigger than the bed Lenore sleeps in. She's pale, even against the whiteness of the sheets. I shut the door behind me. A needle in her hand attaches her to tubes and the IV. Besides the steady drip of fluid into her veins, the only sound is the low hum of the fluorescent lights above her.

There's a folding chair next to the bed, but I stand and study Lenore. Somewhere, there's a photo of her, maybe six or seven years old, asleep. She looks remarkably like she does now, hair fanned out wildly around her, like a crooked halo.

I watch her eyes twitch beneath her eyelids. When Lenore was smaller, just a baby really, I used to creep to her bed and pull her eyelids up, ever so gently. I was sure that I'd be able to see her dreams, as if they were movies, projected onto her eyelids. I was disappointed. For a moment, I want to do it again, but I know I still won't find out what she dreams about.

I notice a mark on her arm, just underneath the paper gown she's wearing. I wonder briefly, angrily, if the mark came from the clinic. I lift the sleeve higher for a closer inspection, and I'm surprised to see that it's not a bruise, but a tattoo. It's maybe three inches high, a black cat with an arched back, Halloween style. I wonder how long it's been there.

I listen to Lenore breathing, deep but disturbed. Every now and then, I think I hear a whimper, but it might be me. I sit down against the cold metal of the chair and sip my lukewarm coffee. When Lenore opens her eyes, I'll be there, waiting.

How It Works

1. Which sister do you sympathize with more, Angie or Lenore? What positive, negative, and neutral information does the writer convey about each sister in order to create a well-rounded character?

2. How does Angie feel about Lenore? How does the writer convey these feelings? How would you characterize this narrative voice? What personality traits does it convey?

3. The character of Manny provides comic relief and helps show Lenore's sensibility and situation. If you were discussing this story in a workshop and someone encouraged the author to develop him further, what would you say? What would be the advantages and disadvantages of doing so?

4. How would you describe this story's central conflict? Underline places where the writer deepens that conflict or makes it more complex by developing other sides of the issue. Now reread the story, leaving out those places. What is different about it?

Eudora Welty

Eudora Welty was born in Jackson, Mississippi, in 1909. She graduated from the University of Wisconsin in Madison and also studied at the Columbia University School of Business. She returned to Jackson in 1931, when her father died. There, she worked for the local radio station and wrote society news for the newspaper. In 1935 and 1936, she worked as a "junior publicity agent" for a U.S. government agency, promoting road building, new airstrips, canning factories, and other efforts to bring economic progress to poor and remote rural areas of Mississippi. Her stories began to be published shortly thereafter. Welty's fiction portrays small-town life in the South and is characterized by delicacy, wit, a sense of human loneliness, and, occasionally, fantasy. It contains vivid characters and voices, and a strong sense of place. Her numerous stories and novels include The Robber Bridegroom *(1942),* The Ponder Heart *(1954),* Delta Wedding *(1946),* Losing Battles *(1970),* The Optimist's Daughter *(1972), and* The Collected Stories of Eudora Welty *(1980). Her nonfiction books include* The Eye of the Story *(1978) and* One Writer's Beginnings *(1984).*

The Key

It was quiet in the waiting room of the remote little station, except for the night sounds of insects. You could hear their embroidering movements in the weeds outside, which somehow gave the effect of some tenuous voice in the night, telling a story. Or you could listen to the fat thudding of the light bugs and the hoarse rushing of their big wings against the wooden ceiling. Some of the bugs were clinging heavily to the yellow globe, like idiot bees to a senseless smell.

Under this prickly light two rows of people sat in silence, their faces stung, their bodies twisted and quietly uncomfortable, expectantly so, in ones and twos, not quite asleep. No one seemed impatient, although the train was late. A little girl lay flung back in her mother's lap as though sleep had struck her with a blow.

Ellie and Albert Morgan were sitting on a bench like the others waiting for the train and had nothing to say to each other. Their names were ever so neatly and rather largely printed on a big reddish-tan suitcase strapped crookedly shut, because of a missing buckle, so that it hung apart finally like a stupid pair of lips. "Albert Morgan, Ellie Morgan, Yellow Leaf, Mississippi." They must have been driven into town in a wagon, for they and the suitcase were all touched here and there with a fine yellow dust, like finger marks.

Ellie Morgan was a large woman with a face as pink and crowded as an old-fashioned rose. She must have been about forty years old. One of those black satchel purses hung over her straight, strong wrist. It must have been her savings which were making possible this trip. And to what place? you wondered, for she sat there as tense and solid as a cube, as if to endure some nameless apprehension rising and overflowing within her at the thought of travel. Her face worked and broke into strained, hardening lines, as if there had been a death—that too-explicit evidence of agony in the desire to communicate.

Albert made a slower and softer impression. He sat motionless beside Ellie, holding his hat in his lap with both hands—a hat you were sure he had never worn. He looked home-made, as though his wife had self-consciously knitted or somehow contrived a husband when she sat alone at night. He had a shock of very fine sun-burned yellow hair. He was too shy for this world, you could see. His hands were like card-board, he held his hat so still; and yet how softly his eyes fell upon its crown, moving dreamily and yet with dread over its brown surface! He was smaller than his wife. His suit was brown, too, and he wore it neatly and carefully, as though he were murmuring, "Don't look—no need to look—I am effaced." But you have seen that expression too in silent children, who will tell you what they dreamed the night before in sudden, almost hilarious, bursts of confidence.

Every now and then, as though he perceived some minute thing, a sudden alert, tantalized look would creep over the little man's face, and he would gaze slowly around him, quite slyly. Then he would bow his head again; the expression would vanish; some inner refreshment had been denied him. Behind his head was a wall poster, dirty with time, showing an old-fashioned locomotive about to crash into an open touring car filled with women in veils. No one in the station was frightened by the familiar poster, any more than they were aroused by the little man whose rising and drooping head it framed. Yet for a moment he might seem to you to be sitting there quite filled with hope.

Among the others in the station was a strong-looking young man, alone, hatless, red

haired, who was standing by the wall while the rest sat on benches. He had a small key in his hand and was turning it over and over in his fingers, nervously passing it from one hand to the other, tossing it gently into the air and catching it again.

He stood and stared in distraction at the other people; so intent and so wide was his gaze that anyone who glanced after him seemed rocked like a small boat in the wake of a large one. There was an excess of energy about him that separated him from everyone else, but in the motion of his hands there was, instead of the craving for communication, something of reticence, even of secrecy, as the key rose and fell. You guessed that he was a stranger in town; he might have been a criminal or a gambler, but his eyes were widened with gentleness. His look, which traveled without stopping for long anywhere, was a hurried focusing of a very tender and explicit regard.

The color of his hair seemed to jump and move, like the flicker of a match struck in a wind. The ceiling lights were not steady but seemed to pulsate like a living and transient force, and made the young man in his preoccupation appear to tremble in the midst of his size and strength, and to fail to impress his exact outline upon the yellow walls. He was like a salamander in the fire. "Take care," you wanted to say to him, and yet also, "Come here." Nervously, and quite apart in his distraction, he continued to stand tossing the key back and forth from one hand to the other. Suddenly it became a gesture of abandonment: one hand stayed passive in the air, then seized too late: the key fell to the floor.

Everyone, except Albert and Ellie Morgan, looked up for a moment. On the floor the key had made a fierce metallic sound like a challenge, a sound of seriousness. It almost made people jump. It was regarded as an insult, a very personal question, in the quiet peaceful room where the insects were tapping at the ceiling and each person was allowed to sit among his possessions and wait for an unquestioned departure. Little walls of reproach went up about them all.

A flicker of amusement touched the young man's face as he observed the startled but controlled and obstinately blank faces which turned toward him for a moment and then away. He walked over to pick up his key.

But it had glanced and slid across the floor, and now it lay in the dust at Albert Morgan's feet.

Albert Morgan was indeed picking up the key. Across from him the young man saw him examine it, quite slowly, with wonder written all over his face and hands, as if it had fallen from the sky. Had he failed to hear the clatter? There was something wrong with Albert. . . .

As if by decision, the young man did not terminate this wonder by claiming his key. He stood back, a peculiar flash of interest or of something more inscrutable, like resignation, in his lowered eyes.

The little man had probably been staring at the floor, thinking. And suddenly in the dark surface the small sliding key had appeared. You could see memory seize his face, twist it and hold it. What innocent, strange thing might it have brought back to life—a fish he had once spied just below the top of the water in a sunny lake in the country when he was a child? This was just as unexpected, shocking, and somehow meaningful to him. Albert sat there holding the key in his wide-open hand. How intensified, magnified, really vain all attempt at expression becomes in the afflicted! It was with an almost incandescent delight that he felt the unguessed temperature and weight of the key. Then he turned to his wife. His lips were actually trembling.

And still the young man waited, as if the strange joy of the little man took precedence with him over whatever need he had for the key. With sudden electrification he saw Ellie slip the handle of her satchel purse from her wrist and with her fingers begin to talk to her husband.

The others in the station had seen Ellie too; shallow pity washed over the waiting room like a dirty wave foaming and creeping over a public beach. In quick mumblings from bench to bench people said to each other, "Deaf and dumb!" How ignorant they were of all that the young man was seeing! Although he had no way of knowing the words Ellie said, he seemed troubled enough at the mistake the little man must have made, at his misplaced wonder and joy.

Albert was replying to his wife. On his hands he said to her, "I found it. Now it belongs to me. It is something important! Important! It means something. From now on we will get along better, have more understanding. . . . Maybe when we reach Niagara Falls we will even fall in love, the way other people have done. Maybe our marriage was really for love, after all, not for the other reason—both of us being afflicted in the same way, unable to speak, lonely because of that. Now you can stop being ashamed of me. For being so cautious and slow all my life, for taking my own time. . . . You can take hope. Because it was I who found the key. Remember that—I found it." He laughed all at once, quite silently.

Everyone stared at his impassioned little speech as it came from his fingers. They were embarrassed, vaguely aware of some crisis and vaguely affronted, but unable to interfere; it was as though they were the deaf-mutes and he the speaker. When he laughed, a few people laughed unconsciously with him, in relief, and turned away. But the young man remained still and intent, waiting at his little distance.

"This key came here very mysteriously—it is bound to mean something," the husband went on to say. He held the key up just before her eyes. "You were always praying; you believe in miracles; well, now, here is the answer. It came to me."

His wife look self-consciously around the room and replied on her fingers, "You are always talking nonsense. Be quiet."

But she was secretly pleased, and when she saw him slowly look down in his old manner, she reached over, as if to retract what she had said, and laid her hand on his, touching the key for herself, softness making her worn hand limp. From then on they never looked around them, never saw anything except each other. They were so intent, so very solemn, wanting to have their symbols perfectly understood!

"You must see it is a symbol," he began again, his fingers clumsy and blurring in his excitement. "It is a symbol of something—something that we deserve, and that is happiness. We will find happiness in Niagara Falls."

And then, as if he were all at once shy even of her, he turned slightly away from her and slid the key into his pocket. They sat staring down at the suitcase, their hands fallen in their laps.

The young man slowly turned away from them and wandered back to the wall, where he took out a cigarette and lighted it.

Outside, the night pressed around the station like a pure stone, in which the little room might be transfixed and, for the preservation of this moment of hope, its future killed, an insect in amber. The short little train drew in, stopped, and rolled away, almost noiselessly.

Then inside, people were gone or turned in sleep or walking about, all changed from the way they had been. But the deaf-mutes and the loitering young man were still in their places.

The man was still smoking. He was dressed like a young doctor or some such person in the town, and yet he did not seem of the town. He looked very strong and active; but there was a startling quality, a willingness to be forever distracted, even disturbed, in the very reassurance of his body, some alertness which made his strength fluid and dissipated instead of withheld and greedily beautiful. His youth by now did not seem an important thing about him; it was a medium for his activity, no doubt, but as he stood there frowning and smoking you felt some apprehension that he would never express whatever might be the desire of his life in being young and strong, in standing apart in compassion, in making any intuitive present or sacrifice, or in any way of action at all—not because there was too much in the world demanding his strength, but because he was too deeply aware.

You felt a shock in glancing up at him, and when you looked away from the whole yellow room and closed your eyes, his intensity, as well as that of the room, seemed to have impressed the imagination with a shadow of itself, a blackness together with the light, the negative beside the positive. You felt as though some exact, skillful contact had been made between the surfaces of your hearts to make you aware, in some pattern, of his joy and his despair. You could feel the fullness and the emptiness of this stranger's life.

The railroad man came in swinging a lantern which he stopped suddenly in its arc. Looking uncomfortable, and then rather angry, he approached the deaf-mutes and shot his arm out in a series of violent gestures and shrugs.

Albert and Ellie Morgan were dreadfully shocked. The woman looked resigned for a moment to hopelessness. But the little man—you were startled by a look of bravado on his face.

In the station the red-haired man was speaking aloud—but to himself. "They missed their train!"

As if in quick apology, the trainman set his lantern down beside Albert's foot, and hurried away.

And as if completing a circle, the red-haired man walked over too and stood silently near the deaf-mutes. With a reproachful look at him, the woman reached up and took off her hat.

They began again, talking rapidly back and forth, almost as one person. The old routine of their feeling was upon them once more. Perhaps, you thought, staring at their similarity—her hair was yellow, too—they were children together—cousins even, afflicted in the same way, sent off from home to the state institute. . . .

It was the feeling of conspiracy. They were in counter-plot against the plot of those things that pressed down upon them from outside their knowledge and their ways of making themselves understood. It was obvious that it gave the wife her greatest pleasure. But you wondered, seeing Albert, whom talking seemed rather to dishevel, whether it had not continued to be a rough and violent game which Ellie, as the older and stronger, had taught him to play with her.

"What do you think he wants?" she asked Albert, nodding at the red-haired man, who smiled faintly. And how her eyes shone! Who would ever know how deep her suspicion of the whole outside world lay in her heart, how far it had pushed her!

"What does he want?" Albert was replying quickly. "The key!"

Of course! And how fine it had been to sit there with the key hidden from the strangers and also from his wife, who had not seen where he had put it. He stole up with his hand and secretly felt the key, which must have lain in some pocket nearly against his heart. He nodded gently. The key had come there, under his eyes on the floor in the station, all of a sudden, but yet not quite unexpected. That is the way things happen to you always. But Ellie did not comprehend this.

Now she sat there as quiet as could be. It was not only hopelessness about the trip. She, too, undoubtedly felt something privately about that key, apart from what she had said or what he had told her. He had almost shared it with her—you realized that. He frowned and smiled almost at the same time. There was something—something he could almost remember but not quite—which would let him keep the key always to himself. He knew that, and he would remember it later, when he was alone.

"Never fear, Ellie," he said, a still little smile lifting his lip. "I've got it safe in a pocket. No one can find it, and there's no hole for it to fall through."

She nodded, but she was always doubting, always anxious. You could look at her troubled hands. How terrible it was, how strange, that Albert loved the key more than he loved Ellie! He did not mind missing the train. It showed in every line, every motion of his body. The key was closer—closer. The whole story began to illuminate them now, as if the lantern flame had been turned up. Ellie's anxious, hovering body could wrap him softly as a cradle, but the secret meaning, that powerful sign, that reassurance he so hopefully sought, so assuredly deserved—

that had never come. There was something lacking in Ellie.

Had Ellie, with her suspicions of everything, come to know even things like this, in her
way? How empty and nervous her red scrubbed
hands were, how desperate to speak! Yes, she
must regard it as unhappiness lying between
them, as more than emptiness. She must worry
about it, talk about it. You could imagine her
stopping her churning to come out to his chair
on the porch, to tell him that she did love him
and would take care of him always, talking with
the spotted sour milk dripping from her fingers.
Just try to tell her that talking is useless, that
care is not needed . . . And sooner or later he
would always reply, say something, agree, and
she would go away again. . . .

And Albert, with his face so capable of
amazement, made you suspect the funny thing
about talking to Ellie. Until you do, declared
his round brown eyes, you can be peaceful and
content that everything takes care of itself. As
long as you let it alone everything goes peacefully, like an uneventful day on the farm—
chores attended to, woman working in the
house, you in the field, crop growing as well as
can be expected, the cow giving, and the sky
like a coverlet over it all—so that you're as full
of yourself as a colt, in need of nothing, and
nothing needing you. But when you pick up
your hands and start to talk, if you don't watch
carefully, this security will run away and leave
you. You say something, make an observation,
just to answer your wife's worryings, and everything is jolted, disturbed, laid open like the
ground behind a plow, with you running along
after it.

But happiness, Albert knew, is something
that appears to you suddenly, that is meant for
you, a thing which you reach for and pick up

and hide at your breast, a shiny thing that reminds you of something alive and leaping.

Ellie sat there quiet as a mouse. She had unclasped her purse and taken out a little card
with a picture of Niagara Falls on it.

"Hide it from the man," she said. She did
suspect him! The red-haired man had drawn
closer. He bent and saw that it was a picture of
Niagara Falls.

"Do you see the little rail?" Albert began in
tenderness. And Ellie loved to watch him tell
her about it; she clasped her hands and began to
smile and show her crooked tooth; she looked
young: it was the way she had looked as a child.

"That is what the teacher pointed to with
her wand on the magic-lantern slide—the little
rail. You stand right here. You lean up hard
against the rail. Then you can hear Niagara
Falls."

"How do you hear it?" begged Ellie, nodding.

"You hear it with your whole self. You listen with your arms and your legs and your
whole body. You'll never forget what hearing is,
after that."

He must have told her hundreds of times in
his obedience, yet she smiled with gratitude, and
stared deep, deep into the tinted picture of the
waterfall.

Presently she said, "By now, we'd have been
there, if we hadn't missed the train."

She did not even have any idea that it was
miles and days away.

She looked at the red-haired man then, her
eyes all puckered up, and he looked away at last.
He had seen the dust on her throat and a needle
stuck in her collar where she'd forgotten it, with
a thread running through the eye—the final details. Her hands were tight and wrinkled with
pressure. She swung her foot a little below her

skirt, in the new Mary Jane slipper with the hard toe.

Albert turned away too. It was then, you thought, that he became quite frightened to think that if they hadn't missed the train they would be hearing, at that very moment, Niagara Falls. Perhaps they would be standing there together, pressed against the little rail, pressed against each other, with their lives being poured through them, changing. . . . And how did he know what that would be like? He bent his head and tried not to look at his wife. He could say nothing. He glanced up once at the stranger, with almost a pleading look, as if to say, "Won't you come with us?"

"To work so many years, and then to miss the train," Ellie said.

You saw by her face that she was undauntedly wondering, unsatisfied, waiting for the future.

And you knew how she would sit and brood over this as over their conversations together, about every misunderstanding, every discussion, sometimes even about some agreement between them that had been all settled—even about the secret and proper separation that lies between a man and a woman, the thing that makes them what they are in themselves, their secret life, their memory of the past, their childhood, their dreams. This to Ellie was unhappiness.

They had told her when she was a little girl how people who have just been married have the custom of going to Niagara Falls on a wedding trip, to start their happiness; and that came to be where she put her hope, all of it. So she saved money. She worked harder than he did, you could observe, comparing their hands, good and bad years, more than was good for a woman. Year after year she had put her hope ahead of her.

And he—somehow he had never thought that this time would come, that they might really go on the journey. He was never looking so far and so deep as Ellie—into the future, into the changing and mixing of their lives together when they should arrive at last at Niagara Falls. To him it was always something postponed, like the paying off of the mortgage.

But sitting here in the station, with the suitcase all packed and at his feet, he had begun to realize that this journey might, for a fact, take place. The key had materialized to show him the enormity of this venture. And after his first shock and pride he had simply reserved the key; he had hidden it in his pocket.

She looked unblinking into the light of the lantern on the floor. Her face looked strong and terrifying, all lighted and very near to his. But there was no joy there. You knew that she was very brave.

Albert seemed to shrink, to retreat. . . . His trembling hand went once more beneath his coat and touched the pocket where the key was lying, waiting. Would he ever remember that elusive thing about it or be sure what it might really be a symbol of? . . . His eyes, in their quick manner of filming over, grew dreamy. Perhaps he had even decided that it was a symbol not of happiness with Ellie, but of something else—something which he could have alone, for only himself, in peace, something strange and unlooked for which would come to him. . . .

The red-haired man took a second key from his pocket, and in one direct motion placed it in Ellie's red palm. It was a key with a large triangular pasteboard tag on which was clearly printed, "Star Hotel, Room 2."

He did not wait to see any more, but went out abruptly into the night. He stood still for a moment and reached for a cigarette. As he held the match close he gazed straight ahead, and in his eyes, all at once wild and searching, there was certainly, besides the simple compassion in his regard, a look both restless and weary, very much used to the comic. You could see that he despised and saw the uselessness of the thing he had done.

How It Works

1. What does Welty's choice of the second-person point of view contribute to this story? Look for places where the point of view particularly affected your experience as you read. Now imagine these passages presented in first- or third-person point of view. How is the effect different?

2. Writing teachers (including me) warn students about depending on adjectives and adverbs in their descriptions. Underline all of the adjectives and adverbs in the first few paragraphs of this story. Do they add to or detract from the story? How? What other descriptive choices might the author have made, and what would have been the effect of each?

3. Underline passages that refer to the key. How does Welty use this symbol? How often is it mentioned, and how much space is devoted to it? How does the author keep the key in the reader's mind?

4. Beginning students are often discouraged from using metaphors and similes. Underline metaphors in this story and others. How often do authors use them, and for what purpose? Now look back through some scenes or stories you've written and identify some metaphors and similes. If you received comments on the story, how did readers react to these particular devices? Experiment with alternatives: try substituting a concrete description for a simile; and on the other hand, look for metaphors that might suggest a new perspective or convey a meaningful comparison.

Kelly Zavotka

Kelly Zavotka was raised in Pataskala, Ohio. She earned her BFA in writing at Emerson College and is currently at work on her MFA at Columbia University. "What Killed a Girl" is loosely based on a real murder but began as a freewrite. Although Kelly intended it to be her first nonautobiographical story, she wound up "characterizing what I saw as the innocent self and the guilty self—what I liked and didn't like about myself." As that thought took hold, she developed the story by consciously exaggerating these traits in the form of characters that became "almost caricatures. But what kept them from being flat, if that would be given to me, is the emo-

tional or psychological connection I felt to them." As she worked on the story, Kelly discovered the importance of "differentiating myself from my characters and yet maintaining enough of a link so that I was not just coldly portraying something that I thought was clever or bizarre, but exploring something." Although Kelly developed these characters intuitively, she explains that she felt that the story's integrity depended on its thematic content. "I still struggle with that—letting the character be whole and releasing control to readers to feel it however they will." Below is the first of "What Killed a Girl"'s three sections.

What Killed a Girl

The first time I got naked in the woods I was twelve. I took the short cut home from school and stopped to sit under an American Hornbeam and wait for a sign of God or a vision of my dead mother, when I got the sudden urge to take off my clothes. I was naked when Mom died—when I was born—and after that I was naked a lot. Then, God knows why, I started to think I had to keep my clothes on.

It felt weird at first, like my skin might float off of me. My body breathed. My stomach, my ass, they felt like they were being born. Touched air, leaves, dirt. The wind rolled over me so tenderly, like soft dry waves lapping, leaving their sweet and musty perfume. I smell it in my sheets now when I fall into bed with dirty feet and hair. It smells like a kid before his evening bath, stained with dirt and a light salty sweat. My entire body discovered the joys of rain beating my muscles soft, my skin silky.

I can stay naked a lot longer now. I've learned things to do, things to be—like a wood nymph. I saw a picture of one once and realized that they are supposed to have wings. Mine are invisible.

Today in my freshman English class, I heard the rain slapping the concrete outside, quieting the voices of Romeo and Juliet that came from the tape recorder on our teacher's desk. Thunder purred far away, raising the hair on my arms. My skin, impatient. By lunch the rain had stopped and I could smell the bloated worms warming in the sun. I knew I would get naked after school; the ground had turned to mud. I love mud, the way it dries on my skin, pulling everything real tight and then cracking in a bunch of lines like the veins on a leaf or the bark of a tree. It was a damp kind of day and the mud wouldn't have dried if I hadn't been running real fast, pretending I was a warrior in training, then a squaw escaping her French captors—that sounded more dramatic. I collapsed on a bed of moss on the other side of the creek. I felt silly, like someone who wouldn't understand at all was watching me. Then I saw a little snatch of blue peaking up out of the ground and I was an archaeologist as I crouched down beside the mysterious object. I pulled and uprooted a pair of Osh-Kosh-B-Gosh overalls. Little ones. That's how I learned that sometimes when I'm not here, there's a little kid who does what I do. I'm happy to know it, but a creepy feeling came over me. This forest was not completely mine. I folded the overalls and placed them neatly on the moss so the kid could find them. I walked back to my own pile of clothes to put them on and go home.

It's about 5:30. The sun's going down. Through the trees, a pink light is glowing off the aluminum blocks of Pine Creek Trailer park. It's time to run home before Daddy gets there, clean up and make some dinner. I'm thinking about what to cook as I throw my dress back over my dirty skin and head home. I part the low branches at the forest's edge, springing off fat drops of rain, and I step onto the wetted ash gravel of the trailer park. The whine of a small engine cuts through the dense September evening. It's Bobby Winston, revving his bright purple crotch-rocket. As I approach his body straddling that humming machine I wish we had lasted until spring so I could've ridden with him. I swear he notices me creeping towards him. He's probably just ignoring me so he won't have to acknowledge that I'm covered in mud. I try to catch his eye but with a scream he becomes a purple blur weaving and slashing through the gravel.

Bobby and I went out last winter, snowmobiling. Well, it wasn't a real date. He didn't ask me out then pick me up at the door, but it's the closest thing I ever had. I was in our field making snow angels and Bobby almost ran me over on his snowmobile. That's how I ended up back at his trailer a couple hours later, my slushy boots and snow pants in a heap on his floor and me tangled up with him in his mom's bed, both of us in only our underwear. Bobby wore silk boxers.

I never got to see it. I still haven't seen one in real life. But I felt it. We went in the room to get some dry clothes of his mom's for me to wear and I had to take my clothes off at the door or else I would have gotten slush all over the fire-colored carpet. It all happened so fast. When I saw that Bobby was half-naked too, I thought he was also changing, but he started kissing me, pushed me back on the bed. It was my first horizontal kiss. His mom, Karen, came home and saw us making out in her bed and starting crying and screaming, calling me a whore. She totally freaked. She was as mean and scary-looking as the lunch ladies at school. Bobby's never talked to me since then. But he never talked to me before that either.

I'm standing in the highway's grassy median. It's taking me about five minutes to cross Route 40, the National Trail. Rush hour, sort of—cars going by, drivers looking at me through water-beaded windows. I'm all drenched and a mud puddle is forming at my bare feet. My dress is sticking to me, my hair in tight wet tangles. I'm just hoping that Daddy won't drive by and see me like this. But he's never been early. I could cross if I ran real fast, but I guess I kind of enjoy being a spectacle. Through the gray sky, fluorescent pink flashes signal my temporary home. "Vacancy," the sign says, just below a glowing green Shamrock and the words "Shamrock Motel." The old

farm lies about a quarter-mile to my right. A landscape of cornhusk brown, sopping wet death. It's a color like dried leaves or bran flakes but not so crisp. Dad sold it to some developers for millions, more than we'd make farming for the rest of our lives. He said that sometimes you just have to move on and there's no stopping it. Still, I don't think he's dealing well. Every day he meets with the architect and takes a room off the house or moves the windows around. All we really have is some property in town, an expensive architect, and the promise of money.

I've finally crossed over and have decided on heating up some leftover ham, potato and green bean soup, and a few rolls. The big Shamrock's about three houses up. A man could stop his car on the highway and run after me to ask if I'm okay, if I fell or something and where am I going and am I cold 'cause of the rain? Of course he'd be real good-looking and he'd seem very nice. He even offers me his jean jacket to wear. I can tell right off he's full of good intentions. And I say out loud what I was doing and that I'm fine, I just like getting in the mud. And I tell him about what mud does when it dries on your skin, till he gets all excited. He's a gentleman, of course, but I see *it* in his eyes, and then I point to where I live and tell him he's welcome to dinner but he has to wait and come back in half an hour when my Daddy gets home because I'm not allowed to have boys over without supervision. He says he'd love to.

Finally at home, last room on the right. Our front door is crowded by the things that used to be in our garage. Everyone at the Shamrock has stuff overflowing their rooms—except for the few that have been empty ever since the drag races at National Raceways. I strip down inside the door and try to run as lightly as I can to the shower so I don't get mud all over. I wash real fast—I want that extra time to get dressed for Rick, my deejay. My light pink dress comes to my ankles and buttons down the front, all the way from top to bottom. I pull my hair up 'cause there's no time to dry it but I take a moment for lipstick. The microwave door slams shut and I turn the dial to seven. The warm yellow glow lights up the room. The ceiling is too low, or the windows too high. I feel big and crowded here and I duck even though I don't really need to. The other room, the bedroom, doesn't feel this way, but I don't like to be in there either 'cause they've got brown paint splashed on the window, blocking out light, so it looks like someone smeared a diaper over it. New carpeting, the same kind of brown, covers the place. But beneath my feet the floor feels like a warped cookie sheet and I wonder what's lying in the hollow pockets between the dirt and the old boards. I lie down on the floor and close my eyes. I wonder how Daddy will react to a strange man at dinner.

Daddy's upset. He asks me who the man is, where I met him, how he knows where I live, why'm I wearing that dress?

I answer all but the last two but Daddy doesn't trust my intuition. And he doesn't trust anyone who wears dark sunglasses, especially inside. He tells the man to leave. And I say I'm going with him, just like something on MTV.

We run out of the house. Daddy doesn't say anything till we're already outside getting in the man's car, a Thunderbird. I know 'cause it's got a big gold eagle-like bird on its black hood. Dad stands at the door and yells something. I don't know what, we have the radio up so loud.

Five miles down the highway a cop spins out of the Methodist church and starts chasing us. But we don't stop, we just keep on going at 90 miles an hour. We don't even slow down for

Outville or New Cairo. Now we just got to keep on going. The man's kind of mad 'cause it's all my fault, but you can tell he's glad it's happening so long as he isn't held responsible. But he's the one driving, I know he is loving it. By now we've got five cops behind us and Metallica, "Ride the Lightning," vibrates the dashboard and blasts out the windows. I've got my left hand wrapped around his hard denim thigh and my right hand hanging out the open window. It's holding one of his cigarettes. My hair blows out of its loose bun and the top two buttons of my dress fly open.

I ask him what his name is, where we're going. He waits to answer 'cause we're running a red light in the middle of Summit Station. We make it through but a big semi cuts off all the cops and we take a moment to scream and yell.

"Rick," he says, "and we're going wherever you want to go."

"Well, do you have a job or anything you have to be at tomorrow?"

Rick puts his arm around me. "I'm a deejay, but I don't care if I ever go back to work. I really just want to be a bounty hunter."

It's a good stopping point. The door of Daddy's trunk just slammed closed outside. I jump up off the floor and run to the microwave to stir the soup. Daddy grumbles through the door and goes over to the sink, where he lathers up his arms and hands with green dish soap. I tell him we're having leftovers. He sort of grunts and starts setting the table.

"What the hell do you do after school that you don't have time to cook a real dinner." He drops his cigarette to the floor and crushes it beneath his shoe.

"I play naked in the mud and then get chased by cops down the highway with a future bounty hunter." I laugh but of course he doesn't. I pick up his cigarette butt between my toes and drop it under the table, then rub the ashes into the carpet with my heel, one hand on the table's edge for balance. I feel like I'm standing too close to Daddy so I go into the kitchen for an ashtray.

"Daddy, what do you do all day since we don't have the farm?" I set the ashtray in front of him.

"Business things." He leans forward, stretching out one massive, freckled arm towards the T.V., which sits on top of two boxes in the corner. His face strains as he leans closer to dial, his chair resting on its two front legs. He gets his evening sports channel and then thumps his chair back to all four legs. He exhales, big, and stares at the T.V., while I set our bowls of soup down on the table. No placemats. They're still packed.

During dinner, Daddy doesn't say a word, he never does. I don't know why we even eat together. I just sit and chew and stare ahead of me at the side of his face. I know every pore of his left cheek, every crease in his thick neck and around his cloudy eyes. The neck lines go up and sideways, the eye-lines downwards and they meet somewhere behind his ear. His hair starts about five inches back from his eyebrows and the skin on his forehead is tight and shiny like a wet potato. So, instead of talking I have a private contest to try to chew louder than he does. When I was little I used to stand on my chair and sing Joan Jet and try and stop the quiet. He'd send me away if I did that now. A girl gets too old for certain things.

I wonder where I ought to tell Rick we're gonna go, the Grand Canyon maybe. I think about what we're going to do when we get there but then I feel weird with Daddy in front of me

and I start thinking, "Daddy if you can read my mind, blink right now," but he doesn't blink at the right time. I wonder if he's bluffing, so I think the nastiest thoughts to see if I can get a wince out of him. I don't, so I go on dreaming about Rick and the Grand Canyon and how that red dust will look on my skin.

The phone's ringing from the bedroom, the red light next to the numbers flashing on each time. I see that Daddy's not going to answer, so I get up. He's got no hope, always assuming it's a salesman or someone he doesn't want to talk to.

"Hello?"

"Cupcake?"

"Hi, Shell."

"How'd you know it was me?"

"Psychic," I lied. Shell's the only person who has my phone number and I just gave it to her today in Biology because Mrs. Hurt made us lab partners.

"Really. That's interesting. I just wanted to know if you got those five signs of life or whatever." Shell always sounds so bored.

"No, I'm going after I finish dinner. Um, Shell, if you pick a leaf would that make it a dead thing?"

"You're going out tonight? Don't you walk that way to school?"

"I want to get out. All my stuff is in boxes."

"Oh your toys? Fingerpaints? Play-Doh?"

"No, you know. Everything. It's all still packed."

"Sure. Whatever. Just have some signs of life for me before class tomorrow. 'Kay?"

"Sure."

"Look. It's been lovely chatting but my boyfriend's here. Got to go."

"Bobby?"

"Yeah. Bobby."

"Did he ride his bike over?" I'm stalling. I can hear Bobby singing Quiet Riot, "Cum on Feel the Noise," in the background. I want to hear him say "get wild wild wild." "It's just that it's been raining."

"Nothing stops him from getting some."

"Bye," I say to the dial tone because she hung up just like that. I feel sorry for Shell even if she does have a hot boyfriend. She's got really bad acne and she always seems so sad.

I turn from the night table and move back to the other room through the space between Daddy's bed and my cot. Dinner's warm salty smell has faded and the room's usual odor is coming back. It's a strange smell, like sweat and Grandpa's curtains. All the rooms at the Shamrock smell this way.

Daddy's looking at me, excited because someone he knows got close to a real phone call.

"Bobby Winston?" he asks. I sit down. I'm surprised he's talking. Asking a question for that matter. It could be considered conversational.

"What about him?

"Nice kid."

"Yeah?" Hot, yes.

"He came by last Saturday afternoon when you were out fucking around, as usual. Asked if I needed any blades sharpened." Daddy stopped and inhaled like he was catching his breath. "Said he was working in town for Jim's Tool Grinding."

"Did you give him anything?" I'm hoping he might have to return whatever Daddy might have given him.

"Some scissors and some kitchen knives. I figured, why not? Kid's trying to make a buck." He stands up from the card table, dragging some of the mint-green cloth under his elbows. The table looks messy, the bowls no longer centered, their bottoms covered in green bean sludge, and paper napkins rising up out of the swamp. Daddy's lying on his bed packing his Doral's against his wrist. "Turn up the volume, will ya?"

I turn it up to halfway, grab my blue satin jacket by the door and leave.

The damp night makes my finger joints feel tight, but anything's better than being inside with Daddy. God, he sucks the energy out of me. I can't wait till I'm eighteen and can move out. I'm going to be an artist. I'll make things out of clay that I dig up from the ground. My house will be beautiful with big open windows and lots of plants and I'll spread dirt into the carpet, water it and grow moss. I'll put big rocks inside for furniture and I'll paint the walls bright blue and wear a pair of wings that I made from dove feathers and cardboard.

Oh! Conversation with my future self: on your mark, get set (I squint my eyes real tight) go!

"Hi, Cupcake." I say.

"Hi, Cupcake," she says, "You look good."

"I wish I could see you. Do you look good?"

"Of course I do. My hair's gotten really, super long. It's past my butt. And things are really great. Our husband just got back from climbing Mt. Everest and the baby said Mama for the first time an hour ago."

"The baby? How old are you?"

"Twenty-five."

"Made any neat sculptures lately?"

"I made a clay pot the size of the kitchen."

"Wow. I'm glad you're happy."

"Why wouldn't I be? I have a fabulous husband. I sit around and play with mud all day and I have a beautiful baby girl that talks."

"How's Daddy?"

"He's dead. But it's okay because I have Rick."

"Is that our husband?"

"Yep. And he's so cool."

I walk through the trailer park. The rain's soaked the road and the mud beneath has swallowed up the gravel. I follow the tracks of a single fat tire. It goes straight through the park and into the forest. A bright light shines from behind the blackberry bushes, which are near the center, breaks through the leaves and trunks of the trees, and ends up on my chest.

I crouch low so I'm not standing in the light. I want to find out what it is before it sees me. I creep over to my right, stand back up in the dark, and move alongside the light, without making a noise, just like a deer. Before I can see anything I hear a whine, a noise I recognize from this afternoon, Bobby.

"Cupcake," he says before I can quite make him out. He turns the front wheel so the light shines on me again. I can't see a thing but on the periphery I sense little giggling shadows running away from Bobby's voice.

"This isn't quite the sign of life I was expecting." I'm surprised I could think up something to say like that, but I think maybe Bobby's coolness is rubbing off on me. I step out of the light again. "I thought you were at Shell's."

"Climb on." He's smirking. A chilly breeze is rustling everything. I look down at my legs, bare beneath the pink cloth clinging to them, at my water-stained cowgirl boots, over to the patterned wheels of Bobby's bike. Nettles and dead things are sticking out of the spokes and the purple paint and the denim of his calves are spotted with mud, my mud.

"Get on the bike, Cupcake."

I'm just staring at his hands resting on his thighs 'cause I can't stand to look into his eyes and I can't speak. Just standing here picking off blackberries and pressing them against the roof of my mouth. I press slow so that one little cir-

cle bursts at a time. Sweet. I want to tell him I've never ridden before but I'm wondering why he's here, why he wants me to ride, how he could be at Shell's five minutes ago—and what were those little beings that I sensed, fairies? This is all very strange. My tongue is covered with little seeds.

Live, Cupcake, I keep reminding myself. It's not every night you're going to meet a hot guy on a motorcycle in the middle of the woods. I pull my dress up around my thighs and climb on.

I don't know what to do with my hands or feet and I'm resisting an urge to just wrap them around him when he reaches back and grabs my wrists and pulls them in front of him.

"Put your feet on the exhaust, that metal thing," he says. He pauses like he's thinking and then turns around and smiles at me. He's pulling my hands down from his waist and putting them on the inside of his thigh. I feel it hard along the inseam.

"Maybe we ought to stay here for a while," he says.

I grip and try to think at the same time. This has never come up in my fantasies, at least not at the very beginning, and when it does it has never happened like this, where I don't know what's going on or what I ought to do. My instincts say go home, but I compromise.

"Let's take a ride, first." I emphasize the word "first" so he thinks we're definitely gonna. I wouldn't want him to get mad and leave before I get a chance to ride.

He shrugs his shoulders and nods. "It's your night, Cupcake." We scream out of the mud and I hold on tight as we turn around and drive away from the trailer park, deeper into the woods.

I'm so afraid we're going to hit a tree or get stuck in the mud I shut my eyes against the base of his neck. He's steering with one hand. The other one's on top of mine, moving it back and forth. I feel kind of dirty. I mean, I guess it's a little cool, but it doesn't seem at all romantic. I'm nervous. Where is he taking me? But the sleepy moans that vibrate out from between his lips, and the jostling of the bike, make it really hard to think. We break out of the forest into the field, where this group of kids called the subhumans parties in the summer. Only it's fall, and the field was sold to the country's largest steel mill. They've started building already, and up ahead, through the dark, I can see large sheets of metal clinging to towering steel beams. The light rain, like hot needles, pricks me but it's bringing me out of my trance, enough to drive me crazy with indecision. Instinct or adventure? I pull myself to Bobby, tight as I can without melting into him, bury my mouth deep into his skin, close my eyes and try to squeeze my ears shut. I give up breathing. I can't. I'm hiding. I'm giving myself over to him. I'm on a roller coaster, at the top of the first hill.

We've nearly reached the single metal wall which has grown larger and larger by the millisecond. He stops his bike. I have to get off first and it's hard to pull my body from his. I keep one hand on his thigh. I just can't seem to let it go but he peels my hand off him so he can walk. I follow him to the other side of the steel wall, onto the concrete foundation. I really want to hold on to him but I don't want to be annoying.

"*Pull!*" a woman's voice yells from somewhere not too far from us. I look in the direction of the voice and see a small glowing circle catapult through the black air. Then, the bang of a gun as the circle shatters to the ground like a falling star. A second voice laughs and cheers. I've grabbed onto Bobby's arm. Nothing seems real. I want to trust him but he's smiling in the direction of the laughter.

"Nice one, Mom!" he yells as she and Shell walk toward us. Mrs. Winston has a shotgun over her shoulder and Shell's carrying a cardboard box. I try to act like I know exactly what we're doing here, or at least like it's all natural.

"These glow-in-the-dark clay pigeons are pretty fucking cool. You ever shot a gun, Cupcake?" Mrs. Winston's voice is gritty-sweet like raw sugar. Her hair sticks out from her face in plaits of steel wool. Her expression is animal. She looks like something that walked out of an image on tree bark or rose up out of dust. Her lips are pulled back to mid-smile; her teeth connecting in deep, crazy lines. Her skin makes me think of roasted chicken, and it scares me.

"Yeah. Once," I say.

"Let's smoke a jay." Shell has sat on the box and is taking a pack of cigarettes out of her sweat jacket. I have absolutely no idea what to do. I can't cling to Bobby with Shell and his mom here. I'm trying to forget about Mrs. Winston calling me a whore. This is normal for them, Cupcake. That's what I'm telling myself. Shell takes a joint out of the cigarette pack, sticks it in her mouth, and Mrs. Winston lights it with a Zippo. They're smiling like they've got a secret, or maybe it's just 'cause they're going to get high.

"Have a seat, Cupcake." Bobby sits next to Shell's box, leans against the sheet metal and pats his lap as an invitation. I look at Shell, she smiles at me. I want to feel like I did on the bike so I walk over to him but Mrs. Winston grabs my arm.

"So, babyface, you want to fuck Bobby? All girls want to fuck Bobby. Even Shell, but Bobby wouldn't have her." She looks over to Shell and smiles. "You know I like you, don't you?"

Shell blows the smoke out through her nose and nods. "If I thought you didn't like me, would I shoot targets with you?" Everybody but me laughs and Shell hands the joint to Bobby.

Mrs. Winston closes her mouth, swallowing her gruff laughter behind a soft grin. Her eyes fade back into their deep wrinkled sockets, and she reaches a hand out toward Bobby. "Come sit with your mother, sweetheart," she says.

"Naw." Bobby looks nervous. "I'm fine right here, Mom."

"He'll learn," Mrs. Winston says to the steel wall.

"I think maybe I ought to go home," I say. I knew Mrs. Winston was a little crazy but now she's scaring me, and geez, I feel sorry for Bobby. He must be totally embarrassed.

"Bobby, give her the jay." Shell smiles. She's got brown stuff between her teeth, which somehow makes her smile more friendly. Humble.

Bobby hands me the joint and I put it between my lips and inhale like I watched Shell do. I've never smoked a joint before. It's hurting my throat more than a cigarette, burning. But I heard some girls in school talking about how you don't get high if you don't hold it in. I hand the joint back to Bobby, afraid to come anywhere near his mom. "Well, I guess I'll stay for a while," I say, although I don't think anybody thought I was really leaving to begin with.

"You ever smoked before, Cupcake?" I don't like the way Mrs. Winston says my name. She says it like she doesn't think it should be my name, like she's making fun.

Shell laughs. "Right. Karen. Does she look like a stoner to you?" Mrs. Winston laughs. Smoke rolls out of her mouth, over her head and into her coarse yellow hair like it was trained to do that.

Karen starts asking Shell if she has a boyfriend and Shell's telling Karen that she doesn't. I look for Bobby's reaction but he just stares at me with those eyes again and I get stuck by them. I feel like at any second red beams will shoot from them onto my chest, push me up into the sky and nail me to a cloud.

Karen's still talking about how it's best to stay away from men and about how sex only gets you in trouble. I'm wondering if all this means Bobby and Shell broke up. Maybe they broke up because Bobby loves me, but then wouldn't Shell be mad at me? Something's moving below Bobby's eyes. He's touching himself and looking at me. I look at Karen and Shell, who seem pretty absorbed in this guy-bashing stuff. Karen's talking about how there's nothing a man can do for a woman that a woman can't do for herself. Shell smiles and drops her head between her knees. The back of her neck is decorated with pink scars, lines, that reach under her jacket. Her fingers run hard over the concrete like she's trying to smooth out its pattern.

"What are you staring at?" Karen asks me.

"She's high, Karen. Just spacing out. Right, Cupcake?" Shell's being so nice to me tonight.

"She can't be high. It's her first time. Everyone knows you can't get high your first time."

"Well, this is my special blend." Shell whispers something to Karen that makes her eyes creep out like two turtles' heads. "You little shit!" she says to Shell. "Well, we're gonna have a good time tonight! Yeehaw. Ya hear that Bobby? Bobby? Stop playing with yourself, sweetheart. It doesn't look nice."

"What?" Bobby doesn't stop. "What's the big deal?"

"We're partying with the fungi tonight." She looks back and forth from me to Shell, smiling. "I hope your daddy's not waiting up for you."

Bobby sighs like he's real pissed off now. I'm confused. It was bad enough not be able to say that I'd smoked a joint before. I hate to keep asking what people are talking about. As far as my dad goes, an invisible daughter doesn't get a curfew. Besides, I'm feeling kind of weird about sharing a room with him tonight. I'd just rather not go home.

Karen's talking about her period now and describing her cramps in detail. "Like someone's in there, poking around with a butterknife," she says. You'd think she enjoyed them and was trying to make Shell jealous. Bobby hands me the joint and I suck it in once again. I think the Indians smoke this stuff for ceremonies so I'm trying to get in the spirit of things. Maybe I'll turn into a jaguar before the night is over. Bobby grabs the joint from my hand and gives it to his mom.

"So Shell, you see, women are either whores or they're whores who are too tired to act like whores." Karen brings the joint to her mouth.

"Whatever, Karen," Shell says. "Does any of this really matter?"

Bobby grabs my arm, hard. "The clock's ticking, Cupcake," he says, pulling me around the metal wall to the field. "Pretty soon I'll be so fucked I won't be able to move a muscle." He winks at me. Thank God he's taking me away. Karen was just starting to talk in detail about her body being old and wrinkly.

I'm feeling kind of lightheaded, not like when I'm sick but like the world is beautiful and I'm a beautiful part of it. I want to take Bobby back into the woods with me. Even though it's a little chilly, I want to show him how it feels to be covered in mud. I'm pulling my jacket off and throwing it behind me. I'm running ahead of Bobby and I can't believe how great my breeze feels, like I went right from the desert into the mountains. I've reached the woods and I pull off my dress. Bobby stops dead behind me.

"Whoaaa." He says. Whoa is so right. The trees. They look like a storybook and the lights, like tiny candles, they're decorating the trees.

"We're tripping' now, Baby," he says. "Damn. I wish. . . . You look so pretty. Like I can't touch you but I want . . ." He reaches for me really slowly. I grab his wrist and slowly draw his hand down to the mud. His fingers slide in like the earth is sipping him through a straw and he keeps. He's moving. Down. I had no idea marijuana was like this.

"It feels so cool!" he says.

He pulls mud up from the ground like it's tar and smears it over my thighs. It's cold and stiff. He's smearing brown all over me. Cold and stiff. I ask him to kiss me.

"Not yet," he says. Please, I want to feel warm. I beg him as he smears mud over my face, in my mouth, in my hair. He scoops a big handful. My skin is cracking to pieces. Now he's kissing me and his spit is wet-warm and makes my mouth the only movable part of me. He keeps kissing me as he presses his handful of mud between my legs. I bite his tongue. He steps back. He looks at me and smiles angry like his mom does. The corners of his mouth stretch off of his face. His teeth look red.

"Trippin' hard?" he asks. I don't answer. I can't open my mouth without his pressed against it. The air is too cold. "Lightweight." He laughs. "I've got a good five, ten minutes before I'm useless."

He unbuttons his jeans and pulls out the thing that I'd been touching, imagining. Look at the trees. My forest. My mud. My forest. My mud. Covering me. Not pretty. He points it at me and it seems to grow longer. He puts his mouth on mine. I can open it. I'm screaming into his mouth forever. He takes his mouth away.

"Bitch!" he yells. Bobby turns in one big blur.

Karen's coming. Open my mouth. No sound. She's yelling all by herself. "Sonfucker!

Cradle robber! Little miss innocent!" Metal barrel two inches from my chest. She must think she's hunting and I'm an animal. I must look like one. Metal looks soft. I wrap my hands around it but it won't bend. Solid.

Quiet is loud. I hear my skin crack.

I fell when it got louder. "Well, that was a fucking blast," Shell says. Her voice comes from inside me laughing.

How It Works

1. This story contains a lot of vivid imagery. Reread it, underlining these passages. Think about how each one affected you emotionally as you read. What does the imagery add to the story?

2. The author mixes fantasy and reality in this story. How can you tell what is real? Underline the transitions between the fantasy sections and the real ones. How does the author move back and forth between them?

3. Underline passages that convey the characters' important traits: class, race, educational level, age, and economic status? How does the writer convey these things without stating them directly?

4. Kelly Zavotka devoted much of her final semester in college to writing this story. Although the characters and setting were familiar to her, the murder itself was not and she found it disturbing to become intimate enough with the character of Shell, particularly, to write through her voice. Experiment with "sympathy for the devil." Think of a person you abhor, and try writing a paragraph in that individual's voice. Use the first-person point of view. What difficulties do you encounter? On the other hand, is there anything that comes easily as you write this character?

Redefinition

The definitions in the introductory section of this book (pp. 2–4) are as simple as I could make them—but the concepts they refer to are not. They are ideas that should grow and develop as you keep thinking about them. To help you do so, the original definitions are repeated below, along with questions designed to provoke more questions and to deepen your understanding.

Abstract description: Description that does not involve the senses but instead relies upon an interpretation or judgment. For example, "The honey was good" is abstract. "The honey was Greek" is concrete. We can all agree on "Greek," but "good" depends on the narrator's interpretation. See also **Concrete description**, below.

1. In the example above, the concrete description is objective, while the abstract description is subjective, or opinion-based. Are abstract descriptions always subjective? Can you think of some that are not?
2. Are metaphors abstract or concrete?
3. What are the uses of abstraction? What can an abstract description do that a concrete description cannot do? What makes good abstract description?

Anecdote: A brief retelling of a single incident. Anecdotes lack the formal plot structure of short stories and novels.

1. Is there a place for anecdotes in fiction? If so, what is that place?
2. Are stories intrinsically more aesthetically satisfying than anecdotes? Why or why not?
3. What kind of structure do anecdotes have?

Author: The person who wrote the story. *Not* the same as the narrator, unless the story is nonfiction.

1. Is it always true that the author is not the same as the narrator?
2. Does this definition of "author" hold true for all cultures and times?
3. How important are the storyteller's conscious decisions? What other factors might contribute to the writing of a story?

Character: The nature of the story's main actors.

1. Choose a main character from this book and consider that character's actions and traits. Do these aspects ever conflict or contradict one another? How does the author portray ambiguities or ambivalences while still retaining the character's and the story's unity?

2. As you consider your answers to the question above, have you touched upon any of the other elements of fiction—for instance, plot, point of view, setting, subtext, or theme? How do these elements influence or reflect upon character?

3. Over and over, this book asserts that character is central in contemporary fiction. But to what extent is it really possible to separate character from a story's other elements? In what sense would you say that character is central—or is it?

Characters: The people or other main actors in a story.

1. How developed does a character have to be in order to emerge as an individual rather than fading into the story's background?

2. How are major characters developed differently from minor characters?

3. Must all characters be human? This book's anthology contains stories with nonhuman characters. (See Gabriel García Márquez's "A Very Old Man with Enormous Wings" (pp. 293–298) and Robert Olen Butler's "Jealous Husband Returns in Form of Parrot" (pp. 244–249). Can you imagine a story in which the main character is, say, a rock, or water? Can the setting of a story be a character? What about an unnamed but distinctive third-person narrator, such as the one in Darrell Spencer's "Park Host" (pp. 418–431)?

Characterization: The way a writer conveys characters' personalities and other attributes.

1. Is characterization always an intentional effort on the author's part?

2. In what sense does the plot of a story contribute to characterization? What about setting, dialogue, and other elements?

3. Pick a story from the Anthology in this book. As you consider the elements above as well as others that make it a story—point of view, time structures, subtext, and theme—are there any that clearly do not contribute to characterization?

Cliché: An overfamiliar phrase, concept, or image that has, as George Orwell expressed it, "lost force." For instance, the beautiful heroine and the dashing hero are clichés.

1. So what if you've seen it before? Some people like familiarity. Why should this be a negative quality? Do expressions ever *gain* force as they become more familiar?

2. Can clichés be used well? (Look, for instance, at Robert Olen Butler's *Tabloid Dreams*, which uses actual tabloid headlines as story titles; or at Norman Rush's *Mating* and Joseph Connolly's "Hard Feelings" (pp. 260–270), both of which play on class, cultural, gender "markers" to great comic effect.)

3. In your own work, when do you find yourself slouching toward clichés? What seems to prompt the impulse, and how can you avoid it?

Concrete description: Description using one or more of the five senses: sight, hearing, smell, taste, or touch. See also **Abstract description**, p. 475.

1. How does a writer decide which concrete details to employ?
2. What else, other than the physical characteristics of the thing described, does a concrete description convey? What do the narrator's words convey about him or her?
3. What kinds of description does this definition exclude?

Dialogue: Characters' speech. **Direct discourse** refers to speech enclosed within quotation marks; **indirect discourse** refers to summarized or unquoted speech.

1. What kinds of information are appropriate in dialogue? What kinds are inappropriate?
2. How might you be able to tell that you're using too much dialogue? Too little?
3. Are there ways other than dialogue by which characters can communicate?

Events: Incidents that occur in a story.

1. What constitutes an event or incident? How dramatic or physical does an occurrence need to be in order to constitute an event in the story's narrative arc?
2. Look at one of the stories from this book's anthology and underline everything in it that is *not* an event. How much of the story have you underlined? What kinds of elements have you underlined? Try this with a second story; is the kind and proportion of underlined material similar? What differences and similarities do you see from story to story? What are the effects upon the stories of emphasizing events or nonevents?
3. What incidents do authors leave out of their stories? Read a few stories and make a list of events that are suggested but not dramatized. How would you characterize these "untold" events? What is achieved by leaving them out— how would the stories be different if the authors had included these events?

Fiction: A made-up story.

1. What about stories that make use of dreams or family history? Where is the line between what is made up and what is not?
2. What is the difference between fiction and personal essay?
3. What is the difference between fiction and memoir or biography?

Fictional present: The time frame in which the story's main action takes place.

1. Have you ever read a book or story in which past events were more important than current ones?
2. Have you ever read a book or story in which the most important events were passed over quickly and mundane ones drawn out? Is the amount of space on the page given to an event always proportional to the event's importance? What other forms of emphasis do writers employ?
3. Are time frames always easily defined? Where is the "nonfictional present" in Brenda Miller's essay "A Thousand Buddhas" (pp. 329–334)?

Foreshadowing: Hints, early in a story, about its eventual outcome. See Flannery O'Connor's "A Good Man Is Hard to Find" (pp. 362–372) for excellent examples of foreshadowing.

1. What does foreshadowing add to a story? What emotions does it create in you as you read?
2. What kinds of events are foreshadowed in stories you have read?
3. What else, other than events, might be foreshadowed?

Frame story: A story in which the writer begins at a point late in the narrative arc (see **Narrative arc**, p. 479), or even outside it entirely, and then flashes back to earlier events, building up to and often past those recounted in the first scene. Thus, external events or those that occur later "frame" the rest of the story.

1. Consider some frame stories in this book: Andre Dubus's "A Father's Story" (pp. 272–286), Joseph Moser's "Close Enough" (pp. 335–346) and Raymond Carver's "The Calm" (pp. 249–252). In what specific ways does enclosing one story within another affect the story's focus? Which events are presented as central and which as secondary?
2. If these authors had chosen to tell their stories chronologically, how else might they have emphasized the important events and kept others in the background?
3. Aside from emphasis, what other aspects of the stories are affected by the frame structure? Consider the stories' emotional impact, the rhythm of the language and the scenes, and your sense of the story as a complete action.

Image: A vivid sensory detail.

1. What do images contribute to the stories in this book? Compare, for instance, Ernest Hemingway's "Hills Like White Elephants" (pp. 320–323) with Gina Berriault's "A Dream of Fair Women" (pp. 239–244). How do these authors use images differently? What is the effect of dense, precise imagery? What is the effect of spare, minimal imagery?
2. Because we receive so much sensory information through our eyes, most images are visual. What is the effect of emphasizing other senses? For examples, try looking at a memoir by a blind person, such as Ved Mehta's *Sound Shadows of the New World*.
3. Is there such a thing as a nonsensory image?

Melodrama: A story in which plot predominates over character and characters are somewhat flat or "stock."

1. What is your emotional reaction when you read a contemporary novel or story that contains flat characters? Are flat characters ever useful in contemporary literary fiction? If so, how do their authors avoid alienating intelligent readers?
2. Many great nineteenth-century novels (such as Emily Brontë's *Wuthering Heights*) are melodramatic, yet we still consider them great. Is this a double standard? What's the difference between such novels and modern soap operas? What are the similarities?

3. Can you think of contemporary novels or stories that you would call melodramatic? Why would you call them melodramatic?

Memoir: An autobiographical work of prose, usually novel-length and often similar to a novel in form.

1. Most memoirists exercise some poetic license. Where is the line between autobiography and autobiographical fiction? What can be changed, and what must remain intact?

2. As a reader, is it important to you to know which details have been fictionalized and which are historically accurate? Why?

3. Is there such a thing as pure nonfiction? If so, what is it, and what is its value?

Narration: What the narrator tells the reader directly, as opposed to what the characters convey through speech and action.

1. Can you think of a story that uses no narration? How would any one of the stories in this book be changed if it had no narration? What would be left if you removed all narration? (Think of the difference between the narrative mode and the scenic mode. Would a story without a narrator be fiction, or would it slip into some other genre?)

2. What would be the effect of telling a story entirely in narration? Which stories in this book rely most heavily on narration?

3. How do different authors use narration? For example, consider Darrell Spencer's "Park Host" (pp. 418–431), Flannery O'Connor's "A Good Man Is Hard to Find" (pp. 362–372), and Brenda Miller's essay "A Thousand Buddhas" (pp. 329–334). How would you describe the narration in each of these? How would these texts be different if the authors had traded narrative methods?

Narrative: A telling of events.

1. Where is the line between a story's events and its characters, setting, or other elements? Think about this line as you identify the narratives within each story in this book.

2. Do a little reading of stories from other times and cultures; (for instance, Native American stories such as Leslie Marmon Silko's "Yellow Woman", pp. 406–413. How do the events in these narratives differ from one another and from most of those represented in this book?

3. How are narratives told? What kinds of techniques does an author use to create the voice that tells the events? How do these techniques differ among various ethnic or cultural groups?

Narrative arc: A simplified way of describing a story's shape in terms of an arc, within which the highest point is the story's *climax*, at which point the main character changes significantly. The arc's upward slope includes *exposition* (background information) and *rising action* (the events that lead up to the climax); its downward slope, after the climax, comprises the falling action or denouement.

1. Are all narrative arcs proportioned similarly? Compare the shapes of several chronological stories in this book.

2. Do the elements of narrative arcs always occur in the same order? For example, can you think of stories in which exposition occurs during or after the rising action?

3. Can you think of other shapes that might be used as visual outlines for stories? What would a narrative spiral look like, or a narrative circle? What about a narrative Möbius strip?

Narrative bridge: Narration used to create a transition between two scenes.

1. What is the difference between a scene that contains a lot of narration and a narrative bridge? Can you think of an example of a scene that is rendered entirely in narration?

2. What kind of territory does a narrative bridge traverse? Can you find examples of narrative bridges that carry the reader through time? From place to place? From point of view to point of view?

3. Are there other ways of crossing those divides? What methods do authors use to move from scene to scene, shift from mood to mood, or accomplish other necessary passages in their work?

Narrative tension: The momentum that impels the reader into and through the story.

1. What creates this momentum? What do plot, character, setting, dialogue, subtext, and theme contribute to its development? How does the answer differ from story to story? For example, compare Flannery O'Connor's "A Good Man Is Hard to Find" (pp. 362–372), Andre Dubus's "A Father's Story" (pp. 272–286), and Mary Austin Speaker's "The Day the Flames Would Stop" (pp. 413–418).

2. Is narrative tension always the same thing as suspense? What emotions does narrative tension evoke? What is the feeling that keeps you turning the pages? How does this differ from story to story?

3. What kind of tension occurs in stories without much action, such as Seth Pase's "The Father" (pp. 373–375)?

Narrative voice: The personality, tone, or sensibility conveyed by a story's language.

1. How would you describe the voices in several different prose pieces—for instance, Brenda Miller's "A Thousand Buddhas" (pp. 329–334), Joseph Connolly's "Hard Feelings" (pp. 261–270), and Joe Moser's "Close Enough" (pp. 335–346)?

2. What techniques contribute to these stories' voices? How do the authors achieve their effects?

3. Compare the third-person voice in Ernest Hemingway's "Hills Like White Elephants" (pp. 320–323) with that in Darrell Spencer's "Park Host" (pp. 418–431). How do these two voices differ from one another?

Narrator: The person or voice that tells the story.

1. Is it possible for the narrator to be the only person in the story?
2. Is it possible to write a story with no narrator?
3. How many narrators can a story or novel accommodate? What factors influence the answer?

Nonfiction: A telling of real events; prose that isn't fictional.

1. What kinds of writing does this definition include? Can you think of ways in which genres such as personal essay or autobiography might be called fictional?
2. On the theoretical continuum between pure fact and pure fiction, reportage and art, where do these forms fall?
3. Do you agree that these distinctions are merely theoretical? Is there such a thing as pure fact or pure fiction? What is it?

Novel: A long, fictional work of prose. Contemporary novels generally—but not always—fall between 150 and 500 pages in length, with many at or around 300 to 350 pages.

1. In what ways, other than length do novels differ from short stories?
2. What does the length, of a novel imply? How would you expect elements such as character and plot to differ from their counterparts in short fiction?
3. Are there structures or subjects that work better for novels than for short stories, and vice versa?

Novella: A short novel, usually around ninety pages. Examples of the novella include Thomas Mann's *Death in Venice* and Andre Dubus's *Voices from the Moon*.

1. What are the differences between a novella, a short novel, and a long short story?
2. What, besides its length, are the intrinsic qualities of this form? What can a novella do that a short story or novel cannot?
3. What are the limitations of the novella? What can't it do?

Plot: The pattern of a story's action; what happens; events. These incidents combine with character and other fictional elements to create narrative tension.

1. Does "what happens" always consist of events? What, other than events, happens in stories?
2. What is the result when a story contains no major events? For example, in Seth Pase's story "The Father" (pp. 373–375) a young man picks up a young woman at home and they drive through town together. Where does the narrative tension come from in this story?
3. Does retelling the plot always convey the story? What, other than the events themselves, contributes to your experience of a story? Try summarizing the events in Joseph Connolly's "Hard Feelings" (pp. 261–270), Raymond

Carver's "The Calm" (pp. 249–252), or Gina Berriault's "A Dream of Fair Women (pp. 239–244)." Would a listener come away having fully experienced the story? What would be missing?

Point of view: The perspective from which the story is told. The most obvious examples are the "I" narrator, called first person; the usually anonymous narrator describing "he" or "she" (third person); or the usually anonymous narrator describing "you" (second person).

1. Does a writer have to switch points of view in order to suggest another perspective?
2. Point of view determines which events can be depicted; in that way, it is like a camera. In what other ways does a story's point of view suggest a narrative sensibility?
3. Can you think of other possible points of view than those listed above?

Prose: Straightforward, direct writing that is not controlled by meter or rhyme as poetry is. Novels and short stories are written in prose.

1. Is it true that novels and short stories are always written in prose?
2. Are all poems controlled by meter and rhyme?
3. What is the difference between poetry and prose?

Scene: A significant part of a story, specifically located in time and place, and in which characters interact.

1. Look at some of the stories in this book's anthology, and underline the parts that are not scenes. What elements of the stories, and what proportion, have you included? What is the effect of including proportionally more or less scenic material in a story?
2. French neoclassical dramatists believed that the entrance or exit of a major character—that is, a duo becoming a trio or a trio becoming a duo—constituted a scene change. Do you agree? Read a few of the stories contained in this book. When do you sense the action of scenes beginning and concluding? How would you define a scene? Does the definition change at all from story to story?
3. Must a scene include characters? Can you think of any that do not? (Hint: Look for a segment that includes highly detailed description and conveys the story's sense of time without specifically acting as a transitional passage.) What about a scene that includes only one character, such as the scene in Henry James's novel *Portrait of a Lady*, in which Isabel sits up all night brooding in her room? What makes that sequence a scene?

Sentimentality: In writing, an appeal to the emotions by using trite or overfamiliar devices; relying on familiar conventions to evoke feeling rather than achieving it through fresh, accurate writing.

1. What if you like being manipulated by a novel or story? Is there anything wrong with that?

2. Can you think of any situations in which sentimentality should be allowed in fiction?

3. Flannery O'Connor wrote that pornography is essentially sentimental. Do you agree? Does sentimentality always have to be sweet?

Setting: The environment in which the story takes place.

1. Consider the setting in several different stories—for instance, Gina Berriault's "A Dream of Fair Women" (pp. 239–244), Flannery O'Connor's "A Good Man Is Hard to Find" (pp. 362–372), and Joseph Connolly's "Hard Feelings" (pp. 261–270). What does setting contribute to each of these stories? How would each be different if the setting were changed?

2. In what specific ways does the setting in each of these stories relate to the plot?

3. How does setting reveal and affect character?

Short short: A very short work of fictional prose, usually 1,500 words or less.

1. Look at the short shorts in this book—"Survivors," by Kim Addonizio (pp. 232–233), "Instructions on How to Sing" by Julio Cortázar, (p. 271), "The Halo," by Michael McFee (pp. 327–328), and "City of Dreams," by Lisa Usani Phillips (pp. 386–387). What, other than their length, differentiates them from longer stories?

2. How are plot, character, setting, dialogue, subtext, and theme affected by the brevity of these stories?

3. How short can a story get and still be a story? Why?

Short story: A relatively short work of fictional prose, usually between 1500 and 20,000 words.

1. What are the intrinsic qualities of the short story form? Other than its length, how does a short story differ from a novel?

2. What uses do these differences suggest? What kinds of material are particularly suited to the short story form?

3. What do unconventional short stories like Juan Rulfo's "Macario" (pp. 388–391) or Robert Olen Butler's "Jealous Husband Returns in Form of Parrot" (pp. 244–249) have in common with more traditionally told stories such as Flannery O'Connor's "A Good Man Is Hard to Find" (pp. 362–372)?

Story: A telling of a sequence of events resulting in a change in the main character.

1. Do stories always focus mainly on events?

2. What else, other than events, might provide a story's central elements?

3. Look at some of the stories in this book and identify who changes and how. What kinds of changes do stories chronicle? How do the other events and details in these stories relate to the central change?

Subtext: Emotional content that is unsaid but present in a story; unspoken feelings, particularly when the characters are talking to or about each other.

1. How hidden are the meanings contained in stories and their subtexts? Consider several different stories. How much in each is hidden, and how much is overt?

2. How is subtext conveyed? Think about scenes you've read. What comes across that is not directly stated? Trace your answers to aspects of the scene.

3. When is it appropriate to discuss emotion overtly?

Tags (also called *attribution*): The words with which the author tells the reader who is speaking when. Example: "he said" or "she said." Gestures or description may function indirectly as tags.

1. How do tags affect a scene? What can they convey in addition to logistical information?

2. How do tags affect a reader? How would the experience of reading be different without them?

3. Are there ways of attributing dialogue that do not rely on specific phrases added to the speech?

Theme: The main idea or ideas in a story, usually conveyed indirectly.

1. State the theme in several different stories; for instance, Flannery O'Connor's "A Good Man Is Hard to Find" (pp. 362–372), Andre Dubus's "A Father's Story" (pp. 272–286), Ernest Hemingway's "Hills Like White Elephants" (pp. 320–323), and James Leon Suffern's "When the Summer Ends" (pp. 432–443). Is it hard to put in words? Are some stories' themes easier to identify than others'?

2. When you can't state the theme, can you feel it? As you read the story what general ideas do your feelings suggest?

3. How do authors suggest theme? Trace your impressions to details in the stories.

Voice: See **Narrative voice**.

Surviving on Your Own

Most of this book deals with writing as a creative and technical effort—with the work itself. But always, when writers talk about how they work, practical problems come up: a writer's needs for time, privacy, silence, solitude; how to make others understand and respect those needs; the writer's own doubts about them; and how to find and maintain creative relationships. It's not realistic to talk about the writing process without acknowledging these human needs. The first section in this chapter discusses some of the logistical problems you will face, or already do, as you seek out the solitude that is necessary in order to write, and the second addresses the need for artistic community.

The Logistics of Writing

Bending Time: Writing in Real Life

Most writers—students as well as those further along in their careers—write when they can. They might prefer to work every day from 9 to 11 a.m., or from 10 p.m. to 2 a.m., or all night long, but they're limited by school and work schedules, by the needs and habits of those around them, and by when and how long they can stay awake. Writers often complain that writing, since it doesn't usually bring in much money, has to be fitted into the bits of time between the activities that do.

This isn't entirely a bad thing. Given the chance, some writers can actually sit down at their desks, stay there, and write for seemingly endless stretches of time. Yet for a lot of people, twelve free and silent hours can be as daunting and ultimately unproductive as five hundred blank pages waiting for the novel to appear on them. Many writers visit artists' colonies—creative paradises that allow them to work every hour of every day and night. They live like that for two or three weeks, and then most of them are ready for a break.

All creative types wish that art were valued more—that more benefactors would appear, enabling writers and other artists to have the time to do their work. Still, perhaps the rareness of the creative moment can make it more valuable and more intense. The relief you get from wandering to the refrigerator, playing computer games, or going out for snacks or cigarettes—that necessary break from intense mental effort—might also be supplied by the scarcity of time. If you find yourself wasting time, it could be that you have too much of it on your hands.

Paying the Bills   In order to pay the bills, almost all writers have to do something other than write. Some teach at universities, colleges, or public or private high schools. These careers provide some flexibility (less than outsiders might think, if tenure is a goal) and proximity to other writers and artists. They also present potentially limitless time commitments and tend to pay so little that many teachers are forced to take on yet more work.

Other writing-related careers include working at a publishing house or literary agency, or becoming a technical writer. If you have the skills, these jobs can pay you well while allowing you to write or work with the writing of others and perhaps meet fellow writers. But writing-related careers are not the only option. Some writers have advised students to stay away from universities and publishing companies and to work instead in non-writing-related jobs, getting out among "real people" and gaining the experience of life outside the realm of words. Even in a time when they were much more likely to be able to earn a living as writers, William Carlos Williams, T. S. Eliot, Wallace Stevens, and others chose careers unrelated to writing. And certainly, many writers, including the author of this book and several of those whose stories are contained in the anthology, have cared for children as they've worked on stories, novels, or poems. In non-writing fields, you will likely make more money than you would in a writing-related field, and money, if used well, can translate into time for writing. In such settings it will, however, be more difficult to meet like-minded people, and you may find that you need to work hard to create opportunities to associate with other writers. You will also, in any career, have to sacrifice some prestige and accomplishment. Allowing the time needed to make your way to the top probably will preclude a second career—like writing.

Q: What if your writing just isn't good enough?

A: Everyone has a variation of this question. Do I have talent? How long should I invest my time and energy in this before I move on? You have to ask yourself why you're writing. The only real reason to write is because you love it and because you have to. Don't worry about success, which everyone defines differently anyway. Find your version, try to articulate it and to hell with being good. Just try to get better than you are right now. If you take your desire seriously, then you'll read a lot, study the craft, and you'll write; and you are bound to become a better writer. Especially if you don't sabotage yourself with questions like this.

—*Kim Addonizio,*
poet and writer

Balance: Art and Life   It has been said that the lack of time and support for their work makes writers and poets, by definition, people who neglect others around them and use them up in the pursuit of art. Writing is a demanding discipline and will take a toll on you and on anyone close to you—but before romanticizing that notion and rationalizing or compartmentalizing your life in the name of your work, it's worth considering the personal and creative consequences. As one of my first writing teachers, Bruce Jorgensen, said to me, "To the extent that your writing harms those you love, your writing has become corrupt." Realistically, a writing life is a hard one, but it's usually possible to cut out some other activities in the interest of emotional well-being.

Rather than becoming frustrated by the limitations on your work, check again on reality: everybody has financial obligations, schedules, distractions, commitments, deadlines, and physical limitations. It's extraordinarily unlikely that even the most successful writers will ever be free to forge their own schedules. So start from the fact that you can't, and work within what's possible. This is a skill that women have had forever: you write while the children are asleep or in school, stop writing when they wake up or return from school and start writing again the next time they fall asleep. Because the arts are not much of a priority in this country at this time—and because of the difficulty, in general, of getting by—it's more and more necessary for anyone who wants to do creative work to learn this kind of flexibility. People who practice flexible writing often discover its virtues as a way of creating tension and urgency—of forcing them to make the most of their time, and of turning pressure to desire.

Making Time   There are a number of ways to create time. The most basic is to use whatever free time is available during odd hours: early mornings, late evenings, lunch breaks. Admit to yourself what you can do without, and make some choices: cut down on television, computer games, and other recreational activities that take hours out of most people's weeks. Use vacations and weekends. Make the most of insomnia—it usually doesn't work to lie in bed fuming anyway, so try getting up and working. If you are a person who doesn't require a lot of sleep, you may find that this solves your time problems. Make writing a priority. Don't be persuaded by the general belief that the arts are frivolous or irrelevant. If writing is what you want to do, do it instead of whatever else isn't absolutely necessary, and don't apologize.

You can also enlist the help of others. Time is space. Make a schedule with roommates or family members that ensures you time alone with the computer. If you have small children, arrange for hours when they'll be out of the house. Even a private office isn't private with a two-year-old banging on the door or screaming in the background. This sort of time-sharing isn't neglect; others will do a better job if they know you're not around to take over, and usually children are less frustrated by actual absence than by knowing you're home but inaccessible.

Agree and get others to agree to clear out of the apartment, keep the noise down, not invite people over, or simply not bother you while you work. Trade time with your spouse or roommates; arrange for privacy. Taking this kind of stand often requires strength of character because people who don't write usually find it hard to understand the need for silence and solitude—the need to write. If you expect to keep working, you're going to have to accept these legitimate needs, and you must expect and help others to understand them, without taking unfair advantage of the people around you.

It's equally important to learn to work well in whatever time you have. Some of this comes naturally if your time is limited—ideas build up in your mind, along with the desire to write, so writing sessions are often more intense, though shorter. Ernest Hemingway found that stopping each session when the writing was going well and he knew what he would write next enabled him to maintain momentum for the following day—a method that may be particularly helpful if you have to work in short bursts. An alternative is to write yourself a note when you stop, summarizing what you've written and what comes next, so that when you continue you won't have to pause and collect yourself and remember where you are. It can also help not to clean up your work space—leave your notes out to remind you of where you were when you stopped. And this is another reason to carry a notebook: so you don't miss ideas that come to you during the times when you can't write.

Choosing Well   If you're just beginning as a writer, it's wise to think over your life decisions carefully, being realistic about the demands of any chosen path. The conventional methods of moving up in the world may not always fit an artistic life. A large apartment or condo, for instance, may be much better for some writers than a house, a yard, and all the maintenance involved in both. But be careful about cutting off your options; dramatic choices in one direction may preclude those in another.

The people around you will be one of the more important influences on your work. Writers need companions who will understand, accept, and support what they've chosen to do with their lives. If a spouse or partner competes with your writing for your attention, you'll be miserable. On the other hand, sometimes writers feel they can live only with other writers or artists. The problem then becomes competition for work time. This can translate into conflicts over who takes care of household, parenting, and social obligations—a situation that is hard for anyone but potentially career-ending for a woman, who will probably earn less money and bear more child-related responsibilities.

It's very important to realize just how much time, emotional energy, and focus creative life can consume. Any person who lives with you must be able, with your help, to coexist with your work as more or less a third partner in the relationship. If they too have an art habit, that makes four of you. Writing is not a particularly easy vocation for anyone to live with, but one note of reassurance: these conflicts are much more intense at certain times of life when you're loaded with responsibilities: graduate school, the early years of marriage and parenting, crucial career moments.

Creating Space: A Room of One's Own

Creating a good work environment can be a particular problem for students, people living with others in limited space, parents of small children—most people, actually. The best situation for writers is a separate room to work in. If you can't get one, set yourself up in the quietest part of the house. Is there a closet, pantry, attic, or basement room that you can use? Try the living room, if it's not centrally located—often it's used least. Sometimes, if the kitchen or living room is big enough to eat in, the dining room can be blocked off as a work space. A screen or curtain is not as good as a wall, but it's better than nothing.

Create some rituals around the writing you do to prepare—the same notebook, the same pen, the same chair or clothing or time of day will stimulate associations in your mind and can be a kind of nest-building or conditioned response, so that whenever you re-enter the environment your brain will be more inclined to shift into a creative mode. It's important to consider those around you. (Don't spend more than your share of the available time or income on yourself, and remember that empathy will make you a better writer.) But recognizing what you need in order to work well is not self-indulgence.

A friend of mine wrote this about her own need for writing space:

> I regret being less assertive about my need for space. When we first got married, my husband bought an expensive set of office furniture that took up so much space that he got the extra room in every place we lived. I chose to write on a folding card table and so I was usually in the living room or a bedroom, stuck in a corner where people wandered in and out. It put a huge dent in the amount of work I could do, especially once we had kids.

There's no need for the extremes of expensive furniture or a top-of-the-line computer, and you may find that the rhythm of no rhythm works best for you. Many writers, particularly in the beginning, prefer the freedom of not having a particular setting or routine, or of having one that shifts from time to time. But whatever your preferences, you must take your need for solitude seriously, or you won't be able to work.

Walls and closed doors are not the only necessary boundaries. At the very beginning, you'll need to make some ground rules: your desk and writing materials are off-limits to children, pets, spouse, and roommates. All can be trained. If possible, avoid sharing your computer. The issues here include time, privacy, and possible loss of work or other technical problems, including viruses. If you must share (for instance, with a spouse), put passwords on important files. This is not lack of trust—you simply need to know that you have privacy in order to feel really free to experiment. Look at it this way: writers are fortunate that unlike some other artists, they don't have to buy and maintain lots of equipment and materials, or rent extra space to house such things. A computer, printer, and paper are really their only necessary tools, but that much *is* necessary. Consider them—and their privacy—professional requirements.

If you're unable to make your home an adequate place to work, you may have to go elsewhere. If you don't find libraries stifling, they may afford you quiet space and time. Crowded restaurants or cafés can offer another kind of solitude—especially if you can find a back table, close out the commotion, and work without being bothered. Sometimes being in a public place will keep you from distracting yourself with television, music, telephone calls, or whatever is your preferred method of time-wasting when you're at home. If you do work outside of where you live, consider getting a laptop—it will allow you to write anywhere. If you use one in public, be aware of laptop etiquette. While it is often fine to plug in a computer in a public place, you should ask first. Don't leave your laptop out of your sight, do insure it, and always back up your work. Also, any time you write in a café or restaurant, order something more than coffee, leave a decent tip, and don't keep other customers waiting for a table.

Connecting with Others

Although—or perhaps because—writing is a solitary pursuit, many writers need artistic companionship, guidance, or direction. There are various ways of finding other writers to work with. The suggestions that follow are a starting point, but probably the best way is simple word of mouth. When you begin with someone you already know and with whom you share some history, or whose sensibility seems compatible with yours, you're much more likely to find what you're looking for and to avoid what you're not. Sometimes such groups form spontaneously out of sudden mutual need, but often the most enduring alliances grow slowly from developing artistic compatibilities or common interests. So, keep the venues below in mind, but never overlook the real starting point: empathy and insight, creative connection and exchange.

Starting Your Own Group

If you are comfortable creating and working with others and already know writers in your area, you may be able to form your own writers' group. There are a lot of different approaches—groups that work on specific genres; groups for women, men, gays or lesbians, or other minority writers; restricted groups and open groups; beginning and advanced groups. The main thing is not to commit yourself to anything you'll regret. Unless you are certain that all of you want a group open to any genre, critical approach, schedule, setting, or protocol, consider carefully whom you invite to join your group and whether or how to publicize the meetings. If you're considering forming a group, it's a good idea to at least think about some of the issues discussed below. Each of them will affect not only the group's work itself but your own writing process.

- *How large do you want the group to be?* Small groups of from three to five people are obviously more intimate and usually easier to organize and predict. But they can also get ingrown, cliquish, or just boring, particularly if the members have histories with one another. Including more members or adopting an open attendance policy makes for spontaneity and also unpredictability. Writers will receive more varied responses, and everything from the length and time of meetings to refreshments to the tone of the criticism may be up for grabs. Occasionally, personal conflicts between group members may damage or destroy small groups. Joining a large group will allow you lots of time between workshops—good for slower writers, frustrating for those who are in a prolific phase.

- *How will you make decisions?* Will you require unanimity? Near-unanimity? A vote or consensus? Secret ballot? Veto power for all members? A written constitution is probably not necessary. Still, these issues are worth discussing in order to avoid confusion and hurt feelings once a conflict has arisen.

  Who, if anyone, is in charge? The answer to this question can define the nature of the group. Will there be one acknowledged leader? If so, who, and

for how long? Will the leader set the schedule, assign responsibilities, conduct the meetings, preside over any conflicts that arise, and decide and enforce how discussions should be conducted? Some leaders ask questions of readers or writers, present or assign a lengthy critique, or simply take charge of the logistical arrangements and say enough to keep the discussion going. In other groups, the writer whose work is under discussion takes charge, asking readers for their responses on whatever issues are important to the discussion. Sometimes discussion leadership rotates.

Whether or not your group has a leader, you should discuss the ground rules, if any. Aside from logistics, will the group agree on procedures such as circulating manuscripts before the workshop, providing written critiques to writers, answering authors' questions as supplied with stories, requiring the author to remain silent during discussion of her work, or observing time limits per story? Particularly if group members have worked in other groups before, they may have unspoken assumptions about how things should be, and these can lead to conflicts if they're not understood.

Aside from interpersonal relations, a workshop's ground rules will affect how you work. Does your need for a particular kind of exchange match the group's approach? Some writers know what they want from readers and chafe at being silenced during discussions. Others don't know what to ask, or wish to avoid influencing the remarks and so prefer to rely on readers to lead the discussion of their work. Time limits and scheduling can also interfere with your work habits. When choosing or forming a group, think ahead to anticipate any such conflicts.

- *How often and when will you meet?* Some groups have a standing weekly, biweekly, or monthly meeting time; others plan as they go. Often the first type of scheduling deteriorates into the second. It will be necessary to find people whose needs and lifestyles can blend well enough to agree on common times and on how much flexibility to allow in the schedule. It's a good idea to think about how often you will need a reader and can provide readings, and whether a proposed schedule will leave you feeling frustrated or pressured.

- *Where will you meet?* Sometimes one member's schedule, location, or living situation causes her to want to host the group regularly. Do you want to meet at the same house every time? Is the location realistically convenient for everyone? Is there enough privacy and comfort for a workshop? Whoever decides to host the group regularly should be prepared for the usual downside to entertaining. It may be helpful to discuss ahead of time such issues as refreshments, cleanup, starting and ending times, and parking. Other possibilities include rotating the location or choosing a neutral spot such as a restaurant or other public area. In any case, the surroundings need to be comfortable enough for everyone to speak and read freely.

- *What type of work will you read?* Does everyone in the group write the same sort of thing? If not, do group members feel qualified to critique out of their genre? Often it can be refreshing to get a poet's perspective on prose, and vice versa. On the other hand, it's important to be realistic about your expectations and whether, in the long run, the group's combined skills will be helpful to you.

- *How many manuscripts, and of what length, will you discuss at each meeting?* The biggest factor here may be logistics. How much time are group members willing to spend, both at meetings and outside them, reading? Would you prefer a regular schedule, perhaps with the option for members to pass up a turn when they have nothing ready to discuss, or something more open-ended, which may mean the more prolific writers will submit quite often? Whatever you decide, it's a good idea to make the ground rules clear to avoid misunderstandings and to control for individuals who may be aware of their own needs more than they are those of others.

- *Will you submit manuscripts ahead of time for written comments, or read aloud on the spot?* Receiving a manuscript ahead of time allows readers to consider it carefully, to read it more than once, and to catch visual cues such as quotation marks, double-space breaks, or italics. But if you will be critiquing a large or unpredictable number of stories, submitting ahead of time may overburden readers. Listening to a story helps both readers and writer catch repeated words and unintentional rhymes, and ensures that readers get a sense of the whole picture rather than getting lost in the details. The spontaneity of an on-the-spot critique can also be useful, particularly for comparing readers' immediate emotional responses. In many cases, this logistical decision is made by group members' lack of time to read beforehand, or the difficulty of exchanging manuscripts. If you decide to read on the spot, providing copies to group members will allow them to make a few written comments as you read and to get a better sense of paragraphing, spacing, and punctuation.

- *How and when will the group welcome new members?* Will people be allowed to drop in, or will you agree on a size limit, inviting new members only as old ones drop out? Will new members be admitted only upon unanimous consent, or by majority vote? Will members have veto power? Will there be a trial period for new members? What if they don't fit into the group as well as hoped? These are all delicate issues and can cause groups to fall apart if they're not resolved mutually and *before* they must be put to the test.

- *Will you allow alchohol or drugs to be consumed during meetings?* Refreshments can attract people to the meetings, but be realistic. Can everyone in the group handle this? Will it result in second-rate critiques that appall you the morning after, or in an atmosphere that is more social than creative? Will anyone be uncomfortable? One of my students returned from a campus writing group in disgust, saying the members all sat around a gallon jug of wine and drank till they couldn't read coherently. Fun, maybe, but it wasn't primarily a writers' group. Will refreshments suit the time and place of your meetings? If they are served, be sure to rotate responsibilities and share cleanup and expenses. Don't use inebriation as an excuse to trash each other's houses or stories.

- *Will guests, children, or pets be accommodated?* Surprisingly enough, this innocuous question can be one of the most troublesome, perhaps because so many people consider such contradictory answers self-evident. Some factors to consider include the time and length of meetings, availability of extra space, adequate supervision of children or pets, allergies, potential interruptions, tensions within the group over these issues, and the preferences of the host. It's not unreasonable to draw the line at children or pets. Some groups accommodate guests, if the writers whose work is under discussion feel comfortable with them present. Many groups allow members veto power over decisions like this.

- *How important is regular attendance?* Informal groups don't usually impose penalties. Still, the host needs to know who and what to expect, and when. Can the group commit to its next date before disbanding for the evening? Is someone willing to organize and reorganize via e-mail or telephone? This can be a time-consuming and annoying responsibility and may need to be shared. You should also discuss the procedure for canceling or rescheduling meetings.

- *How often do you need readers?* As you consider forming a writers' group, think carefully about your own needs and what kind of arrangement can best answer them. Will a large group give you frequent enough readings, or would you be happier in a smaller, more intense group—maybe even just meeting weekly with a friend? Would you feel pressured by the demands of a small group? Are you comfortable sharing work in progress with everyone involved? Do you have time to meet others' expectations? Remember that a writers' group is not primarily a social occasion. In fact, participating in a group can help clarify your own methods and preferences by contrast. It is important not to become more committed to the group than to your own writing—if the group is not working for you, you could probably do better, artistically and socially, elsewhere.

Joining a Class

Most colleges, junior colleges, universities, private schools, and adult education programs offer some kind of creative writing courses. Many individual teachers freelance as well, offering courses or leading groups independently. Formal classes of whatever kind typically meet at a specified time and place for a stipulated number of sessions, and require specific fees as well as assignments and projects upon which the final grade is based. Some offer course credit that can be applied toward university writing programs, while others do not. Such courses present a very good option for those who feel they will benefit from the structure, consistency, leadership, and community a class offers.

Writing classes offered at nonaccredited schools and community education or arts centers, and increasingly also the more typical classroom settings, often attract nontraditional students who may be combining education and career or be returning to school after an absence. Though sometimes such students feel self-conscious among younger writers, they are becoming more and more numerous and often their skill at absorbing and creatively using criticism, their well-developed technical abilities, and their life experience make them promising students. Less experienced writers tend to appreciate their helpful comments and can also offer their own perspective.

You may be surprised to find that many community colleges and local adult education centers offer courses as high in quality and more diverse than those at universities. Because almost all writers, including and especially those who teach, have to do what they can to make ends meet, these courses are usually taught by published writers who may also teach at a local university or college. Often, you can get essentially the same course that the instructor would teach at a university, for less money and on a more flexible schedule.

Cultivating and Maintaining Relationships with Other Writers: Basic Etiquette

Working in solitude so much of the time, writers sometimes find it difficult anticipating and adjusting to the demands of a group. Whatever setting you choose for group work, it's a good idea to keep in mind a few things about communication and consideration. If you want help with your work over time, then when you find someone whose comments have been consistently useful, hold on to them, be good to them, and do whatever you have to do in order to keep them working with you.

If you're in school, be thoughtful of others in your classes. Don't trash their work or blow it off. Don't skip their workshops. Pay close attention to their stories and give them your best honest and constructive criticism and praise. Outside of class, be careful not to wear out readers. If you overuse them, not only will they get tired, but they'll lose perspective on your work and become less useful to you. It's considerate not to ask friends, classmates, or teachers to read extremely long manuscripts or to read the same manuscript more than once or twice. It helps to be understanding of others' schedules and limitations and to communicate clearly about when manuscripts will be returned. It's even better if you can learn to recognize when readers may be telling you passively or nonverbally that they just can't help you right now. If—outside of a classroom situation—they keep not returning your work, take the hint and don't take it personally.

Always offer to return the favor of a reading. When you read someone else's work, be clear about when you will return it, and stick to your promise. If there are delays, communicate about them. When possible, trade work and try to give back what you get, page for page. Spend the time to deliver an honest and sensitive reading with detailed comments. Find some other way to compensate readers who are nonwriters. Say thank you. Especially, let readers know when their suggestions helped you.

A final suggestion from one of my finest teachers:

Here is the best writing advice I ever read, from Henry James's essay "The Art of Fiction." Not the famous "Try to be one of the people on whom nothing is lost!" (see, Henry James uses !s too, once in a while) but something a whole lot better right at the end of the essay: "Be generous and delicate and pursue the prize."

—*Bruce Jorgensen,*
writer and teacher

Beyond these basic considerations are a number of procedural issues that will affect any group of writers. These are discussed in Chapter 11, as they apply also to formal workshops, but many of the suggestions can be applied as well to informal groups.

Like a lot of habits, writing is more than an act—it's a way of life. Unfortunately, it's not always understood or supported by nonwriters. Most writers will never make much money from their writing, and many will never publish. Why do it, then? The German poet Rainer Maria Rilke answered a young writer's questions with this advice, published later in his book *Letters to a Young Poet*:

> You ask whether your verses are good. You ask me. You have asked others before. You send them to magazines. You compare them with other poems, and you are disturbed when certain editors reject your efforts. Now (since you have allowed me to advise you) I beg you to give up all that. You are looking outward, and that above all you should not do now. Nobody can counsel and help you, nobody. There is only one single way. Go into yourself. Search for the reason that bids you write; find out whether it is spreading out its roots in the deepest places of your heart, acknowledge to yourself whether you would have to die if it were denied you to write. This above all—ask yourself in the stillest hour of your night: must I write? Delve into yourself for a deep answer. And if this should be affirmative, if you may meet this earnest question with a strong and simple "*I must*," then build your life according to this necessity; your life even into its most indifferent and slightest hour must be a sign of this urge and a testimony to it.

"Must I write?" is a very personal question. A writing life isn't for everyone, and there's no reason it should be. No one can guarantee that you'll ever publish or create enduring art. But if you're willing to make space in your life for writing, it is possible to learn and to improve, and to give and receive help from others along the way.

More Books and Stories

This list includes the readings that helped me as I wrote this book, as well as those suggested by friends, teachers, students, reviewers, and other writers. I've added meditations on creativity and craft, interviews with writers, autobiographies, books of letters, and even a little philosophy. What they all have in common is that they helped someone along the way as they learned to write. Those that are currently out of print may be found at libraries or through rare book dealers or online bookstores.

The Stories

Addonizio, Kim. "Survivors." Kim Addonizio. *In the Box Called Pleasure*. San Francisco: Black Ice Books, 1999.

Baxter, Christine. "If You Ever Want To Have a Fling. Student story, 1997.

Berriault, Gina. "A Dream of Fair Women." *Women in Their Beds*. Washington, D.C.: Counterpoint, 1996, first paperback edition 1997.

Butler, Robert Olen, "Jealous Husband Returns in Form of Parrot." *Tabloid Dreams*. New York: Henry Holt, 1996.

Carver, Raymond. "The Calm." *What We Talk About When We Talk About Love*. New York: Knopf, 1981. Reissued by Vintage Books, 1989.

Chekhov, Anton. "Gooseberries." Ed. Ralph E. Matlaw. *Anton Chekhov's Short Stories*. New York: W. W. Norton, 1979.

Connolly, Joseph. "Hard Feelings." Ed. Anne Bernays and Pamela Painter. *What If? Writing Exercises for Fiction Writers*. Revised and expanded edition. New York: HarperCollins, 1995.

Cortázar, Julio. "Instructions on How To Sing." *Cronopios and Famas*. Copyright 1962 by Julio Cortazar and the Heirs of Julio Cortázar. Translation copyright 1969 by Random House, Inc. New York: New Directions, 1962.

Dubus, Andre. "A Father's Story." *Selected Stories*. New York: Vintage Contemporaries, 1999.

Finkelstein, Rachel. "Awakening." Student story, 1999.

García, Márquez Gabriel. "A Very Old Man With Enormous Wings." *Leaf Storm and Other Stories*. New York: HarperCollins, 1954.

Grimm, Jakob and Wilhelm. "Little Red-Cap." Ed. James Stern. Tr. Margaret Hunt. *The Complete Grimm's Fairy Tales*. New York: Pantheon Books, 1976.

Hall, Garnette. "8 Mountains." Student story, 2000.

Hawthorne, Nathaniel. "The Minister's Black Veil." Ed. Thomas E. Connolly. *The Scarlet Letter and Selected Tales*. New York: Penguin, 1978.

Hemingway, Ernest. "Hills Like White Elephants." *The Complete Stories of Ernest Hemingway*. New York: Scribner Paperback Fiction, published by Simon & Schuster, 1987.

Joyce, James. "Araby." *Dubliners*, by James Joyce. New York: Vintage Books, 1993.

McFee, Michael. "The Halo." Ed. Jerome Stern. *Microfiction*. New York: Norton, 1996.

Miller, Brenda. "A Thousand Buddhas" (personal essay). Ed. Bill Henderson. *The Pushcart Prize, XIX: Best of the Small Presses*. Wainscott, New York: Pushcart Press Distributed by W.W. Norton, NY NY., 1995.

Moser, Joseph. "Close Enough." Student story, 1999.

Munro, Alice. "Lichen." *Selected Stories*. New York: Vintage Contemporaries, 1997.

O'Connor, Flannery. "A Good Man Is Hard to Find." *The Complete Stories*. New York: Noonday Press, 1996.

Pase, Seth. "The Father." Student story, 1996.

Phillips, Jayne Anne. "Souvenir." *Black Tickets*. New York: Delecorte Press, 1989.

Phillips, Lisa Usani. "City of Dreams." Previously published in *The Beacon Review*, vol. 12, no. 1.

Rulfo, Juan. "Macario." *The Burning Plain*. Austin: University of Texas Press, 1996.

Sharma, Akhil. "Cosmopolitan." Ed. Larry Dark. *Prize Stories 1998: The O. Henry Awards*. New York: Anchor Books, 1998.

Silko, Leslie Marmon. "Yellow Woman." *Storyteller*. New York: Arcade Books, 1989.

Speaker, Mary Austin. "The Day the Flames Would Stop." Student story, 1997.

Spencer, Darrell. "Park Host." *Caution: Men in Trees*. Athens: University of Georgia Press, 2000.

Suffern, James Leon. "The End of Summer." Student story, 2000.

Thibodeau, Jeannine. "Close." Student story, 1997.

Welty, Eudora. "The Key." *The Collected Stories of Eudora Welty*. New York: Harcourt Brace, 1982.

Zavotka, Kelly. "What Killed a Girl." Student story, 1997.

More Fiction

Banks, Russell. *Affliction*. New York: HarperCollins, 1989.

Busch, Frederick. *Don't Tell Anyone*. New York: W. W. Norton, 2000.

Butler, Robert Olen. *Tabloid Dreams*. New York: Henry Holt, 1996.

Cartland, Barbara. *A Runaway Star*. London: Severn House, 1987.

Cather, Willa. *Death Comes for the Archbishop*. New York: Vintage Classics, 1990.

Cather, Willa. *Youth and the Bright Medusa*. New York: Random House, 1975. (Out of print.)

Cheever, John. *The Stories of John Cheever*. New York: Vintage Books, 2000.

Connell, Evan S. *Mrs. Bridge*. San Francisco: North Point Press, 1981.

Danford, Natalie and John Kulka, eds. *Scribner's Best of the College Fiction Workshops*. New York: Scribner's, 1997-1999.

Diaz, Junot. *Drown*. New York: Penguin Putnam, Inc., 1996.

Dorris, Michael. *A Yellow Raft in Blue Water*. New York: Warner Books, 1987.

Dubus, Andre III. *House of Sand and Fog*. New York: W. W. Norton, 1999.

Drury, Tom. *The End of Vandalism*. New York: Houghton Mifflin, 1994.

Ellison, Ralph. *Invisible Man*. New York: Random House, 1947.

Fitzgerald, F. Scott. *The Great Gatsby*. New York: Scribner, 1995.

Henry, DeWitt. *Breaking into Print*. Boston: Beacon Press, 2000.

Ingalls, Rachel. Mrs. Caliban. Boston: Harvard Common Press, 1986.

Lahiri, Jhumpa. *Interpreter of Maladies*. New York: Houghton Mifflin, 1999.

Leavitt, David. *Family Dancing*. New York: Houghton Mifflin, 1997.

Plath, Sylvia. *The Bell Jar*. New York: Harper & Row, 1971.

Rush, Norman. *Mating*. New York: Vintage, 1992.

Salinger, J. D. "Uncle Wiggily in Connecticut," in *Nine Stories*. Boston: Little, Brown, 1981.

Salinger, J. D. "Seymour: An Introduction." in *Raise High the Roof Beam, Carpenters*. Boston: Little, Brown, 1963.

Stevick, Philip, ed. *Anti-Story*. New York: Free Press, 1971.

Toomer, Jean. *Cane*. New York: W. W. Norton, 1989.

Twain, Mark. *Huckleberry Finn*. New York: Penguin, 1986.

Walker, Alice. *The Color Purple*. New York: Washington Square Press, 1998.

Yorgason, Blaine, and Brenton Yorgason. *The Krystal Promise*. Salt Lake City: Deseret, 1993.

About Writing and Fiction

Allen, Walter. *The Writer on His Art*. New York: McGraw-Hill Book Co., 1949.

Allott, Miriam. *Novelists on the Novel*. New York: Columbia University Press, 1949.

Atchity, Kenneth. *A Writer's Time*. New York: W. W. Norton, 1986.

Barzun, Jacques. *On Writing, Editing, and Publishing*. Chicago: University of Chicago Press, 1986.

Baxter, Charles. *Burning Down the House: Essays on Fiction*. St. Paul: Graywolf Press, 1997.

Behn, Robin, and Chase Twichell. *The Practice of Poetry*. New York: HarperCollins, 1992. Though written for poets, many of the exercises in this book are very adaptable for fiction writers.

Bell, Madison Smartt. *Narrative Design: A Writer's Guide to Structure*. New York: Norton, 1997.

Bernays, Anne, and Pamela Painter. *What If? Writing Exercises for Fiction Writers*. New York: HarperCollins, 1995.

Bly, Carol. *The Passionate, Accurate Story*. Minneapolis: Milkweed Editions, 1990.

Booth, Wayne C. *The Rhetoric of Fiction*. Chicago: University of Chicago Press, 1961.

Borges, Jorge Luis. *Borges on Writing*. Ed. Norman Thomas di Giovanni, Daniel Hallpern, and Frank MacShane. New York: E.P. Dutton, 1973.

Bowen, Elizabeth. *Collected Impressions*. New York: Alfred A. Knopf, 1950.

Bradbury, Ray. *Zen in the Art of Writing*. New York: Bantam, 1992.

Brande, Dorothea. *On Becoming a Writer*. Los Angeles: Jeremy Tarcher, 1981.

Brown, Kurt, ed. *Writers on Life and Craft*. Boston: Beacon, ongoing.

Brown, Rita Mae. *Starting from Scratch: A Different Kind of Writer's Manual*. New York: Bantam, 1988.

Burroway, Janet. *Writing Fiction*, 5th ed. New York: HarperCollins, 1995.

Busch, Frederick. *A Dangerous Profession: A Book about the Writing Life*. New York: St. Martin's Press, 1998.

Busch, Frederick, ed., *Letters to a Fiction Writer*. New York: W. W. Norton, 1999.

Cather, Willa. *On Writing: Critical Studies on Writing as an Art*. New York: Alfred A. Knopf, 1949.

Cohn, Dorritt. *Transparent Minds: Narrative Modes for Presenting Consciousness in Fiction*. Princeton: Princeton University Press, 1978.

Dillard, Annie. *The Writing Life*. New York: Harper and Row, 1989.

Elbow, Peter. *Writing without Teachers*. New York and Oxford: Oxford, 1973.

Epel, Naomi. *Writers Dreaming*. New York: Vintage, 1993.

Fitzgerald, F. Scott. *The Notebooks of F. Scott Fitzgerald*. Ed. Matthew J. Bruccoli. New York: Harcourt Brace Jovanovich, 1978.

Forster, E.M. *Aspects of the Novel*. New York: Harcourt, Brace & World, 1954.

Frank, Thaisa, and Dorothy Wall. *Finding Your Writer's Voice*. New York: St. Martin's Press: 1997.

Friedman, Bonnie. *Writing Past Dark*. New York: HarperCollins, 1993.

Gardner, John. *On Moral Fiction*. New York: Basic Books, 1978.

Gardner, John. *The Art of Fiction*. New York: Alfred A. Knopf, 1984.

Gass, William. *Fiction and the Figures of Life*. Boston: David R. Godine, 1979.

Goldberg, Natalie. *Writing Down the Bones*. Boston: Shambhala, 1986.

Harvey, W.J., *Character and the Novel*. London: Chatto & Windus Ltd., 1965. (Out of print.)

Heffron, Jack, ed. *The Best Writing on Writing*. Cincinnati: Story Press, 1995.

Hemingway, Ernest. *Ernest Hemingway on Writing*. Ed. Larry W. Phillips. New York: Charles Scribner's Sons, 1984.

Hemingway, Ernest. "On Writing." *The Nick Adams Stories*. New York: Scribner's, 1972.

Hersey, John, ed. *The Writer's Craft*. New York: Alfred A. Knopf, 1974.

Hills, Rust. *Writing in General and the Short Story in Particular*. Boston: Houghton Mifflin Co., 1977.

Huddle, David. *The Writing Habit: Essays*. Layton, Utah: Peregrine Smith Books, 1991.

Hughes, Elaine Farris. *Writing from the Inner Self*. New York: HarperCollins, 1990.

Hugo, Richard. *The Triggering Town*. New York: W.W. Norton, 1979.

James, Henry. *The Art of Fiction*. New York: Charles Scribner's Sons, 1948.

James, Henry. *The Art of the Novel*. Oxford: Oxford University Press, 1947.

James, Henry. *The House of Fiction*. Westport, Conn.: Greenwood, 1973.

James, Henry. *The Notebooks of Henry James*. Oxford: Oxford University Press, 1947.

Jason, Philip K. and Allan B. Lefcowitz. *Creative Writer's Handbook*, 2nd ed. Englewood Cliffs, N.J.: Prentice-Hall, 1994.

Kaplan, David Michael. *Revision: A Creative Approach to Writing and Rewriting Fiction*. Cincinnati: Story Press, 1997.

Kennedy, Thomas, "Realism and Other Illusions." In Heffron, Jack, ed. *The Best Writing on Writing*, vol. 2. Cincinnati: Story Press, 1995.

Kercheval, Jesse Lee. *Building Fiction: How to Develop Plot and Structure*. Cincinnati: Story Press, 1997.

Lamott, Anne. *Bird by Bird*. New York: Pantheon, 1994.

Lodge, David. *The Art of Fiction*. New York: Penguin Books, 1992.

Lubbock, Percy. *The Craft of Fiction*. New York: Viking Press, 1957.

Macauley, Robie, and George Lanning. *Technique in Fiction*, 2nd ed. New York: St. Martin's Press, 1987.

Madden, David. *Revising Fiction: A Handbook for Fiction Writers*. New York: New American Library, 1988.

McCarthy, Mary. *On the Contrary*. New York: Farrar, Straus & Cudahy, 1961.

McCormack, Thomas, ed. *Afterwords: Novelists on Their Novels*. New York: Harper & Row, 1969.

Minot, Stephen. *Three Genres*, 4th ed. Englewood Cliffs, N.J.: Prentice-Hall, 1988.

Muir, Edwin, *The Structure of the Novel*. London: Brill Academic Publishers, 1963. (Out of print.)

Nelson, Victoria. *On Writer's Block: A New Approach to Creativity*. Boston: Houghton Mifflin, 1993.

O'Connor, Flannery. "The Church and the Fiction Writer." *Mystery and Manners*. New York: Farrar, Straus & Giroux, 1969.

O'Connor, Frank. *The Lonely Voice: A Study of the Short Story*. Cleveland: World Publishing, 1963.

O'Connor, Frank. *Mirror in the Roadway*. New York: Alfred A. Knopf, 1956.

Olsen, Tillie. *Silences*. New York: Delacorte Press, 1978.

Orwell, George. "Politics and the English Language." *Shooting an Elephant and Other Essays*. New York: Harcourt Brace, 1984.

Nosakovich, Josip. *Fiction Writer's Workshop*. Cincinnati: Story Press, 1995.

Pack, Robert, and Jay Parini, eds. *Writers on Writing*. Middlebury, Vt.: Middlebury College Press, 1991.

Petracca, Michael. *The Graceful Lie: A Method for Making Fiction*. Upper Saddle River, N.J.: Prentice-Hall, 1999.

Plimpton, George, ed. *The Writer's Chapbook*. New York: Viking, 1999.

Plimpton, George. 1953-1989. *Writers at Work: The Paris Review Interviews*. New York: Viking Penguin.

Pritchett, V.S. *The Living Novel and Later Appreciations*. New York: Macmillan Co., 1959.

R.S. Crane, ed., *Critics and Criticism Ancient and Modern*. Chicago: University of Chicago Press, 1954. (Out of print.)

Rico, Gabriel Lusser. *Writing the Natural Way*. Los Angeles: J.P. Tarcher, 1983.

Rilke, Rainer Maria. *Letters to a Young Poet*. New York: Norton, 1993.

Shelnutt, Eve. *The Writing Room*. Marietta, Ga.: Longstreet Press, 1989.

Skelton, Robin. *The Poet's Calling*. London: Heinemann Educational Books, 1975. (Out of print.)

Skelton, Robin. *The Practice of Poetry*. New York: Barnes & Noble, 1971.

Sloane, William, and Julia Sloane, ed. *The Craft of Writing*. New York: Norton, 1979.

Stafford, William. *Writing the Australian Crawl*, ed. Donald Hall. Ann Arbor, Mich.: University of Michigan Press, 1978.

Stern, Jerome. *Making Shapely Fiction*. New York: W.W. Norton, 1991.

Strunk, William C., and E.B. White. *The Elements of Style*, 3rd ed. New York: Macmillan, 1979.

Ueland, Brenda. *If You Want To Write*. St. Paul: Graywolf Press, 1987.

Welty, Eudora. *The Eye of the Story*. New York: Random House, 1977.

Welty, Eudora. *One Writer's Beginnings*. New York: Belknap, 1995.

Wharton, Edith. *The Writing of Fiction*. New York: Charles Scribner's Sons, 1925.

Willis, Meredith Sue. *Personal Fiction Writing: A Guide to Writing from Real Life for Teachers, Students, and Writers*. New York: Teachers & Writers Collaborative, 1984.

Willis, Meredith Sue. *Deep Revision: A Guide for Teachers, Students, and Other Writers*. New York: Teachers & Writers Collaborative, 1993.

Willis, Meredith Sue. *Blazing Pencils: A Guide to Writing Fiction and Essays*. New York: Teachers & Writers Collaborative, 1990.

White, E.B. *The Elements of Style*. New York: Allyn & Bacon, 2000.

Woolf, Virginia. *A Writer's Diary*. New York: Harcourt, Brace & Co., 1954.

Woodruff, Jay, ed. *A Piece of Work: Five Writers Discuss Their Revisions*. Iowa City: University of Iowa Press, 1993.

Ziegler, Alan. *The Writing Workshop*. New York: Teachers and Writers Collaborative, 1984.

Books of Letters

Bruccoli, Matthew J., *The Only Thing that Counts: The Ernest Hemingway—Maxwell Perkins Correspondence*. New York: Simon & Schuster, 1995.

Merton, Thomas. *The Hidden Ground of Love*. New York: Farrar, Straus & Giroux, 1985.

O'Connor, Flannery. *The Habit of Being*. New York: Vintage, 1980.

Stuhlman, Gunther, ed. *A Literate Passion: Letters of Anais Nin and Henry Miller, 1932-1953*. New York: Harcourt Brace, 1989.

White, E. B. *The Letters of E. B. White*. New York: Harper & Row, 1976. (Out of print.)

Credits

Kim Addonizio. "Survivors" from *Micro-fiction,* ed. Jerome Stern, pp. 52–53. Reprinted by permission of author.

David Ambrosini. Unfinished short story. Used by permission of author.

Russell Banks. Excerpts from *Affliction,* pp. 15, 16, 32. New York: HarperCollins, 1989.

Christine Baxter. "If You Ever Want to Have a Fling." Student story. 1997. Used by permission of author.

Gina Berriault. "A Dream of Fair Women" from *Women in Their Beds,* pp. 34–41 Washington, DC: Counterpoint, 1997.

Jenna Blum. Unpublished essay. 2000. Used by permission of author.

Penelope Bone. Personal correspondence. 1999. Used by permission of author.

Robert Bosnak. Excerpt from *A Little Course in Dreams,* by Robert Bosnak, © 1986, p. 27. Reprinted by arrangement with Shambhala Publications, Inc., Boston.

Robert Olen Butler. "Jealous Husband Returns in Form of Parrot" from *Tabloid Dreams* by Robert Olen Butler, © 1996 by Robert Olen Butler. Reprinted by permission of Henry Holt & Co.

John Cage. Quotation. Used by permission of Merce Cunningham.

David Carkeet. "Dear Reviewer" from *The Best Writing on Writing,* pp. 155–157. Cincinnati: Story Press, 1995.

Barbara Cartland. From *A Runaway Star,* pp. 155–56. London: Severn House, 1987.

Raymond Carver. "The Calm" from *What We Talk About When We Talk About Love,* pp. 115–121. New York: Knopf, 1981.

Anton Chekhov. "Gooseberries" from *Anton Chekhov's Short Stories,* ed. Ralph E. Matlaw, pp. 221–35. New York: Norton, 1979.

Joseph Connolly. "Hard Feelings" from *What If? Writing Exercises for Fiction Writers,* eds. Anne Bernays and Pamela Painter, pp. 360–72. New York: HarperCollins, 1995. Reprinted by permission of author.

Ryan Conroy. Personal correspondence. 2000. Used by permission of author.

Julio Cortázar. "Instructions on How to Sing" from *Cronopios and Famas,* p. 7. New York: New Directions, 1962.

Michael Dorris. Excerpt from *A Yellow Raft in Blue Water,* pp. 3–17. New York: Warner Books, 1987.

Andre Dubus III. Excerpts from *House of Sand and Fog,* pp. 15, 34, 357. New York: Vintage Contemporaries, 1999.

Andre Dubus. "A Father's Story" from *Selected Stories,* pp.455–76. New York: Vintage Contemporaries, 1989.

Rachel Finkelstein. "Awakening." Student story. 1999. Used by permission of author.

Gabriel García Márquez. "A Very Old Man with Enormous Wings" from *Leaf Storm and Other Stories,* pp. 105–12. New York: HarperCollins. 1954.

Leon Golden, trans., and O.B. Hardison. Excerpt from *Aristotle's Poetics: A Translation and Commentary for Students of Literature,* p. 14. Tallahassee: Florida State University Press, 1981.

Jakob Grimm, and Wilhelm Grimm. "Little Red-Cap" from James Stern and Margaret Hunt, *The Complete Grimm's Fairy Tales,* pp. 139–43. New York: Random House, 1972.

Brewster Ghiselin, *The Creative Process.* Berkeley: University of California Press, 1985.

Garnette Hall. "8 Mountains." Student story. 2000. Used by permission of author.

Nathaniel Hawthorne. "The Minister's Black Veil" from *The Scarlet Letter and Selected Tales,* ed. Thomas E. Connolly, pp. 299–314. New York: Penguin, 1978.

Ernest Hemingway. *Ernest Hemingway on Writing*. Ed. Larry W. Phillips. New York: Scribner's, 1972.

Ernest Hemingway. "Hills Like White Elephants" from *The Complete Short Stories of Ernest Hemingway*, pp. 211–14. New York: Simon & Schuster, 1987.

Ernest Hemingway. "On Writing." *The Nick Adams Stories*. New York: Scribner's, 1972.

Bruce Jorgensen. Personal correspondence. 2000–2001. Used by permission of author.

James Joyce. "Araby" from *Dubliners*, pp. 21–27. New York: Dover Books, 1991.

Ross Kilburn. Personal correspondence. 2000. Used by permission of author.

Bret Lott. Personal correspondence. 2000. Used by permission of author.

Robie Macauley and George Lanham. *Technique in Fiction*. New York: St. Martin's Press, 1987.

Michael McFee. "The Halo" from *Microfiction*, ed. Jerome Stern, pp. 40–41. New York: Norton, 1996.

Brenda Miller. "A Thousand Buddhas." Originally published in the *Georgia Review*. Reprinted by permission of the author.

Joseph Moser. "Close Enough." Student story. 1999. Used by permission of author.

Alice Munro. "Lichen" from *Selected Stories*, pp. 351–73. New York: Vintage Contemporaries, 1997.

Flannery O'Connor. "A Good Man Is Hard to Find" from *The Complete Stories*, pp. 117–33. New York: Farrar, Straus and Giroux, 1946.

Dennis Packard. Personal correspondence. 2000. Used by permission of author.

Seth Pase. "The Father." Student story. 1996. Used by permission of author.

Jayne Anne Phillips. "Souvenir" from *Black Tickets*, pp. 175–96. New York: Simon & Shuster, 1984.

Lisa Usani Phillips. "City of Dreams." *The Beacon Review*, 1998, v. 12, no. 1, pp. 86–88. Reprinted by permission of author.

Henri Poincaré. Excerpt from "Mathematical Creation." From Brewster Ghiselin, *The Creative Process: Reflections on the Inventions of Art*, p. 26. Berkeley: University of California Press, 1996.

Juan Rulfo. "Macario" *The Burning Plain*, pp. 3–8. Austin: University of Texas Press, 1996.

Norman Rush. *Mating*, pp. 173–77. New York: Vintage, 1992.

Michelle Sarrat. Interview. 1999. Used by permission.

Akhil Sharma. "Cosmopolitan" *The O. Henry Awards, The Best of 1998*, pp. 273–96. New York: Anchor Books, 1998.

Leslie Marmon Silko. "Yellow Woman" from *Storyteller*. New York: Arcade Books, 1989.

Mary Austin Speaker. "The Day the Flames Would Stop." Student story. 1997. Used by permission of author.

Darrell Spencer. "Park Host" from *Caution: Men in Trees*, pp. 1–25. Athens: University of Georgia Press, 2000.

Darrell Spencer. Personal correspondence. March 2000. Used by permission of author.

Janet St. John. Personal correspondence. 2000. Used by permission of author.

James Leon Suffern. "When the Summer Ends." Student story. 2000. Used by permission of author.

James Leon Suffern. Interview. 1999. Used by permission.

James Leon Suffern. Personal correspondence. 1999. Used by permission of author.

Jeannine Thibodeau. "Close." Student story. 1997. Used by permission of author.

Trevor, William. Interview. Ed. George Plimpton, *The Writer's Chapbook*. New York: Random House, 1999.

Alice Walker. Excerpt from *The Color Purple*, pp. 3–17. New York: Washington Square Press, 1998.

Eudora Welty. "The Key" from *The Collected Stories of Eudora Welty*, pp. 29–37. New York: Harcourt Brace Jovanovich, 1980.

Kelly Zavotka. "What Killed a Girl." Student story. 1997. Used by permission of author.

Index

Advance Praise for

Where the Stories Come From: Beginning to Write Fiction

by Sibyl Johnston

"Look at this book. It offers you a way to do hands-on workshops, student run workshops—with lots of nuts and bolts stuff on the basics. Plenty of space devoted to process, and equal emphasis on technique. The stores in the anthology are great. This book . . . has an informed and strategic sense of the writer as a work in progress. . . . While it has become standard in composition textbooks, this focus on process is new and necessary in a creative writing text."

—Heather Sellers, Hope College

"I would describe this book as the most comprehensive and creative text on the market that addresses both the technical and process issues of what it is like to be a writer."

—Willard Cook, New York University

"This is a groundbreaking text! Never before have so many real student concerns been so capably addressed, with creative guidance and worthwhile exercises. Students will be guided into generating story material, into leading their own student-centered workshops, and into making the most of their stories through revision. This text will ensure that our students will benefit from the workshopping process, and it is bound to make better teachers of fiction of us all."

—Connie Wasem, University of Texas at El Paso

"Since reviewing this book twice I have become aware of the need to change my approach in this direction. . . . The text balances professional advice, awareness of a student audience, and attention to the craft of fiction . . . As I read I kept thinking, 'This is good. This is really good.' . . . Shifting from a traditional creative writing workshop to a student-centered workshop is bound to be energizing, effecting change for all concerned. . . . I predict that this book will set the standard for a long time."

—Nancy McLelland, Mendocino College